THE CELTS

The Celts

A MODERN HISTORY

IAN STEWART

PRINCETON UNIVERSITY PRESS
PRINCETON & OXFORD

Published by Princeton University Press
41 William Street, Princeton, New Jersey 08540
99 Banbury Road, Oxford OX2 6JX

press.princeton.edu

Library of Congress Cataloging-in-Publication Data

Names: Stewart, Ian B., 1990– author.
Title: The Celts : a modern history / Ian Stewart.
Description: Princeton : Princeton University Press, [2025] | Includes bibliographical references and index.
Identifiers: LCCN 2024036107 (print) | LCCN 2024036108 (ebook) | ISBN 9780691222516 (hardback) | ISBN 9780691222530 (e-book)
Subjects: LCSH: Civilization, Celtic. | Celts—Intellectual life. | Pan-Celticism. | BISAC: HISTORY / Europe / Western | HISTORY / Europe / Great Britain / Wales
Classification: LCC CB206 .S78 2025 (print) | LCC CB206 (ebook) | DDC 941—dc23/eng/20240824
LC record available at https://lccn.loc.gov/2024036107
LC ebook record available at https://lccn.loc.gov/2024036108

British Library Cataloging-in-Publication Data is available

Editorial: Ben Tate, Josh Drake
Production Editorial: Elizabeth Byrd
Jacket: Chris Ferrante
Production: Danielle Amatucci
Publicity: Alyssa Sanford (US), Carmen Jimenez (UK)
Copyeditor: Arielle Lewis

Jacket Credit: Aleksandr / Adobe Stock

Printed in the United States of America

10 9 8 7 6 5 4 3 2 1

MIX
Paper | Supporting responsible forestry
FSC® C008955
FSC
www.fsc.org

To my mom and dad

CONTENTS

LIST OF ILLUSTRATIONS

PREFACE AND ACKNOWLEDGEMENTS

MORE THAN A CENTURY AGO, the Irish historian Eoin MacNeill pointed out that 'the modern Celtic consciousness' had a 'somewhat academic origin'. Although 'the Celts of Ireland, Britain and Gaul' must have once recognised 'that they were nearer akin to each other than to the Germans and Italians', this 'knowledge perished altogether from the popular memory and the popular consciousness' and had to be 're-discovered and re-established'.[1] We don't know whether these ancient peoples did in fact recognise any such familial relationship, but the assumption that they did has meant a great deal to many people across Europe for several centuries. This book begins with that 'somewhat academic origin', the rediscovery of the Celts in the European Renaissance, and tells the story of how 'the modern Celtic consciousness' developed up to today.

If not quite all things to all people, 'the Celts' are and have been many different things to many different people. This is a history that connects those meanings and explains how and why the people and places we understand as Celtic came to be thought of in that way. It links the ancient Celts, who stretched across ancient Europe, with the modern Celts, who now live on its north-western 'fringes', by showing how the ancient Celts became glorious ancestors sought after in many European nations from the early modern period onwards. Most of my attention falls on the eighteenth and nineteenth centuries, bridging the three areas that have received most historical notice: the early modern French and German vogue for Celtic ancestry, the so-called Celtic Revival in eighteenth-century Britain and further afield, and the Yeatsian 'Celtic Twilight' of the late nineteenth and early twentieth centuries, which was international but Irish above all. Readers will find these more familiar subjects portrayed within a much broader and more detailed picture than that in which they are usually observed.

This book has taken nearly a decade to write, and I could have easily spent the rest of my life researching the subject, learning all of the languages inside-out, and refining the text. But there are other things I want to write about before I die. I am therefore acutely aware of its limits, and for that reason my aim has not been to provide a comprehensive history of the modern idea of the Celts, but to present a coherent account of the trajectories of varying ideas of the Celts and their intellectual, cultural, and political ramifications in the modern era. This is a history of 'Celticism'—or ideas about the Celts and the histories and qualities ascribed to them—not a history of the ancient Celts, or a history of modern Celtic studies.[2] I hope Celticists find it interesting and illuminating, but I set off in a very different direction. Rather than focusing on the ancient Celts and the 'afterlives' of the texts and traditions in which they are located, I am interested in the intellectual and cultural histories of Britain, Ireland, France, and Europe more generally, and why the Celts became and remain important to them.

The text is divided into three parts, reflecting the three major intellectual shifts with which (I believe) ideas of the Celts changed. Part I focuses on the recovery of knowledge about the ancient Celts in early modern Europe in the context of the formation of modern nations and national identities. Part II examines how the idea of race—which crystallised in European thought toward the end of the eighteenth century—changed ideas of the Celts and generated new political arguments about them during the nineteenth century. Part III follows the rise of a pan-Celtic consciousness and the forms it took over the nineteenth century, into the twentieth, and down to the present day. Ultimately the book is a history of ideas, but the histories of scholarship and knowledge play a dominant role in Parts I and II—where the history of political thought is also present—while Part III includes more cultural history. In effect, then, the book is a case study for how collective identities were constructed over the modern period, and follows the ways in which the idea of the Celts was recovered by scholars; honed by intellectuals, politicians, and other thinkers of various stripes; and adopted by cultural revivalists and activists. Sometimes all of these roles were played by one person, but it is also possible to follow how ideas changed incrementally as they were picked up and refashioned over time, across borders, and in different languages. Beyond the Celts, the relationship at the heart of the whole book is that between knowledge-making and popular culture.

The geographical scope is large, though it focuses primarily on the Celtic nations—albeit with much more weight given to Ireland, Wales, Scotland, and Brittany than to Cornwall and the Isle of Man—and France (whose Celticity is both obvious and complicated). Events, thinkers, and themes in England are often discussed, and I also look occasionally at developments in Germany, the Netherlands, Switzerland, Austria, and the United States. Each of these has its own historiography with its distinctive concerns and character. Trying to get them to speak to each other, even where there is the common thread of Celtic interest to follow, has been one of the greatest challenges in writing this book.

Because it is fairly wide-ranging, I hope that there is something for everyone in this book. But the flipside is that there might be chapters that don't appeal to individual readers. Although I think chapters 2 and 6 are, from a scholarly standpoint, two of the best and most original, and help to rewrite the history of Celtic philology, they are comparatively technical. Despite my best efforts in chapter 3, the Druids remain a mystery, and in the later chapters I deal hardly at all with the international Celtic diaspora. There was so much material with which to work that I have had to make a number of difficult choices about what to include. Many make sense to me but will seem arbitrary to others, but hopefully some of the ones that seem arbitrary to me might make sense to others who know better.

Sometimes in Celtic studies—as in other fields—errors or emphases are mistaken for biases, whether conscious or unconscious. To put my cards on the table, I hope to have avoided the 'ancient, deep-seated, almost wholly unconscious English prejudice against "Celts" and all their works' by being American (and therefore gripped by a different set of prejudices entirely).[3] Still, I have lived in Britain, and mostly London, for many years and have developed new preoccupations and partialities, though most of these have to do with the narcissism of small academic differences and methods of humanistic study. Occasionally I am asked whether I chose this subject out of an interest in my 'heritage', but the truth is that it happened almost completely by accident, and I pursued the topic because I was curious and found it interesting. However, I am very aware that the ideas, traditions, and people in this book were not created for scholarly dissection, and that they have meant and still mean a lot to many people. I find Celticism just as interesting as when I started, and much of that has to do with the people—academic and lay—who care deeply about these subjects. I hope they all find something of interest in this book.

More than anything else, writing this book has been a lot of fun, and I am grateful to all of the people and institutions that have made it possible. These include the London School of Economics and Political Science (LSE); Sciences

Po; Queen Mary University of London (QMUL); Cambridge University; University College London; the University of Edinburgh; the Leverhulme Trust; and the British Academy. I would also like to thank the staff of the many libraries and archives in which I worked—many of which are listed in the bibliography—especially those of the British Library (particularly in Rare Books & Music), the Bibliothèque nationale de France, the National Library of Scotland, and the National Library of Wales. I am also grateful to Christine Fournier d'Albe for hosting me in 2017 and giving me access to her grandfather E. E. Fournier d'Albe's papers—an experience which was a historian's dream.

I have been extremely lucky to have excellent mentors since I was an undergraduate. I did not realise it at the time, but the seed for this project was planted at Durham University in Anthony Parton's lectures (still among the best I have ever heard) on art in the French Third Republic, and especially the weeks focusing on Pont-Aven in Brittany. My notes became part of an essay on Celticism in late nineteenth-century Cornwall with links drawn to Brittany, which I wrote for Paul Readman's popular MA module 'Patriotism and National Identity in Modern Britain' at King's College London. This interest in Celticism was translated into another essay on the subject in 1880s Scotland, which became the basis of my MA thesis supervised by Paul, which in turn developed into my first article. Expanding my focus to the other Celtic nations, I was fortunate that Heather Jones and John Hutchinson agreed to supervise the doctoral thesis that I envisaged on Pan-Celticism at the LSE—this ultimately morphed (and greatly expanded) into this book. In addition to providing valued support and feedback, Heather and John allowed me a great deal of intellectual freedom. Joep Leerssen and Ian McBride have both been generous supporters since they examined the PhD thesis in 2017.

Since then, this book and my work more generally have benefitted from many colleagues. In addition to those at the LSE already mentioned, I would also like to thank Tim Hochstrasser, Paul Keenan, and Paul Stock, all of whom read parts of the early work. Similarly, at QMUL I am particularly grateful to Andrew Fitzmaurice, Colin Jones, Andrew Mendelsohn, Miri Rubin, Rob Saunders, Gareth Stedman Jones, and Georgios Varouxakis, who read drafts of the work at various stages or offered advice.

Discussions with historians of adjacent subjects have helped me to build up larger contexts and arguments. Among them are Agnes Arnold-Forster, Oliver Carter-Wakefield, Alessandro D'Arcangelis, Sarah Dunstan, Joshua Ehrlich, Margot Finn, Laura Forster, Adela Halo, Colin Kidd (whose chapter 'Constructing the Pre-Romantic Celt' I have read probably two-dozen times—

its insights permeate Part I of this book), Paul Kurtz, Avi Lifschitz, Hélène Maloigne, Robin Mills, Tuva Nodeland, Jessica Patterson, Mark Philp, Tom Pye, Michael Rupp, Silvia Sebastiani, Floris Solleveld, Martin Spychal, Martha Vandrei, Brian Wallace, Matthew White, and all the members of Paul Readman's Modern British History Reading Group at King's College London.

Celtic studies is an idiosyncratic field, but a beguiling and exceptionally rigorous one where real scholarship is still highly valued. I have learned so much from conversations and correspondence with Mary-Ann Constantine, Rhys Kaminski-Jones, John Koch, Patrick Sims-Williams (who also supplied a generous selection of offprints), and Mark Williams, among others. Alderik Blom has been a source not only of enlightening and entertaining conversation but also of offprints and some hard-to-get publications.

I am grateful to all of my friends who have shown interest—real or feigned—in my work for a long time now. Special thanks to Tom Agnew, Ted Arnold, Amadea Bentheim, Pete Duff, Ben du Feu, Michael Harrison, Michael Horrocks, Lara Hughes, Pete Hughes, Sam Johnston, Yu-Michael Kato, Jim Kitchen, Keaton Lora, Phoebe Luckhurst, Tom Miller, Simon Prosser, Sean and Amber Sarafilovic, Lukas Schmitz, SCP, Cara Southworth, Pete Stephens, Alice Stiles, Thatcher Svekis, Katy Tencor, Ruth Turvey, Matthew Wright, the B-Team Social, and many others I haven't mentioned here. Sam Ritchie and Nic Hargreaves have always been engaged listeners and generous hosts. Some of my earliest ideas on this subject were formed while driving across the Continent with the Davies-Tsagkadakis family, exploring Europe ancient and modern.

There are several people without whom this book would not exist. Most obviously, Ben Tate at Princeton University Press met the idea behind it with great enthusiasm. It has been a pleasure to work with him and the rest of the team at the press, including the anonymous readers they recruited at various stages, who all offered helpful suggestions. Christian Melby is my greatest intellectual comrade. We coaxed each other into academia, and I want to thank him for his patience, his sense of humour, and his great friendship. Max Skjönsberg has always been encouraging and helped introduce me to the history of ideas—he has been a great guide to the field of the history of political thought, in particular. For their camaraderie and healthy cynicism about all aspects of the academic world, I am grateful to Anne Irfan and Alex Mayhew. Toon Van Hal introduced me to the exciting field of the history of linguistics and has helped me with many things in this arena since I was a first-year PhD student. John Considine has also been a generous guide and read several early chapter drafts. Margaret Crump has been a friendly and invaluable source of knowledge on all things James Cowles Prichard. Roy Foster has supported this book and its author from an early stage, and I am proud to call him a friend. My greatest thanks in the academic sphere I owe to Paul Readman, who changed my life. I hope he will forgive this cliché, because the counterfactual would have been worse.

Because this might be the most public forum in which I ever get to do so, I would like to thank those who early on encouraged me to study history: J. B. and Sandy Stewart, Margaret Hiple, Lee and Teresa Harrison, Peter de Manio, Tramm Hudson, and Marina Keegan. Scott Wolfinger let me subject the rest of my eighth-grade U.S. history class to my first lecture (a global history of World War II). My work is now far away from the subjects that we bonded over, but our shared enthusiasm for history is the same as it ever was.

No one shares this interest more than the Ghosh family. Helen, Peter, and William have all in different ways helped this book finally come to fruition. Olivia, who has also assisted with points of French and German translation, has been endlessly patient and supportive. I have talked through many ideas with her, and she has usually at least pretended to find them interesting. I couldn't ask for more.

I owe the most to my parents, Leslyn and Bill Stewart. I would not be who and what I am without their unwavering support. Trying to here put into words the depth of my gratitude has been more challenging than writing anything else in this book, which I dedicate to them with love.

A NOTE ON THE TEXT

I HAVE TRANSLATED from all foreign languages directly into English. My translations are very literal, and I have occasionally provided tricky passages in the original in endnotes.

Dates before 1752 have been adjusted to New Style (1 January signalling the start of the new year instead of 25 March).

Readers may assume that, unless a specific work is cited, I have drawn biographical information from the *Oxford Dictionary of National Biography*, the *Dictionary of Irish Biography*, and the *Dictionary of Welsh Biography*. I have also frequently consulted John T. Koch's *Celtic Culture: A Historical Encyclopedia* (5 vols., Santa Barbara, CA, 2006). I have often used Wikipedia but always verified the information contained there.

A NOTE ON THE CELTIC LANGUAGES

THE **CELTIC LANGUAGE FAMILY** is a branch of the Indo-European language family, and it is broken into two mutually unintelligible groups. The **Brittonic** group is comprised of Welsh, Breton, and Cornish.[1] The **Goidelic** group is comprised of Irish, Scottish, and Manx Gaelic. **Continental Celtic** refers to extinct languages once spoken by the ancient Gauls, Celtiberians, Galatians, and whoever the Lepontic people were. These all descend from a common source, usually called 'Proto-Celtic', though this may have never existed. It is unattested in writing but has been reconstructed through the techniques of modern historical and comparative linguistics.

ABBREVIATIONS

BGE	Bibliothèque de Genève
BL	British Library
BNF	Bibliothèque nationale de France
BSAP	*Bulletins de la société d'anthropologie de Paris*
CMCS	*Cambrian Medieval Celtic Studies*
CUL	Cambridge University Library
EHR	*English Historical Review*
EMLO	*Early Modern Letters Online*
EUL	Edinburgh University Library
IHS	*Irish Historical Studies*
JHI	*Journal of the History of Ideas*
JMH	*Journal of Modern History*
NLI	National Library of Ireland
NLS	National Library of Scotland
NLW	National Library of Wales
OED	Oxford English Dictionary
P&P	*Past & Present*
RIA	Royal Irish Academy
SHR	*Scottish Historical Review*
THSC	*Transactions of the Honourable Society of Cymmrodorion*
TRHS	*Transactions of the Royal Historical Society*
UCD	University College Dublin
ZCP	*Zeitschrift für celtische Philologie*

THE CELTS

Introduction

IN THE SUMMER OF 1898 the Welsh National *Eisteddfod* was held in the picturesque slate-mining town of Blaenau Ffestiniog in northern Wales. There on 20 July a map was published and circulated depicting the very northwestern corner of Europe, including most of Britain, all of Ireland, the Isle of Man, and Brittany (Fig. 1). A note at the top reads 'Map of the Celtic Countries, showing the distribution of the living Celtic languages', and areas are shaded according to the concentration of individuals speaking a Celtic language.[1] Boldly titled 'Celtia', the map pays little attention to the contemporary borders of the United Kingdom—England is not even labelled—instead delineating an imagined community consisting solely of the 'Celtic countries'. Few probably would have suspected that the cartographer was an Englishman, a physicist named Edmund Edward Fournier d'Albe (1868–1933), who at the dawn of the twentieth century led the international Pan-Celtic nationalist movement. Fournier founded the Dublin-based group, named the Celtic Association, and edited its journal, also titled *Celtia*, which began appearing from 1 January 1901. The map appeared on the inside front cover to remind its readers of the future for which they were striving. This vision of 'Celtia' was the amalgamation of a number of ideas—some ancient, some modern—whose origins, interactions, and consequences it is this book's purpose to examine and understand. It accounts for how and why these places and peoples came to be called Celtic, why that mattered then, and why this idea is still meaningful today.

The 'Celts' and all things 'Celtic' are of perennial interest in both academic and popular culture.[2] This is despite the fact that there is only a hazy understanding of the peoples called Celts in antiquity, and that there is considerable disagreement over whether the modern Celtic nations—Ireland, Scotland, Wales, Brittany, the Isle of Man, and Cornwall—and their cultures bear any direct relation to their purported ancient forebears. Popular authors like to

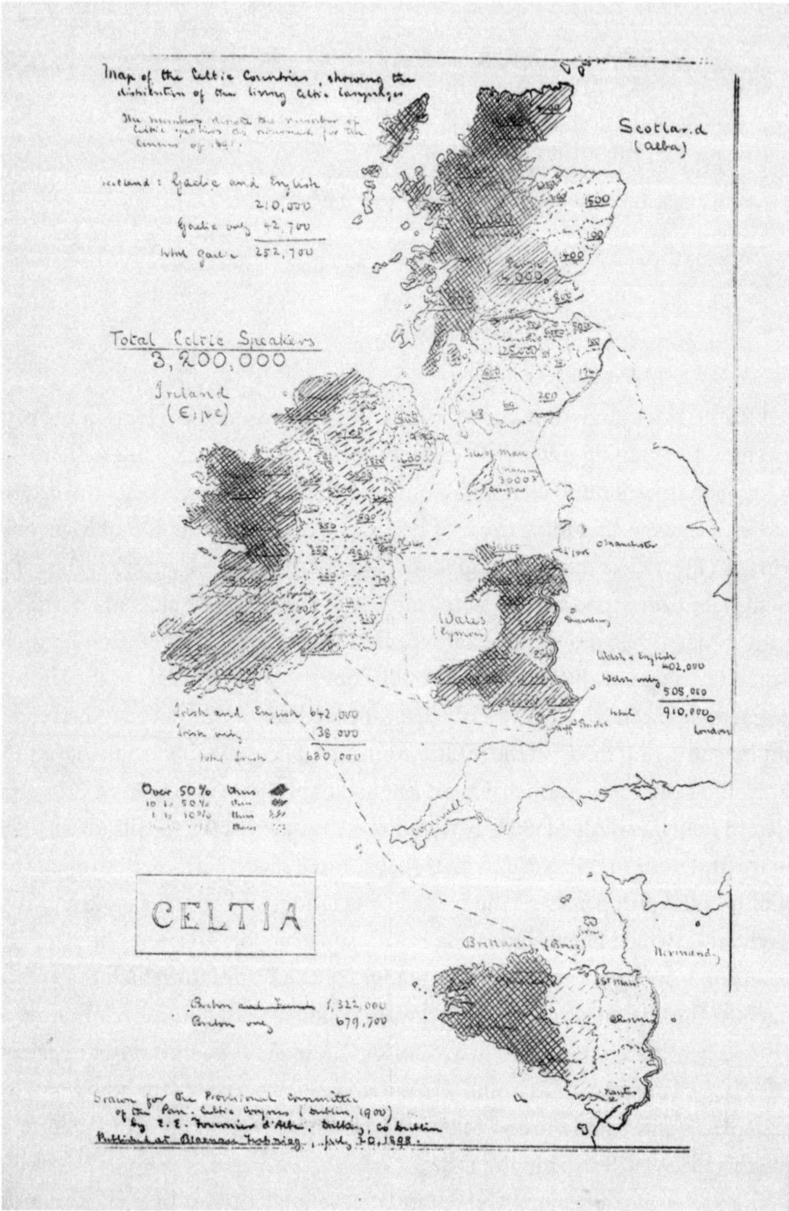

FIG. 1. 'Celtia', National Library of Wales, Sir John Rhys Papers, A4/10, Box 99, folder: Maps. By permission of Llyfrgell Genedlaethol Cymru/The National Library of Wales.

suggest that the Celts are a lost people we might 'discover' if we resolutely 'search' for them, but if books published in English are anything to go by then we probably do not need to look very hard.[3] Arguably, we know more about the Celts now than ever before. Nearly every year scholarly books based on the latest scientific research in linguistics, archaeology, and genetics are published;[4] popular studies of Celtic mythology and art appear just as frequently.[5] A bumper year was 2015, when a major exhibition titled *The Celts: Art and Identity* opened at the British Museum (and then in 2016 at the National Museum of Scotland), and during which the BBC aired a television series called *The Celts: Blood, Iron, and Sacrifice*.[6] France, as the territory of ancient Celtic Gaul yet also the medieval kingdom of the Germanic Franks, has had an ambivalent relationship with Celtic subjects, yet there appear seemingly every year new books in French playing upon the idea of the Celts.[7] The classic two-volume work by Henri Hubert (1872–1927), *Les Celtes* (1932), remains in print almost a century after its first publication; however, this might have more than a little to do with the fact that it was edited and introduced by Hubert's more famous collaborator Marcel Mauss (1872–1950), and that they were both disciples of the founding father of French sociology, Émile Durkheim (1858–1917). Probably better known than all three of them combined are the comics of *Astérix le Gaulois*.

The Celts also have a broader European popularity, as reflected in a range of exhibitions and publications on art and antiquity, sometimes with more than a hint for European unity embedded in them. The largest of these—*I Celti: La prima Europa*—took place in Venice in 1991, in the run-up to the Maastricht Treaty that forged the European Union in 1992.[8] *Keltenmuseums* are dotted around the alpine regions of Germany, Austria, and Switzerland, while Germanic scholars have been responsible for some of the most scrupulous studies on the Celts and their languages.[9] In Spain, Celtic interest stretches from the academy—and a strong archaeological focus[10]—to popular culture, especially in Galicia, where *Celta de Vigo* are a solid mid-table football team in *La Liga*. The question of whether Galicia—whose Celtic language died out in the Middle Ages—still qualifies as a Celtic 'nation' has recently been a contentious subject within activist Celtic circles,[11] and a novel academic theory posits Iberia as the place where the Celtic language family might have been born.[12] There are also transatlantic dimensions to the Celtic idea, linked particularly to the Irish and Scottish diasporas and the North American obsession with heritage.[13] American Celticism is often presented with a New Age spiritual twist, but it would be difficult to think of many things further from this affected mysticism than the Boston Celtics, a storied and sometimes gritty franchise in the National Basketball Association, named for the city's large Irish population. Therefore, if not quite all things to all people, the idea of the Celts is a highly changeable one with international resonance; but, as the historian Joep Leerssen has pointed out, it is probably the very ambiguity related to things Celtic that has allowed the idea to take so many forms and achieve such popularity.[14]

One thing seems clear: despite widespread interest in the various understandings of the Celts, attention remains concentrated on the ancient Celts. There has been comparatively little interrogation of how and why the Celts became known as such during the modern era. What is the link that binds those who called themselves Celts in ancient Europe to those who now claim Celtic heritage? Most of the many overviews of the ancient Celts will contain a chapter or two dedicated to the ways in which ideas of the Celts inspired modern literary, religious, and cultural developments, and became foundational components of modern national identities in Britain, Ireland, and France.[15] But these are usually highly impressionistic, and a sustained focus on the modern period is rarer.[16] This book, on the other hand, takes the modern manifestations of Celtic ideas as its central focus. It shows how, from about the sixteenth century, the Celts became one of the most popular ancestral groups across Europe. Over the next few centuries scholars from most European nations claimed Celtic ancestry for their peoples at one point or another and fought in the Republic of Letters over the claim to the purest Celtic provenance. The Celts featured in the great intellectual shifts that resulted from movements like the Renaissance and the Enlightenment, and in political upheavals like the French Revolution. The nineteenth-century onset of nationalism and racialism invested ancestral origins with even more weight and found an important place for the Celts in the developing identities of different European nations. Yet, by the middle of the nineteenth century, the Celts had to a large degree been intellectually and physically relegated to the 'fringes' of Western Europe, as apparent victims of political impotence and racial prejudice.[17] If the idea of the Celts and who could claim to be one became clearer, the power of that idea had dramatically weakened and has arguably been in decline ever since, despite twentieth-century events like the Irish Revolution, and the rise of separatist nationalisms in Scotland, Wales, Brittany, and even Cornwall. But the idea of the Celts has proved remarkably resilient and it is perhaps the lack of a certain kind of political import behind it that ironically allowed the Celts to weather the twentieth century: if one can still proudly and publicly identify as a Celt, the same cannot be said for the Anglo-Saxons, Teutons, or Aryans. Though E. E. Fournier d'Albe's imagined Pan-Celtic polity never came to pass, his Celtic Association and its emphasis on language learning and shared culture remain the model for groups in the Celtic imagined community to this day.

Questions and Constructions

Who were the Celts? This seemingly innocuous question has actually been ideologically fraught for centuries. Running from the speculative ethnography of classical antiquity, through early modern *Celtomanie*, the nineteenth-century *Keltenfrage*, and today's 'Celtoscepticism', it remains a touchy subject. Helping to account for the tension that has characterised attempts to correctly identify the Celts are a number of related issues wrapped up in that question: Where did the Celts come from, who were they related to, what languages did they speak, what was their culture like, how was their society organised, and, perhaps most importantly, where are they now? These questions were certainly posed in antiquity, especially during the millennium stretching from roughly 500 BCE to 500 CE, but then they seem to have mostly disappeared from the textual record until the Renaissance, when scholars began to ask them again with renewed vigour. For the answers now came loaded with implications for early modern peoples and their institutions. Early modern thinkers were especially concerned with the extent to which nations preserved the virtues and vices of their ancestors, but the arrival of racial theory toward the end of the eighteenth century led to the overarching nineteenth-century question: Who *are* the Celts? Underpinning this shift to the present tense were several new questions: Did modern national characters preserve the unique moral qualities of ancient races, and if they did, then what were the political and cultural consequences for European states with Celtic populations? Who could claim to be a Celt? If the Celts had once formed an ancient European polity or even an empire, could they do so again?

These are the questions this book addresses. They have been asked and answered in many ways at different times and places, but the root question, 'Who were the Celts?', has remained constant.[18] As far as the ancient Celts go, we have textual, linguistic, and material evidence, and their centrality has remained stable over the last five hundred years, though methods have evolved, disciplines have become specialised, and there has been considerable dispute over whether evidence from one discipline should be cross-borrowed into another.[19] Textual evidence—in the form of observations recorded in writing by classical authors—formed the first layer of available information, but it was subject to charges of hearsay and so needed to be corroborated with more neutral sources like linguistic evidence—both in the form of written samples and the spoken Celtic languages—and the evidence of physical remains. These approaches prevailed throughout the early modern era, before major progress in the quest for Celtic origins seemed to have been made with the professionalization of history, linguistics, archaeology, anthropology, and other related disciplines in the nineteenth century. Archaeology—grafted onto linguistic models—dominated the field for most of the next century, before its explanations were cast into doubt in the 1980s. After a period of impasse, the revolution in the sequencing of ancient DNA over the last decade or so seems poised to break the deadlock between linguistics and archaeology and reshape things again.[20] However, because of the limited nature of the evidence, a definitive answer to the question 'Who were the Celts?' has never been given and probably never will be. As a result, scholars have had to either reduce the scope of their claims or rely on a potentially hazardous level of conjecture. For these reasons the Celts are, and have always been, constructions.[21] Especially in the modern era, the Celtic picture is held together by much interpretative glue. This is neither to say that the Celts are simply invented or imagined, nor that they are primarily the product of an identitarian centre's need for a peripheral other.[22] Rather, it is to claim that the images of those peoples and cultures that have been called 'Celtic' are the result of more than two-and-a-half millennia's worth of negotiation in different places and cultures, with various kinds of evidence.

Dedicated to examining that process is the field of Celtic studies, a sophisticated multidisciplinary venture with a focus that stretches from prehistory to the present. Emerging in the nineteenth century, 'Celtology' sought to attain a scientific understanding of the Celts and drew in scholars from across Europe, especially Germany and France, as well as Britain, Ireland, and the United States, in order to write the history of the Celtic peoples. That history begins about halfway through the first millennium BCE, when peoples called Celts (κελτοι/Keltoi/Celtae and Γαλάται/Galatae/Galli) inhabited a considerable portion of the European continent, and therefore also occupied a prominent place in the mental maps of classical Greece and Rome.[23] Yet the Celts are elusive. Because they lacked their own literate cultures until the early medieval period, we depend almost completely on classical sources for textual evidence of who the ancient Celts were, where they lived, and what they were like. Those accounts are often vague at best and contradictory at worst. For example, the two most significant Roman ethnographies of Northern Europe—the *Commentarii de bello gallico* of Julius Caesar (100 BCE-44 BCE) and the *Germania* by Cornelius Tacitus (c. 56–c. 120 CE)—both allude to the relationships between the Gauls (part of whose territory was called 'Celtica') and the Britons and Germans, but leave their ethnic affiliations undetermined. A millennium and a half later that grey area would lead to acrimonious disputes—particularly between French and German scholars—and, a few centuries after that, those classical accounts would provide many of the negative stereotypes employed at the height of Franco-German nationalist antagonism.[24] This scholarly quarrel, which began in the sixteenth century and ran for over four hundred years (!), revolved primarily around language, and whether ancient Gaulish or ancient German had been spoken by the Celts. Language—preserved in place names, personal names, recorded ancient words, and in the surviving Celtic tongues—formed the main pillar of investigation into the identity of the ancient Celts for most of this period. Yet just as the linguistic debate was finally settling in the 1850s, the rapidly professionalising field of archaeology seemed to offer a new key to unlocking the mystery of Celtic origins once and for all. After some remarkable discoveries, a consensus emerged that the fount of the European Celtic civilization had been in the centre of Europe, specifically in present day Hallstatt (in Austria) and La Tène (in Switzerland), rather than anywhere else in the arc running from Ireland to India that had been proposed over the preceding centuries.[25]

After holding the field for more than a century, that consensus has been eroded over the last four decades by scholars whose position has been named 'Celtoscepticism', a term borrowed into English by Patrick Sims-Williams.[26] This may be summed up as follows: the Celts were widely mentioned in classical sources, but so vaguely and inconsistently that it becomes difficult to say much more than that they referred to peoples—often the barbarous foil to the civilized Greeks and Romans—in west and central Europe. Driven by the archaeologist John Collis since the 1980s, this position points to larger problems with the cultural mode of archaeology that rose to prominence in the nineteenth century and assumed that material remains could be straightforwardly aligned with particular cultures based on a shared style. In the Celtic case the most glaring incongruity was that, even though no ancient sources survive that refer to the inhabitants of Britain and Ireland as Celts, nineteenth-century scholars uncritically adopted the assertions of some earlier thinkers—particularly the Scottish humanist George Buchanan (1506–1582) and the

Welsh antiquary Edward Lhwyd (1660–1709)—that, based on historical and linguistic evidence, these peoples were Celtic. The Celtosceptic critique turned on questions of methodology, but in the mid-1990s it caused a heated exchange in the journal *Antiquity*, in which defenders of the traditional interpretation accused Collis and his followers of being motivated by a latent English nationalism.[27] Linguists, perhaps more acutely attuned to the dangers of casually linking languages and material cultures to particular ethnic groups because of an awareness of the wild excesses of their predecessors—one variant of which was labelled 'Celtomania' and held that the Celts spoke the earliest human language from which all others descended—also noted the problems of aligning the linguistic and archaeological records. The meticulous Celticist Patrick Sims-Williams has been the most important voice urging restraint in this respect, but the critique has roots stretching back to the nineteenth century; however, Sims-Williams cautiously links some of the textual evidence to linguistic remains, especially place names, and suggests we can carefully refer to an ancient Celtic linguistic culture in parts of west and central Europe.[28]

At the same time as ideas of ancient Celtic identity were beginning to be picked apart by archaeologists and philologists in the 1980s and 1990s, modern ideas of the Celts came into focus with the critical study of nations and nationalisms. As part of a general examination of the phenomenon of nationalism, individual national identities and their supposed ethnic and cultural bases came under scrutiny. Naturally, the 'Celtic nations' were placed under the microscope, and with them the very idea of the Celts and whether a Celtic identity had ever existed. The main early catalyst was Hugh Trevor-Roper's (1914–2003) stimulating, if mean-spirited, 1983 essay on the invention of Highland traditions, in which he argued that Scotland's identity as a nation whose traditions stemmed from the Celtic Highlands was predicated on a series of recent and, cruelly, English fabrications.[29] Trevor-Roper was warned by the classicist Nan Dunbar (1928–2005) against using 'Celtic' and 'Saxon' to delineate the Highlands and Lowlands, and against using the word 'Scotch', but he did so anyway, clearly enjoying trolling proud Scots.[30] Some Celtosceptic archaeologists and anthropologists followed Trevor-Roper's lead in the 1990s, seemingly exposing the apparent modern manufacture of the entire Celtic tradition. In 1999 the controversy reached its height with Simon James's *The Atlantic Celts: Ancient People or Modern Invention?*, a flawed work relying on a crude reading of the 'invention of tradition' thesis and seeking to introduce the Celtosceptic debate to the public with provocative rhetorical questions implying that 'the Ancient Celts of Britain and Ireland are an essentially bogus recent invention', which made waves in newspapers and predictably met with approval in places like the *Daily Telegraph*.[31]

However, the work of most lasting significance in this vein is Malcolm Chapman's wide-ranging *The Celts: The Construction of a Myth* (1992), which argued that the only point of real continuity running from the ancient to the modern Celts was that they were peripheral cultures effectively othered by a dominant metropolitan core.[32] Of concern to many was that Chapman's model eliminated Celtic agency, but as Patrick Sims-Williams suggested several years before his book appeared, impressions of the Celtic countries have often been made with the help of individuals from those places, who may have had something to gain from their role as intermediaries.[33] This mediated vision extends back to the classical accounts of the Celtic peoples in Britain which, as Francesca and Rhys Kaminski-Jones and their collaborators have shown, tied together the classical and Celtic worlds from that point forward.[34] It was the Celtic presence in Greek and Roman sources that allowed them to reemerge in the European imagination during the Renaissance, when these texts were rediscovered, published, and widely disseminated and studied. From that point forward, anyone moderately well-educated would have likely encountered the Celts many times over in their reading. But, with the eighteenth-century interest in vernacular poetry, many modern readers were for the first time presented with material translated from the Celtic languages, the one indisputable link between the ancient peoples called Celts and those modern cultures that have wished to claim their inheritance.

For all the flaws with his centre-periphery model, Chapman made the first extended attempt to deal with the creation of the Celts in the modern period. It was clear by this time that the Celts were to some extent a construction, but also that this was the case for all ancient peoples given conceptual cohesion by Greek and Roman works, like the classic Celtic foil the *Germani*. Recognition of these wider patterns helped to weaken the purchase of the value judgments that had accompanied historical criticism, and scholars turned to the much more interesting question of the ways in which the Celts had been reimagined in modern European culture.[35] This constructive approach became enshrined in a landmark volume, *Celticism* (1996), in which Joep Leerssen named the enterprise and defined it: Celticism is 'not the study of "the" Celts and their history, but rather the study of their reputation and of the meanings and connotations ascribed to the term "Celtic"'.[36] This book is a study of Celticism from the early modern era to the present. I am interested in what people meant by the terms 'Celt' and 'Celtic', why they wanted them to mean what they did, and how those ideas changed over time as the result of negotiation in all manner of texts, traditions, and wider cultural and intellectual movements.

To summarise, Celtic studies has shifted focus over the last several decades as the idea of the Celts as a monolithic ancient people with an obvious territory and clear national descendants has fractured and given way to a more granular examination of the component parts of the Celtic image. Historical criticism in this respect has moved from a rigid deconstructionism to a more sympathetic appreciation of the ways that those ideas and images were constructed over time. Because the ancient Celts lacked extensive documentation, imagination stepped in to fill the void. Studying the vivid ways that humans imagined the past—for whatever purpose—tells us far more about the patterns of historical thought, memory, and identity over the last several centuries than does determining whether particular texts and traditions are true or false. Moreover, doing so does nothing to damage the ancient Celts or modern Celtic traditions. As a result of recent archaeological and philological criticism, the Celts are in now flux. And as this book shows, this has always been the case.

Key Ideas: Nations and Nationalism, Race and Racialism

Although some Celtosceptics point to the obvious modern construction of the Celts as the smoking gun that makes their case, the notion that the Celts have to some extent always been a construction would not have been much of a surprise to the founding fathers and mothers of Celtic studies, who were only too aware of the patchy evidential record. Yet what began as an intradisciplinary methodological dispute spilled into the popular press and was reduced to the crude (and wrong) idea that Celtoscepticism is a denial that the Celts ever existed, a mischaracterisation that now seems to generate more headlines than anything else about the Celts.[37] For the historian of the modern period, however, the greatest problem with the Celtosceptic discussion is that it presents Celticism as the sterile product of academic debates and scholarly paradigm shifts that are mostly methodological in character. Overlooked are the wider ideological movements coursing through the public sphere over the last several centuries, especially nationalism—arguably the most powerful political force unleashed in modern times—and racialism, an idea just as pervasive and maybe more damaging. The ubiquity of these two gargantuan forces meant that many of their assumptions were baked into the hardening dough of the professionalising academic disciplines in nineteenth-century Europe, including Celtic studies. As will be seen throughout this book, the barrier between scholarly and public understandings of the Celts has been extremely porous, but there has normally been a casual assumption by Celticists that ideas flow one way: from scholarship into the public sphere. This book, on the other hand, takes popular attitudes and ideas as seriously as it does the academic debates.[38] Figures like Ernest Renan (1823–1892), Matthew Arnold (1822–1888), Douglas Hyde (1860–1949), and in his own way W. B. Yeats (1865–1939)—four thinkers who, among other men and women, disproportionately shaped the modern image of the Celts—all straddled the line between private scholar and public moralist. Their work was suffused with racial theory, which obviously shaped their conceptions of the Celts. Accordingly, it is one of my central arguments in this book that it was neither the professionalisation of archaeology nor even of Celtic studies itself that was the most important development in the history of Celticism, but the onset of national thought and race theory. The extent to which these shaped scholarly and public understandings of the Celts remains largely unrealised.[39]

The evolution and fluctuations of these two ideas—nation and race—are kept firmly in view throughout this book.[40] At the risk of extreme oversimplification, we might think of 'nation' as having two broad meanings here; both are 'imagined communities' but are based on different constituent elements.[41] The first sense used here is the natural understanding of nation: nations are seen as kinship groups held together by language, culture, and the supposition of a common descent. Celtic ideas featured quite heavily in early modern European discussions about nations, but their influence was indirect because no one called themselves 'Celts' and there was no 'Celtic' nation. Instead, the Celts were seen as prestigious ancestors whose legacy was up for grabs if it could be proven that a modern nation descended from them. To assert Celtic lineage was to make a political claim to be descended from one of the earliest known European peoples whose conquests had stretched from Ireland to Anatolia. Establishing these claims required the tools of scholarship: textual philology, linguistic comparison, the study of physical remains (archaeology), and the collection of supposed remnants of Celtic culture (folklore). These are the subjects of Part I, in which we will see how the vague picture of the Celts left by the ancients became sharper through developing scholarly techniques and the argumentative force of political necessity.

The Celts acquired more importance over the course of the eighteenth century as the second, political, sense of the nation strengthened: nations, it was argued, are entitled to certain rights and to independently pursue their own destinies. Although national thought had flourished since the Renaissance, and although nation-builders gathered their materials together from a past that stretched from their own age back into antiquity,[42] it was only really during the eighteenth century that the nation changed 'from a fact of nature to a product of political will',[43] in step with the rise of social contract theory, the idea of popular sovereignty, an accompanying rehabilitation of democracy, and other developments in the history of political thought, as well as the rise of the middle classes and the expansion of the 'public sphere' in the form of a burgeoning press and rising literacy rates.[44] The issue of national sovereignty (where did it reside?) was the overriding concern during the first phase of the French Revolution in the summer of 1789; as will be seen in chapter 5, the ultimate resolution to this question as the Third Estate, or '*le peuple*', as *la nation*, had dramatically positive consequences for Celtic ideas in France.[45] In Ireland too, this period saw significant Protestant interest in Ireland's Celtic past for the first time, as that island's political claims grew louder and a neutral, idealised ancestor was needed in order to circumvent religious sectarianism.

The onset of nationalism during this period—which we might understand variously as the pursuit of sovereignty or self-determination for a particular nationality, the advancement of interests of one nation *vis-à-vis* others in the international nation-state system, or a chauvinistic belief that a particular nation (almost always one's own) was intrinsically superior to all others[46]—also saw the Celts firmly established as a foundational element of national identity in three out of the 'four nations' that made up the United Kingdom following the Act of Union of Great Britain and Ireland in 1800.[47] They also won out as the predominant national ancestor of the French in the early nineteenth century. This story of the rise of modern national identities over the course of the eighteenth and nineteenth centuries is essential to the history of Celticism.[48] But it is far from straightforward. Although early moderns might have had a sense of their *gens*, or even a linguistic identity, 'national identity' in our terms would probably have made little sense to them.[49] As Colin Kidd has argued, they were much more concerned with religious, dynastic, and social (class) identities than they were with 'national' identities—the 'nation' had not yet become a salient consideration in European politics. Once this occurred, national identities were compounds that varied based on their constituent elements, of which ethnic ancestry was only one, and they reacted differently to other national identities composed of separate elements. For example, while Ireland's Catholicism was its standout feature, tension between

Scotland and England also came more from the religious sphere than those of ethnicity or culture; not only did Scots play a leading role in the British Empire, but the predominant ethnic identity in the nineteenth-century Lowlands was Germanic, which meant that Lowlanders felt entitled to share in the glory of the Gothic ancient constitution of England.[50] The dynamics of international politics also mattered more for some nations than for others. Whereas the English and, eventually, the British seem to have by and large considered themselves locked in eternal combat with the French—famously analysed in Linda Colley's *Britons* (1992), which argued that Anglo-French conflict helped to forge a modern British identity at the end of the eighteenth century—the French seem to have been more preoccupied with their relationship to Germany and to Rome.[51] The idiosyncratic trajectory of French Celticism stands out, because it is the only case in which the Celts—usually but not necessarily equated with the Gauls—became embraced by a state, until they were elevated by Ireland in the twentieth century.[52] This included a process catalysed by the Franco-Prussian War by which French republican nationalism, up until this point predominantly left-wing, folded in the right-wing, a development largely complete by the 1890s and crystallised in the Dreyfus Affair.

Reflecting and reinforcing the sense of distinct national identities are the disparate historiographies of the nations under consideration here. As is well recognised, history writing has been more intimately related to nation-building than perhaps any other intellectual pursuit, and even though historians have discarded many of the assumptions that prevailed when their discipline professionalised in the nineteenth century, most still investigate the history of a particular 'nation', a focus often called 'methodological nationalism'. The result is a set of strikingly different historiographies with different interests, moving at different rhythms. The 'national question' has been an important subject in the historiography of each of the Celtic nations, but it has a different character in each of them. Studies cutting across the boundaries of the Celtic nations have, in part because of this, been rare, and pulling these strands together has been one of the main challenges of writing this book.[53]

Race is the other idea that transformed perceptions of the Celts in nineteenth-century Europe. For most of the early modern period it meant something like common descent or lineage, and Samuel Johnson (1709–1784) noted that it could be used to describe families of humans, animals, or plants, among other things.[54] However, over the course of the eighteenth century a discursive shift took place wherein 'race' gradually came to preponderate as the term of choice for denoting a distinct, *natural* human population classifiable by physical features that (usually) accorded with geographical position. The crucial move in the transition to racialism that occurred in the decades around 1800 was the increasing alignment of external features with inner qualities, of physical appearance with moral character and intelligence; whereas these things were previously thought to be mutable and produced by climate and prevailing institutions, the new racialism often held them to be immutable products of nature. It was assumed that when members of the same race reproduced, both their physical and moral characteristics survived in their offspring.[55] Although 'race' had similarly benign beginnings to 'nation' and was often interchangeable with it, it had much more dramatic consequences for ideas of the Celts, who began to be treated as a distinct population *naturally* different from the Germanic nations next to whom they lived. For the Celts, this meant that a particular set of qualities—like sensitivity to nature and emotional volatility—was thought to correspond with particular face shapes, skull forms, stature, and hair and eye colouring. These biological qualities made up the Celtic race out of which the Celtic nations and their particular characters and institutions had grown. According to the logic of nineteenth-century racialism, because of their natural racial character the Celtic nations had to be governed differently from other populations, and they were frequently portrayed as needing to be civilized by the Anglo-Saxons. So by 'racialism', I mean the idea that humanity is divided into populations distinct by virtue of natural differences, which often entailed separate political treatment. However, it must be noted that nation and race remained interchangeable in many cases throughout the nineteenth century, and it is therefore often necessary to outline the position of a particular thinker. In Parts II and III of this book, we will see how these conceptions played out in scientific and political debates over the course of the nineteenth century.

Empire is not an immediate context for this book, but as the term 'Celticism' suggests, post-colonial criticism accompanying the 'cultural turn' in the humanities and social sciences—probably associated above all with Edward Said's *Orientalism* (1978)—strongly influenced the study of the Celts and the Celtic nations in the 1980s and 1990s.[56] The Marxist sociologist Michael Hechter's *Internal Colonialism* (1975) inspired a number of post-colonial treatments of the 'Celtic' nations, which, though they show the ways literature in particular encoded reactions to the creeping British state, have tended to flatten people, ideas, and texts into two-dimensional pieces in the politics of identity formation.[57] Here again the centre-periphery model is visible in studies that depict a fairly rigid dichotomy between England and the Celtic nations, whose identities supposedly developed primarily as a response to English hegemony.[58] Historians and literary scholars have pointed out the many problems with this model and have shown how Celticism was often harnessed in support of British state- and nation-building.[59] Moreover, historians have been alert to a tendency of applying post-colonial models 'to project onto the early modern period racial notions of selfhood and otherness that were not crystallised until much later', in Ian McBride's words, a particularly noticeable anachronism in the case of Celticism.[60] As Parts I and II show, there was no shared sense of Celticity among the different nations of Britain and Ireland until the nineteenth century, and when this developed it was integrally linked to the development of racial theory. As Part III shows, the upshot is that race was an idea also harnessed by activists who felt kinship with their 'Celtic' neighbours, not simply an othering device used by the *Sassenach*. A version of liberal racialism was at the heart of E. E. Fournier d'Albe's Pan-Celtic project, for example. Yet it is essential not to fall into the trap of thinking that Celts shared an innate fellow-feeling, despite Oscar Wilde's (1854–1900) suggestion in 1884 that 'all Celts gravitate towards each other'.[61] Celticism was 'one of the strangest things on *this* earth', according to a Welsh critic of Fournier's project, a sentiment shared by many Irish nationalists of the time, who preferred the vision of an independent Gaelic Ireland to synthetic Pan-Celticism.[62] This book therefore rejects the tendency to equate Ireland with the other Celtic nations on that racial basis, collapsing the varying experiences of people in these different nations.[63] The post-colonial approach has been fruitfully applied to Ireland and has shown how anti-Celtic racial discourse operated in the British-Irish relationship, which became increasingly fraught over the course of the nineteenth century. However, as chapter 8 shows, the other Celtic nations were not subjected to denigration on the same basis, and even Welsh people and Scots who proudly identified as Celtic often viewed the (Catholic) Irish as something other entirely. Trying to place Ireland, its history, and the experience of its peoples in the 'correct' interpretative framework has been an ongoing point of contention, but I think any attempt beyond simple historicism might be futile. The history of Ireland is like a platypus: it has many recognisable features but is something wholly its own. Unlike the platypus, however, Irish history's classification is still undecided.[64] Aspects of this book will help to show that Ireland is nearly always a special case; understanding it requires careful empirical work and not ingenious theorising.

With the ideas and contexts discussed so far in mind, my argument is that appreciating the history of Celticism in all its complexity requires serious attention not only to ideas of and attitudes toward the ancient Celts, but to the history of knowledge and scholarship across early modern and modern Europe, as well as the histories of the scientific and political concepts of nation and race, and the ideologies they spawned. The development of knowledge about the Celts did not proceed insulated from the political imperatives of drawing genealogies in the early modern period, and the nineteenth-century formation of Celtic studies was pursued in a European context saturated with nationalism and racialism. These contexts obviously shaped enquiries into the Celts and their legacies, which varied in their emphases depending on which national or racial context in which an author was writing. At the same time, those who wanted to draw on the conceptual resources of Celticism in the pursuit of political and ideological goals were circumscribed by the available source base and limits of what scholarship would allow. Traditions can be invented and memories manufactured, but it is the factual base produced by scholarship—itself obviously the changing product of multiple variables over time—that determines the coherence of these crucial components of national myth-making.

The Shape of This Book: A New Narrative

Like ancient Gaul, this book is divided into three parts. These reflect the three major intellectual forces that (I believe) shaped modern Celticism: national thought, racial theory, and pan-nationalism. These ideas were part of the wider intellectual currents flowing through European culture over the last several centuries. As they did so they swept the idea of the Celts along with them. Those ideas changed over time as they were adapted to new contexts, and those contexts reshaped the collection of Celtic ideas in kind. Yet the book is essentially ordered chronologically. It provides a history of Celticism from the Renaissance to the present, but the bulk of the text focuses on the eighteenth and nineteenth centuries, when the idea of the Celts crystallised in the context of democratic revolutions, the rise of nation-states, and the global expansion of empires.

Defining the relevant geographical territory is trickier. Rather than any particular nation, my focus is ultimately on ideas: their genesis, circulation, and manifestation in different contexts, as well as their effects on those contexts. Most of this intellectual energy pertained to the ancient and modern inhabitants of the six core Celtic nations: Ireland, Scotland, Wales, Brittany, the Isle of Man, and Cornwall. However, depending on the criteria one chooses, certainly the French and even the English can make Celtic claims, and many have done so. Much of this thinking was done in places like Edinburgh, Dublin, London, Oxford, Cambridge, Paris, and Berlin, often by those who considered themselves Celts, but equally as often by those who wanted nothing to do with them, or others who were neutral. Germany—not itself considered a Celtic country, although this question generated debate for centuries—has made a huge contribution to our understanding of the Celts, and German thinkers will appear frequently throughout these chapters. Early modern Dutch scholars were also very important in the recovery of the Celts from the classical record, and archaeological discoveries in Austria and Switzerland in the middle of the nineteenth century initiated a major shift in the study and understanding of ancient Celtic geography and material culture. Ideas from even further afield are accounted for as they appeared and became woven into modern Celticism, including from India and North America. My approach emphasises movement and the permeability of historical borders, whether linguistic, geographical, political, intellectual, or cultural.

With these geographical and chronological parameters established, the book tells a new story about the Celts, showing how they transformed from a two-dimensional yet prestigious people from Europe's ancient past into a living and breathing, yet marginalised, people living on the continent's western periphery in the European present. This protracted shift, the primary focus of Parts I and II, was the result of intellectual, cultural, and political flux, but the changing idea of the Celts helped to reshape the very contexts in which it was altered. Part III, which focuses on pan-Celticism, shows how individuals and groups then used these ideas to fashion new 'Celtic' cultural and political identities. It would be impossible to give a comprehensive account of an idea so large, protean, and diffuse; my aim therefore has been to present one that is coherent. The result is the new narrative drawn here.

The Celts: A Modern History

As outlined in chapter 1, the Celts were widely recorded in classical sources from about 500 BCE to 500 CE. Depicted as a fearless warrior people, the Celts marauded across Europe and penetrated well into Asia Minor. One Celtic tribe even sacked Rome. Broadly, though, the Celts were associated with the west of Europe, and especially Gaul. Although they did not offer definitive proof, Caesar and Tacitus surmised strong links among the Gauls, the ancient Britons, and the Hibernians. The Celts gradually vanished from the textual record during the early Middle Ages, but a thousand years later they were rediscovered by Renaissance humanists mining the classical sources for ammunition to fire in the inter- and intranational scholarly conflicts that raged across early modern Europe, where new historical origin myths were devised to suit the political and religious needs of the time and place. Generally speaking, the Celts enjoyed great prestige during the early modern period. To claim Celtic lineage was to claim descent from the oldest known inhabitants of Europe, who were fierce warriors ruling large territories, and perhaps even a Europe-wide empire. Scholars from France, the Holy Roman Empire, the Low Countries, England, Wales, and Scotland held views like these over the sixteenth and seventeenth centuries, arguing over which nation was the closest descendant of the ancient Celts, which they would have encountered countless times in the course of reading the classics by Caesar, Tacitus, and many others discussed in the following chapter.

The Celts as we now understand them became more clearly delineated in the period from about 1690 to 1710 through developments in linguistic scholarship, which are examined in chapter 2. Important steps had been made to recover the remnants of the Gaulish language by seventeenth-century scholars, above all by the Dutchman Marc Zuer van Boxhorn (1612–1653), who linked it to modern Welsh, and these attempts were built upon in different ways by the Breton monk Paul-Yves Pezron (1639–1706), the Welsh scholar Edward Lhwyd, and the German polymath Gottfried Wilhelm Leibniz (1646–1716). While Pezron associated the Celts more firmly with Brittany and Wales and the related languages spoken there than anyone previously did, Lhwyd demonstrated that these Brittonic languages were related to the Goidelic languages of Scotland, Ireland, and the Isle of Man. These two language branches—the Brittonic and the Goidelic—together made up the Celtic language family, which strongly suggested that the peoples who spoke these languages in Britain and Ireland were related. As shown for the first time in this book, Leibniz had already speculatively drawn this conclusion, though for separate reasons and by different means, but his suspicion turned to resolution after reading Lhwyd's work. Though Leibniz was particularly influential in the French and German discussions of the Celts, and his contribution to debate in Britain and Ireland should not be underestimated, Pezron and Lhwyd more than any others shaped the parameters within which ideas of the Celts became understood in the eighteenth century and, in Lhwyd's case, beyond.

The Celtic areas of Britain and Ireland thus became firmly established as those nations and regions where English was not spoken. Yet, it was recognised that Celts had once occupied the entirety of Britain and most of Western

Europe. As shown in Chapter 3, there were features of the landscape across England, Wales, Scotland, and Ireland, which antiquarians thought could also be identified with the ancient Celts and especially their priestly class, the Druids. Even though Caesar had noted that Druidical ceremonies took place in oak groves, megalithic monuments like Stonehenge, Avebury, and the many similar structures that could be found around Britain, Ireland, and the French coast became associated with the Druids and their ceremonial practices. Although the English antiquary John Aubrey (1626–1697) was an important seventeenth-century precursor, the key decades in which the early 'archaeological' approach to antiquities flowered and yielded an association of megalithic structures with prehistory and the Celtic Druids were the 1710s and 1720s, and the antiquaries who did the most to achieve this were John Toland (1670–1722) and William Stukeley (1687–1765). Concurrent developments in France, where reconstruction work on Notre-Dame de Paris yielded the famous *Pilier des Nautes* (Pillar of the Boatmen) in 1711, helped scholars to get a better sense of the gods unmentioned in classical sources who were worshipped by the ancient Celts and their Druids across Europe.

The poems of Ossian and the controversy they stirred up are the subjects of chapter 4, for they completely reshaped the debate over the ancient Celts in Britain and Ireland. Their 'translator' and composer James Macpherson (1736–1796) was manipulative, disingenuous, and fraudulent, but he was also fiercely clever, and his poems of Ossian were not only a European literary sensation but an ingenious attempt to rewrite the ancient history of Britain and Europe. For by collecting oral poetry and whatever manuscript sources were available, Macpherson sought to recover historical information available only in Gaelic, which he then combined with frameworks more familiar to his non-Gaelic audience. He intuited Enlightenment ideas of civilization, savagery, and society better than almost anyone and wielded them as weapons to attack rival historical interpretations. His version of Celtic history ignited an antiquarian civil war over national histories in Scotland, England, Wales, and Ireland, and which nation could claim most plausibly to be the true descendants of the ancient Celts and first inhabitants of Britain and Ireland. Ironically, while Ossian sowed historiographical discord in Britain and Ireland, the poems raised the reputation of the ancient Celts to new heights across the European continent.

By the outbreak of the French Revolution in 1789, the background for the events and ideas examined in chapter 5, scholars had access to vital linguistic, archaeological, and literary evidence of Celtic culture that they had not possessed a century earlier. All of this could be drawn upon in the long-running battle over French national origins waged between two scholarly camps, one tracing French national descent from the Germanic Franks, the other arguing for more ancient origins in Celtic Gaul. With the Revolution came the triumph of the Gaulish interpretation, symbolised above all by the Abbé Emmanuel Sieyès's encouragement to the French nobility to return across the Rhine to their 'Franconian Forests'. The importance of the Celtic past attained such heights in the Napoleonic period that a Parisian antiquarian society patronised by the empress named itself the *Académie celtique* and dedicated its efforts to illuminating the Celtic origins not only of the ascendant French nation but of the entirety of Europe. This period also witnessed important breakthroughs for the Celtic past in Ireland, where for the first time Anglo-Irish institutions such as the Royal Irish Academy embraced the ancient Celts for historical, political, and religious reasons. In Wales too, the events of the revolutionary period stimulated attempts by patriotic antiquaries—above all the mad genius Iolo Morganwg (1747–1826)—to claim Wales as the birthplace of ancient Celtic civilization and the original home of Druidism. Iolo forged medieval Welsh poetry and integrated it into a philosophical system supposedly inherited from the Druids, inventing traditions in the process that remain integral to popular Celticism to this day.

Part I thus focuses on the ways in which a convincing picture of the Celts was drawn in the early modern period—primarily through a recovery from the classical record, but also as the result of innovative linguistic, archaeological, mythographical, folkloristic, and historiographical techniques—which could then be drawn on in the vital period of national identity formation during the late eighteenth and early nineteenth centuries. In Part II the narrative moves into the nineteenth century and is underpinned by the inception of the idea of race in European thought. By fundamentally altering the conceptual foundations of nations and their characters—which, depending on the thinker, could be seen as determined partially or entirely as a result of racial composition—this new understanding of people and populations transformed the picture of the Celts.

As examined in detail in chapter 6, one of the main subjects of contention that arose with racial theory was whether the Celtic race belonged to the wider European family or not. Significant developments in the field of comparative philology—the most important discipline for racial classification well into the nineteenth century—showed that most of the European languages, and therefore peoples, were related and descended from a common ancestor. Yet some hostile scholars alleged that the Celts were a separate—and likely inferior—race entirely. However, the English scientist James Cowles Prichard (1786–1848) realised by at least 1813 that the Celtic languages could be classed within the Indo-European language family, though he did not publish definitive proof until 1831. Several years later he was followed by the Genevan Adolphe Pictet (1799–1875) and the German Franz Bopp (1791–1867), who each illuminated new aspects of the historical development of the Celtic languages in support of their Indo-European credentials. However, the most important work of the century, which appeared in 1853, was by a German teacher named Johann Kaspar Zeuß (1806–1856). Basing his scholarship on the oldest known Irish manuscripts—stashed away in the monasteries of central Europe—Zeuß was able to trace the history of the Celtic languages in greater detail than ever before. His scientific study laid the foundation for the academic field of Celtic studies.

At the same time as these impressive linguistic works were being composed, writers were refashioning national identities in large historical and literary works that drew on the latest scientific research. Chapter 7 teases out their political implications. Sometimes these were fairly subtle, as in the case of Scotland, where Walter Scott (1771–1832) promoted reconciliation between Highland Celts and Lowland Saxons as important members of the British nation; or, in the case of Wales, where a few scholars sought to hold their compatriots and national mythologies to increasingly rigorous scientific standards and had no political line to pursue beyond cultural patriotism. However, embracing the Celtic past had dramatic political implications in other places. In politically volatile France, for example, where liberals and republicans looked to the example of their warlike Celtic ancestors the Gauls; and in Ireland, where the nationally minded Young Ireland group embraced the Celts and their laudable qualities in the face of Anglo-Saxon racism during the years of the Great Famine, before their dismal failed rebellion in 1848. In Switzerland, Austria, and Germany, archaeological breakthroughs and the theory of 'Celtic Art' played into the consolidation of national and regional identities, supporting centralisation in some places and federalism in others. Coming at the subject from racial and literary angles, Ernest Renan penned his famous essay 'La poésie des races celtiques' in 1854, which catalysed the study of Celtic literature and contributed to the rise of the pan-Celtic movement.

The question of race is at the heart of chapter 8, which shows how ideas of the Celts were fashioned and deployed in relation to the 'Irish Question' that dominated British politics throughout the nineteenth century. With the racialisation of nations and peoples, new ideas of the Celts were promulgated, both by those who identified as Celts and those who despised and demonised them. If taken to its logical extreme, the idea of race could cut through the Gordian knot of religion, class, and politics—in other words, of history. The question, therefore, is to what extent the idea of the Celtic race was a *causal* explanation of, or an answer to, the Irish Question. The answer is not to any great extent, and to a lesser degree than some have argued. Instead, I show how a range of different thinkers deployed the idea of the Celts as it suited their other arguments, and that although monolithic anti-Celtic racism did exist, it was a minority position. This was almost inevitable after the key decade of the 1860s, when scientists started to argue that all nations were racial hybrids, an idea applied to the literary culture of the Celtic nations by Matthew Arnold in his *On the Study of Celtic Literature* (1867).

With the recovery of the Celts as prestigious national ancestors through a variety of developments in scholarship—the subject of Part I—and the shift in ideas about the Celts that occurred through the rise of racial theory—examined in Part II—the final third of the book is the first thorough and scholarly examination of pan-Celticism.[65] I employ two loose definitions of pan-Celticism.[66] The first (lower-case p) 'pan-Celticism' denotes an informal series of networks, journals, and correspondence, ranging across scholarship, cultural groups, and occasionally politics, that accepts a shared Celtic descent and therefore racial, cultural, and linguistic links among the Celtic nations. Often this kind of pan-Celticism is mobilised in pursuit of common political goals. The second (Upper-Case P) 'Pan-Celticism' denotes the enshrinement of pan-Celticism in a formally organized movement with its own institutions, mobilized in pursuit of stated pan-Celtic cultural and political goals. In other words, pan-Celticism is merely an awareness by 'Celtic' peoples of shared links among them; Pan-Celticism is a self-conscious pan-national movement mobilized to promote and strengthen those links. The goal of Pan-Celticism *is* Pan-Celticism, often envisioned politically in a federation of the Celtic nations, or culturally, as by E. E. Fournier d'Albe in *Celtia*.

The origins of pan-Celticism are traced in chapter 9 to the 1830s and the Celtic *Eisteddfod* of 1838, where the influential Welsh cultural group *Cymdeithas Cymreigyddion y Fenni* hosted a deputation of five Bretons to Abergavenny. Welsh-Breton links remained intact throughout the century and were strengthened by French nationalists, who viewed Brittany as the Celtic spiritual repository of the French nation. Together they hosted a *Congrès celtique international* at St. Brieuc in 1867. The 1838 Abergavenny *Eisteddfod* only involved the Bretons, while the *Congrès celtique* aimed at true pan-Celtic participation but only drew a handful of participants from Wales and Cornwall. Yet both these events transcended their ephemerality and became lodged in the pre-history of the later Pan-Celtic movement.[67] The links among Wales, Brittany, and France were also vital in the emergence of the first Celtic studies journal and the professionalisation of Celtic studies as an academic field, a subject first discussed in chapter 9 and revisited throughout Part III.

National identities in Britain and Ireland also progressively consolidated around Celticism in the last quarter of the nineteenth century, when pan-Celtic ideas became mobilised in order to demand reform from a British parliament dominated by English interests. Chapter 10 examines pan-Celticism within the political framework of land reform across the 'Four Nations', which was intimately linked to nascent nationalist movements. Congresses remained popular forums in which to explore pan-Celticism, but whereas the Cambro-Breton exchanges had been culturally focused, political organising was the main goal of the land-based pan-Celtic movement, culminating in the Pan-Celtic League founded in 1886. The literature on the land question is huge—particularly in the case of Ireland—but while studies have noted the existence and occasional manipulation of Celtic links between nations,[68] these have not as yet been considered within the context of a developing pan-Celticism, which is the purpose of this chapter.

Chapter 11 returns us to E. E. Fournier d'Albe and his Celtic Association, which I consider the first real Pan-Celtic society. The Celtic Association was the first to promote the closer association of all of the Celtic nations as an end in itself, rather than as a booster movement for a particular nationalist group or goal. It sought to create a distinctive Celtic future to be realised in a new Celtic polity: *Celtia*. The Celtic Association organised three congresses—in Dublin, Caernarfon, and Edinburgh—and attracted the (usually brief) involvement of many of the leading cultural figures interested in Celticism. Though it was short-lived, the Celtic Association drew the blueprint for the forms that the twentieth-century Pan-Celtic movement would take, and in which it still exists.

As even this cursory sketch will show, ideas of the Celts have shapeshifted through time, and continue to do so to this day. For this reason, I have decided not to give this book a traditional conclusion and instead follow several threads down to the present in chapter 12. The main narrative concerns the rise of Ireland in the world of Celtic studies and the decline of Germany, where the mobilisation of Celtology by the Third Reich nearly destroyed it there as a real science. It was in the twentieth century that the history of Celticism itself began, when Eoin MacNeill noted that the 'modern Celtic consciousness' had a 'somewhat academic origin'.[69] This fact is ironic in the context of the story of Celticism in the second half of the twentieth century. For at the same time that Celtic studies became firmly established as a scholarly field producing major advancements in knowledge, the growing Celtic popular movements became increasingly untethered from the scholarly record. Whereas in previous centuries scholars of the Celts and Celtic revivalists had often been one and the same, that connection weakened as scholarly rigour increased and the Celts became circumscribed by their existence in the sources, while Celtic revivalists needed material that was inspiring and malleable. Instead, leading Celtic scholars are turning the tools of modern science to answering the almost timeless question: Who were the Celts? The story of Celticism is evolving all the time, and that is the reason why the chapter with which this book ends is not a conclusion.

Part I

1

Source Traditions

THE CELTS FROM ANTIQUITY TO THE EARLY MODERN ERA

'THUS I HAVE ATTEMPTED to depict europe, or Old Celtica', wrote the Flemish geographer Abraham Ortelius (1527–1598) at the top of his 'new map of ancient Europe' in 1595 (Fig. 2).[1] With 'Celtae' stretching across Europe from Iberia to Crimea, this map encapsulates the prevailing early modern view of the Celts: they were an ancient people whose territory had been so extensive that 'Celtica' and 'Europe' were basically synonyms. Before the rise of the Greeks and the Romans the Celts ruled ancient Europe. Ortelius was just one of a number of figures who thought along these lines, according to the English antiquarian Thomas Pownall (1722–1805). Exactly two centuries later he complained that Ortelius had believed 'all the nations of Europe were originally *Celts*', that the humanist giant Joseph Scaliger (1540–1609) and the German geographer Philipp Clüver (1580–1622) held that 'the Celts inhabited the greatest part of Europe', and that the polymath G. W. Leibniz similarly thought the Celts encompassed the ancient peoples of Gaul, Germany, and Western Europe.[2] Clearly, the Celts as they were imagined in the early modern period inhabited a very different world—mentally and geographically—from our own idea of the 'Celtic fringe', and were of central importance to European history. This chapter's purpose is to reconstruct that early modern vision of the ancient Celtic world, from the Renaissance until about 1700, highlighting the major points of debate that would continue to resonate in later centuries. The basic questions are: Why did the Celts matter to scholars, from where did they get their information, what sort of works did they compose with it, and what was the collective Celtic picture drawn as a result?

FIG. 2. Abraham Ortelius, *Europam sive Celticam veterem*—'Europe or Old Celtica' (1595). Courtesy of Osher Map Library, University of Southern Maine.

Though considered barbarians, the Celts were enveloped in the classical worlds of Greece and Rome.[3] The large corpora of Greek and Latin texts were the most important historical sources for studying the ancient Celts, and contained lyrical descriptions of their virtuous qualities—that they were fearless warriors and gracious hosts, for example—which made them attractive ancestors to scholars beginning to write national histories. Patriotism had to fit with religious imperatives, and so the information gleaned from classical works was reconciled with the sacred history contained in the Bible, the ultimate authority for European histories of the world until the nineteenth century. Classical texts and biblical narratives provided the ancient historical foundation on which the medieval rise and fall of various European kingdoms, as well as the vicissitudes of the Church, needed to be traced out before the histories of particular nations, regions, cities, churches, or dynasties could be written. Although the evidentiary record remained quite stable over the sixteenth and seventeenth centuries, the Celts were wrapped up in the political and religious quarrels of the day, as nation-states came into being and knowledge buttressed power. Therefore, while the shift from the early view of the ancient European Celts to our own idea of the Celtic nations on the 'fringes' of Western Europe relied on certain developments in knowledge and scholarship (outlined over the following chapters), during the sixteenth and seventeenth centuries views of the Celts fluctuated more as a result of the purposes to which knowledge was applied.

The Classical Inheritance

The classical record containing references to 'Celts' spans a thousand years, from the fifth century BCE to the fifth century CE.[4] Groups of peoples speaking languages we now know, or strongly suspect, to have been Celtic were at the beginning of this period concentrated in Western Europe—in Iberia and Gallia, and the islands Britannia and Hibernia—but over the next few centuries they expanded through migration and conquest to portions of southeast Europe, from Dacia south to Thracia, and even to what became Galatia in the centre of the Anatolian peninsula. With the expansion of the Roman Empire from the third century BCE, however, Celtic territory contracted. By the time of the major Roman decline and rampant Gothic migrations that began in the fourth century CE, the Celtic languages and cultures were under severe strain. Nevertheless, Celtic peoples made a considerable mark on ancient Europe for at least a thousand years and, accordingly, on the classical literary record. In the absence of an ancient native literary tradition, this is the primary corpus for the history of the ancient Celts. This section sketches an outline of the main sources, lingering on the characteristics attributed to the Celts that would make them appealing ancestors to early moderns.

Although the most famous classical texts featuring Celtic peoples were written by Romans—Caesar and Tacitus—they appeared frequently in Greek sources from about 500 BCE, when travellers and ethnographers like Hecataeus of Miletus (*fl. c.* 500 BCE) and Herodotus (*c.* 484–*c.* 430 BCE) mentioned the *Keltoi* as inhabitants of the far west of Europe.[5] According to these writers, Celtic territory stretched from the Greek settlement of Massalia (Marseille) to beyond the Pillars of Hercules (the Straits of Gibraltar). By the middle of the following century, Western Europe was so well established as Celtic that the geographer Ephorus of Cyme (*c.* 400–330 BCE), in his *Universal History* that survived only in later fragments, assigned major peoples to the four points of the compass: Indians in the east, Ethiopians in the south, Celts in the west, and Scythians in the north.[6] With the Celts positioned in the west and northwest of Europe, one common theme in classical sources came to be that the Celts lived in a cold, harsh climate that made them hardier. Yet things were far from clear-cut, despite the blanket use of terms in these sources, and authors often did not know the territory firsthand. Sometimes the precise relationship of Celts to other peoples was unknown, producing hyphenated ethnonyms in classical sources, for example the Celt-Iberians, Gallo-Grecians, or a name that would be consequential in the early modern period, Celto-Scythians.[7] These earliest references have featured heavily in the modern debate over the Celtic 'homeland', but for our purposes the point is the fluidity of antiquity, and that Celts could be found across the European Mediterranean, from Iberia to Asia Minor, in their own communities or in the Hellenistic city-states.

These first Greek references were fleeting and devoid of any real detail about the Celts themselves. Once the Celtic tribes began to impinge upon Hellenistic Europe in the fourth century BCE, however, references ballooned. After a tribe led by Brennus (*fl.* 387 BCE?), chief of the Gaulish Senones, sacked Rome around 387 BCE, the Celts began to register as a people who were, above all, bellicose. Xenophon (*c.* 428–*c.* 354 BCE) and Plato (*c.* 429–347 BCE) both mentioned the Celts as mercenaries with a 'warlike' culture.[8] Aristotle (384–322 BCE) also spoke of Celtic reverence for 'martial ability' but claimed that barbarian bravery was based not on honour but on extreme passions, as with the Celts who were unafraid of earthquakes or who 'take up arms against the waves', which might be called 'mad or insensible'.[9] Strabo (*c.* 63 BCE–*c.* 21 CE) later reported that when Alexander the Great (356–323 BCE) asked a group of Celts what they feared most—anticipating that they would say him—they surprised him by saying nothing except for the sky falling, and that they valued the friendship of great men like him more than they feared anything.[10] Linked, therefore, to the picture of the Celts as a warlike and fearsome enemy was their perceived irrationality. According to Livy (64 BCE–17 CE), wrath was 'a passion which their race is powerless to control', along with 'religious awe'.[11] The point seems clear: the Celts possessed many of the right qualities for the wrong reasons. Though not to be underestimated, their bravery stemmed from emotional volatility, not strength of principle. Conventional wisdom would regard these features as inherent parts of the Celtic character well into the twentieth century.

Considerable attention was devoted to the Gaulish invasion of Italy and sack of Rome. Accounts of these events by the Greek historians Polybius (*c.* 200–*c.* 118 BCE) and Diodorus Siculus (*fl.* first century BCE), and by the

Roman historian Livy, form some of the earliest extended accounts of the Celts.[12] Polybius's came first, followed by Diodorus's and then Livy's, both of which added considerable but often differing details.[13] Polybius recounted how the Gauls crossed the Alps and established themselves in Northern Italy to such an extent that it became known as Cisalpine (as opposed to Transalpine) Gaul;[14] Livy later added that (Transalpine) Gaul had been a land of such wealth and plenty that it became overpopulated, and so the young warriors Bellovesus and Segovesus—important characters who would later reappear in French sources—were sent out to settle new lands, implanting themselves in Italy (where they supposedly founded Milan) and Germany, respectively.[15] These tribes lived in simple villages, 'were exclusively occupied with war and agriculture,' and 'had no knowledge whatever of any art or science'.[16] Although they were portrayed as fierce warriors afflicted by 'a sort of epidemic of war', the Gauls were reportedly drunkards who often fought amongst themselves. Nevertheless, as both writers discussed at length, the Gauls were a powerful people, and in 387 BCE a tribe named the Senones rampaged down through Italy and sacked Rome; notoriously, they agreed a ransom of one thousand pounds of gold, but used a rigged scale to collect it, and when the Romans protested a Gaul threw his sword onto the scale, underling the point that those who were conquered could not expect fair treatment.[17]

Celtic tribes continued to expand eastward and harassed Greece. One warband laid siege to Delphi in 279 BCE, while others went on to establish themselves in Anatolia.[18] A turning point seems to have come in 225 BCE, when they were decisively defeated by Rome at the Battle of Telamon. Persistent battles between Romans and Cisalpine Gauls—who joined the Carthaginian side when Hannibal (247–*c.* 183 BCE) crossed the Alps in 218 BCE—occurred over the next two decades, until the Gauls were finally subdued in Italy during the 190s BCE. Subsequent Roman expansion eastward meant that they encountered the Celts who had settled in the Balkans and Asia Minor, and a speech reportedly made by Gnaeus Manlius Vulso in 189 BCE and related by Livy highlights just how deeply the Gauls had imprinted themselves in the Hellenistic mind:

> Of all the peoples that live in Asia the Gauls have the preeminent reputation in warfare. They are a fierce tribe that has wandered virtually throughout the world doing battle. . . . They have tall frames and long, red-dyed hair, huge shields and long swords. In addition there are their chants as they go into battle, their yells and war dances, and the frightening clash of arms as

> they strike their shields following some ancestral custom—all deliberately contrived to instil terror.[19]

Livy thus vividly painted the Celts as a proud people and fierce enemy—foes worthy of being defeated by the Romans. Similarly, while Polybius was contemptuous of what he saw as the hallmarks of Celtic barbarity, he placed much importance on the Celtic wars in helping Rome to hone its military prowess against a daring if undisciplined enemy.[20]

The expansion of the Roman Empire produced some of the most illuminating sources through the invasion and occupation of Celtic territory. Without doubt, the most important classical text that discussed Celtic peoples was Julius Caesar's *Gallic Wars,* in which he mixed his own observations in with those of the lost ethnography of the Greek Stoic philosopher and traveller Posidonius of Apameia (*c.* 135–*c.* 50 BCE), which included details of Celtic religion, politics, and society. Caesar's book is crucial not only because of the material it contains—including the first substantial account of Britain, as a result of Caesar's forays there in 55 and 54 BCE—but also for its later reception. Caesar's memoir of the Gallic wars survived in multiple manuscript copies through the medieval period, unlike Tacitus's *Germania,* and formed half of one of the earliest *editiones principes* printed in 1469. From this point Caesar's passages on the Gauls, Britons, and Druids would be endlessly parsed, and often interpreted very liberally, by all manner of investigators for centuries.

Gaul was a whole divided into three parts, according to Caesar's famous opening line, one of which was inhabited by 'a people who in their own language are called "Celts", but in ours, "Gauls"'.[21] The *Gallic Wars* is a lively memoir of Caesar's decade fighting these people, mixing adventure and ethnography. The barbarous and frequently treacherous Gauls were a useful foil to Caesar's civilied Romans, but there were many positive examples of the Gaulish character; for example, in Caesar's Druid friend Diviciacus (*fl.* 58 BCE), who was brave and loyal. The Gauls were also presented as freedom-lovers willing to fight the largest power in the known world to regain their independence.[22] They were, in short, a worthy adversary, 'once pre-eminent among all nations for their excellence in war'.[23] Caesar was supported in this impression by Cicero (106–43 BCE), who argued that the Celtic peoples had always been Rome's greatest enemies. The final conquest of Gaul—including the suppression of countless rebellions, a decisive naval battle, two expeditions into Britain, and the defeat of Vercingetorix (later ceremonially executed in

Rome)—took nine years and is presented by Caesar as a major and arduous achievement. Later scholars would know the text virtually by heart.

One of the most important parts of the book is the famous sketch of Gaulish society, contained in Book Six. Politically, Gaul is presented as exceptionally factious; alliances change frequently as different tribes jockey for power, but there is not a clearly preeminent tribe. Socially, aristocracy predominates, and the masses exist in an almost slave-like relationship to those in power, who are divided into two groups: Knights and Druids. The Druids are the clerisy holding both religious and secular power. There is a supreme Druid, either elected by the other Druids or sometimes decided by combat, and there is an annual Druidic assembly, once held in Britain—which Caesar conjectures might have been the home of Druidism—but now in central Gaul. Beginning from a young age, some Druids trained for as long as twenty years, during which time they presumably memorised poetry and philosophy—the principal doctrine of which was transmigration of the soul after death—for it was forbidden for this knowledge to be written down. However (and this is crucial for our story), Caesar reported that 'for almost all other purposes, including public and private accounts, they use Greek characters'.[24] This passage would be endlessly parsed in later centuries: Did the Druids use Greek letters to write in their own language, or did they write in the Greek language?[25] The Druids were also responsible for performing notorious human sacrifices, including the custom of burning victims inside wicker figures designed to resemble the Gods.[26] The Druids were exempt from taxation and military service, which was directed by the knightly class, the other aristocratic faction in Gaulish society, about which Caesar was either much less interested or had less information.

After Caesar's forays into Britain, Rome descended into civil war and its armies remained away from Britain for decades. Only during the reign of the emperor Claudius (10 BCE–54 CE) in 43 CE did Romans return to Britain in numbers large enough to establish a foothold, flushing out resistors and then quashing the revolt of the Iceni and neighbouring tribes led by Boudica (*fl.* 60 CE) about ten years later.[27] This information comes to us primarily from Tacitus, whose *Agricola*, though ostensibly a biography of his eponymous father-in-law, contains an important early history and ethnography of Britain.[28] Tacitus was uncertain as to the origin of the inhabitants of Britain, and conjectured that the Caledonians—with their 'reddish hair and large limbs'—could have been German, while the 'swarthy' complexion and curly hair of the Silures in South Wales might suggest an Iberian origin. Yet he resolved with

Caesar that it seemed likely that Britain was populated from Gaul because the language, religion, and character of the people was very similar, though the Britons remained a bit wilder as they had not yet fully succumbed to Roman rule.[29] The importance of Caesar and Tacitus together cannot be overstated; their passages about the manners, religion, and language of the Gauls and Britons would be redeployed, usually together and often exclusive of other sources, almost endlessly.

The *Agricola* also contains a short note on the similarities of character and civilization between the Britons and Hibernians, though without more specificity than that; this was an important point because much less was known about Hibernia and its people than most other places in Europe. The lack of Roman colonisation was in this way a double-edged sword for the posterity of the Hibernians: while patriots could later boast that Ireland had not been colonised by Romans while Britain had been, the lack of close Roman contact meant that very little was actually known about the island and its people. And in the absence of solid intelligence, sensationalist hearsay often filled in the gaps. Strabo, for example, who never went to the island, reported that the inhabitants were cannibals more savage than even the Britons. Ideas like these lived long afterlives. The Irish were plagued by accusations of barbarism into the twentieth century, and while much of this kind of abuse could be attributed to political instrumentalization, the lack of information proved a serious stumbling block for scholars.

A vital non-Roman source written in the first century was the *Antiquities* of the Jewish historian Josephus (*c.* 37–*c.* 100), who did not discuss the Celts at all but linked up many of the peoples of antiquity with supposed descent from Noah. His line that '*Gomer* founded those whom the Greeks now call *Galatians*, but were then called *Gomerites*', would be of huge importance for early modern scholars seeking to establish Celtic national genealogies (discussed below).[30] As John Collis notes, in the second and third centuries Roman authors were more likely to write about the Celts in the past tense and to provide accounts that were mostly derivative of earlier sources.[31] Cassius Dio (*c.* 155–*c.* 235) is one of the more important sources; he describes Vercingetorix's execution in Rome and Boudica's revolt in Britain. The Celts also occasionally featured in poetry, such as in Callimachus's 'Hymn to Delos', where 'barbarians' bring 'Celtic war' from the 'West'. One of the major sources of late antiquity that would become a standard 'textbook' in the Middle Ages was the *Etymologiae* of Isidore of Seville (*c.* 560–636), where it is noted that the Gauls were called after the Greek word for milk (γάλα); however, shortly afterward Isidore notes that the Gauls were also called Celts, but gives no etymology for the word.[32] His lack of attention probably suggests the waning of discussion about ancient Celts and their subsequent disappearance from the literary record.

Importantly, however, the Gauls did not disappear in the same way. Contemporary scholarship concerned with Celticity has debated how straightforwardly aligned the Latin *Celtae/Galli* and Greek *Keltoi/Galatae* of antiquity really were.[33] For our purposes, though, this terminological confusion can be sidestepped. As early as the fourth century BCE, Greek writers like Aristotle were identifying the *Galli* who sacked Rome with the *Keltoi* known by earlier Greek writers. Since this sort of elision was common in classical sources, early modern scholars did not trouble themselves much with trying to make a distinction; in fact, it often suited their purposes to be able to search for evidence under all of the different ethnonyms. Instead, this is a modern problem of scholarly exactitude. Trying to pin down the who, what, and where of the Celts of antiquity was a point of dispute even in antiquity itself, and the point to grasp is therefore that 'Celts', or peoples considered synonymous with them like 'Gauls,' were mentioned, often favourably, in a wide range of sources over the course of the millennium from 500 BCE to 500 CE. That textual treasury would be an alluring source for erudite humanist raiders when they came to it a thousand years later.

The Absence of the Celts in the Middle Ages

In the meantime, ideas of the Celts entered into the ironic limbo of the Middle Ages. Ironic because while the Celts of antiquity were sealed in the textual amber of classical sources—some of which, like Caesar's *Gallic Wars*, survived and were known during the Middle Ages—their descendants who spoke Celtic languages and retained remnants of their respective cultures lived on in their own kingdoms or became absorbed by larger powers. There was no self-consciously Celtic tradition in any of these places, whether the Celtic language had survived, as in Britain and Ireland, or perished, as happened in Gaul.[34] As Patrick Sims-Williams has stressed, not only were the Welsh and Irish languages mutually incomprehensible, but there was little mutual literary influence; in fact, 'medieval and early modern Welsh and Irish had absolutely no idea that they *were* fellow "Celts"'.[35] To this relationship of non-recognition can be added the other inhabitants of Britain, the occupants of the territory of Gaul, and those living in the other 'Celtic' areas of the Continent. Instead, the cultural glue connecting these peoples, to each other and to others, was Latinate

Christianity. While medieval scholars—mostly monks—were unconcerned with the Celts of antiquity, they were interested in those places where the Celtic peoples still lived or where they belonged to a larger polity. The histories they wrote of these peoples and places would eventually come to be connected to the classical texts—which contained Celts—by later scholars, so it is important to take note of the major sources.

Medieval origin myths tended to follow two prominent traditions. The first was the classical model laid out by Virgil (70–19 BCE) in the *Aeneid,* in which Aeneas and his family flee Troy and ultimately go on to found Rome. The Trojans factored into most origin myths from late antiquity until about the sixteenth century, when they were discarded for more particular, if sometimes no more plausible, ancestors. The other major tradition was the Mosaic history laid out in the Book of Genesis, in which Noah's three sons—Ham, Shem, and Japhet—populated the three known continents after the Flood. This dispersal of nations and the subsequent confusion at the Tower of Babel—where it was held that seventy-two peoples and languages were created—remained universal reference points through the early modern period. As Edward Gibbon (1737–1794) later put it: 'Among the nations who have adopted the history of the world, the ark of Noah has been of the same use as was formerly to the Greeks and Romans the siege of Troy.'[36] They provided the framework in which history developed over the next thousand years, and the biblical account at least was still in play by the time Gibbon wrote near the end of the eighteenth century. To this basic framework would be added a variety of fabricated narratives and characters, who would be traced back to Noah's son Japhet, one of his elder sons like Gomer or Ashkenaz, or an invented descendant of Noah not recorded in the Bible. Mark Williams's description of the Irish variant of these stories as characterised by a 'Tolkienesque enthusiasm for the family trees of imaginary persons' can be extended to the other national traditions in the Middle Ages.[37]

The bases of the myths that would shape national conceptions in Europe until the Renaissance were primarily fashioned in the sixth and seventh centuries by the first historians of the barbarians, and of Europe more broadly.[38] The Frankish invasions of the fifth century saw the establishment of the Merovingian dynasty in Gaul and the birth of the kingdom of Francia. Their origin stories were first written down by Gregory of Tours (*c.* 539–594) and then in the Chronicle attributed to Fredegar. Gregory's *History of the Franks* placed them in a universal history, beginning with the biblical creation story and recounting the upheaval in Gaul that followed Rome's fall and was eventually stabilised by the Franks. Fredegar—though using an abridged version of Gregory—is famous for deriving the Franks from Troy.[39] In fact, according to the Chronicle, King Priam himself was a Frankish king whose descendant Francio founded a settlement on the Rhine—this legend held pride of place in France until the reentry of the Gauls onto the historiographical stage in the fifteenth century.

In Britain, which was split into a number of small kingdoms, the three most important origin accounts of the early Middle Ages were those attributed to Gildas (500–570), whose *De Excidio et Conquestu Britanniae* (*c.* 540?) portrays the Britons as a weak and sinful people who foolishly brought the Saxon inundation upon their own heads instead of dealing with the invading Scots and Picts themselves;[40] to Bede (673/4–735), who identified the Britons, Picts, Scots, and Saxons as successive settlers of Britain; and to Nennius (*fl. c.* 770–*c.* 810), though it is now doubted that he authored the *Historia Brittonum*, which introduced Brutus as the eponymous founder of Britain, whose descendants were nevertheless subdued by the Picts, Irish, and ultimately Saxons.[41] However, this author included one crucial detail—probably drawn from Josephus—that would be carried into the early modern period, which identified the Gauls as descendants of Noah's grandson Gomer.

Building on Gildas, Bede, and Nennius, Geoffrey of Monmouth (d. 1154/5) composed his *Historia regum Britanniae* in the 1130s. It became the standard British history for most of the next half millennium. Geoffrey claimed it was a Latin translation of an old Welsh source (still missing) tracing the kings of Britain from Brutus to Cadwallader, about 1500 BCE to 689 CE.[42] In this account, after fleeing Troy, Aeneas's great-grandson Brutus gave his name to Britain after he and his followers arrived there and subdued the native giants. He divided the kingdoms of England, Scotland, and Wales among his three sons, and his descendant Brennus later sacked Rome. The Britons reached the height of their power in the mid-sixth century under King Arthur, who conquered the whole island, Scandinavia, and Gaul, before defeating the Roman emperor. They were finally undone by the Saxon invasion and civil wars. Not only did Geoffrey's British history provide a usefully complete historical picture, it also gave the British monarchy a noble and heroic genealogy, and ancient Britain the sheen of high culture. For all of these reasons, it maintained its authority in both England and Wales into the sixteenth century and resonated in popular consciousness long after that.

In comparison with its history of subordination for much of the second millennium—following the world-shattering Anglo-Norman Invasion of

1169—Irish culture was rich and self-confident during the earlier Middle Ages. Literacy only came with Christianity and it is therefore impossible to access a purely 'Celtic' tradition; instead, Irish mythology and early culture has to be distilled from texts written by Christians and thus imbued with their worldview.[43] Nevertheless, vernacular Irish texts survive from the seventh century in monasteries in the German-speaking lands and Northern Italy, while written sources in the other Celtic languages do not start appearing in much volume for at least another five hundred years.[44] Striking is the bullishness regarding the Irish language in the seventh-century *Auraicept na n-Éces*, a grammatical primer, in which Gaelic is described as cobbled together from the best linguistic remnants of the Confusion at the Tower of Babel by Fenius Fársaid, Magog's descendant: 'What was best then of every language and what was widest and finest was cut out into Irish.'[45] By the seventh century, then, there existed native Irish figures mixed in with the biblical account in a tradition of origins often called 'synthetic history.'[46] The myths of Gaelic Irish origins were known beyond Ireland and feature, for example, in the ninth-century *Historia Brittonum*.[47]

Around the end of the eleventh century, these various accounts of Irish origins, most of them in verse, were synthesised in a prose account called the *Lebor Gebála Érenn*, literally 'Book of the Taking of Ireland.'[48] The narrative is straightforward enough and tells the story of how Ireland was populated by several waves of supernatural invaders, each one replacing the group that came before it.[49] After the extinction of the first settlers of Ireland by Noah's (non-biblical) granddaughter Cessair, Ireland had been overrun by the Partholonians, Formorians, Nemedians, Fir Bolg, and finally the semidivine Tuatha Dé Danaan, before the arrival of the Scoti, the mortal heroes of the story who originated in Scythia and descended from Japhet's son Magog. After the confusion at the Tower of Babel, Fenius Fersiad created the Gaelic language, which was spoken by his son Nel, who went to Egypt and married the Pharoah's daughter Scota—whence Scoti—and fathered Goídel Glas, eponym of the Gaels. After several peregrinating generations, the Gaels sailed to Spain and settled there before conquering Ireland under Míl Espaigne (hence the adjective 'Milesian,' often used to describe the Gaelic Irish population). Although the *Lebor Gebála* has achieved an essential place in Celtic studies as a native account of the origins of a Celtic people and society, it bears repeating that there is nothing self-consciously Celtic about it. In fact, the Galli and Celtiberi are mentioned as other peoples descended from Japhet but not related to the Irish. The book only became retrospectively synthesised into the Celtic canon during the eighteenth century, when the Gaelic Irish were recognised as a Celtic people.

The mythology of the Irish was conveniently also the basis for that of the dominant people of medieval Scotland: the Scoti, a Gaelic-speaking tribe who had invaded from Ireland and were settled in the west by the early sixth century. Their kingdom, *Dalriada,* spanned the Irish Sea before it became incorporated into the larger Kingdom of Alba in the middle of the ninth century, after Kenneth Mac Alpin (810–858) conquered the (probably) Brittonic-speaking Picts and absorbed their territory. The other considerable populations—the Strathclyde Britons, the Angles, and the Norse—were gradually folded into Alba over the next few centuries, and while there is little surviving manuscript material, this is beside the point, as much of the same master narrative of invasions as that contained in the *Lebor Gebála* provided the foundations of what can be called 'Scottish' national mythology in the early centuries of the second millennium. For example, elements are featured in the eleventh-century *Duan Albanach,* and in the famous 'Declaration of Arbroath' (1320), which traced the nation of the Scots from Scythia via Spain to Scotland, where they smashed the native Britons and Picts, and then fought off Norwegians, Danes, and English.[50] The crucial Scottish innovation came in the fourteenth century, when in his *Chronica Gentis Scottorum* (1371–1385) John of Fordun (d. 1363 or after) systematised the origin myths and added on top of them forty apocryphal kings, beginning with Fergus I, who supposedly landed in Scotland in 330 BCE.[51] Scottish antiquity was thus pushed back about six hundred years and undercut English claims to originality and supremacy through Geoffrey of Monmouth's Brutus. We will see below that while alternatives existed, Fordun's work provided the main shape of later humanist histories of Scotland; for now, it is only necessary to note that there is again nothing self-consciously Celtic in them.

Renaissance, Reformation, and Early Modern Scholarship

The Celts were well-positioned to benefit from the humanist currents of the Renaissance, as forgotten ancient sources were rediscovered, emended with new critical tools, and circulated across Europe. Humanists aimed to recover the entirety of classical learning, or at least as much as the manuscripts stashed away in monasteries and municipal buildings allowed for. Although they were 'scholars' in what might be considered the normal sense of the word—that is, occupied with the accrual and advancement of knowledge and the publication of learned texts—or at least were regarded as such by their contemporaries, these people were activists in a way their modern descendants are not (or pretend not to be). The confessionalisation of Europe in the wake of the Reformation drew the major ideological battle lines within which scholarship was undertaken,[52] but the crystallising sense of nationhood occurring during this period also stimulated research.[53] Scholarship was undertaken for overtly political and apologetic purposes, and historical studies were often designed to consolidate civil and religious power.[54] Scholarship could also be subversive in its aims and practices; if, for example, the Roman Catholic Church's claims for legitimacy rested on historical authority, then new Protestant histories were needed to challenge established institutional narratives. Adducing new evidence—then as now—was a straightforward way to shift debate, and forgery was a relatively common early modern practice;[55] as will be seen, it remained a factor in the Celtic case well into the nineteenth century.

One of the most exciting developments in European intellectual history has been the recent appearance of a range of studies concerned with the histories of scholarship and knowledge, associated above all with the historian Anthony Grafton.[56] Close attention has been paid to scholarly practices, especially the philological recovery of information from ancient texts, and the centrality of the text to early modern scholarship has been underlined.[57] The many ways in which European expansion and deepening engagement in the Americas led to new knowledge creation (often through violence), as well as profound challenges to aspects of the Christian and, to some extent, European world view have been thoroughly excavated.[58] Intellectual historians have also examined the early modern turn to the East and the origins of 'orientalist' scholarship.[59] For a number of reasons, the Celts have not featured much in these recent overlapping historiographical waves, but they can nevertheless help us to understand more thoroughly the early modern contexts in which they were investigated, the sources of information upon which scholars drew, and the aims of their work.

To begin with, the Celts had no obvious place in the overriding subject of early modern scholarship: the history and truth of Christianity. The Holy Land and the sacred and 'oriental' languages formed the objects of primary concern, and universities across Europe had chairs in these subjects and in sacred history. There was an abundance of texts written in Hebrew, Arabic, Syriac, Persian, Greek, and Latin, which it was thought might contain precious information on the history of early humanity and its true religion given by God. The history and languages of the Britons did not attract the same level of attention, though Old English received support while the Celtic languages did not. The first lectureship in Anglo-Saxon was founded at Cambridge in 1638 and there was also a flurry of Anglo-Saxon activity around Oxford in 1700; by contrast, the first Celtic chair was filled at Oxford only in 1877, following Matthew Arnold's publicity campaign. Because of ancient Celtic illiteracy, there was no obvious native textual tradition for scholars to investigate; the few medieval manuscripts dating from when these cultures finally did become literate are glosses on Christian scripture, and they only began to be systematically mined in the nineteenth century. As the Scottish scholar John Leyden (1775–1811) wrote in 1805: 'The revival of modern literature was chiefly derived from Greece and Rome yet the Celts and Goths seem to have had peculiar laws manners and institutions if not a literature of their own, the loss of which has rendered many parts of European history obscure.'[60] This was the challenge to be overcome.

Why, then, were the ancient Celts of interest to early modern scholars? After all, there was no Celtic nation or polity in early modern Europe and there is no evidence that early modern individuals identified as Celtic. Scholars of the period did not write histories of 'the Celts' as such; instead, they composed a variety of works ranging from universal histories to philological commentaries on particular texts, in which information about the Celts could be employed in support of whatever goal they pursued. The predominant approach to history—whether universal, national, or local—was genealogical, and in the context of Renaissance and Reformation, the origins of nations, regions, cities, dynasties, and other institutions took on huge importance in establishing legitimacy. Scholars devoted considerable energy to tracing the migrations and conquests of ancient peoples, thereby endowing their subjects with prestigious pedigrees. Because of their extensive presence in classical texts, the Celts, especially through their close association with the Gauls, retained an important place in the European historical imagination. When Italian humanists recovered their ancient Roman forefathers, they also recovered their ancient Gallic enemies—the ancestors of their modern French rivals—as can be seen in a Florentine painting from the 1470s depicting a battle likely inspired by Caesar's *Gallic Wars* (Fig. 3). This example is significant because it was likely painted after the publication of the *editio princeps* in 1469, showing that the Celts were already registering in historical consciousness decades before the major synthetic humanist histories that are the subject of the following section.

When those histories were written, the new critical tools of humanist scholarship were used to dismantle old myths, like the descent from Aeneas and the

FIG. 3. Detail from 'Battle between Romans and Gauls', *c.* 1470, tempera and oil on wood, The John and Mable Ringling Museum of Art, Sarasota, Florida. The Gauls have cocks (Latin *Gallus*) drawn on their shields and are depicted in line with classical descriptions. There is even a 'dying Gaul' *avant la lettre.*

Trojans, but also to create new ones. As outlined above, the two main source traditions were the biblical and the classical, which were then mixed with whatever national material an author deemed relevant. It was a commonplace that Europeans descended from Japhet, and Celtic descent was usually then either claimed from Gomer or Magog, but sometimes Ashkenaz. Caught up in this pushing and pulling over ancestry, the Celts often served as a bridge spanning the sacred history of the Bible with the profane history of the classical sources. An important link between the Bible and the Celts was Paul's Letter to the Galatians, the ninth book of the New Testament, in which Paul preaches to the descendants of the Gaulish invaders of Asia Minor. Anchored in sacred history and vouched for by classical authorities, the Celts could then be mixed with a specific *mythistoire* and used to support almost whichever national system an author desired. Jean Bodin (1530–1596) pointed out this popular pattern in 1566:

> After the Gauls had filled Germany, Italy, Spain, Britain, Greece, Asia Minor, and even farthest Scythia with colonies, founded cities, cultivated the areas, established laws, they stirred up such a reputation among all

> peoples that all races of Europe boasted that the fame and the splendour of their stock descended from the Celts, as though they were Trojans.[61]

With enough hermeneutic ingenuity, a prestigious pedigree could be drawn from the major textual sources for just about any modern people. Scholars therefore looked for other sources of information to give their exegeses more authority.

It was very widely agreed that, in the absence of written testimony, languages contained the key to national origins.[62] Believed to be almost inherently linked to the nations that spoke them, languages were treated as historical objects in and of themselves in early modern thought: by comparing ancient linguistic remains to modern languages, which were also compared with one another, it was thought possible to follow early migrations of peoples, delineate between different populations, and trace their modern national descendants, all in the absence of written historical accounts. The problem was that there was little linguistic material available in the ancient Celtic languages, because these had not been written down until well into the medieval period. By this time Gaulish was long extinct, and even though linguistic evidence existed in epigraphical inscriptions, and personal and place names, these were not methodically studied until the nineteenth century. Instead, the classical sources were combed again and again until they were exhausted.

Celtic Claims on the Continent

The major resurgence of the Celts began with one of the most consequential and controversial works of the Renaissance. One of the fundamental needs of early modern scholarship was to establish a reliable chronology in which the history of European culture could be aligned with the dates of events and reigns of monarchs in non-European cultures.[63] One particular chronologer, a Dominican named Annius of Viterbo (*c.* 1432–1502), established a popular system by combining the biblical account, the recently rediscovered *Germania* of Tacitus, and forgeries of his own passed off as lost fragments by real ancient historians such as the Chaldean Berosus and Egyptian Manetho.[64] The Pseudo-Berosus fragments in *Commentaria fratris Joannis Annii Viterbensis* (1498) provided a new account of the peopling of the world after the Flood, riffing off of the biblical account of origins while providing grist to the mill of developing national identities.[65] The Pseudo-Berosus fragments derived all European kingdoms from the descendants of Japhet, who were the patriarchs of their respective peoples. The Celts came from Japhet's son Samothes (invented), who Annius said was also known as 'Dis'—the God identified by Caesar as the founder of the Druids.[66] Thus the Celts married the classical and the biblical in a supposedly secure chronology that could anchor different national histories. Because of the use he made of the Gauls and Celts, Annius's work became especially popular in France, but it was widely influential and 'perverted the early histories of every country in Europe', in Grafton's words.[67] Annius either went insane or was poisoned by Cesare Borgia (or both), but his works continued to pour off the presses in Italy, the Netherlands, France, and Germany, and by 1551 there were at least twenty-five editions, which remained points of reference long beyond their demasking.[68] Through their important place in Annius's book, the Celts became woven into the early histories of most European nations.

However, some scholars felt their nations had better claims to the Celtic legacy than others. The major dispute was between French scholars and their counterparts in the Holy Roman Empire.[69] Although Caesar actually delineated between Germans and Gauls quite clearly, there was enough ambiguity about Gaulish language and culture, and the significance of the Rhine as a border, for both French and German speakers to contend for the prestigious legacy of the ancient Celts.[70] Generally, it was easier for German scholars to claim the more neutral Celtae than the Galli, who were more firmly associated with France (in Latin *Gallia* is both Gaul and France), though there were plenty of attempts to do so.[71] There were often local dimensions to ancient claims, with humanists claiming direct descent from the specific tribes mentioned in classical sources, such as the Helvetii. Although Gaul remained a geographical idea throughout the Middle Ages—known from Caesar, Livy, and Isidore, among others—the historical Gaul was only reconstructed from about the fourteenth century and, in Colette Beaune's memorable line, by 1480 a Frenchman had Gaulish ancestors that he had not possessed in 1400.[72] A major sticking point was usually the Gaulish language, which generated real problems for humanists.[73] Although a few passages by classical authors seemed to shed light on the language spoken by the Gauls, these could be easily bent to a scholar's ulterior motives. In the absence of Gaulish manuscripts, scholars were forced to cull Gaulish words from classical texts, but these yielded less than a hundred lexical samples, and many German-speaking scholars confidently linked them to the Germanic languages.

The major historiographical development in France was the usurpation of the place of the Franks by the Gauls, both of whom were still derived from

Trojans.[74] The book normally identified as most important in supplanting the Franks with the Gauls is the *Illustrations de Gaule et singularitez de Troye* (1511–1513) by the Frenchman Jean Lemaire de Belges (1473–1524). He reconciled the Gaulish myth with the Trojans by giving them a common descent and making them cognate peoples; once Troy fell, some of the young refugees settled in Gaul and became princes there. Drawing on the 'tresdiligent historiographe' Annius, as well as classical sources, the biblical tradition, and several contemporary Renaissance works, Lemaire traced a universal history through euhemerism, etymologically tracing the names of tribes back to individual people; he derived the kingdom of France from King 'Jupiter Celte', who had given his name to the third of Gaul called 'Celtica', and whose daughter Galatee 'mere des Gaules', married Hercules.[75] A slew of works followed Lemaire's Gaulish patriotism, and therefore Annius's fabrications, across the century, including Guillaume Du Bellay's (1491–1543) *L'Epitome de l'antiquité des Gaules et de France* (1556) and Noël Taillepied's (1540–1589) *Histoire de l'estat et republique des druides* (1585).

Lemaire's work was part of a widespread tendency that both revived the Gauls as the progenitors of the French nation and identified the French language with Greek, thus bypassing Latin and Italian, as well as German, claims for influence and perhaps ancestral primacy.[76] Annius's Pseudo-Berosus fragments had identified Samothes as the creator of the alphabet that the Gauls then supposedly passed to the Greeks,[77] a move which probably inspired the widespread idea that it was the Celtic Gauls who had birthed Greek civilization, and not vice versa. Although the careful classical philologist and lexicographer Henri Estienne (1531–1598)—who recognised the Celts as the ancestors of the French—only suggested that French and Greek bore many similarities related to being the most refined languages of their day, others derived French directly from Greek. These included Joachim Périon (1499–1559)—whose dialogues showed a warmth for the Gauls/Celts and an annoyance with overemphasis on the Franks—Jean Bodin, and Léon Trippault (1538–?), who traced the roots of French to Greek in his etymological dictionary, *Celt'-hellenisme ou, Etymologie des mots françois tirez du græc* (1580).[78] Trippault—like Isidore and Lemaire—derived the name of the Gauls from γάλα and relied on liberal readings of classical passages, especially Caesar's, to argue that the Druids and Gauls spoke and wrote in Greek.[79] The *Prisca celtopaedia* of Jean Picard (life dates unknown) went even further in deriving the Greek language and attendant intellectual culture *from* Gaul.[80] Even humanists who now have higher reputations, like Guillaume Postel (1510–1581) and Pierre de la

Ramée (1515–1572), thought Greece owed more to Gaul than vice versa,[81] but as time went on authors abandoned much of the Trojan and Annian props, while retaining a Gallo-Frankish patriotism, as for example in the *Recherches de la France* of Etienne Pasquier (1529–1615), or in the works of François de Belleforest (1529–1583), in which the Trojans were discarded in order to consolidate France's Gallic foundations.[82]

German claims to Gaulish were not just simple Francophobia but part of a long, wide, and complicated debate about the *imperium* of the Holy Roman Empire, as well as the relationship of the German-speaking peoples to one another, that was omnipresent in the era before the collapse of the empire in 1806 and German unification in 1871. The main targets of German antagonism in the sixteenth century were Italian scholars, but the French came to occupy this role over the seventeenth and eighteenth centuries. Around 1500, humanists began articulating a 'Germanic' national myth, revivified by the information gleaned from Tacitus's recently rediscovered *Germania*, the *editio princeps* of which appeared in 1472.[83]

There was also a religious calculus for German humanists to claim Celtic associations. Druidism was seen as a remnant of the *prisca theologia*—the ancient religion of humanity that existed before God revealed true religion to Moses—probably taken to Europe by Japhet and his sons (see chapter 3). According to some humanists, such as Conrad Celtis (1459–1508), the Druids had been driven out of Gaul during the reign of Tiberius and brought both their religion and their Greek learning to Germany.[84] Because the *prisca theologia* that they practiced was seen as a precursor to revealed religion, the Druids seamlessly adopted Christianity and helped to convert Germany during the time of Charlemagne. According to Celtis and others, since the ancient Germans had Druids and their language was related to Greek, they were not such barbarous heathens after all.[85] In fact, according to Johannes Aventinus (1474–1534) in his *Bayerische Chronik* (1533), the ancient classical authors had been confused by northern geography, so 'wherever one finds in Old Greek and Latin the words Galli Galate Celtae, must be understood German'.[86]

Although this Celto-Germanic equation was the dominant tendency among German humanists, there were important exceptions, chief of which was the Alsatian scholar Beatus Rhenanus (1485–1547), who displayed a superior critical acumen. He dismissed the Trojans, outed Annius as a forger, and already in 1519 concluded that Gaulish was a separate language from German and had 'perished', rather than survived in any modern language (though he noted it might bear some relation to Welsh).[87] In his important history of the

Germans, Beatus included an insightful section on language, identifying Frankish as Germanic and forthrightly declaring that Gaulish was extinct.[88] The Germanic tribes were valorous and famous enough without needing to steal the identity of the Gauls, according to Beatus, who firmly separated Celts from Germans.[89] At the time this was an outlying position—held also, for example, by the minor Swiss scholar Johannes Müller or 'Rhellicanus', (*c.* 1478–1542)[90]—but one which gained traction over the century, particularly among French Calvinists.[91]

By mid-century, enough ink had been spilled over the Celto-Germanic question that accumulated opinions could be grouped together. In his well-known *Cosmographia* (1544), Sebastian Münster (1488–1552) merely noted the existence of the controversy without weighing in himself.[92] The famous Swiss humanist Conrad Gessner (1516–1565), who published what is recognised as the first major linguistic catalogue, *Mithridates* (1555), discussed the issue at much greater length.[93] The question remained whether Gaulish had been distinct from modern French and German, or was originally Germanic, but after summarising the views of the two camps and adducing much new linguistic evidence gleaned from his own reading, Gessner too abstained from judgment, although he seems to have leaned towards the Germanic explanation.[94] However, he included other important ideas illustrating his knowledge of the 'Celtic' languages, such as the theory that Welsh had been the language of the ancient Britons and was identical to Breton, and that the Scottish Gaelic language, moeurs, and clothing were the same as those of the Irish.[95]

In the second half of the sixteenth century, histories were increasingly politicised in the context of the religious conflicts ripping Europe apart.[96] Remarkably, in France, Protestants and Catholics both appealed to the ancient Celtic past, but emphasis differed regarding the identity of the Franks and the Rhine's border status. Often the differences between the Gauls and Franks were simply elided in claims that the Franks were descendants of Gauls who had settled across the Rhine. In one striking instance, the orientalist Guillaume Postel identified the Gauls as the first post-diluvian people, the 'Loi Gallique,' as the first in the world, and the Frankish 'Loi Salique' as but a corruption of its first letter.[97] The great humanist Jean Bodin was likewise keen to assert the continuity between the ancient Gauls and the Franks in his important historiographical treatise, the *Methodus ad facilem historiarum cognitionem* (1566). He argued that the 'plainly Celtic' name of the Franks was adopted after they crossed the Rhine (still as Gauls) to escape Roman slavery, only to go 'back again to their fatherland as soon as they could, when they had shaken off the

Roman yoke'.[98] Bodin was annoyed that some German authors had tried to strip the French of the Gaulo-Frankish pedigree, but he made an original linguistic argument that etymology made it 'plain that the Germans originate from the Gauls, not the Gauls from the Germans'.[99] On the other side of the religious coin, the Calvinist Pierre de la Ramée—killed in the St Bartholomew's Day Massacre in 1572—was keen to show that the ancient Gauls had possessed all the 'arts libéraux', including literacy, before the arrival of the Romans, clearly implying that their modern descendants could also do without Roman influence.[100] The classical accounts of the Gauls as freedom-loving warriors with limited monarchy were grist to the mill of the Calvinist lawyer and political theorist of resistance, François Hotman (1524–1590), whose *Francogallia* portrayed the Gauls as having willingly invited in the Franks to help deliver them from Roman tyranny; however, his account made the modern French a mongrel people and divested them of the Celtic pedigree present in the works by Postel and Bodin.[101] Yet the important thing to emphasise is that wherever an author came down on one or the other side of the tricky Gaulish/Frankish relationship, there was a notably consistent wider insistence on the Celtic origins of France across the confessional divide.[102]

The claims of Bodin and other Frenchmen for the Celtic mantle, and often a related Franco-Greek descent, rankled scholars beyond Germany, particularly in the Low Countries, where linguistic scholarship was arguably most advanced.[103] Among these was the physician Johannes Goropius Becanus (1519–1573)—famous for identifying his local Antwerpian Dutch as humanity's primeval language—who posited a Germano-Gaulish unity and described French as Latin bastardised by Frankish.[104] In his posthumously published *Batavia* (1588), Goropius's friend Franciscus Junius (1545–1602) noted that the identity of the ancient Celts had caused a dispute between French and Germanic scholars, both of whom wanted the 'glorious past of the Celts'. But Junius argued matter-of-factly that the Celtic mantle belonged to the Germans, 'and not to the French'—he named Bodin explicitly—who had purposely manipulated the confusion around 'Gallorum', 'Celtarum', and 'Galatarú [*sic*]'.[105] The youthful Joseph Scaliger adhered to the idea of Celto-Germanism, but in his later influential work *Diatriba de europaeorum linguis*, written in 1599, he kept Germanic separate as a major language family, and identified Irish and Welsh as separate minor families with no genetic overlap; a letter of 1606 shows that he associated Welsh with Breton and firmly separated them from Teutonic, but Irish was more confusing and Scaliger was unsure whether the Irish had once spoken Danish (because of the Viking invasions).[106] But Scaliger was the exception, and Toon Van Hal has shown that most of the major humanists in the Low Countries subscribed to some idea of Celto-Germanic unity well into the seventeenth century.[107]

The Germanic claims for Celtic reached a sophisticated peak with the Danzig-born historical geographer Philip Clüver (Philippus Cluverius), a widely travelled member of the great late humanist network around Leiden, where he studied under Scaliger before being himself appointed to a position there in 1616.[108] His most significant book, *Germania antiqua* (1616), opens with his own edition of Tacitus side-by-side with that of Justus Lipsius (1547–1606), and an earlier foreword describes it as really a commentary on and extension of Tacitus. This foundational text had to be reconciled with the biblical genealogies and, if possible, show that the Germans were not such pagans as the Romans had taken them to be. Clüver settled on Ashkenaz, Japhet's grandson, as the progenitor of the Celts (*Celtarum pater*), who sometimes went by 'Celta' and who stormed all of Celtica directly after the Flood, understood as the Balkans, Germany, France, Iberia, and the British Isles (*Britannicas insulas*).[109] These first Celts spoke one language, 'lingua Celtica', which had varied by dialect, but which was preserved most completely in modern 'Teutsch', contrary to the claims of figures like Bodin, against whom Clüver aimed a chapter and challenged his idea that the Germans were 'drawn from the Gauls, and the Gauls from the Greeks'.[110] Clüver was well respected for his geographical works and a textbook introduction to geography was translated into English, in which can be found the same theory about ancient Celtic Europe.[111] Clüver's critical standards are still appreciated, and where many sixteenth-century German humanists had quietly relied on Annius for their ancient chronology, Clüver angrily dismissed his forgeries along with those of the Abbot Trithemius (1462–1516).[112] His Celtic theory would be convenient for scholars looking to aggrandise the Celts—for various reasons—through the eighteenth and nineteenth centuries, and it will appear again later in this book.

Although Clüver weaponised the prestige of the lingua Celtica in support of high claims for German, his idea of a European Celtic parent language was a relatively common one among seventeenth-century scholars. At Leiden, where Cluverius had been based, an idea now called the 'Scythian theory' emerged in the middle decades of the seventeenth century; according to this hypothesis, the European languages descended from a parent language, referred to variously as 'Japhetic', 'Scythic', 'Celtic', or 'Scytho-Celtic', which might have gone extinct.[113] Although its originator seems to have been the physician Johannes Elichmann (*c.* 1601–1639), the Leiden historian Marc Zuer van Boxhorn articulated the theory at its most complete in the late 1640s and early 1650s, after the statue of the goddess Nehalennia was uncovered on a beach at Zeeland and prompted an etymological debate (discussed further in chapter 3).[114] We can set its details aside, but in a pamphlet on the matter—in which he began to outline his linguistic theories—Boxhorn incorporated Welsh into the Scythian family. Fixating on Tacitus's comments on the similarity of the languages of the Britons and Gauls, Boxhorn compared Welsh specimens with Greek, and drew the following line of reasoning: British was similar to Gaulish, Gaulish was the language of the Celts, the Celtic language was the same as that of the Germans, and the Germans were definitely Scythian.[115] In his *Originum gallicarum liber*, posthumously published in 1654 by his colleague Georg Horn (1620–1670) at the request of Boxhorn's children, Boxhorn spelled this out at greater length (though not necessarily with greater clarity).[116] Arguing against those who denied that any trace of Gaulish survived, he reiterated his argument about Gaulo-British linguistic identity and included an extensive set of lexical proofs from John Davies's *Dictionarium Duplex* (though he rejected Davies's theory on the Hebrew roots of Welsh).[117] Admittedly, he mistakenly assumed German and Celtic were the same, but the point here is that Boxhorn developed the idea of a European parent language and included Gaulish and what he asserted were its related dialects—Welsh, Cornish, and Breton—under its auspices, two points of critical importance for the emergence of Celtic comparative philology in the next chapter.[118]

Calling this language Scythian or Celtic gave it a more neutral sense because neither of these two ancient peoples now had their own easily identifiable nation. Confusingly, Welsh and (more rarely) Irish were sometimes included in these relationships, but there was as yet no necessary equivalence between them and 'Celtic'. Generally speaking, in the half-century before 1700 the ancient Celts remained sought-after ancestors and the *lingua Celtica* a very catholic option for scholars across Europe.

England, Wales, Scotland, and Ireland

Although standing somewhat apart from the main areas of humanist development on the Continent, scholars from England, Wales, and Scotland were nonetheless well integrated into the networks of European scholarship.[119] Many were educated on the Continent, asked and answered the same questions in the Republic of Letters, and welcomed counterparts from abroad either travelling through their countries or fleeing the wars that ravaged

Europe over confessional and dynastic issues. This section sketches the wider patterns of Celticism on the island of Britain, which fit between an interest in recovering the works of classical antiquity and the instrumentalization of them for political and religious reasons. It was imperative that national mythologies be based upon a glorious past, and here the Celts entered into the equation, though their utility varied in England, Wales, and Scotland. As on the Continent, nationally minded scholars argued over their own national descent and whose language best preserved the original Celtic tongue. For our purposes the most significant development in this period was the gradual acceptance that ancient Britain, and perhaps also Ireland, had been populated from Gaul, though this was not universally accepted.

Our starting point is to recall that neither classical nor medieval writers referred directly to Britain as Celtic, and that Geoffrey of Monmouth's Trojan Brutus provided the main British history at the outset of the sixteenth century. Geoffrey's British history was useful for the historical pretensions of the Welsh, whose status as the descendants of the original Britons remained intact; for the political ambitions of the English monarchy, who used the narrative to support claims to sovereignty over Scotland and Ireland (because Brutus had passed on each of the three kingdoms to a separate son); and for the religious purposes of the Reformed Church, many of whose partisans traced the conversion of the ancient Britons to the second-century King Lucius mentioned by Geoffrey.[120] The sharper tools of humanist criticism were brought to bear on this myth when in 1534 the Italian scholar Polydore Vergil (*c.* 1470–1555) published *Anglica historica,* in which the foundations of Brutus and Geoffrey's British history were undermined, though they lingered on in historical accounts for centuries.

As in France, Annius's forgeries were useful for scholars with varying purposes.[121] For the Protestant polemical historian John Bale (1495–1563), who cited Annius directly in his *Illustrium maioris Britanniae scriptorium* (1548), Samothes the giant and his followers practiced 'philosophy and theology', astronomy, jurisprudence, and other arts and sciences long before the Greeks did, but this Eden was corrupted by the giant Albion; Brutus's rout of the latter restored true monarchy and religion, a story that clearly allegorised and celebrated Henry VIII's recent behaviour. We should note that Samothes and his family lived in 'the Celtic lands, which were afterwards called Britain and Gaul'.[122] A handful of scholars adopted Bale's interpretation for their own works, by the far the most important of which was the *Chronicle* (1577) of Raphael Holinshed (1525–1580).[123] Here, William Harrison's (1535–1593)

'Description of Britaine' reported that originally Britain 'seemed to be a percel of the Celtike Kingdom' founded by Samothes; he included linguistic arguments, derived from Tacitus, that the 'speach of ye auncient Britons, and of the Celtes had great affinitie one with another, so that they were either all one,' or they could easily understand each other with the help of an interpreter.[124] The Annian version of the Celts also featured in more popular works, such as *The Triumphes of re-vnited Britania,* staged for the lord mayor's pageant of 1605. Here using the Brutus myth to emphasise James I and VI (1566–1625) as ruler of a newly unified Britain, Anthony Munday (*c.* 1560–1633) depended on Annius and John Bale for information about Britain's pre-history as part of the 'whole country lying between the Ryver of Rhene and Pyrenian mountains' ruled over by Samothes, who 'founded his kingdome of Celtica ouer his people called Celtae, which name, by the opinion of Bale our Countrey man, was indifferent to them of Gallia, and vs of this Isle of Britaine.'[125] This was the normal understanding of the Celts in Britain through much of the seventeenth century, which associated the ancient Britons with the Gauls, with whom they had likely shared a language, religion, and wider culture. Thus, the maintenance of Annius allowed authors in Britain a smooth connection between the native inhabitants and the customs of their island and Gaul.

While English historians were rewriting their national histories with the help of Annius's Celtic kingdom, Scottish historians were likewise searching for new historiographical foundations, writing in the shadow of growing English claims for overlordship of Britain. Since English pamphleteers writing in the 1540s still relied on Brutus to support their demands for Welsh and Scottish submission to England,[126] the task for Scottish writers was clear: craft an alternative account of Scottish and British origins that legitimated their independent national existence.[127] Scotland's distinctive medieval traditions, including its fictive king lists, were recycled into refined humanist narratives justifying the independence of the Scottish monarchy and church by cosmopolitan scholars such as Hector Boece (*c.* 1465–1536), author of the *Scotorum historiae* (1527), and George Buchanan, whose *Rerum Scoticarum historia* was published in the same year that he died. While Boece retained the myth of Scottish origins from Scota, daughter of the Pharoah, and fleshed out the king list from the mythical Fergus I in 330 BCE to Fergus II in the fifth century CE, Buchanan—one of the premier European humanists but also perhaps a native Gaelic speaker—disposed of the Greco-Egyptian origins of the Scots and instead derived them from the Celtic Gauls.[128] In fact, although they had arrived from Spain, Gaul, and Germany, according to Buchanan *all* the ancient nations of Britain were originally Celtic Gauls. This he deduced with the help of his formidable erudition, with which he made full use of the classical record of extensive Celtic migrations, arguing that the overcrowding of Celtica meant that the Gauls sent colonies into Spain, Italy, Greece, Asia Minor, and Germany. Importantly, he included the ancient Irish in this scheme, arguing that they derived from Spanish Celtiberians and therefore 'spoke the *Celtick* Tongue'. The Scots therefore were Celts, as were the Britons who, according to Tacitus, had spoken a language similar if not identical to Gaulish; indeed, as were the Picts, who descended from Gaulish tribes that had penetrated into Germany. Buchanan's analysis of place names was pioneering and impressive: he traced the European extent of Celtic migrations by noting the similarities of place names in these different countries, including the classic example of *dunum* (fortified town or hill) and several more.[129] Thus, Buchanan used aspects of the Celtic past to argue for Scottish institutional continuity, the core of which was maintained by Royalists and Whigs alike through the seventeenth century, though aspects were challenged. The resulting incongruous situation in which the 'Scottish nation', Germanic speaking (Scots and English) and demographically centred in the Lowlands, relied on a Celtic tradition for its political arguments and national identity is an intriguing and variable relationship to be kept in mind throughout this book.[130]

The landmark history and survey of Britain, *Britannia* (1586), appeared shortly after Buchanan's Scottish History. Its author was the leading English humanist William Camden (1551–1623), who was headmaster of Westminster School and the node around which antiquarian studies developed in England.[131] His *Britannia* began as an investigation into Roman-era Britain (he was encouraged by a visit from Abraham Ortelius in 1577) but turned into a large antiquarian compendium of the different peoples who had inhabited Britain. He dismissed Annius, Brutus, and the Scottish myths, and instead opted for the simple idea that Britain was populated by Gauls, who Josephus had shown were the progeny of Japhet's son Gomer.[132] Camden thought this was provable by 'name, site, religion, maners, and language', the most important proof. As opposed to Buchanan's Gaelic, Camden famously instead learned Welsh, employing a Welsh servant in order to teach him the language, and found that 'the ancient Gauls and our Britans used one and the selfe same language' and therefore 'had the same beginning.'[133] Although he was not the first to draw a link between Gaulish and Welsh, his investigation was particularly thorough and would be influential for later writers, British and continental, in the conceptualisation of the 'Celtic' language family.[134]

Camden's special attention highlights the importance of Wales and the Welsh, who were generally treated as the remnants of the original ancient Britons. First, there was the myth of the original British monarchy founded by Brutus, and even when Brutus was set aside the myths of the ancient constitution made space for the Britons. Second, and no less importantly, the original 'Celtic' church—founded apostolically by St. Paul (*c.* 5–*c.* 65 CE) and independently of Rome—had supposedly survived in Wales into the eleventh century, before being incorporated by the Anglo-Normans but then ultimately restored by Henry VIII (1491–1547).[135] The Welsh were proud of their language and claimed a distinguished status and ancient descent for it.[136] Although humanists like Camden and Scaliger linked Welsh to ancient Gaulish, ironically, the best native scholars preferred to give it what they saw as a more prestigious history because of its supposed pious descent from Hebrew. According to the leading seventeenth-century Welsh scholar, John Davies of Mallwyd (*c.* 1567–1644), it was 'clearer than the mid-day sun' that the language of the ancient Britons had an Eastern origin and bore little relation to the other European languages, and certainly not Gaulish.[137] Davies's own opinion was that Welsh was closely related to Hebrew, the original and archetypal language, which he laid out in his Welsh Grammar of 1621 and his *Dictionarium Duplex* (1632) of Welsh and Latin, where he censured 'Those who conjecture [Welsh] to have originated from Gaulish, i.e. Celtic' and laid out his Hebrew theory at greater length.[138] The publication of this work was easily the most important development in Welsh linguistic scholarship in the seventeenth century. It was a godsend for those who believed that Welsh was a remnant of extinct Gaulish, and Boxhorn was so pleased to receive the book that he kissed it, though he did not think much of Davies's Hebrew theory.[139] But Davies's ideas on Welsh-Hebrew kinship remained popular in Wales for centuries, evident in works like the puritan Charles Edwards's (1628?–*c.* 1691) *Hebraismorum Cambro-Britannicorum specimen* (1676) the works of Edward Davies (discussed in Ch. 5), and well into the nineteenth century, largely because it helped Protestants to draw a close line to the original Church independent of Rome. However, throughout the seventeenth century there were some, including the grammarian John Wallis (1616–1703), who supported the idea that Welsh and Irish were related, believing that Camden had more or less proven the matter, and refuting Scaliger.[140] Still, a firmer association of the Welsh with the Celts was still far from assured and a long way away. According to the textual record, the Celts were not discussed in Welsh until the eighteenth century. The *Geiriadur Prifysgol Cymru* identifies Edward Lhwyd as the first to use 'Celt' in Welsh in

1707, and Lewis Morris as the first to refer to the 'Celtae, neu'r Ceiltiaid' ('or the Celts').[141]

As on the Continent, where Germanic speakers claimed a Celtic lineage as assiduously as others in more historically attested Celtic areas, English scholars could also see themselves as part of a European Celtic heritage and were eager to do so for civil and religious reasons. A healthy tradition of English Celticism existed into the eighteenth century, assisted by the logic of kinship inherent in the Noachic genealogies and a shared Japhetan descent. Many seventeenth-century legal scholars, exemplified by Sir Edward Coke (1552–1634), thought the immemorial constitution extended back to the original Britons and that parliamentary tradition remained unbroken through the successive waves of invasion.[142] England's Anglo-Saxon origins were well documented, but although Gothic political myths eventually came to dominate ideas of English national origins, as Colin Kidd has shown, early modern origins' accounts were fairly ethnically flexible and the idea of Celticism and Gothicism as antithetical did not develop until the nineteenth century and its racialist ideologies.[143] The pioneering Anglo-Dutch philologist Richard Verstegan (*c.* 1548–1640) was able to link the English to the Celts because the Gauls and Germans apparently spoke one language, and were referred to by the Greeks under the joint name of Celtae.[144] The position of the ancient Cimbri—often etymologically linked to the *Cymri* (Welsh)—between the Gauls and Germans was of great help here. Although Camden had suggested that the Britons/Welsh descended from the Cimbri, but separated them from the Germans, others adopted the view that they were all basically Germanic. In 1611 John Speed (*c.* 1552–1629) drew the Welsh and English from the Cimbri, 'whose sonnes, and our fathers, were the Celts and Gaules'.[145] This tendency continued through the seventeenth century and in 1670 the English philologist Robert Sheringham (*c.* 1604–1678) argued that the English derived from the Cimbri—on the Northern European shore between Germania and Gaul—who were 'sometimes called Celts, sometimes Germans, sometimes Gauls, and sometimes Galatians' by the ancients.[146] This sort of promiscuity continued until the Celts and Germans were firmly separated in the eighteenth century.

Ireland's national myths stand out for their idiosyncrasy, but one striking aspect needs to be stressed immediately: their utter lack of interest in or identification with the ancient Celts. Despite today's popular conception of Ireland as the quintessential Celtic country, for most of the early modern era the Irish seemed to prefer descent from almost any other people—Scythians, Egyptians, Phoenicians, or Greeks, for example—before Irish thinkers finally accepted the idea of Celtic descent in the eighteenth century, while still making room for their traditional ancestral stories. As late as 1750, the philosopher Bishop George Berkeley (1685–1753) attributed the alleged laziness of the native Irish to the 'Spanish or Scythian Blood, that runs in their Veins. . . . The Scythians were noted for wandering, and the Spaniards for Sloth and Pride; our Irish are behind neither of these Nations from which they descend, in their respective Characteristics.'[147]

Berkeley was a Protestant bishop writing about Irish Catholics, and his example highlights the important issues of conquest, colonisation, and the resulting fractures in Irish society. Religion was paramount and the sixteenth-century cleavage between settler Protestants and native Catholics profoundly reshaped the political relationship between Ireland and Britain. There were knock-on effects for Irish scholarship and, as Clare O'Halloran has shown most thoroughly, through the eighteenth century, 'religious affiliation . . . was the governing factor in all [historiographical] interpretations and controversies'.[148] Still, while Gaelic learning was confined primarily to native Irish families, there was some Protestant scholarly interest in Irish and its relationship to the languages of Europe. James Ussher (1581–1656), the orientalist Archbishop of Armagh most famous for dating the Creation to 4004 BCE, was aware of the Leiden philological school, and a Leiden-based correspondent named Louis de Dieu (1590–1642) asked him in 1636 for Irish materials so that Elichmann could review the 'essential nature of Irish' and see if it came closer to Persian than the Germanic languages or Greek and Latin.[149] Ussher did what he could, sending an alphabet and a New Testament, but the lack of printed material in Irish was a problem and it would continue to be for the rest of the century.[150]

The seventeenth century saw the composition of two major works by Catholics, though neither of them made it into print until much later. The first was a compilation of annals by four clerics known since as the 'Four Masters', which circulated primarily in scholastic circles.[151] The second, and the standout, in early modern Irish historiography was by Geoffrey Keating (*c.* 1580–1644), an Old English Catholic priest.[152] His *Foras feasa ar Éirinn* (Compendium of wisdom about Ireland) was completed by about 1634 and circulated widely in manuscript. Keating's was a patriotic history defending Ireland from charges of barbarism made by invaders like Gerald of Wales (*c.* 1146–*c.* 1223) and more recent Tudor colonisers like Edmund Spenser (1552?–1599). Keating's decision to write in Irish surely reflects his pride in the language.[153] The work is divided into two books, the first of which reformulated the traditional origin stories found in the *Lebor Gebála* and other annals into a modern scholarly prose, mixing in and refuting recent scholarship by, for example, Camden and Buchanan. He took particular issue with their use of linguistic arguments, asserting instead that the reason there were Irish words in so many languages—including Welsh—was because Ireland was the ancient seat of European and Druidic learning, and carried on commerce with its neighbours.[154] If there was any correspondence between them it was because they borrowed from Irish, not because there was any 'Celtic' affinity. Keating's book remained the dominant history of Ireland, consulted by Protestants and Catholics alike, into the eighteenth century, and while English authors in particular would reject Ireland's traditional histories, there would not be a sound genealogical connection established between the inhabitants of Britain and the inhabitants of Ireland until Edward Lhwyd published his *Archaeologia Britannica* in 1707.

Conclusion

To return to the basic questions raised in the introduction about why the Celts mattered to early modern scholars and whence they derived their information, we can see that the ancient Celts were of widespread importance to early modern scholars for political and religious reasons, as well as for reasons of national and historical pride. Like Ortelius, many scholars across Europe believed that the Celts were the first tribes to inhabitant the Continent and its northwestern islands; after all, classical sources did not indicate that any people had been there before the Celts, and the medieval traditions listed only mythological figures, monsters, and giants. Because 'the Celts' were synonymous with the original Europeans, and because little was known about their language, Germanic scholars made claims to be their descendants that seemed just as valid as those made by French scholars, who thought they had firmer claims to Celtic ancestry based on their descent from the Gauls. Thus, claims to be descended from the ancient Celts were advanced more forcefully by continental scholars—French and German—than by scholars on the island of Britain, including even in Wales. Irish thinkers rejected the idea of Celtic lineage outright, in deference to their native origin traditions drawing them from the Scythians, Egyptians, Greeks, or Iberians, or some combination of these. The main source of information from which scholars drew was the large corpus of classical works throughout which the Celts were sprinkled liberally, which were matched up with biblical narratives and more particular medieval traditions. However, the novel techniques of philology were beginning to be put to use in tracing Celtic migrations and demonstrating their affinity to various populations, ancient and modern.

It is sometimes suggested that Britain and Ireland only became 'Celtic' around 1700,[155] due primarily to linguistic arguments that form the subject of the following chapter, but this is not the best way of understanding either the early modern significance of the Celts or the impact of linguistic developments at the outset of the eighteenth century. As this chapter shows, over the sixteenth and seventeenth centuries scholars from the different nations of Britain—though rarely Ireland at this point—participated in a pan-European discussion about the identity of the ancient Celts and a competition over their national legacy. What happened in the eighteenth century is that breakthroughs in comparative philology helped scholars to add the nations of Britain and Ireland more confidently to the wider European Celtic story traced in this chapter.

2

Celtic Linguistic Antiquarianism

PAUL-YVES PEZRON, EDWARD LHWYD, G. W. LEIBNIZ, AND THEIR LEGACIES

WHILE SITTING IN a York jail cell awaiting trial in 1759, a prisoner asked for some books to help pass the time. Along with the poems of Catullus (*c.* 84–*c.* 54 BCE), he requested a history of Christianity in Yorkshire—John Burton's *Monasticon Eboracense* (1758)—and 'any one Welsh Dictionary'.[1] Soon afterwards this man, a middle-aged schoolmaster named Eugene Aram (1704–1759), drafted a prospectus titled 'An Essay Towards A Lexicon Upon An Entirely New Plan'. It identified the 'ancient Celtae'—descendants of Noah's grandson Gomer—as either the aboriginal Europeans or their conquerors, who spoke the ancient language from which Latin and Greek descended: 'polished by Greece, and refined by Rome,—only with dialectic variation', Celtic 'flowed from the lips of Virgil, and thundered from the mouth of Homer'.[2] The ancient Celtic language was now preserved most completely in the 'dialects' of Wales, Brittany, and Ireland. Unfortunately for Aram and Celtic scholarship, he was found guilty of murder and hanged at Tyburn outside York on 16 August 1759. His trial caused a sensation and the writer Tobias Smollett (1721–1771) went so far as to suggest, 'if ever murder was entitled to indulgence' Aram deserved it, as his Celtic dictionary 'might have thrown some essential light upon the origin and obscurities of European history'.[3] This chapter therefore departs from the obvious question: Could a Celtic dictionary be so valuable that its compiler should be allowed to get away with murder?

If the dictionary in question were the *Glossography* of the Welsh scholar Edward Lhwyd, Celticists might be tempted to say yes.[4] For, on the basis of this work, Lhwyd has often been identified as the founder of Celtic studies. In it he proved for the first time that what we now call the Brittonic languages—Welsh,

Breton, and Cornish—were related to the Goidelic languages of Ireland, Scotland, and the Isle of Man. Lhwyd was not only answering a linguistic question, but contributing to the historical discussion about the origins of Britain, Ireland, and Europe, as well as the European debate over the Celtic mother tongue, whose outlines we saw in the previous chapter. The French scholar Paul-Yves Pezron had recently reinvigorated this conversation in a book identifying his native Breton, together with Welsh, as the closest survivors of Europe's original Celtic language, from which most others descended. Although Lhwyd's *Glossography* is now taken to be the foundational work of modern Celtic studies, it has been agreed that Pezron's book was better received in the eighteenth century.[5]

Their works differed considerably, but Pezron and Lhwyd concurred on the imperative of linguistic study. After recorded historical accounts, languages were the most useful evidence for determining the origins of peoples and their relationships to one another. Alongside the material remains dug up by antiquarians, languages were treated as historical objects in and of themselves by philologists. Often these two pursuits were undertaken by the same person as part of a historical study,[6] and I occasionally use the term 'linguistic antiquarians' to describe scholars who used linguistic evidence primarily for historiographical purposes. A common linguistic antiquarian pursuit was the hunt for the original language of Europe, which was often called 'Celtic'. Pezron and Lhwyd were aware of and indebted to earlier works in this vein, but their distinct contributions lay in tying the term 'Celtic' and its associated antiquity firmly to the Brittonic languages and peoples, and in linking these with the Gaelic languages and peoples, respectively. G. W. Leibniz, a proponent of the Celto-Scythian theories pioneered in seventeenth-century Leiden, was also intrigued by Welsh and Irish, and observed these developments from his library in Wölfenbuttel. Although he objected to Pezron's arguments, he welcomed Lhwyd's findings and incorporated the Celtic languages into his sophisticated diffusionist scheme for the European language family, which was influential on the continent. Pezron, Lhwyd, and Leibniz all developed their ideas independently of one another in the 1690s—and Lhwyd was apparently speculating in the late 1680s, before Pezron—but their relevant books appeared, respectively, in 1703, 1707, and 1717, and that is therefore the order in which I have treated them here. Leibniz was only the most famous spectator, and beyond him a range of figures in Britain, Ireland, and Europe also paid close attention to the Celtic works of Pezron and Lhwyd. In 1759, when the news about Aram broke, the Welsh antiquarian Richard Morris (1703–1779) described him as a 'most surprizing genius!—master of most languages, and like Edward Llwyd and Pezron of the Celtic dialects'.[7] The masters were clear, and they and their legacies over the half-century before the appearance of Ossian—who changed everything—form the focuses of this chapter.

Paul-Yves Pezron and the Titanic Origins of Europe

The two decades between 1690 and 1710 were crucial for the foundation of the modern understanding of the Celtic languages and peoples. At the beginning of this period the relationship between the Irish and Welsh languages, and therefore peoples, was still undecided; however, by the end of it their linguistic kinship was firmly established, and along with it their link to the ancient Gauls and related Celtic civilizations of antiquity. The first large step taken in this direction was the secure association of the ancient Gauls with the modern Brittonic speakers in Wales, Brittany, and Cornwall. As far back as the twelfth century, Gerald of Wales had observed in his *Descriptio cambriae* (1194) that Welsh, Cornish, and Breton seemed to derive from a common language, and in the sixteenth and seventeenth centuries scholars like Camden and Boxhorn elaborated on this idea.[8] Pezron, however, drew new attention to the Welsh-Breton connection, and argued that these languages had been spoken by the ancient Celts or Gauls (for him the same people), and that a Celtic tranche could be found in most European languages. This argument was spelled out in *Antiquité de la nation, et de la langue des Celtes, autrement appellez Gaulois* (1703), which can be seen as a fulcrum between the early modern idea of the Celts as the earliest European people and progenitor, and the narrower modern idea of the Celts as the extant populations inhabiting the areas of Northwest Europe and speaking a set of related languages.

Paul-Yves Pezron is often identified as the first 'Celtomaniac', and in the latter half of the eighteenth century the Swedish philologist Johan Ihre (1707–1780) joked, 'As whatever Midas touched became gold, so whatever came under the hand of Pezron thereby became Celtic'.[9] Although his zeal for the Celts eventually made him a figure of ridicule, it also helped to make him, in the historian Prys Morgan's words, 'in all probability the inventor of the modern Celts, and thus of Celticism'.[10] He was born in 1639 in the walled town of Hennebont on the southern coast of Brittany, and after studying with the Jesuits at Rennes he was selected to continue theological studies at the Cistercian Collège des Bernardins in Paris, where he received his doctorate in 1682. In 1694 Louis XIV (1638–1715) appointed him commendatory Abbot of

Charmoye—his moniker in the Republic of Letters—but he renounced the position in 1703 to focus on scholarship and died a few years later in 1706.[11]

Pezron's work on the Celts came near the end of a long scholarly career investigating ancient history, primarily of the Near East, and he was well known for his erudite works arguing for an extended chronology based on the Greek (Septuagint) as opposed to the Hebrew (Pentateuch) biblical text, in order to more easily reconcile people and events recorded by different civilizations—mainly Egyptian and Chinese—with biblical history.[12] What became his Celtic book began as a commentary on the dispersal of nations outlined in *Genesis* 10, which he announced to the world in a letter written on 23 February 1699 to the Abbé Claude Nicaise (1623–1701), who sent it to Leibniz as well as to the *Nouvelles de la république des lettres*, which published it in June 1699.[13] Aiming principally at Samuel Bochart (1599–1667) and his Phoenician scheme of universal history, Pezron initially planned a larger work—which he might have been working on before his death—that would examine all of the nations descended from Noah's other sons, but the book published in 1703 focused principally on Japhet and his son Gomer's descendants, the Celts, as they migrated west into Europe from Central Asia.

The book was divided into three parts. The first presented his grand narrative of Celtic migrations; the second examined the Celtic origins of the Greek, Latin, and Germanic peoples and languages specifically; and the third was a collection of Celtic etymologies for Greek, Latin, and Germanic words.[14] Essentially the narrative ran as follows: the Celts/Gauls/Galates were the descendants of Gomer who settled in Bactria after the Flood. Here the Gomerians were known as Sacae before they migrated to Phrygia, farther into western Asia Minor, and then to Thrace, Crete, and all of Greece, where they were known as the Titans of mythological fame. They were led on these migrations and conquests by a series of princes named Uranus, Saturn, and Jupiter who had then been euhemerised into the Gods of classical antiquity. Branches split off and formed great civilizations: the Cimmerians migrated northwards to the Chersonese peninsula (Jutland), but the Spartans stayed on the Peloponnese and invented the Olympic Games.[15] Other branches split off and became the progenitors of the Umbrians and Sabines in Italy, but when the Gomerians settled in France they were known either as Celts or Gauls.[16] By the first millennium BCE Celtic peoples formed an 'empire' that stretched from the Euphrates to Iberia. Although they developed over time into different nations as they migrated—Gomerians, Sacae, Titans, and then Gauls—what remained constant was their language, which then fused with the languages spoken by those who migrated after them into Europe. This language, 'the language of the Titans, which was that of the ancient Gauls, is still preserved by us [the Bretons], after the revolution of more than four thousand years'.[17]

It has been well recognised that Pezron's silver bullet was his native Breton. The entire book is shot through with dubious etymologies tracing the names of figures in ancient history and classical mythology to Breton, which is presented as a key to unlocking their true meaning. These were at the heart of the second part of the work—devoted to proving the supposed Greek, Latin, and Teutonic derivatives of Celtic—which basically recapitulated the master narrative, but with special attention to language.[18] Here Pezron revealed that he was fully aware of the Scythian parent language theory that had been expounded in Leiden during the middle of the seventeenth century (see the previous chapter for details).[19] He cited Claudius Salmasius's (1588–1653) *De Hellenistica commentarius* (1643)—where an early version of the theory was laid out—multiple times and also indicated his awareness of Boxhorn's work, if perhaps only through Brian Walton's (1600–1661) reference to him in the Polyglot Bible.[20] However, Pezron rejected Boxhorn's Scythian hypothesis, opting instead for a descent from the more obscure Daæ (Dahae) people around the Caspian Sea, which he claimed to have adopted from Salmasius.[21] Moreover, Pezron was cagey about direct linguistic filiation, probably trying (vainly, it turned out) to avoid charges of 'Goropianism' (see chapter 1). The Celtic language, he argued, was one of a number of original languages that arose out of the Confusion at Babel, and its supposedly greater collection of monosyllables proved it was older than the other European languages.[22] But it was the huge extent of the Gomerian/Celtic migrations that meant that Celtic populations were present across Europe and mixed with later invaders. Accordingly, there was a Celtic substratum to most of the major European languages that was easily revealed with Pezron's etymological tables.

Pezron was of course not the first to draw attention to Breton, nor to give it an exaggerated world-historical importance. In 1659 the Jesuit missionary Julien Maunoir (1606–1683) published the first substantial Franco-Breton grammar. He made it perfectly clear in a prefatory essay 'On the excellence of the Armorican language' that Japhet's children brought 'the ancient language of the Celts or Gauls' to Europe, and that it was the same as 'the language of the Armorican Bretons' in his own time.[23] However, Pezron skilfully wove Breton into the complicated tapestry of universal history, mixing classical, Christian, and Near-Eastern sources into a substantial narrative with political and religious edges.

Apart from his emphasis on Breton as the modern exemplar of the Celtic language, another factor setting Pezron apart from many prior authors was that his book took the ancient Celts as its central focus, pinpointing their origin and following their migrations to Gaul.[24] Whereas many authors began with Gaul in recorded classical history, Pezron was interested in prehistory, and the settlement of the Celts in Gaul was his ending rather than starting point. This was in part because he aimed at the major seventeenth-century universal history, Bochart's *Geographia sacra*, in which the Gauls and their language served as just another plank for the author's Phoenician theory. In *Geographia sacra*, Bochart argued that many Gaulish words had Phoenician etymologies, most importantly the names of gods, but also the names of chiefs like Brennus, terms of war, clothing, animals, plants, and geography; however, he decided these similarities were the result of commerce and word borrowing and not genetic relation.[25] Bochart's work in turn inspired a refutation from Boxhorn, whose *Originum Gallicarum liber* (the second chapter of which is a reprint of Bochart's essay on Gaulish) placed Gaulish in the Celto-Germanic family identified as part of the Scythian group, but Pezron argued that these terms could instead be explained by Breton etymologies. Apart from these erudite works of ancient history, the Gauls and Celts reliably appeared at the beginning of French national histories, but after a fleeting reference that normally regurgitated Caesar and perhaps Livy or Tacitus, the author would move swiftly on to their real focus: the origins and early history of the monarchy.[26] By the time Pezron wrote, therefore, the ancient Gauls had been discussed in various important works, but these usually merely reviewed the classical evidence.

Yet Pezron dismissed Caesar and Tacitus—the former for being a propagandist, the latter for his heretical idea that the ancient Germans were indigenous—and asserted that the Celtic successes in Europe were nothing as compared with their accomplishments in Asia during the time of Abraham and Nimrod. The key to ancient Celtic history was not the accounts recorded by their conquerors, but their illustrious language, which was preserved in Breton and Welsh. Pezron essentially grafted the Celts onto the more firmly established ideas of Eastern antiquity with the use of shaky Breton etymologies. In practice this usually meant breaking down a proper name into parts that were then traced to similar-sounding words in Breton. To take only one example, 'Jupiter', which has a well-attested Indo-European etymology meaning something like 'Sky-Father', was actually 'taken from the Celts, who called him *Jaou*, & *Jou*, which means *young*, because he was the youngest son of

Saturn.'[27] However, Pezron also included a considerable amount of historical evidence, and he stood apart by relying on Greek and other Eastern sources rather than the usual Latin material. The most important association that allowed Pezron to construct his historical scheme was Josephus's identification of Gomer as the father of the Galatians, and by extension the Gauls (see chapter 1).[28] Pezron then padded this out with lines from Pseudo-Eustathius's commentary on the Hexameron and St. Jerome's *Hebrew Questions on Genesis* (both of which were just following Josephus, however, creating a feedback loop), as well as Isidore's *Etymologies* and the Chronicle of Alexandria.[29] But elsewhere Pezron simply invented. For one of his central arguments—that the Gomerians changed their name to 'Titans'—Pezron posed the rhetorical question 'Where are the authors who wrote it down?'. Instead of answering, he simply shrugged and admitted he could not produce a single author who did so, but asserted that the names of 'Princes and Princesses' were all taken from the Celtic language and this was proof enough.[30]

Pezron's book served several patriotic purposes at once, bringing glory to the French, the Bretons, and the Welsh. In addition to making a forceful argument that the French descended from the Celtic Gauls, with his lengthy chapter arguing that Greek and Latin were descended from Celtic, Pezron returned to the long-running question about the relationship of the classical languages to French. As seen below, this idea became the subject of animated debate in the *Académie des inscriptions et belles lettres* in the 1730s and 1740s. Pezron's book was translated into English in 1706 and reissued at several points, including in an edition of 1809 that contained a biographical sketch.[31] His ideas went on to have a major impact on Celticism over the course of the eighteenth century, and one of those stimulated by his ideas—even if he ultimately rejected them—was Edward Lhwyd.[32]

Edward Lhwyd, the *Archaeologia Britannica*, and the 'Celtic Languages'

Edward Lhwyd's *Glossography*—a collection of comparative dictionaries and accompanying essays—was really the first instalment of a much larger book project called *Archaeologia Britannica*. Intended as a multivolume work on the antiquities and natural history of Britain, it was ultimately left unfinished at Lhwyd's early death in 1709 at the age of 49. So, while Lhwyd is famous for his linguistic achievements—and his genius and most striking originality did lie in the study of languages—this work was really a buttress to his more comprehensive interests in the civil and natural histories of Britain, Ireland, and Europe. He was a member of the concentric circles of antiquaries and natural philosophers around the second generation of the Royal Society, and he made important contributions in the fields of what are now called archaeology and palaeontology.[33] This training imbued his linguistic work with an empiricism that prioritised data collection, often directly from the mouths of those who spoke the languages. The resulting focus on sounds—phonology—is what allowed him to make his famous breakthrough regarding Celtic linguistic kinship.

Lhwyd was born in Shropshire on the border with Wales around 1660.[34] He was the illegitimate child of two members of the minor gentry and attended Oswestry School before matriculating to Jesus College, Oxford, in 1682, initially to study civil law. But he never graduated. Instead Lhwyd became preoccupied with natural history and started working at the Ashmolean Museum in 1684, publishing about its collections in the Royal Society's *Philosophical Transactions* before being appointed the museum's second keeper in 1691. Although natural history took pride of place in his early work and correspondence, it was closely linked with the study of antiquities, and in 1693 Lhwyd was recruited to write some of the Welsh entries in the updated edition of Camden's *Britannia* (1695). Ultimately, he was responsible for all of Wales, and the fieldwork he undertook for the project in the early 1690s set him further on the path to working on the history and languages of Britain and Ireland.

Yet already in the late 1680s, Lhwyd's correspondence reveals linguistic interests that would stretch across the rest of his life. Clearly manifest in these early letters are the seeds of some of his later innovations concerning the identity of the ancient Gauls and their language, as well as the Irish language and its relationship to Welsh, but also to the other European tongues. The Hebraic credentials of Welsh had been challenged since John Davies's death, notably by Boxhorn, who Lhwyd read probably in 1687. In a letter to the antiquarian John Aubrey, Lhwyd asked after Edmund Wyld (1618–1695), who had recommended a French work to him 'that treats of the origin of the Galles', as he had just read 'Boxhornius upon [Wyld's] recommendation, & to me [Boxhornius's] arguments (tho the author seems sui plenus [full of himself]) were very plausible.'[35] In other words, Boxhorn's etymologies suggested to Lhwyd that Welsh was probably related to Gaulish rather than to Hebrew.

What was the Irish language's relationship to Welsh, as well as to the other European languages? On the one hand, Joseph Scaliger had identified Irish as one of the seven minor original languages of Europe, meaning it bore no relation to the other mother tongues including Welsh, and he had been followed in this assertion by scholars in Britain like Edward Brerewood (*c.* 1565–1613) and Stephen Skinner (1623–1667). On the other hand, figures like Clüver and Boxhorn had conjectured that Irish was part of the European family, and the grammarian John Wallis had suggested its affinity to Welsh in particular.[36] But this was all speculation, and in 1695 the English historian William Temple (1628–1699), perhaps channelling Scaliger, summarised the general puzzlement:

> [the Irish language] is neither known, nor recorded to have been used *any where else* in the world besides Ireland, the Highlands of Scotland, and the Isle of Man, and must be allowed to be an *original* language, without any affinity to the old British [Welsh], or any other upon the continent.[37]

John Toland, the famous Irish deist, later claimed that he had convinced Lhwyd of the link between Irish and Welsh when he visited Oxford in early 1694, but Lhwyd's letters show he was already entertaining the idea in the late 1680s.[38] In his Irish tour of 1688 he observed that Irish 'hath many primitive words common with our [Welsh] language', and speculated that it was a mishmash of European languages: 'I belive its composd of old British, old Danish, Biscay, & perhaps several others'.[39] His belief in the affinity between Welsh and Irish strengthened in response to the prefatory letter of Edward Bernard's (1638–1697) *Etymologicon Britannicum*, written to the Saxonist George Hickes (1642–1715), in which Bernard blithely asserted that Welsh borrowed half of its words from Latin and a quarter from English.[40] In a pseudonymous letter designed to be read in response at the Oxford Philosophical Society, Lhwyd cited Boxhorn's assertion that despite some similarities, Welsh was not derived from Latin or Greek.[41] He argued instead that Welsh was 'co-originall' with Latin, and listed Welsh words with equivalents in other languages not derived from Latin such as Irish, Gaulish, and German.[42] Therefore, although he had yet to advance a strong genetic link, Lhwyd was already in 1690 pointing out affinities between Irish and Welsh, and including them within a European group *à la* Boxhorn.

A stumbling block in these early years was the lack of access to materials in Irish and Cornish. In 1692 Lhwyd wrote to a correspondent that he was learning Irish—principally because it would make him a 'better critic in the British'—but could find no 'Dictionary, Vocabulary or Grammar . . . nor one man in this Town that can read it'.[43] John Toland's arrival in early 1694 was therefore propitious. Lhwyd wrote to Aubrey in January that he had not met 'Mr. Tholonne', but that he was in Oxford composing 'an Irish dictionary & a dissertation to prove Ireland a colony of Gauls'.[44] They certainly met and discussed these subjects, but it is difficult to know what Toland's real influence was. Decades later, Toland claimed that he demonstrated the kinship of Irish and Welsh to Lhwyd, but we have seen that Lhwyd had been speculating about it already for several years.[45]

In 1695, after the completion of his portions of the *Britannia*, Lhwyd expanded his view and began fundraising for a huge project on the history, natural and civil, of Britain. It was to be divided into three parts and was summarised in a subscription proposal, entitled 'A design of a British dictionary, historical and geographical; with an essay, entitled, *Archaeologia Britannica*: and a natural history of Wales'.[46] Essentially Lhwyd intended a sort of national biography, an essay on ancient history and antiquities (the *Archaeologia*), and a natural history. The project was firmly focused on ancient Britain and the Britons, the ancestors of the Welsh, and would give the study of Wales a solid modern scholarly foundation. What became the *Glossography* was only intended as one division of the second part, *Archaeologia Britannica*, in which he would compare 'the Modern Welsh with other European Languages; more especially with the Greek, Latin, Irish, Cornish, and Armorican'.[47] Distributed among the Welsh gentry, the proposal was also circulated among politicians at Westminster and the learned.

It met with remarkable support and Lhwyd won enough funding for himself and several assistants to undertake fieldwork from May 1697 to March 1701.[48] He had for years been searching out manuscripts and dictionaries in Welsh and Cornish, as well as a Breton dictionary, but had very little success, and so from a linguistic point of view the trip would allow him to actually gather the data he needed. The tour began with two years in Wales, from May 1697 to August 1699. Lhwyd then arrived in Dublin and travelled north into Ulster before sailing for Scotland in late September or October, where he trekked around the western highlands and islands, before returning to Ireland in January 1700.[49] He toured Ireland for the next seven or so months before crossing over into Cornwall by August, where he stayed until January 1701. The expedition ended on a sour note when Lhwyd arrived in Brittany at the outbreak of the War of Spanish Succession (1701–1714) and was swiftly accused of being a spy. He and his assistants were imprisoned, had their manuscripts confiscated, and were deported shortly thereafter, ruining their plans to go on to Paris and perhaps the Netherlands.[50]

Lhwyd made his epochal linguistic finding in the middle of the tour. As John Considine has recently discussed, Lhwyd's breakthrough came as a result of compiling a Welsh-Irish-English wordlist while travelling through Scotland in late 1699, and he dates the realisation probably to November of that year, though no later than January 1700.[51] Lhwyd's famous discovery was to show that specific sounds in Gaelic reliably corresponded to specific sounds in Welsh. The most famous of these is Welsh *p* and Irish *kw*—which gave rise to the *P-Celtic* and *Q-Celtic* distinction—as in *pen* and *ceann* (head), or *pedwar* and *cathair* (four). Lhwyd provided a demonstration of these sound shifts that he allowed to be included in *The Scottish Historical Library* (1702) of his friend Bishop William Nicolson (1655–1727), and wrote in a letter of 1703 that he was 'troubled with an Hypothesis of C. Britons and P. Britons. . . . I cannot find the Irish have a word (purely their own) that begins with a P. and yet have almost all ours, which they constantly begin with a C'.[52] This phonological observation and its consistency put Lhwyd more than a century ahead of his time, and was a startlingly brilliant innovation at a time when etymology consisted for many of culling random words from various dictionaries and looking for similarities across languages. As David Cram has shown, Lhwyd was well versed in the classical grammatical understanding of *permutatio litterarum* (basically an explanation for sound changes over time), and developed further his own method for determining which classes of letters could be shifted and whether such cases could be concluded to be accidental or forced a new rule, as was the case with the Celtic P and C change.[53]

Following several practical delays, and fatally testing the patience of its funders, the *Glossography* was finally published in 1707. It might be thought of as primarily a large comparative dictionary, but the book is divided into ten parts and comprised of various vocabularies, essays, and prefaces written in English, Welsh, Irish, and Cornish. But its chief historical purpose was straightforward enough: 'to contribute not a little towards a Clearer Notion of the First Planters of the Three Kingdoms, and a better Understanding of our Ancient Names of Persons and Places'.[54] A better understanding of the ancient languages of Britain and Ireland would help illuminate the history of their peoples and cultures, not least because it would make intelligible various ancient manuscripts, some of which Lhwyd planned to include in subsequent volumes. Linguistic knowledge would also help those 'Curious in the Antiquities of the Ancient Gauls', because Gaulish was proved to be related to Welsh and now, crucially, Irish:

> I am sensible Mr. Camden, Boxhornius and others have long since taken notice of the Affinity of our British with the Celtic; but there being no

> Vocabulary extant of the Irish (or Ancient Scotish) they could not collate that Language therewith, which the Curious in these Studies, will now find to agree rather more than ours, with the Gaulish.[55]

This often-quoted line is significant because it not only tied Irish and Welsh together, and to Gaulish, but contained Lhwyd's opinion that Irish was more closely related to the latter. This assertion reverberated through the eighteenth century. While Lhwyd did not quite put it in such terms, later linguistic patriots read this as an assertion of the greater antiquity of Irish—an important aspect at a time when greater antiquity more or less equalled greater prestige, and partisan scholars jostled for the primacy of their subjects.

We have already seen that Lhwyd's major innovation was to prove the kinship of Welsh and Irish, but how did he relate them to the other European languages? Here Lhwyd's ideas are murkier and need to be patched together from his various unpublished and published writings, as they changed over time. His early engagement with Boxhorn provides some clues about how his thoughts developed over the 1690s, when he was trying to determine the relationship of Irish and Welsh to one another and to Latin and Greek. Did Irish and Welsh derive from them, originate alongside them, or merely borrow words from them? Boxhorn had repeatedly stressed that those who thought Welsh derived from Latin or Greek erred,[56] and Lhwyd seems to have found this persuasive, citing Boxhorn directly (though a little inaccurately) to this effect in his letter of 1690 refuting Bernard:

> Marcus-Zuerius Boxhornius saith in his Origines Gallicæ p. 86.
>
> Gracorum [*sic*] Romanorumque sermoni quin plurima simillima Britannicus habeat, negari non potest, neque tamen ex eo sequitur vel a Græcis vel a Romanis sermonem suum Britannos accepisse.[57]
>
> [It cannot be denied that the British language resembles that of the Greeks and the Romans in many regards; however, it does not follow from this that the Britons adopted their language from the Greeks or the Romans.]

Instead, for Lhwyd, Welsh appeared to be 'co-originall' with Latin, but Greek was more difficult to pin down. He returned to the issue in his letter to Lister that contains his famous passage about first learning of Pezron:

> [Pezron's] Notion of the Greek, Roman & Celtic Languages being of one common origin agrees exactly with my observations. But I have not advanced so far, as to discover the Celtic to be the Mother Tongue, thô per-

> haps he may not want good grounds (at least plausible arguments) for such an Assertion. The Irish comes in with us, & is a Dialect of the Old Latin, as the British is of the Greek. But the Gothic or Teutonic thô it has also much affinity with us must needs make a Band apart.[58]

These lines have been picked apart for all sorts of reasons, one of which is for the possible influence that Pezron might have had on him. Yet here Lhwyd also appears to be thinking about Boxhorn, for in the same paragraph from which Lhwyd borrowed his rejoinder to Bernard eight years previously, Boxhorn had written that the most likely explanation for linguistic similarities of Greek, Latin, Welsh, and Germanic was that 'those peoples descend from one and the same tribe, as if from a mother, namely the Scythian tribe, and that they have learned the same language from her, which differs only in dialect'.[59] Lhwyd seems to have adopted most of Boxhorn's findings—principally that there were lexical similarities between all these languages through borrowing, that Welsh did not come from Latin, and that German was separate from them as well—but he never seems to have entertained the 'Scythian theory' or any idea of a lost parent language.[60] More perplexing is Lhwyd's assertion that Irish was a dialect of 'Old Latin' and Welsh of Greek, but he may have just meant that they shared vocabularies;[61] in any case, by 1704 he had decided that 'the Greek, Celtic & Roman seem to have been anciently but much the same Language'.[62] He wrote in the prefatory letter to the 'British Etymologicon'—itself primarily Welsh and Greek words—that the curious would find a 'great Number of words . . . agreeing with the Greek, and not at all with the Latin'.[63] The implication was that there were many root words in the modern Romance languages with Celtic etymologies—as opposed to Greek or Latin—so European antiquities could not be studied with only a knowledge of the classical languages.

Two more linguistic opinions—one wrong, one right—need to be highlighted. The first was his mistaken assumption that Basque was related to the Celtic languages, one all the more bizarre because in his prefatory letter to the 'British Etymologicon', Lhwyd noted that Basque numbers did not match up with those of any other European language.[64] John Aubrey had notified Lhwyd of some Welsh words in the Pyrenees, and Lhwyd perhaps also assumed a relation because he placed some stock in the Irish myths of Iberian origins—despite ridiculing Irish historians like Keating—but one wonders whether he would have made the error if he had been able to travel to the Basque country and gather the linguistic data orally.[65] However, Lhwyd made the correct determination on the fundamentally important issue that Celtic and Germanic were separate, the opposite of the continental consensus shared by scholars like Boxhorn and Leibniz. A letter to Ray in 1690 shows he was considering whether similarities in northern English dialects to Welsh meant they were borrowed from it or whether 'the ancient British language had much affinity with those of Germany, Denmark, &c'.[66] Trusted opinions in his network coalesced around the idea of difference. John Ray (1627–1705) followed Cluverius's idea that Celtic had once been spoken in Germany, but now 'the present Dutch or Teutonick language is originally different from the ancient Celtick or British & Gallick, being nothing but a dialect of the Gothick. How the Celtick came to be lost in Germany & the Teutonick introduced I know not'.[67] The master of Old Germanic languages, George Hickes, also separated the 'Celtick, or ancient British' from the Gothic family, the Greek, and the Slavic, in a letter of 1694 that was apparently given to Lhwyd.[68] By 1698 Lhwyd was writing to Lister that although there were similarities between 'Gothic or Teutonic' and the 'Celtic Languages', ultimately they 'must needs make a Band apart', a view reinforced by letters from later correspondents.[69] Lhwyd pointed out sound changes between Teutonic, Greek, Latin, and the Celtic languages, but famously left the mother tongue 'modestly undecided'; although his caution was laudable, his hesitation to draw a clearer picture would leave the door open for a century of misguided theorising.

Instead, many opted for Pezron's thesis that Celtic was the European 'mother tongue'. The relationship of Lhwyd and Pezron is one of the more famous aspects of this foundational episode in Celtic linguistics, but any influence of the latter on the former has been overplayed.[70] It is occasionally assumed that Lhwyd was referring to Pezron when he wrote about his interest in a book on Gaulish antiquities in 1691,[71] but this is unlikely, both because Pezron's chronological works of those years included nothing about the Celts or Gauls, and because Lhwyd wrote to Martin Lister in 1698 that he was 'such a stranger to [Pezron's] works that I never heard of his name'.[72] After Lister attempted to put them in contact, Lhwyd spent years trying to reach him, to no avail, though Pezron and his theories appeared constantly in his letters.[73] Yet Lhwyd's comments are mostly sceptical of Pezron's Celtic thesis and of the nationally minded motivations behind it.

Although he never presented a clear summary of his view of linguistics and history, Lhwyd's linguistic, and therefore historical, picture of ancient Britain and Ireland can be synthesised as follows. A colony of ancient Gauls brought their Celtic language to Britain, where they left evidence in place names across the west and northwest of the island, before migrating to Ireland, though circulation continued between Ireland and the west of Scotland. Celtic died out in Gaul but Irish survived, though it received an influx of Basque when the Scots arrived from Spain—as preserved in Ireland's medieval annals. Meanwhile, another Gaulish colony had arrived in Britain and developed a dialect of Celtic, but once enough words changed in sound and signification a new language developed: Welsh. Both descending from Gaulish, Irish and Welsh shared the same 'genius' and many words differing only by their initial sounds. The origins and relationships of Celtic with other languages were more obscure. Lhwyd was certain that Celtic and Latin were 'co-originall' and that the Teutonic family was separate from the Celtic, but Greek posed a problem and Lhwyd seems to have vacillated about whether Celtic derived from it or whether they originated together, though he was adamant that Celtic was closer to Greek than Latin was. In any case, because Celtic had been spoken across much of ancient Europe, etymologists had to learn Irish and Welsh because these languages preserved roots of Latin and Greek words whose origins were obscure. Whether there was some higher genetic affiliation between Celtic and Greek (from which he believed Latin derived) or their similarities resulted from borrowing is unclear, for though Lhwyd was familiar with Boxhorn's Scythian idea, he never adopted it or advanced the idea of a lost European parent language, despite having a clear understanding of the dynamics of language change and death.

The *Glossography* met a mixed reception.[74] Learned 'linguists and antiquaries' like his friends William Baxter (1650–1723) and Bishop William Nicolson appreciated it, but many 'gentlemen'—crucially most of those who had funded the project—did not.[75] Lhwyd was forced to print the *Glossography* at his own cost and two years later he died penniless. Still, it was enough to achieve his reputation, and one of those who quickly grasped its brilliance was G. W. Leibniz.

G. W. Leibniz and the European 'Celtic' Family

Among his myriad interests, the German polymath G. W. Leibniz paid close attention to linguistic scholarship throughout his life, but especially from the early 1690s, when he began working on a prefatory dissertation to the history of the House of Guelf, his patrons, that would reveal their origins and migration into Europe.[76] For the purposes of reconstructing ancient history and tracing the early movements of nations, Leibniz repeatedly attested to the unrivalled utility of linguistic evidence, and it is well known that he was a proponent of the Scythian theory.[77] He was also a patriotic advocate of the German vernacular and inherited the common European view that the ancient Gauls and Germans spoke related languages that could be grouped together as 'Celtic'. Yet until the middle of the 1690s he was unsure whether Welsh and the Brittonic languages belonged to this group or not, and he was even more trepidatious about Irish until about 1704. However, ultimately Leibniz accepted that all of them did—independently of Lhwyd—and he developed a sophisticated theory of a European language family he often referred to as 'Celtic'.

Interestingly, Leibniz' curiosity about Welsh seems to have been stimulated by the same work that spurred Lhwyd: Edward Bernard's *Etymologicon*.[78] After reading about it in October 1691, Leibniz enquired after the work and Bernard himself, 'For I also often reflect on these things. We may note many things in British or Armorican, Greek, Latin, and German. . . . I do not doubt that all of these languages no less than Slavic flowed from the same source'.[79] Just before he learned about Bernard's work, Leibniz had inspected the extract of Davies's Welsh lexicon in Boxhorn's *Originum Gallicarum* and detected similarities between Welsh and the Germanic tongues.[80] For the next several years he deepened his enquiries into Welsh and Gaulish.[81] Boxhorn's book cropped up repeatedly in his letters of this period, and Leibniz agreed with him and Camden that Welsh, Breton, and Cornish were remnants of Gaulish.[82] And because Welsh was a remnant of Gaulish, it too could be referred to by the word under which Leibniz understood German and Gaulish: 'Celtic', which increasingly appeared in his letters from about 1693.[83]

Leibniz's ideas developed and solidified on this point over the next few years, but his use of 'Celtic' was highly variable, at different times referring to the Brittonic languages specifically, or used as a synonym for Germanic. In 1695, for example, he wrote to Antoine Verjus (1632–1706) that 'our Germanic peoples and apparently also the Celts came from Scythia',[84] but in 1697 he wrote to another correspondent that 'the old Celtic or Gothic language received many words and terms from Greek'.[85] In 1697 he introduced these findings into his essay on the use and improvement of the German language, separating the Gauls and Celts: 'the old Gauls, Celts and also Scythians had common roots with the Germans'.[86] Yet in 1698 Leibniz began to use Celtic more frequently as an umbrella term for the languages of Western Europe that encompassed primarily Germanic, Gaulish and the modern Brittonic languages, and Latin. For example, in two different letters—one in Latin the other in German—he wrote:

> That which is common to German, Latin, even Welsh, is Celtic to me: Latin, I say, wherever it differs from Greek.[87]

> I call German and Gaulish, *Celtic*. And I look for ancient Gaulish partly in Welsh or British, and partly in Latin and the languages corrupted from Latin . . . I suspect, however, that the original German was nearer to Welsh and Latin than it is now, and that Gaulish was, as it were, intermediate between German and Latin. By Latin, I understand the part of the language not derived from Greek.[88]

Written in quick succession, these two letters show that Leibniz was now not only referring to the affinities of these languages as Celtic, but also trying to account for words in Latin that did not appear to come from Greek, and therefore came from Gaulish or Welsh, exactly the thesis Lhwyd was articulating around the same time.

Pezron's letter of 1699 written to Nicaise, which the latter sent to Leibniz as well as to the *Nouvelles de la république des lettres*, was evidently of great interest. For a genius, Leibniz was fairly patient with inferior thinkers and their works, and he sent out five copies of Pezron's letter to correspondents in order to collect opinions.[89] He saw much to recommend Pezron's theory, in particular his idea that the Titans may have been allegorised Celtic or Scythian invaders, but ultimately he disapproved of Pezron's instrumentalization of Breton, which to him smacked of 'Goropianisme'.[90]

The year 1704 was a turning point. Leibniz learned about Lhwyd's ongoing work, though even before this he had reached the conclusion that Irish was part of his Celtic group of languages. Erich Poppe has examined Leibniz's inquiries into Irish, and what he calls Leibniz's 'first phase' was characterised by puzzlement over whether Irish was related to Welsh or the other European languages more generally.[91] In 1694 Leibniz speculated about a connection between Irish and Welsh—as he knew John Wallis had suggested[92]—but rejected the notion upon examining the Lord's Prayer in both languages. However, after Thomas Smith (1638–1710) reported that he had been present when a Welsh bishop and an Irish bishop had found commonality between their languages, Leibniz turned agnostic and lamented the lack of reliable Irish materials which would allow him to decide for himself.[93] When the trail in his correspondence picks up again in March 1704, Leibniz had accepted Irish's Celtic credentials. As he wrote to Andrew Fountaine (1676–1753), 'The dictionaries, grammars and notices of the languages of Wales and Ireland have always interested me greatly, because I consider Welsh as ancient Gaulish and

I consider Irish as a still more ancient Celtic'.[94] Again, this was the same as Lhwyd's idea at the time. In July, Leibniz expanded further, writing that because of the remoteness of the Isles they likely preserved traces of the 'ancient languages' better than the languages of the Continent, and therefore '[Irish] shows something of the oldest language of the Celts and Gauls'.[95] It was during these years that Leibniz composed the *Nouveaux essais sur l'entendement humain*—only published posthumously in 1765—and formulated the Irish relationship to the other Celtic languages in a more lapidary form than the scattered remarks in his letters:

> Ancient Gaulish was even more different [than Old Gothic was to modern German], judging by the language most approaching true Gaulish, which is that of Wales, Cornwall, and Brittany; but Irish is still more different and gives us traces of an even older Britannic, Gaulish, and Germanic language. Nevertheless these languages all come from one source and can be taken for alterations of a single language, which could be called Celtic.[96]

If Leibniz's ideas bear some resemblance to Lhwyd's, this might be because he was in part stimulated by them. In the March 1704 letter to Fountaine, Leibniz wrote that 'It struck me one day reading your *Transactions* [*of the Royal Society*] that one of your learned men had perceived some connection between Latin and Irish, even independently of the Romans'.[97] He was referring to Lhwyd's letter to Lister that had mentioned Pezron, as well as the line that 'The Irish comes in with us, & is a Dialect of the Old Latin, as the British is of the Greek'.[98] There is too little in this remark for Leibniz to have borrowed for his own theory that Irish was an older dialect of Celtic, but he may have been encouraged by the idea. Lhwyd entered more firmly into Leibniz's consideration later that year, when the English scholar William Wotton (1666–1727) wrote to him about philological work in Britain and announced that 'the Cambro-Briton Edward Lhuyd . . . labors at a work . . . in which whatever pertains to the languages and antiquities of the Cambro-Britons, Irish, and Armoricans, will be explained and illustrated most accurately'.[99] Leibniz eventually wrote back that he read the news about Lhwyd with 'great pleasure', but in the same letter he wrote that he believed 'the Irish originate from the ancient inhabitants of Britain and that they are witnesses to an even greater antiquity'.[100] In a letter written shortly before this one, reporting on Lhwyd's work to another correspondent, Leibniz stated his suspicion that the Irish had migrated west earlier than the Britons and 'would mark a Celtic still more ancient'.[101] What all of this shows is that Leibniz came to the same conclusion as Lhwyd without having read him.

That Leibniz eventually saw Lhwyd's work is certain, for there exists a short set of manuscript notes on it in the Leibniz Bibliothek in Hanover.[102] It is undated, but a remark in the 'Brevis designatio' that a 'learned Englishman' was investigating Irish and Celtic, but nothing more specific, suggests that Leibniz still had not seen the *Archaeologia* by 1710. When he did finally see it, the notes Leibniz made were wordlists and etymologies taken from the various vocabularies included by Lhwyd, or passages copied verbatim about sources mentioned or drawn upon by Lhwyd; unfortunately, there is little metacommentary on Lhwyd's ideas in their own right. Yet what Leibniz chose to note is revealing. Of course, as he had hitherto lacked specimens, Leibniz was interested in Irish, and the first page contains about thirty words beginning with 'A' in Irish. However, the most substantial notes are taken from the 'Essay on Comparative Etymology', particularly the sections about the permutation of letters. Leibniz noted the famous *P-Q* Celtic distinction, copying two sections remarking on the correlation of *P* and *C* in British and Irish respectively, once amid an extended paraphrase of Lhwyd's summary of the permutation of letters, and in another section on the P and C distinction specifically.[103] In line with what we know about his interests, Leibniz also noted passages that explained similarities between the Celtic, Latin, and Germanic families.[104]

The relationships across these families, and the information on Gaulish, British, and Irish, helped him to fill out the picture of his 'Celto-Scythic' theory of the origins of the European peoples and languages during his last years.[105] He had explained this clearly in his *Nouveaux essais*, where he suggested that common roots in Celtic, Latin, Greek, and Germanic were due to 'the common origin of all the peoples descended from the Scythes', who then settled in different parts of Europe.[106] His theories for linguistic origins were fleshed out more fully in his inaugural address to the Berlin Academy of 1710, where he outlined how Europe had been populated by a series of Celtic invasions coming east from Scythia.[107] Basically, the farther west one travelled, the more archaic the language they would encounter; this was helped especially by the remoteness of Britain and Ireland, and therefore Irish was closer to the original Celtic than was Welsh, both of which were closer than most modern European languages. The 'Celtic' languages comprised one large portion of the 'Celto-Scythic' family, which fanned out from the Atlantic Ocean all the way to the Sea of Japan and was itself one of the two branches that had developed from the *Ursprache*. One of Leibniz's most elegant statements to this effect, which contained his most well-known reference to Lhwyd, came in the section 'Celtica', in his posthumously published *Collectanea etymologica* (1717):

> I consider it necessary for the perfection or, indeed, the real advance of Celtic Studies to include a careful study of Irish, in the way especially begun by Lhwyd [*Lloydius*] . . . the Irish are an offspring of the ancient inhabitants of Britain, anterior to the many colonies of the Celts . . . if beyond Ireland there is another Celtic-speaking island, it would lead us like a thread to things more ancient still.[108]

Leibniz's more deductive approach and macroscopic view of the European languages was very different from Lhwyd's careful empiricism and study of cognate dialects, but they nevertheless reached very similar conclusions about Celtic. One of the key differences was Lhwyd's concern with delineating the Celtic family as that descended from Old Gaulish; although he saw connections with German, ultimately it had to make a 'band apart'. Leibniz, on the other hand, was trying to determine the affinities of European languages to one another and the relative ages of languages, which could help to draw a more accurate picture of ancient history and human migrations; therefore, he was more concerned to connect the language families of Europe to one another and thereby get past the Scaligerian idea of mutually exclusive *linguae matrices*. Here Leibniz's concern aligned with the longer tradition of European scholarship that conflated ancient Gauls and Germans under the concept of 'Celtic'. That Celtic and German are related is technically correct, but only on the broadest level, and it was out of step with the notion of the particular language family that was beginning to be called 'Celtic' in Britain and Ireland. The precise relationship between the Celtic and Germanic languages was yet to be determined, but the continued use of 'Celtic' as an umbrella term—as Leibniz used it—ultimately occasioned a negative reaction in Britain, explored further in chapter 4.

Celtic Linguistic Studies in Britain and Ireland, after Pezron, Lhwyd, and Leibniz

The remainder of this chapter focuses on the reception of the works by Pezron and Lhwyd, as well as Leibniz where relevant. As we have seen above, before its publication Pezron's work was anticipated by word of mouth, and reported in publications such as the *Nouvelles de la République des lettres* in 1699, which was 'Englished & read by J.J. at Gresham Colledge ye 10th May 1699'.[109]

Whatever his other failings, Pezron hammered home the affinity of Welsh, Breton, and Cornish, and after his work was published the question became the relationship between this group and the Gaelic family. Although Lhwyd's rather unwieldy book provided an answer, it did not present a coherent broader historical outline—only bits and pieces that had to be stitched together—and so left the field open for Pezron. Generally speaking, historians agree that Pezron's work was more influential in Britain, but this should be qualified by the recognition that Brittonic proponents made greater use of it than Gaelic antiquarians did. In part this must be down to the fact that Lhwyd averred that Gaelic was closer to ancient Gaulish and was therefore the older language.[110] This was hard for Welsh patriots to take. Scott Mandelbrote points out that English theologians also preferred Pezron's work for the purposes of linking the English to the Welsh (as the original Britons), stressing the supposed continuity of the ancient British (Celtic) Church to strengthen independent claims from Rome.[111] It was these national and religious biases and the ulterior motives they engendered that plotted the salient points within which Celtic linguistic research developed over the eighteenth century.

While Lhwyd is now seen as one of the greatest Welsh scholars ever and a pioneering Celticist, Pezron was the polestar for eighteenth-century Welsh antiquarians. One reason is probably because subsequent writers did not compose highly technical works like Lhwyd's, but more straightforwardly narrative histories like Pezron's. His book was obviously useful for proud Welsh patriots who were nevertheless sceptical of the traditional Brutus myth.[112] One of these was the vicar Henry Rowlands (1655–1723), who developed ideas in correspondence with his friend Lhwyd. In 1703, for example, he accepted with Lhwyd and Leibniz that Irish and Welsh were related to each other as well as to the other languages of Europe.[113] Rowlands's magnum opus, *Mona Antiqua Restaurata* (1723) was nominally a history of Anglesey—which he held to be the island 'Mona' mentioned in Roman sources, against antiquaries who argued that it was the Isle of Man—but placed the island within the wide sweep of universal and sacred history.[114] Tracing the Celts westward from the Flood, Rowlands thought place name evidence revealed that they arrived directly from Babel, though he also accepted a later Celtic arrival stipulated by Pezron.[115] In a long essay on linguistic relationships appended to the main text, Rowlands praised Pezron, 'that great light of our British antiquities', for his historical narrative and agreed with him that 'Celtick' was the European 'mother-language', which Lhwyd left 'modestly undecided'.[116] Lhwyd was also lauded, but mainly for having outlined the correct approach to etymological study. Rowlands accepted that Irish and Welsh were related, but his own purpose was closer to Pezron's: to show that the 'Celtic or British' bore a closer relationship to Hebrew than Greek, Latin, English, and Gaulish put together, meriting consideration as the 'most ancient and least corrupted language in this western part of the world'.[117] While Rowlands's was the most sophisticated English-language history of Wales in the eighteenth century, the most important Welsh-language history also relied on Pezron. This was Theophilus Evans's *Drych y Prif Oesoedd* (Mirror of the first ages), a popular Welsh vernacular history first published in 1716, updated in 1740, and reprinted through the nineteenth century.[118] Evans retained Geoffrey's Brutus myth, but mixed it with Pezron's account of the direct descent of the Britons from Gomer, deriving Cymraeg from 'Gomeraeg'; this book might be thought of as an eighteenth-century popular history and as such there is not much room in it for careful scholarship like Lhwyd's.[119]

The later mainstream currents of Welsh scholarship did not pursue Lhwyd's philology much further. Instead, the dominant thread, followed by the Morris Circle—named for the remarkable Morris brothers, Lewis (1701–1765), Richard (1703–1779), and William (1705–1763), who were the leading Welsh scholars of the mid-eighteenth century—was literary, focusing on the recovery and publication of Welsh medieval poetry and establishing its history. Of course, Lhwyd was interested in Welsh literary manuscripts, but primarily for philological and historical purposes: What could these manuscripts tell him about the ancient Britons, the European Celts, and their histories? The differences of emphasis here are subtle but important. Welsh scholars of all stripes and backgrounds were proud of their language, and they were naturally eager to learn the lessons Lhwyd had to teach them. His work was read and cited reverently; however, in general, Welsh scholars preferred the work of Pezron for the higher universal significance he gave to the Celtic language. In 1763 Lewis Morris wrote to a correspondent about the pedigree of Welsh, 'the principal remains of the *Celtic* Tongue, which made formerly so great a Figure in the World . . . as has been sufficiently proved by *Pezron*, and other learned Men'.[120] As seen in the introduction to this chapter, Richard Morris had identified Lhwyd and Pezron as the twin masters of Celtic, but his older brother Lewis was a little more circumspect. In his own magnum opus, *Celtic Remains* (unpublished until 1878), Morris criticised Lhwyd for neglecting Welsh verse and accused him of wild etymological guesses; Morris said that by contrast, Pezron was more careful, and he drew copiously on ancient authorities, only dressing up his etymologies as 'mere guesses and probabilities'.[121] Scholars now recognise the opposite was in fact the case. But language was not highly valued for its own sake in the eighteenth century, and Lhwyd's book merely seemed to tediously prove what everyone already knew: that the Welsh language had a prestigious pedigree and an ancient history. There was nothing unscholarly in the subsequent Welsh focus on its literature. A huge corpus of material preserved in manuscripts hidden away in the libraries of the gentry needed to be excavated, carefully studied, and published.

Those sympathetic to Scots Gaelic brimmed with confidence following Lhwyd's statement that it appeared to be closer to ancient Gaulish. Although Irish scholars would protest that Irish Gaelic was the purer version of the language, Scottish scholars by and large did not differentiate between the two. In the 1730s, the Scottish Presbyterian minister David Malcolme (d. 1748) wrote a series of letters and essays in which he outlined a model positing Gaelic as the parent not just of the European languages but of all those stretching around the world from the Isthmus of Panama to China. He mentioned Pezron but praised Lhwyd as the 'Prince of the antiquaries of his age', and he also approvingly cited Leibniz several times and seemed to allude to him when he stated his own desire 'to proceed in a Way as near that of the Mathematicians, as the Nature of the Thing would allow'.[122] Although the geographical scope of his Celtic theories was excessive, Malcolme understood better than most of his contemporaries the Lhwyd-Leibniz synthesis, as he translated Leibniz's approving passage in the *Collectanea* mentioning Lhwyd and sought to build on it by identifying St. Kilda as the island 'beyond Ireland' where the oldest form of Gaelic would be found.[123]

Gaelic lexicography and poetry increased in popularity during the 1740s. Alexander MacDonald (*c.* 1698–*c.* 1770) published the first Gaelic-English dictionary (stimulated by Lhwyd's research) in 1741 and ten years later produced a collection of verse inspired by the Jacobite Uprising of 1745 titled *Ais-Eiridh na Sean Chánoin Albannaich* (The resurrection of the ancient Scottish language), which featured a similar diffusionist scheme in a preface indignant at the persecution that Gaelic had undergone in the supposedly enlightened eighteenth century.[124] MacDonald's justification for cultivating the language centred around its historical value as a remnant of the 'greatest monument' of the ancient 'Celtic nation' and 'the depository of the manners, customs, and notions of the earliest inhabitants of this island.'[125] In these years there were also several antiquarians collecting Gaelic verse,[126] but for our purposes the most significant figure in the pre-Ossianic context was the Dunkeld schoolmaster Jerome Stone (1727–1756), who combined an emphasis on the intrinsic worth of Gaelic poetry with a linguistic antiquarian framework in several letters to the *Scots Magazine*.

Of inauspicious birth and circumstances, Stone taught himself Hebrew and Greek successfully enough to impress the Rev. Thomas Tullidelph (d. 1777), principal of the newly created United College of St Andrews University, who helped to enrol him there in 1748 and remained a patron for the rest of Stone's short life.[127] In the early 1750s, Stone took up the position of schoolmaster in the village of Dunkeld—on the border of the Highlands—and in 1754 set about learning Gaelic, announcing its utility as an antiquarian tool to the *Scots Magazine* a year later. Stone lamented the Germanic etymological follies of Goropius Becanus, and argued instead that the European languages derived from ancient Celtic, now preserved in Welsh and Irish.[128] Another letter to the magazine announced that in the Irish language could be found poetry 'of very great antiquity . . . which for sublimity of sentiment, nervousness of expression, and high-spirited metaphors, are hardly to be equalled among the chief productions of the most cultivated nations',[129] and in a letter to Tullidelph, Stone suggested that because the Highlands and Ireland had long remained free of foreign admixture, there was 'no People on the Globe of the Earth, whose Language may be proven to have Undergone less Change'.[130] Here, then, we see Stone connecting the strands of continental linguistic antiquarianism to some of the patriotic Gaelic sentiments beginning to be aired, as well as several of the themes that would dominate the Ossianic controversy several years before James Macpherson met any of the Lowland literati.

Stone's public campaign for Gaelic came to an abrupt end with his premature death at the age of 29 in 1756, but it is clear that he intended to publish a full-scale linguistic antiquarian work.[131] Titled 'An Enquiry Into the Original of the Nation and Language of the ancient Scots, with Conjectures about the primitive State of the Celtic, and other European Nations', the manuscript contains the standard lines that 'Conformity of Language was the Strongest Proof of the Kindred of Nations' and 'the ancient Language of our Country [Gaelic]' was the 'best Help in the World for clearing up [Scotland's] remote Antiquities'.[132] Citing Lhwyd, Leibniz, and the English political theorist Sir William Petty (1620–1687), Stone argued that Gaelic preserved 'the Old Celtic' of Europe, whose speakers had crossed from Gaul to Britain and from there settled Ireland—this play would be remade to great effect by James Macpherson.[133]

It is well established that Lhwyd's work was decisively influential in Ireland, and that Leibniz also made an impact, but it took some time for the full implications of their conclusions to be realised.[134] Ironically, Lhwyd's most important correspondent in Irish matters explicitly warned him not to associate Irish with 'the Celtic', which he thought to be Germanic, 'as the Celtae came from Germany', therefore 'I advise you not to touch that allusion of Celtæ, & gaiḋel'.[135] This was the dispossessed Gaelic aristocrat Roderick O'Flaherty (1629–1718), who lived a secluded scholastic life at Cois Fhairrge west of Galway. Although he wrote in Latin and English, O'Flaherty maintained the veracity of the traditional myths of Irish origin in the Gaelic annals and aligned them with biblical and classical chronology.[136]

Of course, one Irishman—perhaps the first—to appreciate Lhwyd's achievement was John Toland. Already in 1694 he was certainly convinced of Ireland's Celticity and later wrote that the only thing more ridiculous than the Irish belief in an Egyptian descent was the British myth of Trojan ancestry; however, his Celtic work, which was planned to include a dissertation on the languages, remained undeveloped for another quarter century and unpublished for several years after that (see discussion in the following chapter).[137] Instead the Anglican clergyman Anthony Raymond (1675–1726), a fairly well-known antiquarian in the Ascendancy Ireland of his day but now obscure, played a more direct role in transmitting Lhwyd's significance to Ireland.[138] He is notable as one of the earliest Protestants to take an interest in the Irish language for scholarly purposes, though he probably picked it up either during his childhood in Kerry or for the practical purpose of administering to his congregation in Trim, County Meath. It is possible he met Lhwyd during the latter's trip to Ireland in 1699–1700, and it has been suggested that he translated Lhwyd's Irish preface.[139] Although he finished none of them, Raymond planned a number of works on Irish history, antiquities, and linguistics. Instead of suspicious medieval origin myths, Raymond described the 'Affinity of Languages' to be 'a certain method to discover from whence any Nation derives its Original'. Yet like almost everyone else, the relationship of Irish to the other European languages puzzled him until he 'examined the Irish with the Celtick, by Mr. Edward Loyd's and Pezrons' Celtick Vocabularies' and 'found almost an universal Agreement amongst them'. In a clever move, Raymond pointed to Strabo's use of 'Scythoceltae', which allowed him to keep the essential outline of the Gaelic account while benefitting from the findings of Lhwyd and Pezron: the Irish still hailed from the Scythians, but their language was best explained with reference to the Celtic languages.[140] Raymond also followed Lhwyd (and perhaps Leibniz) in arguing that where Greek and Latin words had mysterious etymologies, they were likely to be Celtic.

After reading Lhwyd and Raymond, Charles O'Conor (1710–1791), the most eminent Irish Catholic antiquary of the eighteenth century, fully embraced the notion of Ireland as 'descended from the most humane and knowing Nation of all the old Celts'.[141] In his *Dissertations on the Antient History of Ireland* (1753), O'Conor drew upon Boxhorn, Cluverius, Pezron, and Rowlands to cast 'Celtic' as the original language of the Gomerians. This primeval language had split into the 'various Dialects of the Gauls, Teutones, Persians and Spaniards' but was 'to this Day, a living Language in Ireland'.[142] Although he acknowledged Welsh as ancient, O'Conor denied its claims to Celtic purity because it did not have an ancient alphabet, whereas the Irish alphabet's supposed antiquity proved for O'Conor that pre-Norman Ireland had been a land of high civilization rather than barbarism, which meshed with the Irish Catholic argument that the Norman invasion destroyed the Irish golden age, an issue that Norman Vance and Clare O'Halloran have shown remained salient from the antiquarian scholarship of the eighteenth century through the Irish cultural nationalism of the nineteenth.[143] The Irish could be proud of their native language, on which the English had cast so many aspersions, wrote Father John O'Brien (1701–1769), because it was 'asserted by very Learned Foreigners to be the most ancient, & best preserved Dialect of the old Celtic tongue', and therefore 'the most useful for Investigating & Clearing up the antiquities of the Celtic nations in General'. Those 'Learned Foreigners' were 'the great Leibnitz' and 'the Learned & Candid Mr. Eward [*sic*] Lhuyd'.[144]

One often forgotten chapter of eighteenth-century antiquarianism is that a number of English antiquarians were influenced by Pezron and Lhwyd and believed their own language came from Celtic. The major reason for this was the continued conflation of the ancient Germanic and Celtic peoples and cultures. This appeared, for example, in the antiquarian history of Europe by the Bodleian librarian Francis Wise (1695–1767), which extolled Pezron's research and called ancient Celtic the 'Titan Language':

> Antiquaries are sufficiently justified in calling these dialects Celtic, because they are the first known in Europe or Celtica. Perhaps they may deserve a much higher title, namely that of the Universal Language of the postdiluvian world.[145]

In his quite mad work on comparative etymology, John Cleland (1709–1789), better remembered as the author of the erotic novel *Memoirs of a Woman of Pleasure* (1749), or 'Fanny Hill', found English to be the purest dialect of the ancient Celtic. It certainly explained the classical world: 'Lycurgus . . . in the

Celtic, is a *maker* of *laws*'; 'Hercules. One who does great execution with a Club'; 'Homer is not a proper name, but a general one, for Bard or Man of Song'.[146] Similarly, an eccentric Welsh-born London lawyer, Rowland Jones (b.1722–1774), thought English was the purest form of Celtic, which should be restored to its 'primitive state' for use as 'an universal language': 'If then the English should appear to be the best Celtic dialect and the original language of the Europeans, why should it not be restored as the general language of those countries?'[147] Finally, in the first major work on Cornish antiquities, the Cornish antiquarian William Borlase (1696–1772)—predictably enough—followed Rowlands and Pezron more closely in the argument that Celtic (and therefore Cornish) was close to Hebrew and at the base of most European languages, including the Germanic. The ancient Celts—traceable by their language—were a sought-after ancestor in every nation of the Isles, even England, well into the eighteenth century, and for some even pointed the way to a universal language.[148]

The *Académie des inscriptions* and the Debate over the French Language

Lhwyd made little impact in France. His book was 'despised at Paris and elsewhere' for being written in English instead of Latin, suggested Thomas Hearne (1678–1735), and it is indeed difficult to find references to it in French works.[149] Although Pezron's work was better known, William Baxter reported to Lhwyd that already in January 1703 the Cistercian was being treated as 'a Visionaire, which is a Lazy way of confutation, as well as a very rude one'.[150] Pezron's work was only used selectively and his argument did not penetrate very far into the lively debate about French national origins that occurred during the first few decades of the century, the most important context for understanding the importance of the Celtic past—and with it ideas of the Celtic languages—in pre-revolutionary France.

Pezron's work did, however, fit comfortably into the patriotic Breton linguistic tradition. Building on Pezron and his predecessor Julien Maunoir, Breton missionary-lexicographers of the early eighteenth century continued compiling dictionaries from the oral material they recorded in their evangelist roles. The Capuchin monk Grégoire de Rostrenen (1667?–1750) reiterated Pezron's major points in highly condensed form in his dictionary preface in order to provide a historical framework for Celtic—preserved in modern Breton—a 'langue matrice' whose roots provided the building blocks for longer word forms in Greek, Latin, and German.[151] Rostrenen used this demonstrated antiquity to contribute to the long-running debate over the ontology of language that stretched back to Plato's linguistic dialogue *Cratylus*, subtly refuting the idea of a natural origin for language by suggesting that the 'barbarous' words identified in Greek were really Celtic and had been borrowed by the Greeks directly from Noah's offspring.[152] Dom Louis Le Pelletier (1663–1733), a Benedictine monk of the scholarly Congregation of Saint-Maur, took a different approach. As his editor explained, Pelletier's dictionary was an etymological 'History of the Breton Language', and his more rigorous comparative method allowed him to reclaim Celtic words that had been borrowed into Latin, French, and Greek.[153] Rostrenen had made exactly this point in his *Grammaire François-Celtique* (1738) where, having consulted the seventeenth-century dictionaries of Antoine Furetière (1619–1688), César-Pierre Richelet (1626–1698), and the *Académie Françoise*,[154] he called out its contemporary members who vainly searched for the origins of French words in Latin, Greek, Arabic, and Teutonic, when they were available closer to home in the Celtic language of Brittany, an argument similar to those made by Pezron, Lhwyd, and Leibniz.[155] If their Celtic theories were not always embraced, the Breton dictionaries of this era intrigued scholars of various nationalities and were widely appealed to for Celtic etymologies.

The attention to Breton underscores the increasing interest in the Gaulish/Celtic language for the purposes of historical enquiry into the French national past—a paramount issue in eighteenth-century French political debate.[156] French scholars and philosophers were trying to decide which of the available ancestors—Celts or Gauls, Romans, Germans or Franks—were the real foundation of the French nation. The results varied according to the thinker and had as much to do with their political proclivities as the information available to them, but generally speaking the nobility—or 'Second Estate'—argued that their special privileges arose out of the right of conquest, which their Frankish ancestors had inflicted upon the Gauls, ancestors of the commoners or 'Third Estate'. After a lull in the seventeenth century, there was a burst of new historical attention given to the Gauls in the eighteenth century, reflected in raw publishing numbers as well as in the number of debates in which they featured in journals, institutions, and academies devoted to studying the national past.[157] From the 1730s, Raymond Mas notes, there was increasing use of the terms 'nos ancêtres' or 'nos pères' when referring to the Gauls, and this decade also saw the foundation of the huge state-sponsored compendium of sources—the *Recueil des historiens des Gaules et de la France*—aimed at a 'perfect understanding of the Gauls' before the Frankish invasion, undertaken by the Benedictines of Saint-Maur.[158] Despite renewed interest in the ancient Gauls, in the pre-revolutionary period they were still very much the underdogs in historical and political debate.

One of the most famous manifestations of this ongoing dispute was what is called the 'Romanist' versus 'Germanist' debate that took place in and around the *Académie des Inscriptions et belles lettres* in the middle decades of the century.[159] These arguments sought to establish the ethnic basis of France's ancient constitution, and thus the proper history and role of the monarchy and three estates. After the theories of Henri de Boulainvilliers (1658–1722), Count of Saint-Saire—which argued that noble privileges came from the Frankish conquest and the imposition of feudalism[160]—were posthumously launched in the late 1720s and early 1730s, the Abbé Jean-Baptiste Dubos (1670–1742) responded with a large history arguing that the Gallo-Romans had allowed the Franks into France, where the two peoples merged relatively peacefully.[161] The Baron de Montesquieu's (1689–1755) demolition of Dubos and critique of Boulainvilliers in the final books of *De l'esprit des loix* (1748)—supporting the Frankish origins of a limited monarchy—reinvigorated the origins debate, which lasted into the next century and the final Gaulish triumph in the 1830s.[162] Even if famous names like Boulainvilliers and Montesquieu supported the Frankish interpretation (both were, after all, nobles), and have therefore somewhat stood out in the historiography, there were many others who supported the idea that the true origins of the nation lay with the ancient Gauls. To take the most famous of these, though he was scathing about their barbarity, Voltaire (1694–1778) nevertheless acknowledged in his 1757 article on 'Les Francais' in the *Encyclopédie* that the ancient Celtic families of Gaul remained the foundation of the eighteenth-century nation, in which the Gaulish character still survived.[163] As the century wore on, the political edge of the Gaulish interpretation sharpened (see chapter 5).

Language was an important part of the origins debate.[164] Did French descend from Celtic, Latin, or Germanic Frankish? Igniting the argument in 1740, one of the *Académie*'s leading historians, the Breton Charles Pinot Duclos (1704–1772), mixed the Romanist-Germanist debate into his moderate argument for the Latin descent of the French language. Making use of the understanding of the Gauls and Germans as both Celtic peoples, Duclos argued that the Franks spoke a 'Celtic' language and therefore did not have to force it on the Gauls: the fifth century was one of cultural assimilation not conquest.[165] The main opponent of the—quite orthodox and correct—view of French Latinity was the antiquarian Pierre-Alexandre Lévesque de la Ravalière (1697–1762), who decided that this was the hill he was prepared to die on. However, despite being a member of the *Académie des inscriptions*, where he delivered papers on the subject, Ravalière was not allowed to publish his opinion that Latin had remained a learned language in contrast to the Gaulish vernacular through most of the first millennium. Pierre-Nicolas Bonamy (1694–1770), historiographer of Paris, stepped forward to clear things up on 10 December 1750, arguing that most French words came from Latin and that the *génie* of their grammatical structures were consonant. Ravalière would not concede, but the *Académie* adopted Bonamy's position, and in a report on the dispute published in 1756 it wrote that Ravalière would not admit French had 'any obligation to the Latin language . . . fearing this origin as like a title of vassalage. . . . He envisions that the Celtic language of the ancient Gauls has been preserved down to us, that we speak Celtic to this day.'[166] Ravalière embarrassed some of his colleagues in the *Académie*, but as we will see throughout this book, the idea that Celtic played a considerable part in modern French remained a common belief well into the nineteenth century. It appeared, for example, in the *Encyclopédie*, where Anne Robert Jacques Turgot (1727–1781) noted that 'our French language has taken many roots' from 'le Celtique'.[167] The academician Nicholas Beauzée (1717–1789) agreed, and wrote that French syntax appeared to be non-Latinate and, like most other European languages, likely descended from a primitive Celtic tongue.[168] There was one lone voice in the *Académie* arguing during these years that Celtic and Germanic were separate and that similarities resulted from borrowing, and it belonged to the best historian of the *Académie*, Nicolas Fréret (1688–1749). Droixhe concludes that Fréret had read Lhwyd's book, and it is notable that he included the Gaelic branch together with the Brittonic as part of the Celtic family, but in all of these things it seems that Fréret is the exception proving the rule.[169]

The most influential work examining French origins through a purely linguistic lens, and one on which Nicolas Beauzée and others drew, was the three-volume *Mémoires sur la langue celtique* (1754–1760) composed by the dean of Besançon University, Jean-Baptiste Bullet (1699–1775). Bullet certainly read Pezron's book and likely Lhwyd's as well; Richard Morris wrote to his brother Lewis that it was suspected that Bullet 'made great use of the Archaeologia Britannica without acknowledging his obligations to the author'.[170] Through an essay on the history of Breton, a long list of European toponyms and their etymologies in Breton/Celtic, and a two-volume dictionary, Bullet purported to show that Celtic/Gaulish/Breton (to him they were all the same) had been preserved as the national language until the tenth century and was the primary base of modern French as well as the *patois* of different regions. Not only did Bullet reject the cultural and political effects of the Frankish invasion, he completely denied Latin's influence on French.[171] His diminution of Latin meant that Bullet's work only snuck through the censor, who felt Bullet's 'système' put the Breton cart before the Latin horse.[172] Bullet's works also help to reveal the potential political import of linguistic research, as in his monarchist *Dissertation sur les Fleurs de Lys* (1759), where he revealed his key for unlocking the secrets of French antiquities unavailable to other scholars: 'la Langue Celtique'.[173] This, for instance, showed that the *fleur-de-lis* had nothing to do with lilies or the Franks, but was drawn from the Celtic word *ly* for 'king' in Breton, Welsh, and Irish—a lexical root that was also the source for the absolutist *lit de justice*. The political point seems hard to miss: the French monarchy owed more to native Celtic traditions than to those of the country's Germanic invaders. Although they were not highly thought of, Bullet's volumes would be cited in Britain, Ireland, and France over the next few decades.[174]

German contributions also continued to stimulate debate over Celtic origins, following distinctly in the Cluverian and Leibnizian tradition of viewing the Celts as one ancient people, from which the modern French and Germans descended. The Huguenot Simon Pelloutier (1694–1757), librarian of the Berlin Academy, authored the most significant mid-eighteenth-century European work on the ancient Celts, in which he conceived of them as the first inhabitants of the Continent, who had branched off into the various nations across Europe that had developed over time. He sought to bolster this with a chapter on language, arguing that there had once been a single Celtic language, which then split into a number of dialects (the languages of modern Europe), and that German was a remnant of the ancient Celtic language.[175] However, he again drew mostly on classical hearsay, including only a few pages of actual linguistic evidence and excusing himself from anything further that would be 'as fatiguing for me, as it would be boring for my reader', whom he referred instead to Leibniz's *Originum gentium*, Cluverius's *Germania antiqua*, and Johann Wachter's (1663–1757) 'excellent' *Glossarium Germanicum* (1737).[176] Pelloutier did include seven words, some of which ('brig' or 'dun') are indubitably Celtic, but then he dubitably claimed they were just as present in German. Finally, he argued not only that German descended from Celtic but that of all the surviving languages it best preserved ancient Celtic.[177] In sum, Pelloutier's 'Celtic History' is really a history of ancient Europe, in which the Celtic peoples (as we understand them) featured heavily because there was a wealth of testimony about them, but they were connected by the author to other people that we would not consider Celtic. Perhaps nothing is more revealing than the fact that Pelloutier envisioned his *Histoire des Celtes* as a prelude to an intended history of Germany.[178] The book generated discussion for decades, leading to its reissue in 1771; it was important not only in continental discussions, but in Britain and even America, where Thomas Jefferson (1743–1826) read it in addition to Montesquieu in the 1770s.

Another member of the Berlin Academy, Johann Peter Süssmilch (1707–1767), was better acquainted with the actual Celtic languages, but still understood 'Celtique' to follow the Leibnizian label of the pan-European language spoken by the Continent's inhabitants before they split into Gauls, Germans, and other early nationalities.[179] J. G. Herder (1744–1803) indicated in his *Treatise on the Origins of Language* (1772) that he too understood German to descend from 'old Celtic'.[180] Despite the crucial work, above all by Lhwyd, but also by Pezron and Leibniz, continental authors largely did not grasp the specificity of the 'Celtic' languages, preferring to think in terms of a single ancient European people who were called 'Celts'. Although incorrect from a strictly linguistic point of view, that idea of the ancient Celtic *Urvolk* would help to determine German success in the development of nineteenth-century comparative philology (see chapter 6), and their interest in the Celts through the twentieth century.

Conclusion

Returning to the flippant question with which this chapter began—Could a dictionary of Celtic be so important that its compiler should be entitled to get away with murder?—we can now better understand the importance of linguistic work in establishing the prominent place of the Celts in the early modern European historical mind. Even though the Celtic languages were spoken by peoples confined to the Atlantic fringes of Western Europe and submerged within larger states dominated by England and France, they were seen by many as the key to ancient European history. As Pezron had stressed, the Celtic language—in his mind Breton and Welsh—had been spoken not only by the Gauls but by the earliest inhabitants of Europe and the Titans of Greek mythology. Edward Lhwyd showed in his remarkable fieldwork that this 'Celtic' language group included not just the Brittonic languages but the Gaelic languages of Ireland, Scotland, and the Isle of Man too. After reading 'Lloydius', G. W. Leibniz became even more certain in his conviction that these were some of the oldest surviving remnants of the ancient Celtic language of Europe, though he differed on some of the particulars. So, if the etymologies in the dictionary promised by Eugene Aram could have been trusted, they would be a linguistic key to Europe's ancient history because they would reflect the ideas, culture, and history of the first Europeans. The problem is that much eighteenth-century etymologising was quite spurious. As we have seen, linguistic antiquarianism was bent strongly towards national pride, theological orthodoxy, and political expediency. Scholars often found what they wanted to find within the languages they examined. In Part II we will see how the dawn of 'scientific' historical and comparative linguistics completely transformed Celtic linguistic scholarship from the 1830s, but until then things remained in the mould examined in this chapter. There was Celticism before Pezron and Lhwyd; it was just very different from the modern version that arose in large part as a result of their work.[181]

3

Gods, Druids, and Stonehenge

MYTHOGRAPHY AND ARCHAEOLOGY

DIOGENES LAERTIUS (*fl.* third century) opened his *Lives of the Eminent Philosophers* with the now famous suggestion that philosophy was born with the barbarians:

> There are some who say that the study of philosophy had its beginning among the barbarians. They urge that the Persians have had their Magi, the Babylonians or Assyrians their Chaldaeans, and the Indians their Gymnosophists; and among the Celts and Gauls there are the people called Druids or Holy Ones.[1]

However, Diogenes knew very little about the Druids, merely that 'they uttered their philosophy in riddles, bidding men to reverence the gods, to abstain from wrongdoing, and to practise courage'. As we have seen, one of the dogmas of Druidic philosophy was that it was forbidden to be written down and was passed along orally instead. Information about this priestly philosopher caste was therefore extremely scant, but even what the Greeks and Romans managed to glean had 'no better foundation than vulgar rumour', wrote the Unitarian minister William Enfield (1741–1797) in his rendering of Jacob Brucker's (1696–1770) *Historia critica philosophiae*.[2] While Diogenes doubted that philosophy was of barbarous provenance, there were many early modern thinkers who wanted to prove him wrong, vindicate their ancestors, and claim a prestigious origin for their own religious philosophies. Facing the same lack of material, however, they 'filled their accounts of the Celtic theology with idle tales and extravagant fables'.[3] Understanding the philosophy and religion of the ancient Celts has therefore been one of the greatest challenges in Celtic studies for centuries. Although the Druids are the standout figures of Celtic otherworldliness and we have a few descriptions of them, conjuring up the pantheon of Celtic Gods—to the extent that one existed[4]—and the devotional practices they inspired has been more difficult.

With the classical record so limited, early modern scholars were driven to try and find alternative forms of evidence.[5] Etymology could be of some use, especially in light of the linguistic developments explored in the previous chapter; however, since ancient Gaulish was extinct, its closest descendant, Welsh—according to scholars like Camden and Boxhorn—was thought to be the best etymological source. For example, Henry Rowlands put it succinctly that 'we the Celtae came to call our first masters of knowledge Druids, from the Celtic word *Derw*', which means 'oak', an interpretation that had appeared in Davies's *Dictionarium Duplex*, been popularised by John Selden (1584–1654), and was supported by Rowlands's friend Edward Lhwyd.[6] Because Caesar had recorded that Druidic ceremonies took place in oak groves, this explanation seemed eminently plausible. Etymology was especially useful in the continental study of the Celtic religion, but the major innovation across Britain, Ireland, and Europe during this period was the investigation and use of material remains, or what we could call 'archaeology', to supplement the written record about the Celts.

Could 'archaeological' evidence be straightforwardly aligned with classical accounts of the Druids? It would have to be if scholars wanted to learn anything more than what the Greek and Roman sources provided. The antiquarian William Stukeley justified his own pioneering archaeological studies on the basis that scholars who confined their focus to written texts had made little headway, 'since authors only transcribe from one to another, the few remaining scraps to be found in classic writers'.[7] Stukeley was one of a number of antiquarians who expanded his field of Celtic vision to the most impressive megalithic structures in Britain: Stonehenge and Avebury. Although the material remains of ancient Britain had long been of interest to antiquaries, learned opinion seemed to prefer a Roman, Saxon, or Viking origin for these stone circles—in other words, anything but a Celtic one. John Aubrey, John Toland, and William Stukeley were the key figures who made some of the first systematical studies of these structures as well as strong arguments for their Celtic provenance.[8] They had different ulterior intellectual motives—to be discussed below—but each aimed to make a comprehensive study of all such physical antiquities in Britain. They were united in their belief that stone circles were Druidic monuments, and while Aubrey was hesitant to describe them as Celtic, Toland and Stukeley were not. They therefore firmly tied the Celts and their Druids to eighteenth-century ideas on the origins of Stonehenge, Avebury, and the megalithic monuments of Britain, Ireland, and much of Western Europe.

Yet even though learned opinion in Britain and Ireland began to accept stone circles as the settings of Celtic religious ceremonies, what happened in them and in whose honour remained matters of speculation. They may have involved human sacrifices—ideas of which captured the imaginations of antiquaries and artists—but other less violent, if still 'barbarous', rituals were often imagined.[9] If the frame was assembled, much of the picture remained to be painted, and one of the key missing details was the gods which the Druids worshipped. There were the scraps left by Caesar—who had identified native Celtic Gods like Dis, the eponymous father of the Druids—and in his *Pharsalia* the poet Lucan (39–65 CE) had mentioned the Gallic Hercules 'Ogmios', who defeated his enemies with rhetoric rather than a club, as well as a mysterious god named Esus. However, a series of archaeological discoveries made on the European Continent over the early modern period gradually revealed a host of ancient Celtic gods. One of the most important findings was the *Pilier des nautes* (Pillar of the Boatmen), found underneath the choir of Notre Dame Cathedral in Paris during renovations in 1711. This monument and others like it were so significant because they provided evidence of Celtic gods not mentioned in the extant classical sources, as well as images and details of gods known only as names in text; Esus, for example. 'Every day we unearth monuments which teach us about the gods of [the Gauls], and of particularities mentioned neither by Caesar nor any other author', wrote the Maurist historian Bernard de Montfaucon (1655–1741) when he reviewed these discoveries.[10] This chapter therefore shows how scholars in Britain and Ireland situated their accounts of ancient Celtic religion within the stone circles of the European landscape, and how at the same time their continental counterparts revealed a new picture of the Celtic gods worshipped in these places.

Already difficult due to the patchy evidential record, research into the Druids was further complicated by the variety of uses to which information about them was applied in the early modern period. As R. E. Asher wrote, every age invents its own Druids for its own purposes, and in early modern Europe these reasons were primarily religious, patriotic, and political.[11] For German and French Renaissance authors, accounts of the Druids proved that their 'barbarous' ancestors had practiced philosophy; if the rumour that the Druids taught Pythagoras was true, then they might even have helped to create classical philosophy, and were therefore probably not so barbarous after all. Following the

Reformation, polemicists on both sides of the confessional divide claimed the Druids. Drawing on the Church Father Origen (*c.* 185–*c.* 253), British Protestants wrote that the Druids prepared a smooth landing for Christianity. Because they preserved knowledge of humanity's primeval religion practiced by Adam, Noah, and his descendants,[12] the Druids readily received the Gospel and then established a Church, 'even before Rome itself'.[13] The upshot was that there existed an independent version of British Christianity that merely needed to be restored by the Reformers. Patriotic concerns were tied up with this religious interest, and British scholars made much of Caesar's note that Britain was the centre of Druidic learning. Following on from John Selden, important figures like John Milton (1608–1674)—who praised 'our ancient Druides, by whom this Island was the Cathedrall of Philosophy to France'—and William Stukeley recast Britain as a mecca of ancient religion and learning superior to the barbarous pagans of the Continent.[14] But the Druids were also politically useful. For the freethinker John Toland they provided a 'complete history' of the evils of 'Priestcraft', while for the Jacobite historian Thomas Carte (1686–1754), the joint civil and ecclesiastical power of the Druids supported his patriarchal argument that power resided with the king and not Parliament.[15] In short, because of their various uses for early modern intellectual argument, the Druids were of much greater significance than simply being the Celtic priestly class; and, because of the source limitations, imagination had to step in.

The Druids, Ancient Theology, and the Comparative Study of Religions

If the practices of the Druids were unclear, their historical origins were generally agreed upon and were deduced from the biblical account of human dispersal and the classical sources. The standard early modern narrative of the Druids ran something along the following lines. The Druids arrived in Europe as part of the ancient Celtic migrations that happened long before the era of recorded history. Descending directly from Noah's grandson Gomer, the Celts spoke a language and practiced a religion that did not differ much from Noah's.[16] But over time idolatrous practices crept in, and they forgot the original faith. The Druids oversaw those practices, and as the philosopher-governor class of the Celts were widely influential across much of the ancient European Continent. The main seat of Druidic learning was probably in Britain, until the Romans cracked down on them there and in Gaul. The massacre of the Druids on the island of Mona (Anglesey) and the burning of their oak groves, as described by Tacitus, signalled their demise in the first century CE. Not all of the Druids were wiped out, however, and their ultimate vindication came—in the eyes of early modern authors writing from a Christian and often also ecclesiastical viewpoint—when they recognised the truth of Christianity once missionaries arrived and helped to convert their countrymen. In Britain the important result was a native form of Christianity that flourished before the establishment of the Roman Catholic Church, while in France the same conversion narrative existed but the emphasis was on continuity between Druids and the first bishops of the Catholic Church. The Druids were celebrated by both patriotic and pious writers in early modern Britain and France, however, often because their joint civil and ecclesiastical authority was useful for supporting arguments that the state should have power in religious matters.

Understanding the significance of Druidism to early modern thinkers therefore requires an acquaintance with some of the central theological issues of the period. One of those was the nature of the *prisca theologia*, the pristine or ancient religion which the first humans had practiced and which Noah and his family preserved before true religion was revealed to the Hebrews.[17] One fairly popular idea was the 'Neoplatonic' one stretching back to late antiquity and positing that everything in the universe proceeded from an immanent first cause, thus squaring pagan philosophy (at least that of some pre-Socratics and Plato and his followers) and Christian theology. Thus, it was thought, ancient humanity had shared a common religion, but once the Confusion of Tongues occurred at Babel and the peoples had scattered, their inability to communicate with one another accelerated their mental and spiritual degeneration. They forgot the Old Testament religion common to humanity and descended into idolatry. As time went on and different civilizations evolved their own cultures with distinctive religious features, the panoply of ancient pagan religions evident at the dawn of recorded history came into existence. Only the Jews preserved the original religion in its purity and were rewarded with revelation, the true principles of which were then adopted by the Christians. Still, optimistic theologians and historians thought that the corruptions of the original religion that they encountered in the different religions of the world's peoples might still contain vestiges of that original system, which could be forensically reconstructed if enough data was gathered and commonalities identified.

Druidism was one of those corrupted religions and was of special interest as, supposedly, the pagan philosophy of much of ancient Europe. But whereas ancient Eastern philosophy and religion could be systematically investigated because there were many surviving texts to examine, as far as anyone was aware there were no such Druidical texts. It therefore seemed unlikely that investigating the Druids would be of much help in composing a history of the original ancient religion, and so interest paled in comparison to that in ancient Near Eastern languages, texts, and philosophy.[18] Still, the Druids were the religious-philosopher caste of the ancient Celts and were accordingly of interest to those nations which claimed descent from them, regardless of their brand of Christianity.

Like the Celts more generally, the Druids fell out of the classical literary record in late antiquity. They survived in Irish and Welsh medieval texts, although the links between the use of the word *Druid*—to mean something close to 'magician'—and the ancient Druids are unclear,[19] and these were mostly unknown to early modern scholars. In any case, there was little room for Druids in medieval texts celebrating Christianity, noble families, military distinction, or chivalry, and they only reappeared in more texts with the rise of Renaissance humanism. Scholars across Europe appropriated the Druids for their own various purposes. Conrad Celtis and the Abbot Trithemius in Germany both contributed to their favourable impression, while French interest in the Druids was also high in the sixteenth century (see chapter 1).[20] To take only one example, Noël Taillepied's little book about the history of the Druidic Republic recounted an Annian-inspired history of France, which from the time just after the Flood had been a justly governed monarchy, and then been converted into an aristocratic republic—during whose duration the three estates were created—which lasted for more than a thousand years until the Roman conquest. The ulterior message, aimed at various heretical Protestant groups, was that the republic had fallen when it started slipping towards democracy.[21] Owen and Hutton suggest that because of the time he spent in Paris, the Scot Hector Boece would have picked up on the French Druidical interest, which might explain their appearance in a favourable guise in his *Scotorum historiae* in 1525 (also published in Paris); however, by (perhaps intentionally) confusing the Isle of Man with Anglesey as the home of the Druids (called 'Mona' and described by Tacitus), Boece set off a controversy that lasted over two centuries but was ultimately decided in favour of Anglesey. The Druids are also present in the works of English Renaissance historians and chroniclers such as John Bale, Raphael Holinshsed, and John Caius (1510–1573)—who claimed the Druids founded the University of Cambridge—as well as in the more critical scholarship of William Camden. In these

Renaissance accounts the Druids hold an ambivalent position, where patriotic pride in their philosophical advancement has to concede the reality that they were superstitious pagans.[22]

With increasing European expansion, the seventeenth century saw a refreshed interest in paganism and the history of idolatry, and the Druids benefitted accordingly. Camden's work served as a bridge for the philologists of the seventeenth century, and was the stepping-off point for John Selden; he was, like Camden, deeply interested in the history of Britain, but embedded this within a much more expansive view of world history made possible by considerable linguistic talent.[23] He gave a succinct but fairly comprehensive account of the Druids with the help of a range of comparative etymologies in his notes to the *Poly-Olbion* (1612), in which he used Greek and Welsh etymologies to derive their name from 'oak', identified them as the philosopher magistrates of ancient Britain and Gaul who believed in Pythagorean doctrines, and proclaimed that Britain was 'their mother: whence, as from a seminary, Gaul was furnish'd with their learning'.[24]

A relatively similar picture of the Druids appeared in the great religious compendia of the seventeenth century. For example, in his important survey of the history of idolatry, *De origine ac progressu idololatriae* (1641), Gerardus Vossius (1577–1649) noted that 'Druid' came not from Greek but from the 'Celtic language', by which he meant 'Old British and Gaulish', though he followed Caesar's suggestion that Britain was their seat.[25] A less thorough account appears in the Scot Alexander Ross's (1591–1654) compendium *Pansebeia, or a View of all the Religions of the World* (1653), where he included the Druids as the gods of the ancient Gauls and Britons but merely regurgitated Caesar.[26] This tradition is also the appropriate one for understanding the first major work on the Druids themselves, the *Syntagma de Druidum moribus* (1664) of Thomas Smith—the same man who would later inform Leibniz that Welsh and Irish might be related languages (see chapter 2). Following well-established precedent, Smith preferred the etymology from the 'Celtic word Deru', or oak, and followed this etymology back to Abraham, the source of their doctrines that had then descended through the Kabbalah, Pythagoras, and finally the Druids.[27] Smith's book appeared with the flowering of Anglican historical scholarship of the Restoration, which tended to find space for Druids as precursors.[28] As impressive as these works are, with their many comparative etymologies drawn from a range of languages, they are not interested in the Celts as such, and were all pursuing various kinds of Christian apologetics, primarily united in their accounts of the Druids' crypto-monotheism. For studies on Celtic religion, their importance lay rather in recovering the relevant passages from the classical authors—they are almost all there in Selden's few pages and discussed at length in Vossius—and identifying the Celtic gods.

Of all the seventeenth-century works on the Druids, arguably the standout text was actually a novel, the immensely popular *L'Astrée*. Written by Honoré d'Urfé (1568–1625), comte de Châteauneuf, the work is a sprawling pastoral novel published in six parts from 1607 to 1628. The plot involves two lovers—a shepherdess, Astrée, and her shepherd partner Céladon—who live in fifth-century Gaul as the Romans depart and the Franks arrive. Druids are stock characters and d'Urfé presents a version of freedom-loving Gauls based on his reading of historians examined in the previous chapters like Fauchet, Pasquier, and Taillepied.[29] The historian Charles Pinot Duclos admitted in a footnote to his essay on the Druids (see below) that he had been tempted to use some information he picked up from the novel, which shows that more than a century after they first appeared, the volumes of *L'Astrée* helped to keep the Druids and the question of French national origins in mind at a time when the 'Germanist' thesis was at its height.

The point to take away from this is that, despite the dearth of primary textual evidence, the volume of scholarly information about the Druids increased greatly over the early modern period, and was substantial by the end of the seventeenth century. There were several now-common assumptions: that the Druids were philosophers whose learning was either drawn from the East or associated with ancient Eastern philosophy; that their theology was in some way monotheistic; and that this led to the easy conversion of Druidic societies to Christianity. However, we have seen that the Druids were largely still adrift in the discourse, conveniently floating around for almost whatever use towards which an author wanted to put them; the limitations of the textual record were apparent, and in the search for alternate sources of information antiquarians turned increasingly to physical remains embedded in the landscape, which finally began to tie the Druids more firmly to particular times and places.

John Aubrey and Stone Circles

Various opinions regarding the architects of Stonehenge had been advanced since at least Geoffrey of Monmouth, who wrote that Merlin had magicked the stones over from Ireland for use as a royal tomb. During the seventeenth century, opinion was divided among ancient British, Roman, Saxon, or Danish interpretations. John Aubrey has been appreciated for being willing to push the era of their assemblage further into prehistory, making them knowable only through 'archaeological' investigation.[30] Stonehenge and other megalithic monuments had, according to Aubrey, likely been built by the ancient Britons for use by their Druids.[31]

Born in 1626, Aubrey was from a cash-poor gentry family in Wiltshire. He studied at Oxford and the Middle Temple, but spent his time on his estates researching and writing. He was a well-connected member of the Royal Society and the author of the famous collection of seventeenth-century English biographies, known as the *Brief Lives*. Although his archaeological ideas were well known, Aubrey never published his magnum opus *Monumenta Britannica*, though its first section, 'Templa Druidum,' was finished by 1690. In the preface, he explained that he had been familiar with Stonehenge as a child but had been entranced by Avebury when he stumbled upon it while hunting in early 1649. He developed theories for its origin as well as that of Stonehenge and was invited to share them with Charles II (1630–1685), with whom he visited Avebury in 1663.[32] The king's brother, the future James II (1533–1701), instructed Aubrey to write up his ideas, which became the 'Templa Druidum'.

Among those who had suggested Druidic associations with megalithic monuments were important predecessors such as William Camden and John Selden,[33] and Aubrey's Druidic theory ultimately extended, he explained, from 'Mr Camden's Kerrig y Druidd' (lit. 'Stones of the Druids'), a monument in North Wales that is now lost.[34] Thus, these stone circles were Druidic temples, but so old 'that no Bookes doe reach them: so that there is no way to retrieve them but by comparative antiquitie'.[35] In other words, there was no textual evidence for the origins of such monuments—whether there had ever been any or it had been destroyed by the Saxons or Danes was an additional question—and therefore 'the Stones' would need to 'give Evidence for themselves', and the best way of doing this would be through a comparative study.[36] The rest of 'Templa Druidum' examines the major stone monuments, including Avebury, Stonehenge, Boscawen-Un in Cornwall, and dozens more besides. Since these monuments were found in Ireland and Scotland (where the Romans had not penetrated), as well as Wales (where the Danes had not gone), it seemed likely they were 'erected by the Britons: and were temples of the Druids'.[37] Aubrey determined that they were spread across Britain and Ireland, and that monuments of a similar nature might be found in 'the less frequented places of Germany, France, and Spain, if not also in Italy', but noted carefully that similar structures were not to be found in Scandinavia, seemingly drawing a division between ancient 'Celtic' and 'Gothic' cultures in Europe.[38]

One puzzling feature of the work that must be noted, and which appears to be standard across Aubrey's oeuvre, is the absence of the adjective 'Celtic' to refer to any of these things. This is despite the fact that many of his correspondents used it, and that his references to ancient and modern authors, particularly in his sections excerpting classical material about the Druids and Bards, show that he was interested in what we would understand as ancient Celtic society.[39] Furthermore, remarks made later in the *Monumenta Britannica* and elsewhere show that he was more or less operating with the same post-Boxhorn, pre-Lhwyd understanding of ancient Gallo-British society and its survival in aspects of Welsh culture, especially its language. One note—probably written before 1670—shows that Aubrey wanted 'some Welsh gentleman' to examine French dictionaries for examples resembling Welsh words, which would likely be remnants of Gaulish. 'Buxhornius' had hinted at this but not completed it, and Aubrey predicted that it would show that Welsh had once been 'spoken from the Orcades [and] Ireland, to the Appennine hills', and noted additionally that Archbishop Ussher had 'averred the Irish language and British to be the same; and differing only in dialect'.[40] Thus, Aubrey seems to have been anticipating Lhwyd's project long before their acquaintance, and their letters show how close their views on this were. Aubrey's notion that people from the same ancient culture had built the stone monuments common to Britain and Ireland, and probably further afield, would have easily squared with Lhwyd's Celtic theory, which was developed just after Aubrey's death in 1697.

In any case, by strengthening the argument for the Druidic origins of monuments like Stonehenge and Avebury, Aubrey prepared the ground for them to be folded more easily into the Celtic past imagined in the eighteenth century.[41] With the Celtic places of worship and the languages spoken by them established, later authors could be left to investigate Celtic philosophy and theology.

John Toland and the Irish Druids

John Toland began studying Celtic antiquity in the 1690s just before John Aubrey's death, but he only published his findings a quarter-century later, just as Stukeley was beginning his research. Though Toland responded to many of the same intellectual and religious issues that they did, his wider philosophical project differed substantially and has been the subject of a considerable literature.[42] It might be crudely sketched as the idea that human reason was all that was necessary to understand true religion, but that 'crafty priests' had obscured this simple fact in order to keep the people ignorant and themselves in power. Politically, he was a republican who believed in religious toleration. These views—which made him an intellectual renegade often on the move—would feature in his *Specimen of the Critical History of the Celtic Religion and Learning*, whose 'design' was 'form'd several years ago at Oxford' in the 1690s but only presented in a prospectus over three letters to the Irish Whig Robert, Viscount Molesworth (1656–1725), in 1718–1719.[43]

Each of the letters are wide-ranging essays on different aspects of Toland's programme.[44] The first is a synoptic overview of the subject matter, themes, and historiographical methods, with special attention to the place of the Druids and their religious system. The second zeroes in on an area of novelty: the Druidic pedigree of megalithic monuments. The third is an antiquarian and philological inquiry deep into European prehistory attempting to prove that the mythical Hyperborean philosopher Abaris—who visited Plato in Athens—was a Druid from the Hebrides. With this identification, Toland teased that the relationship between Pythagoras and the Druids would finally be nailed down in the projected book. Partially because of this synoptic character, the work is a strange one and contains several of the irregularities and occasional inconsistencies that have led to Toland's characterisation as 'Janus-faced'. The most fundamental of these is that the *Specimen* was at once a work of serious erudition and a philosophical weapon aimed at the historical phenomenon of priestcraft. Toland intended to smooth this out by confining the philological and antiquarian discussions to a *Dissertation concerning the Celtic Language and Colonies*—which would supersede Pezron's—but they remained mixed together in the *Specimen*.[45] But destroying philosophical and religious arguments with critical erudition was Toland's calling card, so perhaps this would have remained in the final version. Yet the irreconcilable inconsistency arising from this is that the evils of priestcraft are basically confined to the first letter, in which Toland praises Druidical philosophy and science—especially in comparison to that of the monks who superseded them—but nevertheless condemns the Druids for crafting a system 'calculated to beget Ignorance and an Implicite disposition in the people'.[46] In the second and third letters, however, the Druids and Celts more generally are repeatedly lauded and priestcraft goes unmentioned. This is perhaps the result of a patriotic Irish streak in Toland, a feature clashing with his claim to write as an ideal historian should, that is as 'a man of no time or country, of no sect or party'.[47] Aspects of this might be true, but the last thing that could be said of Toland is that he was in any way neutral.

Born into a Catholic family in Derry, Toland converted to Protestantism and studied in Glasgow, Edinburgh, Leiden, and Utrecht, but he was a free-thinking republican radical by the time he moved to Oxford in the mid-1690s to pursue Celtic research. It is unclear to what extent his Celtic research played a role in his wider philosophical project at the time. This is because, although he was about to make his name with his *Christianity not Mysterious* (1696), Toland's project at Oxford consisted of the more antiquarian aspects of compiling vocabularies and accruing information about stone circles and other megalithic structures. Already he harboured advanced views on the Celtic languages and culture, and he benefitted from his native education in Gaelic. As described by Lhwyd, in 1694 Toland laboured to prove Ireland was a colony of Gauls well before the general realisation that Irish was a Celtic language. This he did straightforwardly enough through a comparison of Irish, Breton, and Latin words, apparently believing that Breton was degenerated Gaulish, but nevertheless making the correct and very early determination that Irish was related to them.[48] His later understanding of language families in the *Specimen* was very accurate;[49] he clearly separated Celtic and Gothic, and in his assertion that 'not one single word' of Irish was related to Basque he was right where Lhwyd was wrong.[50] In the 1690s Toland was also advanced in his views of physical remains, the subject of the second letter of the *Specimen*. He met John Aubrey at Oxford and praised him as 'the only person I ever then met, who had a right notion of the Temples of the Druids'.[51] Surveying many of the same stone circles as Aubrey, Toland expanded the Druidical view to include Irish, Scottish, and Manx cairns and forts. Bolstering his own talents was Toland's wide reading in just about all of the available literature—most of which I have already surveyed in the foregoing chapters—as shown by Justin Champion.[52] The erudition upon which the work was based was therefore solid and the conclusions were genuinely original in several places.

Much of this originality came from what Toland (not unreasonably) pitched as his comparative advantage: his native knowledge of the Irish language. With the Irish sources he claimed to be able to fill in and correct the incomplete and occasionally erroneous classical record.[53] With his very first footnote Toland illustrated his etymological prowess with an example drawn from his native Inishowen: Derry had originally been a 'Grove and School of the Druids', deducible by the Irish word *daoire* for 'oaks'.[54] This school had been part of ancient Ireland's advanced civilization, of which Toland painted a patriotic picture: ancient Ireland had been a peaceful land of liberty, where Druids taught belief in the supreme being or first cause, and religious differences were tolerated.[55] The Druids were not only literate but had their own alphabet, which Toland etymologically deduced from the myth of Gallic Hercules. According to Lucan, the Gauls had revered Hercules not as a strapping young warrior but as an old rhetorician able to lead people by the power of his words alone. Although Gaulish Hercules was dressed in the same clothes and carried a club, bow, and arrows—which had allowed Lucan to identify him—he was called 'Ogmius'. According to Toland this was 'pure Celtic' and meant 'the Secret of Letters' and was the same as the 'Ogam' writing system of ancient Ireland.[56] Thus, Celtic etymologies would, Toland claimed, allow him to paint a much fuller picture of Druidism than had hitherto been done, one akin to Thomas Hyde's *Historia religionis veterum Persarum* (except better, he claimed), especially once he was able to study the ancient Irish law codes.[57] What had happened to this advanced ancient civilization? It withered away with the arrival of Christianity. Toland thus transformed the usual hero of medieval Ireland—Saint Patrick—into a villain.[58] Because of ancient Ireland's 'Tolerating principle, this *Impartial Liberty*', and because the Druids had fallen into priestcraft, the Irish people were docile and brought to Christianity quite easily.[59] Patrick and later monks had destroyed most of the Druidical records, and even though some manuscripts existed, now virtually the only thing left of ancient Celtic advancement were the megalithic monuments of Ireland and Britain. The cairns dotted around the Isle of Man, Wales, and Ireland were beacons dedicated to Belenus, the sun god (discussed below),[60] while the many hillforts around the Isles were folded into the picture of the ancient Celtic civilization.

Toland's was the key work on Celtic religion into the nineteenth century. It went through multiple editions and was translated into French and German. Even those who objected to his subversive irreligiosity, like Stukeley, still found much of value in the work.[61]

William Stukeley and the Patriarchal Religion

William Stukeley is not only the vital figure in the popularisation of eighteenth-century Druidism, but also an important pioneer in the history of British archaeology.[62] A physician, member of the Royal Society, and eventually an Anglican clergyman, Stukeley became fascinated with megalithic monuments in the late 1710s, and eventually, in the 1740s, he published books arguing that Stonehenge and Avebury were Celtic temples of Druidic worship. Following on from the archaeologist Stuart Piggott's once classic—but now very dated—biography of Stukeley, recent debate has focused on whether a religious epiphany inspired his ordination in 1729, and the extent to which this arose from his antiquarian interests. Supposedly, Stukeley was afflicted by 'Druidomania', which led to a retreat from 'archaeological' objectivity into a Casaubonish project to reconcile the religions of the world to the patriarchal natural religion.[63] Stukeley himself stated that his interest in Celtic antiquities led him to the view that the Trinity was based upon natural reason: 'my disquisitions into the history of our Celtic ancestors, & their religion, have . . . given me the opportunity of discovering some notions about the Doctrine of the Trinity . . . that 'tis deducible from reason itself'.[64] Yet it seems clear that he was a committed Christian his entire life, that his historical and mythological ideas long predated his ordination, and that these remained consistent until his death. I am therefore unconcerned with Stukeley's religious convictions, and instead focus here on the information on which he drew in constructing his Druidic theories for the origins of Stonehenge and other megalithic structures, and the picture that he painted of the Celts as a result. In contrast to those who smeared the ancient Britons as barbarous, Stukeley patriotically envisioned them as part of an ancient Celtic society as advanced as any of the great civilizations, practicing the original patriarchal religion that was both natural and rational.

Born in Lincolnshire in 1687, Stukeley studied medicine at Cambridge and London in the early 1700s. His friends included many of the major natural philosophers of the time, including Isaac Newton (1642–1727), and after moving to London he was elected to the Royal Society in 1718. At Cambridge Stukeley 'began to conceive a passionate love for Antiquitys', which he explored from at least 1710 on annual walking tours. In the first of these through Oxfordshire, Stukeley expressed his delight at the Rollright Stones, which he surmised were Druidic temples.[65] A strong sense of patriotism is discernible in these early years, and in a letter of 1714 Stukeley wrote that he was not yet ready to cast off the Brutus myth, and resented those who began British history only with Caesar, who had told 'lyes to depreciate the honour of his Enimys the Britons'.[66] By the following year he was reading Lhwyd, and in 1716 Stukeley was meditating on the origins of Stonehenge. At the end of 1718 he transcribed large sections of Aubrey's *Monumenta Britannica* into his own commonplace book, and in 1719 he visited Stonehenge and Avebury for the first time.[67] Finally, before the beginning of his systematic study of Stonehenge from 1721 to 1724, Stukeley read Pezron, where he learned that 'the Celts' were

> as is admirably well shewn in Monsieur Pezron's Antiquities of that Nation, the first, at least most considerable Inhabitants of the Body of Europe. . . . It is observable that the ancient Celtic Nations, of which the Inhabitants of these Countries are Part, erected all their Temples in a circular Form and of dry Stones, where innumberable Examples are still to be seen in all the British Islands.[68]

In short, many of the pieces for Stukeley's Celtic theories were in place before his major period of work began.

The 1720s were a crucial decade for Stukeley, beginning with his annual excursions to Stonehenge and Avebury and ending with his Anglican ordination. Through these years Stukeley also participated in early Enlightenment sociability; he joined the Freemasons, and in 1722 co-founded a society to honour the Romano-British past, which admitted women. Each member took a pseudonym, and Stukeley settled on 'Chyndonax', supposedly an ancient Archdruid mentioned on a Greek inscription found by Jean Guenebault (d. 1629?) on his estate near Dijon in 1598.[69] Discoveries at Stonehenge, the 'most curious Antiquity of Great Britain, & at present, as far as we know [the] only one of its sort in the World', bolstered Stukeley's enthusiasm.[70] His research notes made between 1721 and 1724 show that he clearly considered Stonehenge to be a Celtic construction based upon sacred geometrical principles. The crux was the unit of measurement, or 'cubit', which all the great ancient civilizations had used:

> We see as clear as daylight that the whole [of Stonehenge] is an imitation of Abury. & was made by the same people upon the same Celtic measure or cubit of the Hebrew . . . the Hebrew or Egyptian cubit, the very same that the pyramids of Egypt, & other their works, the Temple of Solomon & as I verily believe by which the construction of Noahs Ark was performd. & by this mesure I find all the works of the Druids in our island are performd.[71]

Stukeley left open the question of which Celtic tribe had built Stonehenge—the ancient Irish or the Belgae were options—but he concluded with the patriotic assertion that 'the greatness &. The beauty of these Works' proved that Britain had been the centre of ancient Druidic culture, and condemned the opinions of 'German or French writers' who argued otherwise because they 'would have nothing said to the honor of Britain'.[72] A drawing Stukeley made in August 1722 depicted his theory in visual form, showing a Druid (Fig. 4) next to the altar at Stonehenge (Fig. 5).[73]

FIG. 4. 'A British Druid', in William Stukeley, *Stonehenge, a temple restor'd to the British Druids* (London, 1740). Reproduced with permission of University of Glasgow Library.

FIG. 5. Illustration from William Stukeley, *Stonehenge, a temple restor'd to the British Druids* (London, 1740). Reproduced with permission of University of Glasgow Library.

These remarks were made during the years that Stukeley undertook his tours of Britain, and in 1724 he published his observations in a book titled *Itinerarium curiosum*.[74] At this point he envisaged a great work on the Celts:

> What I shall next trouble the reader withal, will be my intended work, of the history of the ancient Celts, particularly the first inhabitants of Great Britain, which for the most part is now finished. By what I can judge at present, it will consist of four books in folio. I. The history of the origin and passage of the Celts from Asia into the west of Europe, particularly into Britain; of their manners, language, &c. II. Of the religion, deities, priests, temples, and sacred rits [*sic*] of the Celts. III. Of the great Celtic temple at Abury in Wiltshire, and others of that sort. IV. Of the celebrated Stonehenge.[75]

However, no Celtic magnum opus appeared. Stukeley was distracted by other things, including a move to his native East Midlands, marriage, and his ordination. To concerned friends he wrote that his 'studys into the antiquitys of our Druids forwarded my religious intentions', but he promised he would complete his Celtic works.[76]

Eventually, in 1740, Stukeley published his book on Stonehenge. Its self-explanatory title—*Stonehenge, a temple restor'd to the British Druids*—somewhat hid his 'ultimate view' in service of religion. This was to harmonise the original patriarchal religion with Druidism, and both of these with Christianity—what they, as well as all of the great ancient religions, had in common was their basis in nature and therefore their comprehension through reason. This is why the Druidic cubit mentioned above was so important: geometry was a way of linking individual physical remains scattered around Europe, Africa, and Asia to one another through universal natural principles set out by the Divine.[77] Supporting Stukeley's syncretic religious argument was a scheme of sacred history tracing the ancient Celtic migration from the East: they 'came hither as a Phoenician colony . . . during the life of the patriarch Abraham,' and 'brought along with them the patriarchal religion, which was so extremely like Christianity'.[78] In fact, the only difference was that whereas the Druids had anticipated the Messiah's arrival, Christians lived in a world in which he had arrived; inherent within this was a patriotic vindication of the ancient Celtic Britons, whose Druidic philosophy corresponded almost exactly with Christianity.

As to the more terrestrial question of who had built Stonehenge and for what purpose, Stukeley was clear. The 'primitive Celts who built Stonehenge, were the Picts, Scots, Highland and Irish, all the same people, tho' perhaps differing somewhat in dialect'; 'the old Britons or Welsh . . . had a notion of its being a sacred place, tho' they were not the builders of it', and were instead a later arrival who had pushed the original Celts west and northward.[79] Mixing the sacred geography of Samuel Bochart and Aylette Sammes with the Celtic findings of Lhwyd and Toland, Stukeley summed up that 'Irish therefore, or ancient Scottish, is the remnants of the Phoenician language, mixt with old Biscayan and Gallic, dialects of Celts . . . they are the descendants of the people who built Stonehenge', and their migration from the East, which harmonised conveniently with native Irish myths, explains why similar monuments could be found in North Africa, Egypt, and farther east.[80] Stonehenge was the seat of the 'Chief Druid of Britain', the place of major ceremonies and sacrifices, and where Gauls and other ancient Europeans came to learn at the fount of Druidical knowledge.[81]

The Druids continued to fascinate Stukeley through the 1740s and 50s. In 1743 he published his work on Avebury, which extended his theories for Stonehenge but contained a great deal of speculation on what he believed was the serpentine design of Avebury and its reflection of ancient Celtic religious belief. Ten years later some workmen digging canals in Kew for the residence of Anne (1709–1759), Princess of Wales, unearthed some 'Celts', or axe heads, normally bronze or brass. After inspecting them, Stukeley wrote a letter to the princess in June 1754, but since she did not respond he ambushed her at the gardens a few months later.[82] They talked about the instruments, the Druids, and their easy transition to Christianity. Stukeley reported that Anne was particularly pleased that the 'patriarchal religion' was 'exactly parallel to [the Church of England], and in every particular'.[83]

Stukeley continued drafting plans for large works until his death in 1763, and was working on a book about the origins of Britain, which placed it as a 'parcel of [the] Celtic Kingdom', inhabited by Celts, along with 'southparts of Europ as part of Germany, Italy, all Illyria, Spain and Gaul'.[84] However, at this point Stukeley was a known eccentric, and his mythological and historical ideas were no longer taken seriously. Still, while Stukeley's abstruse mythological and historical theories exhausted contemporaries, through his archaeological work he firmly established that stone circles like Stonehenge and Avebury had been built by the prehistoric inhabitants of Britain, not the Romans, Saxons, or Vikings. To eighteenth-century Britons this meant the Celts, and as both Ronald Hutton and Rosemary Sweet have shown, Stukeley's worked proved decisive in transforming opinion about these places.[85]

Europe: Digging Up the Gods

European literature on the Druids followed similar patterns as those found in the works outlined above. For some, the Druids were benevolent guardians of the corrupted patriarchal religion, while for others they were a bloodthirsty tyrannical class who 'delighted in all that affirmed their power and subjugated men, hope and fear'.[86] Ongoing intra- and international historiographical disputes examined in previous chapters added to the religious dimension. Their archaeological focuses differed considerably, however. Toland, for example, repeatedly complained that the continental literature on Druids was defective because it failed to recognise the Druidic identity of megaliths.[87] This should not be surprising, given that none of the classical sources associated the Druids with these monuments; indeed, they were explicit that the Druids performed their ceremonies and sacrifices in oak groves. The Druids had 'no need for other temples' than the thick of the forest, wrote the future French *historiographe du roi* Charles Pinot Duclos (1704–1772) in 1746.[88] However, the gods who were worshipped in these places remained mystifying, and this was a subject of increasing discussion on the Continent following the piecemeal discovery of objects depicting Celtic deities. In many cases these were quite literally the detritus of ancient civilizations and communities, and though they were less impressive than Stonehenge, they provided evidence that was much more definitive.

Information about the Celtic pantheon beyond what was known from the classical sources gradually came to light over the sixteenth and seventeenth centuries.[89] Among the many statues and antiquities displayed in the Palazzo Grimani in Venice, an inscription caught the eye of the Dutch traveller Stephanus Vinandus Pighius (1520–1604) in 1548. Rather than the Roman gods strewn around the palace, this engraving mentioned 'Belenos', and had come from the ancient Roman port town of Aquileia. Pighius quoted the Grecophone Roman historian Herodian's (*c.* 170–*c.* 250) description of Belenus as the local god equivalent to Apollo, who had been seen flying through the air and aiding the Aquileans in their victory against the Dacian Roman emperor Maximinus Thrax (*c.* 173–238), who died in the siege.[90] The inscription became widely discussed in the Republic of Letters, attracting commentary from figures like Joseph Scaliger, who noted that the Gauls called the herb with which they coated their arrows 'belenium' [henbane], and William Camden, who found an ancient British coin bearing the name of 'Cunobelinus'.[91] It was therefore concluded that Belenus was an ancient Celtic god worshipped across Europe. The next discovery of major significance was uncovered on a beach on the coast of Zeeland in 1647. It was a collection of stones and statues with votive inscriptions to 'Nehalennia', a local goddess usually depicted with a dog by her side. Nehalennia played a starring role in Marc van Boxhorn's articulation of the Scythian linguistic theory, but his etymological guess for the statue was the relatively simple one that 'Nehalennia' was the Latinised version of the place name given by the local German tribe. It is to this day uncertain whether Nehalennia was a Celtic or Germanic goddess, but because of the assumption of close Celto-Germanic links by European scholars, the question was unimportant and Nehalennia was often included among the Gaulish gods.

However, of all the Celtic archaeological finds from the period, the most dramatic discovery was the *Pilier des nautes*, uncovered on 16 March 1711 in an old wall of Notre Dame during renovations.[92] Five stone blocks remain of what would have stacked up to a pillar of about four metres in height. One of the surviving pieces bears the dedication of the 'Nautae Parisiaci' to Jupiter during the reign of the Roman emperor Tiberius (42 BCE-37 CE, r.14 CE-37 CE).

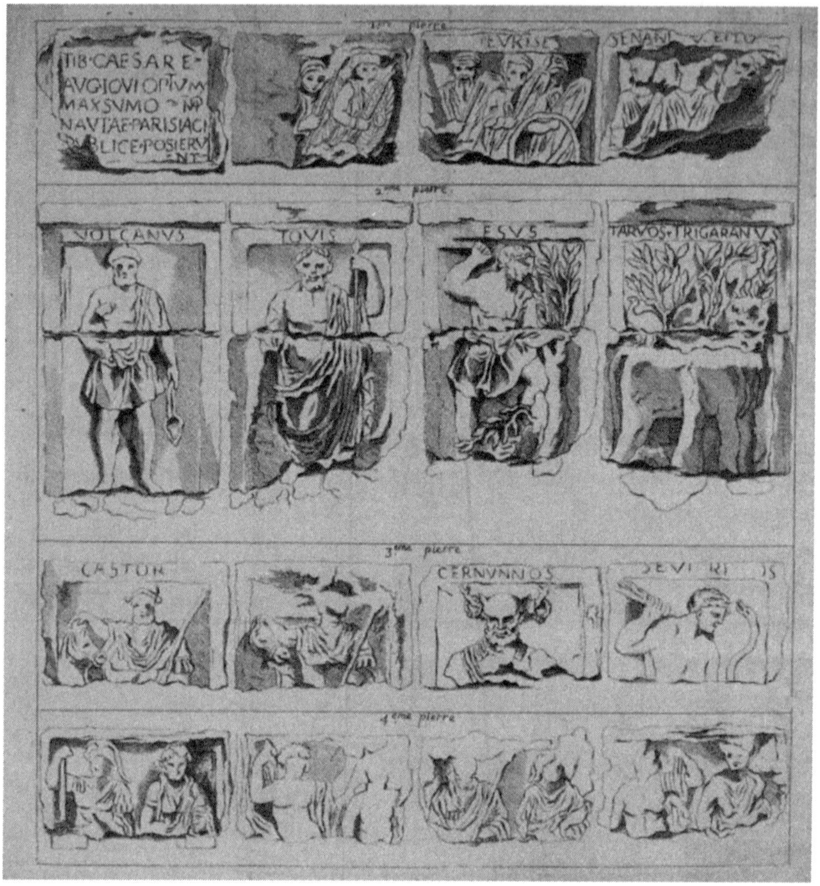

FIG. 6. Reliefs from the *Pilier des nautes*, illustration in Moreau de Mautour, *Observations sur des monuments d'antiquité trouvez dans l'eglise cathedrale de Paris* (Paris, 1711).

Other blocks depict familiar figures of Roman mythology, but the prize findings were the Celtic deities Esus and Cernunnos, and the bull Tarvos Trigaranus (see Fig. 6). The pillar was probably a votive offering to Jupiter made by the boatmen of Lutetia; it is the oldest Gallo-Roman monument that can be dated with some precision. It now retains pride of place in the Musée de Cluny on the Left Bank and has been identified as significant not only for helping to fashion civic and national identities, but for the development of archaeology itself.[93]

The monuments created huge excitement. 'All of Paris has been to see them', wrote the antiquary Charles-César Baudelot de Dairval (1648–1722), who was one of the first to publish on them, in addition to his friend Philibert-Bernard Moreau de Mautour (1654–1737), in July 1711.[94] Both agreed that the unfamiliar figures were Gaulish gods or perhaps Druids, for which they tried to draw Celtic etymologies with the help of the works by Boxhorn, Maunoir, and Pezron. Of course, they also relied on classical descriptions. Baudelot wrote that it was well known that Esus was the Celtic name for the god Mars—presumably drawing on Lucan and the commentaries upon his *Pharsalia*, where human sacrifices made to Esus were stabbed and then hung from trees to bleed to death—but Cernunnos was a mystery.[95] Baudelot thought the pillar depicted religious ceremonies, while Moreau ventured that the figures holding spears and shields might represent the Gauls who raided Asia under Brennus.[96] Whatever they were, the monuments brought honour to Paris and the nation, wrote Mautour, whose pamphlet was reviewed in the *Journal des Sçavans*, and thereby made the discovery known throughout the Republic of Letters.[97]

Leibniz certainly read it as well as Baudelot's pamphlet by late 1711.[98] In a letter to Louis XIV's niece the Duchesse d'Orléans and printed in his *Collectanea etymologica*, Leibniz interpreted the monuments within his Celto-Germanic historical framework, bemused that Baudelot had separated 'les Allemands des Celtes'. The 'Bardes' depicted were 'Gaulish and German poets and singers', and he was perplexed as to why Baudelot wanted to claim that the word *barde* had entered into German from Gaulish, when 'the Gaulish language and nation' had come from the Germans in the first place.[99] As for the names of the gods, Leibniz largely agreed with the two Frenchmen that Esus was Mars and that Cernunnos was analogous to Bacchus or Pan, pointing out that in 'old Celtic, & still today in Armorican *Quern* or *Kern* is *cornu*, corne; the Germans say *horn*, Latin, Greek, and Hebrew agreeing with it'.[100] In another letter, he animatedly discussed Belenus, Nehalennia, Cernunnos, and Ogmios, showing that there was, if not exactly a pantheon, then a collection of Gaulish gods now known largely through antiquarian recovery.

Although the first reports of the pillar were made at the *Académie des Inscriptions*, the Benedictine monks of Saint Maur were of course also interested in the monuments and folded them into their huge erudite works.[101] The new composite picture of ancient Gaulish religion assembled from text, sculpture, and inscription was probably best represented in the Maurist Bernard de Montfaucon's monumental *Antiquité expliquée* (1719–1724). In addition to discussing Belenus, Nehalennia, and other gods known from classical texts, as well some of the standard passages from Caesar and Pliny on the Druids, Montfaucon devoted an entire chapter to the *Pilier des nautes*. This was 'one of the most beautiful discoveries, concerning the religion of the Gauls, that has been made for a long time', and was so important because it provided, among other new gods, images of Esus for the first time.[102] Another Maurist, Dom Michel Félibien (1665–1719), tackled the unanswered question of the monument's purpose shortly thereafter: it had been built by the boatmen's guild responsible for river commerce.[103] Writing at mid-century in his impressive and authoritative *Receuil d'Antiquités* (1756), the Comte de Caylus (1692–1765) commended Félibien's interpretation and reminded his readers that the monument proved that ancient Paris was a city of 'splendour' and commerce.[104] The Gauls had been a commercial people with their own religious identity, not a barbaric group of warring tribes.

Though he also made use of archaeological and linguistic evidence of this kind, another Maurist named Dom Jacques Martin (1684–1751) sighed that the main recourse in studying the ancient Gaulish religion was still to 'leaf through the [classical] authors', an enterprise that was 'as large and broad' as it was 'dry, boring, and often fruitless'.[105] Martin trudged through them anyway and became the most erudite historian of the Gauls in the eighteenth century. Born in the countryside near Toulouse, he spent most of his life in the southwest of France before encountering Montfaucon in 1724 and moving to Paris, where he spent the rest of his life at the Abbey of Saint-Germain-des-Près. Martin best highlights the orthodox apologetic approach to the Celtic religion. Although the Gaulish religion, argued Martin in his *La religion des Gaulois* (1727), had degenerated into something different, it had come directly from the ancestor of the Gauls (Gomer) and resembled closely the religion of the patriarchs and the Jews, and the philosophical theologies of the peoples mentioned by Diogenes Laertius: the Persian mages, the Chaldean sages, and the Indian Gymnosophistes.[106] Martin dismissed Pezron's euhemeristic explanation but kept all of his historical authorities. He also added the patriotic twist that, though the Gaulish religion had almost certainly originated in Gaul and then spread to Britain, the Gauls sent their youth to Britain because—Britain being a backward place on the edge of the world—the religion remained purer there than in dynamic Gaul at the crossroads of European civilization.[107] We can see, therefore, that differences of this sort aside, the Catholic view of the ancient Celtic religion and the Druids was one that shared the same basic narrative as the Protestant one. The popularity of Martin's work also helped to make the pillar finds known in Britain; for example, coming across the antiquity *Bryn Cornyn Jau* in Gwynedd, the travel writer Thomas Pennant (1726–1798) linked it etymologically to 'the horned deity *Cernunnos*, who was venerated by the

Gauls', and since the Gauls and Britons shared a religion, '*Cernunnos* might as reasonably be supposed to have a place here as in France'.[108]

Ideas of the Druids among the *philosophes* normally associated with the main currents of the Enlightenment were mixed and relied almost entirely on the classical sources and their depiction of *moeurs*, customs, and culture, rather than the information that could be speculated upon from physical remains. There was a general revulsion at the—following Toland—priestcraft of the Druids, the superstition they promoted, and their barbaric practice of human sacrifice; however, patriotic impulses often caused scholars to overlook such foibles. The two approaches can be summarised in the dispute between Charles Pinot Duclos and Nicholas Fréret (1688–1749), the two leading historians at the *Académie des inscriptions et belles lettres*, that took place in 1746.[109] At a meeting on 4 February, Duclos read an idealised and highly contoured paper on the Druids that depicted them as the civic and religious leaders of a civilized aristocratic republic. He sidestepped the issue of human sacrifice, writing that they instead offered mistletoe and bulls to the Gods, and denied they were either polytheists or idolators: above all, he wrote, the laws of the Druids were designed to honour the Supreme Being (*souverain Être*).[110] Duclos's rose-tinted picture was due to the fact that he thought that he could see lines of continuity between ancient Gaul and modern France. 'To understand well what a nation was in the most distant times, is a means to understand what she still is to this day' and studying the Druids 'could even serve to make known the spirit of the first laws of our nation, and even those that we follow today.' For example, the origins of the three estates lay not with the Germans but with the Gauls, who were divided into the three orders of 'the Druids, the Knights, and the People'.[111] The paper provoked a heated discussion, from which Fréret apparently came away the victor. He zeroed in on Duclos's denial that the Druids sacrificed humans, showing that immolation was almost universal among ancient pagans—Romans, Greeks, Phoenicians, Israelites, Carthaginians—and since there were several testimonies from classical authors to this effect, it could not be doubted that the Germans and Gauls also practiced human sacrifice by this method.[112] In another paper, Fréret responded to Duclos's suggestion that the Gauls were not polytheists or idolators—at least before the Romans arrived—by pointing to the archaeological evidence discussed above and the depictions of different gods such as Esus and Belenus, among others, and their seemingly Celtic etymologies.[113]

A similar system prevailed in the *Encyclopédie*, where three noticeable patterns stand out: the conflation of ancient Gauls and Germans under the umbrella term 'Celtes', the general disdain for Celtic barbarity, and the absence of almost any awareness of the philological and archaeological work that had begun to change perceptions of the Celts.[114] As we have seen, it was still common to subsume the Gauls and Germans under the name 'Celts', but the additional misstep taken in many articles of the *Encyclopédie* is the assumption that the Norse pantheon was part of the larger Celtic one; by this mistake Odin became a Celtic god. This blunder is evident in all of the articles written by the famous *philosophe* Paul-Henri Thiry, Baron d'Holbach (1723–1789) on the mythology of the 'Scandinavian Celts', but they can be traced to his reliance on the *Monuments de la mythologie et de la poesie des Celtes, et particulierement des anciens Scandinaves* (1756), by the Genevan Paul-Henri Mallet (1730–1807), who is discussed in the following chapter. The second pattern is the general disdain for ancient Celtic society and especially the Druids. The Abbé Yvon (1714–1789), in his article on the philosophy of the ancient Celts, declared that the Druids were not philosophers but 'impostors, uniquely occupied with their interest, their glory, their reputation, working to enslave their imbecilic nation under the yoke of shameful ignorance', which they did by the 'double doctrine'.[115] Yvon's article also serves as an example of the third pattern, which is that it is based solely upon classical accounts. By ignoring the erudite works—in English, Latin, and German—of the type that the *philosophes* of the *Encyclopédie* disdained, they produced a relatively flat picture quite out of step with the best scholarship available at the time.

Conclusion

With the examination of physical remains, an increasingly clear picture of the ancient Celts and their religion quickly came into existence in the eighteenth century. However, ideas of the Druids were still flexible enough to be twisted in almost any direction that an author wanted to take them. Greater attention to the Druids resulted in a corresponding general increase in interest in the ancient Celts, and announced their entry into cultural outlets more popular than their usual erudite settings. While one could see art in various media or read about Celtic themes in poetry and prose, those with the means were also keen to see the supposed monuments in which the Druids performed their rites and the dramatic landscapes in which the ancient Celts had lived. There was a corresponding increase in travel during the middle decades of the century, and we now have excellent studies by Mary-Ann Constantine and Nigel Leask showing the ways in which reading Tacitus and Ossian, among other classics, inspired travel through Wales and the Scottish Highlands and Islands during this time.[116] Through the eighteenth century the Druids became quite fashionable. As Ronald Hutton has chronicled, they had gained enough purchase in the British imagination that sociable groups began to name themselves after the Druids, but this probably has more to do with a strengthening British identity, the celebration of native ancestry, and a desire for fun than anything historically or philosophically significant about the Druids.[117]

They acquired more serious implications in France, however, where the Gauls and Franks were associated with the Third Estate and the nobility, respectively. In his reactionary *Considérations sur la France* (1797), Joseph de Maistre (1753–1821) saw the origins of the civil and ecclesiastical roles of the monarchy as originating in ancient Gaul. One of the secrets to the monarchy's longevity, he wrote, was a theocratic element in it particular to France's history: 'There is nothing so national as this element. The bishops, successors to the Druids in this respect, only perfected it'.[118] In his classic essay *On the Liberty of the Ancients and the Moderns* (1819), Benjamin Constant (1767–1830) used basically the same interpretation to argue against the notion that there was any national precedent for representative government in ancient Gaul. Their regime was, on the contrary, 'theocratic and warlike. The priests enjoyed unlimited power. The military class or nobility had markedly insolent and oppressive privileges; the people had no rights and no safeguards'.[119] Even on the other side of the revolutionary caesura, the limited information about the Druids and the religion of ancient Gaul meant that the pattern wherein they could be nearly all things to all people, and deployed to support many different and often conflicting arguments, remained intact.

4

Civilization, Savagery, and the Celts

OSSIAN, THE SCOTTISH ENLIGHTENMENT, AND CELTIC LITERATURE

ON 12 MAY 1763, the old English antiquarian William Stukeley wrote to the young Scottish Highlander James Macpherson (1736–1796) to congratulate him on Ossian, the third-century Caledonian bard whose epic poetry Macpherson had 'translated' from Gaelic into English and published between 1760 and 1763 to thunderous acclaim.[1] Stukeley was delighted with the poems, for they seemed to prove what he had been arguing for decades: that the ancient Celts were a virtuous people whose Druids practiced the 'patriarchal religion' within the great monuments at Stonehenge and Avebury.[2] Stukeley was famous for investigating these sites, but in publishing supposedly ancient poetry Macpherson had also recovered other 'valuable remains of our old Bards, and Druids'.[3] The letter therefore symbolises the passing of a torch, for although he had become something of a laughing stock in British letters, Stukeley, probably more than anyone else, had shaped popular perceptions of the ancient Celtic inhabitants of Britain during the first half of the eighteenth century, and Macpherson indisputably had that effect in the century's second half. Ossian was a European sensation, and the story of the publication and reception of the poems is one of the great literary episodes of the eighteenth century. Yet the poems also incited a scholarly civil war among the Celtic nations in Britain and Ireland, which in some ways damaged the reputation of the Celts and helped to catalyse an exclusionary Anglo-British Gothicism. As we have seen in previous chapters, most early modern thinkers to this point assumed that the Gauls and Germans could be grouped together under the term 'Celtic', but one of the most significant developments examined in this chapter is the realisation by Macpherson, his collaborators, and his opponents that this was incorrect.

The Ossianic controversy has echoed on for over 250 years, generating a huge literature in the process. Most of it has focused on the issue of authenticity, but putting this matter to one side, Ossian is considered the key text in the early history of European Romanticism, and it is well-known, for example, that Johann Wolfgang von Goethe (1749–1832) had young Werther translate the poems, and that Napoléon Bonaparte (1769–1821) supposedly carried both of these works on campaign with him.[4] But my focus here is on Ossian's effect on ideas of the Celtic past. The controversy is especially useful for surveying ideas of the Celts at the time, because just about everyone who claimed special expertise in Celtic matters had something to say about Ossian. Several major works of literary history have also had important things to say about Ossian and the Celts. The most influential of these stretches back to 1923, when Edward Snyder published *The Celtic Revival in English Literature*, which showed that the period from about 1750 to 1800 saw 'a real movement among English men of letters . . . to infuse into English poetry the mythology, the history and the literary treasures of the ancient Celts'.[5] Snyder's interpretation has basically been universally accepted, but as I have argued elsewhere, it relies on a metaphysical view of Celtic literature—inherited from Arnold and Yeats—and tells us little about ideas of the Celts at the time.[6] More recently, one influential work has argued that Ossian and the Celts helped to forge a sense of Britishness through literary expression, but another significant book sees Ossian as part of a wave of 'Bardic nationalism', through which individuals from the Celtic nations expressed their opposition to British cultural imperialism.[7] Eschewing these totalising lenses, in this chapter I examine how scholars from the other Celtic nations reacted to Ossian and to the historical interpretation in which James Macpherson embedded the poems. What were the issues that mattered to them, how did they argue those points, and what effect did this have on ideas of the Celts? The picture that emerges is one of strident disagreement.

Although the enmity between Samuel Johnson and Macpherson is famous, the most unrelenting criticism came from other Celtic scholars, who objected fiercely to Macpherson's historical framework.[8] He was trying, among other things, to give Scotland a new national origin story and to solve the 'Pictish Problem', and in order to do so he had to dismiss the Welsh and Irish accounts of British and Irish antiquity. The central historical issue was the ancestral primacy Macpherson gave to the ancient Caledonians—whose language and, supposedly, manners were still preserved with his kin in the Highlands—who he identified as the first branch of the Celtae in the Isles (as opposed to the Welsh) and 'the founders of the Irish nation'.[9] These were incendiary claims, and to support them Macpherson deployed the traditional antiquarian tools of textual philology and linguistic comparison, but also the new stadial model of civilization emerging as part of the 'science of man' of the Scottish Enlightenment, whose thinkers turned their attention to the questions of the origins and progress of civil society.[10] Macpherson played into these trends, situating Ossian within the stadial model while turning the rhetoric of civilization and savagery against rivals from other Celtic nations, who pushed back against his accusations with evidence from their own historical traditions for the next half century.

This was an especially sensitive issue for the Irish, who had long been castigated as savage or barbarous and therefore felt strongly compelled to refute Macpherson's charges. Yet Colin Kidd and Clare O'Halloran have shown that they were largely talking past each other. For although the idea of an 'Irish Enlightenment' has started to gain some currency, with its own strands of the science of man and political economy developed at mid-century, Irish historical scholarship remained in an older mould, advancing political arguments through historiographical proxy and viewing the historical dynamics behind social change in terms of cycles or 'revolutions' brought about through external shocks—as had happened to Carthage, Rome, and pre-Norman Ireland, for example.[11] The Scottish stadial model—focusing on the progression of a society through stages—was somewhat out of step with Irish approaches, which depicted ancient Celtic Ireland as a civilizational 'golden age' that gave rise to the 'island of saints and scholars'.[12]

Stepping back from the conflict, we can also see how material from the vernacular cultures of the Celtic nations at this time became accepted as legitimate evidence of ancient Celtic society. It was suspected that Druidic practices might have survived in the superstitions and manners of the eighteenth-century peasants who inhabited the 'Celtic' areas, and that perhaps the 'folklore' (to use the anachronism) of these peoples preserved direct evidence or at least clues of Celtic religious and civic life. It was in this context that Ossian exploded onto the scene with a carefully calibrated historical framework and claims by Macpherson, among others, that the poems could 'contribute to finish the picture of our ancestors, of which the outlines have been drawn by the writers of Greece and Rome'.[13] Rival scholars agreed with this point at least and looked to Wales and its literature for a challenge to the Scots. The Mancunian historian John Whitaker (1735–1808) impressed upon the Welsh scholar Evan Evans (1731–1789) that 'considered in an Historical view', the Welsh tradition contained 'invaluable remains, being the only particular accounts of the transactions within the island during the 5th and 6th centuries'.[14] Such claims were strengthened by the very real bardic culture that had existed in the medieval Celtic nations and seemed to connect ancient bards to modern poets. Even though this institution was basically extinct, bardic material was salvaged and used to construct new histories of Celtic Britain and Ireland.

James Macpherson's Celtic History

James Macpherson brought a renewed interest to the question of Celtic origins and history when he published the poems of Ossian in the early 1760s, but he also tainted the debate over British and Irish antiquity for decades. The complicated nature of the texts and the controversy that arose over their authenticity almost immediately means that Ossian cannot be straightforwardly studied like other literary classics. Scholars have had to pay unusually close attention to the contexts of the production and reception of the poems, and it is now recognised that a genuine culture of 'Ossianic' poetry had long existed in the Highlands—ultimately rooted in the Irish Fenian Cycle best exemplified by the Middle Irish *Acallam na Senórach*—and that Macpherson drew from it but altered and added to the material quite freely in line with his own views and those he thought would appeal to his audience. Yet, although a detailed report on the subject essentially concluded this already in 1805, the debate degenerated into a reductive dichotomy between outright forgery or entirely authentic.[15]

The nineteenth-century view tended toward forgery—an accusation levelled by some of the leading Celtic authorities, who thought Macpherson had polluted Scottish Gaelic tradition[16]—especially after Ludwig Christian Stern (1846–1911) dismantled the Gaelic 'originals' with the tools of advanced philological criticism. But after Derick Thomson (1921–2012) published a study in 1952 on Gaelic ballad culture, a revisionist view took hold in the 1980s that sought to move beyond the authenticity debate.[17] We now better understand that the poems were based primarily on medieval Gaelic oral tradition—a fact Macpherson never covered up—and on only a few manuscripts, none of which contained material that was supposedly fifteen-hundred years old. Still, there remain many unanswered questions, and complicating everything is the mercurial character of James Macpherson—at times dour enough to fluster easygoing David Hume (1711–1776) and at others bombastic enough to annoy manic James Boswell (1740–1795)—whose motivations have never been clear and whose personal papers were lost sometime in the nineteenth or early twentieth century.[18] By their very existence, the poems of Ossian seemed to give Highland Gaels claim to a tradition of epic poetry nearly as prestigious as that of the ancient Greeks—Ossian was sometimes only half-jokingly called the 'Highland Homer'—but Macpherson also laid out a distinctive historical vision favouring the ancient Celtic Caledonians at the expense of all the other Celtic nations—not to mention England—in the dissertations and notes that accompanied the published poems, which were fleshed out in 1771 as *An Introduction to the History of Great Britain and Ireland.*

Born in the Highlands near Badenoch in 1736, James Macpherson was old enough in 1745 to have witnessed the outbreak of the Jacobite rebellion, and then the torching of the army barracks near his native village of Ruthven and the disintegration of the Jacobite army after the Battle of Culloden the following year. But we are unsure exactly what, if anything, he saw and what effect it might have had on him.[19] He was an illegitimate nephew of Ewan 'Cluny' Macpherson (1706–1764), chief of the relatively minor Clan Macpherson of Badenoch, who had rallied around the Jacobite pretender to the British throne Charles Eduard Stuart (1720–1788), and afterwards remained on the run for nine years before finally escaping to France. Stamped by these experiences and a strong sense of Highland identity, Macpherson attended King's College and then Marischal College, Aberdeen, in the early 1750s. As Fiona Stafford has shown, there he would have been exposed to a variety of intellectual influences that shaped his later works, including enlightened primitivism, the Aberdonian humanist legacy, and the Scottish science of man.[20] Following a short stint in the Divinity Hall at the University of Edinburgh in 1755, Macpherson returned to the Highlands, where he taught and tutored, collecting fragments of poetry and composing his own (in English) during his spare time—he managed to publish some of these in the *Scots Magazine* and their themes foreshadow those found in Ossian.[21] Tiring quickly of his life as a schoolmaster, Macpherson secured the post of tutor to a young nobleman—Thomas Graham (1748–1843), the future war hero Baron Lynedoch—and moved south in 1758.

Accompanying his tutee to Logierait sometime in early 1759, Macpherson met the philosopher Adam Ferguson (1723–1816), an important member of the blossoming Edinburgh intellectual scene and the only Gaelic-speaking literatus of the Scottish Enlightenment.[22] Ferguson introduced Macpherson to his friend, the famous playwright John Home (1722–1808), who he met in

September 1759 at the spa town of Moffat.[23] Impressed with Macpherson's translations of Gaelic poetry, Home introduced him to other members of the Edinburgh 'Moderate' Circle—the leading group of Scottish Enlightenment thinkers—including Alexander Carlyle (1722–1805), William Robertson (1721–1793), and Hugh Blair (1718–1800). Blair took the greatest interest in the poems and convinced Macpherson to publish some of them, adding a short preface and helping them through the press as *Fragments of Ancient Poetry, Collected in the Highlands of Scotland, and translated from the Galic or Erse language* in June 1760. The results impressed other Scottish literati, including David Hume, Adam Smith (1723–1790), and Henry Home, Lord Kames (1696–1782), and a subscription fund was set up to send Macpherson on a collection tour.[24] He undertook two of these with a kinsman in 1760–1761, meeting with ministers and poets around the Highlands and Western Islands, asking them for manuscripts and recording any Ossianic poetry they might know.[25] At Sleat on the Isle of Skye, he met the Rev. John Macpherson (1713–1765) and his son, the future Sir John Macpherson (*c.*1745–1821), who would both become close allies.[26] Macpherson collated the material back in Badenoch before returning to Edinburgh, where he lived below Hugh Blair, and polished the final manuscript of *Fingal: An Ancient Epic Poem*, which was published in December 1761.

Fingal was met with—mostly—great enthusiasm by the polite literary worlds north and south of the border, though not across the Severn and definitely not across Saint George's Channel.[27] Invigorated by his success, Macpherson published yet another epic poem, *Temora*, in 1763. Although he promised to produce the Gaelic 'originals', in fact this was Macpherson's last major Ossianic work, though he remained a formidable presence in the antiquarian field for the next decade.[28] Washing his hands of Ossian, Macpherson—together with John Macpherson—became a hired pen for successive governments, a Member of Parliament, and a London agent of Muhammad Ali Khan (1717–1795), the Nawab of Arcot; he died a rich man with four illegitimate children of his own at the mansion called Belleville, or Balavil, which he had the Adams brothers build a few miles from Ruthven, where he was born and raised.

At the heart of the Ossianic enterprise was the connection between Highland Gaelic culture—where the traditional clanship system was disintegrating but still a point of great curiosity to the rest of Britain—and the enlightenment occurring in the lowlands. There are two points to stress about the Highland context. The first is that, as the Highland Society's *Report* emphasised, the

Ossianic tradition of Gaelic poetry was a genuine part of Highland culture: having been preserved by Gaelic bards over the centuries, it was *believed* to be ancient and that Macpherson was only the first to publish a substantial slice of it.[29] As the Rev. John Macpherson summarised it:

> Ossian was the Homer of the ancient Highlanders, and at the same time one of their most illustrious heroes. . . . The poems of that author would have been emulously studied by the bards of succeeding generations, and committed at the same time to the memory of every one else who had any taste for these admirable compositions . . . it seems plain enough that the compositions of that poet might have been transmitted orally from one generation to another, until letters began to flourish in some degree in the Highlands and Isles.[30]

Once the poems were written down, Rev. Macpherson assumed, they would have been transmitted easily across the centuries, and there was no necessary reason to think they would have become corrupted. The second point is that there was already an established Gaelic scholarly culture, primarily among Kirk ministers, who collected Gaelic poetry and composed works on Scottish history and antiquities—civil and ecclesiastical—as well as on the ancient Celts and their languages.[31] We encountered one of these figures in chapter 2, Jerome Stone, the Dunkeld minister who had written most of a manuscript history of the Celtic languages and published Gaelic translations in the *Scots Magazine*—which Macpherson almost certainly read—before his early death in 1756. Highland Kirk ministers were among the few who achieved the fine balance of being acquainted with Gaelic society and being conversant in the idiom of the European Republic of Letters. Macpherson was clearly aware of this culture but was drawn to the intellectual powerhouse that was Edinburgh at this time.

The Scottish Enlightenment setting is absolutely crucial to understanding the manufacture and success of the poems, which are now seen as a collaborative venture between Macpherson and the literati—Hugh Blair went so far as to say that the poems were virtually 'extorted' from a reluctant Macpherson.[32] The 1750s and 60s were extraordinary decades in Scottish intellectual life, when key works were published by Hume, Smith, Ferguson, Robertson, and Kames, among others, on traditional subjects like the histories of England and Scotland, as well as on more adventurous topics like the foundations of morals and the origins of civil society. It was during this vital period that the 'science of man' assumed its characteristic 'stadial' form, which posited a series of stages through which human societies advanced.[33] As Adam Smith formulated them, they were '1st the Age of Hunters; 2dly, the Age of Shepherds; 3^{rdly} the Age of Agriculture; and 4^{thly}, the Age of Commerce'.[34] Among other things, the literati were using these theories to reshape Scotland's sense of itself in the aftermath of major changes like the Union of 1707, the demolition of Scotland's patriotic historical tradition by Thomas Innes in 1729, and the Jacobite defeat at Culloden in 1746, at the same time as they addressed the embedded question of how to best maintain martial virtue in their luxurious modern society.[35] Macpherson's timing was perfect: Ossian provided an idealised picture of ancient Scots who lived primitively virtuous lives in nature during the 'Age of Hunters', fighting off waves of Roman and Danish invaders. The stadial framing was crucial because it simultaneously validated the authenticity of the poems—the content depicted was consonant with the social theories of the time—and allowed them to be used as further evidence supporting those very theories with which the Scots were making a major contribution to European intellectual life. In the preface to the *Fragments,* Hugh Blair wrote that the reader would find in the 'spirit and strain of the poems', the 'ideas' and 'manners, that belong to the most early state of society'.[36] These themes are captured immediately in the first lines of the *Fragments*:

> My love is a son of the hill.
> He pursues the flying deer.
> His gray dogs are panting around him;
> His bow-string sounds in the wind.

Blair leaned on this internal evidence as proof of authenticity both here and in his *Critical Dissertation* in 1763, and Macpherson made the same point almost word for word in his preface to *Fingal*. In his *Lectures on Jurisprudence,* Adam Smith placed the Ossianic Caledonians 'much in the same state as the [Native] Americans', and in the early fragment of *The Wealth of Nations,* he asserted that 'Ossian plainly describes the exploits of a nation of hunters', before civilizational advancement introduced the division of labour.[37] Macpherson introduced his own three-stage theory—which accorded closely with that of Adam Ferguson at the time[38]—in the preface to *Temora* which, as much as a structural device, also provided Macpherson with a weapon to attack his critics and a shield to defend the poems' authenticity.

The controversy over authenticity began as soon as the poems appeared and has dominated discussion ever since. It is more complicated than might first appear and was not really about whether the poems were 'forged within these five years by James Macpherson', as Hume put it, although there were those like Samuel Johnson who believed this from the start.[39] The issues tended to centre around antiquity, orality, and literacy: Could verse like this be preserved orally and remain uncorrupted for nearly 1,500 years? Macpherson thought so and used stadial theory and the particularity of Highland geography to argue that, since the Highlands were difficult to reach and had remained free from commerce, the poems and the Gaelic language in which they were spoken were preserved in their antique purity. He was helped here by the mysteries of the Celtic languages and his fellow Scots. In the *Critical Review*, Tobias Smollett noted that 'the Celtic tongue' was by its complexity suited to memorisation, because its many declensions combined for a naturally fluid language thereby easier to remember.[40] David Hume, who had raised doubts over the use of 'memory and oral tradition' for historical evidence in the *History of England*, had similar concerns about *Ossian*; however, he initially supported the venture and gave Macpherson the benefit of the doubt because, like other Scots, he had heard of the existence of such poems from others, including his friend Adam Smith. They were 'in every body's mouth in the Highlands', Hume told David Dalrymple (1726–1792) in 1760, including that of 'a country surgeon somewhere in Lochaber, who, he says, can recite a great number of [Ossianic poems], but never committed them to writing; as indeed the orthography of the Highland language is not fixed, and the natives have always employed more the sword than the pen'.[41] The uncertainties of Gaelic and the best means of rendering it in Roman script would remain an issue for decades, but because of the orthographical difficulties memory was supposedly a more certain tool.

Still, Hume warned Hugh Blair that many did not believe the poems were authentic, and it was primarily in their defence that Blair published his *Critical Dissertation on the Poems of Ossian* in 1763, which became a bestseller in its own right and also favourably contrasted the ancient Celts with the Goths.[42] Poetry, asserted the newly appointed Regius Professor of Rhetoric and Belles-Lettres, was likely where the most ancient traditions and manners of nations would be found, because it was 'handed down from one race to another' and preserved in memory in the absence of writing.[43] Even though, according to the universal principles of stadialism, poetic refinement was more a function of civilization than a quality that particular nations possessed, 'the Celtic tribes' were 'addicted in so high a degree to poetry' and devoted so much attention to it that 'generous sentiments and tender affections' were found in *Ossian* where they would not otherwise be expected from savages.[44] These unique features of Ossianic poetry distinguished the ancient Celts and their modern Scottish descendants. 'The Celtae' had been 'a great and mighty people' who 'once extended their dominion all over the west of Europe', and were not 'altogether a gross and rude nation', but 'possessed from very remote ages a formed system of discipline and manners'.[45] Importantly, the Celts were 'altogether distinct from the Goths and Teutons' and, if Ossian was anything to go by, their poetry was much more refined in contrast to the 'blood and slaughter' (as he later put it) of Gothic poetry.[46] Macpherson made similar points to Blair in his notes and dissertations, and it is clear that they were reading from the same hymnal. When *Temora* was published, Blair wrote to their joint publisher that 'Mr Macpherson's notes too are many of them very useful & many of them amusing' (he might have written some of them), but he also noted the sales of his own *Dissertation* would be 'quickn'd by [the publication of] Temora'.[47] Authentic or not, the poems were good for business, and were a major part of the reason that Blair died famous across Europe and one of the richest clergymen in eighteenth-century Scotland.

Beyond the poems and the superficial debates over their authenticity—tied up in politics and patriotism—there was a much more expansive historical vision idealising the ancient Celts and their Caledonian descendants, which Macpherson laid out in the prefaces and dissertations to *Fingal* and *Temora*, his preface to Rev. John Macpherson's *Critical Dissertations* (1768), and in his later *Introduction to the History and Antiquities of Great Britain and Ireland* (1771).[48] The poems of *Ossian* were also part of this historical vision, for even though the 'Celtic nations' had once been 'the masters of Europe', stretching from Russia to Spain, theirs had been an oral culture and not a literate one, and so the poems were believed to contain important evidence of ancient Celtic manners. In the preface to *Fingal*, Macpherson suggested that the poem was 'genuine history . . . embellished by poetry', and therefore 'not less valuable' as a historical source than as a piece of poetry.[49] As Colin Kidd and Dafydd Moore have shown, Macpherson explored some complex issues of political theory in a brand of 'Celtic Whiggism'—that is, that the ancient Celts shared in the same European tradition of liberty as the Gothic peoples—by connecting the classical ethnographical tradition of Tacitus and Caesar with evidence from his own Gaelic culture. The Celts, according to Macpherson's preface in *Fingal*, were a group of decentralised tribes sharing one language and a set of customs, who united in times of danger for mutual defence under one king; in times of peace kings were elected, but 'legitimate power was entirely in the hands of the Druids', who were a laudable priestly class that never abused their power.[50] However, Macpherson explained, the early model of elective kingship gave way to a hereditary system when the kings refused to give up their power and instead turned on the Druids, who became outcasts. Supposedly because of this exile, there is not much about the Druids in the poems—and the general absence of religion, pagan and Christian, was claimed by Macpherson and Blair as proof of their antiquity—which were said to be composed as Druidry was declining and Christianity was just beginning to reach the Caledonians, but in his later work Macpherson suggested that there had been some idea of a 'supreme being' at the base of the Druidical system.[51]

Macpherson helped John Macpherson publish his father's essays in 1768, but he had been working on a few of his own when in 1770 the 'dull' John Whitaker started advertising his 'two immense quartos'—which contained a system in opposition to that of James—forcing Macpherson to polish off his own work 'in order to get the start of the heavy rogue'.[52] The *Introduction to the History of Great Britain and Ireland* was described by an early biographer as 'a mere glorification of the Celts', and the extent to which Macpherson went to prove that the Celts were the first inhabitants of Europe, who had profoundly shaped its early development, is indeed remarkable. The book is divided into two halves, with the first entering the dry antiquarian debates over national migrations and primacy, and the second exploring the religion, manners, languages, and institutions of the ancient Celtic and Germanic (he used the term 'Sarmatian') nations of Europe. Although Macpherson cites classical sources almost exclusively, it is clear that he was familiar with contemporary scholarship, and Irish scholars accused him of plagiarising Geoffrey Keating. Despite some idiosyncratic and confusing terms, his historical system is actually quite straightforward: the Celtae had been one of the three ancient stocks of Europe, along with the Sarmatians who occupied Scandinavia and invaded the Roman Empire as the Goths and Vandals, and the Slavi in the far east of Europe. The Celts occupied 'the immense track of country . . . of Celtica. . . . From the pillars of Hercules to the mouth of the Danube, from the Hellespont almost to the Baltic', where 'one language, though in a great variety of dialects prevailed', and had therefore given rise to all the nations of Western Europe, though their homeland was Gaul.[53] Controversially, and likely derived from his reading of Jean-Baptiste Bullet (see chapter 2), Macpherson argued that Rome itself was of 'Celtic stock', and therefore that 'the French, Italians, and Spaniards speak, in some measure, to this day, the tongue of their Celtic ancestors'.[54] However, unlike many earlier advocates for an ancient *Europa Celtica*,

Macpherson found no indication that 'the present language of Germany is the remains of the old Celtic', and therefore clearly separated Celts and Germans.[55] As for the all-important question of British and Irish origins, Macpherson argued that the Isles had been populated by three successive waves of Celtic invaders—Gaels (Scots and Irish), Cimbri (Welsh), and Belgae (who ultimately settled in Brittany)—before the Anglo-Saxons arrived. The Gaels had crossed over into Britain from Gaul and, following the laws of stadialism, hunted the herds of deer into the north of the island—Caledonia—*and then* crossed over into Ireland.[56] The Scottish Highlanders were therefore the oldest inhabitants of the Isles and had preserved vestiges of ancient Celtic culture—including the purest version of the language—most completely, because the Caledonians had repulsed wave upon wave of invaders, as celebrated in the poetry of Ossian, and remained free of commerce thanks to the harsh Highland landscape. Importantly, as Kidd has stressed, the Celts had similar institutions and shared the same ancient sense of liberty as their barbarian neighbours the Scandinavian Sarmatae, implying that 'North Britain' (a term Macpherson used repeatedly) shared with England the same ancient constitution that now held together Great Britain.[57]

Although Macpherson drew a flattering portrait of the ancient Celts, he treated the other Celtic nations, especially Ireland, with thinly veiled disdain. It has been pointed out that Macpherson's historical intentions are illuminated most revealingly by his treatment of Ireland.[58] Already in February 1760, even *before* the publication of the *Fragments*, Macpherson was aiming at Irish historical tradition, representing it in a letter as 'fables' and asserting that the Caledonians had conquered Ireland, forcefully rejecting the notion that the poems were of Irish derivation or that Scotland owed any cultural debt to the Irish nation, who 'lost their liberty . . . long before the English invasion', whereas the Scots 'have ever been a free people' and repelled wave upon wave of foreign invasion: by the Romans, Picts, Britons, Danes, and Saxons.[59]

The key historical issue at stake was whether the ancient Scots came from Ireland and populated Scotland sometime in the fifth century, or whether the Irish came from Scotland and crossed over at some point in the prehistoric past. It had been a point of contention between scholars from both countries for centuries, until the Catholic Jacobite Father Thomas Innes (1662–1744) settled the dispute for a time with his *A Critical Essay on the Ancient Inhabitants of Northern Britain or Scotland* (1729).[60] Among other things, Innes aimed to demolish the forty mythical Gaelic kings from which Scots claimed their monarchy descended. Macpherson targeted Innes directly on this in his preface to the Rev. John Macpherson's *Critical Dissertations*:

> The Scots of this age saw with unconcern, if not with pleasure, forty of their ancient list of Kings expunged at once by Innes. This furious regicide, endeavoured to make amends to his countrymen, by giving them forty great Pictish monarchs for the long list of the petty Princes of Jarghaël, of whom he deprived them.[61]

This was, according to Macpherson, rejected with the 'scorn it deserved'. Macpherson was thus unbothered by the superficial issue of the king list, because the real issue was one of ethnic descent. Macpherson claimed that Ossian was a third-century Gaelic bard, but if Innes's account was allowed to stand then no Gael had arrived in Scotland until the fourth century.

Because Innes's interpretation of the Pictish origins of Scotland was expedient for the Irish in their dispute over Gaelic primacy, they adopted it willingly. This helps to explain the anti-Irish kernel—inherited from prior generations of Scots antiquarians and Highland tradition—at the centre of Macpherson's historical apparatus throughout his published work. It was the main focus of the dissertation affixed to *Temora*. Here Macpherson began his campaign against the 'idle fabulists' Keating and O'Flaherty, first among a list of Irish antiquaries 'credulous and puerile to the last degree' who claimed the poems of Ossian for the Irish and claimed an Irish origin for the Scottish Highlanders.[62] Language was the key for Macpherson:

> That dialect of the Celtic tongue, spoken in the north of Scotland, is much more pure, more agreeable to its mother language, and more abounding with primitives, than that now spoken, or even that which has been writ for some centuries back, amongst the most unmixed part of the Irish nation. A Scotchman, tolerably conversant in his own language, understands an Irish composition, from that derivative analogy which it has to the *Gaelic* of North-Britain. An Irishman, on the other hand, without the aid of study, can never understand a composition in the *Galic* tongue.—This affords a proof, that the *Scotch Galic* is the most original, and, consequently, the language of a more antient and unmixed people.[63]

Because Scottish Gaelic appeared to be older and purer, it stood to reason that the poems preserved in that language were also purer than any that might exist in Ireland.

It was in attacking the historical traditions of the other Celtic nations that Macpherson's stadial theory came in most handy. Introduced in the preface of *Temora,* it was comprised of three stages: in the savage stage humans drew together out of 'consanguinity' and 'natural affection'; in the barbarous second stage private property was established, violence increased, and humans entered into society for 'mutual defence'; at the third stage society trusted the 'safety of their persons and property' to 'certain laws and subordinations of government'.[64] While the first stage was 'formed on nature' and noble, the second stage was one of 'compleat barbarism and ignorance'.[65] This stadial interpretation allowed Macpherson to do several things. First and foremost, it helped him to undermine Irish historical tradition by consigning its sources to the second stage of 'barbarism and ignorance', an era of 'idle fabulists'. Second, Macpherson's stadialism accounted for the defeat and subjugation of the more civilized Picts by their savage warlike Celtic brethren the Scots, thereby implicitly dismissing Innes's case for the Pictish origins of the Scottish monarchy.[66] Third, it assisted his case for the plausibility of poetry surviving in its antique purity. The Highlands were isolated and the landscape was 'only fit for pasture' and not commerce, therefore its inhabitants had little contact with the outside world and remained a contained population that had managed to preserve its ancient traditions: 'their language is pure and original, and their manners are those of an ancient and unmixed race of men'.[67] Because language became refined and corrupted with the advancement of civilization, the fact that the Highlands had remained isolated and in a low stage of development meant that the Highlanders' language had remained 'pure and original' for much longer; therefore, their oral poetic tradition was much more trustworthy than Ireland's manuscript tradition, which relied on the introduction of writing by Christian missionaries (this was a clear swipe at Charles O'Conor, discussed below). Although writing allowed memory to be preserved, it was introduced along with a different religion, language, and accompanying *moeurs,* and thus completely perverted the very memory it sought to preserve.

The Welsh are barely an afterthought for Macpherson. They had arrived in Britain after the Caledonians as the 'Cimbri, which signifies a band of robbers', and had been in the second stage of violent barbarity.[68] But the Welsh had then been conquered by the Romans, elevated and enervated by their civilized luxury and then—unable to defend themselves from the Caledonians in post-Roman Britain—forced to invite the Saxons to fight in their stead, which had ultimately ended in their marginalisation. Macpherson did not think much of the Welsh language and bragged that he could learn it well enough to translate poetry out of in six weeks—a claim that infuriated Welsh scholars.[69] However, the absence of any real attention to the Welsh in his works about the ancient history of Britain probably speaks louder than any of Macpherson's verbalised slights.

Staying with the Scottish Enlightenment for a moment, it is easy to see that Ossian generated a greater interest in the ancient Celts, who come off rather well in many of these works. In his final volume of the *History of England*—published after the *Fragments* and *Fingal* had appeared—David Hume spent hardly any time on them at all, but echoed Macpherson in noting the 'governments' of the ancient Britons, 'though monarchical, were free, as well as those of all the Celtic nations'.[70] In his important *Essay on the History of Civil Society* (1767), Adam Ferguson used Celtic society as an example of martial virtue at the foundations of chivalry, and whereas the priestly class of other barbarous societies like the Tartars used their influence to institute 'an early taste of despotism and absolute slavery', the Druids had rather given the 'first rudiments of civil government' to 'the ancient Gauls and Britons'.[71] Lord Kames was a fierce defender of the poems and wrote to the bluestocking Elizabeth Montagu (1718–1800) that he believed Ossian 'a true historian', and that 'the manners described by Ossian were the genuine manners of his country. Such refined notions . . . of a people in the first stage of society, approach to a miracle', and yet Kames thought he had corroborated this evidence in his great work *Sketches on the History of Man* (1774).[72] John Millar (1735–1801) was also struck by Ossian's portrayal of the Caledonians with manners expected of a society at a higher level of civilization,[73] before Edward Gibbon noted the same philosophical puzzle, but rolled it into his critique of Roman luxury, contrasting the 'untutored Caledonians, glowing with the warm virtues of nature, and the degenerate Romans, polluted with the mean vices of wealth and luxury'; it seems significant that he adopted James and Rev. John Macpherson as his guides through 'the dark and doubtful paths of Caledonian antiquity'.[74]

Ossian was a huge success outside of Britain and remained a popular subject in European art and literature well into the nineteenth century.[75] In America too, Ossian fascinated Thomas Jefferson, who had a keen interest in the language and origins of nations and believed there might be an originally Celtic tribe of Native Americans somewhere beyond the frontier, and who wanted to learn Gaelic in order to read the Ossianic originals, which he requested from a relative of Macpherson's along with a grammar and dictionary.[76] Macpherson replied through the intermediary that it would be too arduous to send the originals (which did not exist) and that his 'manner' and 'spelling' differed from others but was, he thought, correct, so a copy by someone else was also out of the question.[77] He gave a similar response several years later to the auditor-general of Bengal, John Murray (1745–1822), who had requested to see the Gaelic originals in order to compare its alphabet to the Persian. Suggesting that the letters Julius Caesar had seen the Druids use were Gaelic letters, Murray was 'sure the Arabic letters, borrowed by the Persians, are most perfectly adapted to the Gaelic' and would help rid Gaelic orthography of its superfluous consonants.[78] Like everyone else's, Murray's request was futile, but he helped to force the issue by his involvement with a group of Scots in Bengal, who raised a large sum in order to cover the cost of publishing the originals. Yet by the early 1770s Macpherson had—except for the flare-up with Johnson that would come in 1775—basically washed his hands of the whole episode and, though he worked on reverse-engineering the poems into Gaelic, they remained unpublished at his death in 1796.

The Welsh Response to Ossian

Scholars from the other nations of the Isles objected to different parts of the Macphersonian project. Samuel Johnson led the English charge against the poems as outright forgeries, Welsh antiquarians rejected Macpherson's claims for Gaelic linguistic primacy and his attempt to speak for all the Celts, while Irish historians were furious that Macpherson had—as they saw it—usurped their heroes and toppled their historical tradition. While it was possible for Irish and many English readers to admire the poems even if their authenticity seemed dubious, according to Mary-Ann Constantine no Welsh writer of note found the merits outweighed the problems.[79] The Welsh poetic tradition was *the* point of national pride to Welsh scholars—to be a scholar of Welsh antiquities was to be a poetic patriot in this era—and so to find favour with Macpherson and Ossian would have been to admit they were only second-best in their preferred arena. As Rice Williams (1689–1766) put it to Thomas Percy, 'the welsh poetic genius, if properly ushered on the stage, would make a much better appearance than any of the pigmy race of the Caledonian muses'.[80] Still, Welsh scholars recognised that Macpherson had opened up new interest in Celtic subjects, but before they could rightfully take the stage he and Ossian would have to be pushed off of it.[81]

Some of the first reactions came from the Morris brothers, the dominant Welsh scholars of the mid-eighteenth century. Before he even read the poems,

Lewis Morris—annoyed by Macpherson's boast that knowing one Celtic language was like knowing them all and that he could learn Welsh well enough to translate from it after a few weeks—suspected they 'may be an original of his own contrivance', and dismissed them as 'but a modern song' when he finally did see them.[82] The Morrises disseminated Macpherson's boast to their network and Rice Williams passed it on to Thomas Percy, noting that it made him 'really afraid the world is grossly imposed upon'.[83] Evan Evans was convinced that 'Mackpherson is a downright cheat', and that the other Scots could not be trusted to corroborate his account because they had made it a 'national affair'.[84] The Welsh wanted to see the Gaelic originals, but when some supposedly original specimens appeared with *Temora* these did nothing to assuage their concerns. Yet while English commentators tended to dismiss the idea that oral tradition could stretch uncorrupted from antiquity to the present, Welsh critics equivocated.[85] Lewis Morris was sceptical in the Ossianic case, but he had been making similar claims for Welsh for decades, averring in 1738 that setting verse to music had helped it to become 'timeproof . . . being sung to the harp from age to age and seldom if ever committed to writing. This is one of the plainest marks I can see of the Druidical Learning left among us, perhaps not to be met with in any other nation'.[86] He made a similar point to Thomas Carte in 1745, and returned to it twenty-five years later in the midst of the Ossian controversy, suggesting that Druids had preserved their religious teachings through song, some of which were 'supposed to be as old as the Druidical times; for the same Verses are remembered in every County in Wales, and are common in the Mouths of the Populace, and scarce ever committed to Writing; but retained by Tradition from Father to Son'.[87] Switch 'Wales' for 'Scotland' and this line could have been written by Macpherson or any of the Highland Kirk ministers. The Welsh were therefore treading a fine line, but for all of their opposition, they did recognise that Ossian opened up space for them to promote their own scholarly activity and to highlight the historical authority of the Welsh language, poetic tradition, and manuscript caches.

The prospect of literary treasures, and possibly even an epic, hidden in Welsh manuscripts had excited the British antiquarian world throughout the eighteenth-century, but Ossian's publication finally catalysed the translation and publication of much Welsh verse. By the 1760s the aged Lewis Morris had relegated poetry to only secondary importance behind his linguistic projects, but his wayward protégé Evan Evans stepped forward to answer the patriotic call in 1764 with *Some Specimens of the Poetry of the Antient Welsh Bards*.[88]

Something of a tragic figure, Evans had studied at Oxford and was an Anglican curate known to be one of Wales' finest scholars at the time, but he was hampered by alcoholism and was never completely trusted by the Morrises or other cultural brokers, though he attracted the positive attention of Thomas Percy and Samuel Johnson.[89] Evans was passionately devoted to Welsh history and culture, but especially the language, and shared the Morrisian desire for a new Welsh dictionary; he was well read and his letters are peppered with references to Davies, Pezron, and Edward 'Llwyd of the Museum'.[90] In the late 1750s, Evans was in search of patronage, pitching his Latin dissertation on the history of the bards to the Morrises and to Daines Barrington, who also promised to show Evans's work to Thomas Gray (1716–1771).[91]

The appearance of Ossian helped Evans to realise he could generate interest in his own work at the same time as it prompted Percy to reach out in search of a Welsh champion.[92] The pair shared an interest in ancient history and the question of how much the Celts and Goths had overlapped, but Percy was a Germanic specialist and knew none of the Celtic languages, so he queried Evans about Welsh historical sources and repeatedly exhorted him to publish 'British literature' translated from 'the ancient Language of this island'.[93] Like the Scots, they treated vernacular poetry in historical as much as literary terms, and Ossian loomed over their correspondence. Each doubted Ossian's authenticity—although Percy relented on this question for a few years in the mid-1760s—and Evans was especially irritated at Macpherson's historical claims. He rejected the assertion that Gaelic was the primary Celtic tongue because the Irish and Scottish Highlanders were 'mixed with numerous colonies of other nations . . . in so much that their language is very much corrupted. So that the Welsh and the Bretons are the most pure dialects of the Celtic this day extant'.[94] It will be recalled that Lewis Morris was at the time advancing Welsh as 'the principal branch and chief remains of the ancient Celtic tongue', and Evans referred Percy to Morris's manuscript history on the 'Celtic Empire', which flourished before Greece and Rome, when 'the Celtae were the greatest men for learning and arms in the known world . . . as you may see in *Pezron's antiquity of nations*'.[95] In his own 'Poem on the Love of Our country', Evans placed the Celts on an equal artistic footing with ancient Greece:

> Nor did this genius shine in Greece alone
> In other nations equally it shone
> Witness the Bards that grac'd the Celtic clime,
> Whose images were bold and thoughts sublime.[96]

Percy set Evans up with his bookseller friends the Dodsleys, who published the *Specimens* in 1764. It had several purposes, including meeting the antiquarian demand for material to rival Ossian, advancing the Welsh patriotic aim of promoting their native language and traditions, and finally securing a place for Evan's Latin dissertation on the bards. The book was broken into three sections: a preface and translations of the poems in English; the Latin *De bardis dissertatio*; and a preface and the originals in Welsh. The poems concern typical medieval subjects like eating and drinking, the exploits of heroes, and odes to great leaders, and were presented with a thorough critical apparatus. Although he swore that he was not inspired to publish the poems as a result of Ossian, and that he did not wish to put them in competition, Evans repeatedly attacked Macpherson in all three languages and most reviewers put them in direct competition anyway.[97] Evans was particularly dubious that Highland Gaelic could have been preserved in its purity from antiquity, considering that neither he nor any of the other leading Welsh scholars could easily understand early medieval Welsh poetry, which they did not pretend to be as old as Ossian.[98] Evans—following Lhwyd—did think that some pieces had pagan Druidic origins, which included a pattern of beginning by invoking the 'Supreme Being', as well as the use of alliteration for the purposes of memorisation, but he recognised that these reflected Christian and classical influence—Julius Caesar is even named in one of them.[99] Called *Englynion*, these are now held to date at least to the ninth or tenth centuries. But Evans did not think the Scots shared in the bardic inheritance—at least independently of the Irish—and his line in the *dissertatio* that 'traces [of the bards] remain only with the Welsh and Irish, the posterity of the Celts' is a dig at the Highlanders, who he indicates in the Welsh preface 'did not come to settle in Scotland . . . before the year 503' as a breakaway colony from Ireland.[100] Macpherson and the Scots, according to Evans (who agreed here with the Irish historians), were therefore trying to use Ossian to craft an alternative national history, casting themselves as the primary Celtic nation of Britain rather than one of its offshoots. Evans died in poverty and obscurity a few years after he published it, but the *Specimens* were an important piece of literary scholarship that introduced Welsh material to the reading public.

Welsh scholars mostly opposed Macpherson on Ossianic grounds, but criticism also came in historical terms from those who thought the English Constitution extended directly from the ancient Britons, direct ancestors of the Welsh, and had nothing to do with the Scots. The most notable objection in this respect came from the Anglican scholar John Whitaker, who in his *History of Manchester* had defended the ancient Britons from the aspersions of barbarity cast on them by people like Hume, valorising them as a refined and commercial people, whose institutions formed the basis of the British Constitution: British feudal tenures were, according to Whitaker, native and not Norman in origin.[101] He was in the middle of this large and ultimately unfinished work when Macpherson's *Introduction* appeared in 1771, prompting Whitaker to respond the following year with a tedious point-by-point refutation of Macpherson's theories of British origins and Caledonian primacy that stretches to over 300 pages. This sharp reaction is interesting, because in his *History of Manchester* Whitaker had enthusiastically accepted the authenticity of the poems of Ossian: 'The whole body of the Highland Scots are living witnesses of their authenticity'.[102] Furthermore, and even more importantly, Whitaker shared the Macphersonian assertion that Britain had been populated by Celts from Gaul who then spilled over into 'the uninhabited isle of Ireland', and he later attacked the traditional Irish account of Milesian origins.[103] Yet Whitaker's idealised commercial Britons differed starkly from Macpherson's barbarous Cimbri, and Whitaker was at pains to refute this 'imaginary' etymology in the midst of his long work that ultimately rejected not only Macpherson's historical explanation, but Innes's Scandinavian Scots, and upheld the Scots as 'transplanted natives of Ireland' (though originally from Gaul via Britain), who conquered Scotland under none other than Ossian.[104] Gibbon was for a time friends with both men and reportedly tried to reconcile them with 'a very excellent dinner', which ended 'in a very singular dispute, Whitaker maintaining the authority of Ossian, and Macpherson disputing it'—perhaps it was over this very point about Ossian conquering Scotland from Ireland.[105] Yet there was an interesting overlap between Macpherson and Whitaker: both believed that the ancient inhabitants of Britain and Ireland had possessed political institutions more or less in step with those of their Germanic counterparts, and therefore that the ancient constitution had Celtic as much as Gothic origins.[106]

Patriotism was at the bottom of the Welsh dispute with Macpherson. For Welsh antiquarians had basically all made similar claims for Welsh and the Welsh literary tradition to those that Macpherson made for Gaelic and Ossian. Welsh scholars not only felt that they had stronger links to the ancient Celts but that, with their extensive manuscript tradition, they could prove it. There was one important point of overlap: the European extent of ancient Celtic power, or the 'Celtic Empire' as both Morris and Evans called it. But beyond this vague appreciation of the extent of ancient Celtic power and influence, there was nothing holding Welsh and Scottish antiquarians together.

Ireland's Outcry

In September 1763, David Hume warned Hugh Blair about the suspicions over Ossian's authenticity and noted that he 'was told by [Edmund] Burke [1729/30–1797], a very ingenious Irish gentleman . . . that on the first publication of Macpherson's book, all the Irish cried out, *we know all these poems, we have all heard them from our infancy*'.[107] Ireland stood to lose the most by an uncritical acceptance of Macpherson's Ossian, whose contours and main characters it was alleged that Macpherson had stolen.[108] The Irish backlash was well under way by the time of Hume's letter—in fact it started even before *Fingal*'s publication[109]—but Macpherson poured fuel on the fire in the prefatory dissertation to *Temora*, devoted primarily to refuting Irish claims to Ossian and undermining the Irish historical tradition. Irish antiquaries tended to see Macpherson as the newest iteration of a long conspiracy to steal from and subvert Irish history; as Sylvester O'Halloran later put it, 'McPherson's Fingal and Temora, were published, in order to destroy the authority of Irish history; and, on its ruin, to raise up a system of Caledonian Antiquity'.[110] The conflict's intensity increased over the next few decades, occurring amidst simmering religious factionalism and a wider Irish historiographical effort to push back against the classic imputation of Irish barbarism, exemplified most recently and prominently by Hume, who had written that the situation of sixteenth-century Ireland was closer to savagery than barbarism.[111] As Clare O'Halloran has most clearly shown, Ossianic primitivism—championing the poems *because* they depicted the simple manners of savages—was a direct threat to Irish historians invested in proving the refined dignity of native Irish society before English colonialism.[112] Macpherson therefore faced trenchant criticism almost immediately, in works published in Paris, London, and Dublin, by Irish authors seeking to show that Macpherson had not only stolen their history but completely mangled it by depicting the Irish as a barbarous cadet branch of the Gallic Scots, when they all knew Ireland had been home to a Celtic society that was one of the most advanced in Europe.

Early protests, like *Fingal Reclaimed* (1762) and Sylvester O'Halloran's articles on 'Caledonian plagiary' in the *Dublin Magazine*, focused on Macpherson's supposed theft—not only did he borrow from and conflate the Ulster and Fenian cycles, but most of *Fingal* takes place in Ireland—but sophisticated historical critiques also appeared almost immediately.[113] Surprisingly enough, one of the first came from an Anglican cleric, Ferdinando Warner (1703–1768), who spent most of his life around London but was drawn to Irish antiquities when writing an ecclesiastical history of the English Church, and had decided to expand his findings into a separate general *History of Ireland* (1763). In the zero-sum game of historical truth, Macpherson's novel Caledonian system posed a direct threat to Warner's history, so he responded in a short pamphlet. The point was simple: the poems were 'undoubtedly the Production of very high antiquity', but because Macpherson probably recorded them from 'the Mouth of an old Highland Bard', they were corrupted versions of the original Irish manuscript sources and could not be used as the basis for a new historical system as Macpherson had done.[114] Brushing off Macpherson cleared the way for Warner's *History*, which regurgitated O'Conor's modified interpretation of the seventeenth-century historians in a more systematic form;[115] if nothing else, Warner wanted to prove that 'poetical romance' was no basis for 'historical truth', and 'that Ireland was the parent country of the Scotch'.[116] As for the Irish, Warner followed a moderated Milesian line corroborated by Genesis, Josephus, and Cluverius to derive them from the Gomerian Celts, one branch of which came from Britain and another from Spain—the 'pride and sloth of the common people' of both Ireland and Spain seemed to prove this—and spoke the 'original Celtic . . . universally spoken over Europe at that time', which was related closely to 'Hebrew and Phenicien'.[117] Essentially Warner followed O'Conor, but before we come to him one further writer needs to be taken into account: John O'Brien, Bishop of Cloyne, who we met in chapter 2 as the compiler of an Irish-English dictionary. O'Brien also published the most learned and interesting Irish refutation of Macpherson in the *Journal des Sçavans*, the leading periodical in the European Republic of Letters.

O'Brien had spent much of his life on the Continent, having been educated at Toulouse and Paris, and in Ireland he had a formidable reputation and a missionary zeal.[118] Elements of this character poked through in Ossianic dispute, which had remained free of confessional tension until O'Brien blamed Calvinism for inciting the kind of 'enthusiasm' he thought characterised Macpherson's poems—which he thought were outright forgeries—and made them resemble productions of Asiatic nations.[119] In six substantial articles, totalling around 40,000 words and published over the course of 1764, O'Brien charged Macpherson with 'Héro-cleptisme' in order to support his 'nouveau Système d'Histoire', which he had taken from David Malcolme, who in turn had pilfered its main elements from Lhwyd.[120] Basically, since he thought the poems were forgeries designed to subvert Irish history, there was nothing worth salvaging from Ossian. Like most of the other Ossianic critics, O'Brien was writing a history of Ireland, and therefore we can assume that Macpherson's interpretation posed a direct challenge to his own; this study never appeared but O'Brien laid out a historical explanation and alluded to his essay in the *Journal des Sçavans* in the long preface to his important Irish-English dictionary published at Paris in 1768.[121]

Macpherson's allegation of Irish and Scottish Gaelic illiteracy posed the most serious challenge to the historical system of Ireland's leading Catholic antiquary, Charles O'Conor. As we saw in the second chapter, O'Conor's interpretation relied on classical testimony and the medieval Irish historians to prove that the Iberian Celts had brought an advanced, literate, commercial society to Ireland in pre-Christian times; he adhered to the traditional interpretation that a breakaway colony of 'Scots' from Ireland established a monarchy in northwest Britain around 503 CE. His and Macpherson's histories were therefore directly opposed.[122] In 1766 O'Conor published a new edition of his *Dissertations* with a separate appendix containing a direct onslaught on Macpherson, to 'remove all his objections out of the way of the Dissertations'.[123] Other Scottish writers had tried to steal Irish material before but, as O'Conor explained, Macpherson knew their systems were untenable because they lacked evidence and so drew on the genuine tradition of Ossian, but misrepresented him '(*very wisely*, for his Scheme) *as an illiterate Bard, who lived in an illiterate Age*!'[124] He showed that Macpherson manipulated the sources by mixing the Fenian and Ulster Cycles, and—contra Macpherson's claims for Gaelic purity—poured scorn on 'Erse' as a corrupted form of purer Irish Gaelic; O'Conor also used Bullet to show that Macpherson's place-name etymologies were indecisive because they were all 'of Celtic original, as most of the antient Names of Towns, Rivers and Districts in Europe, are, to this Day'.[125] But O'Conor came up against the same problem as Macpherson, lack of manuscript evidence, and considering his system revolved around the notion of ancient Celtic literacy, this was even more troublesome for him.

The Ossian debacle came at a bad time for Irish Catholics like O'Conor, who had founded the Catholic Committee in 1756 and was preoccupied with refuting David Hume's treatment of Ireland in his *History*. Taken together, the works of Hume and Macpherson depicted the native Irish as an untrustworthy nation that had remained mired in a state of savagery since antiquity. According to O'Conor, in the 'ages of bad government the Irish were barbarians, but not in a greater degree than the other nations of Europe during those periods. Savages they were not'.[126] Accusations of savagery past and present needed to be refuted at all costs, but O'Conor recognised that it would be useful to have a Protestant vindication of the Irish, not least because they would have better access to historical materials kept at Ascendancy bastions like Trinity College. The Irish were also sensitive to the fact that they lacked—as Hume claimed—a philosophical historian.[127] A native Dubliner and Trinity Fellow, Thomas Leland (1722–1785), was identified by both Burke and O'Conor as the man for the job, and in 1772 he published a bland refutation of Macpherson's *Introduction,* not exactly vindicating the Milesian account while still defending it from Macpherson. But in the end, Leland reverted to the Protestant status quo and blamed Catholics for 1641 and the situation in which they found themselves under the penal laws, to the fury of O'Conor and the disappointment of more neutral observers.

Yet if Leland produced a philosophical history without redressing Catholic grievances, the self-appointed Irish Catholic champion Sylvester O'Halloran (1728–1807)—a prominent Limerick eye surgeon educated in Paris and London—also did not move things forward, producing a more extreme version of the Milesian system with overtly political purposes.[128] Publishing only scientific and medical works prior to the 1760s, O'Halloran was induced to enter the field of Irish antiquities by Macpherson, for he greatly admired the poems but thought they had been stolen by Macpherson, until O'Conor convinced him they had mostly been 'Calculated for the [historical] System'.[129] O'Halloran spent the 1760s fleshing out his own system with the help of O'Conor, but the result was even more grandiose than Macpherson's, claiming Ireland as the site of the most advanced civilization of ancient Europe, which had been at once martial, moral, pious, and possessed of a powerful commercial empire. O'Halloran stated that 'With their liberties were destroyed, the early History of the antient Celtae', while at the same time in their medieval annals the Irish preserved the only records that could illuminate that ancient golden age.[130]

O'Halloran first teased these claims in *Insula Sacra* (1770)—where he embellished the Milesian account and implied that the Scythian Irish gave hieroglyphs to ancient Egypt and the Olympic Games to Greece, before establishing a commercial empire in Ireland—and expanded them in his first major work on Irish antiquities, *An Introduction to the Study of the History and Antiquities of Ireland* (1772), and then in his *General History of Ireland* (1778).[131] His overriding purpose in these works was to vindicate Ireland, ancient and modern, from aspersions cast by Hume, Voltaire, Macpherson, and others; he was relatively uninterested in Celtic ancestry apart from what positive light it could shine on Ireland, and he managed to accommodate the traditional Milesian system with the Celtic theory. Ireland had been the centre of Celtic civilization and European commerce, where the Druidical universities were located, and whose ancient constitution formed the basis of European laws. Studying ancient Irish history, O'Halloran boasted, would illuminate 'the antient laws and customs of the Celtic nations of Europe . . . as our legislation was the great reservoir, from which they borrowed their systems of Government'.[132] There were presentist political allusions interspersed throughout his work too, such as, 'To hope by severe & penal laws, to make mankind better and juster, the History of all times denies'.[133] Although he aided O'Halloran, when the *Introduction* was published O'Conor admitted to another antiquary that despite O'Halloran's zeal the work made no positive progress and was 'destitute of the proper proofs. . . . I mean [of] the early use of letters in Ireland'.[134] Ultimately O'Halloran was a poor scholar, and it seems remarkable that he thought there might still be valuable hints in Annius's long-discredited Pseudo-Berosus.[135] In the press, both British and French, his work was met either with mockery or silence.[136] Yet despite his overblown claims and overwrought system, O'Halloran would play a direct role in the translation of native Irish poetry into English (*à la* Macpherson), and therefore in a reconciliation of the Anglo-Irish with the Gaelic past, when he assisted Charlotte Brooke in the 1780s (see the following chapter).

By the 1770s, O'Conor was increasingly uncomfortable with O'Halloran's uncritical enthusiasm, in part because he himself now doubted portions of the traditional interpretation—principally the Greek and Egyptian parts—whose 'genuine truths' had been 'obscured by forged adventures on sea and land'.[137] They broke with each other after O'Conor publicly criticised O'Halloran in 1775 and O'Halloran responded in kind in his *General History* of 1778.[138] At the same time, O'Conor was supporting a new entrant to the field of Irish antiquities, Charles Vallancey (*c.* 1726–1816), an English military officer of Huguenot extraction passionately devoted to the Irish language. Whereas O'Halloran doubted the use of linguistic comparisons but used superficial etymologies like tentacles to seize particular points of ancient history that could bring credit to ancient Ireland, Vallancey was chiefly interested in the Irish language, which he thought was the original Celtic language that seemed to share an 'affinity with almost every language of the known world', and therefore 'we might conclude with Boullet, that it was the primaeval language'.[139] Vallancey also lectured Macpherson on Gaelic and thought his corrupted Celtic was 'strong evidence of the novelty of this poem, or if it be ancient, it is a proof of the unlettered ignorance of the ancient Gaolic Scots'.[140] As Clare O'Halloran explains, Vallancey's famous 'discovery' provided O'Conor with a workaround for the problem of proving ancient Irish literacy without ancient Irish texts: if Irish was 'pure Phoenician', and the Phoenicians were famously lettered, then it stood to reason that the Irish were too (this is discussed further in the following chapter).[141]

None of this interested the Scots, who were trying to explain the progress of society to its present commercial stage, and Macpherson never bothered to respond to Irish challenges. In fact, it was John Whitaker who reacted most vocally to O'Halloran's *Introduction*, equating it with that of 'their brethren and antagonists of the Highlands. . . . True history can only subsist upon the destruction of both . . . in order to maintain the dignity of the [British] national identity'.[142] This prompted another pamphlet from O'Halloran.[143] Whitaker was met by O'Conor's refutation in 1775, but rather than rehearse these squabbles, what should hopefully be clear is that in the 1770s the Celtic past was a point of contention within and without Ireland. 'Celtic' scholars from Scotland, Wales, and Ireland—not to mention England, Brittany, and France—essentially all made exclusive claims to an ancient Celtic provenance. Ossian had certainly stirred new interest in the ancient Celts and in the distinctive national pasts of the British and Irish nations, but there was as yet no agreed upon version of the Celts upon which all those who identified with them could embrace, and even the frameworks employed greatly differed.

Anti-Ossianic Gothicism: Thomas Percy and John Pinkerton

The English response to Ossian was ambivalent. Although he admired them, the English poet Thomas Gray thought the poems too good to be true, and was one of many unconvinced of their antiquity in 1760.[144] His friend Horace Walpole (1717–1797) similarly doubted that the *Fragments* and *Fingal* were genuine, and by 1763, Hume reported to Blair that the imputation of forgery had become very common among men of letters in London.[145] Samuel Johnson led the charge and thought they were not only fake but also stylistically worthless.[146] His famous trip to the Highlands with James Boswell in 1773 was undertaken in part to investigate whether any of Macpherson's account could be verified; the publication of Johnson's travelogue in 1775 infuriated Macpherson and opened the old wounds of the authenticity controversy. Macpherson and

Johnson exchanged verbal hostilities and subsequent commentators cried wolf that Macpherson threatened Johnson physically, but Fiona Stafford has shown that this is doubtful.[147] This story is well known, and in this section I am instead interested in the historical controversy, and principally in the work of Johnson's friend Thomas Percy, at the time Rector of Easton Maudit in Northamptonshire, the publisher of *Reliques of English Poetry* in 1765, and the future Bishop of Dromore.[148] Percy was also close to Edward Lye (1694–1767), the best Gothic scholar of the age,[149] and himself became an expert in Gothic antiquities, poetry, and languages. These interests underpinned his most significant historiographical contribution: his definitive separation of the Germanic and Celtic language families, and therefore the ethnic affiliation of those ancient peoples. After Percy it was no longer possible—in Anglophone writing at least—to conflate ancient Celts and Goths without censure.[150]

Percy had a complex relationship with Ossian; although he vacillated on the question of the poems' authenticity, he was clearly inspired by them and produced several verse collections after their example, not least the famous *Reliques of English Poetry*, the most important eighteenth-century collection of Old English verse.[151] It was in 1761, while he was planning a set of 'specimens of the poetry of various nations in a series of literal translations', that Percy reached out to Evan Evans (as discussed above). Early in the course of their correspondence, Percy announced to Evans his plan to translate a work by the Genevan historian Paul-Henri Mallet, *Introduction à l'histoire du Dannemarc* (1755), a work on Scandinavian antiquities.[152] Importantly, it contained the first translation into a modern language of the prose Edda; however, Mallet had made the serious blunder of describing it and other northern antiquities as 'Celtic'. This cardinal error indicated Mallet's subscription to the common European idea that the Celts and Goths were the same people: 'Being ignorant of all the modern branches of the real Celtic Language; and very little acquainted with those of Gothic Origin: he has every where confounded them: a mistake which I shall endeavour to rectify in my translation'.[153] In his reply to Percy, Evans pointed to the root of the problem: Cluverius's assertion that the Celts had once controlled all of Europe, compounded by continental misreadings ever since (examined in chapters 1–3). While the separation of Celts and Goths had been digested in Britain since the works of Lhwyd and Hickes—and, to be fair, was well recognised and accepted by Macpherson—on the Continent there was still a strong tendency to identify the ancient Celts as the first settlers of Europe who spoke its first language, which meant that the Celtic and Gothic families were intertwined.[154]

Percy published his translation in 1770, with a critical preface delivering the great blow to the idea that Celts and Goths were the same people. He asserted that this assumption had been

> a great source of mistake and confusion to many learned writers of the ancient history of Europe; viz. that of supposing the ancient Gauls and Germans, the Britons and Saxons, to have been all originally one and the same people; thus confounding the antiquities of the Celtic and Gothic nations.[155]

In fact, the description of the preface indicated, 'the Teutonic and Celtic Nations were *ab origine* two distinct People'.[156] Percy blamed Cluverius as the originator of this error, which had then been taken up by a series of eighteenth-century European authors.[157] He adduced several types of evidence but relied most heavily on language, which 'amounts in questions of this nature almost to demonstration'.[158] To this end he first presented Hickes's genealogical tree of Gothic languages together with a Celtic family tree—likely derived from his extensive reading of Lhwyd—and then several specimens of the Lord's Prayer in the different derivative languages, whose comparison proved decisively the 'radical dissimilitude' of the two families.[159] Percy's understanding of language families was more sophisticated and his proofs more systematic than most of the authors thus far examined, but rather than target his countrymen directly, Percy instead chose to expose the weaknesses of the work of Jean-Baptiste Bullet, which may have been an oblique attack on some of the more extravagant Celtic antiquarians, most of whom relied on Bullet's *Mémoires de la langue celtique*.[160] Percy's work was undoubtedly influential and led to the Gothic-Celtic uncoupling in Anglophone writing, which we will see play out over the next few chapters.

Following Thomas Percy's spur to English Gothicism, Lowland Scots grew increasingly interested in their own potential Gothic inheritance. A young acolyte of Percy named John Pinkerton (1758–1826) developed the main contours of this argument and shifted the antiquarian debate in the 1780s, placing himself at the centre of the post-Ossianic moment.[161] Although he seems to have been a thoroughly unpleasant man, Pinkerton was one of Scotland's best scholars in the last decades of the eighteenth century. His erudition so impressed Gibbon that he designated Pinkerton heir to his project for an edition of the English medieval historians.[162]

After trying his hand at poetry in the 1770s, Pinkerton undertook a dense programme of study that formed the basis for several of his most important works, published from 1785 to 1789.[163] Pinkerton first aired these theories in 'An Essay on the Origin of Scottish Poetry', prefixed to his collection *Ancient Scotish Poems* (1786). His narrow purpose was to prove that Lowland Scots was a Gothic dialect descended from Pictish and distinct from English, and that Scottish poetry derived chiefly from Pictish, rather than Celtic (Welsh and Irish) or Saxon sources. Thus Pinkerton established a nobler Scottish linguistic and poetic tradition distinct from English influence, but also one that undercut Celtic claims.[164] Macpherson provided Pinkerton's great target, though not for his imposture—Pinkerton admired Ossian as a modern work—but rather 'for the singular embarrassment he has thrown upon the antiquities of Scotland, by his dreaming essays, and prefaces to [Ossian]',[165] in other words, Macpherson's historical interpretation. Pinkerton took particular issue with what he saw as Macpherson's linguistic mistakes, censuring him for deviating from Lhwyd and believing that Highland Gaelic was a purer version of Celtic than Irish, and for the graver error of deriving the Goths from the Sarmatae in his *Introduction to the History of Great Britain and Ireland*.[166] Macpherson 'ought to have known that the languages prove the contrary. The Gothic, Getic, and Scythian are all one tongue'.[167] The implications of this assertion were spelled out at length a year later in Pinkerton's *Dissertation on the Origins and Progress of the Scythians or Goths* (1787).

Pinkerton's main purpose in the *Dissertation* was to show that the ancient people called 'Scythians' by the Greeks and 'Goths' by the Romans originated in Persia and spread to the Euxine Sea, formed an empire stretching from Egypt to the Ganges around 2,200 years before Christ, and were altogether distinct from the ancient Celts and Sarmatians. Relying on linguistic evidence and the authority of ancient writers, Pinkerton put his erudition to remarkable use, not only pointing out the mistakes of modern authorities such as Cluverius, Grotius, Lipsius, Scaliger, Salmasius, Vossius, Ihre, and Robertson, but also correcting the ideas of the ancient Gothic historian Jordanes (*fl.* 551 CE), who had led Gibbon and Montesquieu astray in their belief that the Gothic invasions proceeded from the North (read: Scandinavia) rather than from Asia.[168] An understanding of stadial theory assisted his case; the 'wandering nature' of the Scythians, who were still in the pastoral stage, explained their eruption westwards into Europe, rather than a want of northern space.[169] The waves of ancient Scythian invaders meant that modern Europe was almost wholly populated by Gothic descendants, and that 'the origin of government, manners, laws, in short, all the antiquities of Europe' could be traced beyond Montesquieu's German woods and to the ancient Scythians of Asia.[170]

Pinkerton also famously developed a polygenetic racial theory—whose implications will be discussed further in chapter 6—and deployed it against the Celtic nations. As it stood, Pinkerton declared that there had been four 'Grand Races of Men' in ancient Europe: the Celts, the Iberians, the Sarmatae, and the Scythians. They were all of distinct origin and could be differentiated by linguistic families. Pinkerton was particularly irked that the Scythians/Goths had been confused with the Celts, despite the fact that no 'tongues [could] be of more different form than the Celtic and Gothic'.[171] As Patrick O'Flaherty notes, between the publication of *Ancient Scotish Poems* and the *Dissertation* in June 1787, Pinkerton's tone turned bilious toward the Celts.[172] This appears to have been chiefly a result of his disdain for Macpherson, whose *Introduction* Pinkerton demolished, exposing not only that Macpherson quoted his authorities out of context but, in the case of Procopius, was unable to read him in the original Greek.[173] His disdain for Macpherson's Celtic interpretation boiled over into a disdain for the Celts in general, who he asserted were still in the savage state when the Scythians invaded Europe and 'fled to the extremities [of Europe]; Britain and Gaul appear to have been the final receptacles of almost all the Celts'.[174] To be fair, the stadial interpretations by the Scottish literati *and* Macpherson had all placed Ossian in the savage, hunter state—one reason the poems were celebrated was in fact because of this—but divorced from the Scottish patriotic mood of the 1760s, Pinkerton could exploit the ambivalence about the savage state frequently highlighted with reference to Native Americans.[175] However, Pinkerton's nascent racialism meant he pitched the Celts as a separate, deficient race who even in his own time were

> mere radical savages, not yet advanced to a state of barbarism; and if any foreigner doubts this, he has only to step into the Celtic part of Wales, Ireland, or Scotland, and look at them, for they are just as they were, incapable of industry or civilization.[176]

He also blamed scholars who 'chuse to sicken the publick with their dreams concerning the Welch language and antiquities . . . a phrenzy also general in Ireland'.[177] But Pinkerton merely swapped one ancient people for another—Scytho-Goths for Celts—and his theories were no less spurious than Macpherson's. In the words of the Scottish schoolmaster and journalist Robert MacFarlan (1734–1804): 'Pelloutier could see nothing but what was Celtick, and Pinkerton, as a counterbalance, finds nothing but what is Gothic'.[178] While some approved of his treatment of the Celts, Pinkerton ultimately suffered from it and later tried to walk back his comments, explaining that his stridency was directed at Macpherson and that ultimately he pointed out the lack of Celtic civilization in the hopes it would spur improvement (note, however, this was a dodge and not a retraction).[179]

Conclusion

This chapter has only covered some of the more prominent interpretations of the ancient Celtic past advanced in the wake of Ossian. Beyond these was a multitude of minor works, some simply continuing the controversy, others seeking to make a real contribution to scholarship and capitalising on the vogue in which Celtic antiquities found itself, and some doing both. The antiquarian Rev. James McLagan (1728–1805) wrote to the president of a new Gaelic Society in 1771 that it was the opportune moment to make a Gaelic dictionary, while 'the Nation seems to be in some humour for relishing things of this Nature'.[180] An English-Gaelic Grammar and a Dictionary were produced by William Shaw (1749–1831), a linguistic patriot whom Johnson convinced that Macpherson was a fraud and pushed to publish a challenge; however, Shaw's linguistic criticisms of Macpherson fell flat when it was later revealed that Shaw had requested his help for the Gaelic grammar.[181] Other editors published English translations of 'Ossianic' fragments and in 1786 John Gillies omitted a historical dissertation to his collection because so much had already been written on Gaelic poetry.[182]

When James Macpherson died in 1796, he left unfinished the Gaelic 'originals' that he had been promising to publish for several decades.[183] He had undertaken this as his retirement project, but was obviously still trepidatious, complaining to Adam Ferguson about Gaelic orthography and returning to an old theme: 'The result of the whole is, that I have resolved to follow the example of the old Druids, in writing the Celtic language in Greek characters'.[184] Ferguson seemed to see the wisdom in this, or at least he humoured Macpherson and agreed that the Greek characters might be preferable to the 'barbarous orthography' of Gaelic written in the Roman script, which he could not read.[185] In the end, the poems were finally printed in Roman characters with a Latin translation in 1807, but this was largely beside the point as the Highland Society's *Report* had been published in 1805.

Walter Scott urged peace, stressing in the *Edinburgh Review* that one could recognise the poems were contrived while still enjoying their literary merits, and that Scotland could be proud of them even if they were not third-century fragments. Whatever his intentions, Macpherson had generated a wider interest in the Celtic cultures of Britain and Ireland, and fuelled a tourist boom to the Highlands and Islands.[186] Travellers wanted to see the Highland landscape, to hear Ossianic verse recited by the Gaelic peasantry, and to search for vestiges of ancient paganism and Celtic heroism themselves. The Scottish Highlands had long suffered from accusations of barbarity, with commentators pointing to their language and customs, as well as the region's rugged landscape and lack of commerce. Macpherson cleverly turned that negative discourse to his advantage, arguing that the purity of the language, a lack of literacy, and the absence of commerce that resulted from the impenetrable landscape all made it more likely that poems could have survived in the national memory for over a thousand years. By mixing this interpretation with an enlightened idealisation of Celtic noble primitivism, Macpherson squared the circle by producing an account of Scottish national origins that conformed to contemporary theories of socioeconomic development, but of which Scots could nevertheless be proud. This was all completely antithetical to the understanding and aims of the Welsh antiquarians—who took pride in being the first Britons—and the Irish Gaelic patriots, who needed an account of ancient Irish civilization as advanced and admirable yet still theologically and politically neutral. Admitting that the ancient Celts had been barbarous would have subverted their main historiographical intention of vindicating their own culture in the face of centuries of slander, which had justified the English right of conquest. Rejecting this narrow political justification by force in preference of the broader rights of the nation would shortly help some French revolutionaries to place the ancient Celtic past at the centre of their own national story.

5

Celts in the Age of Revolution and Empire

SOMETIME TOWARDS the end of the French Consulate, Jacques Cambry (1749–1807) hosted John Pinkerton at his estate just south of Paris at Arcueil.[1] The pairing was an odd one. The Breton Cambry, author of the popular *Voyage dans le Finistère* (1799)—a travelogue sponsored by the revolutionary government[2]—was a famous Celtic enthusiast, a co-founder and the first president of the *Académie celtique*, precursor of the *Société nationale des antiquaires de France*. Pinkerton, on the other hand, was perhaps the shrillest Celtophobe in all of Europe. As we saw in the previous chapter, he argued that the Celts were an inferior race compared to the Goths, who alone were responsible for European civilization. After the meeting Pinkerton attacked Cambry as overzealous and under-learned, while Cambry accused the 'English government' of hiring Pinkerton to subvert ancient Celtic, and therefore modern French, power and prestige.[3] While this exchange occurred at the height of modern Franco-British antagonism, we have seen in previous chapters how a sense of Celticity—often linked to Brittany, the Breton language, and ancient Gaul—increased in France over the course of the eighteenth century. But it was during the Revolutionary and Napoleonic years that the idea of Gaulish, and therefore Celtic, national origins finally displaced the constitutional importance of a Frankish, and therefore Germanic, national descent.

When the Revolution broke out in 1789, the prevailing issue was sovereignty and where it lay: with the people, with the nobility, or with the king? Who really constituted *la nation*? The Abbé Emmanuel Joseph Sieyès answered the question resoundingly in favour of the people, or 'Third Estate', and in a famous passage he encouraged the nobility to return to their 'Franconian forests', because the nation were 'descendants of Gauls and Romans'.[4] Sieyès's invocation was rhetorical and part of a larger critique of the equation of historical tradition with political legitimacy, but by tapping into the long-running historical debate on the composition of the nation, he added weight to his rejection of 'privilege'.[5] The first section of this chapter is intended to show how claims of this sort were connected to interpretations of France's national past and resonated not just due to their political implications, but also because people from around France believed themselves to be descended from the Gauls. It was suspected that elements of the Celtic language existed in the various *patois* around France, that Gaulish customs might have survived in the manners of the people, and even that peasant superstitions could preserve Druidic beliefs. If ordinary French men and women were descendants of the Gauls, then there was a deeper significance to Napoleon's epithet 'Emperor of the Gauls' than just a wry statement about his raw power.[6] These ideas found their most prominent expression in the *Académie celtique*, a scholarly society founded in the wake of the Napoleonic Empire's proclamation in 1804.

At the same time that France's constitutional crisis was deepening in the 1780s, Irish patriotism increased in strength, symbolised above all by the reinstallation of Ireland's parliament in 1782. This movement was led by 'Patriot' Anglo-Irish Protestants who, crucially, started to adopt Ireland's Celtic history as their own. Many of them were involved in the foundation of the Royal Irish Academy in 1785, which is the point normally taken as signifying the Protestant embrace of the Celtic past. Although the bloodshed and failure of the 1798 Uprising dampened patriotic activity and celebration of the national past—Celtic or otherwise—we can nevertheless see that, as in France, the 1780s and 90s in Ireland witnessed the general embrace of the ancient Celtic past as the historical foundation of Irish nationhood.[7]

The French Revolution captivated Europe, but fascination turned increasingly to fear, especially once war broke out between France and the other European powers in 1792. Although the Republic declared on 22 September of that year had its admirers in Britain and Ireland—including among some Welsh radical antiquarians examined below—by and large the response was a predictable British patriotism, stoked by a fear of invasion. The Revolution registered differently in the four nations, but it had its clearest effect on Celtic ideas in Wales, particularly with Iolo Morganwg, one of the leading cultural figures and a committed republican. Revolutionary anti-clericalism and ideas of natural religion inspired Iolo's writings and his *Gorsedd Beirdd Ynys Prydain* (Congress of the bards of the Isle of Britain), a neo-Druidic clerisy that staged its first ceremony on Primrose Hill in London on 21 June 1792. Iolo's invented texts, ceremonies, and philosophy—publicised through a sympathetic network in London—would have a huge impact on the development of Celticism in the nineteenth century, in Wales and Britain but also in France.

Iolo and his friends, many members of the Royal Irish Academy, and the scholars of the *Académie celtique* all attacked the same problem that we have seen appear in previous chapters: aspersions of ancient Celtic barbarity made by classical authors and seemingly proved by the lack of civilizational markers such as a native alphabet and a corpus of texts written in it. As Iolo's antagonist, the Rev. Edward Davies (1756–1831) wrote, when it was 'recollected . . . how unwilling the learned are to allow *the Celtae* any degree of knowledge, but that which had arisen from the contact of strangers', the antiquarian hunt for Celtic remains took on a new significance.[8] Even the slightest evidence of civilizational advancement might lead to a favourable change in opinion. At the heart of this chapter, therefore, are questions about the nature of evidence still plaguing Celtic studies today: How could a history of the Celts be written without relying on Greek and Roman sources?

One answer was to make it up. Despite his many genuine contributions to Welsh scholarship, this was the level to which Iolo occasionally stooped. Another answer was to turn to evidence from the other Celtic nations, which could be used to make inferences about the culture of the ancient Celts as a whole. Communication increased along these lines, and it was during the Napoleonic Wars that the first scholarly stirrings of pan-Celticism can be detected, when William Owen Pughe (1759–1835) contacted leading scholars from the different Celtic nations of Britain with the aim of creating a Celtic Society for the study of antiquities. Although this group never seems to have come to fruition, its plans were known to the founders of the *Académie celtique*, the focus of the final section of this chapter. This French antiquarian society dedicated itself to the study of the ancient French past through novel linguistic, folkloric, and ethnographic approaches, aligning its scholarly mission to the expansion of the French Empire.

Running through this chapter, therefore, are several imperial threads. The new context created by the Napoleonic Empire is the most obvious one, but it should be remembered that the ideas and personalities examined in this chapter lived against the backdrop of the 'Second Age of Exploration', when the European empires tightened their grip on the rest of the world, sending out scientists and scholars to survey the lands, peoples, and languages they encountered in places like the South Pacific or the North American frontier. In fact, one of the first inductees into Iolo's *Gorsedd y Beirdd* was the physician

David Samwell (1751–1798), who had travelled with Captain Cook on his third voyage and recorded his famous death on Hawaii. The material recovered and published on these voyages was grist to the Celtic mill, which allowed enthusiastic Celtic scholars to make increasingly dramatic claims for the significance of the Celts to world history. These were aided by the *Asiatick Researches* edited in Calcutta by Sir William Jones (1746–1794), who in his famous discourse of 1786 wrote that Sanskrit shared grammatical and lexical features with the European languages, including Celtic. Finally, the Celts had lain dormant in texts for centuries, but in the form of the French *grande armée* they awoke and seemed bent on resurrecting their ancient European empire.

The Gauls and the French Revolution

In the years just before the outbreak of the French Revolution, debate swirled around the nature of France's constitution and what to do about it.[9] Should it be regenerated—a situation that would necessitate a historical examination of what exactly France's ancient constitution *was*—or should a new constitution be designed? By August 1789 it was obvious that the revolutionaries would devise a new constitution based on the principles of natural right. In the early phase of the Revolution, therefore, there was not much scope for historical appeals to ancient national ideals, which might have fixated upon the Gauls, because revolutionaries were self-consciously challenging the idea that modern political societies could be founded on tradition and precedent alone. Yet, although historical theories did not play any real role in the outbreak or early ideology of the Revolution—despite the rhetorical Gaulishness of Sieyès—in the last decades of the century there was an increasing recognition of the ancient Celtic Gauls as the forefathers of *la nation*.[10]

This played out in a variety of scholarly genres and was embraced by figures of greater and lesser importance, but for the French *cognoscenti* the idea of the Celts may have been linked with one man above all others: Jacques le Brigant (1720–1804), a Breton lawyer and *parlementaire* zealously devoted to claiming the prestige of the ancient Celts and their language for his beloved Brittany and Breton. Despite promoting linguistic theories that were outrageous even in his own time, Le Brigant was an energetic Celtic propagandist who promoted his ideas in elevated social circles—he was once a guest of Louis XVI (1754–1793) at Versailles—and gained his own followers. Moreover, there is evidence to suggest that his ideas had more influence in some provincial areas of France than among the *philosophes* of Paris.

Le Brigant's linguistic thesis remained consistent throughout his published work: that the Celtic language, spoken by the *Gomérites* when they peopled Europe, was the primitive language of the entire world, and could be found preserved in its entirety in modern Breton, specifically in the dialect of his hometown Pontrieux. His earliest works focused on proving that Celtic/Breton had once been spoken from Finistère to the Hellespont[11]—an assertion not hugely out of the ordinary for the time—but eight years later he expanded this idea to argue that all languages derived from Celtic, and included comparisons to the Semitic languages, Chinese, Sanskrit, Galibi (Carib), and Tahitian.[12] So convinced was Le Brigant of Celtic's linguistic universality that when some of his antiquarian peers paid a Parisian of swarthy complexion to pretend to be Tahitian and to speak gibberish to him, Le Brigant claimed to understand him and that it confirmed his findings.[13] The story spread through polite society and to the King's cousin Louis Philippe, Duc d'Orléans (1747–1793), the future Philippe Égalité; but, instead of retreating, Le Brigant published an abridged Celtic grammar lesson offered to Orléans as a response.[14]

Le Brigant was an assiduous propagandist, and he did more than anyone to popularise the idea that Breton could be the primeval human language. He met and corresponded with Voltaire, who clearly thought him ridiculous but used him for inspiration in parts of the novel *L'ingénu* (1767).[15] Nevertheless, Le Brigant remained hopeful that Voltaire would accept his conclusions, sending him a chart comparing modern European languages and arguing they were simply dialects of the original Celtic Breton. In 1780 Benjamin Franklin (1706–1790) received a similar chart, along with Le Brigant's best wishes for the colonists against 'les pirates Saxons' and the assertion that the American colonies' language descended from that spoken by the ancient Gauls, whose love of liberty still existed with the colonists.[16] Le Brigant reportedly won the support of Catherine the Great (1729–1796) as well as that of the financial ministers Charles-Alexandre de Calonne (1734–1802) and Jacques Necker (1732–1804), the latter of whom convinced Louis XVI to patronise Le Brigant.[17] Louis's joke that Le Brigant was 'the most learned man in my kingdom' suggests that amused contempt rather than respect was the overriding sentiment of most who encountered Le Brigant.

Yet he remained undeterred in his mission and gained some followers. A young physiocratic Baron, Claude-Urbain de Retz de Servières (1755–1804), alias 'Reth', wrote excitedly to Le Brigant that his work supported the idea that 'an exact understanding of the origin and filiation of languages would be the key to all human knowledge'.[18] Later, the Marquis de Condorcet (1743–1794) graciously responded to one of Le Brigant's letters with a hope that his research might contribute to a better understanding of the French language and history,[19] and a year after that Olympe de Gouges (1748–1793) referred excitedly to Le Brigant's linguistic discoveries in a pamphlet criticising Rousseau.[20] But the frustration with Le Brigant's work is epitomised in a letter by the ecclesiastical historian the Abbé Grandidier (1752–1787) to the Strasbourgeois polymath Jéremie-Jacques Oberlin (1735–1806). Several years before William Jones set foot in India, Grandidier related that Le Brigant wanted 'to prove that the language of Indian scholars named Samskrete or Hanscrite has much in common with the ancient Celtic language of the Bas-Bretons'. However, Grandider then noted that Le Brigant was 'so occupied with his system that he sees in all idioms presented to him, the language of his friend Gomer'.[21] The point here is that, while Le Brigant anticipated later developments in comparative linguistics, this was really the result of an all-encompassing system rather than a critical acumen.

A similar project focused on the ancient Celtic language, though one with a much stronger philosophical foundation, was undertaken by Antoine Court de Gébelin (1719/1725–1784), a Protestant *philosophe* associated with the physiocrats and prominent in Paris until his death in 1784. He sought to uncover the primitive natural language of humanity as a key to all human knowledge and believed that the ancient Celtic language was the closest to it.[22] If the original, true meanings of words could be discerned, then all ancient allegories would be deciphered and lead to the secret to understanding the natural laws of human happiness.[23] He pursued this project through his nine-volume *Le Monde Primitif analysé et comparé avec le monde moderne*, in which he stated that he understood the original language to be Celtic, from which descended Gaulish, Teutonic, Greek, Latin, and the other European languages.[24] Gébelin was one of those who played the 'Tahitian trick' on Le Brigant, but his view that Breton was probably closest to the original language was not that far off from his target's.

If, as affirmed by Guiomar, theories of Celtic origin did not carry much ideological weight during the early phase of the Revolution,[25] we can nevertheless detect ways in which they were useful for revolutionary polemicists. In the same way that Rousseau and other *philosophes* could be invoked for the purposes of policy legitimation, versions of the French past were deployed depending on the writer's position and purposes. Although the wily Sieyès provided the most famous example in *Qu'est-ce que le tiers état?*, the same trick appeared in a number of contemporary works, usually written by those who would later be associated with the Girondins.[26] The Celtic linguistic antiquarians would occasionally be cited to bolster their theories. For example, the founder of the Girondist *Cercle social,* Nicolas de Bonneville (1760–1828), described the ancient Celts as a warlike, free, and democratic people with weak kings—an obvious example for a constitutional monarchy. He praised the contributions of Le Brigant and also recommended the project of Court de Gébelin.[27] Another Girondin associate, Jacques-Antoine Dulaure (1755–1835), wrote several scathing anti-nobility tracts, depicting the Germans as a race of barbaric thieves who subdued the Gauls through treachery.[28] As a future member of the *Académie celtique,* he would go on to publish a paper purporting to prove that a Gaulish senate had existed independently of Rome, arguing that Gaul's native Celtic government was republican.[29]

Although origins accounts dipped in importance following the toppling of the nobility, language issues became red-hot during the radical phase of the Revolution.[30] Yet while the revolutionary government policed language and shut down the *Académie française* as a conservative relic of the *ancien régime,* it also recognised linguistic patriotism. At the end of 1794 the Convention awarded Le Brigant three-thousand *livres* on the recommendation of the Committee of Public Instruction.[31] Le Brigant also made a cameo appearance in the Abbé Grégoire's (1750–1831) famous 1794 report to the Convention, in which he called for the French language to be 'revolutionised' and for the 'annihilation' of *patois.* Grégoire demonstrated a clear grasp of the linguistic terrain and cautiously accepted the Celtic theories. He affirmed that 'Celtic' was 'the first idiom of Europe' and cited the 'rather astonishing facts revealed' by 'Peloutier, Bochart, Gebelin, Bochart, Lebrigand [*sic*]', which included among other things the relationship between Irish, Punic, and ancient Celtic, which was preserved in its primitive purity in Northern Scotland and had recorded the masterpieces of Ossian.[32]

David Bell has drawn attention to the inclusion of figures like Gébelin, noting that their presence makes the report read like a prize essay;[33] their inclusion also shows the extent to which Celtic theories permeated France's educated elite. Michel de Certeau et al. found that Celtic 'obsessed' the respondents to Grégoire's 1790 linguistic survey, on which the 1794 report was built;[34] while this assertion might overstate the case somewhat, there is nevertheless considerable evidence of knowledge of the Celtic theories in the responses. For example, the correspondent from the department of Haute Vienne referred to the ancient peoples of Europe as 'Celtes', whose language had been spoken by the Gauls and survived the Frankish invasion to form the base of

French patois. He cited Pelloutier and Grégoire as sources on the French language, but remarkably found that Limousin patois agreed with Tahitian, specifically the word *Aipà* (*il n'y en a pas*)—an almost sure sign he had read Le Brigant's prospectus, which featured this exact word as taken from the vocabulary recorded during Louis-Antoine de Bougainville's (1729–1811) voyage to Tahiti in 1767.[35] Unsurprisingly, the correspondent from western Brittany also cited Le Brigant's work to show that Breton was the original Celtic language of Europe, while on the other side of the country, in the Franche-Comté, a correspondent dutifully reported that the local patois derived from Celtic, as demonstrated in the dictionary of Jean-Baptiste Bullet.[36] The letters to Grégoire therefore suggest that while the linguistic conclusions of figures like Le Brigant and Bullet were basically discounted in intellectually dynamic Paris, they seem to have had more staying power in provincial France.

Used for the purposes of anti-aristocratic polemic in the early years of the Revolution, the Gallo-Celtic interpretation was ascendant from the establishment of the Directory in 1795.[37] Guiomar points to the Celtic interests of some of the *Idéologues*, particularly Constantin de Chasseboeuf (1757–1820), Comte de Volney and Amaury Duval (1760–1808), founder of the *Décade philosophique*, which featured a number of Breton contributors.[38] A particularly striking example of the political uses of Celtic history was provided by the future co-founder of the *Académie celtique*, Michel-Ange de Mangourit (1752–1829), who penned an allegorical *roman à clef* in defence of the Coup of 18 Fructidor against the director Lazare Carnot (1753–1823), *De la Tyrannie de Carnot, ou les Carnutes: Anecdote druidique, écrite il y a 2000 ans* (On the tyranny of Carnot, or the Carnutes: A Druidic anecdote written 2,000 years ago). The narrative is set in Celtic Gaul during the Wars with Rome, and the Gaulish republic is riven by internal factionalism, as the tyrant 'Carnutorix' and his corrupt circle attempt to crush Gaulish liberty and deliver the republic to Caesar—the sequence of events corresponds roughly to the period from the fall of Robespierre through Fructidor (September 1797). The parallels drawn between the ancient Roman incursion and the foreign and royalist threats facing the modern French Republic are obvious, but Mangourit included 119 notes precisely identifying his targets by name, just in case.[39] Strongly republican in tone, the pamphlet shows the strengthening association of ancient Gaul with the modern French Republic—a historical connection that had been highlighted in an important scholarly work published in December 1796 by Mangourit's friend Théophile Malo-Corret de La Tour d'Auvergne (1743–1800).

La Tour d'Auvergne was the consummate revolutionary hero, combining soldierly virtue with unquestioning loyalty to the Revolution (despite his nominal links to the nobility), whose fame drew attention to his historical project. A proud Breton and career soldier, La Tour d'Auvergne had studied languages in his various postings, and in 1783 he had asked for a transfer to Asia in order to study the connection between European and Asian tongues and above all his native 'gauloise, ou le Bas Breton'.[40] He was a popular man in revolutionary Paris, where his friend and former teacher Bishop Claude Le Coz (1740–1815)—who later joined the *Académie celtique*, declaring 'I am a Celt, I confirm it'[41]—encouraged his scholarship, which in 1792 resulted in the publication of *Nouvelles recherches sur la langue, l'origine & les antiquités des Bretons*. La Tour d'Auvergne was a student and close friend of Le Brigant but cautiously distanced himself from some of the latter's excesses. He dispensed with a biblical descent from Noah's family—making only one oblique reference to the Ark in Armenia—but was nevertheless bullish on Breton as the mother language of Europe.[42] There was one notable recognition: La Tour d'Auvergne identified that Basque was neither related to the other Celtic languages, nor to any of the other European languages (this is today's scholarly consensus, though it was rare at the time).[43] Criticism could therefore curb the patriotic excesses of early modern antiquarianism, and La Tour d'Auvergne was sure of his conclusion because he had spent many years in the Basque country.

La Tour d'Auvergne published a new, retitled edition of his major work in 1796, upon returning to France after a year as a prisoner of war in Bodmin, Cornwall.[44] Retrofitted for the increasing nationalism of the French Republic, the book had more than doubled in length and featured a new, more inclusive title, *Origines gauloises*. He skirted the Frankish foundation of the monarchy by claiming they were a warlike Celtic people whose eighteenth-century descendants transformed their kingdom 'into a republic, which from the very dawn of its days proves itself to be a match for Rome at the height of her splendour'.[45] The work struck the right tone for the insecure French Republic; in its review, *Le Moniteur* declared that 'Latour d'Auvergne no longer belongs to himself; he belongs to the *Patrie*'.[46] He received congratulatory letters from the Directors for his military and scholarly service to the *patrie*,[47] but his fame exploded after he volunteered for active duty in 1797 at the age of fifty-four, taking the place of Le Brigant's twenty-second, and youngest, child. After La Tour d'Auvergne refused election to the Senate in 1800, Napoleon made him a living legend, naming him the 'Premier Grenadier de la France', shortly be-

FIG. 7. François Anne-Louis Girodet de Roucy-Trioson, *Ossian Receiving the Ghosts of French Heroes*, 1802, oil on canvas, 192 × 184 cm, Musée National du Château de Malmaison, Rueil-Malmaison. La Tour D'Auvergne is the first from the right in the middle row (with the aquiline nose).

fore he was killed with a lance through the heart at the Battle of Neuberg. His heart was carried around in an urn by his regiment (it now occupies its own sepulchre in the *Invalides*), his sword was gifted to Garibaldi, and his ashes were eventually Pantheonised in 1889.

Celtic themes also increased in French artistic nationalism.[48] In 1802, Anne-Louis Girodet (1767–1824) immortalised La Tour d'Auvergne in his overwrought painting of dead French military heroes for Napoleon's palace at Malmaison (Fig. 7). Fittingly, it is Ossian who welcomes the fallen into the heavens. Incidentally, it was also during the Napoleonic era that the famous sculpture now known as 'The Dying Gaul' came to be recognised as such. A staple on the Grand Tour, the masterpiece had been, and sometimes still is, identified as a gladiator; however, after Napoleon's brilliant victories in Italy and the signing of the Treaty of Tolentino, the statue was seized and sent to the Louvre, where two antiquarians seemingly independently argued that, on the basis of the figure's hair, moustache, and torque necklace, it was likely a barbarian. For one of them, Antoine Mongez (1747–1835), the traits most likely resembled those of the 'Gauls our ancestors'.[49] This interpretation was endorsed in the catalogue of the renamed *Musée Napoleon* (the Louvre) and as it gradually became accepted over the course of the nineteenth century it gave the public a powerful new visual representation of the Gauls.[50]

Spurred by the Revolution and installation of the Republic, the Celtic interpretation of the French past grew in importance throughout the 1790s. Linguistic antiquarian works underpinned some of the more overtly political writings, and even if they were not always directly cited, figures like Le Brigant and La Tour d'Auvergne were fairly well known in revolutionary Paris and their ideas were reported in the press. La Tour d'Auvergne's correspondence features a range of prominent characters of the time, and his heroic death helped to reinforce a web of association linking Brittany, the ancient Celts, and the newly historicised French nation—connections that would continue to strengthen through the early 1800s.

Embracing the Celtic Past in Ascendancy Ireland

Only slightly less dramatic than the French revolutionary period, the 1780s and 90s were fraught decades in Ireland and culminated in the failed United Irishmen Rebellion of 1798. Inspired by the American and French Revolutions, patriotic Irish demands for political rights rose alongside religious tensions and occurred amidst the background of popular disturbances in the countryside. As Leerssen and O'Halloran have shown, we can see the self-conscious adoption by patriotic Anglo-Irish men and women of a past that was national instead of just Gaelic or Anglo-Irish.[51] When we consider how this past was beginning to be embraced just as Gaelic scholars were coming to accept native Irish Celticity—as discussed over the last few chapters—we can see how space was made for the adoption of the ancient Celts as Ireland's national ancestors.

One antiquary stands out for the outrageousness of his beliefs, for the symbolism of his having adopted them, and for the industry with which he promoted them. This was Charles Vallancey, encountered briefly in the last chapter. Of Huguenot descent, he grew up in England and joined the British Army, coming to Ireland in 1750 as part of the Royal Engineers and settling there permanently.[52] After beginning to study Irish he came to the fervid belief that it was Europe's primeval language, a view normally only held by Gaelic or 'Old English' antiquaries. Though very aware of Vallancey's scholarly deficiencies, Charles O'Conor assisted him and probably recognised the political benefits that might come from befriending a Protestant English officer. Vallancey brought O'Conor into closer association with the various antiquarian groups he started and then achieved what was previously unthinkable by securing O'Conor a place in the Royal Irish Academy in 1785.

In his work Vallancey took the Irish theory of Milesian origins and ran with it, building on O'Conor's Hiberno-Phoenician hypothesis. He announced his major breakthrough to O'Conor in 1772: a passage written in Carthaginian speech in the Roman playwright Plautus's (*c.* 254–184 BCE) play *Poenulus* bore a striking resemblance to Irish.[53] By this logic, Vallancey circumvented the problem of the lack of proofs for a lettered ancient Irish civilization: if Irish and Phoenician were the same, then Phoenician specimens could stand in as proofs of antiquity for Irish specimens. As it was known the Phoenicians were the transmitters if not the inventors of the alphabet, this also played positively into the debate about pre-Roman Celtic literacy. Vallancey published an essay on the topic in his journal *Collectanea de rebus hibernicis*, and then reprinted it as a standalone pamphlet titled *An Essay on the Antiquity of the Irish Language* (1772), in which he razed the idea (supported by Lhwyd) that Irish was related to Basque, but in its place raised the new chimera that Irish was a 'Punic-Celtic Compound'.[54]

While Vallancey's political motivations are ambiguous, he was intellectually committed to the Gaelic version of Irish history, and in the *Grammar* included a 'Postscript. Proving that the History of the Milesian Expedition from Spain to Ireland is founded in true Facts'. His collocutor O'Conor appreciated that Vallancey's participation increased the ranks of those resisting the Macphersonians, and in a 1772 letter to the *London Chronicle* he (ironically) placed Vallancey in the sound tradition of Lhwyd and Leibniz, as opposed to the spurious one of Goropius Becanus and Macpherson.[55] His questionable work aside, Vallancey played an important role as an enthusiastic networker. He was in 1772 the main foundational force behind the 'Select Committee' of the Dublin Society that would inquire into ancient Ireland, as well as the

Hibernian Antiquarian Society (1779–1783).[56] His journal *Collectanea de rebus hibernicis* served as a semi-official journal for the group, but it bore the scars of conflict that ultimately led to that society's breakdown, in part because several of them rejected Vallancey's theories.[57] Finally, Vallancey was yet again a leading light in the creation of the Royal Irish Academy.

The foundation of the Royal Irish Academy in 1785 is normally accepted as symbolising the point at which a substantial swathe of the Protestant Ascendancy embraced Ireland's pre-conquest Celtic history.[58] Importantly, it admitted Catholics, even if there were only two among its first eighty-eight members.[59] It had normally been left to Catholic Irish scholars to write the history of pre-conquest Ireland using the medieval Gaelic sources, but Charles Vallancey, among others, had been drumming up enthusiasm since the 1770s by emphasising that Ireland's history was worth appreciating, if not exactly on its own terms, then for the light it could shed on the ancient history of Europe and the World. Medieval Irish sources and especially the Irish language—considering that, in Vallancey's opinion, it *might* have been the primaeval language of the world[60]—contained historical information unavailable elsewhere, and in recognition of this the academy committed to collecting and publishing Irish manuscripts at the same time as the *Gwyneddigion* Society was doing the same with Welsh materials (see below).[61] Through the intermediary of Edmund Burke, Vallancey also managed to secure the permanent deposit of Edward Lhwyd's Irish manuscripts in the library of Trinity College Dublin.[62]

One of the early disputes at the society was on a familiar theme: the existence of a native Irish alphabet. It all started on 24 June 1784, when Charles Vallancey read his paper on an ogham inscription on the tomb of *Conan Colgac*, said to be slain in 295 CE, more than a century before St. Patrick's—and therefore the Roman alphabet's—arrival in Ireland. He enquired about it to Theophilus O'Flanagan (*c.* 1762–1814), a young Irish scholar from County Clare, who went to inspect the monument and wrote back, confirming with his own research that *Conan Colgac* had died around 296. According to Vallancey, this showed straightforwardly enough that 'the ancient Irish had an alphabetical character before the arrival of St. Patrick'.[63] A year and a half later, O'Flanagan published his own paper on the subject, in which he advanced the idea that ogham was the 'secret writing' of the Druids, based upon a native script that already existed.[64] Unfortunately the carving was a forgery, and critics—including even Charles O'Conor—doubted both that it could have survived fourteen centuries in such pristine condition, and that O'Flanagan could read it with such ease.[65] We will see in subsequent sections how similar themes played out in Wales and France.

The academy context also provided the backdrop for the unquestionably most important work that crossed the Gaelic and Anglo-Irish divide, Charlotte Brooke's *The Reliques of Irish Poetry* (1789), which made a significant body of Irish Gaelic poetry readily available in an English translation.[66] The daughter of a Protestant lawyer, man of letters, and landowner who became both more liberal and poorer with age, Brooke learned Irish from the peasantry in County Cavan and history from O'Conor, O'Halloran, and Vallancey. Following their arguments for an ancient Irish enlightenment, Brooke wrote in her self-effacing introduction that the poems reflected a 'spirit of elevated heroism, sentiments of pure honor, instances of disinterested patriotism, and manners of a degree of refinement, totally astonishing, at a period when the rest of Europe was nearly sunk in barbarism'.[67] Ossian was an obvious influence but the critical apparatus included with the work emphasised Irish distinctiveness within the Celtic nations. In his introduction to the first poem, Sylvester O'Halloran clucked that if more scholars bothered to learn the ancient history and language of Ireland, the ancient Celts more generally would be better understood because, alone out of the Celtic areas of Europe, the Romans had not wiped away their 'laws, customs, legislation and manners'.[68] His immediate point was to argue that chivalry—as demonstrated in the four cycles of Irish mythology—had a Celtic origin, but more generally that the feudal system and military tenures 'flourished among the Celtae in those days of politeness and erudition, which long preceded the conquests in Gaul' and survived in Ireland long afterward.[69] Brooke made a compelling case for the historical importance of Celtic poetry, because 'nothing amongst those people went unsung: Poetry was their darling science' and therefore it shed light on 'the obscurest periods of Celtic antiquity'.[70] She also drew a favourable contrast between Celtic bards and Scandinavian skalds: whereas the latter sang before battle, the former heroically led the charge and sang his warriors through the fight.[71]

An appreciation for Ireland's native culture also increased among Irish 'patriot' politicians. When the leading patriot Henry Flood (1732–1791) died, his will contained a bequest for the foundation of 'a professorship of and for the native Irish or Erse language' at Trinity College—earmarked for Vallancey—as well as for the foundation of an annual essay or poetry contest in Irish, and for purchasing books and manuscripts in that language.[72] Because the endowment was successfully contested by his family, the chair was never created. But the bequest—as Leerssen has shown—tells us that leading Anglo-Irish patriots approved of Gaelic linguistic antiquarianism, especially the type that aggrandised the lustre of Ireland's national past.[73] Illustrating these points, the patriot Lawrence Parsons (1758–1841) defended Flood's intentions by arguing for the utility of the language in illuminating ancient history. He repeated the main narrative of the annals, tracing the Irish from Scythia to Ireland via Phoenicia—where they invented the alphabet—and repeating Vallancey's discovery that the Carthaginian speech in Plautus's *Poenulus* was really Irish.[74]

With figures like Vallancey, Brooke, and Parsons, among others, we therefore have a number of Anglo-Irish figures intellectually committed to Ireland's Gaelic past for historical and political reasons. There was also the religious expedience of linking the Gaels to the ancient Celts—who were pagans—which meant they could more readily be embraced in common by Anglicans, Catholics, and Dissenters. After the Rebellion of 1798 and the Union of 1800, confidence in this past wobbled and the antiquities section of the Royal Irish Academy was disbanded in 1810. Other societies were short-lived, such as Theophilus O'Flanagan's Gaelic Society of Dublin, whose aim was preserving and cultivating the 'most ancient, copious, and elegant [language] of Europe', the 'Mother Tongue of all the Languages in the West', by publishing 'every Fragment existing in the Gaëlic Language' and investigating the history 'natural, civil, and ecclesiastical' of Ireland as well as 'its sister Scotland'.[75] An Iberno-Celtic Society was founded in 1818 but it still showed signs of dissension because its assistant secretary, the Gaelic lexicographer Edward O'Reilly (1765–1830), had been a United Irishman, though he strenuously claimed it was a decision taken in self-defence because he was a Catholic.[76] O'Reilly stressed he had always been committed to the Crown, and when George IV visited Ireland in 1821 he wrote the Irish address which presented the Society's labours as elucidating the antiquities of the lands over which he ruled, as well as 'the origin of many Celtic Tribes which inhabit Europe'.[77] The Union, the Celtic past, and Ireland's links with Scotland also shaped Irish fiction in the early decades of the century.[78] In the most famous novel in this vein, the *Wild Irish Girl* (1800), Sidney Owenson (1783–1859) included a critical apparatus drawing on the scholars and antiquaries of the previous century. With the Ascendancy embrace of the Gaelic past, and the increasing linkage of the Gaels with the European Celtic past, the space was made for Ireland to eventually become seen as the most Celtic of nations.

Iolo Morganwg and the Invention of Modern Druidism

When Iolo Morganwg led several of his compatriots up Primrose Hill on the sunny morning of 21 June 1792 in order to induct them into his Bardic Congress, or *Gorsedd y Beirdd Ynys Prydain*, even he—an eccentric egomaniac—probably had little inkling that he was creating the most important invented tradition in the modern Celtic world.[79] Although Iolo depicted the *Gorsedd* as an ancient clerisy whose tenets were jealously guarded, he clearly wanted everyone to know about it and (in a great favour to future historians) produced a copious paper trail. That corpus has been a major focus of research in recent decades, the collective result of which is a fantastic multifaceted portrait of Iolo Morganwg set against the cultural landscape that he helped to fashion.[80] The *Gorsedd* is unquestionably the most important invented Celtic tradition; it has been a key part of the Welsh *Eisteddfod* for nearly 150 years, and a Breton spinoff—the *Goursez Vreizh*—is almost as old. Yet the *Gorsedd* was only one aspect of an entire bardic philosophy crafted by Iolo based on a romantic Celtic historical vision and radical political and religious principles. 'Bardism' was designed to distinguish his native county of Glamorgan and Wales more generally, where, in his opinion, 'Celtic civilization began' and then spread to the rest of Europe.[81] However, as Mary-Anne Constantine contends, Iolo has been overlooked in considerations of Celticism, and the international consequences of his neo-Druidic religion have been insufficiently elaborated.[82] If, as Ronald Hutton has argued, Iolo did more than anyone else to link Wales and the Druids, then to this affiliation must also be added the Celts, for Iolo's bardic system remained a deep well for nineteenth-century Celtic revivalists, especially in France, and helped to shape Celtic ideas into what they are today.[83] This influence will be elaborated further in subsequent chapters, but here we are primarily interested in Iolo's views on language, his bardic system, and the ways these wrapped elements of genuine Welsh history and literature in the mostly synthetic blankets of Druidism and Celticism.

Iolo was born Edward Williams in Glamorgan in 1747 and followed his father into stonemasonry, but he was also a brilliant autodidact, a rational dissenter, a poet, and the era's foremost collector of Welsh manuscripts, which he doctored and forged quite freely.[84] Although he put it to idiosyncratic use, Iolo hoovered up information from wherever he could and had an excellent understanding, not only of Welsh historical tradition,[85] but of the scholarly landscape in Britain; he recognised, for example, that historians like David Hume, William Robertson, and Edward Gibbon had raised the bar for historical work, while he thought that James Macpherson and John Pinkerton had polluted the antiquarian landscape with Gaelic chauvinism and Celtophobia, respectively, and hated them for it.[86] But Iolo's patriotism was regional as much as national, and although friendly with northwalians from the *Gwyneddigion* Society during his youthful years in 1770s London, Iolo eventually fell out with them and claimed his native Glamorgan as the site of purest Welsh tradition.[87] He turned on Edward Lhwyd too—the scholar who young Edward Williams had followed as his polestar—seemingly because Lhwyd had not devoted much attention to Welsh poetry, a tradition of which Iolo was intensely proud and protective.[88] Iolo may also have resented Lhwyd's assertion that Gaelic was the elder Celtic language. He argued the opposite in an early letter to the Welsh lexicographer John Walters (1721–1797), responding to Macpherson's Gaelicism by pressing Welsh's claim to linguistic primacy: 'the names of all the countreys that were ever inhabited by the Celtic nations are very naturaly accounted for in the British [Welsh]'. Not content with controverting the argument, Williams also (characteristically) mocked the Scottish accent: 'Well said, mon! The Deel tack me, mon, thou art a muckle bony loon'.[89] In a later essay on the Welsh language, Iolo refuted Pinkerton's aspersions on the Celts but could not resist a kick at the Gaels in an etymology of 'Cymmry' (Welshmen) that casts it as 'civil communities, compatriots, a name assumed by the civilized Celtae in distinction from *Gwyddelod* (Irishmen), savages, wildmen, woodmen, barbarians &c'.[90] Like the Breton *Celtisants* Pezron and Le Brigant, Iolo looked beyond the Isles, claiming the Celtic descent of other European languages, including English and Latin, which would upon examination 'be found to be only a dialect of the Celtic', an assertion he made with increasing confidence over the next couple decades.[91]

The last decades of the eighteenth century were an exciting time for Welsh scholarship. After a lull that came with the deaths of the Morris brothers and then the fizzling out of the Cymmrodorion Society in 1787, figures like Owen Jones, or 'Owain Myfyr' (1741–1814) and William Owen Pughe were keen to reinvigorate the cultural scene through their North Walian group *Cymdeithas y Gwyneddigion* (Society of the Men of Gwynedd).[92] Iolo seduced both of them with his bardic vision.[93] A wealthy furrier passionate about Welsh literary culture and manuscripts, Myfyr was eager to finance their publication, a long-awaited initiative greeted with enthusiasm by Welsh cultural activists who had long had the materials and the inclination but lacked the means to do so.[94] Pughe, a grammarian and lexicographer, was one of those who benefitted from Myfyr's largesse. In the early

1790s Pughe edited the sixth-century poet Llywarch Hen in a work that included an introductory essay on Iolo's neo-Druidic philosophy of Bardism (discussed below). It is a great irony that Iolo was supported most by these North Walians, because he was committed to wresting Welsh cultural prestige away from them. This was evident as early as 1777 when, travelling home from London, he stopped off at Avebury to examine the stone circle and subsequently wrote to Owain Myfyr that it, and not Anglesey, had been 'the grand seat of the Druids'. By the 1790s, however, Iolo's resentment had grown to the point that he began to claim his beloved Glamorgan was actually the centre of Druidism and always had been.[95]

Iolo had already published forgeries of the fourteenth-century poet Dafydd ap Gwilym (*fl.* 1330–1350) in 1789, but his most famous and largest-scale deception came in the three-volume *Myvyrian Archaiology of Wales* (1801–1807), undertaken with Pughe and financed by Owain Myfyr, whose name is honoured in the collection's title. Organised chronologically, the first volume contained poetry from the sixth to the fourteenth centuries; the second, prose; and the third collections of aphorisms and proverbs.[96] The second volume contained some of Iolo's most notorious forgeries in the form of the 'Third Series' of the *Trioedd Ynys Prydain* (Triads of the Island of Britain), a genuine corpus of three-line mnemonic verses once passed down orally by the bards and surviving in late medieval manuscripts. They contain much information about the peopling of Britain by those who eventually became the Welsh and were considered by them to be almost sacred historical authority for the origins and early history of Britain. The first two series were based on known manuscripts, but the third was purported to be from another manuscript dated 1601 and later discovered to be Iolo's own riffs upon the first series. Iolo filled in gaps and rounded out the overall picture of Britain's foundation by the Cymry, who were led by their (apocryphal) King Hu Gadarn from Anatolia to Britain, where they set up an elective monarchy and devised just laws.[97] The triads would be of widespread interest across Europe, but Iolo's famous third series has been very well covered by great scholars of Welsh literature, so I will move on to discussing his bardic philosophy and its implications for Celticism.[98]

Iolo began putting together the elements of his bardic system in the 1780s and continued to work on it for the rest of his life. It fluctuated based on his caprices—which were not aided by his addiction to laudanum[99]—but it can be summed up as a manufactured philosophical system underpinned by an intellectual genealogy that traced the origins of Welsh, and specifically

Glamorgan, poetry back to the sixth-century school of Taliesin (*fl.* sixth century) and a supposed Druidic tradition.[100] According to Hutton, Iolo's significance lay in fully integrating 'the ancient Druids with the medieval bards', thereby linking 'Druidry firmly to the Welsh national tradition'.[101] This was summarised in one of his most cherished works, '*Cyfrinach Beirdd Ynys Prydain*' (Secrets of the bards of the Isle of Britain), which Iolo composed while imprisoned for his debts in Cardiff Gaol during much of 1786 and 1787.[102] He began to feed bits of this philosophy along with poetic impostures to his friends in London, who were particularly taken with it. One of the earliest and clearest expositions is in his essay in Pughe's edition of *Llywarch Hen*. According to Iolo, Bardism was a sort of civil religion: it was based on a social compact and regulated ancient British society with laws, civic ceremonies (of which memorised poetic triads were an important component), and a tripartite social order.[103] This is a mishmash of Caesar, Rousseau, and genuine Welsh poetic convention, held together by Iolo's imagination. The theology of Bardism was 'a system embracing all the leading principles which tend to spread liberty, peace, and happiness amongst mankind'.[104] Because he swore Bardism was the Welsh heir of Druidism, Iolo was able to imbue his system with the spiritual gravity of the original patriarchal religion. Since the 'patriarchal religion' was likely 'the foundation from whence [Bardism] flowed', modern Welsh bards preserved a remnant of the patriarchal religion, since their philosophy 'is now exactly the same that it was two thousand years ago'.[105] But if that was the case, then what did bards do? Welsh society had long been regulated by English laws. So, with the philosophy taken care of, Iolo still needed to bring the system to life, which he did with the *Gorsedd*.

The *Gorsedd* is now an established and prestigious part of the national *Eisteddfod*, but it began as a sort of rival to the revived *eisteddfodau* organised by the *Gwyneddigion* Society from 1789.[106] Like the rest of Iolo's Bardism, the *Gorsedd* mixed elements of fact and fantasy together, and he made sure to bolster its provenance with an illustrious genealogy, but the crucial point is that the *Gorsedd* is what made Bardism real, because it granted the system a ceremonial sacrality in which others could participate. This came together gradually. In 1789, Iolo had announced to the world his status as one of only two living members of the order of 'Ancient British Bards', then in 1791 he indicated he would be opening it to selected new members, and, after the first *Gorsedd* on 21 June 1792, he published reports of the following ceremonies in the English press.[107] *The Times*, for example, dutifully printed an account of the third meeting:

> Last Friday, being the first day of the Bardic New Year, the winter solstice, and, consequently, one of the solemn Druidic Days; the Welch Bards assembled in Congress, on Primrose-Hill, according to ancient Druidical manner, which requires that it should be held under the canopy of Heaven, in the open air, and whilst the sun is above the horizon.[108]

It was also specified that the *Gorsedd* should take place within a stone-circle—this had allegedly once been the purpose of 'that *Bardic Circle Stone Henge*'[109]—where the sheathing of a sword (symbolising peace) began the initiation rites that included poetry recitals and various invocations designed to bind inductees to a supposedly sacred ancient British tradition.[110]

The public presentation of Iolo's Bardism occurred in the frenetic context of the 1790s, when Iolo embraced the Revolution. He nourished his republicanism with the writings of Thomas Paine (1737–1809), and in the company of the circle around the radical bookseller Joseph Johnson (1738–1809), which included figures like William Godwin (1756–1836).[111] Most of the early initiates into the *Gorsedd* had radical sympathies. There were also clear links to the French Revolution and the Girondins. In his unpublished manuscripts, Iolo often translated *Gorsedd* as a Bardic 'convention' or 'congress'—echoes of French and American legislatures—a rendering fairly subversive, considering that calls for a British convention were met with prosecution for sedition at the time.[112] Iolo's fixation on 'Truth', for example in the *Gorsedd*'s motto '*Y gwir yn erbyn y byd*' (The truth against the world), has parallels to the *Confédération des amis de la vérite*, a radical republican society and publisher, associated most with Paine's friend Nicolas de Bonneville, mentioned above. Both Paine and the Girondin leader Jacques Pierre Brissot (1754–1793) were among the impressive list of subscribers to Iolo's *Poems, Lyric and Pastoral* (1794).[113] Iolo penned a poem in 1793 called 'Breiniau Dyn' (Rights of Man), which was firmly republican, but had to suppress it for several years because, following the declaration of war against France in 1793, British authorities cracked down on known radicals and activity that could be construed as seditious, and the London *Gorsedd* met no more. Instead, Iolo moved back to Glamorgan, where he held *Gorseddau* several times a year from 1795 to 1798, and a secret (and only North Welsh) *Gorsedd* in 1799, but the climate remained suspicious, and it was not until 1814 that the ceremony was revived.

As Charnell-White has discussed, Iolo's Bardism was crafted in part as a defensive casing around Welsh poetic tradition, which he asserted had reached civilized refinement before the Romans and had preserved that chain unbroken to his own day. In one revealing note titled 'Bardism' and aimed at 'Goth Pinkerton', he savaged the 'barbarous hodge podge languages, that had . . . no existence five centuries ago' (i.e., English), unlike superior Welsh, which 'became fixed in the first centuries' and descended in its purity from this 'first great enlightened period'.[114] In another fragment Iolo named the targeted language as Saxon, simultaneously praising the 'singular trait . . . in the Welsh National Character, they have for 1600 years at least been a literary people, have authentic MSS [Manuscripts] of nearly that age'.[115] A number of things can be drawn from these jottings, but in short Iolo directly refuted Pinkerton's (and others's) accusations that the lack of a written tradition proved Celtic barbarity, instead claiming Welsh had reached a higher level of perfection at least a thousand years before English, as proven in its manuscripts.

The actual existence of Welsh manuscripts allowed Iolo to claim a civilized native literary tradition; however, this argument only went so far, given that the manuscripts were much younger than their content and were written in the Roman script. So Iolo devised an 'ancient' alphabet of the Bards, *Coelbren y Beirdd* (Fig. 8), which he claimed the ancient Druids had invented.[116] All letters supposedly derived from three characters '/ | \', which together made up every other letter; the figure itself would become known as the 'mystic mark' and a common symbol of the nineteenth-century Welsh cultural revival and neo-Druidism. It was elaborated in his *Barddas* notebooks, where Iolo linked the alphabet to his wider claims to Welsh linguistic purity by connecting it to famous classical sources. The most important was Caesar's account of the oral culture of the Druids, who could use Greek letters but had no alphabet of their own—an assertion that could be used to besmirch the Druids and ancient Celts more generally as unenlightened.[117] Iolo's invented alphabet countered this notion. It had supposedly been engraved upon wooden billets by the Druids and was still preserved by the modern bards, *viz.* Iolo. He sent out samples to his correspondents, placing his bardic characters alongside the Latin alphabet to bolster ancient claims by way of comparison: '[Welsh and Latin] were twin sisters born of one common parent, the primitive Celtic'.[118] If one accepted this assertion, then the physical resemblance of the bardic letters to the Latin characters suggested the ancient provenance of the Celtic alphabet, with the implication that it perhaps even antedated the Latin alphabet. Iolo soon added comparisons to the pre-Roman alphabet of the Etruscans—who he identified as 'a Celtic people'—which he found similar to the Greek; the implication was that when Caesar noticed the Druids using Greek letters he had been mistaken: it was really the ancient Celtic alphabet

COELBREN Y BEIRDD, OR BARDIC ALPHABET *.

Rad.	Der.
A	â
E	ê u û
I	
O	ô w ŵ y
B	f m
P	b ph mh
Ff	
M	f
C	g ch ngh
G	— ng
D	dd n
T	d th nh
N	
Ll	l
Rh	r
S	
H	

FIG. 8. *Coelbren y Beirdd*, in *Cambro-Britain* I (1820), 240.

he supposedly saw Druids reading and writing, which was still preserved by the modern bards.[119]

The alphabet was not simply a harmless bit of invented tradition; it was a serious intervention into the scholarly record. Iolo's relative tepidity probably suggests he knew it was a risky claim, and so he created a provenance from a sixteenth-century bard named Llewellyn Sion. Initially it met with enthusiasm. Harbouring no suspicions, William Owen Pughe communicated the alphabet to his own network, among them the English typographer Edmund Fry (1754–1835), who included the characters in his *Pantographia, containing accurate copies of all the known Alphabets of the World* (1799).[120] Pughe himself sought to supplement the alphabet's authority by comparing it to the Devanagari characters used to write Sanskrit. He made the (un)surprising discovery that the *Coelbren* agreed with the Sanskrit alphabet 'exactly in arrangement, number of vowels, consonants and classes,' as well as in its 'structure, idiom and words', and that hundreds of individual analogies could be produced.[121] Proud of Welsh orthography before Roman letters, he opened his Welsh dictionary with the *Coelbren* as it was 'absolutely necessary' to give a clear view of how the Welsh language had been constructed.[122] The *Coelbren* was reprinted and adopted across Welsh publications—in Welsh and English—and we will see in a later chapter that it survived well into the nineteenth century.[123]

However, already sceptical of Iolo's Bardism, some immediately suspected invention, and over the 1790s and early 1800s concerns grew among the Welsh antiquarian community.[124] Iolo riled the forces of state, religious, and scholarly orthodoxy throughout his career, but while state and church had their own methods for dealing with this upstart, those who sought to delegitimise his system on scholarly grounds faced the problem that Iolo was considered by many to be the best Welsh scholar alive. The powers that be found a champion in the schoolmaster and curate Edward Davies (1756–1831), who won the moniker 'Celtic' for his eponymous work *Celtic Researches* (1804). Iolo's work perplexed Davies, who was suspicious of Bardism almost immediately; he and Iolo's old mentor John Walters agreed in 1793 that Bardism was 'cooked up,' and he later wrote that it was concocted with French revolutionary doctrines in mind.[125] But if Davies was unsure about the dish, he appreciated many of the ingredients. He had unknowingly translated some of Iolo's forgeries of the medieval poet Dafydd ap Gwilym, but he was extremely taken with *Coelbren y Beirdd*, which supported his own hypotheses and which he suspected to be the 'original alphabet of Europe'.[126] However, Davies was developing a very different view of ancient and medieval Celtic history than Iolo and his associates, one deriving in large part from Edward Lhwyd. As he explained in a letter to Pughe, he had little time for the oriental syncretism connecting the mythologies of East and West, and instead adhered to the traditional view that Welsh resembled Hebrew because of the Noachid descent of Europeans.[127] However, for his *Celtic Researches* Davies relied heavily on material contained in the *Myvyrian Archaiology*, thereby unknowingly contaminating his work; and, while he was much more sceptical in his *Mythology and Rites of the British Druids* (1809), he was not able to weed out all of Iolo's interpolations even though he clearly thought him a fraud.

However, for most people Iolo was the grand old man of Welsh antiquities from the 1810s until his death in 1826, made more pathetic by the abject poverty in which it was known that he lived. Iolo had long threatened to write a new history of Wales based upon unique manuscript sources, but he never got beyond the prospectus, which was finally published in 1819.[128] However, most important for our purposes is Iolo's resurrection of the *Gorsedd*—which had been banned by the government since 1799—in 1814 and then finally 1819 alongside the provincial *Eisteddfod* at Carmarthen.[129] Although Iolo was invited to the festival in order to defuse tensions between Anglicans and Dissenters, he took full advantage of the situation, initiating the archbishop into the *Gorsedd* and staging several ceremonies within a stone circle, all of which would provide a blueprint for later Welsh and Celtic revivalists to this day. As examined comprehensively by Marion Löffler, his influence in the century after his death was staggering, and it has proved extremely difficult to weed out his forgeries.[130] Incorporated into the *Eisteddfod* and spread to the other Brittonic nations, the *Gorsedd* has taken on a life of its own as the quintessential modern Celtic ceremony.

The First Celtic Society in Britain

The formation of what can be considered the first Celtic Society was born out of controversy. Around 1800, as the Highland Society's report on Ossian was coming together, Gothicist Scots following John Pinkerton again attacked the authenticity of early Celtic poetry. This time they also impugned the traditions of the Welsh, but in contrast to the Ossian debacle, the challenge was deflected rather easily and with the considerable assistance of English antiquarians. William Owen Pughe, the industrious Welsh lexicographer who played second fiddle to Iolo, but who was better able to maintain cordial links with antiquarians from other nations, helped with several of these, including Sharon Turner's

A Vindication of the Genuineness of the Ancient British Poems (1803), and an anonymous *Vindication of the Celts* (1803).[131] Pughe was himself working on the *Mabinogion* at the time, and was encouraged by the English poet George Ellis (1753–1815) and by John Leyden, who agreed that they were 'more valuable, as pieces of antiquity tending to illustrate history, than all the volumes of pretended historians put together'.[132] Such activity, Pughe wrote excitedly to Iolo, portended 'the dawn of a splendid day of Cymbrian lore, when Pinkerton and his disciples will be in the shades of oblivion'.[133]

With all of the interest in the early histories of Britain, Europe, and their first Celtic inhabitants, it seemed a propitious moment to found a group dedicated specifically to Celtic antiquities. All of the organisation was undertaken by Pughe.[134] The idea might have arisen in conversation with some other antiquaries based in London, but Pughe—probably anticipating the kind of answer it would receive—described it as someone else's idea in a letter to Iolo of 9 December 1802, noting the group would discuss nothing 'but what relates to Cymbric matters'.[135] Iolo's response was sourly ambivalent. On the one hand, he was glad to hear of Pughe's intentions and hoped 'to see amongst its members some intelligent Welsh, Irish, and Highland Celtae, and possibly a Breton or two', thus envisioning a truly pan-Celtic group, before despairing at finding those who might be sound members with a critical knowledge of a Celtic language, and then predictably spiralling into a diatribe against the savage lower classes and 'diabolical' upper classes until he forgot the Celtic society altogether: 'But why should I now make so much mention of this kind of d–d stuff?'[136]

A better description of the society's intentions was given in a letter written to the Scottish scholar George Chalmers (1742–1825)—who attributed the plan to Pughe—dated about a month later, on 10 January 1803, which included a one-page handwritten prospectus and a list of suggested members.[137] The Celtic Society prospectus lists as its object 'to bring together materials, from which eventually may be furnished a history of the primitive population of Europe'. It would hold monthly meetings discussing relevant subjects and would aim to first cover the earliest periods before moving systematically onward. It is uncertain whether the first meeting, slated only five days later for 15 January, ever took place, but the members Pughe anticipated being there included himself and Chalmers, Turner, and a couple others. Proposed corresponding members included William Coxe, John Whitaker, Walter Scott, John Leyden, and at the bottom 'Mr Ed. Williams'. It might just be a coincidence, but below Iolo's name was the note 'I have not mentioned the society to anyone but Mr Turner, so that any name may be struck out'. An exciting cast of characters, but it seems that even if it did manage to get off the ground, the Celtic Society did not last long. Yet whatever the group's fate, it was noted shortly thereafter in Paris that several 'enlightened men had formed the Celtic Society of London'.[138] Inspired, a number of patriotic Frenchmen would shortly do the same.

The *Académie celtique*, 1805–1813

The *Académie celtique* and the Celtic origins narrative that it promoted at the beginning of the nineteenth century signalled the point at which the Celtic past was first embraced by the modern French state. With the creation of the French Empire in May 1804 came the need for national histories stressing imperial antecedents. Since the Celts were known to have rampaged across ancient Europe, the Gaulish narrative that had triumphed with the Revolution only needed to be tweaked to fit this new geopolitical setting. *Académie celtique* members were some of those most responsible for drawing up this retrofitted version of the national past.[139] The *Académie celtique* therefore forms an important hinge in the narrative of this book, for it harnessed all of the innovative scholarly approaches examined in the previous four chapters in support of the overtly political project of building the French nation.

The *Académie* was the brainchild of three men: Éloi Johanneau (1770–1851), Michel-Ange de Mangourit, and Jacques Cambry. In 1804 a few informal meetings took place in Cambry's house in the Place de la Vendôme, while the group waited for official sanction—apparently delayed because the *Institut national* opposed its creation[140]—that eventually came in the summer of 1805 along with meeting space at the Louvre. Eventually, however, the *Académie* settled into the appropriate setting of the *Musée des Monuments français*, a national history museum run by Alexandre Lenoire (1761–1893), who had almost single-handedly saved many of France's important cultural monuments from revolutionary vandalism, displaying them at the *Musée* in a chronological history of the nation through its art and architecture.[141] The proceedings of the *Académie*'s bimonthly meetings were printed along with research articles in the group's journal, the *Mémoires de l'Académie celtique*. The two thousand pages published between 1807 and 1812 are a testament to the editorial industriousness of the permanent secretary Johanneau.

The *Académie* boasted an impressive membership. Of the founding trio, Johanneau was a professor and *érudit* who became an imperial censor in 1811,

Mangourit had travelled widely as a diplomat under the Convention and the Directory, and Cambry was a bestselling author, man of letters, and governmental administrator.[142] There were several former Girondins, including Mangourit, Volney, Dulaure, and the former Director Louis Marie de la Révellière-Lépeaux (1753–1824).[143] Another Girondin associate was the *Académie*'s third president, the jurist and orientalist Jean-Denis Lanjuinais (1753–1827), who had been president of the Convention just before Thermidor and was an imperial senator. The *Académie* also accumulated some distinguished foreign members, including Paul-Henri Mallet, Christian Gottlob Heyne (1729–1812), both Humboldts (Wilhelm [1767–1835] and Alexander [1769–1859]), and eventually Jacob Grimm (1785–1863) and Friedrich Carl von Savigny (1779–1861), both of whom joined in 1811. The cosmopolitan Italian scholar Carlo Denina (1731–1831), former librarian to Frederick the Great (1712–1786), also joined the *Académie* in 1805, having relocated to Paris the previous year at Napoleon's behest. There was a strong Breton contingent in the *Académie*, and La Tour d'Auvergne was elected an immortal member, a shrewd choice that simultaneously aligned the Académie with the military glories of *la nation* while flattering Breton pride. Composed of some notable figures, the group had serious scholarly aspirations as well as political goals.

The members of the *Académie* worked to further establish the Celtic origins of the French nation and to draw out historical antecedents for the Empire.[144] Napoleon's decade of victories had ignited a desire to recover the glories of the nation's forefathers—summarised in its motto '*Gloriae majorum*' (Glory of the Ancestors)—according to the *Académie*'s dedication to its patron Empress Joséphine (1763–1814).[145] Drawing on the popular idea that Gaul had been the centre of ancient Celtic Europe, Joseph Lavallée (1747–1816)—author of a travelogue depicting republican Brittany—made the connections between imperial past and present perfectly clear:

> The idea to found a Celtic Academy must naturally owe its birth to the epoch where French glory draws all attention to it. . . . The country in which we live was the metropole of [the ancient Celts], whose surplus population colonized many distant lands. . . . If the Celts were the ancestors of Bellovesus and Sigovesus, are we not still today these same Gauls whose forefathers followed these illustrious voyagers?[146]

The group's secretary Éloi Joheannu delivered a memorable speech at the first official meeting (30 March 1805), laying out the implications of this view: 'Almost all the peoples of Europe are descendants of the Celts, almost all are the children of Celtica [*la Celtique*]: newly reunited, they almost all form, still today, a single and great family under the same federal government'.[147] However, Cambry noted with alarm in 1805 that 'After centuries of confusion, modern peoples want to usurp the name of the Celts, and to appropriate for themselves all the glory of these ancient conquerors of Greece, Rome, of all Europe, and almost all of Asia'.[148] It was one of the *Académie*'s goals to restore France's exclusive claim to the Celtic legacy and to rehabilitate the view of the ancient Celts as a powerful and refined civilization, a fact obscured by a disproportionate scholarly focus on Greece, Rome, and, more recently, Egypt.[149] This it sought to do through an extensive research programme.

However, these scholars faced the same obstacle that their predecessors had come up against repeatedly over the last two centuries: the lack of native Gaulish, or any Celtic, written records. How, then, to retrieve the Celtic past? We have seen how this same problem prompted developments in philology, archaeology, mythography, and literary antiquarianism over the eighteenth century, all of which the members of the *Académie* adopted while adding some new approaches of their own. The *Académie* set itself two broad goals—to write the history of the ancient Celts, and to do so primarily through a comparative linguistic project—which remained consistent though their wording occasionally changed. Johanneau provided the most complete formulation:

> 1o. to recover the Celtic language in ancient authors and monuments; in the two dialects of this language that still exist, Breton and Welsh, and even in all the popular dialects, the patois and jargons of the French Empire, as well as the origins of languages and place names, of monuments and customs which derive from them, and to give dictionaries and grammars of all these dialects, whose inventorisation must be hastened before their total destruction.
>
> 2o. to collect, write, compare, and explicate all the antiquities, all the monuments, all the usages, all the traditions; in a word, to make a statistical study of ancient Gaul [*faire la statistique antique des Gaules*], and to explain ancient times by modern times.[150]

These projects were pursued through different committees and research groups. The most famous of these was concerned with gathering information about the French peasantry and its customs, which it was thought might preserve remnants of ancient Gaulish customs and Druidic superstitions.[151] This interest has led to the *Académie celtique* being identified as the pioneering institution for the study of French folklore and ethnography.[152] The centrepiece of this interpretation is a questionnaire of fifty-one queries devised by a committee comprised of Cambry, Johanneau, Denina, Dulaure, and the geographer Edme Mentelle (1730–1816) and sent out to the different communes of France. A number of local dignitaries responded with details of customs preserved in their communes, which were printed in the *Mémoires* and usually accompanied by Johanneau's endorsement that such traditions were of Druidic origin.[153] Just as Lenoir's museum preserved the physical monuments of the French past, the questionnaire was designed to record and therefore preserve knowledge of the more unstable 'monuments' of Celtic language and thought retained by the French peasantry.

For the *Académie*, then, 'monuments' were much more than just physical remains of the past.[154] Cambry and Johanneau outlined this in their *Monumens celtiques* (1805), which used the menhirs (standing stones) of Carnac—one of the largest megalithic sites in Europe—as a jumping-off point for the investigation of ancient Celtic history more generally. Although Cambry's focus was ostensibly on the standing stones, these physical monuments were only the raw material to be examined using 'the true science of etymologies', which would see 'a new geography born in France' through the comparison of place names.[155] Johanneau made the point more clearly: 'words are precious monuments when we can understand them, because through them we can recover the *moeurs*, habits, religion [*le culte*], and finally the history of a people, even if they have left no other monument than the names of places, people, and things'.[156] Whether in physical monuments, folklore, or mythological remnants, 'words are the most durable and most numerous monuments of the most distant times'.[157]

There was therefore a strong etymological aspect to all of the Académie's research, and I have argued elsewhere that language played the central role in the group's scholarly project.[158] The *Académie*'s approach to language was shaped chiefly by Johanneau, who reconciled physical antiquities and Celtic mythology through etymology. Johanneau's investigations into alphabets provide an example of the way these different approaches supported each other. We have already seen that the hunt for the origins of alphabets was a common scholarly pursuit, but as we saw above with Welsh and Irish, it had potentially huge consequences for views of the Celts: the discovery of a native alphabet would be the smoking gun that would prove the sophistication of Celtic civilization before Roman incursion. Recent Spanish research into Celtiberian origins therefore interested Johanneau, who published a French translation of the antiquarian Juan Bautisto Erro's (1773–1854) *Alfabeto de la lengua primitiva de España* (1806), which sought to prove that ancient Celtiberian inscriptions on medals and coins were written in an early Basque alphabet, which could be used to decipher all Iberian inscriptions.[159] For Johanneau, the exciting conclusion was that if Gaulish monuments were compared to the ancient Celtiberian letters in Erro's book, it would be possible, with the aid of the Breton and Welsh languages, to finally 'read and to decipher all the inscriptions of Gaul in characters regarded as unreadable and unknowable until now . . . this discovery, so desired, so often hoped for by the best scholars of Europe, opens a very vast field for the reform of history'.[160] Among other important linguists such as Volney and Lanjuinais, the *Académie* also featured the leading Breton scholar of the first half of the nineteenth century, Jean François Marie Maurice Agathe Le Gonidec (1775–1848), who in 1807 published the most important French-Breton grammar for a century.[161] He dedicated it to the *Académie celtique*. He eventually became a vice-president of the society, and placed several of his research papers in the *Académie*'s *Mémoires*. He will reappear later in this book as an important figure in the early history of pan-Celticism.

In spite of the great flurry of activity in the *Académie celtique*, its pioneering scholarly techniques, and its novel mission as a society dedicated almost purely to the study of national origins, it crumbled with Napoleon's Empire. The group metamorphosed into the *Société royale des antiquaires de France* between 1813 and 1814, and with this transformation came a more conservative membership and approach. This rapid transformation has been something of a puzzle to scholars, but one prominent interpretation has been that it was plagued by 'Celtomania', or a fanatical belief that the ancient Celts were the first inhabitants of Europe, spoke its first language, and that all European nations descended from them.[162] A fatal conflation of the *Académie celtique* with some of its overenthusiastic 'Celtomaniac' predecessors, and most of all with Jacques Le Brigant, plagued it from the beginning.[163] However, while this is certainly true to some extent, Johanneau repeatedly went out of his way to target the excesses of patriotic linguistic antiquarians. He ridiculed the Jacobin secret policeman Pierre Bacon-Tacon (1738–1817), who published two volumes arguing that the south-eastern region of Bugey was the cradle of the Celts and the original language, and though he respected Le Brigant's zeal did not spare him censure: this 'célèbre celtomane' had 'abused the Celtic language' by seeking to explain all languages through Breton, and did not produce one etymology admissible by Johanneau.[164] Johanneau argued that if French bore resemblances to Breton it was because Celtic and Latin had both developed from the same root. If French preserved a number of words whose etymology derived from Breton, it was therefore likely down to filiation as much as borrowing.

It is therefore of considerable irony that the word 'Celtomanie' was coined within the *Académie* and that Johanneau himself used it to criticise such exuberance.[165] It would shortly be turned against them and many others with Celtic interests. Celtomanie provided a convenient scapegoat in 1814, when the *Académie* was renamed the *Société royale des antiquaires de France* and its programme became more archaeologically based in a conscious rejection of the previous dominance of etymology and a general linguistic approach. At the session of 18 October 1814, the new secretary Antoine-Jean Saint-Martin (1791–1832) noted that from its origin the *Académie celtique* had adopted a 'singular and bizarre system', with 'audacious suppositions' and 'absurd etymologies', complaining of its 'mania for rendering all parts of the ancient world Celtic'—Saint-Martin was an orientalist.[166] He was also a Christian and a monarchist, and proclaimed the new society's loyalty to the Bourbons; after surveying the destruction of ancient Europe by pagan barbarian tribes—the Celts included—Saint-Martin celebrated the fall of the French Empire, which had threatened to plunge Europe back into barbarism once more.

Conclusion

At the end of the Napoleonic era, the Celts were much more quiescent than they had been at the beginning of the Revolution. In Restoration France, the Frankish *thèse nobiliaire* returned with the aristocracy and the monarchy. After the Union came into effect in Ireland, the island's ancient Celtic history suffered along with the study of antiquities more generally.[167] The reactionary atmosphere in Britain had stifled Iolo Morganwg's politically inflected literary undertakings and put a stop to the *Gorsedd*. Set against these changes was an increasing emphasis on the Germanic past in Britain and Europe. All of this was temporary, however, and in Part II we will see the Celts overtly politicized to a far greater extent than in this chapter, a process that thrived off of the new idea of race.

Over the several chapters of Part I we have seen how the Celts were recovered as national ancestors over the early modern period, primarily through developments in scholarship. While the classical record provided evidence of the Celts for straightforward historical narratives, novel linguistic, archaeological, mythographical, literary, and folkloristic approaches illuminated many new angles of the ancient Celts, and revealed important relationships between peoples in the nations of Europe that could now confidently be called 'Celtic'. However, the extent of Celtic influence was about to be whittled down considerably as it became realised that the Germanic and Celtic peoples were not identical, and that the Celts were not the ancestors of most Europeans, as we saw that Abraham Ortelius and many others believed in chapter 1. The 'Celtomaniacs' examined in this chapter—Le Brigant, Vallancey, and others—lived during the last period in which extravagant claims like theirs could be made for the Celtic provenance of all languages of the world. The nineteenth century would see the birth of a 'scientific' approach to Celtic studies, one based above all on comparative philology and the birth of the Indo-European idea.

Part II

6

From Philology to Ethnology

THE CELTIC RACE AND THE INDO-EUROPEAN IDEA

ONE EVENING IN 1807 two friends hiked around Loch Katrine in the Trossachs, soon to be famous as the setting for Walter Scott's poem 'The Lady of the Lake'. Medical students at the University of Edinburgh, the pair happened upon 'a Highlander' dramatically situated 'amidst the wildest scenery . . . on a distant crag'. For one of the students, James Cowles Prichard, the effect was reportedly 'magical: fatigue was felt no longer, and he at once resumed all his powers of mind and body, and poured out a most splendid dissertation on the history of the Celtic nations'.[1] Prichard's entire scholarly life as Europe's leading ethnologist was still ahead of him, but his warmth for the Celts was already evident and would help him contribute to a series of developments in knowledge that took place across Europe in the first decades of the nineteenth century that, taken together, can be seen as the beginning of 'Celtology'—or the study of the Celts and their languages on a 'scientific' basis—which is the subject of this chapter.

The formation of Celtology took place against the background of a huge epistemological shift then underway in European thought: the crystallisation of the modern idea of 'race'. Race had existed in early modern thought primarily as a genealogical idea, but in the eighteenth century this merged with the classificatory mode of natural history to form the idea that there existed distinct populations of humans with naturally and correspondingly varying physical, mental, and moral characteristics.[2] It was an open question to what extent racial characteristics were mutable—and it was still the orthodox view to see them as the product of climate, among other external factors—but the central point is that perceived differences between peoples could now be attributed to differences of 'race'. 'Race' and 'Civilization' developed at the same time in Enlightenment thought, and racial theorists arranged races according to the civilizational scale.[3] It is no coincidence that these concepts crystallised with European imperial expansion, as the civilizing mission was formulated in terms of helping less developed races to reach maturity.[4] However, racialism—the idea that the human species was divided into identifiably distinct races—was just as prominent *within* Europe, where older notions of national character became aligned with newer theories of biological and moral fixity. The Celts became swept up in these developments, particularly in the overarching debate over whether there was one human species or several. Did all races come from one common source (monogenesis), thus rendering their particular characteristics, institutions, and culture a product of climate or some other factor? Or did each race originate separately (polygenesis), meaning there were natural differences among them that existed from their point of origin and were therefore permanent?[5] In short, did all humans belong to the same species, or were separate races separate species? The cantankerous Scot John Pinkerton was one among many who considered races to be distinct species, and he held the Celts to be separate from and inferior to the Goths. His ideas were taken seriously even if he was not much liked and, as will be seen, other important thinkers held similar opinions and doubted the place of the Celts in the European family of nations.

The main problem in classifying the Celts was the uncertain relationship of the Celtic languages to the Indo-European linguistic family, because determining linguistic affiliation remained the overriding method of categorising nations and races until the latter half of the nineteenth century. Although Sir William Jones had suggested in 1786 that Celtic was likely related to Latin, Greek, Gothic, and the Asian languages Sanskrit and 'old Persian', this assertion remained unproven until the 1830s.[6] Moreover, it was actively opposed by scholars like Pinkerton, Conrad Malte-Brun (1775–1826), and the German philological giant August Wilhelm Schlegel (1767–1845), among others on the Continent, who reacted against what they saw as an unscientific exaggeration of ancient Celtic influence in a tendency they called 'Celtomania'.[7] It was Prichard, the impromptu lecturer at Loch Katrine, who first substantiated the Indo-European credentials of the Celtic languages, and therefore 'the relation of the Celtic people to the rest of mankind,' with the publication of his comparative philological work *The Eastern Origin of the Celtic Nations* (1831).[8]

The histories of Celtology's origins confine themselves quite strictly to the linguistic context, in which Prichard, Adolphe Pictet, Franz Bopp, and Johann

Kaspar Zeuß stand out among a range of mostly German philologists.[9] The vital context of the gelling of 'race' and the development of a set of practices for comparing and classifying different human races has tended to be overlooked. This chapter therefore puts the rise of racial theory at the centre of its account of the formation of Celtology. The following section contextualises Celtic theories within the strengthening currents of racial thought, and the subsequent three sections then examine the main settings in which the Celts became the object of modern scientific study. The first is Prichard's linguistic proof within his wider ethnological project; the second is the linguistic, physical, and moral anthropology of the French physiologist William Frédéric Edwards (1776–1842); and the final context is the German setting in which Zeuß produced his epochal work, *Grammatica Celtica* (1853). Zeuß's work has often been taken to be the foundation of modern Celtology, but it would be better seen as a critical turning point that set a new scientific standard; as later chapters will show, it was impossible to ignore from a scholarly point of view. Prichard, Edwards, and Zeuß all had 'ethnological' motives, and by examining their scholarship we will see how Celtic linguistic study helped to shape the idea of the Celtic peoples as a coherent race sharing linguistic, physical, moral, mental, and cultural characteristics.

The Celtic Race

The discussion of the Celts in the developing human sciences of comparative philology and ethnology was primarily but not solely a continental one. Even if British and Irish scholars were not as disconnected from the comparative philological context as has often been assumed, there can be little doubt that there was much more attention devoted to the topic in continental Europe, and especially Germany, than in Britain and Ireland at this point. However, the important results did trickle back into the islands. The main questions were: Did the Celtic languages, and therefore peoples, belong to the wider Indo-European family? If so, then to what degree were the Celts and other peoples, especially Germans, related? Finally, what was the relationship between the two branches—Goidelic and Brittonic—of the Celtic family?

As we saw at the end of Part I, there was still a great deal of confusion in the early nineteenth century about who the ancient Celts really were and which modern nations descended from them. In Britain and Ireland, the Celtic nations had been identified as those whose 'mother tongue' was a branch of Gaelic or Brittonic, largely through the work of Paul-Yves Pezron and Edward

Lhwyd. Although some still confused the Celtic and Germanic peoples throughout the century, Thomas Percy put the final nail in that coffin with his 1770 translation of Paul-Henri Mallet's *Histoire de Dannemarc*, before John Pinkerton smashed it in with his *Dissertation on the Origin and Progress of the Scythians or Goths* in 1787. After this point, it was difficult in Anglophone writing to confuse the Celtic and Germanic families or to claim Celtic as the *Ursprache* without facing ridicule. Even if they did not go as far as Pinkerton in thinking the Celts a separate race, Scottish philologists like Alexander Hamilton (1762–1824), Alexander Murray (1775–1813), and John Leyden took turns flaying Charles Vallancey, a thinker commonly associated with the theory of a Celtic *Ursprache*, in the literary periodicals around 1800.[10] Yet this is not to say that a 'correct' consensus was reached; Celts and Germans could be separated, but other errors were still often made. The Welsh cleric Peter Roberts (1760–1819), for example, understood that Celtic and German were not closely related, but also thought Welsh and Gaelic were '*radically* different' in their grammatical structures and therefore unrelated.[11] One of the most prominent Irish antiquarians of the time, Sir William Betham (1779–1853), drew the same conclusion—*viz.* 'those nations who are not Gael, are not Celtae'—in his reheated version of Vallancey's Celto-Phoenicianism, a tradition that remained alive in Ireland until it was finally displaced by the insights of comparative philology around the middle of the century.[12] In general, Irish contributions do not feature much in this chapter. This is partly because, as one Irishman bluntly put it in 1863, 'Irish scholars, with very few exceptions, have not hitherto done anything in Comparative Philology', but also because the Irish Question is the subject of chapter 8.[13]

The situation on the Continent was quite different at the outset of the nineteenth century. As we have seen, the Franco-Germanic dispute over Celtic identity had raged from the sixteenth century. In the decades before 1800, the French tendency to *celtomanie* was embodied by figures like Court de Gébelin, Jacques le Brigant, and la Tour d'Auvergne, who all believed in different ways that Breton was either the original Celtic language of mankind or its purest descendant. The latter pair partly inspired the formation of the *Académie celtique*, some of whose members harboured similar views, even if more prominent members like Volney, Johanneau, and Lanjuinais did not. The latent *celtomanie* was attacked by critics like Malte-Brun, A. W. Schlegel, and Rasmus Rask (1787–1832), all of whom denied Celtic's Indo-European credentials, although Rask wavered on this point, puzzled by the initial mutations (as many were).[14] Yet this denial of Celtic's Indo-European affiliation was an overreaction and a major error, and there was plenty of confusion about these issues among scholars from other nations, especially Germany, where the Celto-German question was still being worked out. German philosophers like Christoph Meiners (1747–1810) had confused the issue by holding to the old tendency of using 'Celtic' as a blanket term for the ancient stock of people from which the modern European nations descended. In his *Grundriss der Geschichte der Menscheit* (1785), Meiners followed Cluverius, Leibniz, and Pelloutier, among others, in calling one part of the 'Caucasian' stem the 'Gothische oder Celtische Race'.[15]

It is worth briefly dwelling on Meiners, who pushed a positive racial view of the Celts as the fount of Western Europe into the nineteenth century. In Meiners's aesthetic ethnology, humanity was one species but composed of two racial stocks, Caucasian and Mongol, beautiful and ugly:

> there are beautiful and ugly nations, as well as beautiful and ugly individuals. Beautiful are all the Celtic, and many of the Sclavonian nations, as well in Asia and Africa as in Europe: ugly, on the other hand, are all or most of the Mongole nations.[16]

The 'Mongole' nations were innately ugly and inferior regardless of climate or diet. But clearly at the head of the human race were the Celts, easily superior to the other, Slavic branch of Europeans. Meiners's work was influential in revolutionary and imperial Paris. Britta Rupp-Eisenreich discovered that Louis-François Jauffret (1770–1840), co-founder and perpetual secretary of the *Société des Observateurs de l'homme* (1800–1804), the first French anthropological society, delivered lectures from a set of notes that borrowed heavily from Meiners's work.[17] Among the selections included in the volume are pronouncements that the Celts had invented alphabetic writing, while the Mongoles were stuck with more barbarous hieroglyphics; the Celts honoured virginity, while the Mongoles detested it; and the Celts differed from, and were superior to, the Mongoles in colour, size, strength, beauty, intelligence, religion, laws and government, clothing, houses, domestic comportment, and their ideas of decency and honour.[18] Julien-Joseph Virey (1775–1846) drew clearly on Meiners in his *Histoire naturelle du genre humain* (1800) when he identified two principal human stocks: 'beautiful and white' and 'ugly or brown and black'. These stocks were further divided into different races, with the Celtic comprising 'most European nations'—including the Germanic—who were 'the pinnacle of the human race'.[19] Therefore, it was through natural history and the growing scientific study of race, as well as the ironic channel of a popular German philosopher, that the old idea of Celto-Germanic unity survived in French thought into the nineteenth century.[20]

Philologists fought back. Johann Daniel Schöpflin (1694–1771) had already separated Celts and Germans in the 1750s, and at the beginning of the nineteenth century Johann Christoph Adelung (1732–1806) lambasted his peers in the first volume of his posthumously published *Mithridates.* It was 'completely inexcusable', in his opinion, for modern scholars equipped with 'infinitely better tools' to confuse the ancient Celts with other peoples like the Iberians, Germans, or Thracians.[21] But even those equipped with such tools and familiar with some of the newer linguistic work still made errors, as Toon Van Hal has shown of the Belgian canon Martin-Jean de Bast (1753–1825), who in 1815 made the old argument that 'Celtic, German, and Gaulish', all stemmed from the same root.[22] Some scholars, like Christian Gottlieb von Arndt (1743–1829), who accepted that Celtic belonged to the European family and separated Celts and Germans, still made the dubious connection between Celtic and Finnish, and it was still common to see Basque as a Celtic language.[23]

Confusion about the Celtic languages led to a reaction against the excesses of the eighteenth-century linguistic antiquarians, and to a recalcitrance on the part of some scholars to accept the Celtic nations as part of the wider European family. Vans Kennedy (1784–1846), a Scottish official of the East India Company stationed in Bombay, followed Pinkerton in his strictures on the Celts and the 'Celtic writers,' who Kennedy accused of manipulating whatever sources they had. He admitted in a footnote that he did not have 'any knowledge' of Celtic, and instead formed his opinion on the writings of Bullet, Court de Gébelin, John Davies, and John O'Brien, seeking mostly to prove not only that the 'Celtic hypothesis' that other European languages descended from Celtic was wrong, but that it seemed unlikely Celtic had any affinity to another set of languages.[24] Instead, Kennedy decided that 'Celtic . . . is a perfectly original language', and the Celts were savages conquered by 'a perfectly distinct race of men'.[25] Assertions like these exemplified a trend that worried Prichard, that once the error of conflating the Celts and Germans had been noticed, 'it became the custom to go to the other extreme'.[26]

At this time it was universally accepted that proving linguistic kingship was tantamount to proving ethnic kinship and common descent, so what was needed was a sober study demonstrating these links. Sir William Jones, proud of his Welsh heritage, picked up on some of the more advanced linguistic theorising coming out of the Low Countries—he was clearly aware of the Celto-Scythian paradigm in the 1770s—and wrote to a correspondent in 1779 of the opinion of some scholars that 'a very old and almost primaeval language was in use among these northern nations, from which not only the Celtic dialects, but even Greek and Latin, are derived.'[27] It was obvious to Jones that the Celtic languages were related to the other European tongues, and he seems to have decided in favour of this position by 1786 when he delivered the famous 'philologer passage', a key paragraph in the history of linguistics that succinctly formulated the Indo-European idea, in which he suggested that 'both the Gothick and the Celtick, though blended with a very different idiom, had the same origin with the Sanscrit', as well as Greek, Latin, and 'old Persian.'[28] But Jones's premature death precluded his ever confirming these suggestions with the proof required, and although the leading British Sanskritist Henry Thomas Colebrooke (1765–1837) took an interest in the question in 1796, he was probably stymied by the lack of adequate dictionaries in Calcutta.[29] Scottish scholars who followed in Jones's steps, like John Leyden and Alexander Murray, both accepted Celtic as part of the Indo-European family, and Murray included some proofs in his large *Philosophical History of the European Languages* (1823). However, both men died early, and when Murray's book appeared ten years after his death the speciousness of its central thesis—that the origins of all language could be reduced to nine sounds—outweighed the many good subsidiary points that he made.

As is well known, the discipline of what became historical and comparative linguistics developed primarily in early nineteenth-century Germany.[30] The focus in the major early works was firmly on Sanskrit, but cursory opinions on Celtic were often aired. In his important work *Über die Sprache und Weisheit der Indier* (1808), Friedrich Schlegel (1772–1829) paraphrased William Jones and included the Celtic family within the European group, but criticised those who confused Celtic and German, alluding especially to those (Celtomaniacs) who saw this connection in traces of Breton.[31] However, there was nothing more substantial advanced beyond these sorts of comments. Franz Bopp's *Conjugationssystem* (1816), along with the important works of Rasmus Rask and Jacob Grimm shortly thereafter, are normally taken to signal the start of *Vergleichende Grammatik*. Only Rask covered the Celtic family, formulating a basically correct view in his now-celebrated *Undersögelse om det gamle Nordiske eller Islandske Sprogs Oprindelse* (1818), but his Celtic opinions were not really picked up on by contemporaries, and therefore I have not discussed him here.[32] This is not to say that they were uninterested in Celtic. Jacob Grimm had tentatively suggested Celtic's Indo-European credentials in the mid-1820s, but noted that it was further away from the Germanic family than even Slavic was;[33] however, he later accepted and praised Prichard's Celtic proof immediately. Bopp hinted at the same thing around the same time and then revisited the Celtic family systematically in the late 1830s. Generally speaking, scholarly interest in the ancient Celts remained high in Germany through the nineteenth century because early modern Germano-Celticism still survived, especially in the debate around the origins of Bavaria, the context in which Zeuß was situated.[34] However, one problem was the lack of older forms of the languages, which were unavailable in extant contemporary dictionaries of Irish and Welsh; it was Zeuß who got around this problem by ferreting out Old Irish glosses from monasteries around central Europe.

In sum, ideas on the ancient Celts and their languages still diverged widely in the early decades of the nineteenth century. In 1815 Prichard complained that 'notwithstanding the attention which has been directed to this subject, there is scarcely any point of importance relating to Celtic history which is not still involved in obscurity'.[35] Evidence was hard to come by, but because no one had firmly tied the Celtic languages to the rest of the Indo-European group, it remained uncertain whether the Celtic peoples themselves shared the same origin as the rest of the European nations. Could the Celts be a separate race? And because it was an open question at the time whether different human races actually constituted separate species, could the Celts actually be a separate species from their Germanic neighbours? As we will see in subsequent chapters, these questions had important political and social implications, but they had to first be addressed in the scientific realm.

James Cowles Prichard and the *Eastern Origin of the Celtic Nations*

If polygenesis emerged as a minor yet resilient trend in eighteenth-century thought, it was kept in check in Britain through the first half of the nineteenth century almost single-handedly by James Cowles Prichard.[36] He was born to Quaker parents in Herefordshire in 1786 and grew up there and in Bristol, tutored privately at the preference of his strong-minded father. Because Dissenters were unable to graduate from Oxbridge at the time, Prichard studied medicine at Edinburgh between 1805 and 1808; but an anguished conversion to Anglicanism around this time meant he fleetingly attended the University of Cambridge before switching to Oxford, where he studied into 1810. Thereafter he set up a medical practice in Bristol, where he also worked at several medical institutions, before moving to London in 1846, two years before his death in

1848. Prichard was civically engaged in Bristol and more generally in the scientific life of Britain, but his overriding passion during these years was scholarship, undertaken in the early morning and late evening hours that sandwiched his busy medical days. He published a variety of works, the two most important of which for our purposes are his magnum opus, the repeatedly augmented *Researches into the Physical History of Mankind* (1st ed: 1813, 2nd ed: 1826, 3rd ed: 1837–1846) and his *The Eastern Origin of the Celtic Nations* (1831).

Upon Prichard's death, his friend and hiking partner around Loch Katrine, Dr Joseph Arnould (1786–1859), wrote that from their student days 'the history of his book is the history of his life, for it was the continual occupation of his mind'.[37] First written up as a Royal Medical Society dissertation,[38] it was then published as a slim MD dissertation, *Disputatio inauguralis de generis humani varietate* (1808), before being expanded into the single volume *Researches into the Physical History of Man* in 1813, which swelled to two volumes in 1826 and included the slight title change to *Researches into the Physical History of Mankind,* before ballooning to five volumes in the 3rd edition published between 1836 and 1847. Prichard's great aim throughout was to reconcile the evident physical diversity of the human race with the monogenetic account laid out in the Bible and embraced by Christians. He resolutely opposed the polygenist idea that different human races constituted separate species. Yet he admitted in the first iteration of his *Researches* that he found the polygenist argument seductive because, as he elaborated in subsequent editions, it cleared up awkward questions about why humans looked different, spoke numerous languages, and varied in their manners. According to this simple logic, human populations simply originated separately and developed independently of one another. Yet Occam's razor could not be trusted here, principally because it would mean contradicting scripture, historical evidence (though this could also be a stumbling block), and the comparison of languages and religions.

However, the main problem of human physical variation remained vexing, especially because the 'environmental' or 'climatic' explanation was waning in its influence and had been discarded by Hume, Kames, Pinkerton, Voltaire, Kant, Meiners, and Virey, most of whom Prichard named with alarm. As Arnould later testified, and as the records of the Royal Medical Society in Edinburgh indicate, the topic of human physical variation was a popular source of discussion in Edinburgh around 1800.[39] Prichard had been drawn to the question by the moral philosophy lectures of Dugald Stewart (1753–1828), who supported the climatic interpretation.[40] Yet like the polygenists he abhorred, Prichard was dissatisfied with Stewart's recourse to the environmental interpretation. Accounting for physical variation between the different human races was therefore the main intellectual problem for Prichard when he began his research as a university student.

The mechanism by which variation occurred, or the 'principle of natural deviation', changed in each edition of the *Researches* and, as Augstein shows, Prichard's thinking was often contradictory and vague.[41] In the first edition he introduced a crude system by which skin pigmentation accorded with the level of civilization achieved by a society, in a Eurocentric aesthetic assumption that whiteness equalled beauty and refinement, and blackness its opposite, similar to that found in Meiners.[42] According to Prichard, all humans were originally dark-skinned, but as they ascended the civilizational ladder their outward appearance changed accordingly: 'the process of Nature in the human species is the transmutation of the characters of the Negro into that of the European, or the evolution of white varieties in black races of men'.[43] A crude form of sexual selection was in operation, as Prichard speculated that white varieties were more aesthetically pleasing and therefore more likely to reproduce. However, Prichard was never satisfied with this, and as the book expanded he stopped trying to account for the mechanism by which physical change occurred, reverting back to environmental and hereditarian ideas. Prichard's main purpose was always to show that different races came from one common source, for which there were better proofs than physical evidence.

With this view of Prichard's project in mind, we can examine more closely his treatment of the Celts. Growing up with a Welsh mother close to Wales, Prichard took a special interest in Welsh history and the language. He seems to have understood the language and spoke with Welsh patients. Both Edward 'Celtic' Davies—to whose *Celtic Researches* Prichard subscribed as an eighteen-year-old[44]—and Iolo Morganwg stayed with the family in Bristol, and Prichard later reminisced to Iolo's son Taliesin about time spent 'in the society of your excellent Father, who as [*sic*] was my much esteemed friend'.[45] Like them, Prichard was keen to hit back against James Macpherson and anyone depriving the Welsh of their 'title of ancient Britons'.[46] As will be seen in chapter 9, he remained connected to Welsh cultural circles and participated in some of the first 'pan-Celtic' *eisteddfodau* of the Abergavenny Welsh Society in the late 1830s and 40s. His main contribution to Celticism, however, was his scholarship.[47]

Although he was intensely interested in them from a young age, the Celts initially did not receive much attention in Prichard's work. This is probably because his Edinburgh dissertation and the first edition of his *Researches* were focused specifically on the question of physical variation among humans—especially skin pigmentation—and devoted little attention to white Europeans, who were assumed to be the ideal type; moreover, at the time he considered this the territory of the antiquarian rather than the natural historian.[48] Yet he soon shed these qualms, and the 'Celtic Race' occupied a larger portion of the book as his scholarship developed and his methods of investigation multiplied. What began as only a few comments in the *Disputatio* stretched to 9 pages in the 1813 edition, and then expanded further to 44 pages in 1826, before more than tripling to 150 pages by 1841. He published this final Celtic section as a standalone pamphlet titled *Ethnography of the Celtic Race*.

In the *Researches* of 1813, Prichard noted the lack of information about the ancient Celts, but was mostly concerned with establishing their Eastern, or 'Asiatic' origin, along with the rest of the European nations. Primarily, he followed the standard classical sources; however, at the end of the short Celtic section, Prichard turned to language and argued that linguistic affinities proved the Celtic race and the other European groups to be 'so far allied in their radical elements, that we may with certainty pronounce them to be branches of the same original stock'.[49] He pointed to an essay of 1809 published in the *Edinburgh Review* proving the relationship of most of these languages.[50] This was penned by the abovementioned Alexander Hamilton, a disciple of William Jones who learnt Sanskrit and other Eastern languages in India before returning to Britain and taking up a post at the East India Company college.[51] He sought to prove Jones's fleeting Indo-European suggestion with lexical and grammatical proofs—which Jones had never provided—by demonstrating the affinity of Sanskrit, Persian, Latin, and German.[52] However, as Prichard noted, Hamilton's 'proof would have been much more striking if he had added the Celtic and Sclavonic dialects, and the Greek. I have made an attempt to supply the deficiency, which I intend shortly to make public'.[53] By 1813, therefore, Prichard's Celtic intentions and method were clear: he would prove the European credentials of the Celts through a study of their languages.

Yet the promised work was not immediately forthcoming, and we can only speculate about the reasons for this. One might be that Prichard began to learn German in 1814—with the intention of translating the Swiss Johannes von Müller's (1752–1809) *Vierundzwanzig Bücher allgemeiner Geschichte* (1811)—and quickly became aware of some of the German linguistic scholarship available, above all the *Mithridates* of Adelung and Vater, of which he made profitable use for the rest of his life. He reviewed this work in 1815 in an essay that included much of the Celtic proof for the first time, in the midst of a wider examination of the Indo-European language family.[54] But though he greatly admired *Mithridates*, Prichard harshly criticised its account of the Celtic languages, where he found 'nothing but inaccuracy and confusion'.[55] Here Prichard's special bias for Welsh came through, along with the influence that antiquarians like Iolo and Davies had on him, because Prichard was irritated that Adelung had been duped by 'Macpherson and other Scottish writers', who represented 'the Gaëlic people as the only genuine offspring of the Celtae'.[56] Yet, countered Prichard, 'An appeal to the Welsh language completely refutes this unfounded conjecture. The dialect of the Welsh, as found in the Triads and in the writings of the old bards, is a far more genuine Celtic than that of the Gaëls'.[57] Welsh bore a greater resemblance to Sanskrit, in Prichard's opinion, and already at this point he noticed that they seemed to share the same euphonic principle whereby certain consonants at the end of a word can modify the first letter of the subsequent word (discussed below). Prichard was continuing the Welsh struggle against Scottish Ossianic chauvinism, but the overarching point here was that the Celtic languages were Indo-European—it should be underlined that this was a very early argument in support of that conclusion. The Celtic tribes, among the other European groups, were all 'colonies from India, or from some eastern country not far distant from it'.[58] Prichard reiterated this conviction again in the second edition of the *Researches* in 1826—the Celtic section of which is mostly concerned to claim the Belgae as Celts and the ancestors of the Irish and Scottish Highlanders[59]—but he knew that a demonstrative and definitive answer to the question was still needed and could be given most clearly through a work of comparative philology.

So, after completing the second edition of his *Researches*, Prichard turned again to the Celts. His Bristol Library borrowing records show that in the late 1820s he was reading Pinkerton and the riposte to him published as *Vindication of the Celts*.[60] However, Prichard was now well versed in German scholarship, and in 1829 he visited Göttingen, where he met Jacob Grimm, to whom his *Eastern Origin* is dedicated. Prichard tells us that Grimm encouraged him to publish the work, and when it appeared Grimm swiftly reviewed it quite favourably in the *Göttingische Gelehrte Anzeigen*.[61]

As Prichard indicated in the book's preface, he had planned to publish such a work since at least 1813 and had been gathering material for almost twenty years. The book's full title explains its purpose and method: *The Eastern Origin of the Celtic Nations Proved by a Comparison of Their Dialects with the Sanskrit, Greek, Latin, and Teutonic Languages, Forming a Supplement to Researches into the Physical History of Mankind*. Prichard intended to show the affinity of the

Celtic languages to the other European tongues, which was both intrinsically worthwhile and also an important piece of evidence for his monogenetic system more generally: the 'use of languages really cognate must be allowed to furnish proof, or at least strong presumption, of kindred race'.[62] Languages are proved cognate by correspondence in basic vocabulary and grammatical structure, and since there were large cultural and religious differences between the peoples of Europe, not to mention those of Asia, it was 'only . . . by an analysis of the European languages' that it could be hoped 'to obtain a proof, that these races of people . . . were connected in origin with the nations of Asia'.[63] Yet Prichard noted that, while the Indo-European family had been established through linguistic discoveries, it was still an open question whether the Celtic languages belonged to it, with figures like Georges Cuvier (1769–1832), Friedrich Schlegel, and Malte-Brun all seeming to doubt the proposition, while Pinkerton and Vans Kennedy resolutely opposed it.[64] Prichard had remarked in his review of *Mithridates* that 'foreign writers who touch upon this subject continually involve themselves in perplexity and error', but he was more charitable in *Eastern Origin* and suggested that it was only the lack of Celtic linguistic material that had precluded German scholars in particular from closely studying it.[65] He therefore stepped forward to clear things up.

The first two chapters of the work contained general observations on the Indo-European languages and showed Prichard's competence in comparative philology. He paid particular attention to sound changes: in the way that some language families had certain internal shifts, but also in consonantal sound shifts that occurred across related languages descending from the same source, which took place 'according to certain rules and not by a merely accidental variation or corruption', as famously observed by Jacob Grimm.[66] Prichard noticed that a remarkable similarity existed between the Celtic languages and Sanskrit in the way that certain consonantal terminations altered the first consonant of the subsequent word for euphonic purposes.[67] But the bulk of the work was devoted to examples of comparative vocabulary and grammatical comparisons. The basic vocabularies of Welsh and Gaelic were compared throughout with Sanskrit, but also with examples from Greek, Latin, German, Russian, and Persian where they showed affinity. Prichard believed Welsh was the purest dialect of the Celtic family and so used it as his Celtic exemplar—he was clearly much more familiar with it than Gaelic—focusing in the grammatical sections on verbs and pronominal inflections. He showed that Indo-European languages formed verbs the same way—*viz.* by adding a suffix onto a root—and, following Bopp, suggested that personal pronouns provided the suffixes; however, pronominal inflections in most Indo-European languages made it difficult to reconstruct their earlier forms. The simpler pronominal system of Welsh, compared to other Indo-European languages, led Prichard to argue that it more closely preserved its ancient state than other European languages.[68] Since Welsh apparently followed the same Indo-European rules for verbal construction, it could shed light on early Indo-European morphology more generally because of the purity of the language, argued Prichard. Here he made the fleeting link at the end of the book that made it easily dismissible by some later scholars: he identified Celtic as a possible 'intermediate link between [the Indo-European languages] and the Semitic' family.[69] He had picked up on this connection as early as his Latin dissertation from 1808: 'There is no less a notable agreement, between the languages of the Hebrew and Welsh people, not in words alone, but what is of much more importance, in the composition of speech, and the declensions of verbs'.[70] Quite strikingly, although he did not mention it explicitly, Prichard therefore seems to have been defending the long-standing Welsh tradition of linking the Welsh language to Hebrew, stretching back to seventeenth-century figures like John Davies of Mallwyd but articulated fairly recently by his friend Edward Davies.

The criticisms that Prichard met with in some quarters over his suggestion that Indo-European and Semitic might be linked seems to have convinced his otherwise reliable biographer Hannah Augstein that Prichard's Celtic work made no European impact, but this is manifestly not the case.[71] Prichard's comparative philology was met with general approval on both sides of the English Channel. It was quickly accepted in Britain, even by those known to be prejudiced against the Celts. The Cambridge polymath William Whewell (1794–1866) wrote that Prichard had put the question of the relationship of the Celtic languages to the other Indo-European languages beyond doubt, while the famous 'Teutonist' and modern historian Dr Thomas Arnold (1795–1842) said it was 'the only sensible book on the subject' in English and paired it with 'Bopp's Vergleichende Grammatik' as the best works for showing 'the real connexion of languages'.[72] Richard Garnett (1789–1850), archivist at the British Museum and a leading English philologist who understood the significance of German linguistic scholarship, reviewed the work positively and wrote privately to Taliesin Williams that Prichard 'has the merit of first proving there is a connection between [Celtic and the Indo-European family]'.[73] At the end of the nineteenth century the pioneer of cultural anthropology, E. B. Tylor (1832–1917), noted the importance of Prichard as having 'first proved the position of the Keltic languages as a branch of the Indo-European'.[74]

Prichard garnered similar praise from scholars in Europe. Perhaps most importantly, Grimm appreciated the work and shortly after its publication wrote that Prichard had 'without doubt' proven Celtic to be a division of the Indo-European family, 'more clearly than ever before'.[75] In Rome, the young Irish Catholic intellectual, and future Bishop of Westminster, Nicholas Wiseman (1802–1865) lauded Prichard's work in his influential *Lectures on the Connexion between Science and Revealed Religion* (1835), and declared he had put the matter 'fairly at rest'.[76] The positive reception of Wiseman's lectures in Ireland meant that Prichard's influence would be felt there, and they helped to contribute to the Celtic question in Ireland being firmly answered (see the following two chapters).[77] One of Prichard's chief admirers was the Prussian Minister to Britain, Baron Carl Josias von Bunsen (1791–1860), who in an 1841 letter explicitly acknowledged that 'Dr. Pritchard' was the first to analyse the Celtic family in relation to the Indo-European group 'from the point of view of the present linguistic science', beating Bopp (mentioned in the next sentence) to it.[78] This is important because Augstein's central piece of evidence in her argument for Prichard's limited impact is an ethnological paper given by Bunsen at the 1847 meeting for the British Association for the Advancement of Science in which she claims he ignored Prichard completely.[79] However, I find Prichard mentioned three times in this paper: the first reference is to the general contributions of his comparative philology to ethnology; another lists him alongside Bopp and Carl Friedrich Meyer (*c.*1801–1884) for having proved the Celtic relation to the Indo-European family; and the final reference credits Prichard's *Researches* alongside Humboldt's *Kosmos* (1845–1862) as the two great general works combining physiology with ethnology and history.[80] Given that Humboldt was generally recognised as the premier scientist in Europe, this was high praise indeed. In the subsequent paper Carl Meyer stated that in his work he had actually followed Prichard's table of Celtic language division, and then went on to mention Prichard and Lorenz Diefenbach (1806–1883) as two modern authors proving the identity of ancient with modern Celtic.[81]

Not everyone agreed at first, and in the mid-1830s both A. W. Schlegel and August Pott (1802–1887) rejected Prichard's proof.[82] However, as discussed below, Prichard eventually won out not long after, and in the 1843 *Jahrbücher der Literatur* Carl Meyer presented Prichard's *Eastern Origin* alongside the work of Pictet and Bopp as having finally brought Celtic studies out of the darkness of 'Celtomania' and into the light of 'modern *Wissenchaft*'.[83] Importantly, in his pioneering history of linguistics in Germany, *Geschichte der*

Sprachwissenschaft und orientalischen Philologie in Deutschland (1869), Theodor Benfey (1809–1881) was careful to emphasize that 'the famous author of the *Researches into the physical history of mankind*, J.C. Prichard' had, along with the Swiss Pictet, proved the Indo-European credentials of the Celtic languages before the German Bopp.[84] Prichard was by no means universally extoled for his Celtic researches, but he was not quite the Cinderella to the continental stepsisters that Augstein makes him out to be.[85]

Prichard obviously continued to think about the Celts, because his ideas on their origin developed further, and by the third edition of his *Researches* they occupied 150 pages of their own.[86] By this point the character of the magnum opus had changed quite considerably and was more along the lines of a universal ethnological history rather than an investigation of human physical variation. As for the Celts, Prichard was quite straightforward that 'topographical names . . . the history of languages and . . . the remains of ancient dialects' were the most reliable ways of tracing Celtic origins and migrations. A new section on place names—inspired by Wilhelm von Humboldt's work on ancient Iberia—seemed to show that Britain and Ireland had been populated from Gaul. The preference for Wales and Welsh—which Prichard found to be closer to Old Gaulish than Gaelic—was again evident, but Prichard was kinder to the Irish in this edition and now poured doubt on the assertion—stretching back to Strabo—that the ancient Irish had been cannibals. He had believed this in 1813 because he had precious little evidence to link the Celts to the other Indo-Europeans in an Eastern origin, but now that he had the abundant linguistic proofs dubious hearsay was no longer required. Prichard even went so far as to suggest that, if the Irish had ever been barbarous, they had civilized remarkably rapidly because the Irish were 'highly gifted by nature . . . and so susceptible of the highest culture both moral and intellectual'.[87]

Prichard also contributed to Celtic cultural interest beyond his scholarship. He maintained links with the elite Welsh group, the Abergavenny Welsh Society, and attended their famous 1838 *eisteddfod* before judging essay contests at them in 1842 and 1845. Bunsen was also a member of this group and helped to draw German interest to its essay contests, which he judged with Prichard. Two letters about the 1842 essay contest—on the place of Welsh within the Celtic family and of these in relation to the Indo-European group, a topic set by Bunsen—illustrate some of Prichard's views on the state of Celtic linguistics.[88] Carl Meyer won the contest before becoming (with Bunsen's help) personal librarian to Prince Albert; but Prichard initially thought the anonymised essay was by Karl Richard Lepsius (1810–1884), a leading Egyptologist, and was slightly worried because he thought some of Meyer's ideas on Celtic being near the base of most European languages would encourage the Welsh tendency to 'derive everything from the ancient Britons'. Had Prichard not suspected Lepsius to have been the author, he admitted he would have regarded it 'very much like the nonsense of Sir W. Bentham [*sic*]'. Yet Prichard was ready to defer to what he thought was Lepsius's expertise and in any case thought it gave a 'more comprehensive and I believe true view of the mutual relations of the Sanskrit & European languages than Bopp'.[89] Unfortunately, Prichard found that the essays by Welsh competitors were ignorant of 'Linguistic science' and full of 'absurdities', and he expressed his fear that 'my countrymen, the true-born Britons' would not 'for some time have much chance in competition either with Germans or Englishmen'.[90] To be fair, a contemporary work by the Scot Lachlan Maclean (1798–1848), *The History of the Celtic Languages* (1840), was even wilder than the works of Betham or the Welsh and recovered Gaelic as the original Adamic language. However, the point we see here is that Prichard thought scholarship in the Celtic nations lagged far behind the standard being set in Germany.

By the time of his death in 1848, Prichard had done more than anyone else to apply new scientific methods to the study of the ancient Celts. Crucially, although his most decisive contribution came in the realm of comparative philology, Prichard's methods expanded as new information became available and new analytical techniques developed. The expansion of Prichard's Celtic focus therefore mirrors the development of British ethnology. In the first edition of 1813 he mostly listed and weighed classical authorities, but by 1831 he was doing advanced comparative philological work, and ten years later he was combining these two methods with sophisticated place-name analysis based on Humboldt's work on ancient Iberia. Prichard's *Eastern Origin* showed clearly that the Celtic languages constitute their own family separate from the Germanic group but are still part of the larger Indo-European linguistic family; in doing so he had gone further towards establishing Celtic studies as a field in its own right than anyone since Edward Lhwyd.

William Frédéric Edwards and French Ethnology

In many ways Edwards can be seen as Prichard's French analogue.[91] Both physicians, they also had similar methods, including a thorough familiarity with classical sources and a belief in the centrality of linguistic evidence, with a Celtic focus. Edwards's *Des caractères physiologiques des races humaines considérés dans leurs rapports avec l'histoire* (1829) was probably the most influential French work on race published to that point, and though it did not have much international influence, Edwards's *Recherches sur les langues celtiques* (published in 1844 but written around 1830) reveals a French strand of comparative philology pursued as part of a larger ethnological interest in the ancient Celts.

Edwards was born in 1776 on his family's sugar plantation in Jamaica.[92] We can only speculate on how owning enslaved people shaped Edwards's interest in the study of human races, but he did not stay there long, as the family moved to a comfortable bourgeois life in Bruges. His slaveholding notwithstanding, Edwards's father had been involved in radical circles in England, with whom the family remained connected. In 1792 father and son joined the local Jacobin club in Bruges, and Thomas Paine was only one of a number of radicals who later came to stay. After attending the dissenting Hackney New College, Edwards worked as Bruges' city librarian until he left for Paris in 1808 to study medicine. He received his degree in 1814 and began to practice medicine while continuing physiological research.[93] His scientific works were well-respected and Edwards gained friends like Stendhal (1783–1842)—whose racial ideas were clearly shaped by Edwards—Prosper Mérimée (1803–1870), and Jules Michelet (1798–1874). In 1829 Michelet read Edwards's *Des caractères physiologiques* in order to glean information on the 'question of races' for his lectures on universal history, and the pair met shortly thereafter.[94] They became close friends—Edwards was Michelet's physician—and supported each other's advancement. Michelet helped Edwards get elected to the newly reestablished *Académie des sciences morales et politiques* in 1832, and Edwards repaid the favour six years later.[95] The company he kept reflects Edwards's liberal political sympathies, an important piece of biographical information needed to appreciate his historical and racial studies.

The political situation in Restoration France was particularly fraught as royalists reemerged in numbers and steered the government far to the right, as discussed in the following chapter. The political battle spilled over into all aspects of intellectual life and shaped history-writing in obvious ways. As we saw in the previous chapter, one of the main interpretative splits was whether France owed more to its purported ancient Gaulish liberties or to medieval Frankish laws established by conquest. Liberals claimed that the Revolution had vindicated the Gaulish interpretation, but the *thèse nobiliaire* lingered on zombie-like in the Restoration, and was the target of liberals such as the Thierry brothers, François Guizot (1787–1874), and Jules Michelet. For Edwards, the most important of these was Amédée Thierry (1797–1873), who with his more famous brother Augustin (1795–1856) had recast French history as a narrative of racial conflict between Gauls and then Romans and Franks. Existing debates over France's constitution and newer interpretations of class thus became (re)racialised.[96] In his *Histoire des Gaulois* (1828), Thierry mustered linguistic, historical, and antiquarian evidence—all very traditional at this point—but advanced a brand-new thesis about the racial composition of Gaul: it was composed of two different peoples, the Galls and the Kymris. Although both were originally Celtic, the Galls and Kymris had very different characters, the Galls preferring egalitarian liberty and the Kymris hierarchical rule. Thierry believed in the permanence of both physical and moral characteristics particular to a race but lacked scientific proof; however, he announced at the end of his lengthy introduction that he had just received word that 'a man known by all of learned Europe, M. le docteur Edwards' had brought his scientific expertise to the same racial question and, though working independently, had arrived at an identical conclusion to Thierry.[97]

In the next year, Edwards's findings were announced to the world in *Des caractères physiologiques des races humaines,* which was subtitled a *Lettre à M. Amédée Thierry*. It is a 129-page essay with no headings or breaks, which reads like a travelogue and physiological treatise mixed together and is based on Edwards's travels from Burgundy south to Naples and then back to France via Switzerland, undertaken from 1826 to 1828. Edwards announced at the text's outset that, based on his findings, Thierry was correct about the permanency of racial characteristics, discounting any major climatic, historical (such as conquest), or civilizational modifiers.[98] Physical evidence—chiefly skull shape and facial traits—was the greatest proof of this. Walking the reader through his travel observations, Edwards divided the populations of these parts of Western and Southern Europe into two physical types: the first with a rounded skull, soft facial features, and medium stature, and the second of a taller type with a long, narrow skull with pronounced facial features such as a prominent forehead and hooked nose. The round-skulled type corresponded to Thierry's Galls and the narrow-skulled to his Kymris.[99] Edwards's purpose was historical, and he announced that he was bringing the insights of natural history to bear on the field of civil history. By aligning their conceptual vocabularies, Edwards forged a new, more powerful conception of 'race', one in which the human physical types investigated by naturalists could be linked to historical peoples with perceived moral characteristics.[100] The upshot for understandings of ancient Gaul was that, since racial types were apparently permanent, the moral characters of particular races—attested in historical accounts—were also likely permanent.

One could better understand the modern French nation by studying the history of ancient Gaul, just as one could better understand ancient Gaul by studying the characteristics of the modern French population: 'ancient people can be rediscovered in modern people'.[101]

It is difficult to know when Edwards became interested in Celtic subjects because we are hampered by the lack of any known cache of personal papers. I have been unable to find any signs of specific interest in the ancient Celts before his important work of 1829, and even here it must be stressed that Edwards did not discuss 'Celts' per se, but Galls and Kymris. However, after this point they increasingly occupied his interest, nowhere more so than in his *Recherches sur les langues celtiques,* submitted to the Académie des inscriptions et belles-lettres on 26 December 1831 for consideration for the *Prix Volney,* the highest award in comparative philology. Impressing the Indologist Eugène Burnouf (1801–1852) and the Armenian specialist Antoine-Jean Saint-Martin, among others, Edwards was awarded the medal, worth 1,000 francs in 1834, but the work was only published posthumously—with a great deal of scholarly support—in 1844.[102]

In order to appreciate this long and technical work, Edwards's approach to language should first be sketched. Toward the end of *Des caractères physiologiques,* he turned towards language in order to consolidate his physiological theories and corroborate the Gallic/Kymric split. 'The physiologist must interest himself in [linguistics]', wrote Edwards, for languages provided the best guide to the origins and relationships among races.[103] Edwards noted that comparative linguists studied vocabulary, grammar, and the 'génie des langues'; however, instead of proceeding down this routine comparative philological route, Edwards suggested a new direction: the comparative study of pronunciation. In learning a foreign language, one can arrive at pure grammatical usage, but never purity of speech sounds, as it is impossible to fully escape one's native accent, according to Edwards. Pronunciation thereby becomes hereditary, inasmuch as there are national sounds to do with accent and pronunciation. Edwards sought to apply this idea to the study of people who had adopted the languages of other nations (evidently through conquest and mixing): Was it possible to find the origin of a people through these traces of distinctive pronunciation?[104] That was part of what he would try to do in his work on Celtic linguistics.

The task set by the linguistic committee of the Académie was: 'To determine, by a work both lexicographic and grammatical, the true character of the languages known commonly by the name of "Celtic" in France and in the

British Isles, and to research the nature and importance of what they have borrowed from Latin and other languages'.[105] Edwards stated up front that '[Celtic] languages belong to the Indo-Germanic family' but felt little further need to expand upon that assertion.[106] This is an important point to note, because that conclusion was far from universally held. However, Edwards's real goal was to further develop the understanding of the relationship between the Celtic tongues to one another and to Latin. He applied his theory of comparative pronunciation that he had outlined in the letter to Thierry, seeking to demonstrate the relationship among the Celtic languages and their links to other European tongues. Aiming to distinguish between genuine filiation and simple borrowing, Edwards focused on the 'physiognomie' of words, which were composed of two parts: a root, which expressed the general idea, and an inflection, which determined the grammatical function of the word in a given sentence. It was in the inflections, or varying endings of a word, where a distinctive national pronunciation could shine through, especially when a people borrowed a word from another language and substituted a '*terminaison nationale*' for a '*terminaison étrangère*'.[107] This had dramatic results for the Celts. Examining English, where differences in pronunciation between continental Germanic and Anglo-Saxon (Old English) had arisen, Edwards attributed changes to the Britons 'imprinting their own pronunciation' onto foreign words and bequeathing this new expression to their descendants.[108] Elsewhere, dredging up an example from his physiological essay, Edwards noted the existence of the 'u' and 'eu' sounds in French, which were absent in the other languages of Western Europe and showed that French pronunciation had been shaped by the Kymris, who had spoken Breton or something close to it.[109] In effect, Edwards resurrected the eighteenth-century idea that a Celtic substratum shaped the modern languages of French and English to a greater extent than was usually assumed.

Edwards's Celtic linguistic work made little impact beyond France, but he continued to write about the Celts, and they were the subject of the bulk of his research just before his death. After reading Prichard's *Eastern Origin*, Edwards agreed with Prichard's Indo-European proof, but argued that the Gaelic branch was closer to ancient Gaulish. Edwards had also shown in an earlier essay that, although the Kymric language was spoken in Brittany and the Kymric moral character prevailed, the physical type had remained Gaelic.[110] Therefore, on French soil there was a larger preponderance of the physical Gaelic race, but its moral and linguistic characters did not always align. The character of the modern French was primarily Gaelic and showed great affinity with the

Irish: 'Could there be a race more spiritual, more lively, more gay, more loving of glory and pleasure, but whose bearing is less constant' than the Gaelic Irish and French?[111] Read with appreciation by the Thierrys, Michelet, Stendhal, Prichard, Broca, and Matthew Arnold, Edwards's work shaped Celticism for decades after his death.

The Birth of Keltologie and the Death of Celtomania: Pictet, Bopp, and Zeuß

Although Prichard had shown the Celtic languages to be Indo-European in 1831, and William Edwards had taken this fact for granted around the same time, there were still some holdouts, most importantly A. W. Schlegel. Schlegel had repeatedly criticised eighteenth-century French *Celtomanes* and the *Académie celtique*, and he continued to lambast *celtomanie* throughout the 1830s.[112] In the context of a long paper delivered to the Royal Society of Literature in 1833 that focused on Indo-European history, Schlegel laid out his criticism of the 'Celtic Hypothesis', whose proponents—'Pezron . . . Pelloutier . . . Court de Gebelin . . . Lebrigant'—had birthed 'Celtic chimaeras' by deriving all languages from Breton, using dubious etymologies to cover up their lack of 'method, historical criticism, and philological tact'.[113] However, Schlegel did discuss Prichard's *Eastern Origin* in a note, and while he did not want to 'positively deny' Prichard's thesis, he thought borrowing might explain more than filiation and stated that the subject required more 'exact, extended, and above all historical' investigation.[114] Yet Schlegel never took the matter that seriously, or at least could not get over his long-held prejudices as a result of his utter contempt for French *celtomanie*.[115]

Schlegel's continued denial of Celtic's Indo-European credentials prompted the Genevan Adolphe Pictet (1799–1875) into a public defence in three open letters placed in the *Journal asiatique* in 1836.[116] Pictet—whose father had been a corresponding member of the *Académie celtique*—was a brilliant young scholar who had studied in Paris and Berlin before travelling to London and Edinburgh in the early 1820s.[117] He identified as a 'Romantic' and was deeply influenced by German philosophy, particularly that of Schelling; this romanticism shaped his interest in Celtic subjects which, typically enough, began with Ossian. Pictet probably first encountered Gaelic when he met the young French philologist Jean-Jacques Ampère (1800–1864) in 1820—who at the time was working on a translation with Prosper Merimée (1803–1870)—but he did not begin his own study of the language until his stay in Edinburgh in early 1823, when he began reading the 'original of Ossian's poems' with a dictionary and grammar borrowed from Edinburgh University Library.[118]

Pictet's letters show that he quickly perceived a connection between the Celtic languages as well as a 'rather striking analogy' between them on the one hand and Greek, Latin, and Sanskrit on the other, which all seemed to have an Eastern origin.[119] However, Pictet initially came at Celtic subjects through his German-inflected interest in mythology, and in linguistic matters he was an autodidact; it took a little while to weed out some of the more speculative connections, such as a quickly discarded assumption that Basque was Celtic, and that the Celtic and Semitic families were connected, as well as the languages of Northeast Asia.[120] At this early stage he was more interested in the religious and mythological connections that could be surmised from the linguistic relationships, and in consulting the Triads in the *Myvyrian Archaiology* he found exactly what Iolo Morganwg wanted him to find: 'the debris of a very profound philosophical and religious system which accords with the doctrine of the Indian Brahmins and the systems of Greece'.[121] Intrigued by the possibility of recovering ancient knowledge through these surviving 'national traditions' as the unmined seam for information on the ancient Celts and above all on their religious practices, Pictet published his first book of etymological mythology—*Du culte des Cabires chez les anciens irlandais* (1824)—focusing on a perceived connection between ancient Irish religion and the cult of Cabiri on Samothrace.[122]

Pictet was therefore interested in Celtic from a relatively early date, but he did not produce anything further until his short study illustrating Celtic's Indo-European connections, focusing in particular on correspondences between the modern Celtic languages and Sanskrit. This won the *Institut de France*'s Prix Volney in 1836, but Pictet also used the forum of the *Journal asiatique* to propagandise for the wider significance of Celtic as a window into the earliest ages of the Indo-European race and the potential of reconstructing the *langue mère* (Proto-Indo-European). Already in contact with Schlegel privately, Pictet stated respectfully in his first open letter that he wished merely 'to complete' the excellent work done on Indo-European by Schlegel, who had 'if not formally denied, at least strongly put in doubt the rights of the idioms called *celtiques*' to their place in the 'vast and beautiful' Indo-European language family.[123] Because Grimm and Bopp also left the Celtic languages out of their work, Pictet—who must have been aware of Prichard but did not reference his work[124]—feared the Celtic languages would languish under the errors committed upon them by the *Celtomanes*.[125] In the three letters, Pictet introduces three kinds of evidence, in order: phonological correspondences between Celtic and Sanskrit, including the initial mutations noted by Prichard; similarities in grammatical construction; and morphology. These constituted the main subjects of his Prix Volney essay, published as the standalone book *De l'affinité des langues celtiques avec le Sanskrit* in the following year. Although Schlegel does not seem to have addressed Pictet's challenge directly, in his 1837 translation of Prichard's work on Egyptian mythology, he grunted that there was still more evidence needed.[126]

Pictet's Celtic interest was an early part of his work on the history of the ancient Indo-European, or 'Aryan', race—the family 'out of whose heart have come the masterpieces that most honour the intellectual and poetical genius of mankind'.[127] He wanted to use the 'important and unexplored mine' of information that the Irish and Welsh sources offered into the 'ancient Celtic race'. 'The Celtic Race', surmised Pictet, had likely separated from the Indo-European stem, and was the first branch to reach Western Europe, but the unmistakable correspondences the Celtic languages showed with Sanskrit provided the most ancient evidence of the Indo-European language family and could shed most light on the *langue-mère*.[128] Best of all for Pictet, these comparisons showed the high level of civilization attained by '*le peuple père de toute la race indo-européenne*', including a wide range of terms for materials, animals, and arts which showed social organisation, intellectual life, and religious beliefs. Reconnecting the Celts to the Indo-Europeans not only unified the family but showed its ancient superiority. Pictet was very proud of his work and especially his priority in the Indo-European argument, as shown in a paragraph communicated to John O'Donovan (1806–1861), who had just published the first number of a review series on Zeuß in 1859:

> The notice of Dr. O'Donovan on Zeuss is very well done and very interesting. Only it is wrong of him to attribute the merit of having first demonstrated that Celtic belongs to the Indo-European family; because this proof had been fully furnished by me already in 1837, and confirmed by Bopp the following year. In fact, Zeuss was almost unconcerned, in his *Grammatica*, with the question of affinity, and thought not, rightly, but of reconstructing ancient Irish by means of the inestimable glosses that he collected with so much care. 'No salvation for Celtic philology without Zeuss' is now an incontestable maxim, and one proclaimed openly in Dublin even by M. M. Siegfried and Whitley Stokes; but it would be unjust to take no account of the works of his predecessors.[129]

One wonders whether Pictet was not being a little unjust to Prichard.

Nevertheless, as Pictet evidently knew, his well-publicised campaign prompted Franz Bopp—named in the essays as not having treated the issue in much detail—to finally air his own views on Celtic.[130] Bopp's scholarly stature was gigantic, stemming from his *Über das Conjugationssystem der Sanskritsprache*, which won him Europe-wide recognition and the first chair in Sanskrit and comparative grammar at Humboldt's new university in Berlin. He was the most formal and methodical of the early generation of comparative grammarians, and he devoted most of his time to Sanskrit and its relationships with other European languages, but in his address, 'Über die celtischen Sprachen vom Gesichtspunkte der vergleichenden Sprachforschung' (On the Celtic languages from the viewpoint of comparative linguistics), to the Berlin Academy of Sciences in December 1838, he finally treated the Celtic languages at length.

Bopp began his address by noting that he had pointed out as early as 1823 that the Celtic languages bore similarities to Sanskrit, but that he had not investigated these as thoroughly as other Indo-European languages.[131] Since then, he had read Pictet's 'excellent' Prize essay, but noted that Pictet did not discuss the Celtic system of declensions, which gave it such a stamp of 'alien peculiarity' that Bopp had once doubted it to be Indo-European. Happily, however, Bopp announced he had since been able to 'lift the veil' and reveal characteristics shared by the Celtic family and Sanskrit. In terms of vocabulary, Celtic possessed a 'wealth of words' showing its early identity with Sanskrit; in fact, it preserved some words in common with Sanskrit better than other European languages.[132] Bopp investigated some of these, weaving in phonology—noting the *P* and *Q* split in Celtic[133]—to help explain divergences, before moving on to similarities in noun and verb declensions. But Prichard and Pictet had covered both of these aspects, albeit without the same technical precision, and so Bopp's real contribution was to elucidate the system of initial mutations characteristic of the Celtic languages. These are the shifting consonants that appear at the beginning of many words—each language has its own mutations and triggers—which make the Celtic languages seem so irregular at first glance;[134] they had long confused scholars, and though 'local Grammarians' called this 'strange phenomenon . . . Eklipse' (eclipsis), they left it unexplained.[135] The crux of the issue was that in older forms of the languages some word endings triggered an initial consonant mutation on the subsequent word, but many such trigger endings had become lost over time while the initial mutations remained, so they seemed erratic.

Bopp, however, was able to show that these inflections originally operated by grammatical principles in line with the other Indo-European languages, so 'through comparison with Sister-Idioms' the 'high degree' of Celtic idiosyncrasy could be explained.[136] Bopp spoke highly of Pictet's essay and referenced it throughout, along with a few mentions of Prichard's *Eastern Origin*, but ended the essay suspecting that he had cleared the matter up and there was little more to be done.

At the same time that Celtic was being publicly debated by Prichard, Schlegel, Pictet, and Bopp in the 1830s, a young Bavarian named Johann Kaspar Zeuß was working out his own views. Born in Franconia in 1806, Zeuß studied theology and philosophy at the University of Munich from 1826 to 1831, and then taught at gymnasia there and in Speyer, before a fleeting appointment at the University of Munich, which was cut short by the ill health that led to his death in 1856.[137] Zeuß was an austere figure devoted to scholarship, and the author of several important works, which he self-financed and which became classics in their respective fields.[138] It was once a commonplace that the monumental *Grammatica Celtica* appeared without warning 'fully armed from Zeus's brow' in 1853, but much recent work has shown that Zeuß's interest stretched back into the 1830s and was stimulated by his concern with the history and language of Germany, and a desire to pin down more precisely the relationship between the continental language branches for historical purposes.[139] Already in 1839 Zeuß claimed that '[rigorous and scientific] Linguistics is the light of the history of nations [*Völkergeschichte*], of ancient history [*Geschichte des Alterthums*]', and that anyone without sound linguistic knowledge would be a futile practitioner in these fields.[140]

He had several scholars in mind, advocates of different linguistic theories. Erich Poppe has mapped this mid-nineteenth-century landscape of German scholarly interest in the Celts and outlines three major linguistic paradigms in operation, versions of which we have encountered at different points in this book.[141] The first is the 'Celtomaniac' position, whose proponents argued through dubious etymologising that modern European languages—including German—could be traced back to an *Ursprache* that most closely resembled the modern 'Celtic' languages of the Brittonic and Gaelic branches. A clear motivation for Zeuß was to finally dismantle this brand of Celtomania, whose roots we have seen stretched back centuries, but which was particularly lively in the political upheavals following the Napoleonic Wars.[142] According to Poppe, proponents of the second, 'Germanist', position—scholars like Cluverius and Leibniz—argued that the European *Ursprache* called Celtic was continued in modern German and had little or nothing to do with the Brittonic or Gaelic languages. The scholar probably most identified with this position, the philologist Adolf Holtzmann (1810–1870), stated his two main propositions directly: 'I. The Germans are Celts, II. The Kymris and Gaels are not Celts'. He traced the error back a few centuries and put the blame primarily on French authors.[143] The final paradigm identified by Poppe was the 'Indogermanist' (Indo-European) position with which we are familiar: the Celtic languages of Brittonic and Gaelic constituted a branch of the Indo-European language family, and were related to old Gaulish but distinct from the Germanic family. This was the (correct) position Zeuß adopted, and he turned his considerable firepower on the proponents of the other two paradigms.

In his first major work—*Die Deutschen und die Nachbarstämme* (1837)—Zeuß attempted to sort out the ancient tribal groups by language (*Sprachstämme*) that had inhabited the middle of Europe at the dawn of recorded history. He identified three main groups: Slavs, Germans, and Celts.[144] He had a clear view of the Celts—'a name known in Europe since the beginning of recorded history'—who had once inhabited much of the Continent but whose languages were now confined primarily to the islands of Britain and Ireland. Crucially, Zeuß implicitly accepted that this family was Indo-European: 'Celtic' was one of the extreme northwestern divisions of a 'great language family stretching from India to Ireland'.[145] Although he did not mention Schlegel, a little further on Zeuß noted that doubts about Celtic's Indo-European affiliation were 'surely exaggerated'.[146] So, although Zeuß is remembered, even revered, most for his purely linguistic work, his initial motivations were ethnological in the sense that he was trying to firmly establish the major tribal families of ancient Europe, and he used linguistic evidence as the firmest means of proof.[147]

In his second major work, *Die Herkunft der Baiern von den Markomannen* (1839), Zeuß dropped some of the formality shown in his first book and pursued proponents of different varieties of Celtomania in an aggressive preface.[148] Although aiming one kick at Celtomaniacs like Bullet who had claimed too much influence for the Celtic language family, Zeuß's real targets were the local historians of Bavaria who confused the Celtic and German families and, as a result, gave Bavaria a Celtic origin.[149] He had in mind figures like the Bavarian archivist and academician Vincenz von Pallhausen (1759–1817), who had confused Eckhart's codex of Old Gaulish with Old High German, as well as his successor Andreas Buchner (1776–1854), who thought that Celtic was the basis of most languages of Western Europe, including German and

French.[150] Zeuß's simple counter-theory was that the tribes who settled in Bavaria were the Marcomanni, who spoke an early German language, and because the German language family was separate from the Celtic, the Bavarians were accordingly Germanic and not Celtic.[151] Andreas Hüther has recently suggested there was a somewhat unintended political strain in German Celtomania, in which those who stressed the Celtic origins of their region tended to oppose a Prussian-dominated unitary state.[152] Zeuß's unimpeachable rigour helped the Germanic cause, and gained him a reputation of systematic historical scholarship aided by the cutting edge of comparative philology.[153] The patriarch of German philology, Jakob Grimm, wrote to Zeuß in 1847 complaining of work in a Celtomaniac vein, and Zeuß replied, gratified that Grimm saw his work as a shot against it, but noted that he opposed Slavomania and Germanomania is well.[154]

In 1853 Zeuß published his magnum opus, *Grammatica Celtica: e monumentis vetustis tam Hibernicae linguae quam Britannicae dialecti Cambricae, Cornicae, Armoricae nec non e Gallicae priscae reliquiis construxit*, in two hefty volumes stretching to almost 1,200 pages in total.[155] As in the works examined above, Zeuß affirmed the Indo-European credentials of Celtic—variations on the line 'from Asia to Europe' appear repeatedly throughout and 'indeuropaeam' appears once[156]—but he was able to do so comprehensively and, the key point, historically. The book showed the development from the 'primitive and common forms of Celtic' to the individual Celtic languages, walking the reader methodically through their grammatical systems and the sound shifts, mutations, and declensions that had flummoxed generations of scholars.[157] This Zeuß was able to do because of the 'ancient records' that he mentioned in the subtitle of the book and throughout, primarily the Old Irish codices—which were older, more copious, and survived in greater abundance than Old Welsh and other Celtic manuscripts—that provided evidence for older forms of the language, and which meant that he did not have to rely on dictionaries that rendered only the modern spoken languages in textual form. Why had Irish scholars not used these before? Because most of them were not to be found in Ireland. The Old Irish glosses (of biblical texts) that Zeuß used so fruitfully survived in monasteries around Central Europe, where they had been taken by Irish missionaries at some point, probably before the year 900. In 1843–1844 Zeuß travelled around Germany, Switzerland, and Northern Italy, then to London and Oxford, in search of medieval material, and made use of the three most important Irish glosses at Würzburg, Milan, and St. Gall.[158] As Thomas Charles-Edwards has explained, by gathering this material and presenting it in one place, Zeuß created a map of the Celtic languages that scholars down to the present day still follow.

The *Grammatica Celtica* made an instant impact. Immediately upon its publication, the French poet and philologist Louis Delâtre (1815–1893) grumpily recognised Zeuß's achievement but lamented that 'la gloire' had fallen to a German.[159] It was positively received in Britain too.[160] The reviewer in the *Cambrian Journal*—perhaps the leading philologist Thomas Stephens (see the following chapter), whose extensive notes on the *Grammatica* survive[161]—called it 'an unparalleled acquisition to Celtic literature' and praised Zeuß's 'untiring zeal and diligence' in recovering the historical material in 'a work which no Irish, Breton, or Welsh scholar should be without'.[162] In another Welsh journal, *Archaeologia Cambrensis*, the English philologist Percy Smythe (1825–1869) wrote that Zeuß had finally shone the 'light of science to those uttermost members of the Indo-European family'.[163] The impact was even greater in Ireland, where the German professor of Sanskrit at Trinity College, Rudolf Thomas Siegfried (1830–1863), preached the gospel of Zeuß to native Irish scholars.[164] His friend, the young Whitley Stokes (1830–1909), imbibed the lessons most deeply, but older Gaelic authorities like John O'Donovan were also converted after urging from Siegfried and Stokes.[165] O'Donovan declared in 1859 that Zeuß had solved 'the famous Celtic problem', and his work formed a topic of constant conversation among Irish scholars.[166] They became more familiar with European comparative philology—O'Donovan also owned Pictet's Celtic work—and learned that Germany had its own 'Keltomaniacs . . . who certainly seem great asses in Celtic matters' and were the 'Vallanceys & Bethams of Germany'.[167] As will be seen in later chapters, armed with a model and possessing a wealth of manuscript material on which to draw, Irish scholars soon ascended to a place of high importance in the field of Celtic studies.

The sober tone of Zeuß's scholarship hid his utter contempt for lesser scholars, which is fully evident in his correspondence with Christian von Glück (1810–1866) during his final years. Zeuß's impressive range and his work from older Celtic forms meant that he was able to point out the errors of native Celtic speakers, such as William Owen Pughe, who he warned Glück had too often confused 'fantasy and abstraction' for 'reality and truth'. In between discussions of etymology and sources, Zeuß poured vitriol on Celtomaniac 'Idiotismus' in Bavaria, whose proponents did not know 'what is right or left, Celtic or German'.[168] There were *Keltomanen* beyond Bavaria, such as Christian Keferstein (1784–1866), who published a massive three-volume work on the Celtic origins of Europe and Germany; that he devoted the third volume to arguing that Tactitus's *Germania* was a modern forgery gives an indication of the extent of his radical views, as well as what irritated figures like Glück and Zeuß.[169] Yet the most provocative work was still to come: Adolf Holtzmann's *Kelten und Germanen*.[170] Holtzmann was a philologist of Old Germanic, who essentially reprised the theory associated with seventeenth-century scholars like Cluverius, that the European *Ursprache* was called Celtic and that this language was preserved in German and had nothing to do with the Brittonic and Goidelic language families, despite the claims of the native speakers of these languages and of German *Keltomanen* who wanted to cede their history to the Irish and Welsh. Reclaiming the history of the ancient Celts, meaning the Gauls and the ancient Germans, would restore one thousand years of history to the German nation. Holtzmann knew his theory was controversial and directly attacked Zeuß, whose 'thick and dry book' only offered the illusion of having solved the Celtic problem.[171] Upon being informed by Glück of Holtzmann's challenge, Zeuß immediately set about formulating a response on the 'Celtic nation', but his death shortly thereafter meant it never appeared. Yet Zeuß had already done more than enough, and in the ethnological work normally identified as having separated Celts and Germans once and for all, H.B.C. Brandes (1819–1884) pointed to 'Vor allem Zeuss', but also Prichard, Bopp, and Pictet, for having solved the linguistic question.[172]

Conclusion

'The history of the variation of opinion about the Celtic languages would make a curious and instructive chapter of literary history', wrote the Irish scholar William K. Sullivan (1822–1890) in 1863, surveying most of the work covered above.[173] According to the German-educated Sullivan, that chapter had 'depended rather upon the dictates of passion than of reason' but was now finished, and the work of Zeuß had commenced a 'new era . . . for Celtic Philology'.[174] Historians now generally agree with Sullivan that, with Zeuß's work, a page was indeed turned; but Sullivan was also well aware of the crucial work that had been done in the 1830s.[175] We have taken account of three major developments. First, the internal unity of the Celtic family was established and extraneous languages like Basque were shorn from it. Second, notwithstanding the opinions of Holtzmann and some of his later followers, the Celtic and Germanic language families were finally disaggregated. Third, and most importantly, the Celtic languages were established definitively as Indo-European, and with Zeuß's work scholars at last had a clearer picture of what older forms of the language looked like and how the two branches had independently developed. Taken together, the new work on the Celts established their status as a distinct race and one of the oldest Indo-European populations, with discernible physical characteristics that helped to distinguish them from the rest of the family, as shown in the work of Prichard and Edwards.

We have also seen that Celtomania was a much more complicated problem than Breton-French overexuberance, and that each nation possessed its own brand of the phenomenon. A later review of Prichard's work semi-seriously suggested that one of its main merits was to prove 'that it was possible to treat of Welsh and Irish without becoming temporarily insane'.[176] In the following chapter we will see in greater detail how older antiquarian theories continued to be discarded by scholars and how a more scientific understanding of the Celtic race was beginning to sink in at a more popular level. Prichard and Bunsen had helped bring the new philology to Wales at the Abergavenny *eisteddfodau* in the 1840s, and at the same time scholars in Ireland were finally casting aside the Phoenician theory in favour of the Indo-European idea.[177] The import of Zeuß's scholarship was grasped immediately in both countries and quickly came to inflect historical work. The scientific arrival of Celtic studies would have serious consequences for Celticism that will be felt throughout the rest of this book.

7

The Celtic Past in the Age of Romantic Nationalism

THE PAST BECAME A BATTLEGROUND in Restoration Europe, as the vacuum created by Napoleon's defeat at Waterloo and exile to St Helena in 1815 was quickly filled by new political forces, whose self-conceptions relied on their own versions of history. Scholars, novelists, poets, artists, and musicians all contributed to nation-building, rooting their national community in a past carefully contoured to their ideals and purposes. The political importance of the Celtic past, which had emerged as an important origin narrative for several Western European nations over the early modern period, became firmly cemented over the Revolutionary and Romantic eras. The moral force attributed to the past and present of the national community made the Celtic character of these same nations a prevalent consideration. Nationally conscious intellectuals undertook or sponsored work into the Celtic past, discovering qualities in their ancestors that explained the particular situations in which they found themselves, and often tweaking their image of the ancient Celts to suit their modern ideals. Historians, journalists, and other authors read the work of the philologists and ethnologists examined in the previous chapter and were thus able to align their ideas with the latest scientific thinking about the Celts; and with the invention of the steam press and proliferation of mass print media, they were able to disseminate ideas more easily than ever.

Racialism and Romanticism are normally held to be the two main forces that shaped modern Celticism.[1] Having parsed racialism in the previous chapter by examining the development of Celtic comparative philology, and ethnology more generally, this chapter attempts to peer through the disorienting haze of Romanticism by examining historical and literary writing during the Romantic era. Rather than 'Romanticism' as such—commonly understood as a broad artistic and cultural movement privileging feeling and sentiment at the expense of classical order and rationality—which I find confusing and vague, I am concerned with the onset of what Joep Leerssen describes as 'Romantic nationalism', a phenomenon characterised by 'the celebration of the nation (defined in its language, history, and cultural character) as an inspiring ideal for artistic expression; and the instrumentalization of that expression in political consciousness-raising'.[2] Leerssen, following on from a masterful study by Anne-Marie Thiesse, has vividly illustrated the international context within which various cultural nationalisms arose across Europe during this era.[3] Following on from similar studies by Clare O'Halloran and Mary-Ann Constantine on Ireland and Wales, respectively, I suggest that the causal relationship between Romanticism and Celticism needs to be unpacked and rethought, with closer attention paid to the numerous transnational cultural transfers that occurred at the intersection of the eighteenth-century enlightened context and the development of nineteenth-century Romantic nationalisms.[4] Not only are these patterns clearly visible in the national settings examined here, it is also obvious that cultural exchange accelerated during this period.

The links between literary antiquarianism and nationalism have been most thoroughly examined in the Irish case, where Clare O'Halloran argues that, 'Far from being the eccentric, marginal, and unscholarly productions of cranks, polemicists and enthusiasts', antiquarian texts laid the cultural basis for nineteenth-century Irish nationalism.[5] I would like to suggest that this conclusion also applies in varying extents to the other Celtic nations, where the literary output—antiquarian, historical, novelistic, poetic, etc.—of its foremost Romantic figures generally remained engaged in refuting accusations of past and present barbarity and cultivating a positive national image. However, the gradual medieval turn in the Romantic era presented a major problem to Celtic enthusiasts in France, because there were no Gaulish textual records through which to comb. How was the dearth of evidence to be surmounted? The most sophisticated scholars looked to their neighbouring Celtic nations, and above all Ireland and Wales, for evidence that could fill in the gaps of their own historical record. This period also witnessed a steep increase in the importance of archaeology—which started to break away from the general field of antiquarianism—and finds in Austria, Switzerland, and Germany seemed to greatly clarify and polish the picture of the ancient Celts, who were important to national and regional identities in these countries as well.

This chapter therefore considers developments not only in the core Celtic nations and France, but across the European Continent. I will look at figures who employed Celtic ideas in their development of national identities through the overlapping fields of literature and history (whose boundaries were blurred until the mid-nineteenth century), but also in the archaeological study of antiquities.[6] Some common but complex patterns emerge. The most important is the paradox that this era witnessed both the scientization of the study of the past in history, archaeology, philology, and related disciplines, *and* the instrumentalization of those disciplines for political purposes. New information could be gleaned in these fields, which were seen to be revealing higher truths about the nation, its foundations, and its ultimate destiny. Accordingly, the Celtic past acquired a new, greater moral importance at the same time as it became understood more clearly and concretely thanks to the development of increasingly sophisticated scholarly tools. Many of those responsible for the advancement of scholarship were also employing the fruits of that labour for their own cultural nationalist purposes. Scientific advancement did not in this case (or any other) mean objectivity, and this chapter sees a noticeable shift from those writing analytically about the ancient Celts to those who could be said to be writing from a 'Celtic' perspective themselves. Although differing widely in their backgrounds, political views, religious beliefs, and national identities, the individuals at the heart of this chapter each championed their version of the Celtic past (to greater and lesser extents) and placed it at the centre of their respective nation's modern identity. In this move from championing a passive ethnic descent towards viewing 'the people' as reanimated versions of their ancestors, Celticism became an increasingly coherent international idea, and at mid-century Ernest Renan finally pulled the different strands together and painted a portrait of the Celt as s/he existed in the present.

Walter Scott and Celtic Highlandism

Scottish national identities became wrapped around one another in the nineteenth century. On the one hand, there was the emergence of a strong ethnic origin myth of the Lowlands as Germanic, emphasising the Scots language and a legal tradition compatible with England's ancient constitution; on the other, a myth of Highlandism tied to a Romantic aestheticization of landscape and folk culture became more prominent and allowed Scotland a cultural veneer of distinctiveness from the rest of Britain.[7] This relied on a vague Celticism but posed no ideological threat to the Union; both myths co-existed and fit within a wider Britishness. Therefore, as delineated in works by Marinell Ash and Colin Kidd, nineteenth-century Scotland bucked the common pattern of Romantic nationalism, in which distinctive cultural expression developed into a separatist movement.[8] Graeme Morton has termed this non-ideological Scottish patriotism 'Unionist-Nationalism'.[9] Whatever label one wishes to use, Walter Scott embodied all of these strands in his own complex sense of national identity, which coloured his hugely popular works and permeated European thought.

Scott's Celticism was pursued through two main avenues: his written works—poetry and prose—and his boosterism as a member of various civic and charitable associations, including the Royal Celtic Society, which he joined in its foundation year, 1820. Indisputably the author of the Scottish national tale, Scott's patriotism was nevertheless couched within a wider Unionism: he preferred English 'Gothic' institutions as models for constitutional and social progress, but also drew on the Celtic legacy—historical and mythical—for historical continuity, in a bid to reconcile Scotland's troubled past and progressive present. Scott was always ambivalent about the ethnic basis of Scotland, partially as a result of his close attention to and participation in the antiquarian debates over Scottish origins. It is therefore necessary to dig into some of them to understand the scholarly basis for his Celtic Highlandism of the 1820s, and how he reconciled Celticism to Britishness.

Born in Edinburgh in 1771, Scott grew up in the Borderlands. A Lowland upbringing did not preclude his being 'delighted in all the Highland traditions' which he picked up 'from the old Jacobites who used to frequent my father's house', which must have inspired *Waverley*.[10] Despite the fun he poked at them in the eponymous novel, Scott was an antiquary himself, and very well read in British antiquities. He corresponded with antiquaries from the other Celtic nations and was one of those invited by Pughe to join the Celtic Society in 1803. Around that time, as Scott was beginning his career as a man of letters, one of the major Scottish antiquarian disputes concerned the origins of the Picts: Were they originally Gothic or Celtic? We saw the origins of this conflict in chapter four, when John Pinkerton made a forceful argument that the Picts had come over from Scandinavia speaking a version of Gothic that developed into modern Scots. As the Ossian debacle was coming to a head with the publication of the official report in 1805, the Picto-Gothic champions led by Pinkerton seemed on the verge of a Celtic rout.

Scott equivocated at this point but leaned toward the Picto-Gothic ethnic and linguistic line. In his introduction to the romance *Sir Tristrem* (1804), he went so far as to say that 'the Celtic has everywhere been found incapable of being amalgamated with the Gothic dialects', and therefore had no effect on the modern language of Scotland.[11] However, he also suggested that the Celtic bardic tradition—thought to have died out with Lowland Gaelic—had been preserved by the Lowland minstrels; therefore, the 'treasures of Celtic tradition', if not the language, were preserved by Lowland Scots. Extending this reasoning, Scott suggested that this combination had made the Scots' language more suitable to poetry than English,[12] an assertion not only syncretising Scotland's major historical ethnicities, but also supporting the historical grounding and importance of his recently released *Minstrelsy of the Scottish Border* (1802–1803).

Scott's ecumenicism reappeared in his review of the report of the Highland Society into Ossian's authenticity and Malcolm Laing's *Poems of Ossian* (1805), investigations directly inspired by Pinkerton, to whom Laing admitted he had been 'bewildered with Celtic poetry and tradition' before he read the former's work, and now knew 'not a man, not born a Celt, whom [Pinkerton's works] have failed to convince'.[13] Scott bristled at Laing's stridency and expressed a certain amount of pride that a 'remote . . . almost barbarous corner of Scotland' produced a 'bard' that impressed every poetically oriented mind across Europe.[14] In an 1806 letter to Anna Seward (1742–1809), an English poet and reported initiate into Iolo's bardic order,[15] Scott was even more partial to Ossian and the Celts. He admired the 'Celtic diction & character' of Macpherson, whose style had given the poems a certain sense of cultural, if not historical, authenticity (a paradoxical relationship he fully embraced with his own Celticism of the 1820s). Fascinated by the cultural and political amalgamation of Britain, and rejecting the Celtophobia of Pinkerton and Laing, Scott allowed Celticism a formative role in his novels and prose works. In the fifth canto of the epic poem *Marmion* (1808), the hero wonders at Scottish diversity: 'And much he marvelled one small land / Could marshal forth such various band'.[16] After watching the warlike Borderers file past,

> Next Marion marked the Celtic race,
> of different language, form, and face,
> A various race of man.[17]

Scott even admitted that he had toyed with the idea of composing a Highland poem in order to present 'a real picture of what that enthusiastic race actually were before the destruction of their patriarchal government'.[18] Instead, he vividly evoked these themes in his first novel, *Waverley* (1814).

The roots of Scott's more outward displays of Highlandism in the 1820s were therefore deep and gnarled. Ultimately it was scholarship that allowed

Scott to embrace a more Celticised Scotland, as the Edinburgh lawyer George Chalmers and Northumbrian Joseph Ritson (1752–1803) sunk the Picto-Gothic argument.[19] Chalmers sought to separate fact and fable in his exhaustive (and unfinished) *Caledonia* (1807–1824), a history of Scotland from its earliest times. The work's vital contribution was to make the case for the Celtic ethnic identity of the Picts who, though not Gaelic, were nevertheless a group of original Britons speaking a language similar to Welsh.[20]

If Chalmers ultimately vindicated the Celts in the historical-antiquarian sphere, Scott made sure a palatable message could be wrung from these arcane studies and communicated to the Scottish (and British) people. While in 1802 Scott disagreed with Chalmers's Celto-Pictish interpretation, after the publication of *Caledonia* he changed his mind, inserting a note in the third edition of *Sir Tristrem* (1811) that Chalmers had effectively combatted the Gothic argument.[21] Five years later Scott made light of the various origin disputes in his novel *The Antiquary* (1816), full of sly scholarly references and antiquarian inside jokes. The Pictish dispute featured as the centrepiece of a famous after-dinner argument:

> "Why, man, there was once a people called the Piks"—
>
> 'More properly Picts,' interrupted the Baronet.
>
> "I say the *Pikar, Pihar, Piochtar, Piaghter,* or *Peughter*" vociferated Oldbuck; "they spoke a Gothic dialect"—
>
> 'Genuine Celtic' asseverated the knight.
>
> "Gothic! Gothic, I'll go to death upon it!"—counter-asseverated the Squire.
>
> 'Why, gentlemen,' said Lovel, 'I conceive that is a dispute which may be easily settled by philologists, if there are any remains of the language.'[22]

Scott rehashed this debate in real life over a decade later, in an 1829 review of Joseph Ritson's posthumously published *Annals of the Caledonians, Picts, and Scots* (1828), finally laying out his own views on the Pictish question.[23] Here he again stressed the ethnic variation of the Highlanders, who were Celtic, Scandinavian, and Gothic; but he finally sided definitively with Chalmers and Ritson, who had used linguistic evidence to show that the Picts were a Celtic-speaking tribe of original Britons.[24]

The other half of Scott's lasting Celtic legacy came through his public sponsorship of the Highland myth of Scottish origins. As a number of works have demonstrated, the specific processes which transformed the image of the Highlands in the popular imagination from negative to positive—integration of Highlanders into the British army, a programme of agricultural and economic improvement, and a wave of tourism inspired by the Romantic vogue for the sublime—occurred between the failure of the '45 and the first decade of the nineteenth century.[25] Scott helped to transform perceptions in his novels, but he also championed the Highlands personally and publicly. He was elected president of the Edinburgh-based Celtic Society, a 'National Society' for the promotion of Highland culture, and above all Highland dress,[26] its members being 'obliged to wear the tartan'. This was not just an excuse to wear fancy dress; Highland garb was thought to be a Celtic 'national feature' extending back to antiquity.[27] In his history of the Highland Society of London, Sir John Sinclair of Ulbster (1754–1835) listed the Society's first aim as the 'Restoration of Highland Dress', which he justified by noting Tartan's 'great antiquity. Garments of this chequered cloth were universal among all the branches of the Celtic Nation,' including the 'old Gauls and Celts of Spain'.[28] Scott copied this line in his review of Ritson, and related nonchalantly that the ancient Picto-Scots 'wore the Irish mantle or Highland plaid', so in promoting what he perceived to be authentic Highland dress Scott thought he was drawing on a Picto-Scottish thread that extended back millennia.

Scott's Celtic Highlandism famously reached farcical form in the pageant he organised for George IV's (1762–1830) visit to Edinburgh in 1822, where he outfitted the king in a kilt and organised a series of Highland-inspired spectacles.[29] Scott is usually seen as having masterminded the entire affair, along with David Stewart of Garth (1772–1829), a colonel in the British Army, but a pageant major in 1822. Fresh from making himself the authority on the Highlands and its culture with the publication of *Sketches of the character, manners, and present state of the Highlanders of Scotland* (1822), Stewart led the Celtic Society—which had paid around £7 to a series of sergeants for 'drilling the Celts' on march and formation[30]—during the pageant and organised the kilting ceremony. It was made known to George that 'the ancient dress of the Highlanders of Scotland has been long a badge of loyalty and fidelity to their King' and was a symbol of attachment to 'the constitution of Britain'.[31] For his part, George communicated through Scott his thanks that the 'Gentlemen of the Celtic Society' had helped to give the ceremonies 'so peculiar and romantic a character'.[32] Much has been read into the pageant, and particularly the kilting ceremony, as a reconciliation of the Highlands, the Lowlands, and the rest of Britain, or as an imperial ceremony, but it could be that George IV just liked wearing tartan.[33] While Prince of Wales he had requested to dine with the Highland Society of London (f. 1778) in 1807, having worn Highland dress at a masquerade and hoping to don it again.[34] Whatever the motivation, however, the Celtic symbolism imputed to the 1822 spectacle lodged in popular memory.

Thanks to the efforts of Walter Scott, the Celts retained a place in Scotland's history, repackaged for Unionist ideological purposes. While in some sense Scott defanged the Celts, he also navigated past the still-toxic Ossian controversy, and proved, contra Pinkerton, that the Celtic Highlands could be a repository of Scotland's proud history and still be integrated into a wider Britishness. Scott probably did more than anyone else to neuter any lingering Jacobite associations with the 'Celtic' Highlands; yet, by incorporating (admittedly sanitised) Celtic elements into his novels, prose works, and into Scottish (and British) society more generally, Scott also probably did more than any other figure to make Celtic ideas more mainstream in Britain until Matthew Arnold.

French Romantic Historiography and Celtic Comparative History

History was highly politicised during the Bourbon Restoration.[35] As the political situation stabilised somewhat and a visible left-right spectrum emerged, historians resurrected old ideas and twisted them into new shapes in order to answer the daunting questions posed by the Revolution. The monarchist right adapted a version of the *thèse nobiliaire*—the idea that France's ancient constitution derived from the fifth-century Frankish invasion and aristocratic conquest of Gaul—to repudiate the revolution and justify monarchical rule, as the left crafted a 'liberal' version of history depicting the Revolution as the latest, necessary, stage in the process of restoring ancient Gaulish liberties. Liberal Romantic historians, like the Thierry brothers or Jules Michelet, looked to national origins for the immemorial characteristics of *le peuple,* where the character and philosophy of the Celtic Gauls could, they believed, help to reveal truths about the modern French nation. As part of the search for evidence, they turned to the histories and customs of Britain and Ireland, but most particularly Wales, drawing on the bardic researches of Iolo Morganwg's circle. Since vestiges of ancient Celtic society had, it was claimed, survived into the medieval period and beyond, studying the Welsh material represented the opportunity to get beyond the hearsay of classical sources and recover information left by Celts themselves.

As briefly discussed in the previous chapter, Augustin Thierry set the racialised terms of French historiographical debate in the 1810s and 20s.[36] A former secretary to Henri de Saint-Simon (1760–1825), with whom he had published various essays, Thierry made his first major mark in *Histoire de la conquête de l'Angleterre par les Normands* (1825), which was underpinned by the simple idea that the Norman Conquest was 'at the bottom of everything' in the history of modern Britain. Thierry had come to the conclusion while reading Hume, but he was also inspired by Walter Scott's novels. The key to English liberty and commercial success was the struggle of the commoners against their Norman aristocratic oppressors, which had been secured in a reconciliation of the two nations at the end of the seventeenth century. Thierry thought that what he perceived to be the key to British history, the clash of separate races, was transposable to France—particularly as the Irish and Scots shared the same Celtic racial characteristics as the French people[37]—and was still visible in French history.[38]

Plugging the Gauls into his brother's formula, Amédée Thierry pitched his *Histoire des Gaulois* (1828) as a biography of *le peuple*, arguing that racial characteristics survived over time and that by investigating ancient Gaul, he could illuminate the 'race' from which nineteen out of twenty modern Frenchmen were descended.[39] The Celtic Gauls were framed against the Germans throughout, and were themselves divided into two different types: the freedom-loving Galls and the stable Kymris. It will be remembered that this split was made at the same time by William Edwards, whose research into the ethnological makeup of France and Europe more generally Thierry cited in his introduction as confirming his historical theories in the physiological realm.[40] In order to investigate what he saw as a distinct Gaulish history, Thierry availed himself of three methods: comparative philological enquiry, the historical sources of classical authors, and information from 'national traditions'.[41] What this last meant was a study of the medieval survival of Gaulish *moeurs*, whether in France or other Celtic countries. Here the Welsh evidence stood out, notably the bardic system and poetry collected and published by Iolo Morganwg and William Owen Pughe.

In 1815 the Professor of Literature at Caen, Abbé Gervais de la Rue (1751–1835), published a short work on Breton bards, in which he transposed Iolo's bardic argument onto Brittany: he claimed that medieval Breton poetry, composed in the Celtic language, preserved the ancient Celtic mythology long after Latin Christianity had stamped it out elsewhere in France, essentially mimicking Iolo's Welsh claims.[42] The folklorist Claude Fauriel (1772–1844) likewise saw potential in the Welsh material. In 1818 he reviewed the *Myvyrian Archaiology*, announcing that it finally provided the documentary proof of Wales' claims to national and literary greatness and glowingly praising the editors for their integrity and faithfulness to the manuscripts.[43] Above all, Fouriel stressed the collection as useful for 'l'historien philosophe' because it offered proofs of early Kymric laws, customs, language, and culture.[44] Remarkably, vestiges of the ancient bardic institution 'of these Celtic druids' had survived until very recently and were perhaps even preserved to Fauriel's own day.[45] Deeply impressed by Iolo's work and mindful of the dearth of information on French bardic traditions, Fauriel wrote to him in 1821 for assistance, but received no reply.[46] Nevertheless, Fauriel played an instrumental role through both his review and personal acquaintance, in introducing historians like Amédée Thierry and Henri Martin (1813–1883) to Welsh bardic antiquarianism. Thierry incorporated the major Druidical researches into his work as proofs for splitting the Gauls into two races, listing as sources the *Myvyrian Archaiology* and Fauriel's review.[47] He was most taken with Iolo's now-notorious Third Series, and the personage of Hu Gadarn, who he thought might be related to the Gaulish god Esus from the Parisian *Pilier de nautes* (see chapter 3).[48] Although citing them to prove rather mundane conclusions like the identity of the Welsh and Bretons and the Eastern origins of the Celts, Amédée Thierry's use of Welsh Druidical scholarship showed just how far Iolo's influence extended.

Celticism and Bardism were also incorporated into the monumental history of Jules Michelet. Born to a printer in revolutionary Paris in Year VI (1798), Michelet's republican politics and stirring historical prose made him the most celebrated French historian of the nineteenth century. He toured the Celtic nations in the 1830s while writing his magnum opus, the *Histoire de France* (1833–1867), in which the Celts are presented as a masculine warrior tribe:

> The genius of these Galls or Celts was above all for movement, raiding, and conquest; it is by war that the ancient nations mixed and came together. . . . Peoples of war and noise, they conquered the world sword in hand.[49]

The Celts were the basis of the French nation, though due to lack of evidence it was difficult to pinpoint exactly which traditions and ideas the French had inherited from them, a point he had also made in his *Origines du droit français*.[50] Thierry and Edwards explained French history in terms of racial conflict but, while certainly not denying the importance of race, Michelet emphasised that the modern French genius was a product of race-mixing over time. What exactly was the Celtic contribution?

Michelet included several language tables taken from his friend William Edwards's work, in order to illustrate that at one ancient point there had existed a 'union of the Celtic world', consisting of Gaul, Britain, and Ireland.[51] The Roman invasion of Gaul and the subsequent Germanic invasions had broken any such unity, but like a 'race of stone' the Celts of Britain and Ireland had maintained their *moeurs* and languages.[52] This meant evidence from the British and Irish Celts could be used to fuel conjectures about the Gauls. In a passage citing the *Myvyrian Archaiology*, he acknowledged that while the modern Druidic tradition was doubtless very different from that of the ancients, it nevertheless provided usable evidence.[53] In a later section examining Celtic traditions, laws, and character in Britain and Ireland, Michelet constructed a general essence of Celtic character, lighting on a tendency towards individuality and 'égalité' that gave France its vitality.[54] He also included several appendices explaining Celtic evidence from British sources, including the Triads, an account of Bardism, and the physiological ideas of Thomas Price (for which see below).[55] Thorough examination of the Celts gave Michelet his ideas about the foundations for the modern French nation, and his use of evidence from the British Celts allowed him to paint perhaps the most powerful portrait of the ancient French Celts with strong contemporary implications for the French nation as liberal, warlike, and masculine.[56]

France's second national historian after Michelet, Henri Martin, made even greater use of the Celts and devoted later works entirely to them (see chapter 9).[57] After writing poetry, novels, and plays, the republican Martin composed the first volume of his *Histoire de France* (1833–1860) at the age of twenty-three.[58] Politely acknowledging the work of La Tour d'Auvergne and earlier *Celtisants* but noting they had gone too far in their linguistic claims, Martin's interpretation of the French Celts did not differ all that much from theirs: the warlike Celtic tribes had conquered the whole of Europe, and to them could be traced many of the modern characteristics of the French nation. His wide-ranging interests and ability for synthesis meant that Martin incorporated findings from a variety of fields but was not himself very original. He relied heavily on the work of Amédée Thierry, corroborating the Gaelic/Kyrmic split with the physiological research of William Edwards and the findings of comparative philology. But Martin placed a new emphasis on the Druids and even thought their tenets might form the basis for a modern French secular religion.

It was from his close friend, the Saint-Simonian philosopher Jean Reynaud (1806–1863), that Martin drew his information on the Druids. The pair had a keen interest in ancient religion and philosophy, and together explored, among other things, Judaism, Zoroastrianism, and Druidism. As an editor of the republican and socialist-inflected *Encyclopédie nouvelle* (1834–1841), Reynaud composed the entry on 'Druidisme', whose significance to ancient Gaulish society was spelled out in the title when it was republished as a standalone essay dedicated to Martin: *Considérations sur l'esprit de la Gaule* (1847).[59] Reynaud's work needs to be understood in the context of the spiritual crisis that characterised post-revolutionary liberal France. Something was needed to fill the void opened by the break with Rome, and in the same way that the Gauls had been recovered as national ancestors, perhaps their Druids could be recovered for the spiritual purposes of the nation. Reynaud's conception of the Druids was similar to those we have seen in previous chapters: they were sublime ponderers of immortality and the life to come, not polytheistic idolators or pagan sensualists, and their beliefs were symmetrical to the Judaeo-Christian religious system, which the Gauls adopted easily for precisely that reason.[60] Reynaud ended his book with reflections on modern Bardo-Druidism, which he linked to contemporary French racial theory. He argued that the reappearance of Druidism among the Welsh in 1792 was inspired by what he described as the Gaulish uprising of 1789 against its racial oppressors, and that there was a 'spontaneous solidarity' between the two 'movements' attributable to the powerful spiritual principles that existed organically within their race.[61]

Henri Martin picked up this thread in the 1850s, declaring that the Welsh study of Bardism over the previous sixty years had produced a 'renaissance celtique' and provided evidence of a Celtic spirit untainted by either German or Latin influence.[62] Martin was thus able to draw a direct line from ancient Druidism as the spiritual manifestation of the 'génie celtique' that had largely shaped French morals from time immemorial: 'l'esprit français' was still recognisably 'l'esprit celtique'.[63] He identified himself, for one, as an 'incorrigible Celt'.[64] Martin supplemented the *Myvyrian Archaiology* and the early commentary on it with Adolphe Pictet's recently published translations of Iolo's bardic triads in the second volume of his *Poems Lyric and Pastoral* (1794),[65] for which Martin thanked Pictet for having 'revealed to us the most important monument of the bardic tradition'.[66] Martin's passion for the material and interest in the ancient Celts would only increase, and in 1861 he visited Wales to consult Iolo's manuscripts at Llanover Hall. In 1868 he played his familiarity with Iolo's manuscripts as a trump card in a dispute with another Celticist in the Parisian *Revue Archaeologique*, writing to a Welsh friend that he debated 'with the help of the study I made of the manuscripts of Iolo', and was 'publishing on this subject a few fragments from the Barddas [notebooks] translated into French'.[67] Martin always spoke reverently of Iolo, calling him 'our patriarch old Iolo' in a letter to Pictet in 1869.[68]

As this section has shown, French historians writing their *roman national* devoted new attention to the Celtic origins of France. In their stirring new histories of *la nation*, they were able to give a more colourful account of Druidism and the spiritual succour it had provided because they went beyond the classical sources, incorporating findings from comparative studies of the Celtic languages and Welsh bardic material. Paradoxically, they were able to write such captivating histories and craft the national identity precisely because they looked beyond their nation.[69] Although it encountered resistance from conservative holdouts, the Gaulish theory of national origins triumphed completely during the Third Republic—thanks in no small part to the Germanic racial antithesis—and was enshrined in the school textbooks of Ernest Lavisse (1842–1922), epitomised by the slogan 'nos ancêtres les Gaulois'.[70]

Wales: Between Romantic and Scientific Approaches to the Past

The spectre of Iolo Morganwg continued to hover over the Welsh cultural landscape in the era of Romantic nationalism.[71] The *Myvyrian Archaiology* achieved an important status in European scholarship following its publication in the early 1800s, the *Gorsedd* became associated with *eisteddfodau* in 1819, and after Iolo's death in 1826 his son Taliesin Williams ('Ab Iolo', 1787–1847) guarded his legacy.[72] Truculent and difficult during his own lifetime, Iolo had already attracted a few sceptics, such as Edward 'Celtic' Davies—who soon attracted his own sceptics—but Iolo's bardic philosophy, invented ceremonial traditions, and literary forgeries survived him relatively undisturbed. However, there were several figures committed to a more critical study of Welsh history and literature, and this section focuses on three of them: the Anglican Rev. Thomas Price (1787–1848), the industrialist Lady Charlotte Guest (1812–1895), and the pharmacist Thomas Stephens (1821–1875). Price—the only one who actually knew him—was ambivalent about Iolo and his creations. Guest was respectful but aloof, while Stephens was the first really incisive critic of Iolo's works. In contrast with the other nations examined in this chapter, Wales lacked a university, but this trio nevertheless benefitted from the rich background of Welsh cultural societies—such as *Cymdeithas Cymregyddion y Fenni* (Welsh Society of Abergavenny), the Welsh Manuscripts Society (f. 1836) and the Cambrian Archaeological Association (f. 1846)—and a burgeoning bilingual national press interested in such matters. Importantly, all three figures understood the importance of placing Welsh literature and history in the context of that of the other Celtic nations, and all three paid attention to continental scholarship—particularly German philology—and were recognised on the Continent as Celtic experts.

Thomas Price was the leading Welsh scholar of his age. An Anglican cleric from Brecknockshire, Price was a philologist and historian, and one of the most important figures of the Welsh cultural revival; as we will see in chapter 9, he was also integral to the development of pan-Celticism. In addition to his commitment to Scripture and the traditional Celtic descent from Gomer,[73] Price was caught between the currents of Romantic Welsh tradition, including the Bardism propagated by Iolo, and the emerging 'scientific' approaches to the past. In his school days, Price had been influenced by the judge Theophilus Jones, patron of Iolo's opponent Edward 'Celtic' Davies and himself a sceptic of Iolo's,[74] and in his first publications of the mid-1820s he took up a stance sceptical of the assertions of previous generations, particularly William Owen Pughe.[75] In his first *eisteddfod* speeches of the early 1820s, Price praised Bardism as an agent of civilization, which with Christianity had contributed 'so much towards the civilizing of our rude and ferocious ancestors';[76] however, maddeningly, in a letter to Taliesin a few years later he wrote 'I never studied the rules of bardism—and have no taste for those with which I am acquainted.'[77] This ambivalence characterised his entire career; as he put it in a letter of 1840:

> One thing only appears certain respecting the Druids—they knew how to keep their own secrets . . . there is one person living who professes to be a Druid . . . i.e. Mr Taliesin Williams, of Merthryr Tydfil, son of Iolo Morganwg . . . I assure you I have not been able to form the most distant idea of ancient Druidism from anything he may have said.[78]

Yet Price admitted to being 'staggered' when confronted by 'some ancient Bardic lines, when I have doubted the antiquity of his system.'[79]

Whatever his opinion of modern Druidism, the point is that Price had an almost uniquely critical eye for his time and looked beyond Welsh traditions—real or imagined—and to the best sources and scholarship available to him.

The recurring subjects in his early speeches and writings were the stirrings of Welsh nationality and patriotism and, of course, the nobility of the Welsh language. Price was probably the Welsh antiquarian who best grasped the significance of comparative philology and the Indo-European idea, both for Welsh and for the Celtic family more generally. His first foray into print was a series of letters to the magazine *Seren Gomer* on the Celtic languages,[80] which began with the familiar assertion that 'the Celtic language' had once spread 'not only over Great Britain, but also over all of France, and the greatest part of Europe', before drilling down into the Celtic languages spoken in Britain and their historical attestations in literary remains.[81] Here Price was particularly interested in the relationship between Welsh and Highland Gaelic, and concluded in a letter on Ossian that although any Welshman examining the Gaelic text would be struck by some lexical similarities, they could talk to a Highlander 'from dawn til dusk' without understanding a single word.[82] In a striking contrast with Iolo and most of his generation, Price so admired the sentiments and turns of phrase in the poems that he did not mind whether they had been composed in the third or eighteenth century. Elsewhere Price demonstrated his familiarity with comparative philology. In 1828 he destroyed Vans Kennedy's philological book—in which, it will be recalled from the previous chapter, the author argued that Celtic was not a member of the Indo-European family—in a review that showed Kennedy had deliberately chosen faulty etymologies in order to support his conclusions; for example, in comparing Latin *rex* (king), Kennedy chose Welsh *llywydd* (leader) instead of the obvious *rhi*.[83] Kennedy's deliberate Celtic ignorance impugned the rest of the book, argued Price, who it must be remembered was writing before the publication of the great works of Prichard, Pictet, Bopp, and Zeuß.[84]

Branching out further into ethnology, Price—who owned Prichard's works and might have known him by this point—published one of his most innovative works in 1829. It was intended at a general level to refute the theory of polygenism—for religious reasons—but at a much more specific level it was a forceful refutation of Pinkerton's theory of the separate racial origins of the Celtic and Gothic nations of Britain, and that there were any insurmountable differences of character as a result.[85] Neither the 'Goths and Celts of antiquity' nor 'their descendants at the present day' were 'distinguishable from each other, by any marks of Gothic or Celtic origin, or by any physical difference connected with those races'.[86] Differences of 'national physiognomy and character' were 'perpetually varying under varying circumstances'.[87] Pinkerton, despite possessing 'an irritable and prejudiced mind', had his ideas 'given currency' because of his 'general erudition' and 'laborious historical researches'.[88] Rather than some original divide between races, physical distinctions were the result of diet—both the quantity and quality of food—climate, and habit. The supposed dark colouring of the Celtic nations could, Price suggested, be explained by their proximity to coal-mining areas.[89]

Given Price's familiarity with the newer scientific approaches to the past available in comparative philology and ethnology, and supported by physiology, it is surprising that he embraced a more traditional approach in his magnum opus, the first major critical history of Wales in Welsh, *Hanes Cymru a Chenedl y Cymry* (The history of Wales and the Welsh nation).[90] It was published between 1836 and 1842 in fourteen instalments in order to make the ultimately eight-hundred-page work more commercially viable.[91] In a way, however, Price did write according to contemporary scientific standards, for as Huw Pryce has described in clear detail, Price was at pains to base his history only on reliable primary sources. In letters written to Taliesin Williams at around the same time, Price stressed that scholars had to base their work upon historical authorities and not secondary interpretations; however, the problem was that Price was not critical enough about his own sources. Unfortunately, Price's first quoted authority was a forged line in Iolo's Triads proclaiming that Britain belonged to no one but the 'Welsh nation' (*Genedl y Cymry*), its first settlers.[92] This was also a silent rejection of Edward Lhwyd's theory that a Gaelic population had first colonised Britain.[93] Price, who had in 1823 written an article defending the traditional derivation of 'Cymry' from the 'Gomari'—though he pointed to Josephus and not the Book of Genesis—also included this theory for the arrival of the Welsh to Britain. The other sources for the early history of Britain that Price looked to were Nennius and *Brut y Brenhinoedd*, a bastardised Welsh version of Geoffrey of Monmouth's *Regum britanniae*. Price's reluctance to combine the new sciences of the past in his Welsh history—with which the following paragraph shows he was certainly familiar—seems like a missed opportunity, but probably reveals a hesitancy to depart from Scripture and Welsh historical tradition.

Price played a significant role in the most important Welsh literary production of the century, the *Mabinogion*, translated and published by Lady Charlotte Guest. Guest is not usually discussed among those taking a more critical approach to Welsh history during these years, perhaps because she came at the material from a different angle than most Welsh antiquarians. Unquestionably sharp and intellectually refined, Guest's most important quality was nevertheless probably the accidental one that she was an outsider.[94] Though she loved Wales and its culture, she was inoculated from the powerful patriotic draw of the Romantic cultural tradition. Interested in the origins and history of the Arthurian and chivalric traditions, Guest conceived of Welsh literature and historical culture within the Indo-European framework, and was influenced by Prichard, who she read at the same time as she began to study Welsh. 'Pritchard my solid reading, Welsh my study', she recorded in her diary on 14 November 1833, shortly after arriving in Wales. About four years later Guest announced her intention to translate and publish 'the Mabinogion', taken from the Red Book of Hergest in Jesus College, Oxford.[95] She began work on the 1 January 1838 and relied, at least in the first year, on the help of Price, who would stay with her family at Dowlais for days at a time in order to check and assist with her translations.[96] Like Price's *Hanes*, Guest's *Mabinogion* was published in instalments. Between 1838 and 1845, seven portions appeared, before a three-volume set was published in 1849. In this final version Guest penned an introductory essay suggesting that European chivalric romance proceeded from a 'Celtic nucleus' in Wales and Brittany:

> It might, I think, be shown . . . that the Cymric nation is not only, as Dr. Prichard has proved it to be, an early off-shoot of the Indo-European family, and a people of unmixed descent, but that when driven out of their conquests by the later nations, the names and exploits of their heroes, and the compositions of their bards, spread far and wide among the invaders, and affected intimately their tastes and literature for many centuries, and that it has strong claims to be considered the cradle of European Romance.[97]

The Celts, according to this interpretation that would be picked up on by Ernest Renan and Matthew Arnold, were one of the most important sources of European literature and its style. Guest moved on to greener pastures after publishing the *Mabinogion*, but it was widely recognised that she had performed a service not only to Welsh literature but to Celtic scholarship more generally.[98] But if Thomas Price played a vital role in the publication of Guest's work, Guest likewise played a crucial role in the work of Thomas Stephens.

Although parts of the work of Price and Guest could certainly be considered 'scientific', it is generally recognised that Stephens finally turned the page. Born in 1828 in Pontneddfechan, in the Vale of Neath,[99] Stephens was apprenticed to a pharmacist in Merthyr Tydfil as a teenager, took over the business in 1841, and was soon playing a considerable and sustained role in the civic and social development of his community. Already in 1840, he won his first *eisteddfod* essay contest,[100] but after his defeat in several contests at the 1842 Abergavenny *eisteddfod*, Stephens announced himself on the national stage with a series of acid letters published in *The Cambrian* between November 1842 and March 1843 about what he found to be the puerility of its prize competitions, and the incompetence of its judges and contestants. No one escaped, not Taliesin Williams, Charlotte Guest, or even Thomas Price, whose *Hanes Cymru* was 'disfigured by prejudices, numberless inconsistences, confused and ill-matured views, and unpardonable neglect'.[101] Stephens's attacks provoked written responses from Price, Taliesin, and others, and the whole episode reached a boiling point on 28 January 1843 when Taliesin—also a resident of Merthyr—accosted Stephens at his home.[102] Stephens became known for his stubborn temper, and the letters can be read almost as a hitlist for his future scholarly career.

Stephens's bread and butter was medieval Welsh philology, but this was situated within a modern and sophisticated understanding of Indo-European comparative philology. Stephens's 1841 essay on the 'position which the Welsh language occupies among those of Celtic origin with their branches among the Indo-European'—is probably about as cutting edge as it was possible to be in South Wales at the time. He had clearly read Prichard and embraced his argument that, of all the Indo-European languages, Welsh retained its ancient purity better than 'any language now spoken'. However, Stephens was careful to emphasise that this did not mean the language had remained pristine, which was a common position held by Celtic and especially Welsh linguistic antiquarians, including Iolo. Instead, 'Society is always progressing. . . . in it there is nothing stationary and in proportion as the condition of the Welsh became changed new demands were made upon the language to express new wants.'[103] As the Welsh became civilized, so their language changed to match the needs of their society. The developing human sciences thus showed that Welsh occupied an important place in the Indo-European family yet still adhered to the universal rules of social and linguistic development. The increasing internationalisation of scholarship in this period helped to bring Wales out of some of its national introspection and obsessions. In 1849, a dispute over the purpose of Cromlechs—or 'dolmens', upright standing stones with a 'tabletop' stone creating a chamber—brought Welsh antiquarians into closer contact with Irish scholars, who helped pour cold water on the idea that the stones were Druidic sacrificial altars. Stephens approvingly wrote to an Irish correspondent that Wales, like Ireland, had seen 'an immense amount of quackery,' but he believed 'a better spirit is about to prevail', namely 'more scientific criticism'.[104]

On top of this scientific foundation, Stephens launched his investigations into more technical philological questions. In 1848 he won the Abergavenny *eisteddfod* prize on the 'Literature of Wales during the Twelfth and Succeeding Centuries' offered by the Prince of Wales. In the process Stephens won the friendship of Lady Charlotte Guest and her husband, who financed an extended version of the essay's publication as *The Literature of the Kymry* in 1849. In it Stephens examined Welsh literature from 1080 to 1350, which worked as a lens to 'give a complete account of the mental labours of the Kymry of these centuries'.[105] As Stephens described it: 'the daring spirit of modern criticism is about to lay violent hands upon the old household furniture of venerable tradition'.[106] Stephens was already known as a precocious and pugilistic young scholar in Wales, but *The Literature of the Kymry* made his reputation abroad.[107] As Adam Coward has helped to show, Stephens more than anyone else brought Welsh scholarship to the European stage on a scientific level.[108] The German scholar Albert Schulz (1802–1893) wrote to him that his work 'is the first and only to submit Welsh literature openly and without prejudice to a critique which has hitherto been missing'.[109] La Villemarqué wrote that together Price and Stephens followed in the critical steps of Edward Lhwyd, and he related praise and questions from Augustin Thierry.[110]

Stephens relinquished the sort of ad hominem attacks he made in the early 1840s, but his work retained its critical intensity. Yet although he was driven to ruthlessly expose the manufacture of historical myths, he could not quite bring himself to accuse the Romantic generation of forgery. He was ambivalent about Iolo though veered strongly toward the side of doubt. Fabrications and distortions, Stephens wrote, came from medieval bards rather than Iolo, who merely repeated them.[111] Although he early suspected *Coelbren y Beirdd*, some 'triads of uncertain date, and of unknown origin', and 'Druid tenets, of modern invention', he cited Iolo's *Cyfrinach y Beirdd* as an authority and called him a 'judicious critic' in 1841.[112] Reviewing Elijah Waring's *Recollections and Anecdotes of Edward Williams* (1850), Stephens wrote that although he did 'not consider him to be a safe guide', no one matched Iolo's interest, fervour, and industry in relation to Welsh literature, for which Wales owed him a debt.[113] Nevertheless, Stephens ruthlessly mowed down Iolo's inventions.[114]

Coelbren y Beirdd, Iolo's bardic alphabet that we examined in chapter 5, was widely credited and remained ubiquitous in Welsh cultural outlets.[115] Journals and societies often chose to include a motto—also often one of Iolo's, like '*Y gwir yn erbyn y byd*'—on their official papers in the script, along with the mystic mark (/ | \). From time to time, discoveries of supposedly archaic carvings seemed to prove its authenticity.[116] However, doubts had been expressed since Iolo first publicised the alphabet, and on this issue Price and Stephens were united in their scepticism. Although young Price was inspired by it and even constructed a 'replica' of the wooden frame in which the writing boards were supposed to have been used,[117] in 1830 he announced himself to Taliesin as a 'sceptic' and tried to dissuade him from publishing too hastily, counselling him to gather proofs and that 'a weak defence of the matter would be equivalent to a defeat'.[118] Although, presumably out of friendship, he publicly awarded Taliesin the *eisteddfod* prize on the subject of the *Coelbren* in 1838, privately he did not mince words when Taliesin was preparing the same paper for publication:

> its publication would be detrimental to the character of our national literature—If you have proof to adduce, well & good—y gwir yn erbyn y byd—But if you have not decided & undoubted evidence, it will only be the occasion of much unwarranted detraction, as regards the originality of our Bardic remains.[119]

This was the problem with Taliesin's paper when it was published in 1840. It relied primarily on authorities found only in Iolo's manuscripts and nowhere else.

In his early salvos in the *Cambrian*, Stephens took a more philological tack. Wood carving was common to all ancient tribes, but the question was if the characters bore any resemblance to other early alphabets, and why. Only then would the *Coelbren* 'render efficient assistance to philology, in solving the question of the oriental origin of the Celtic nations. To Grimm, Boeck, and Potts [*sic*], we owe all the information we have on the subject; to the author of this treatise—none'.[120] Many years later, when he wrote the essay that finally dispatched the *Coelbren* from respectable credibility after it was published in 1872, Stephens confined his method to research in Welsh manuscripts and antiquities. *Coelbren y Beirdd* 'hast no pretensions to a high antiquity, and is neither found on sculptured stones nor in old MSS'.[121] 'It claims to be an emanation from Heaven. It is an emanation from the Roman alphabet', and one dating back only to the seventeenth-century bard Llewellyn Sion. Although he included plenty of suspicions, Stephens ultimately accused Iolo of being a poor scholar rather than a forger. Importantly, he couched his criticism within a broader accusation that the bardic Chair of Glamorgan could not be trusted: 'The bards of Morganwg have created a system of bardism bearing inherent evidences of recent fabrication'.[122] Another fabrication was the legend of

Madoc, the Welsh chieftain who had supposedly 'discovered' America and whose descendants lived among Native Americans there. In 1858, Stephens debunked it in a now-famous episode, summed up succinctly by the *Saturday Review*: 'Some Eisteddfod or other offered a prize for the best essay on Prince Madoc's settlement in America. Nobody doubted that Mr. Stephens' essay was the best, but he was refused the prize because he proved incontestably that Prince Madoc never did settle in America.'[123] John Williams (1811–1862), the *eisteddfod*'s organiser, who had himself entered an essay in the contest arguing the opposite side, instructed the brass band to drown Stephens out as he ran onto the stage to protest. The essay was not published until 1893.

Price, Guest, and Stephens existed within a constellation of cultural revivalists, who can be placed along a spectrum running from sober and critical like themselves, to prosaic and credulous, to eccentric and outlandish. The majority were probably somewhere in the middle: respectable yet patriotic and unsuspecting. An interesting example is William Williams (1788–1855) of the gentry family at Aberpergwm, who encouraged Taliesin repeatedly about the *Coelbren*, which he thought might help to decipher ancient Etruscan, perhaps 'a dialect of Celtic', which would create a European sensation.[124] Eighteenth-century Celtomaniacs like Pezron and Vallancey had been onto something and were only 'laughed at through ignorance'.[125] Yet at the same time, Williams sustained one of the earliest campaigns to establish and endow a 'professor of Celtic language & literature at Oxford', which he began around 1832 and revived in 1840. The position would ideally 'embrace all Celtic dialects', as well as the classical languages, Hebrew, and Sanskrit.[126] A professor of Celtic would probably have disagreed with most of Williams's opinions, but he was in no doubt that one should exist for patriotic, religious, and scientific purposes.[127] More zealous were devotees of Bardism such as John Williams (Ab Ithel), an Oxford-educated Anglican priest, who did the most to harmonise Iolo's writings on Bardism with Christianity in works that he published on ecclesiastical history, as well as in the translation and edition of many of Iolo's bardic writings in *Barddas; or, A Collection of Original Documents, Illustrative of the Theology, Wisdom and Usages of the Bardo-Druidic System of the Isle of Britain* (1862).[128] Stephens criticised him frequently and eventually refused to work with him after Williams condemned Stephens's essay on Madoc. Yet Williams had also co-founded the Cambrian Archaeological Association (though he was eventually forced to leave), which produced a serious journal still in existence today. On the outlandish side of the spectrum were those who were so eccentric that they were perhaps on the border of sanity. Evan Davies ('Myfyr Morganwg', 1801–1888), usurped the chair of high Druidism and, though celebrated as an autodidact by some, was cut down to size by Stephens as 'an illiterate man, who professes to be the sole depository of Bardo-Mystic knowledge!'[129] Then there was the famous radical William Price (1800–1893), a sort of cult leader who capitalised on the tradition and discourse of Druidism without being much involved with the post-Iolo mainstream at all.[130]

Iolo's creations thus lived on, despite Stephens's best efforts. They survived the reform of the national *Eisteddfod* in the early 1860s—reformed in large part because of the excesses of John Williams and Evan Davies—and in 1876 one Anglican bishop noted that 'it is said that bardism, as a part of the eisteddfod, actually existed 750 years before the Christian era'.[131] From 1881 the *Gorsedd* opened every subsequent national *Eisteddfod*,[132] and we will see its importance for Celticism as a whole in later chapters. However, Stephens had led the charge against Iolo's fabrications and against the credulity of his most exuberant followers, and new generations followed Stephens's lead in detecting and exposing Iolo's interventions. Many better scholars have considered the question, but my opinion is that Iolo's success lay in his understanding that forging a convincing provenance was just as important as being able to mimic the style of the masters.

Stephens died in 1876, just as Celtic studies was developing its own distinct identity. That Henri Gadoz (1842–1932)—founder-editor of the *Revue celtique*—tried to recruit Stephens as a contributor, and then wanted to include his unpublished essays following his death confirms the assessment of one of Stephens's correspondents that for his iconoclasm Stephens would 'have the thanks of the next race of Celtic Scholars, though you may pass through the fiery ordeal of the present'.[133] One friend wrote bluntly to Henri Gaidoz that Stephens was 'not a popular man'.[134] As James Hadley wrote to Stephens, even in 1865, it was 'rare to find a writer of Celtic birth who knows how to exercise that judicious scepticism which historic truth demands'.[135] More elegant and perhaps appropriate was the phrase of the 'Continental writer', who said that Stephens 'scaled the Celtic mythological heavens and scattered the false gods and goddesses that disported there'.[136]

The Young Ireland Generation and the Scientific Study of Ireland's Celtic Past

Although the Celtic theory of Irish origins had gained strength over the eighteenth century—and achieved a considerable symbolic victory in being accepted by many of the foundational generation of the Royal Irish Academy[137]—it had not triumphed completely. Moreover, it had not entered into the revolutionary thought of the United Irishmen. To take one example illustrative of both of these points, in 1822 the United Irishman Roger O'Connor (1762–1834) published a very amusing two-volume history, *Chronicles of Eri*, vindicating the native Scytho-Iberian myths with what he claimed were direct translations from Phoenician manuscripts that had been destroyed by his English jailers. There was 'no term less understood . . . than Ceiltig, Keltkoi, Celtae, Celts', according to O'Connor, but he was certain that they could not be associated with the Irish, and instead referred to the ancient Gauls and modern Welsh (also unrelated to the Irish in his opinion).[138] Instead, the Celts were not fully vindicated in Irish scholarly and nationalist circles until the 1830s and 40s.

These intense decades witnessed the height of the early movement for repealing the Union led by Daniel O'Connell (1775–1847), the rise and fall of the revolutionary nationalist group Young Ireland, and the Great Famine, an event of devastating consequence in Irish history and for Gaelic culture in particular. Yet Irish scholarship also made considerable strides, discrediting the myths of oriental descent and making room for the victory of the Celtic past. For the youthful Romantic nationalists of Young Ireland, this Celtic past was worthy of study, celebration, and even emulation. The dismal failed rebellion of 1848—mocked as the 'Battle of Widow McCormack's Cabbage Patch'—tends to overshadow the vitality of the movement, but the Young Irelanders were a group of well-educated, intelligent men and women who promoted research into Ireland's history for its own sake as well as for their own political purposes.[139] Even after 1848, Young Irelanders continued their historical work alongside the more orthodox scholars outside of the movement, laying the scholarly foundation for the Gaelic nationalism of the revolutionary era.[140]

Joep Leerssen has outlined how Gaelicism became a central component of Irish nationalism over the course of the nineteenth century, making the crucial point that Anglo-Irish Protestants adopted Gaelic history as their own as a result of increasing discontent with England.[141] Catholic Gaels and Protestant Anglo-Irish met on the field of Celtic studies.[142] Irish scholarship also became more self-consciously scientific, relying more on primary sources and less on annalistic hearsay as archaeology and textual philology were brought to bear on the study of the past. This development is associated primarily with the triumvirate of the Protestant artist and musician George Petrie (1790–1866), the topographer and philologist John O'Donovan, and the historian Eugene O'Curry (1794–1822), both Catholic. We saw in the previous chapter that O'Donovan introduced Zeuß's *Grammatica* to an Irish audience. But many years before this he formed part of this trio that was the backbone of the topographical department of the Irish Ordnance Survey, which also included the Young Ireland poet James Clarence Mangan (1803–1849), from about 1835 until its dissipation in 1842.[143] This was a gargantuan undertaking sponsored by the government, the aim of which was to survey all of Ireland, map its topography, and write histories with the aid of local folklore. These were complex men with their own separate, sophisticated views, but roughly their significance in this case is threefold: they were at the forefront of the generation that severed the link between Irish mythology and attempts to write its history, they developed more rigorous methods for the investigation of the Irish past, and they consolidated the position of the Celtic past at the forefront of cultural nationalist historical thinking.

In the rejection of native Irish historical shibboleths, George Petrie was most important. He was a Protestant artist—of Scottish stock originally—and is generally acknowledged to be the initiator of scientific archaeology in Ireland.[144] He was interested in antiquities from an early age, which he sketched and painted on his tours around Britain and Ireland; through these he came to realise that Irish history had to be based on both the historical record contained in Ireland's medieval manuscripts and on the antiquities, or physical remains, of the country: 'The antiquities of a nation and its history are indissolubly linked together, and to shrine brightly each requires a reflected light from the other'.[145] Alongside his various activities and work on the Ordnance Survey from 1832 to 1842, Petrie produced three prize-winning essays for the Royal Irish Academy in the 1830s. The most important of these was on the origin of Ireland's famous Round Towers, for which he won the Academy's essay prize of 1832 (he had suggested the topic), but which led to a protracted scholarly quarrel that rumbled through the 1830s and 40s between Petrie and several opponents of his theory, chiefly the English antiquarian Sir William Betham, Ulster King of Arms (head of the heralds) and an enthusiastic and prominent, if inept, antiquarian.[146]

The disagreement has been brilliantly reconstructed and analysed in detail by Leerssen, who describes the episode as an important paradigm shift in the study of the Irish past, in which the outmoded theories of an oriental descent were cast aside because they were no longer scientifically sustainable.[147] The Round Towers are unique to Ireland (except for two in Scotland and one on the Isle of Man) and consequently became a distinctive national symbol. We now know they probably date no earlier than the ninth century and were used as belfries and lookouts, but theories abounded as to their origin and symbolism until Petrie sorted things out. Giraldus Cambrensis thought they were built by Danes, but Irish annalistic and antiquarian tradition held they were likely of Eastern Scythian or Phoenician origin; Vallancey, for example, thought they could be Zoroastrian fire temples, a view sustained into the 1830s.[148] The most outlandish idea was that the towers were pagan phallic monuments, an argument advanced by a frenetic Trinity College graduate named Henry O'Brien (1808–1835), who died amidst the controversy.[149] But Petrie proved they were nothing of the sort in 1832, when he submitted his essay, but the long delay before he finally published an extended version as a book thirteen years later meant the Round Towers remained a subject of protracted debate. Then, in 1845, Petrie announced his findings in a lapidary four-page introduction: the towers were of 'Christian and ecclesiastical origin'; they were belfries and keeps, and they could be used as beacons and watchtowers when required.[150]

Further details of the book need not detain us here; what is of chief interest is the light that the controversy sheds on ideas of ancient Irish history. There was as yet little 'Celtic' focus, and one remarkable article in the *Dublin Penny Journal* of 1832, edited by Petrie, doubted whether Gaelic was a Celtic language.[151] But even the propagation of Petrie's theory of the Round Towers did not lead to the dissipation of the oriental story and concomitant triumph of a Celtic, Christian past. Instead, the various traditions in Ireland continued to be elided. For example, Daniel O'Connell's secretary, William O'Neill Daunt (1807–94), wrote a *Catechism of the History of Ireland* for children, in which he sought to vindicate their 'brave and gallant Celtic forefathers', but then stated the 'most probable belief' that Ireland was first peopled by Phoenicians.[152] After all, the Phoenicians had apparently travelled to the Isles to trade for tin, so it was not beyond the realm of possibility that a colony might have settled in Ireland; yet, while in terms of national filiation this was plausible history according to the medieval sources, it was a linguistic impossibility.

The defeat of Irish orientalism in the linguistic sphere came in the late 1830s. Even though Prichard had published his work situating the Celtic languages within the Indo-European family in 1831, it did not immediately register in Ireland. Works still appeared like Betham's *The Gael and the Cymbri* (1834), in which he argued that the ancient Gauls, Irish, and Britons were all Celtae whose 'language, religion, and institutions, not only appear to have been similar, but identical' with those of the Phoenicians; however, according to Betham, 'those nations who are not Gael, are not Celtae', which meant that the Welsh Cymbri were excluded.[153] As he wrote to Thomas Price, 'I find there is no affinity between [Welsh and Irish] beyond the existence of a few words of similar import and sound, and I am, therefore, satisfied they never could have been of the same family of the human race'.[154] Betham's linguistic method was woefully outdated and inadequate. Rather than bothering to learn how grammars worked—that is, how words were formed and their syntactical functions changed—he only identified lexical similarities and attributed them to a shared etymology. Open conflict erupted between him and Petrie, who exposed the speciousness of Betham's etymological method, which soon became the subject of international ridicule by Bishop Nicholas Wiseman.[155] Betham's theories damaged the reputation of Irish antiquarian study abroad, although by the 1840s Petrie was beginning to be recognised as the authority and gaining a European reputation.[156] He remained studiously apolitical, however.

The key figure linking the new scientific scholarship to the political causes of the 1840s was John O'Donovan. He was born to a humble Kilkenny farming family in 1809. Importantly, his father's side had arrived in Ireland during the Cromwellian settlement, while his mother was of native Irish Catholic stock; O'Donovan was acutely aware of his mixed background, and was raised a Catholic, though he was sceptical of the Catholic establishment and those he considered overzealous—he eventually described his brother-in-law Eugene O'Curry this way. His Catholicism notwithstanding, O'Donovan received a good education in Dublin and eventually trained as a lawyer at Lincoln's Inn, but he was an obsessive Irish scholar. He referred to himself as an antiquary and his interests as Irish antiquities, but he was what we would think of as a textual philologist, and he became increasingly interested in comparative philology in the 1850s, especially after his encounter with Zeuß's *Grammatica Celtica*; in other words, his interests changed somewhat from the content of Irish language sources to the Irish language's history and relationships with other languages.

O'Donovan made his name working on the Ordnance Survey, for which he was the man on the road, travelling to every Irish county and recording topographical and ethnographical data from 1834 to 1841. He was scathing about the errors made by eighteenth-century predecessors like Vallancey. His main contribution to the development of Celtic studies was the *Grammar of the Irish Language*, published in 1845, which returned to long-standing questions, such as the origin of writing in Ireland, with a newly critical eye. In this work O'Donovan brought insights from the new comparative philology; for example, in a brief section on the Celtic language family, O'Donovan repeated the observation made by Lhwyd and others that Welsh and Irish had similar vocabularies independent of Latin, Danish, or English influence, but also that

Welsh and Irish had similar grammatical constructions and phonological shifts, referring the reader to Prichard's *Eastern Origin* for further examples.[157] O'Donovan's grammar featured in Zeuß's bibliography and it was surely because of it that Jakob Grimm wrote to O'Donovan in 1856 to notify him that he had been elected a corresponding member of the Berlin Academy on the basis of his study of, among other things, the Celtic languages.[158]

Deeply interested in Irish history, nationalists followed the developments in Irish scholarship, especially those associated with the Young Ireland movement. A derisive epithet given to a group of young nationalists in 1843, but which they eventually embraced, 'Young Ireland' emerged as a subset of the Repeal Association, but it became a splinter group after Daniel O'Connell tried to force all members to disavow violence in 1846. The focal point of the group was *The Nation*, a popular weekly newspaper, founded in Dublin in October 1842 by Thomas Davis (1814–1845), Charles Gavan Duffy (1816–1903), and John Blake Dillon (1814–1866). Although most Young Irelanders were youthful, well-educated Catholics, Davis was a Protestant and the early driver of the group's ideology. After his premature death in 1845 and Young Ireland's break with O'Connell, some of them mounted a spectacularly unsuccessful uprising in 1848, after which the group was proscribed and its leaders eventually exiled.

Young Ireland has traditionally been presented as Ireland's Romantic nationalist movement *par excellence*, and scholars have emphasised how its members were well read in contemporary European literature and history. According to James Quinn, history was seen above all as a moralising force for educating and improving the Irish nation.[159] Yet even though Young Ireland's approach to Irish history was direct and didactic, valuing vivacity and examples of heroism for instrumental purposes, its leaders appreciated the scientific antiquarianism of Petrie, O'Donovan, et al. and were careful to court their approval.[160]

There were clear links between Irish scholars and Young Irelanders, and a marked interest in Irish history and culture as a result. James Clarence Mangan had worked for the Ordnance Survey in the 1830s and during the 1840s published poetry in *The Nation*, both his own and translations from German. Davis and William Elliot Hudson (1796–1853) took Irish with John O'Donovan in 1845, and Davis was a consistent supporter of the language as a key component of Irish nationality, as was William Smith O'Brien (1803–1864), leader of the 1848 uprising. O'Donovan was connected to other members of the group, and he appreciated *The Nation* both because it supported Irish scholarship and because it aimed to represent Ireland rather than any political party.[161]

The Nation is saturated with references to the Celts, conquest, and oppression, and the movement's leaders wrote about their own Celticity. Charles Gavan Duffy conceived of the Irish situation in racial terms in his youth, claiming in his memoirs that he had 'burned with the desire to set up again the Celtic race and the Catholic church'.[162] Since he was the son of a Welsh surgeon in the British Army, Celticity was a particularly useful and important identity for Thomas Davis. Friends were aware of his British origins, and John O'Donovan wrote that he was amused to see his name mistakenly given at one point as 'O'Davis' because he was 'Cymbric and of Alcu[i]th [*sic*—that is, descended of Strathclyde Britons], not Gaelic'.[163] Signing off his early columns as 'The Celt' allowed Davis to claim shared descent, however distant, with the Gaelic Irish.[164] In an article on 'Our National Language' in *The Nation*, Davis used Celticity to fold in the various waves of invasions Ireland had experienced from Britain; adding the 'Celtic Scots' and the 'Celtic Welsh'—who colonised Ireland after the Norman Invasion—to the native Irish Celtic population rendered Ireland 'probably five-sixths' Celtic.[165] Given the relatively recent unimportance of the 'Celtic' past in Ireland, it is a little ironic that *The Nation* thought only the Irish 'seem destined to reproduce on earth a solitary Celtic nationalism . . . the sole inheritance of that people which once covered western Europe, their literature, their poesy, their passion'.

In the following chapter it will be shown that 'Celtic' rhetoric increased in the British and Irish press in 1843, together with assumptions of irreconcilable racial differences between Celt and Saxon. In the exceedingly sharp Irish historical memory, 'race'—standing in for national, religious, cultural, and linguistic differences—was obviously a vexed question, yet as Quinn has emphasised, Davis and the others realised the need to make clear that within Ireland, race had to be subordinated to common nationality. Thomas Davis's poem 'Celts and Saxons' highlights the difference:

We hate the Saxon and the Dane,
  We hate the Norman men–
We cursed their greed for blood and gain,
  We curse them now again.
Yet start not, Irish born man,
  If you're to Ireland true,
We heed not blood, nor creed, nor clan–
  We have no curse for you.[166]

The poem very clearly acknowledges historically rooted conflicts—race and religion are not mentioned but would not need to be spelled out for the audience—which are nevertheless subsumed under an inclusive Irishness.[167] Davis added a note to disavow 'the assumed hostility of Irish Celts to the *Irish* Saxons'.[168] 'Irish nationality', he wrote in an essay on 'Irish ballad poetry', 'must contain and represent the races of Ireland. It must not be Celtic, it must not be Saxon—it must be Irish'.[169] John O'Donovan was one who appreciated the mediation, writing to a correspondent in 1845 that he thought 'the Nation Newspaper has done more to enlighten and liberalize the Irish of all parties, than any Journal ever published'.[170]

It was not to last. After Davis's death in 1845 the group radicalised and splintered. O'Donovan worried in May 1848 that the failure of the potato, the political situation, and 'fear of [John Mitchel]' threatened Irish scholarship, and in July he again wrote that, 'Politics run too high . . . and the non-amalgamation of races has prevented all Irish nationality. The theories about Celts and Teutons have also done harm'.[171] He blamed the Young Irelanders, among others Lalor and Gavan Duffy, but thought the only one capable of leading an uprising was Smith O'Brien. About two weeks later the disastrous uprising quickly came and went. Middle-class Romantic nationalists were scared off. William Elliot Hudson, to take an example, a contributor to *The Nation* and a financial patron to various groups in its orbit, said that Smith O'Brien had 'acted as a lunatic', and considered emigrating.[172] However, even with the exile of the uprising's leaders, *The Nation* continued to be published until its suppression in 1855. An Irishman from North America, Thomas d'Arcy McGee (1825–1868), who had used the pseudonym 'Celt' in his American publications, kept up a steady flow of articles glorifying the Celtic history of Ireland.

While the uprising might have failed, linguistic patriotism bolstered by the popular Celticism of Young Ireland strengthened. Irish finally became a university subject when Celtic positions were endowed at the new Queen's Colleges in 1849. John O'Donovan was appointed to the Belfast lectureship in August 1849,[173] while Eugene O'Curry took the chair of Irish archaeology and history at Newman's Catholic University in Dublin in 1854. These positions were little more than tokenistic in the end—in 1850 O'Donovan had one student—but they symbolise a new acknowledgment of the importance of the Irish language beyond its cultural significance.[174] The Belfast antiquary Robert MacAdam (1808–1895) recognised an increasing interest in such subjects, and encouraged O'Donovan to publish his lectures and asked him whether he was interested in 'starting a periodical connected with Celtic subjects'.[175] He did so himself with the *Ulster Journal of Archaeology* in 1852, which printed O'Donovan's reviews of Zeuß.

The main scholars also participated in the various antiquarian societies—the Irish Archaeological Society (f. 1840); the Celtic Society (f. 1845), which merged in 1854; and the Ossianic Society (f. 1853)—whose primary purpose was the publication of Irish historical manuscripts and materials.[176] Scholars, politicians, unionists, nationalists, Catholics, and Protestants were all involved, but interpretations occasionally split along sectarian and geographical lines.[177] Already there were concerns about German involvement with Irish materials, and in 1858 the poet Nicholas O'Kearney (1800–1865) wrote anxiously to Smith O'Brien that foreign scholars would get the wrong idea of Irish if scribal errors were not ironed out of their manuscripts in new editions. O'Kearney imagined this hypothetical scholar would say:

> those Irish Celts after all that has been said and written to the contrary, had no learning—here is a specimen of their barbarous poetry. We must look amongst the Welsh, Scotch, or native of Man for the real Celtic tongue, if it had been ever spoken in its purity in the Western Islands![178]

Smith O'Brien himself submitted his Gaelic translations to the highest authority in the land, Eugene O'Curry.[179]

O'Curry was from even humbler circumstances than his brother-in-law John O'Donovan. Born in County Clare, he had little formal education, but his father was an amateur Gaelic scholar and manuscript collector at the centre of a small circle of historical and cultural enthusiasts. He worked as a sort of itinerant tutor, smuggled tobacco, and tried to emigrate to America before setting up a shop in Limerick.[180] After debt imprisonment he found work in 'a lunatic asylum', where he was working when John O'Donovan came across him and arranged his job for the Ordnance Survey between 1835 and 1842. O'Curry was a more overt nationalist than O'Donovan, and had been courted by agrarian agitators, the Rockites and Terry Alts, while he lived in Limerick. It was well known that their relationship was strained and ultimately irreparable, as a result of their work on the Brehon laws, but already in 1853 O'Donovan wrote (somewhat affectionately) that his brother-in-law hated to be corrected and had to be treated 'like a big spoilt child'.[181]

As professor at the Catholic University, O'Curry delivered *Lectures on the Manuscript Materials of Ancient Irish History* (1861) and *Lectures on the Manners and Customs of the Ancient Irish* (1873), which together laid the foundation for serious historical study of ancient Ireland based on source material. O'Curry was apparently a more natural Irish philologist than O'Donovan, but he was ignorant of linguistic matters; O'Donovan tried to teach him Latin but 'he could not submit to the drudgery of it'.[182] O'Curry himself wrote that he 'never thought of having any thing to do with etymology or comparison with other languages'.[183] He also apparently hated R. T. Siegfried, the German representative of the new philology at Trinity College.[184] So while his works possessed a wealth of information on Irish sources and history, they were somewhat insular—Rudolf Thurneysen (1857–1940) later introduced them to his students as 'ganz unkritisch'.[185] Perhaps sensing these shortcomings, William K. Sullivan, a former Young Irelander, ensured that O'Curry's *Lectures on the Manners and Customs of the Ancient Irish* were presented within a scaffolding of the best scientific scholarship of the time. His one-volume introduction to O'Curry's work explained the revolutions in geology and archaeology that had recently occurred, and how a scientific examination of the Irish sources would provide a unique window onto the Aryan race and the early history of Europe, assisted by the development of sciences such as comparative philology and ethnology. It is probably the first major attempt to bridge the worlds of Irish and European scholarship, synthesising the Irish material within the master narrative developing for the early history of Europe and its nations.

The rhetoric of Celticism strengthened in Ireland as the nineteenth century wore on. Scholars cleared the ground in the 1830s for the triumph of a Celtic origin story, which acquired a political hue in the 1840s as politics and history became racialised. John O'Donovan, who in 1848 wrote of the harm done by 'theories about Celts and Teutons', dedicated his life to empirical Irish scholarship, and his gravestone explicitly mentions his contribution to 'Celtic Studies'.[186] Similarly, shortly before his death in 1866, Petrie wrote that, although he was of 'an Anglo-Norman descent, and an Irish [*sic*] only by accident of birth', he nevertheless sought 'the ultimate removal of hostile prejudices against that Celtic race'.[187] Both O'Donovan and O'Curry were nationally minded, and in 1861, just before they both died, Jeremiah O'Donovan Rossa (1831–1915)—who discussed O'Donovan genealogies with his namesake and lamented the historical damage done by the 'Saxon engines of Celtic destruction'[188]—told O'Curry that he hoped 'you will both live long, at least long enough to see yourselves laboring in our ancient National literature for a National Government'. Scholarship was thus seen as connected even to the most advanced nationalist politics of the time.[189] It was well-known that O'Donovan and O'Curry fell out, and interested onlookers queried whether their rivalry had stymied Celtic studies in Ireland. Henri Gaidoz wrote to Pictet about it with obvious amusement—'O'Curry et O'Donovan etaient beau-frères; mais c'étaient les beau-frères Ennemis!'—seemingly implying that the Irish were more prone to petty jealousies than most.[190] But whatever their differences, together O'Donovan and O'Curry more than anyone else placed Celtic scholarship on a new critical footing in Ireland, and their deaths in quick succession were 'almost a fatal blow to the progress of Celtic Studies' in Ireland, according to John T. Gilbert (1829–1898).[191]

Ernest Renan and 'La Poésie des races celtiques'

The era of Romantic nationalism witnessed the gradual rise of a Breton consciousness, one that would become separatist and violent in the twentieth century.[192] For reasons discussed in Part III of this book, Breton national consciousness was from the early nineteenth century firmly pan-Celtic in outlook. Therefore, while his 'Bretonisme' was perfectly compatible with his French patriotism, Ernest Renan made an important contribution to both, as well as nascent pan-Celticism, when he first considered Celtic literary culture collectively in his 'La Poésie des races celtiques' (1854). He also reoriented the focus to the present and to the effect that the Celtic sense of place had on the literature of the Celtic peoples. Evident too are some of the most recognisably 'Romantic' elements of the package of modern Celtic ideas, and because of Renan's European popularity some of these became canon, above all the portrayal of the Celts as a feminine, antimodern race. It will therefore be necessary to carefully parse the essay in order to pinpoint the inception of certain ideas.

Born in Tréguier in 1823, Renan confided to his diary that he was 'Born a Romantic . . . I only need my soul, something that pushes me to the brink of the abyss'.[193] Renan's idea of his Romantic soul was intertwined with his Breton upbringing,[194] upon which he often reflected throughout his life. Initially deciding to take holy orders, he studied at the seminary of St. Sulpice in Paris before a crisis of faith inspired him to pursue an academic philological career instead, and he eventually became professor at the *Collège de France*. In Paris Renan mixed with a number of young Bretons, among them Alphonse de Lamartine (1790–1869) and Theodore Hersart, Comte de le Villemarqué (1815–1895).[195]

'La Poésie des races celtiques' was first published in the *Revue des deux mondes* as a review essay of La Villemarqué's *Barzaz Breiz* (1839), Lady Charlotte Guest's *Mabinogion*, and John Williams's *The Ecclesiastical Antiquities of the Cymry* (1844).[196] Renan's essay is above all a plea for recognition of Celtic brilliance as an ancient, united race still loyal to its unique genius, language, memories, and *mœurs*. He feared Celtic extinction in the face of 'the increasing tumult of uniform civilisation'.[197]

Renan is generally credited as one of the first to treat the Celts and their literature holistically; he argued that the Celtic peoples had a unique history, demonstrated through their literature, which attested to the existence of a particular Celtic conscience.[198] This conscience had remained intact through the vagaries of time and helped to explain why all the Celts still existed as an anachronistic anomaly on the edge of Europe. This difference could be physically experienced in the ethereal changes a traveller perceived passing into Celtic lands:

> A cold, turbulent wind full of sadness rises and carries the soul towards other thoughts. . . . It is said that the same contrast is noticeable when one travels from England to Wales, from the lowlands of Scotland, which are English in language and custom, to the Gaelic Highlands, and also, but with a noticeably different nuance, when one travels deep into the parts of Ireland where the race has stayed pure, free from foreign mixture.[199]

The result of physical separation was a race of people isolated from the rest of Europe by virtue of its distinct history, culture, and values, as well as its unmixed blood: 'If racial excellence were judged by the purity of blood, by an unshakeable character, it must be said that none could challenge the nobility of the remaining descendants of the celtic race'.[200]

Renan argued that Celts knew themselves to be distinct and maligned, but that a feeling that the race's salvation was not long in coming—a 'messianisme celtique'—permeated the Celtic mind.[201] He linked the idea of Celtic salvation in Brittany and Ireland to the race's intuitive piety: whereas Christianity had homogenised most areas of Europe, no other race had kept its national characteristics—notably its almost pantheistic connection to nature—so intact and blended them so well with the Christian religion.[202] Where Christianity had elsewhere been destructive, it was edifying in Ireland and Brittany, where Christian themes became grafted onto Celtic mythology, the two becoming symbiotic. There was no mention of Druidism, or the works of Reynaud or Martin, though they had each made similar points lauding the spirituality inherent in the Celtic population, and we saw in earlier chapters how various thinkers had stressed an easy transition from Druidism to Christianity in late antiquity.

Perhaps the most famous strand of thought to emerge from Renan's essay was the 'femininity' of the Celts. As we saw above, Michelet described the Celts as a barbarous, virile, warrior race, which should guard against any trans-temporal idea of Celtic femininity.[203] It seems the idea began with Renan:

> If it were allowed to assign a gender to nations as it is to individuals, it would have to be said that the celtic race, especially when considering the Breton or Welsh branches, is essentially a feminine race. . . . No other has conceived of the ideal of the woman with such delicacy, nor has been more dominated by her. It is a sort of drunkenness, madness, dizziness.[204]

It is seldom possible to point to one thinker as the sole progenitor of an idea, but this seems to be such an occasion. I have found no explicit treatment of the Celts as feminine in any work before Renan's. But here it began in earnest. Renan vividly described the pages of Celtic literature as 'damp, so to speak, with feminine sentiment'.[205] Although Renan favourably cited the translation of the Welsh triads in Iolo's *Myvyrian Archaiology*, the accurate rendering of the feminine sentiment in them required 'the quill of a woman', which made Lady Charlotte Guest's *Mabinogion* 'the pearl of Welsh literature'.[206] The Celtic idealisation of women was also responsible for chivalry, the moral foundations of which were neither classical nor Germanic, but Celtic.[207] This idea of the 'feminine Celt' remained a consistent theme throughout Renan's life and œuvre; the question must be how the two came together in his mind.

Renan's ideas of Christianity were inextricably tied up with his ideas on femininity and race. Robert Priest has shown how Renan's profoundly controversial *Vie de Jésus* (1863) presented a Romantic, feminine Jesus, which derived from Renan's ideas of the religiosity of women garnered from his Breton upbringing.[208] He dedicated the work to 'the pure soul of my sister Henriette'.[209] Renan's Celtic ideas must be considered in the same context, where he thought his Breton childhood gave him special insight into the Celtic race. In 'La Poésie' he described the Celts as 'a domestic race par excellence, formed for the family and the joys of the foyer. . . . Every social institution of the Celtic races was nothing in the end but an extension of the family'.[210] In his early letters, Brittany and his mother were nearly always linked. Reflecting upon his departure for a Breton seminary, Renan regretted having to leave 'my mother, my Brittany, my gilded life';[211] and when he dropped out of the seminary and left for Paris, he lamented: 'Poor mother! . . . and me, my dear friend, do you not think it is as painful to have to say an eternal goodbye to my Brittany!'[212] For Renan Celtic ideas were underpinned by a femininity linked to the religiosity and familial feeling in his Breton childhood. In the last year of his life, he sounded a similar note in an essay reflecting on his sister's piousness and Breton upbringing, where he inserted a brief aside about chastity being a Celtic, rather than Anglo-Saxon, characteristic.[213] Taking all this together, it seems that the feminisation of the Celt has less to do with Romanticism and more to do with the idiosyncrasies of Renan's upbringing and ideas of Breton piety and traditionalism.

Following his reading of Renan, Matthew Arnold introduced the feminisation of the Celts into Victorian culture with his lectures on Celtic literature (Renan's essay was not translated until 1896). Before Renan and his interlocutor Arnold, there was nothing inherently feminine about the Celts or their poetry, but afterwards it became a common trope. This is despite the fact that the word 'feminine' is only mentioned in Arnold's 181-page essay three times, and is confined to a single paragraph.

Though Renan had initially and reluctantly condemned the Celts to extinction, at the end of the essay he offered a glimmer of hope, perhaps inspired by all of the positive Celtic qualities he had described. After all, 'Germany, who began with science and criticism, has finished by poetry; why cannot the Celtic races, which began with poetry, finish by criticism?' In other words, perhaps each nation was destined to follow its own arc of development, rather than facing a homogeneous future of modern European civilization. Renan finished by pointing to the recent rise of individual nationalities—the flowering of Romantic nationalism—as evidence that, rather than being subsumed under modernity, the Celts might yet preserve their unique genius.[214]

Celtic Art and Archaeology

Archaeology emerged as a discipline separate from its broader antiquarian origins in the middle of the nineteenth century,[215] when the examination of its discoveries helped to consolidate Celtic national identities in the countries examined in previous sections. Perhaps more important than the societies, journals, and university chairs that signalled the professionalisation of the subject was the formulation of a new conceptual system for arranging prehistoric materials. The 'Three Age' theory—Stone, Bronze, Iron—was devised in Denmark and Sweden in the 1830s, and then became employed across Europe in fits and starts over the next few decades.[216] Its chief merit was to provide a rough chronology for prehistory where none had hitherto existed, but opinion differed about whether a particular ancient people could be correlated directly with the use of a specific material. In other words, where stone, bronze, and iron objects were all discovered in one location, did this show that a people wielding iron weapons had conquered earlier inhabitants who used bronze weapons, and so on; or, were these three types of materials evidence that a culture had evolved and developed better metallurgy over a long period of time, and probably through interaction with neighbouring peoples?[217] Played out across Europe, this debate bore directly on the Celtic question. The consideration of surviving physical remains had of course long been an important part of investigating the Celts (see chapter 3), but there were several developments in the 1840s and 50s that can together be seen as the beginning of 'modern' Celtic archaeology, which placed artistic styles front and centre.[218] Given the twentieth-century dominance of archaeology in interpretations of ancient Celtic culture, the origins of this approach are surprisingly murky, but in the middle decades of the nineteenth century a number of scholars agreed that there was a distinctive style of Celtic art, most likely dating to the late Iron Age and stretching from Ireland to Austria.

One of the first programmatic statements about Celtic art was uttered in 1846, when Samuel Birch (1813–1885) posed the question 'whether the art-remains of the Celts are sufficient to enable us to fix the position which that people occupied in the scale of nations'.[219] Surveying the wealth of material he had at his fingertips as an assistant at the British Museum, Birch pointed to torques as evidence of a distinctive Celtic style. Rather than trying to trace ancient migrations through slippery linguistic evidence, and incomplete and perhaps unreliable ancient historical testimony, Birch showed that scholars might do better to build their picture of the ancient Celts empirically through surveying physical remains. One major additional benefit of this approach was that archaeological evidence allowed scholars to assess the civilizational refinement, wealth, and general prosperity of now vanished cultures. Nevertheless, despite the beauty of the torques, their relative simplicity led Birch to conclude they were the 'productions of a rude, simple, and unartistic people, and are evidence of their intellectual inferiority to the other great nations of antiquity'.[220] Obsessed instead with Egyptology, Birch left further exploration of Celtic art to others, who held more favourable views of Celtic civilization.

These views were propounded in volume by archaeologists in Central Europe, themselves increasingly under the spell of Romantic nationalism.[221] Anglophone scholarship has remained almost completely ignorant of the history of Celtic archaeology in Germany, Switzerland, and Austria, but as we will see this was the key context for what became the Celtic art theory. There are a few points of interest to be discussed, but for this story the most important figure was Ferdinand Keller (1800–1881), a professor of English at the Technical Institute in Zurich. After studying theology and natural science there and in Paris, Keller had worked for several years as a tutor in England, where he visited Stonehenge, before returning to Switzerland and founding the *Gesellschaft für vaterländische Alterthümer* in Zürich in 1832.[222] Keller was interested in burial mounds, and one of his first published investigations concerned some graves near Zürich, which in 1837 he argued were likely Celtic, both because they did not seem German or Roman, and because the beauty of the site seemed consonant with Druidic locations in England and France.[223] This is a slightly bigger step than it might seem, for the lack of written ancient sources meant that Switzerland's prehistory before the Helvetians—probably but not certainly a Gaulish tribe—was unknown.

Keller's work slotted into the ongoing *Keltenfrage* in Southern Germany (see chapter 6), where the borders with France and Switzerland made the issue more fraught.[224] In 1838 he became friends with a German philosopher from Freiburg, Heinrich Schreiber (1793–1872), an early archaeologist and 'Celtomaniac',[225] who already in 1826 had attributed ancient gravesites around Freiburg to a 'Celtic origin', and extended this interpretation further in 1839 with his study of 'Celtic Graves on the Upper Rhein'.[226] Schreiber and Keller buoyed one another against their opponents, such as the Germans Karl Wilhelmi (1786–1857) and the Lindenschmit brothers, Ludwig (1809–1903) and Wilhelm (1806–1848), who wondered how anyone could celebrate the pederastic and incestuous Celts.[227] Although his published work was sober and restrained, the tone of Keller's private letters to Schreiber matched the allegations of Lindenschmit. In June 1842 he mocked the 'Celteater' (*Keltenfresser*) Karl Wilhelmi and jokingly asked the next month if he and the other 'Germanomaniacs' (*Germanomanen*) should not be 'shot to death'.[228] This came at a particularly tense time, as Schreiber published a work on ancient battle axes (*Streitkeile*)—which he called 'Celtic national weapons' (*keltische Nationalwaffen*)—that painted the iron-wielding Celts as far more civilized than the stone-wielding Germans. The Celts, wrote Schreiber, could be traced through the implements: 'The historic geography of the Celtic people in Europe is the same as that of the iron battle-axe and vice versa'.[229] Given these implements were found across Europe and in Britain and Ireland, Schreiber's theory had implications far beyond his local German context.

However, there were Swiss opponents too, the most steadfast of whom was the Francophone Swiss preacher Frédéric Troyon (1815–1866).[230] Troyon had excavated the gravesite at Bel-Air in Cheseaux and, supported by Keller, had initially preferred his Celtic hypothesis. However, in 1842 Troyon began to suspect instead that these sites were in fact medieval Burgundian remains. Three years travelling around Germany and Scandinavia and meeting leading German scholars fortified this belief. It was the famous historian Leopold von Ranke (1795–1886) who encouraged Troyon to publish his Germanic theory in the *Allgemeine Zeitschrift für Geschichte*.[231] In it, Troyon complained about the tendency in Switzerland and Germany, among other places, to attribute all ancient non-Roman gravesites to the Celts, since the Germans were supposedly inured to stone. According to Troyon, on the other hand, such ancient gravesites in Switzerland, Southern Germany, and Eastern France were Burgundian, Alemannian, and Frankish; in other words, they were medieval Germanic and not ancient Celtic.[232]

Soon afterwards, in November 1846, Johann Georg Ramsauer (1796–1874) came upon a few skeletons in the course of his duties as 'Mountain Master' of the Hallstatt salt mines in Austria.[233] The oncoming winter precluded further work, but Ramsauer began excavating again in May 1847, and by the time he stopped in 1863 his team had uncovered almost a thousand burials. Ramsauer was an engineer and not a scholar, so it was left to others to introduce the findings to the learned world. The first large report came from the antiquarian Joseph Gaisberger (1792–1871), who assumed they were Celtic, and likely part of the ancient Celtic kingdom of Noricum. Gaisberger relied on a work by Matthias Koch (1798–1877), who had argued in 1845 that finds in Fridolfing, Bavaria, were the remains of a Celtic tribe defending their lands, and particularly their lucrative salt mines, from invading Germans.[234] An official in the Habsburg administration and an Austrian patriot, Koch rooted Austria, Tyrol, and the Southern German lands in the ancient Celtic kingdom of Noricum, and—relying on Schreiber's work—had innovatively argued in the leading German paper, the *Allgemeine Zeitung*, that the gravesites in question were Celtic because they bore similarities to finds across Europe and as far away as Scotland, Wales, and Ireland.[235] Gaisberger cited Koch's work, as well as that of Keller and Schreiber, in his argument that the ancient Hallstatt society was Celtic. He offered three reasons: First, the Hallstatt finds seemed to be in line with classical descriptions of Celtic culture; second, they corresponded not only in 'material' but in 'form' to other Celtic archaeological discoveries, such as those written about by Koch and Keller; and finally, the 'Ornamentation' of many of the objects seemed 'genuinely Celtic'.[236] Hallstatt thus slotted firmly into the Celtic interpretation of the origins of Central Europe, and the finds became a popular sensation, bringing to the little town flocks of well-heeled tourists, including Emperor Franz Joseph I (1830–1916) in September 1855. The novelist Wilhelm Raabe (1831–1910) serialised a novel about Hallstatt entitled *Keltischen Knochen* (Celtic bones), in which two antiquarians try to steal bones in their escalating argument over whether the original inhabitants were Celts or Germans, thus bringing the *Keltenfrage* to a popular literary audience.

Returning to Switzerland and Ferdinand Keller, the most significant development in the formulation of the Celtic art theory came along Lake Zürich in the winter of 1853–1854. Fishermen had long complained that their hooks would often snag along the strange wooden pilings visible just below the surface of alpine lakes, and local antiquarians had investigated these from time to time when water levels dipped low enough. But during that particularly dry winter the water receded to the point where the wooden pilings could be systematically investigated. Keller did so and made them famous, quickly publishing an article that became the centrepiece of the Celtic art hypothesis, 'Die keltischen Pfahlbauten in den Schweizerseen' (The Celtic pile-dwellings in the Swiss Lakes).[237] Keller envisioned an ancient civilization where people lived along wooden platforms on the lake, which protected them from invaders, animal and human; unsurprisingly, given his decades-long support for the interpretation, he found the inhabitants of the pile-dwelling villages were 'most likely of Celtic origin.'[238] Surely, such dwellings were not limited to Switzerland, he argued, and would be found in all Celtic parts of ancient Europe.[239] This was the case in Ireland, where in 1857 William Wilde (1815–1876) drew attention to the crannogs as 'Celtic stockades', linking them to Keller's finds in Switzerland and thus firmly connecting 'the Celtic Irish' to the Continent.[240] The finds made a few years later on Lake Neuchâtel at La Tène in 1857 were the richest and largest collection, and eventually became incorporated into the Celtic art interpretation, but Keller's first article was the most important at the time and was widely cited. He continued to report on similar findings, and in 1866 his first six articles were synthesised, translated into English, and published as *The Lake Dwellings of Switzerland*, further bolstering the Celtic theory.

The Celtic origins of France were already well established when the Central European finds were made. Napoleon III (1808–1873) was himself deeply interested in France's Gaulish origins and archaeology, sponsoring several large projects in the 1850s and 60s. The most significant was the monumental *Commission de la topographie des Gaules*, founded in 1858 to survey 'national geography, history, and archaeology' before Charlemagne, and headed by Alexandre Bertrand (1820–1902).[241] Its major success came in 1861 when it located definitively Alésia, where Caesar defeated Vercingetorix. A few years later an article published as a letter to Ferdinand Keller announced to the world that the weapons of Alésia matched those found in the Swiss lakes and typified at La Tène, and were therefore of the same Celtic period.[242] An archaeological map of ancient Celtic Europe was taking shape.

The pile-dwelling civilization was discovered at an opportune political moment.[243] Switzerland's progress as a federal state had been stop-start, and a civil war in 1847 had given way to a new constitution in 1848. Could an origins myth based on the pile-dwelling peoples give a sense of historical stability and continuity to the new state? The question naturally became: Were the remains Celtic, Roman, Germanic, or remains of an even earlier people who had populated Europe such as the Iberians or Finns, or a combination of some of these? The dispute about ancient Swiss remains had been running since the 1830s, with Keller leading the Celtic position and mixing it with a patriotic celebration of the pile-dwellers as an early and advanced ancient civilization.[244] Yet questions of method complicated the discussion. Keller's rival Troyon argued that every material progression—from stone, to bronze, to iron—signalled the invasion of a new people; the Celts had arrived with bronze weapons, he suggested, and then been pushed out by iron-wielding Germans.[245] Keller defended his Celtic interpretation and responded astutely that one could not correlate a material culture exclusively with one people in this way; instead, a single people had probably lived along the lakes and developed their own new technologies or learned them through trade with other peoples.[246] Other archaeologists were more circumspect. Based on the similarities between the La Tène weapons and those found by Napoleon III's excavations at Alésia, Édouard Desor (1811–1882) believed the Iron Age Helvetic inhabitants were Gauls, who probably invaded but came to exist peacefully alongside the Bronze and Stone-using inhabitants about whose origins he would not speculate; he wanted the reader to note that he had 'carefully avoided' using the nebulous 'nom de Celtes' throughout his book.[247] In the following year Troyon argued against the use of the word 'Celt' at all, claiming it was a vague term deployed by everyone but was really a 'nonsense'.[248] Troyon's position is complicated because his determination that the gravesite he uncovered at Bel-Air was medieval turned out to be correct; however, as Keller noted, his model for material shifts primarily through invasions was too simplistic. In any case, Troyon died in 1866 and the *Keltenfrage* rumbled on in Central Europe through the end of the century.

While the 'Celtic art' theory has normally been identified as of British origin, it seems evident that it was really developed in the German-speaking lands of Central Europe. Its popularisation is usually attributed to John Mitchell Kemble (1807–1857), somewhat ironically because he was Victorian Britain's greatest Anglo-Saxonist. A student of Grimm and first and foremost a philologist, Kemble had become increasingly interested in archaeology and was invited in the mid-1850s to curate exhibitions and deliver lectures on the subject. In what turned out to be the last lecture he ever gave, in 1857 to the Royal Irish Academy in Dublin, Kemble identified

> a peculiar development of the double spiral line . . . which is essentially characteristic, not only of the Scoto-Keltic, but the Britanno-Keltic populations of these islands . . . a form of beauty which belongs to no nation but our own, and to no portion of our nation but the Keltic portion.[249]

This style had existed before the Romans came and long after they left, and it was, Kemble argued, indigenous to Britain and Ireland. It was found not only on swords and other metals but also in illuminated manuscripts, 'which is familiar to you in the "Book of Kells" . . . and in the equally beautiful records of Scoto-Keltic self-devotion and culture in the MSS. Of St. Gall, in Switzerland'.[250] In revising Kemble's notes for publication, the Keeper of Antiquities at the British Museum, Augustus Wollaston Franks (1826–1897), decided to term this 'very remarkable class of antiquities . . . Late Celtic'.[251] Importantly, where Kemble thought this style indigenous and confined to Britain and Ireland, Franks—who had visited Switzerland in 1860—wrote that it was in these islands that the best examples were preserved, but still included objects of similar style found in the Swiss Lakes and elsewhere on the Continent in the 'Late Celtic' period, which he dated to about two hundred years before Christ.[252] Franks's theory was grist to the continental Celtic proponents, and Ferdinand Keller himself applauded his theory in his sixth report on the pile-dwellings.[253]

Although Desor had apparently suggested something along similar lines in the 1860s, in 1874 the Swedish archaeologist Hans Hildebrand (1842–1913) identified Hallstatt as the type-site for the early Iron Age of Central Europe, and La Tène as a continuation of that culture and the type-site for the later Iron Age.[254] It was widely assumed not only that these were ancient Celtic settlements but that they were the original home of the Celts, an interpretation that remained robust for over a century and put German nationalists in an uncomfortable position. By the time we get to the French scholar Henri d'Arbois de Jubainville (1827–1910) in 1889, we find a conclusion at first sight unthinkable to prior French generations: 'the Celtic language and nation were formed at the centre of the country that is modern Germany', until the payoff that the Germans, fearing Celtic war prowess, had submitted to Celtic domination for a period that may have lasted longer than the Roman Empire.[255] Jubainville's proofs were linguistic, but in 1914 he was followed by the archaeologist Joseph Déchelette (1862–1914), who argued that the material culture of La Tène spread across Europe wherever the Celts took it. According to John Collis, this is the *urtext* for the coffee table books on the Celts, with the Celtic art hypothesis associated with La Tène at their core ever since. The end of that story is traced out in chapter 12.

Conclusion

The era of Romantic nationalism was a crucial period for the consolidation of Celtic national identities across Europe. Popular histories and literary works were often based upon the latest scientific standards, but these could also be used to connect 'Celtic' cultures conjecturally where precious little evidence existed. With the French linkage to Welsh medieval material, and the archaeological emphases of some Swiss, Austrian, and German scholars who traced connections to Ireland—connections which all had ulterior political motives—we can see how an image of an ancient Celtic Europe was created that is still visible in many accounts of the Celts today.

8

Race, History, and the Irish Question

POLITICS AND THE LIMITS OF ANTI-CELTIC RACISM

ON 31 JANUARY 1848, the Scottish phrenologist George Combe (1788–1858) warned the radical English MP Richard Cobden (1804–1865) about the perilous political situation in France. Phrenology—the 'science' of reading the skull for evidence of the animal, moral, and intellectual characters of individuals, nations, and races—was then extremely popular, and as the leading figure of the movement, Combe was Cobden's guru.[1] He had just returned from France, where, based on his phrenological analysis of the population, he feared the rise of a second Napoleon. The small Celtic brain of the French had overdeveloped propensities for combativeness, self-love, and the need for approbation, leaving its 'moral and intellectual organs resolutely deficient', and therefore vulnerable to demagoguery (Fig. 9). European political tensions posed little threat to Britain—where the larger, steadier Teutonic brain was calibrated to prefer political liberty—but by 'glorying over Waterloo, & over other victories', the English press threatened to drive the French 'Celtic brain to *madness*'.[2] Combe must have seemed like a prophet after the fall of King Louis Philippe (1773–1850) a month later and the rise of Louis Napoleon that ended in his *coup d'état* of 1851.

If conclusions like Combe's were often drawn about the French, they were even more frequently made about the Irish, and usually in harsher terms. Nineteenth-century racial logic made this almost inevitable, and the Celtic basis of both nations meant that political discussions of one often meant comparisons with the other.[3] Reflecting on the revolutions of 1848, for example, the

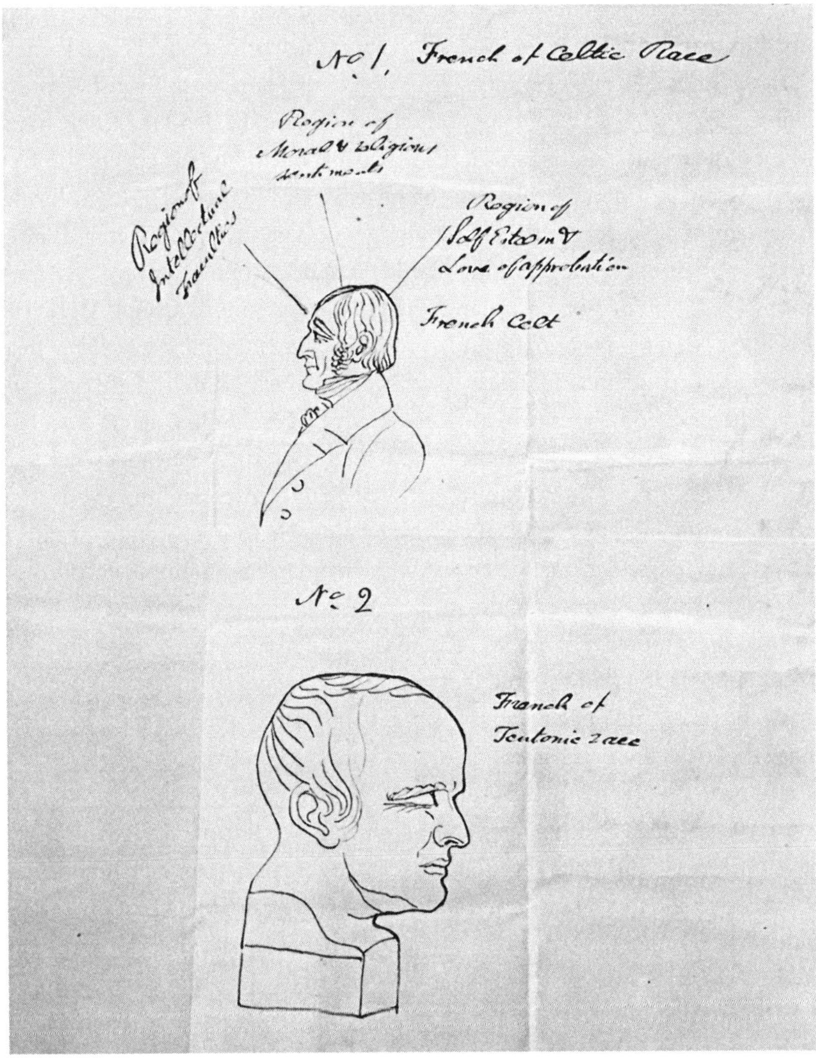

FIG. 9. British Library, Cobden Papers, Add. MS 43,660, f. 96. Reproduced with permission of the British Library.

Economist rejoiced in Britain's steady Saxonism and condemned 'the savage Celt on one side, and the flighty Gaul on the other. . . . The Frenchman is a civilised Celt. The Irishman a Barbaric Gaul'.[4] The leading French ethnologist William Edwards drew the same racial conclusion but in positive terms: 'Could there be a race more spiritual, more lively, more gay, loving glory and pleasure more, whose bearing is less constant; but in here describing the French, is it not obvious that what I have said applies equally to the Irish?'[5] Other liberal French authors had little trouble imputing Irish problems primarily to English oppression rather than racial deficiency. This allowed them to defend the Celtic basis of their own nation and to attack the English. Concluding his chapter on Ireland, Augustin Thierry wrote that the miseries and injustices of English rule had made of 'a pleasant and fertile country, with a naturally sociable and spiritual population, the most uninhabitable place in Europe'.[6] Gustave de Beaumont (1802–1866) toured Ireland with his more famous friend Alexis de Tocqueville (1805–1859) in the 1830s, producing a sociopolitical travelogue that immediately condemned English 'tyranny . . . conquest [and] . . . legal persecution'.[7] Ireland would be interesting 'especially to Frenchmen', as the Irish belonged 'to the same Celtic race, from which the Gauls, our ancestors, are descended'.[8] But for de Beaumont national character seemed the overriding consideration, and was little influenced by race. He took a strongly negative view of the Irish character, which was 'lazy, mendacious, intemperate, prompt to acts of violence'; however, the history of English misgovernment easily explained these moral deficiencies. According to de Beaumont, the pre-conquest Celtic population had suffered from none of the vices that now plagued the Irish character, and neither did the modern Scottish or French; thus, he sacrificed the Irish national character in order to mount a preemptive defence of the Celtic race (and therefore the French).[9]

In the previous two chapters, we examined how ideas of race led to the reclassification of the Celts through the sciences of comparative philology and ethnology, as well as how the racialisation of the Celts sharpened national identities through historical and literary works. This chapter takes a wider approach and surveys the ways in which the idea of the Celtic race functioned in mid-nineteenth-century intellectual discourse, paying special attention to political thought. While the Franco-Hibernian connection is the most prominent one drawn here, the other Celtic peoples were sometimes also sucked into the comparison. Even though they were less politically concerning, the Welsh and the Scottish Highlanders were occasionally discussed in such terms, as in a letter to the editor in the *Caledonian Mercury* complaining of the 'veritable sanscullo-terie of the Mountains' and their infection with the '*rabies Celtica*'.[10] While many such comparisons were drawn in England, this particular comment came from a Lowlander who identified as a 'Pure Saxon'.[11] Intranational tensions are therefore important to keep in mind in this chapter, as are prejudices held by those who themselves identified as 'Celts' against the other Celtic nations, especially Ireland. Racialisation cut many ways, but in British politics the Irish situation and its idiosyncrasies towered above everything else.

The 'Irish Question' dominated nineteenth-century British politics and was an important subject of discussion across Europe.[12] As such, it has shaped virtually all historical writing about Celticism during the Victorian era. Although Ireland had joined Britain in the Act of Union of 1800 that created the United Kingdom, its relationship with the larger island remained strained by the repression of Catholics, widespread peasant discontent, large-scale Irish immigration to Britain, and a general feeling of national subordination instead of equality within the Union. Led by Daniel O'Connell until his death in 1847, Irish politicians pursued their own solutions at Westminster, organising around two major successive causes: Catholic emancipation from the penal laws, achieved with the Catholic Relief Act of 1829, and then repeal of the Act of Union, which morphed into the cause of Home Rule around 1870.[13] Punctuated by periods of unrest and revolutionary activity, the Irish Question reached an early crescendo in 1886 with William Gladstone's (1809–1898) cataclysmic Home Rule proposal, which shattered friendships, networks, and the Liberal Party, and created a rupture that would stretch well into the twentieth century. Crowding around, and sometimes among, the politicians were the mass of 'public moralists' seeking to influence policy or public opinion.[14] This chapter is concerned with them and the ways in which they employed or interpreted Celtic ideas in light of the Irish Question. The breadth of the topic necessitates a selective use of evidence, but I have chosen influential figures and examples that reveal both the complexity of the debate and the dominant themes. My argument is that although a racialised image of 'the Celt' had ripened by about 1820 and was available for politicisation across Britain, Ireland, Europe, and North America, the Irish case was understood to be unique and, though often blended with anti-Celtic racial prejudice, could not be distilled from it.

This conclusion differs from the once-popular and controversial thesis of L. P. Curtis Jr, who in the late 1960s and early 1970s published two thorough studies documenting Victorian anti-Irish prejudice that have remained standard works.[15] In the suggestively titled *Anglo-Saxons and Celts* (1968), Curtis outlined what he called the 'Anglo-Saxonist' attitude, which he identified as an outlook conceived in terms of Germanic racial supremacy and Celtic racial inferiority. 'What really killed Home Rule in 1886 and 1904', according to Curtis, 'was the Anglo-Saxonist stereotype of the Irish Celt'.[16] Curtis viewed the racialised nineteenth-century worldview as a zero-sum game—'In England the idea of race as *the* determinant of human history and behavior held an unassailable position in the minds of most Anglo-Saxonists'[17]—instead of a complicated view of human history in which race played a role that was important if not paramount. Curtis's thesis has since been unpicked in all sorts of ways, most effectively by those pointing out that perspectives of class, religion, and culture were just as salient in British reactions to and depictions of the Irish.[18] There are many examples of these factors being linked to Celtic racial prejudice.

Of course, religion was a major sticking point, and Catholicism further linked the Irish and French while forming a breach between them and the other Celtic nations. In 1866 the *North Wales Chronicle* posed the question, 'Is "Fenianism" essentially Celtic?' The answer was emphatically negative: 'The Irishman, we repeat, is not a rebel because he is a Celt, but solely because he is a Papist'.[19] The religious argument forced British Catholics into peculiar positions. For example, Lord Acton (1834–1902) mixed racial essentialism with a civilizational argument, asserting the Celts could only reach a certain level of social development: 'the Celts are not among the progressive, initiative races'.[20] Here Acton lighted upon another common idea with deep roots, Irish barbarity. Whether racially determined or not, the purportedly low level of civilization in Ireland meant that the Irish were not ready for democracy, and therefore needed benevolent British governance. As George Combe argued, although the British were at fault for not better governing Ireland, the Irish were nevertheless 'not prepared for free institutions'.[21] Likewise, following a formative trip to Ireland, where he notoriously referred to the Irish as 'white chimpanzees', the novelist and Regius Professor of History at Cambridge, Charles Kingsley (1819–1875), declared to a correspondent his belief in the insurmountability of racial distinctions: 'the differences of race are so great, that certain races, e.g., the Irish Celts, seem quite unfit for self-government'.[22] Upon returning from a trip to England, the American critic Ralph Waldo Emerson (1803–1882) suggested that race determined both religious and democratic inclinations: 'Race avails much . . . that all Celts are Catholics, and all Saxons are Protestants; that Celts love unity of power, and Saxons the representative principle'. But Emerson also asserted that civilizational development could refine these natural tendencies.[23]

There were thus many variables at play in analyses of Ireland; however, my main objection to Curtis's argument is that it rolls all of the (very real and virulent) criticism of the Irish into a racial prejudice against the Celts more broadly. These are not the same thing. What we gained by a more focused picture on anti-Irish prejudice, we paid for with blurrier images of Victorian racism and Victorian attitudes to the Celts. There were many self-identified British Celts who considered the Irish to be uniquely troublesome, not because they were Celts but because they were Irish. Moreover, many of those who denigrated the Irish had a more benign view of the other Celtic populations in Britain and France. The peculiarities of Irish history and that country's relationship to Britain explain more than totalising views of race, religion, or class, though these are all of course significant factors in this case.[24] However, Curtis's work was pathbreaking and continues to be referenced because it struck at something real and important, so I am not beating a dead horse by directly challenging his approach to race, instead of further nuancing anti-Celtic racism within a wider range of factors (valid as this approach is and as fruitful as it has been).

This chapter takes a kaleidoscopic approach to views of the Celts in British, Irish, and European discourse. It surveys the attitudes towards the Irish, and the Celts more generally, from a range of thinkers, and revises our understanding of stock 'anti-Celtic' characters such as the historian and 'Celt-hater' Thomas Arnold, Thomas Carlyle (1795–1881), and to a lesser extent Thomas Babington Macaulay (1800–1859). Arnold is usually positioned at or near the beginning of the Victorian trend of 'Teutomania', or the idealisation of the Anglo-Saxons and their imputed legacy within Britain, which has often been presented as the flip side to anti-Celtic racism.[25] Scientists and scholars both contributed to this discourse, which Peter Mandler determines reached its peak in the 1860s.[26] However, as I show below, the increasingly positivistic study of human races—relying on measurements and statistics—helped lead to the view at this time that the British, the French, and even the Irish were hybrid peoples, and that dominant racial characteristics were difficult if not impossible to determine. It is in these contexts that Matthew Arnold made his intervention with his lectures 'On the Study of Celtic Literature' in 1865–1866, the most important text on popular Celtic subjects of the Victorian era. There was no one overriding view of the Celtic race, and the authors examined here modulated the impact which they attributed to race—whatever they determined that to mean—but when it came to Ireland, there was one causal explanation on which most people agreed, even if they differed greatly in their interpretation of it: history. As even the conservative *Globe* newspaper put it in 1841:

> Ireland is a Celtic island commanded by a Saxon island—a Catholic island commanded by a Protestant island. The inhabitants of Ireland consist of the descendants of those who robbed the native inhabitants of

eleven-twelfths of the land, and the descendants of those who suffered the robbery.[27]

If there was a perspective that could fold in race, religion, class, and culture, it was Ireland's unique historical experience, a fact recognised by most of the commentators whose views are examined in this chapter, and none better than Thomas Arnold and Thomas Babington Macaulay.

English Historiography, or, Was Thomas Arnold really a Celt-Hater?

Father of Matthew, famous headmaster of Rugby School, and briefly Regius Professor of Modern History at Oxford, Thomas Arnold has also been remembered as that 'Teuton of Teutons, the Celt-hating Dr. Arnold'.[28] Simply put, this frequently repeated line is a mischaracterisation that was made nearly thirty years after his death, and it has miscoloured perceptions of him ever since.[29] Of course, as he outlined in his famous inaugural lecture, Arnold believed that the Germanic invasions had changed the face of Europe and inaugurated the era of 'Modern History', and that these were the foundation of England and its constitution.[30] Yet, Arnold the Christian classicist obviously recognised the influence still retained by the structures of the ancient world on the modern, and his idealisation of England's Germanic roots did not entail a corresponding hatred of Celts. On the contrary, he lamented England's historical treatment of Ireland, supported Catholic emancipation, and granted the 'Keltic' races an important place in European history.[31]

Arnold wrote directly about the Irish Question in his pamphlet, *The Christian Duty of Granting the Claims of the Roman Catholics* (1829), in which he called for Catholic emancipation and participation in government. The long-term English failure to repair the injustices that arose from conquest made English governance 'a perpetual crime', in which his own generation was just as complicit for failing to palliate it.[32] There was absolutely no racial basis that condemned Irish Catholics to slavery and it was ludicrous for any Christian to adopt that stance because it was a fundamental principle of Christianity that mankind shared a common descent and were united by their sinful nature.[33] Therefore, 'no one race of mankind possesses except from accidental causes such a superiority over another', and England had failed to remedy that accident.[34]

Arnold directly addressed the nature and history of the Celtic race in later works and his correspondence. It is clear that he considered the Celts to be an advanced and important people in European history. In a letter to his friend Richard Whately (1787–1863), Anglican Archbishop of Dublin, on the topic of the process of civilization, Arnold wrote in 1835 that 'some races, e.g. the Keltic, the Teutonic, and the Hellenic . . . we cannot trace back to [a] savage state, nor does it appear that they were savages'.[35] Working on his Roman history, Arnold informed the same correspondent in 1836 that he 'would soon set to work at the Celtic languages', asking for 'a good Erse grammar' and contentedly expressing how 'beautifully does History branch out into all varieties of questions, and continually lead one into fresh fields of knowledge'.[36] This is not 'Celt-hating'.

In the first volume of his *History of Rome* (1838–1843), Arnold included a discussion of the Celtic races when he addressed the Gaulish sack of Rome in the fourth century BCE, bolstering his own formidable classical erudition with the modern scientific approaches of James Cowles Prichard and William Edwards for linguistic and physiological evidence. He praised Prichard's Celtic work and pointed to the kinship between the 'Keltic and Teutonic languages', and argued that the differences in manners and language must have been far less marked in ancient times 'when the Keltic and Teutonic tribes were intermixed with each other, within the limits of what is now Germany'.[37] Arnold had also read the 'clever pamphlet' of William Edwards, and appreciated his argument that the 'original inhabitants of all countries, such as the Celts in Britain, have been much less lost by subsequent conquests than is commonly supposed' (an idea already independently present in Arnold's pamphlet on Catholic emancipation).[38] As he stressed in his inaugural lecture, the Teutonic character was imprinted on the governments of the modern European nations, but for Arnold the European cultural inheritance was also Greek, Roman, Jewish, and 'Keltic'.

I have treated Arnold here because he is the most conspicuous example of someone who has had anti-Celtic racial views imputed to him—most famously by his own son—that do not square with the available evidence. His composite explanation of race, religion, civilization, and their expression through history, is symptomatic of much educated opinion about Ireland, and helps us to see the variables at play and how much more complex they were than simple racism. Though coming at the question from a different historiographical approach, Arnold's contemporary Thomas Babington Macaulay shows how easily a sustained historical consideration of the Irish Question undercut racial explanations while not shying away from the complex and considerable obstacles in the way of reconciliation.

The inception of 'Whig' historiography—the presentation of English history as the story of the progress and triumph of liberty as enshrined in the English Constitution[39]—signalled British historians' abandonment of the Enlightenment's universalist approach to the subject and the increasingly dominant conception of history writing as above all politically focused.[40] Macaulay led the way, considering the thirteenth century—that of Magna Carta—as the origin of the modern English nation and constitution.[41] Widely acknowledged as the greatest English history of the nineteenth century, the first volumes of Macaulay's *History of England* appeared in 1848 and expounded a powerful historical philosophy of national progress, wherein the Glorious Revolution of 1688 marked a major step towards the 1832 Reform Act, the apotheosis of Whiggism.[42] In this account, Scotland proved a shining beacon of progress and the rewards of historical conciliation. Ireland by contrast tripped things up, forcing Macaulay to frequently interrupt the narrative and explain the failure of Irish reconciliation, which has recently led some to miscast Macaulay as a Saxon supremacist.[43]

Macaulay used the comparison of Ireland and Scotland for instructive effect, focusing on differences of race, religion, and civilizational development. There is a Thierry-esque acknowledgment that racial animus arises from conquest, but equally a belief that this can be overcome, as had happened in England and Scotland.[44] The Scottish situation provided 'evidence sufficient to justify the belief that no natural inferiority had kept the Celt far behind the Saxon'.[45] Comparison of Ireland with the Scottish example actually shows how little racial essentialism mattered for Macaulay: 'The Anglosaxon and the Celt have been reconciled in Scotland, and have never been reconciled in Ireland. In Scotland all the great actions of both races are thrown into a common stock, and are considered as making up the glory which belongs to the whole country'.[46] For Macaulay, then, it was the historical fact of irreconciliation rather than the races themselves that was at the root of the Irish predicament. The historical problem of race ossified when religious differences became grafted onto the racial split during the Reformation: 'The new feud of Protestant and Papist inflamed the old feud of Saxon and Celt'.[47] Macaulay is endlessly quotable and digressed frequently on Irish differences, but if such disquisitions were couched in racial terms it is because race as a category of intellectual consideration was common to the point of banality in Victorian discourse, not because of a crude essentialism. For Macaulay, there existed clear variables conditioning the Irish situation, but when added together in the historical relationship between Ireland and Britain the sum was greater than its parts: history collectively embodied and animated all of the factors that set Ireland apart.

The Irish Question and the Social Question

Following Catholic Emancipation in 1829, the Irish Question gathered speed alongside one of the major issues in British politics: the condition of the working class in an industrial society, which formed a component of the wider European 'Social Question'. In the wake of the disappointing Great Reform Act of 1832 and the New Poor Law of 1834, popular discontent boiled over and led to the emergence of Chartism and its domination of working-class British politics in the 1830s and 40s. This was the same period during which Daniel O'Connell's Repeal movement took over Irish popular politics.[48] The plight of the English working poor was the starting point of Thomas Carlyle's famous and controversial commentary on the Irish Question in his 1840 pamphlet *Chartism*: the Irish were flooding into Britain and stealing English jobs by their willingness to work for starvation wages. All the Carlylean racist tropes are present in this work, in which the 'Celtiberian' Irish are presented as ape-like savages intrinsically inferior to the Saxon peasantry of England, yet Carlyle placed almost all of the blame on the English: 'England is guilty towards Ireland; and reaps at last, in full measure, the fruit of fifteen generations of wrong-doing'.[49] Desolated Ireland could not provide for the Irish peasant, who was now outcompeting the already destitute English worker, and therefore 'the Irish population must get itself redressed and saved, for the sake of the English if nothing else'.[50]

Carlyle used to be seen as one of the most prominent Celtophobic racists of the Victorian era, but in blaming centuries of English misrule for Irish problems Carlyle is really emblematic of the much larger range of European thinkers from across the political spectrum who saw history rather than race as the explanation for the existence of the Irish Question.[51] He certainly subscribed to a view of Saxon superiority, and thought there was a species of 'Celtic blockheads . . . who are *past* logic'.[52] Yet he also understood that the cause of Irish distress was infinitely more complex than their race.

Carlyle's treatment of the Irish looks almost mild in comparison with that of Friedrich Engels (1820–1895) a few years later. Throughout his *The Condition of the Working Class in England* (1845), Engels vividly and almost pitilessly depicted the utter deprivation of the Irish in England, recognizable by their Celtic physiognomy and language:

> The worst quarters of all the large towns are inhabited by Irishmen. Whenever a district is distinguished for especial filth and ruinousness, the explorer may safely count upon meeting chiefly those Celtic faces which one recognizes at the first glance as different from the Saxon physiognomy of the native. I have occasionally heard the Irish-Celtic language spoken in the most thickly populated parts of Manchester.[53]

Engels did discern a common racial core among the Celtic nations traceable in history, and one that seemed to account for a continuity in depictions of the Celts stretching from Caesar to the present:

> the Irish Celts and the Gallic Celts have originally resembled each other more than present-day Irishmen and Frenchmen. Therefore we should not be surprised to find in Caesar's description of the Gauls many features which are ascribed to the Irish by Giraldus some twelve hundred years later, and which, furthermore, are discernible in the Irish national character even today, in spite of the admixture of Germanic blood.[54]

However, in the draft chapters and material he collected for his 'History of Ireland', Engels made clear that it was Irish historical experience rather than anything Celtic that explained Irish unrest. After all, the Welsh and the 'Scottish Celts' had been easily reconciled to 'English rule', but even after 'the most savage suppression, after every attempt to exterminate them', the Irish remained resilient.[55] Engels rolled some of his unpublished reflections on Ireland into his *Origin of the Family and Property* (1884), where evidence provided from Celtic sources showed that a Celtic ethnic familial tradition had existed with the Welsh before the English conquest and with the Highlanders before 1745, but was still alive in the Irish consciousness.[56]

Karl Marx (1818–1883) also described Irish immigration in racial terms: 'The revolutionary fire of the Celtic worker does not go well with the nature of the Anglo-Saxon worker, solid, but slow . . . in all *the big industrial centres in England* there is a profound antagonism between the Irish proletariat and the English proletariat'.[57] The language aside, race does not actually do much work in the analysis of either Marx or Engels on Ireland, which posed a singular problem to their sociohistorical theories and revolutionary projections.[58] As they saw it, the immediate problem was that the deplorable system of tenant farming in Ireland had reduced the Irish peasantry to abject poverty at the same time as the rapid industrialisation of Britain had created a labour vacuum. The Irish therefore flooded Britain looking for work—and, in Engel's analysis, because they had sunk into a state of savagery and did not know any better, they brought their filthy habits with them to the slums—and would do it for almost nothing. For capitalists this was a dream, because it gave them cheap labour and created a de facto system of divide and rule wherein the English and Irish proletariats hated one another instead of their bourgeois oppressors. Because of England's parasitical dependence on Ireland, Marx and Engels broke from their normal opposition to nationalism and supported the Irish republican cause, which would strike near the heart of the British Empire, and would lead to the proletarian revolution in England. Once again, the peculiarities of Irish history made it a special case.

More mainstream political economists agreed that unique circumstances had more to do with the problems in Ireland than race. From the time of the famine, John Stuart Mill (1806–1873) roundly condemned the notion that Celtic racial difference was to blame in the Irish situation:[59]

> Is it not, then, a bitter satire . . . to find public instructors of the greatest pretension, imputing the backwardness of Irish industry, and the want of energy of the Irish people in improving their condition, to a peculiar indolence and *insouciance* in the Celtic race?[60]

A Francophile who placed more emphasis on differences of national character, Mill noted that the Irish did have their own particular 'pleasure-loving and sensitively organized' character, 'but they are not less fitted for [labour] than their Celtic brethren the French'.[61] The English political economist George Scrope (1797–1876) had likewise asserted that the 'Scotch Celts' were not more suited for labour than their Irish cousins, but had benefitted from government sponsored public works that raised their 'character for industry',[62] and the liberal historian Henry Thomas Buckle (1821–1862) later drove the point home in his *History of Civilization* (1857–1861): 'the simple fact being, that the Irish are unwilling to work, not because they are Celts, but because their work is badly paid. When they go abroad they get good wages, and therefore they become as industrious as any other people'.[63] Although dilettantish commentators invoked its tenets to berate the Celts, political economy had an egalitarian potential buried within it that could cut through the increasingly psychological approach to poverty and the associated idea of Celtic racial deficiency.

The Great Famine and *The Times*

Keyword searches in the Irish Newspaper Archive and the British Newspaper Archive show a distinct increase in 'Celtic' rhetoric from 1843, the 'Great Repeal Year'.[64] It appears this occurred as the result of the debate over the Irish Arms Bill, during which Lord John Russell (1792–1878)—to take just one example—inveighed against the 'bad example . . . of him who talks about the Saxon and the Celts . . . proclaiming an organic and natural difference between the people of England and the people of Ireland'.[65] By the time of the Great Famine, then, there was already an established tendency to refer the problems between Britain and Ireland to a racial dichotomy.

One of the most famous episodes of Celtophobic racism is *The Times*'s coverage of the famine, where what was perceived to be Irish indolence was declared to be a characteristic common to the entire Celtic race by *The Times*'s 'commissioner' to Ireland Thomas Campbell Foster (1813–1882). Foster spent five months in Ireland in 1845–1846, inquiring into 'the true condition of the Irish people'—identified as a state of 'social disease'—and its causes.[66] He rejected the argument that Irish distress was attributable to misgovernment or the landlords, blaming the Irish peasantry and provoking a public dispute with Daniel O'Connell in the process.[67] Foster identified a lack of industriousness as the chief Irish moral failing—the sort of interpretation we just saw Mill and Buckle rejecting.[68] The differences between the 'orderly and industrious' mixed population of Ulster and the wretched 'Celtic' population of Leinster represented the Irish problem in microcosm: '*race* has more to do with the distinguishing characteristics . . . than either politics or religion'.[69] In a lengthy footnote Foster made clear that he lumped all members of the Celtic race together, criticising the 'excessive vanity' and physical weakness of the Welsh, Scottish Highlanders, and the French.[70] Although he claimed to acknowledge Celtic racial virtues, such as their 'endurance' and 'contentment with almost any lot', in the context of Irish history this proved a weakness as the Irish had endured rather than opposed English domination. When Irish commentators had the temerity to dispute his opinions, Foster retreated to the supposed 'weakness . . . in the Celtic race to be vain'.[71] Thus, in the conventional wisdom of *The Times*, the Celtic race possessed innate qualities that reached their strongest and most negative expression in the Irish national character.

There were different ways of dealing with this kind of Celtophobia. As we have seen, probably the most common route was to point to factors other than race as generative of the Irish predicament. Another obvious but crude strategy was to adhere to the same racialist logic but reverse the charge: the Celtic race was superior to the Saxon. This required some creative thinking to squeeze past the seven-hundred-year-old elephant in the room, the domination of the smaller island by the larger one. The most outstanding example is probably the anthropological work of John McElheran (d. 1859), an Ulsterman who founded the nationalist Celtic Union in 1853 with, among others, Charles Gavan Duffy, before emigrating to America in 1854.[72] McElheran laid his ideas out in 1852–1853 in a one-man war against *The Times* and its worship of the Saxon, who based on McElheran's scientific calculations was really 'A flaxed-haired, bullet-headed, pig-eyed, huge-faced, long-backed, pot-bellied, bad-legged, stupid, slavish, lumbering, sulky boor, whose moral state is a disgrace and regret to England'.[73] *The Times* pleaded innocent to portraying the '"Saxon" or the "Anglo-Saxons" as the rival and contrast of the Celt', but still depicted the Irish peasantry as indolent, filthy, and prone to murder,[74] and *Punch* honoured M'Elheran with a simianised cartoon.[75] Meanwhile the nationalist press in Ireland rallied around McElheran, celebrating the blow he had struck for, variously, Ireland, the Celts, Catholics, and/or the hardworking poor.[76] *The Times* lost interest in the dispute and McElheran later claimed to an American audience that his challenge had 'extinguished Anglo-Saxonism in Britain'.[77] After moving to the United States, McElheran published his masterwork in Boston in 1858. It placed his argument for Celtic superiority at the centre of an idiosyncratic ethnology tracing the ancient tribes from a 'Celtic centre', the cradle of civilization. Among the markers of Celtic civilizational refinement was their largely herbivorous diet, the evidence of the Brehon Laws in Ireland, and the Celtic reverence for women and children; the Goths, McElheran argued, were only too happy to sell their wives and children into slavery. In a clever twist, he capitalised on the theory—articulated in different ways by a range of thinkers including Montesquieu, Gibbon, Burke, and de Staël—that Christianity had helped to civilize Europe, and as the island of 'saints and scholars', Ireland had therefore done more than any other nation in this process. In any case, the great ancient civilizations of Egypt, Greece, and Rome were all at root Celtic anyway. Reviews were mixed. Nationalist newspapers in Ireland praised the book to the roof, but it was largely ignored elsewhere. The same cannot be said for the work of the subject of the following section, George Combe.

Phrenology, George Combe, and the Celts

Phrenology was birthed in Vienna at the end of the eighteenth century by the physician Franz Joseph Gall (1758–1828), who toured the Continent giving demonstrations of his method until his death in 1828. His protégé Johann Spurzheim (1776–1832) took the act to Britain in 1814 and, after some initial resistance, managed to inspire a number of followers, primarily in London and Edinburgh. George Combe became the most important of these and helped to shape the direction and reception of the science around the world more than either of his German predecessors. It was in Britain that the 'system of Gall and Spurzheim' was named 'phrenology' in 1815. Although the scientific establishment treated it with circumspection, phrenology proved immensely popular and sustained interest throughout the nineteenth century. By 1900 Combe's *Constitution of Man* (1828) had outsold Darwin's *On the Origin of Species* (1859) by about 6 to 1.[78]

The Constitution of Man is, above all, a work of moral philosophy. Combe placed it as the latest in the distinguished line of Scottish works on the philosophy of the mind and explained that the point of phrenology was to discern the moral laws that governed the universe. Once these were understood, education could be reformed and human conduct improved. The moral laws governing human behaviour were deduced from external 'readings' of skulls: grooves and bumps were thought to directly mirror the size and development of different areas, or 'organs', of the brain, each believed to correspond to a particular faculty. The larger the organ, the more powerful the faculty. Drawing on the large skull collection of the Edinburgh Phrenological Society, the British movement's flagship organisation, Combe compared and contrasted skulls from different races around the world, determining that European 'brains possess a favourable development of the moral and intellectual organs', while those of the 'Hindoos, and native Americans' were inferior.[79] Since some races 'cannot, with their present brains, adopt European civilization', Combe's answer was hybridity: essentially to breed those from the Global South adapted to warm climates with those from the Global North who had more developed 'moral and intellectual organs'.[80]

The same relationship essentially operated with respect to the Saxon and Celtic populations; the former needed to tame the unstable qualities of the latter. Nine Irish skulls showed the dominant qualities to be 'Amativeness' (a phrenological term for the inclination towards sexual love), 'combativeness', and 'destructiveness'; these matched with the old 'Celtic skull', which showed these 'propensities' to 'considerably overmatch those of the intellect and moral sentiments', while the notable quality of Germanic skulls was 'cautiousness'.[81] Due to its total scientific discredit, phrenology provides a transparent window into how prejudice and racialism interacted: because it was bogus, we are able to see the large extent to which practitioners found what they wanted to find. Combe used phrenological readings when it suited him to explain politics or to cloak his aversion for certain peoples.

High up on this list were the French. Combe travelled to France in 1847 and related his findings in his diaries and letters to friends—such as the one to Richard Cobden with which this chapter opened—when he returned suspecting revolution in 1848:

> Many of [the people] *are* favourably organised; but the great majority have small heads of the Celtic type, moderate in the reflecting and coronal regions, and large in Self-esteem and Love of Approbation, with a relatively predominant development of the organs of the propensities.... The effect of this combination also is that the Celtic Frenchman exists for himself; France is the extension of himself, and hence egotism and patriotism are his polar stars.[82]

Fearful of French republicanism in 1848, Combe wrote to one correspondent that because of these qualities the French people 'may be led to any mischief by big-headed unprincipled leaders' who excited their vanity and lower passions.[83]

Combe's views on the Celtic cousins of the French in Britain and Ireland were muddled. On the one hand he saw the same negative qualities, but on the other he took a historicist line on the Irish Question and tried to persuade Richard Cobden that they should be viewed as victims of four centuries of misgovernment rather than as a deficient race.[84] 'My soul bleeds for Ireland', wrote Combe, 'The Irish are highly emotional, acute in direct perception, but they are deficient in Causality, and their intellects have not been trained to reason'. Ireland needed the support of England, otherwise it might force a social revolution.[85] The Welsh provided a more positive Celtic example:

> The Welsh are the best race of Celts I have seen.... They are industrious, and do not appear in squalid poverty. Still there are strong marks of their Celtic character. They are dirty, i.e., the children have unwashed feet, faces, and hands; their clothes are in general dirty although not ragged; the cottages and humbler houses for tradesmen, shopkeepers, and small

> farmers are destitute of all beauty or taste in form and proportion, exactly like the same edifices in Celtic Scotland. . . . Their brains have the Celtic narrowness in the anterior lower region, and Ideality is deficient. But the population is much mixed, and one sees many finely organised, and some very pretty auburn-haired children with blue eyes, whose brains are of Saxon forms.[86]

This passage shows the increasing reach of hybridity theories, which would change the scientific discussion in the second half of the century, with significant influence from anthropological developments in France.

Craniometry and *la question celtique* in French Anthropology

Craniometry was the central focus of physical anthropology in the nineteenth century. The suite of measurements, techniques, and tools developed to classify the human skull are probably what first comes to mind when 'race science' is mentioned.[87] Like every other human race, the Celts—including skeletal remains found in 'Celtic' areas as well as their presumed living descendants—were weighed, measured, and often but not always found wanting. However, the paradoxical conclusion reached in this section, and vital for this chapter, is that the measurement practices associated with the most heinous and distasteful aspects of racial science led to the eventual breakdown of scientific racism against the Celts. Trying to make the 'science of race' empirical helped lead to its implosion, and although the racialised world in which nineteenth-century people lived continued to exist, it started to lose its scientific veneer.

Skull shape had been an important aspect of the study of race since the eighteenth century, and around 1800 began to overtake skin colour—seen as more liable to the influence of climate—as the major focus of physical race science. William Edwards, for example, had based his entire ethnological thesis on a division between round-skulled and long-skulled populations in Western Europe.[88] This shift was due in large part to the considerable influence of Johann Friedrich Blumenbach (1752–1840) and his massive skull collection in Göttingen, which had a great impact on the race classifiers we looked at in previous chapters such as Prichard and Virey.

Edwards observed only with the naked eye, but shortly thereafter the Swedish anatomist Anders Retzius (1796–1860) devised a more positivistic scheme of classification based on dividing the width of the skull by its length. Multiply-

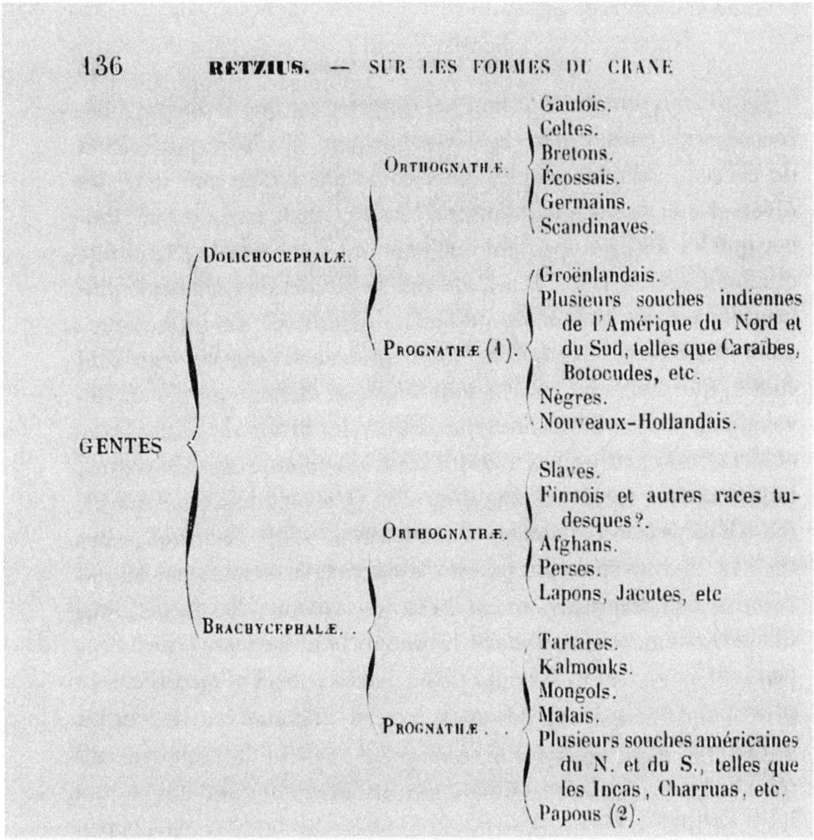

136 RETZIUS. — SUR LES FORMES DU CRANE

GENTES
- DOLICHOCEPHALÆ.
  - ORTHOGNATHÆ.
    - Gaulois.
    - Celtes.
    - Bretons.
    - Écossais.
    - Germains.
    - Scandinaves.
  - PROGNATHÆ (1).
    - Groënlandais.
    - Plusieurs souches indiennes de l'Amérique du Nord et du Sud, telles que Caraïbes, Botocudes, etc.
    - Nègres.
    - Nouveaux-Hollandais.
- BRACHYCEPHALÆ.
  - ORTHOGNATHÆ.
    - Slaves.
    - Finnois et autres races tudesques?.
    - Afghans.
    - Perses.
    - Lapons, Jacutes, etc
  - PROGNATHÆ.
    - Tartares.
    - Kalmouks.
    - Mongols.
    - Malais.
    - Plusieurs souches américaines du N. et du S., telles que les Incas, Charruas, etc.
    - Papous (2).

FIG. 10. Anders Retzius, 'Mémoire sur les forms du crane des habitants du nord', trans. G. Courty, *Annales des sciences naturelles* S3.6 (1846), 136. The Celts remained in this division through the rest of Retzius's work.

ing the quotient by 100 (to round out the numbers) resulted in the 'cephalic index':[89] skulls where the ratio between breadth and length was lower (i.e., the skull was rounder) were called 'brachycephalic', while those where the ratio was higher (i.e., the skull was longer and narrower) were called 'dolichocephalic'.[90] A new set of racial classifications was developed based upon this measurement and then subdivided further by the prominence of the jaw, which Retzius picked up from Prichard (see Fig. 10). Retzius declared from the beginning that the Celts were, along with the Germans but also the Africans, a people 'pre-eminently dolichocephalic', and was further confirmed in his suspicion after visiting all four nations of Britain and Ireland in 1855.[91]

When he encountered increasing evidence of brachycephalic populations in Celtic areas such as Ireland, Scotland, and France, Retzius linked this to the theory postulated earlier in the century that an earlier population, probably related to non-Indo-European linguistic anomalies like the Basques and Finns, had inhabited Europe before the arrival of the major European races.[92] These were held to be short and dark-haired, and generally inferior to the tall, blonde, long-skulled Aryans. Retzius's theories were influential across Europe, and his terms for long-skulled and round-skulled specimens—dolichocephalic and brachycephalic, respectively—became standard terminology.

However, Retzius's theoretical reign was virtually halted in France by the famous neurologist Paul Broca (1824–1880), the main founder of the *Société d'anthropologie de Paris* in 1858 and dominant figure of French anthropology until his death in 1880.[93] Broca is a towering figure in the history of nineteenth-century science—some of his discoveries in neurology have stood the test of time—but his polygenism, and related belief in the inferiority of non-white races as well as women, has today made him notorious.[94] He cast the *Société d'anthropologie de Paris* as a successor to Edwards's *Société ethnologique de Paris,* and paid homage to Edwards's *Des caracterès physiologiques,* which Broca identified as the first text to formulate a complete notion of race as comprised of physical, intellectual, and moral characters.[95] Like Edwards, Broca was also interested in the origins of the races of Europe and the Celtic racial basis of France in particular, and he sought to place Edwards's findings on more solid empirical ground.[96] However, he argued forcefully and repeatedly that physical evidence should take priority over linguistic evidence because physical characteristics were fixed while languages could be learned or forgotten by populations.[97] Broca therefore articulated his own sophisticated view of French ethnology based primarily on physical evidence, one that rejected what he saw as the imprecision of the linguistic theories for Celtic and French origins, and instead embraced the French as a mixed-race nation.

After establishing himself as a leader in the Parisian medical world, Broca made his first real steps in anthropology in the late 1850s when he began to investigate the question of species hybridity. Broca was a devout polygenist, and by showing that different animal species could produce fertile hybrids—the *sine qua non* of species definition associated above all with Buffon—Broca sought to undermine the monogenist argument that humanity was a single species because those of mixed race could procreate.[98] Broca's polygenism intertwined with his belief in the inferiority of non-European races and occasionally brought him into accord with notorious pro-slavery American race scientists;[99] however, in this instance Broca firmly opposed them, along with Arthur, Comte de Gobineau (1816–1882) and Robert Knox (1791–1862), for their fatalistic theories that race-mixing led to the decline and fall of nations.[100] In fact, the opposite was the case: racial mixing led to progress. Nothing proved his point better than the French, who resulted from the combination of Gauls, Kimris, Romans, and Germans, and every day grew in 'intelligence, prosperity, and numerical force'.[101] Broca's findings about species hybridity were so controversial that he was barred from sharing them at the *Société de biologie*, which had been the stand-in group for anthropological discussion since the suppression of the *Société ethnologique* a decade earlier. So Broca conceived of a new society, and once he and his supporters received official permission—with the provisos that the society would be forbidden from discussing politics or religion, and that there was a policeman present at all meetings—the *Société d'anthropologie de Paris* began officially meeting in May 1859.

French national origins, race-mixing, and the Celts were all therefore key subjects of discussion from the very beginning of the *Société d'anthropologie*, and continued to be so over the next few decades. No one contributed more in these overlapping areas than Broca, who incorporated them into the very first paper delivered to the society, on the 'Recherches sur l'ethnologie de France'.[102] Here Broca confirmed the Gallic-Kymric split of Thierry and Edwards, following the conception of the Galls as short, dark-haired, and round-skulled, and the Kymris as tall, blonde, and long-skulled.[103] However, Broca made two argumentative tweaks. The first was to verify the Thierry-Edwards thesis empirically, and the second, resulting argument was that France's population was more mixed than it presented at first glance.[104] Broca followed Caesar's geography of ancient Gaul and split France into three zones: first, a Gallic or 'celtic properly so called' zone pertaining to most of the south and west of France; second, a 'kymric' zone in the northeast; and third and finally, a mixed-race 'kymro-celtique' zone in the middle.[105] Broca then verified this split by drawing on the published statistics of army recruitment heights by department. These confirmed his split: the Gallic/Celtic zone was shortest, the Kymric zone was tallest, and the kymro-celtique zone was in the middle.[106]

In July 1861, arguing further for French racial mixture, Broca robustly challenged the presuppositions of Retzian craniometry in a paper examining skulls excavated on the Isle de la Cité dating from about the twelfth to the nineteenth centuries. Retzius's dichotomous scheme did not fit these skulls, many of which Broca found to fall in between the ratios of 7:9 and 8:10 that Retzius had identified as brachycephalic and dolichocephalic, respectively. Broca thus concluded that Retzius had 'exaggerated the importance' of the cephalic index, and had idealised the dolichocephalic form out of his own racial pride. Instead, Broca argued that the brachycephalic skulls likely represented the purest descendants of the autochthonous inhabitants of France, the dolichocephalic skulls represented the purest descendants of the Indo-Germanic invaders, and those that fell in the middle were 'mixed race' (*métis*). Broca was apparently himself brachycephalic and dark-haired, and so the implication that this was the inferior type was probably difficult for this headstrong and combative man to take. Richard McMahon has pointed out that Broca was one among several physical anthropologists—including William Wilde—who recovered some prestige for brachycephaly.[107] When he eventually began his famous research into skull capacity—or brain size—Broca argued brachycephals were more voluminous and therefore had bigger brains. His arguments along these lines had considerable implications for the identity of the Celts.

In the early 1860s the Celtic Question was batted back and forth in these debates over French national origins, Indo-European migrations, whether races and languages were congruent, and the utility of Retzius's racial classification system. Finally, in 1864 Broca addressed the Celtic Question itself, outlining a position that we can—albeit anachronistically—call 'Celtosceptic'.[108] Broca had already warned about the dangers of arbitrary nomenclature in a paper that prised apart linguistics and anthropology, and in this, his first large statement on the Celts, he indicated his belief that 'Celtic' was one such word used entirely too arbitrarily and therefore misleadingly.[109] In 'Qu'est-ce que les Celtes?', Broca delineated four different understandings of 'Celt': the historical Celts described by Caesar and other classical writers, the linguistic Celts discovered by modern philologists, the archaeological Celts that were included in the three-age system, and the Celts of craniology associated with Retzius and his skull classification system. In subsequent papers, Broca did not hide his opinion that the only proper use of 'Celtic' was to refer to the area and inhabitants of ancient 'Celtica', the middle portion of Gaul identified by Caesar.[110] This was, according to Broca, the only way of making history and anthropology agree. Although Broca implied that the 'race celtique' or population of Gaul that was 'celtique proprement dit' accorded anthropologically with the smaller, darker inhabitants of Ireland and Scotland,[111] he pointed out that the ancients never seemingly referred to the populations of Britain and Ireland as 'Celtic', and that it was an error to do so.[112] Broca articulated most of his Celtic arguments in his early anthropological papers but reiterated them constantly over the next twenty years, trying to empirically verify them as more data became available.

Broca's mixed-race theory of French national origins was widely influential, but his Celtic arguments seem to have been more limited in impact. As he had argued, everyone within and without the *Société d'anthropologie* had different views about the Celts, which he pointed out in 1873 had been a subject of discussion in every single session.[113] His friend the archaeologist Alexandre Bertrand (1820–1902), for example, agreed with Broca that the usage of 'Celts' had been indiscriminate and uncertain since antiquity, but argued that archaeology was the best means of rendering a new picture of prehistoric Europe.[114] The nationalist historian Henri Martin drew on traditions in the vernacular Celtic literatures to argue against Broca that a tall, blond, and blue-eyed race that had arrived in Europe about fifteen centuries before Christ and imposed itself on a shorter, darker race could be called 'Celts', because the groups were bound by kinship, language, and a common civilization.[115] However, Broca's strong belief that anthropology and philology should be separated—that language bore no necessary connection to race—is probably one of the truly decisive factors limiting the reach of his Celtic theories. For this was also the crucial moment in the foundation of Celtic studies as an academic discipline, where philology prevailed. The *Revue celtique*, fundamental in the international establishment of Celtic studies (see chapter 9), was begun in 1869 and bore no trace of anthropological impact. Ironically, Broca's successful quest to establish anthropology as an individual field of study in France had the unintended consequence of ringfencing his Celtic theories. For our purposes in this chapter, however, it should be grasped that Broca's unrelenting argument for racial hybridity helped to dismantle the race purity arguments associated with some of the more strident critics of the Celts and Ireland.

Ethnology and Anthropology in Britain

The debate over hybridity played out in Britain under the shadow of the Irish Question. Broadly speaking, the 'Natural History of Man' broke into two rival factions in Britain, one espousing ethnology, the other anthropology. The 'ethnologicals' of the Ethnological Society of London (ESL)—which was founded in 1843 and had a strong Quaker and evangelical element—maintained the monogenist tradition of Prichard and believed in the importance of comparative philology, before adopting Darwin's theory of evolution by natural selection, which was held to undermine the polygenist position held by the 'anthropologicals' who had founded the rival Anthropological Society of London (ASL) in 1863.[116] After Darwin, the question of hybridity came to the fore.

The Ethnological Society's Christian philanthropic disposition and philological focus annoyed those concerned more with anatomy and physiology, such as Robert Knox, the most famous because the most outrageous British racial theorist of the nineteenth century. Many of his outbursts were directed at the Celts. Trained as a physician in Edinburgh and Paris, he became a leading anatomist in Edinburgh, but lost it all after he was exposed as the purchaser of the bodies of Burke and Hare's murder victims in 1827–1828. He became a pariah in polite society but remained popular in medical and scientific circles, garnering attention for his brusque racial determinism. Knox combatted those, like Prichard, who viewed 'human history . . . as a chapter of accidents', countering that 'human character, individual, social, national' was attributable solely 'to the all-pervading, unalterable, physical character of race'.[117] History was essentially just a series of race conflicts: the Boyne, Culloden, and Waterloo all boiled down to the triumph of Saxon over Celt.[118]

Knox is famous for his bile, and some of his outbursts are genuinely shocking. However, there is a tension in his work between guarded admiration for the French—'all but wholly Celtic'—and his hatred for the Celtic race in the abstract and particularly the British Celtic nations.[119] There was a civilizational chain of being, where the French sat at the top and the Irish at the bottom.[120] Although he claimed to hold the Celtic race in 'the highest regard and esteem', he portrayed them generally as cowardly, bloodthirsty, despotic, uncivilized, illiterate, unathletic, narcissistic, humourless, dirty, irrational, and work-shy.[121] Knox conceded that Celts were fashionable and inventive, but noted with back-handed approval that the Saxons appropriated Celtic inventions for practical use. Yet Knox revered Napoleon and, alluding to France, praised the Celt's muscular strength and pugnacity, which had twice saved 'Europe and the Saxon race' from destruction and 'Asiatic despotism', and would perhaps do so again, this time against the Slavs of the East.[122] Britain and Ireland were another story, where Knox envisioned an approaching conflict between Celts and Saxons, who remained fundamentally distinct: '700 years of absolute possession has not advanced by a single step the amalgamation of the Irish Celt with the Saxon-English', nor the Welsh nor the Scottish Highlanders.[123] He approvingly cited the Encumbered Estates (Ireland) Act (1849), that would achieve the 'quiet and gradual extinction of the Celtic race in Ireland', the only fate 'suitable for the Celtic man'.[124] In the expanded second edition of the *The Races of Men*, Knox extended his prescription to the Welsh and Highlanders: 'Look at Wales, look at Caledonia. . . . The race must be forced from the soil . . . England's safety requires it . . . nations must ever act as Machiavelli advised'.[125] But the contrast with the French Celts was striking. Knox recognised they were entitled to pursue their own racial destiny. In fact, he repeatedly recommended that the 'Celt of France must look to Africa as the continent which he is entitled to seize', as the Saxons had North America.[126] Thus even Knox, racialist and racist *par excellence,* reveals some of the nuances in Victorian racial thought.

The Ethnological Society barred Knox in 1855, only readmitting him at the instigation of his disciple James Hunt (1833–1869) in 1858. Increasingly dissatisfied with the ESL, Hunt and a small cadre around him finally broke away to form the Anthropological Society in 1863. Generally, the position of the Anthropological Society was polygenist, pro-slavery, and pro-Confederacy; that their pretext for leaving the ESL was its admission of women gives some indication of the differences in outlook of the two groups.[127] Hunt's self-published *Anthropological Review* served as the semi-official mouthpiece of the ASL, and he was unabashedly political. Against the smouldering Fenian problem, and in sharp contrast to the reaction of Arnold, Hunt thought fit to resurrect Knox's ideas on the Celtic Race, urging politicians to 'learn their anthropological alphabet' and realise that until different racial characteristics were taken into account, English political attempts to placate the Irish would continue to fail.[128] He even included a Knox-esque diatribe in a footnote aimed at the Quaker Radical politician John Bright (1811–1889), who had claimed the Irish and English were the same people:

> The same people as ourselves! How astonishing then that the Irish will not accept peaceably the laws, government, and constitution which satisfy the English! . . . How long will politicians continue to sing the same song, 'Oh no, we never mention *race*'?[129]

Not all ASL members expressed negative views of the Celts. James Higgin urged the political utility of anthropology and its potential for what he thought was good, declaring the Celtic and Teutonic races to be separate but equal, and therefore suggesting that Ireland be partitioned on racial lines, as the Celtic population of the West required paternalism while the Teutonic population of the North and East needed representative government.[130] The examples of Hunt and Higgin encapsulate the general views of the ASL as regarded the Celts: their positive or negative qualities could be emphasised as the author saw fit, but the essential fact was that they constituted a singular, immutable race that had to be dealt with on those terms.

Meanwhile, the Ethnological Society continued more or less in its Prichardian mould, notwithstanding some members who rejected the equality of races. Darwin's *On the Origin of Species*, though it did not deal with the natural history of man, raised a number of questions for it. T. H. Huxley (1825–1895)—who loved a good fight—was among the first to apply the theory of natural selection to humanity and its origins, and upon becoming president of the ESL in 1868 he engaged in polygenist whack-a-mole, arguing that Darwinian natural selection conclusively proved monogenesis. In the midst of this campaign, Huxley made the most significant defence of the Celt based on race science. Arising from a public lecture printed in the *Pall Mall Gazette*, Huxley addressed the 'antagonism of the Celt and the Teuton' in Ireland and England, investigating whether the ethnological assumptions of politicians and public commentators had any basis.[131] He argued that the isles were mostly a racial mixture of Celt and Saxon and that any difference beyond language was 'a mere sham and delusion'; therefore, 'the sooner we leave off drawing political distinctions between Celts and Saxons the better'.[132] When a 'Devonshire Man' proud of his Saxon blood dared to challenge the assertions, Huxley ripped him apart, accusing him of spewing 'platitude[s], absorbed from a newspaper, and . . . unchanged by even accidental contact with the reasoning faculty'.[133] This was not just blood sport for Huxley, who wrote to Darwin that he would have let 'Devonshire man' off 'if it were not for the political bearing of the Celt question just now', alluding to the acute situation in Ireland in the wake of the Fenian revolt.[134] So while he sought to curtail the erroneous folk racialism of politicians and the popular press, Huxley admitted his expectation that his ethnological opinions be considered politically; thus, his intervention was part Celtic defence and part demand to leave racial questions to the experts.

British racial science, like Victorian scholarship more generally, also became more positivistic, a turn leading to further erosion of the sharp delineation of European races, as attempts to quantify physical racial qualities allowed more scope for mixture. John Beddoe (1826–1911)—who helped merge the Anthropological and Ethnological Societies as the Anthropological Institute in 1871—provided the most comprehensive British work in the new positivistic vein. Given that he was a Saxonist, it is ironic that Beddoe's 'empirical' work ultimately undermined the anti-Celtic position. It is a further irony that the work was developed from a prize-winning *eisteddfod* essay of 1868. It was published later as *The Races of Britain* (1885), and showed by examination of hair and eye colour that Britons became darker the farther west one travelled, which purportedly reflected a greater amount of Celtic blood. Beddoe's famous 'index of negrescence' reduced colour to the equation 'D+2N–R–F = Index'.[135] Beddoe's ultimate point was that there were distinct Saxon and Celtic populations, but his detailed ethnographic maps revealed a much more mixed population than many of his anthropological predecessors would have conceded.

The political implications of the more mixed, positivistic race science were made clear in an 1887 press debate about the ethnological arguments for or against Home Rule, where there existed a racial argument for unionism. Arguing against Home Rulers who he claimed reduced nationality simply to race, the Liberal Unionist MP and former vice-president of the ESL, John Lubbock (1834–1913), cited the findings of both Huxley and Beddoe to prove racial mixture: 'if we recognize the undeniable ethnological fact that the English, Irish and Scotch are all composed of the same elements . . . it would do much to mitigate our unfortunate dissensions'. Following this intervention, a number of prominent figures wrote to Lubbock, including Huxley, who agreed about the 'absurdity of the nationality plea on ethnological grounds'.[136] He joined the fray against the racial basis for Home Rule, referring readers back to his interventions in the early 1870s.[137] The expertise of race scientists made an ironic contribution to a progressively anti-racialist movement in British politics through the end of the century.[138]

Matthew Arnold's Intervention

Finally, we arrive at Matthew Arnold. When considered within all of the foregoing contexts, his *On the Study of Celtic Literature* (1867) is not really a study of Celtic literature. First given as a lecture series at Oxford in 1865–1866 and printed in *Cornhill Magazine*, the work was above all a political intervention to reconcile the Celtic populations of the non-English nations, and particularly Ireland (approaching the height of early Fenianism), to Britain. Interpretations of the text are excessively protean, but a common misguided approach has been to view it as a mere prelude to *Culture and Anarchy* (1869), Arnold's most famous work.[139] However, Rachel Bromwich went too far in the opposite direction, attributing the 'inspiration' behind Arnold's appeal for serious consideration of Celtic subjects almost entirely to continental ideas, those of Renan above all.[140] Undoubtedly, Arnold borrowed much from Renan, but his focus was firmly on Britain and Ireland and, in a broad sense, it was political. He sought to intercede in public debate over the Union by placing the study of

Celtic literature on a scientific basis. Whereas the authors examined in the preceding section stressed some aspect of Celtic difference, whether racial, religious, or civilizational, Arnold emphasised the overarching Britishness of the Celts by noting their racial mixture with the Anglo-Saxons and their resulting shared cultural features. The most significant of these was the modern English literary tradition, which Arnold portrayed as a cultural Saxon-Celtic hybrid. By lending the weight of his name, Arnold forced Celtic ideas more obviously into mainstream debate, arguing that the Celtic element in the British population could do much to 'improve' the Saxon.

One of the towering figures of mid-Victorian culture, Arnold was a critic and eventual professor of poetry at Oxford.[141] He reacted strongly against what he saw as his father's overemphasis of 'the Celt's vices', writing to his sister of his pride in their 'semi-celtic origin', which he thought gave them the ability 'of comprehending the nature of both races'.[142] While Arnold had toyed with Celtic-related subjects in some of his poetry—'Tristam and Iseult' and 'St. Brandan' among others—*Celtic Literature* engaged specifically with English translations of Celtic verse collections. Arguing that, to know a people, 'one must know that by which a people best express themselves,—their literature', Arnold used Celtic verse as a literary base from which to launch an investigation into national characters—English, German, and French—and to what extent they were rooted in Celtic, Saxon, Latin, or Norman racial elements.[143] In this way the essay obviously slotted comfortably into Arnold's ongoing campaign against English 'Philistinism', or the smug tendency of the English middle class towards a Saxonist cultural chauvinism. In order to counter the 'vulgarity', 'coarseness', and 'unintelligence' of English philistinism, Arnold recommended the 'greater delicacy and spirituality' of the Celtic population, which he argued was 'blended' with the English.[144] Therefore he turned the negative conclusions normally drawn from racial essentialism on their head, inverting the moralising language directed at the Celts to argue that it was not they who needed civilizing by the English, but vice versa. Arnold openly called for 'a new Englishman'.[145]

Arnold wanted to inaugurate a new scientific study of Celtic literature, a political act in itself, as some argued the Celtic nations had no real literature to speak of. This had been declared most notoriously in the 1847 governmental commission into Welsh education, or 'Treason of the Blue Books', which found there was 'no literature of any real value and utility in the Welsh language'.[146] Arnold sought to make the first step himself, but freely admitted that he was no expert on Celtic subjects, basing his research largely on secondary material and appealing to the expertise of the philologist Percy Smythe, Eighth Viscount Strangford, who provided corrections and appendices for the book. In a letter to the *Pall Mall Gazette*, Strangford wrote approvingly of Arnold’s venture, agreeing with his suggestion that ‘the English nation’ would benefit by an ‘infusion of the artistic and imaginative faculty through a more complete incorporation of the various Celtic fragments . . . which it . . . has yet to absorb’.[147] Despite his own scholarly deficiency, Arnold wanted the ‘Celtic genius’ to be understood through ‘science and history’, thinking the ‘*science des origines*’ incomplete without an account of ‘the Celts, and their genius, language, and literature’.[148] He believed the increasing proof of the Celts as members of the Indo-European family would lead to the recognition that they were a sibling race to the Saxons and would reverse their estrangement.[149] Arnold’s conclusion mirrored the ongoing debates in race science and the increasing positivism that suggested Britain was comprised of a mix of races.

Although placing much stock in comparative philology, Arnold argued that it only went so far and that the ‘great key’ to a people is ‘what it says in its language, its literature’: ‘The literature of the Celtic peoples has not yet had its Zeuss, and greatly it wants him’.[150] If Celtic literature was treated scientifically, there would be found ‘spiritual kinship, between us and the Celt, of which we had never dreamed’.[151] Citing ethnological and phrenological studies, he disputed the popular opinion that Celts, like the Normans, had been completely subsumed into the Anglo-Saxon population, suggesting the English had a ‘composite’ genius.[152] While the Saxons were steady and staid, ‘sentimental’ most aptly described the Celts, who were ‘always ready to react against the despotism of fact’.[153] The Celt ‘loves bright colours, he easily becomes audacious, overcrowing, full of fanfaronade’; but there was a darker side, ‘undisciplinable, anarchical, and turbulent by nature’.[154] Here also is the introduction to Anglophone writing of the Celt as ‘feminine’, an idea taken from Renan.[155] Only in the final section of the essay did Arnold actually analyse English poetry, diagnosing three things within it that he believed came from the Celtic character: the ‘turn for style’, ‘melancholy’, and ‘natural magic, for catching and rendering the charm of nature in a wonderfully near and vivid way’.[156] Style in English literature had to be Celtic because it was something ‘the Germans are singularly without’; it could be seen in English poets like Byron and Milton,[157] and Keats and Shakespeare also had ‘Celtic powers’.[158] ‘Rhyme’ was a main source of English poetry’s ‘*romantic element*’ and ‘comes into our poetry from the Celts’.[159] Through Ossian—where melancholy particularly factored in—Celtic poetry had touched all of Europe, so the Celtic genius had touched other nations and enriched all of European poetry.[160]

However, Arnold's overriding aim was political: to encourage his English 'brother Saxons' to take a more sympathetic view of the Celtic Irish and the situation in Ireland.[161] Arnold urged the English to consider that 'in the spiritual frame of us English ourselves, a Celtic fibre . . . lives and works'.[162] The book's final line is worth quoting in its entirety:

> Let us reunite ourselves with our better mind and with the world through science; and let it be one of our angelic revenges on the Philistines, who among their other sins are the guilty authors of Fenianism, to found at Oxford a chair of Celtic, and to send, through the gentle ministration of science, a message of peace to Ireland.[163]

Made clear here are the political aspirations of Arnold's scientific approach. However, it was not only the English who needed to change their mentality; the Celts had to adapt themselves to the times as well. Despite his affinity for Celtic culture, Arnold argued that the integration of the isles's populations was inevitable—'a necessity of what is called modern civilization'—and that English should therefore replace Welsh and the other Celtic languages: 'For all modern purposes . . . let us all as soon as possible be one people; let the Welshman speak English, and . . . let him write English'.[164]

The response provoked by Arnold's intervention revealed the kaleidoscopic Victorian understanding of Celtic ideas. In a letter to the *Pall Mall Gazette*, Strangford immediately and approvingly understood that Arnold's aim was to let the literature reflect the spirit of the Celtic people themselves, rather than to relate things in a 'merely rhetorical and suggestive . . . or in a bare dry ethnological way'.[165] As soon as the lectures began to be printed in *Cornhill*, however, *The Times* declared them to be 'arrant nonsense'.[166] But they were widely influential. *The Examiner* stated that the lectures, articles, and book had generated so much interest that it would not bother to summarize their contents as they 'have been in the hands of almost every reader of our current literature'.[167] A Google Books Ngram search shows that since 1800, the word 'Celtic' reached its peak in English language texts during the mid-1860s, an obvious testament to the importance of Arnold's lectures.[168]

Undoubtedly, Arnold's Celtic mediation was crucial to a reckoning with Celtic ideas and their political implications in the public sphere, but with his campaign for a Celtic Chair at Oxford he made a lasting and important contribution to Celtic studies. There had been previous attempts to found chairs in Celtic and Welsh at Oxford, which had been stymied by disputes among the university, the colleges, and the parliamentary commissions formed to deal with these things. Friedrich Max Müller (1823–1900) recommended a Celtic Chair but had 'little hope of anything being done.'[169] However, the chair was eventually funded and taken up by the Welshman John Rhys (1840–1915) in 1877, who dedicated much of his career to illustrating the ethnological origins of Britain and illuminating just how much it owed to the Celtic population.[170] He was the first to make sustained use of the stone inscriptions around Britain and Ireland,[171] which he dated to the fifth and sixth centuries, and which gave him a linguistic corpus older than the manuscripts from which Zeuß had so greatly benefitted. Rhys thus embodied the ideal combination of philology and ethnology that Arnold had envisioned for the Celtic chair at Oxford, which remains one of the field's most prestigious positions.

Conclusion

The scientist T. H. Huxley summed up the Celtic Problem best in 1870:

> A leading article on the affairs of Ireland in any popular English paper is pretty certain to contain some allusions to the Celt and his assumed peculiarities. If the writer means to be civil, the Celt is taken to be a charming person, full of wit and vivacity and kindliness, but, unfortunately, thoughtless, impetuous, and unstable, and having standards of right and wrong so different from those of the Anglo-Saxon that it would be absurd, not to say cruel, to treat him in the same way; or if the instructor of the public is angry he talks of the Celt as if he were a kind of savage, out of whom no good ever has come or ever will come, and whose proper fate is to be kept as a hewer of wood and a drawer of water for his Anglo-Saxon master.[172]

Although the language of Celticism could be deployed in various contexts, it was at its sharpest in Irish matters. While figures like George Combe and Robert Knox sought to prove Celtic inferiority through 'science', the empirical turn in anthropology ultimately undermined the scientific basis for Celtic racial inferiority by creating a more blended image of the British and Irish populations.

This of course did little to preclude popular prejudice against the Celts or the Irish. Moreover, an author could embrace monogenism, a pan-European descent from a common Aryan ancestor, and the close links of certain races—such as the Celts and Saxons—and still be a racist. The historian E. A. Freeman

(1823–1892), for example, recognised the Celts as racial relatives, yet still hated the Irish.[173] Freeman believed all three of these scientific and historical proofs, yet still joked on a tour of America in 1881 that it 'would be a grand land if only every Irishman would kill a negro, and be hanged for it'.[174] Towards the end of his life Freeman paradoxically supported Irish Home Rule *because of* perceived Irish inferiority and a desire to flush Irish MPs from Westminster. Historicising Victorian racialist thought therefore demands an awareness of the frequent incongruity of public statement and private opinion and cognizance of the irrational intangibles that could influence both of these. Wellington's equine opinions of Ireland are well known, but in response to reported seditious activity in 1881 a later Anglo-Irish war hero, Garnet Woleseley (1833–1913), suggested shooting 'some fifty or so' Irish as a deterrent and ruling with an iron fist as 'the Celtic race is not fit for a parliamentary form of government'.[175] I doubt he sought to ground this conclusion scientifically.

Part III

9

Nos ancêtres les Gallois

THE RISE OF PAN-CELTICISM IN WALES, BRITTANY, AND FRANCE

SO FAR THIS BOOK has examined the main intellectual and cultural contexts in which Celticism took shape from the early modern period through the middle of the nineteenth century. This chapter marks the beginning of the third major intellectual shift in what Eoin MacNeill called 'the modern development of Celtic consciousness': pan-Celticism. Although prior to the 1830s there was a vague recognition of Celtic kinship and an increasing sense that the Celtic countries were cognate nations who could be fruitfully studied together, little shared sentiment existed among individuals from different Celtic nations and very few personally identified as 'Celtic'.

By the 1830s, however, there were enough pieces in place for the rise of a genuine, though informal (lowercase p), pan-Celticism, the subject of this chapter. Spurred by the increase and advancement of knowledge explored in the first two parts of this book, pan-Celticism manifested as a greater attention to historical, cultural, and (importantly) racial links among the Celtic nations in works ranging from scientific studies to travelogues. At the heart of this chapter are the travels of Welsh, Breton, and French pan-Celticists to each other's nations and participation in their cultural festivals, above all Welsh *eisteddfodau*, through which they demonstrated their belief in pan-Celtic kinship.

The word 'pan-Celtic' was coined in 1867 to refer to the international *Congrès celtique* in St. Brieuc.[1] However, Celtic fêtes remained rooted in their respective national contexts, where the pan-Celtic element was important but ancillary. This is the major difference—first noted in the introduction of this book—between lowercase pan-Celticism and uppercase Pan-Celticism: while pan-Celticism exists alongside related causes, the purpose of Pan-Celticism *is* Pan-Celticism. Only in 1901 did the first explicit Pan-Celtic Congress devoted to that specific goal take place, where national movements were subsumed under an international Celtic banner with a political purpose. While Pan-Celticism is conscious of itself as a cultural and often political pan-national movement, pan-Celticism is not and only requires recognition of shared Celtic kinship by its practitioners. Pan-Celticism will primarily be discussed in chapter 11, to which this one is an essential prelude.

This chapter must answer some basic questions.[2] Why did pan-Celticism emerge? Who was interested in it? What did they hope to achieve? Another question raised is whether there was such a thing as a pan-Celtic identity. Given that ideas of belonging and self-recognition go to the heart of how nations and nationalisms develop (or whether they even exist), a preliminary explanation should be given here. The short answer is, not really. Despite an increasing academic awareness of Celtic kinship, and perhaps more importantly an eagerness to pursue closer relations among the different Celtic nations, individuals largely approached pan-Celticism through their own national prisms. Implicit in identifying as 'Celtic' at the time was the belief that one belonged to a Celtic 'race', with its own linguistic family, shared culture and customs, a long-buried history, and a common literary tradition. Yet one was a 'Welsh Celt' or an 'Irish Celt', or perhaps simply a 'Celt', but not a 'pan-Celt'. The awareness of deep racial ties is not the same as voluntaristic association with others of the same race. Even in the early twentieth century 'pan-Celt' was rare. The poet Robert Graves (1895–1985) recalled his father arguing with a Merionethshire postman in the early 1900s over whether the noun 'pan-Celt' existed and, more importantly, if it counted as one word in a telegram (it did).[3]

Although we know that linguistic kinship provided the rationale for modern Celticism, in the nineteenth century this became the bedrock of a broader racial idea of the Celts. As we saw in Part II, the idea of race was not simply an 'othering' tactic employed by a hegemonic Anglo-British state to justify sociopolitical control. Peoples also racialised themselves. Although the two Celtic language branches were mutually unintelligible, national customs differed greatly, and anything resembling shared history lay far outside the bounds of living memory, the idea of race allowed members of Celtic nations a new, scientific grounding in which to explore and justify their affinity. Racial theories permeated historical and literary works, which in turn informed pan-Celtic ideas of shared culture. It is no coincidence that many of the scholars who shaped some of the racial ideas discussed in earlier chapters, such as

Thomas Price or Henri Martin, reappear in this one—they were some of the most ardent Celtic cultural nationalists, and their pan-Celticism suggests that in the middle of the nineteenth century Celtic racial ideas were beginning to move beyond mere academic recognition and leading to shared sentiment. Price's biographer, Jane Williams (1806–1885), drew a direct line between scholarship and racial feeling, explaining that the Welsh affinity for their own past stimulated historical enquiries that produced both stronger 'national attachment' and bonds to 'kindred races'.[4]

Scholarship was therefore crucial to pan-Celticism, but something was needed to reify the ideas advanced. The key seam was stitched in the 1830s, when the Abergavenny Cymreigyddion Society focused upon a joint Celtic cultural heritage and welcomed a deputation of Bretons to its *eisteddfod* in 1838. Inspired by the Abergavenny network, similar gestures occurred in different Celtic nations throughout the nineteenth century, with individuals able to participate in a variety of regional and national festivals by virtue of being part of the same Celtic race. While academic papers and addresses were read out, the pageantry and ceremonial aspects of such festivals conferred a sense of immemorial sacrality on the proceedings and substituted for the lack of more tangible links among the participants.

Considering much of it had to be manufactured, Victorian pan-Celticism lays bare the potential of national constructivism. By necessity, pan-Celts invented memories and borrowed traditions. Initial pan-Celtic intellectual exchange drew on shared mythology, poetry, and early religious history—pagan and Christian—all of which could be invoked as common memories of ancient national cooperation or even a prehistoric Celtic Empire. Various national traditions, most of them Welsh, were adopted by other Celtic nations as legitimate expressions of ancient Celtic ceremony. However, there existed one indisputable link to ancient Celtic culture: the languages, which enjoyed a level of authenticity denied to many other European minority languages.[5] The Celtic literary tradition—as discussed by figures like Renan and Arnold—also pointed to links among the nations. Furthermore, invented pan-Celtic traditions were not the state-sponsored attempts at coercion outlined as one of two broad patterns for invented traditions by Hobsbawm.[6] Instead they were counter-hegemonic, aimed at carving out a cultural sphere for modern Celticism where it was denied an overt role in more mainstream political culture, until the last quarter of the nineteenth century, when in the 1870s-1880s cultural nationalists began to employ Celticism for their own political ends, in conjunction with land reform campaigns (see chapter 10).

Although cooperation increased among cultural revivalists from different nations, pan-Celticism was not a coherent project. Activists frequently called for increased collaboration, and occasionally for pan-Celtic unions or leagues, but these were evanescent, and there was little ambition to create a pan-Celtic nation or polity. However, the developments outlined in this chapter built momentum for the emergence of formalised Pan-Celticism, with many of the events and personages themselves becoming *lieux de mémoire* and mythologised heroes for later Pan-Celticists. The nations within the two language branches drew closer together, a necessary step before the great linguistic divide between Brittonic and Goidelic was crossed.

Thomas Price, Jean-François-Marie-Maurice-Agathe Le Gonidec, and the Breton Bible

The story of pan-Celticism begins with the increasing interaction of Welsh and Breton scholars in the 1820s. At this point Wales had the strongest cultural movement of all the Celtic nations, which some scholars have argued was driven by a desire to be accorded greater importance within Britain.[7] Yet for fellow 'Celts', Welsh cultural autonomy was something to aspire to, and when French nationalists sought a Celtic muse, they looked to Wales. One example was the Breton-born Frenchman Alexis-François Rio (1797–1874) who, disenchanted with France after the revolution of 1830, travelled to Wales in search of 'Celtic poetry and history' that would reinvigorate the French Celtic population. As he reported to William Whewell, the French had 'let some of their Celtic spirit and culture slip away from them'.[8] Welsh scholars were likewise interested in their relation to the Bretons, and this section examines some of their initial pan-Celtic exchanges.

Perhaps the first true pan-Celt was Thomas Price, who we encountered in chapter 7 as the leading Welsh scholar of the first half of the nineteenth century.[9] He had heard Breton spoken by French prisoners of war during his childhood in Brecon, and in 1824 won the essay contest at the 1824 Powys *Eisteddfod* on the subject of 'The Causes and Extent of the Early intimacy and Mutual intercourse between the Armoricans and Britons; and the National affinity still existing between their descendants'.[10] Much of the essay was later incorporated into his travelogue 'A Tour through Brittany', which he undertook in 1829 as a representative of the British and Foreign Bible Society in order to discuss the publication of a Breton Bible.[11]

The Breton Bible saga was arguably the first substantial pan-Celtic exchange, and it shows how these scholar-activists spliced religious history with racial and national consciousness in the concoction of pan-Celtic historical memory. It began in 1814 with the secretary of the (newly renamed) *Société nationale des antiquaires*, the orientalist Jean-Antoine Saint-Martin, identifying a Bible in the Breton vernacular as a desideratum unlikely to be filled in France, and suggesting the British Bible Society undertake the project.[12] Yet the matter went unattended until Price raised it after being roused by a passage in the Rev. John Hughes's (1776–1843) *Horae Britannicae* (1819):

> We have the Sacred Scriptures in every language spoken in the British Isles. . . . But the Bretons of France have not so much as the New Testament in their ancient Tongue. There appears to be no one likely to undertake such a work, unless some Welshmen engage in it, and thus make some return, after the lapse of numerous ages, for the labours of Garmon and his associates in our island in the fourth century.[13]

Hughes's final sentence is a reference to Germanus (*c.* 378–*c.* 448), bishop of Auxerre, who travelled to Britain in the 430s and 440s to combat Pelagianism (essentially the denial of original sin), winning a crucial battle for the Britons over the Picts and Saxons in the process. Increased Cambro-Breton cooperation was a stated aim of Hughes's introduction; the above passage was therefore not a casual aside, but a calculated plea supplemented by an appendix on the affinity of their languages, with a brief digression on the related, though defunct, Cornish tongue.[14] Galvanised by Hughes's writing, Price began fundraising for the Bible project in 1824, addressing the Brecon *Eisteddfod* in pan-Celtic terms: Brittany was composed of a 'race of people of Celtic origin . . . who established a Welsh colony in Gaul', and whose descendants 'speak a language so similar to the Welsh, as clearly to show the identity of their origin'. It was their brethren from 'Armorica and Celtic Gaul' who had defeated Pelagianism and secured the British Church; assisting them would therefore 'discharge of a debt, which had lain heavily upon [the Welsh] for more than a thousand years'.[15] Beyond justifying pan-Celtic cooperation through a moralised historical argument, harking back to fifth-century Celtic Christianity also circumvented the Protestant-Catholic split between the modern Welsh and Bretons.

In 1824 the Bible society sanctioned the project and in the following year made Price the chief agent.[16] They put him in correspondence with the foremost Breton scholar, Le Gonidec, probably the most important Breton cultural figure in the first few decades of the nineteenth century. From a minor noble family, Le

Gonidec was ordained as a priest before the Revolution and then imprisoned during the Terror. In 1804 he arrived in Paris and helped to found the *Académie celtique*, to which he sent reports from his travels around France for the French Navy's forestry division. Having already in 1807 published a grammar, in 1821 Le Gonidec published his *Dictionnaire Celto-Breton*, and these two texts became standard works. Le Gonidec had visited Britain in 1802 and also had an interest in Welsh culture.[17] He agreed to translate the New Testament, sending the text to Price for criticisms, which were then incorporated into the one thousand copies printed by Le Gonidec himself at Angoulême in 1828. Ultimately, however, it was a flop. It was ignored by the Breton clergy (who mistrusted its Protestant provenance), and rewarded with a spot on the Catholic Church's Index of Banned Books. Although Le Gonidec completed the Old Testament by 1835 it was not printed. The episode created lasting links between cultural revivalists in Wales and Brittany and was an important spur to early pan-Celticism, but also showed how far apart the Bretons and Welsh were.

Price's own writings reinforce this. In 1829 he travelled through Brittany to Paris and then Angoulême to deliver a copy of Davies's Welsh-Latin dictionary to Le Gonidec. Breton antiquarians gave Price a hearty welcome, asking for the addresses of the 'Celtic literati' in Britain and inviting them to Brittany. Inspired by such enthusiasm, Price suggested to a Welsh friend that they might set up 'a sort of Eisteddfod' in Brittany the following year.[18] However, his writings show that pan-Celtic sentiment was still limited by some common prejudice and ignorance. As well as the obvious Breton differences—nominally French and devoutly Catholic—Price found Brittany the most exotic and barbarous of the Celtic nations he visited. He expected 'something egregiously outlandish and untamed, something between the Esquimaux and the Hottentot. . . . I was thus looking out for my Breton cousins, in their sheepskins and noserings'.[19] Although pleasantly surprised by what he found there, Price still did not see the Bretons and Welsh as identical, as some of his contemporaries wanted to. The Welsh and Bretons were 'both of the Celtic race', but still 'two separate nations'. He was particularly struck by their native costume and complained for several pages about the Breton *sabots*, or wooden clogs, which were a 'disgrace to civilization', and he could not decide which he found more offensive, 'actual barefoot squalor, or this remnant of the rudest and most uncouth efforts of barbarian ingenuity'.[20] Despite the fact that Price acknowledged the Bretons as his relatives and enjoyed his trip through Brittany, his writings suggest that in 1829 pan-Celtic kinship was still more of a scholarly idea than a sentiment shared by many people.

Cymdeithas Cymreigyddion y Fenni

Price's pan-Celtic interests coincided with a wider Welsh cultural revival in the 1830s, in which he played a major part. He helped to found the premier group in 1833, *Cymdeithas Cymreigyddion Y Fenni* (Abergavenny Welsh Society), which sought 'the cultivation of Welsh language and literature, the increase of historical research, the encouragement of national music and poetry, and likewise of native industry', but also made the first institutional move towards pan-Celticism.[21] At its heart was Augusta Hall, Lady Llanover (1802–1896), the most important patron of Welsh culture in the Victorian period.[22] Among other cultural projects—which included designing a national costume and sponsoring a revival of the triple harp—Lady Llanover also understood the importance of Welsh textual tradition, and after co-founding and sponsoring the Welsh Manuscripts Society, she purchased Iolo's *Nachlass* in 1853 and opened it to scholars for consulation.

There was a pan-Celtic dimension to *Cymreigyddion y Fenni* from the start, in the form of Alexis-François Rio. Born on the Breton archipelago of Île-d'Arz to royalist peasant parents, Rio joined the *petite chouannerie* rebellion against Napoleon during the Hundred Days in 1815, before pursuing a career as an art historian in Paris.[23] Although a proud Breton who spoke French with a heavy accent, Rio only had 'la fibre celtique' awakened in him in 1832 at the age of thirty-five, when Lady Llanover's sister showed him some Welsh verse in Rome.[24] Inspired, he left for Britain, where he made a strong impression on, among others, Carlyle, Disraeli, and Gladstone; Rio esteemed the latter, at one point inviting him to Brittany where he hoped to rid him of any anti-Catholic prejudice.[25] Eventually Rio made it to Abergavenny, where he won over the cultural elite with his enthusiasm and erudition. There he married the Catholic Apollonia Jones (1804–?) of Llanarth in 1833 and helped to found the Cymreigyddion Society, staying for several years. Named president of the 1836 *Eisteddfod*, Rio clearly had a sense of ownership in the whole enterprise, referring to the 1838 *Eisteddfod* as 'our Welsh festival' in a letter to Gladstone.[26]

Scholarship was a prominent concern for the Cymreigyddion Society, which made an essay contest the centrepiece of its *eisteddfodau*.[27] Another European scholar was of special importance here, Baron Christian von Bunsen, a German scholar and diplomat mentioned in chapter 6 as a friend of Prichard.[28] Taken to Rome by the historian and diplomat Bartold Niebuhr (1776–1831) as his secretary, Bunsen met and married Frances Waddington (1791–1876)—Lady Llanover's elder sister—there in 1817.[29] When they arrived back in Britain in 1838, the couple spent most of the next two years at Llanover Hall, where Bunsen took an active interest in Welsh culture, language, and history. He solicited entries from German scholars to the essay competition and set the 1842 question on 'The place which the Welsh language occupies among the languages of the Celtic family; and together with the other branches of the same, among the languages of the Indo-European race', which he thought would allow the Cymreigyddion Society to 'take the lead, in one of the most important enquiries of the age' by proposing a question which 'if well answered' would be 'a decisive influence on the science and literature of Europe'.[30] It was won by Bunsen's friend Carl Meyer, who Bunsen then helped to become librarian to Prince Albert from 1847 to 1850.[31] Bunsen suggested that Meyer should occasionally be given leave, 'that he may in Ireland and Scotland study the remains of Celtic antiquity, as he had done already in the matter of the Welsh manuscripts'.[32] Although he initially impressed Queen Victoria (1819–1901) with his 'knowing I don't know how many languages, including numbers of ancient ones such as Welsh & Irish', Meyer ultimately had to step down after harassing too many women at court and stalling on his academic work.[33]

Other scholars who took part in the *eisteddfodau* as judges were the English historian Henry Hallam (1777–1859) and James Cowles Prichard.[34] The Welsh network revered Prichard for his Christian piety and Celtic philology, and his involvement in Welsh cultural circles extended back to Iolo's day. He judged Meyer's 1842 essay but also encouraged the runner-up, A. J. Johnes (1809–1871), to publish his work, welcoming its contribution to the monogenetic argument.[35] Prichard also judged Price's winning essay of 1845 on a pan-Celtic topic comparing the historical utility of the 'Welsh, Irish and [Scottish] Gaelic' languages.[36] Price stressed that the languages descended from the same 'Celtic original' but, in what was characteristic for both him and Prichard, he easily found Welsh the superior language; a comparative table at the end of the essay presented Welsh as having eight superior qualities to the two each of Irish and Scots Gaelic.[37]

Prichard's role and the arguments presented by members of the Cymreigyddion Society illustrate the extent to which Abergavenny revivalists were connected to wider academic currents in Britain and Europe—this was a movement seeking to influence scientific discourse and embed its own ideas into a broader intellectual awareness. A long letter written by the English comparative philologist Richard Garnett to Iolo's son Taliesin Williams may be taken as some proof that they succeeded; among other things, Garnett praised the researches of Le Gonidec, Price, and Prichard, all of whom had convinced Garnett of the 'etymological affinities' and connections between 'Celtic and the great Indo-European family of tongues'.[38] The network provides a striking exception to arguments made by Sinéad Garrigan-Mattar about the old-fashioned 'romantic antiquarian' context of Celtic studies before the inception of Celtology on the Continent in the 1870s;[39] while still operating within a Christian framework like Prichard, the Abergavenny competition and essays conformed to the standards of international philological scholarship and were certainly scientific by contemporary benchmarks. Indeed, as judge of the 1842 essay contest, Prichard applauded 'the liberality of the Association which offers a free competition to the natives of all countries', as philology was underappreciated in Britain and the winning essay 'enlarged the field of philological science'.[40] A number of other notable works arose from the Abergavenny network,[41] and its intellectual legacy lasted beyond the disbandment of the group.

The 1838 *Eisteddfod*

The salient event for pan-Celticism was the 1838 Abergavenny *Eisteddfod*, to which five young Breton noblemen travelled under a mission sanctioned by King Louis Philippe.[42] Rio played a central role, inviting the Bretons 'to renew, after the interruption of many centuries, the ancient relations between the two principal branches of the Celtic family'.[43] He collected them in Brittany, accompanied them across the Channel, and dropped them off at Abergavenny.[44] Price and Le Gonidec also played a role. Although the latter was too ill to attend, he put his disciples—the 'poëte aimable' Auguste Brizeux (1803–1858) and the 'antiquaire très-studieux' Theodore Hersart, comte de la Villemarqué—in contact with Price, who discussed Celtic philology with the latter and encouraged him to submit an essay to the contest.[45]

Villemarqué became a gentleman-scholar and was elected to the *Académie des inscriptions et belles-lettres* and the *Légion d'Honneur*.[46] In the late 1830s he was preparing his *Barzaz Breiz*—a collection of native verse that eventually caused an Ossianic controversy—and was charged with instructions (and given six hundred francs) from the *Ministre d'instruction publique* to search for Breton manuscripts in the major British libraries.[47] Accompanying him were five other young Breton aristocrats.[48] Brizeux had intended to join the deputation, but stayed behind at the last minute to look after Le Gonidec, whose health was rapidly deteriorating (he died during the *eisteddfod*).[49]

Fuelled by mutual national admiration and racial fraternity, the 1838 *Eisteddfod* was full of pan-Celtic nods to shared history and traditions. Taking place over 10 and 11 October, it opened with a morning procession into Abergavenny over two miles long, before a series of opening speeches. In his address, Price painted the event as the culmination of a pan-Celtic odyssey, considering 'the gloomy events that have befallen our race' and rejoicing in the long-awaited deliverance of 'allies and representatives of other nations . . . the sons of the most chivalrous lands in Europe.'[50] Villemarqué composed a song that was the highlight of the gathering for many of the Welsh, who claimed to understand the supposedly Old Breton words, thus legitimating the truth of pan-Celticism. Sufficiently impressed, Prichard jotted off a letter to an American correspondent:

> I had lately the gratification of hearing some Gentlemen from Brittany deputed by King Louis Philippe, sing some Breton songs in their native Armorican before a Welsh assembly termed Cymreigyddion, & of observing that the Welsh understood them & evinced the most enthusiastic pleasure in recognising their common nationality. It is a most curious circumstance that this branch of our old British language should be still preserved to such a degree of purity as to be intelligible after a period of fifteen centuries of separation.[51]

Next Louis Jacquelot de Boisrouvray recited a poem from Alphonse de Lamartine (1790–1869) and gave a speech about the fraternity shared by the 'twin peoples' given by nature, like all twins, 'mysterious ways of communication.'[52]

On the following morning, the *Gorsedd* inducted Villemarqué into its ranks, and gave him a certificate to prove it. He wrote home to his father of both the enthusiasm with which the song he had composed for the occasion had been received and of his pride at being inducted into the bardic order:

> I am now a bard, truly a bard! 'An official bard', and I was received according to the ancient rites of the fifth and sixth centuries, which have been handed down to us. . . . My song won me this honour, of which I am very proud.[53]

Villemarqué's example shows the potency of invented traditions on those already made vulnerable by their own desire to believe. Of course, Villemarqué was not alone, with Price and even Prichard convinced that the event had genuine roots—whether ceremonial or linguistic—stretching over a thousand years into the past. In the same letter to his father, Villemarqué noted his admiration for Prichard, who he described as 'one of the most excellent scholars

I have seen in my life'.[54] He stayed with Bunsen at Prichard's home before visiting Stonehenge, remarking with disbelief to his father at the enthusiasm with which he was received and the eminent company he was privileged to share. Price wrote especially to the Cymreigyddion of Merthyr to greet Villemarqué's visit with 'such attentions as are due to his mission'.[55] They duly complied and tracked him down at the house of Lady Charlotte Guest, who saw through the spectacle: 'There was a great deal of Breton & Welsh talked which I think was but little understood de part et d'autre'.[56] As Mary-Ann Constantine has remarked, all of this special treatment would have been a heady cocktail for a twenty-three-year-old already predisposed to romantic ideas.[57]

It should therefore be no surprise that Villemarqué retained a lifelong commitment to pan-Celticism. He submitted essays to *eisteddfodau*, controversially published French translations of Welsh poetry, and planned to write a travelogue provisionally titled 'Le Dragon rouge ou les Bretons des Galles', though it never materialised.[58] He remained in contact with Welsh scholars and helped to organise the historian Henri Martin's trip to Wales in 1861.[59] His preface to the 1839 edition of the *Barzaz Breiz* was full of pan-Celtic gestures and ended with a flourishing nod to the previous year's *eisteddfod* and shared Celtic memory:

> Recently, in the midst of a family celebration thrown for the Bretons by their Welsh brothers, seeing wave the old flags of our common ancestors, rediscovering moers similar to our moeurs, hearts which answered our hearts, hearing voices which seemed to call out from the grave, awakened as if by miracle by the notes of the Celtic harps, voices we recognised after more than a thousand years, we repeated, with enthusiasm the traditional refrain . . . *No! King Arthur is not dead!*[60]

Villemarqué's works were marked by pan-Celtic sentiment for the rest of his life, and the enthusiasm with which he left Wales helps to explain in part why Bretons carried the pan-Celtic baton in the mid nineteenth century.

Yet it was not just the participants who were enthusiastic about the *Eisteddfod*; elements of the press on both sides of the channel also hailed the event. A letter to the editor in the *Monmouthshire Merlin* praised Rio and lauded Villemarqué's bardic welcome as proof of the 'perfect union', which the correspondent believed 'for all time', would 'exist between our beloved Wales and the renowned land of Brittany . . . Identified as they are in language and ancestors'.[61] The British press made much of the deputation of the French king, and Villemarqué's sister teased him about his label, 'l'envoyé de Philippe'.[62] Predictably, English papers like *John Bull* and the satirical *Figaro in London* scorned the gathering, but even the conservative *Morning Post* could not hide its positive curiosity.[63] French papers also covered the exchange, with the *Gazette de France* noting the high quality of scholarship and pedigree of the Cymreigyddion Society, who had invited the Armoricans out of the 'old links of race, language, and affection', whose participation gave the festival 'a new character of nationality' and the air of 'a grand family celebration'.[64]

What stimulated these early exchanges? Chartier-le Floch has recently argued it was 'la vague romantique' and its obsession with traditional communities and an idealised pastoral life.[65] Perhaps elements of this interpretation were true for Rio, Villemarqué, and the Breton delegation, and it is certain that parts of the shared Celtic past were romanticised, but as a whole this was not a movement looking to the past and retreating into itself. One of the Breton deputation, Auguste François Félix du Marc'hallac'h (1808–1891), suggested that the bonds of kinship illuminated by historical scholarship allowed them to look to the future.[66] Guiomar has argued that the Breton network, far from isolating itself from the world, wanted to share their work and passion with it, and Welsh revivalists operated under the same auspices.[67] If this brought their nations closer together, then so much the better, but pan-Celticism's hold was still weak. Although intellectual exchange continued, another delegate swap would not occur until the 1860s. Still, pan-Celticism was alive from the 1830s.

Charles de Gaulle and *le Congrès celtique international*

The French—often though not always of Breton origin—showed great enthusiasm for pan-Celticism in the three decades between the 'pan-Celtic' *Eisteddfod* at Abergavenny and the *Congrès celtique* at St. Brieuc. This manifested primarily but not solely in tours and literary appreciation for Wales.[68] Villemarqué was the most obvious link between those two events and the network of people interested in them. He drew some of the best Breton scholars around him in the *Breuriez-Breiz* (Brotherhood of Brittany) to meet in Paris and discuss Breton literature and language in the late 1850s, but he also had an international network that included the Celtic countries, and he published pan-Celtic works such as *La légende celtique, en Irlande, en Cambrie et en Bretagne* (Paris, 1859).

The historian Henri Martin was committed to pan-Celticism for the purposes of French nationalism. He sought in the Celtic nations the outward manifestations of a Celtic culture that he perceived in the French character but not its public life. For this reason, as we saw in chapter 7, Martin greatly valued

Iolo's bardic material for the window it seemed to provide onto ancient Celtic culture. Martin travelled to Wales in 1861, where Villemarqué provided him with a letter of recommendation to Thomas Stephens. With Stephens translating, Martin spoke at the Aberdare *Eisteddfod* about how France was rediscovering its Celtic spirit, which he hoped would provide a basis for reconciliation with Britain. In the face of rising Pan-Slavism, which he feared, Martin wanted the West to 'form a Pan-Celtism; all the sons of the Gauls shall unite for the good of civilization and the human race'.[69] Heather Williams calls this speech 'the most rousing call for Celtic solidarity' since the 1838 *Eisteddfod*, and from this point until his death two decades later Martin would reappear favourably in the Welsh press.[70] His main purpose in 1861, however, was to consult Iolo's *Nachlass*, about which he reported excitedly to Adolphe Pictet:

> I have just come back from Wales, and I acquired there the certitude of the existence of many documents analogous to the Cyfrinach [the 'Secrets of the Bards'], which prove what had before been contested, the existence of collective secret doctrines. I was able to browse the precious collection of M. Edward Williams for several days.[71]

Martin wrote in his published account of the trip that the material seemed imprinted with Platonism.[72] He returned the next summer with Alfred Erny (1838–?), who recorded Lady Llanover's lingering pan-Brittonic feelings, and Martin continued on to Ireland to examine the remnants of Celtic traditions there.

The greatest pan-Celtic rejuvenator was an unlikely one: a young man born in the northern town of Valenciennes named Charles de Gaulle (1837–1880; see Fig. 11).[73] He was in fact the uncle of General Charles de Gaulle (1890–1970), future president of the Fifth Republic. Together with a fellow Parisian, the scholar Henri Gaidoz, discussed in the following section, De Gaulle forged new links between Paris, Brittany, and Wales.

Paralysed from a young age, de Gaulle engrossed himself in study and fell in love with Brittany when he read Rio's book on the *petite chouannerie*.[74] He learnt the language and became secretary to Villemarqué's *Breuriez*. Confined to his *fauteuil*, de Gaulle never travelled to Brittany, but the cultural landscape depicted by Rio must have seemed appropriately matched to his Catholic monarchism; he noted that reading Rio's work for the first time made him feel immediately Breton. And like Rio responding to the Revolution of 1830 forty years before him, de Gaulle looked to the Celtic qualities of France for the 'morale renaissance' it needed after its defeat in the Franco-Prussian War.[75] De

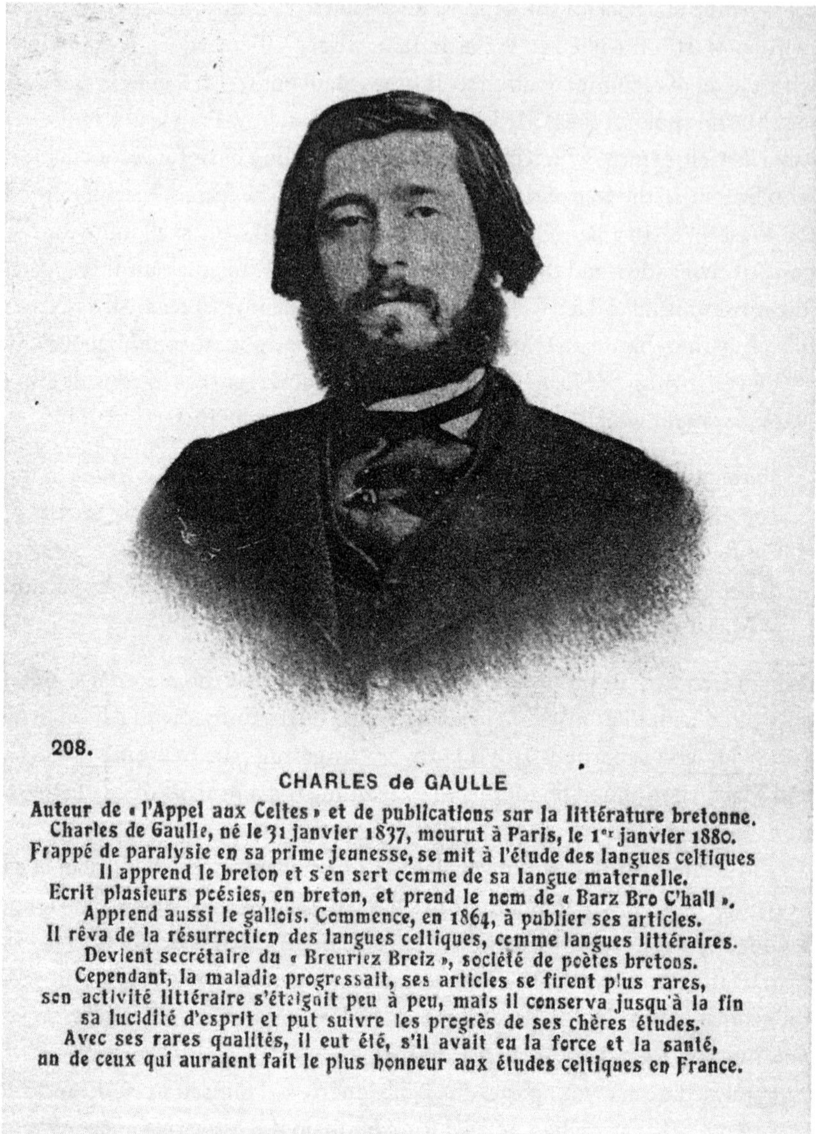

FIG. 11. Charles de Gaulle, Carte postale. Reproduced with permission of Archives municipales de Rennes, 100 Fi 448.

Gaulle was also drawn to Wales, and learnt the language, in which he wrote to Welsh scholars such as John Rhys and his wife Elspeth (1841–1911)—presumably they met when Rhys studied in Paris—signing off as Siarl o Fro'al.[76]

De Gaulle's major contribution was a pan-Celtic essay: 'Les Celtes au XIXe siècle: Appel aux Représentants actuels de la race celtique' (1864). It was first printed in the *Revue de Bretagne et de Vendée,* before republication as a pamphlet that went through four editions and an English translation by 1904. Grounded in contemporary scholarship, de Gaulle's text is nevertheless a clarion call for action: 'Man is born to act, not to know'.[77] De Gaulle divided the essay into two halves and began with an appeal for greater cooperation among the Celtic nations. He claimed they were united by racial affiliation and were the Western vanguard of the original Aryans, and had maintained an advanced 'liberal' civilization—which included the separation of powers—before Roman and Frankish conquest.[78] Sceptical about Thierry's overly rigid French racial divisions, de Gaulle followed Renan in his pan-Celtic vision, refocusing attention on Brittany, Wales, Ireland, and the Highlands of Scotland and away from France.[79] But other than vague calls for the Celtic nations to come together and pursue common goals like language revival and the preservation of popular culture, the first half of the essay is relatively unremarkable. The second half more than makes up for this, featuring calls for a Celtic Union, a new Celtic Atlantic colony, and a neo-Druidic order. This began with an idea for a Celtic *école normale,* where Christian neo-Druids would teach national history, poetry, and music to youths from all the Celtic countries in their native languages.[80] A monthly journal, *La revue celtique,* would give Celts an international forum. The Celtic college would be part of a wider Celtic union to benefit 'the entire race', united by frequent events and a synthetic language composed of 'neo-Celtic idioms'.[81] The essay's finale urged British Celts to stop emigrating to the colonies and propping up the British Empire, and to instead form a new pan-Celtic colony in the Western hemisphere on the model of Welsh Patagonia (*Y Wladfa*).[82]

After the essay's publication, De Gaulle wrote in some excitement to the founder of *Y Wladfa,* Michael D. Jones (1822–1898), noting that news of it had elicited 'the greatest sympathy amongst the Armorican-Britons'; de Gaulle enclosed copies of his essay 'Les Celtes' for 'the bold pioneers of Celtic colonization' and asked if Breton emigrants could join their Welsh brethren in Patagonia, even though he was slightly disappointed the Welsh settlers had accepted Argentinian sovereignty.[83] De Gaulle was known in Wales for his support of the colony, and was kept updated on the venture by friends of Jones.[84]

By outlining common Celtic goals and repeatedly using language like 'our race', de Gaulle went further than any previous figure and may be called the first (uppercase P) Pan-Celt. He sent the essay to the *Cambrian Journal*, which translated and published it as a standalone pamphlet, acknowledging its 'desire to promote the welfare of the Celtic people', but censoring most of the second half as 'repugnant to our feelings of religion and loyalty', thereby foreshadowing cleavages that would reappear in later pan-Celtic groups.[85] Although most of his more ambitious proposals went unheeded by his contemporaries, some were adopted immediately.

One of these was the reestablishment of pan-Celtic contact through a 'general congress of Celtic science', where the 1838 Abergavenny *Eisteddfod* served as a model and pan-Celtic *lieu de mémoire*.[86] However, unlike the Abergavenny gathering, the *Breuriez Breiz* planned to incorporate the Gaelic branch of the Celtic language family—which Martin in particular insisted on—envisaging an event that would reconnect the entire Celtic race.[87] Billing it as the *Congrès celtique international*, the Franco-Breton group sent out invitations to each of the British Celtic nations. Villemarqué, Martin, and de Gaulle devised a particularly emotive proposal to the Welsh, which de Gaulle translated into Welsh. It began by identifying the fraternal bond, 'On the other side of the channel lives a nation whose ancestors are yours, whose name is your own, who preserves the same old traditions, and speaks almost the same language',[88] before appealing to historical memory by invoking the famous 1838 Abergavenny *Eisteddfod* where the fraternal bond had begun to be retied. The congress, they hoped, would tighten it. Martin wrote to Thomas Stephens, along similar lines, that they wanted to 'strengthen the links between the *celtisants* of the two sides of the sea'.[89]

The advertisement piqued the interest of the press in Britain and Ireland, but responses varied. In Ireland *The Nation* hoped that 'the Celts of Ireland' would make an effort to attend and looked forward to 'welcoming to Dublin at some future day, some of our Celtic kinsmen of Brittany'.[90] The English and Lowland Scottish press was more circumspect. One London-based Scottish journalist noted that it had been advertised as 'a great Pan-Celtic Congress', or an 'International Eisteddfod', where 'Breton, Welsh, Scotch and Irish Celts' would be represented, but he half-joked that he hoped the Irish republican delegation would not seek to start a 'Pan-Celtic Republic'.[91] The *Nottingham Journal* also saw the congress in political terms and set it within wider European developments, noting its Pan-Hellenist and Pan-Slavic antecedents, but thought it would be impossible 'to construct a nationality out of the scattered and unabsorbed fragments of the Celtic races'.[92]

The goals of the organisers did not reflect these political predictions. As Martin wrote to Pictet:

> There will take place an international Celtic Congress at St. Brieuc. We hope that this will be a point of departure for outlining the links between our Bretons and the friends of Celtic studies in France and on the continent, on one side, and of the Welsh first of all and then the Gaels, on the other.[93]

After an introductory address hailing Cymro-Breton kinship, the congress rapidly ratcheted up the intellectual gears, as Martin and Villemarqué plunged directly into issues of racial and linguistic scholarship.[94] Villemarqué, still the poster boy for Cambro-Breton cooperation, also discussed the ancient relations between Wales and Brittany, but other than a speech by a Welsh pastor resident in Morlaix, the only real pan-Celtic element was the performance of the blind Welsh harpist Gruffyd and his daughter—both wearing national costume—who had been sent as a friendly gesture by Lady Llanover in lieu of her own attendance.[95] Despite its pan-Celtic aspirations, in actuality the congress was a pan-Cymric event and was well attended only by Bretons. Of the four Welsh delegates two already lived in Brittany, and the lone Cornish participant was not about to reignite Cornwall's extinct Celticity. Nevertheless, its organisers proclaimed the Congress triumphant, and the inclusion of Welsh traditions went a long way towards this conclusion. Martin wrote to Pictet that 'We succeeded in Saint-Brieuc . . . all of this is a very good sign for the introduction of eisteddfodau in Brittany'.[96] However, he later admitted that for future congresses they hoped to 'attract . . . a greater concord of Celts from abroad'.[97] Perhaps the Welsh were scared off by de Gaulle's overenthusiasm. Henri Martin wrote (unsuccessfully) to the Johnes family in Wales before the conference that 'there is nothing to fear from [de Gaulle]', to whom he had made it clear that the congress was not the place for religious discussions, which could create 'invisible divisions in the cause', an interesting insight into French pan-Celtic thought and its aims for the future.[98] The involvement of French Celtic scholars was also curtailed by the controversy then breaking out about the authenticity of Villemarqué's *Barzaz Breiz*, just reissued in a sixth edition. François-Marie Luzel (1821–1895) summed up the new critical mood emerging in French Celtic philology: 'Play at being a bard or an archbard, or even a Druid, if that amuses you, but try not to distort history with your inventions'.[99] Villemarqué protested to his critics that he brought his manuscripts to Saint-Brieuc in order to show them to the ascendant philological critic Henri d'Arbois de Jubainville, but the latter did not bother to turn up.

Though the proceedings were quite esoteric, this congress was nevertheless a political event. With its stated goal of bringing together the Celtic race, its participants were well aware of the analogous movements in Europe and North America seeking the rapprochement of common stocks. The 1867 Congress is a well-known event to cultural historians of Brittany and Wales;[100] however, there seems little awareness that the French group also planned a second *Congrès celtique international* for 1869. Henri Martin wrote to his friend A. J. Johnes about it several times over 1867–1869, hoping to draw Welshmen, 'who have loyally guarded the common traditions' and were interested in the 'continental Celtic renaissance'.[101] Elsewhere, Martin called the event 'our Breton *Eisteddfod*', but it ultimately had to be called off due to political difficulties in France, where Martin expected another revolution.[102] He also suggested the formation of some sort of Pan-Celtic league, about which A. J. Johnes wrote to a correspondent of Scottish extraction that he expected 'Wales will <u>have her due</u> if the Celtic Society is set on foot!'[103] Although the associational attempts were all stillborn, the existence of such correspondence networks reveals that pan-Celticism was becoming real in the minds of cultural figures.

Henri Gaidoz and the *Revue celtique*

The strengthening of Celtic studies and pan-Celticism reinforced one another. As we have seen, the Abergavenny *eisteddfodau* and the *Congrès celtique* at St. Brieuc championed scholarship as both method and medium for connecting the Celtic nations. Thomas Charles-Edwards notes that the period between 1853 and 1913—bookended by the publication of Zeuß's *Grammatica Celtica* and the second volume of Holger Pedersen's *Vergleichende Grammatik der keltischen Sprachen*—was that in which Celtic linguistic scholarship outside of the Celtic countries flourished most vigorously, above all in Germany.[104] In this period of increasing Franco-German antagonism, French scholars were acutely aware of German dominance and sought to make their own mark in Celtic studies.[105] Perhaps more than any other event, it was the foundation of the *Revue celtique*, first envisioned by de Gaulle but undertaken chiefly by his friend Henri Gaidoz from 1869, that marked the inception of Celtic studies as a modern, scientific, and interdisciplinary field. Martin identified Gaidoz as part of a new hypercritical school unwilling to take some received elements of knowledge—such as Iolo's Bardism—at face value.[106] Gaidoz had been educated in Germany, but 'more to learn German than philology', and, like Renan, he was caught between his admiration for German science and his French nationalism.[107] Although he is now often identified as a founder of modern French folklore studies, Gaidoz himself looked back to that discipline's origins with the *Académie celtique*, where he claimed 'Jacques Grimm' had learned his trade.[108] Germano-scepticism is probably also what sometimes led him to huffily dismiss philology as a science unimportant in its own right and only useful for the tools it furnished mythography, ethnography, and literary criticism, as he expressed in a letter to Pictet.[109]

These subjects formed the core of his vision for the *Revue celtique* (Fig. 12), but he also anticipated editions of unpublished texts in the Celtic languages, such as works of history, philology, and 'a bibliography as complete as possible', all made by contributors from across Britain, Ireland, and Europe, in 'French, German, English, Italian, Spanish, and Latin'.[110] If the lack of Celtic languages here seems strange, Gaidoz explained to Pictet that although there was no *revue* of this type in 'les pays Celtiques', one was unnecessary because most of their inhabitants were uneducated and uninterested. That a new scientific page had been turned can be inferred from Gaidoz's encouragement to John Rhys in 1874 to cultivate subscriptions from '<u>noblemen</u> or rich clergymen interested in their national language', because 'La Revue has lost a large number of subscribers since the first volume (undoubtedly they found it too scholarly), British subscriptions have fallen from 80 to 40!'[111] In addition to Pictet, Gaidoz recruited Renan, Stokes (for whom starting a Celtic journal was 'an old dream of mine'),[112] John Rhys, and many of the German scholars about which Gaidoz was somewhat sceptical. It cannot be considered anything other than a striking success and remained a flagship journal for over sixty years. It surely helped Gaidoz to be appointed to a chair for the study of Celtic languages and literatures at the new *École pratique des hautes études* in 1876, where he taught Celtic philology for decades, including to future luminaries such as Rudolf Thurneysen and Joseph Vendryès (1875–1960).[113]

As hinted at, Gaidoz was one of a number of intellectuals whose scholarship sustained a wider concern with French politics. A committed regionalist despite his Parisian birth, he sponsored an 1870 appeal for the protection of regional languages with de Gaulle and the philologist Hyacinthe de Charencey (1832–1916). They hoped the 'decentralisation of languages' would lead organically to national decentralisation, curiously pointing to the Celtic nations of

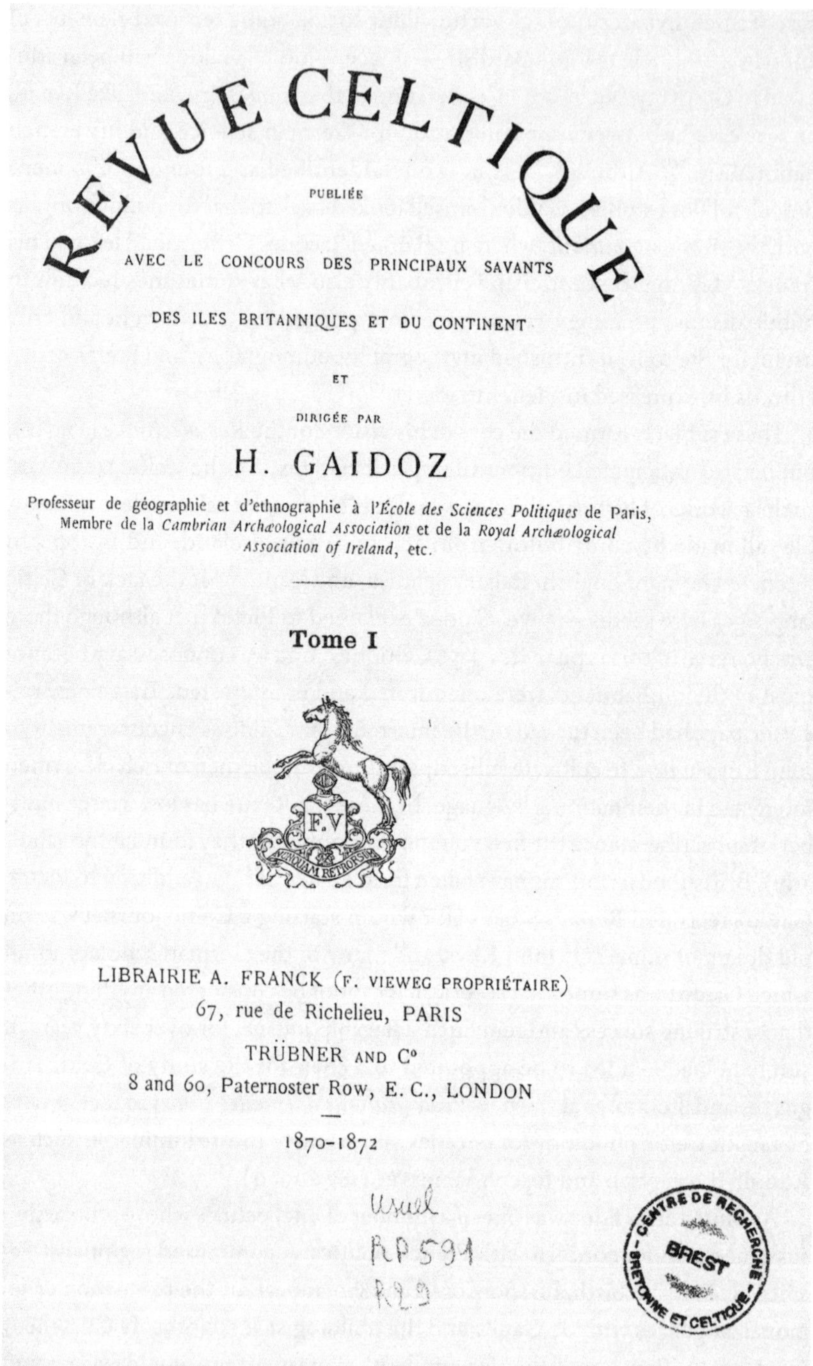

REVUE CELTIQUE

PUBLIÉE

AVEC LE CONCOURS DES PRINCIPAUX SAVANTS

DES ILES BRITANNIQUES ET DU CONTINENT

ET

DIRIGÉE PAR

H. GAIDOZ

Professeur de géographie et d'ethnographie à l'*École des Sciences Politiques* de Paris,
Membre de la *Cambrian Archæological Association* et de la *Royal Archæological Association of Ireland*, etc.

Tome I

LIBRAIRIE A. FRANCK (F. VIEWEG PROPRIÉTAIRE)
67, rue de Richelieu, PARIS
TRÜBNER AND C°
8 and 60, Paternoster Row, E. C., LONDON

1870-1872

FIG. 12. *Revue celtique* I (1870–1872).

Britain as positive examples, perhaps thinking particularly of Wales, where the native language was still robust. Composed during the last breath of the Second Empire, the petition came to nothing, but Gaidoz republished it again in 1903 when the regionalist movement was gaining steam.[114]

Gaidoz, de Gaulle, and Martin all embraced pan-Celticism in the context of wider fears of Pan-Germanism and its bellicosity.[115] During the siege of Paris, de Gaulle wrote despondently to Martin, wondering whether the French would 'succomb in our turn to the fatality which seems to weigh on the entire Celtic race'.[116] Unable to begin the intended *Revue celtique* in 1870 because of the war, Gaidoz penned an analysis of Pan-Germanism, warning that Teutonic pugnacity and an overemphasis on race had infected the German intelligentsia.[117] For a regionalist like Gaidoz, the homogenising centralisation he saw in Pan-German racialism stood in stark contrast to France's racial hybridity and corresponding principle of individual nationalities. On an 1874 trip to (newly German) Alsace, Gaidoz wistfully described it to Rhys as 'a sad sight for a Frenchman', a reminder of the tension between the professionalization of science and the age of high nationalism.[118] Eleven years before Renan's famous lecture, Gaidoz affirmed that it was 'a consciousness, a contract of souls, resting on the participation of free wills which alone makes a nation'.[119] Renan echoed Gaidoz in *Qu'est-ce qu'une nation?*—also aimed at assimilationist Pan-German racialism—and rejected the equation of nation and race, noting that France was Celtic, Iberian, and Germanic.[120] It was for precisely these reasons that figures like Gaidoz and Renan could embrace regional, and especially Celtic, particularity in the context of a wider French nationalism. A rather banal though illustrative set of examples of this kind of cultural nationalism were the *Dîners celtiques* organised by Gaidoz and (until his death) Renan in Paris from 1879–1902. One of a number of regional dinners popular in the capital at the time—there were also Norman and Provençal occasions—the *Dîners celtiques* were open to Bretons and Celtic enthusiasts from France and Britain, and attracted the leading Celtic scholars, who discussed poetry, history, and politics more generally. Renan himself also treated pan-Celticism warmly and had embraced early in his correspondence to John Rhys their 'antique communauté de race'. Sensitive to the international situation, Renan encouraged a contingent of Welsh archaeologists to work for peace, which was 'truly . . . a Celtic work. We are a sympathetic race and for that reason the world readily listens to us'.[121] But the point here is that, by regionalist logic, if what made the French nation great was its heterogeneity, then the celebration of individual regional (or even Celtic national) identities was simultaneously a celebration of France itself.

Conclusion

The pan-Celtic movement as it developed over the nineteenth century fed upon the cultural strengths of Wales and Brittany, and the political power of France. Welsh 'Celtic' traditions seemed to provide the spiritual succour for French political thinkers still negotiating France's national story and character, while European interest strengthened Welsh self-confidence. Brittany also stood out as a subject of interest to French nationalists, but the fact that the Bretons Le Gonidec, Renan, and Villemarqué—not to mention the non-Breton de Gaulle who had never even been there—were all based in Paris shows that Brittany had yet to fully develop its own autonomous cultural movement, though pan-Celticism provided a vital source for the national affirmation to come.

10

Politics and pan-Celticism

LAND AND NATION IN IRELAND, SCOTLAND, AND WALES

AFTER A SERIES of fiery and emotive speeches about the 'Land Question', given in a Sutherland glade in late September 1886, the Scottish sociologist John Stuart Stuart-Glennie (1841–1910) urged the audience that it was time to harness the energy unleashed by years of popular agitation in the Celtic countries.

> That whereas the Scottish Highlanders, the Irish, and the Welsh have now common political objects, it is hereby agreed to form a Celtic League, of which the hereafter-to-be elected Executive shall organise mutual co-operation, with respect to those common objects both in the country, and in Parliament.[1]

A 'Keltic League' was created shortly thereafter to promote an advantageous solution to the Land Question, 'Home Rule all round', and 'a spirit of brotherhood and solidarity . . . between the different branches of the Keltic Race'.[2] We have seen repeatedly throughout this book that recognition of a shared Celtic past was no guarantee of common Celtic sentiment, let alone political cooperation. In fact, it was often a point of contention between members of different Celtic nations who wanted to claim the Celtic legacy primarily for their own people. However, the 1886 Conference and the formation of the 'Keltic League' stand out as an important pan-Celtic moment, when a political cause was finally harnessed to the idea of a shared Celtic history. What had changed?

In short, the Celtic past finally became politically useful. It did so in the context of a long-standing problem in all four nations of Britain and Ireland: the 'Land Question'. Generally speaking, the Land Question revolved around the facts that the vast majority of land belonged to only a few thousand people; that many landlords were absent and merely extracted profit from their estates without proportionate corresponding investment; that the tenant-peasantry was occasionally evicted and forced to emigrate to cities or overseas; and that these populations were angry about it and increasingly willing to use force to assert their will.[3] Although it had been an issue throughout the nineteenth century, the Land Question became increasingly vexed in each nation during its final decades, becoming violent in Ireland and, to a lesser extent, Scotland. The Irish 'Land War' of 1879 to 1882 was a vital moment in the Irish nationalist movement, bringing together the social force of agrarian discontent with the political direction of the Irish Parliamentary Party. The politics of land were also salient in Scotland and Wales—and, as Paul Readman has shown, England too[4]—where an increasing awareness of a shared Celtic past and cultural similarities in the present created a fruitful area for transnational political and cultural exchange, and fertile ground for a political pan-Celticism.

The Land Question had been analysed in pan-Celtic terms at least from the 1840s amid wider political and social developments. For example, an article in the *Leeds Times* from November 1843 averred that

> The Celtic population . . . is by far the oldest portion of the British population; and if anciency of possession gives right, then they have the oldest right of all to a comfortable subsistence on the soil on which they live . . . the Celts of South Britain are in a state of agrarian insurrection, in Wales; the Celts of Ireland are in a state of virtual rebellion to the English government and the Celts of the Northern Highlands, stung by the grinding tyranny of their landlords, are now organising themselves for the maintenance of their rights and the resistance of a most grinding system of oppression.[5]

However, if it was noticed that people in the Celtic areas of Britain and Ireland were agitating, and that they had claims in common because of their history, they were not as yet working together. Pan-Celtic political cooperation would not arise for another few decades, and even then it did not have the intensity that English and Scottish Lowland observers sometimes suspected. As Andrew Newby has shown in detail, they feared that Irish radicals and socialists had infiltrated the Highlands and were responsible for the disturbances there; however, Newby concludes that Irish agitation inspired rather than instigated Highland rebellion.[6] Foremost among those galvanizing activity in the Highlands was the Irish land agitator Michael Davitt (1846–1906), about whom W. B. Yeats later wrote that he had intended if possible to carry 'the land league into the Highlands, and rescue for Ireland as much of Scotland as was still Gaelic in blood and language'.[7] We will see below that Davitt had similar intentions for Wales, and was one of the principal pan-Celtic agents during his lifetime.

The Land Question is a huge, complicated, and well-investigated topic, and so my purpose here must be limited to exploring how its development in the Celtic nations fused with the rhetoric of pan-Celticism. I do not discuss the various legislative solutions advanced, except through the lens that Celtic historicism played in their genesis. As Clive Dewey summarised the historicist case:

> What ancient Celtic literature proved—or was held to prove—was that from time immemorial the whole Celtic race had enjoyed tenant rights such as those contemporary Irish and Scottish tenant leagues were demanding. Presented as an appeal for the restoration of rights only recently, incompletely, and unjustly abrogated, the tenant-right campaign acquired a force it would otherwise have lacked.[8]

It will be seen that Welsh political thinkers conceived of their land campaign in similar historicist terms. Above all, the aim in this chapter is to illustrate how, in pursuing political change, this sense of a distinct Celtic history mixed with pan-Celtic recognition and feeling in Ireland, Scotland, and Wales. The politicised pan-Celticism examined here was an essential step to take before the emergence of the fully-fledged Pan-Celtic movement of the twentieth century, examined in the two subsequent chapters.

The Irish Land War

The Irish Land Question stretched back centuries and it was widely recognised that land relations were ultimately rooted in conquest, the legacies of which still shaped the power asymmetry between landlord and tenants. The O'Connellite *Cork Examiner*, for example, wrote that 'the tenure by which the chief part of the land of the Celt is held, both in Scotland and Ireland, is merely *physical force*, or the right of the strongest'.[9] Famine was a sadly regular occurrence, and we saw in chapters 7 and 8, respectively, how the Great Famine of the late 1840s formed an important part of the background to the politicisation of the Celtic past by the Young Ireland movement, as well as how it provided the setting for a more strident racialisation of Celt and Saxon. The fusion of land issues, radical and revolutionary politics, and Celticism remained a feature of Irish politics and culture for the rest of the century, and eventually led to links with the other Celtic nations on a related basis.

Celticism provided an easy link between historical ideas of the Irish people and the land itself, and searching newspaper databases shows that 'Celt' was increasingly used as a descriptor for the Irish peasantry, with a noticeable spike from the 1840s.[10] This coincided with the rise of Young Ireland, whose paper *The Nation* was—as Michael Davitt identified in his history of the Irish land movement—'a powerful advocate of land reform'.[11] The most historically considered contributions came from Thomas Davis, who James Stafford has recently shown rooted his criticism of land tenure in Ireland in the cutting edge of political economy;[12] he placed the traditional Celtic land system of Ireland within a wider Indo-European pattern, and argued that English feudalism had swept away Celtic land-use practices. A similar critique was central to the more radical politics of John Mitchel (1815–1875) and James Fintan Lalor (1807–1849)—the latter was a 'true Celtic revolutionist' according to Davitt—who paved the way for the peasantry's right to the soil to form a core component of the revived revolutionary tradition.[13] Mitchel introduced the articles of 1854 later collected and published as his *Jail Journal* within a historical framework that depicted British land legislation as 'statutes . . . unknown to the common law of England, and . . . invented for the sole sake of the Irish Celt', who needed to be cleared off the land so that corn and cattle could be provided to English markets and money to Irish landlords.[14]

After the catastrophe of the Irish Famine and the dramatic increase in overseas emigration, these connections were increasingly seen in racial terms. Father J. F. Tormy (1820–1893), who himself emigrated to America for a time, considered in a poem during 'the era of the Irish Tenant League (from 1850–56), when the principles of the land struggle were first defined and formulated': '"What shall become of the ancient race, / The noble Keltic island race?"'.[15] The point to consider here is not the poetic merits of rhyming 'race' with 'race', but the connection of the 'Keltic race' to land politics, emigration, and the American nexus. Building on the Celtic arguments of Young Ireland affiliates, the physician Robert Cane (1807–1858) founded the Celtic Union in Kilkenny in 1853 and began a short-lived journal called *The Celt* in 1857. Cane's organisation was a literary counterpart to the Irish Republican Brotherhood, founded in 1858, and he was friendly with its initiators James Stephens (1825–1901) and the Fenian writer Charles Kickham (1828–1882), a poet and novelist involved with the botched rising in 1848. *The Celt*'s rhetoric matched Fenian intentions, with its inaugural issue announcing the publication's didactic aims of cultivating Irish national 'historic memory' through education; but Irish history not only needed to be written, 'it requires to be acted . . . gloriously and prosperously . . . such is the mission of the CELT'.[16]

In the 1860s, the cause of land reform was linked to the nascent constitutional nationalist 'Home Rule' movement by its founder Isaac Butt (1813–1879), an Ulster Protestant, political economist, and idiosyncratic Tory MP. In his *Plea for the Celtic Race* (1867), Butt argued that 'the position of the occupiers of the soil of Ireland is at present generally that of serfs', who 'have no security for their tenure, no certainty of reward for their industry, and therefore no motive to exertion' and were wholly dependent on the goodwill of their landlord.[17] Laying out an economic case was only superficially useful in this case, argued Butt, who rooted the social and political problem in 'the antagonism which difference of blood, of religion, and of race—the memories of conquest— . . . have produced'.[18] Emigration from Ireland was 'the last scene of the struggle between the "Sassenach" and the Celt. The pressure of conquest and ascendancy is at last crushing them from their homes'.[19] A slew of works from liberal thinkers, notably John Stuart Mill, similarly framed their interventions in terms of economic and political expediency as well as moral necessity.

Linking the Irish rural population with Celticism created space for the cultural politics beginning to surface. Ciaran McDonough argues that the foundation in 1876 of the Society for the Preservation of the Irish Language, by the future Pan-Celts Thomas O'Neill Russell (1828–1908) and George Sigerson (1836–1925), signals a moment when the Irish language changed from being primarily a subject of antiquarian study to an object of cultural revival.[20] Elements of pan-Celticism were present in the society's reports that praised the Welsh commitment to their language and singled it out for emulation, as the Gaelic League later would in the 1890s.[21] On a journey through Wales, Isaac Butt noted that 'we passed through another branch of the Celtic race, and there the Welsh tongue was patronized, was encouraged, was taught'.[22] There was a small early victory for the language revivalists in 1878 when 'Celtic' (i.e., Irish), was granted an extra-curricular place in Irish schools. As Eoin MacNeill later explained,

> A certain amount of enthusiasm, culminating in what is called Pan-Celticism, has gathered around the recognition of this fact that the Irish, the Gaels of Scotland, the Welsh and the Bretons are Celtic peoples. So much favour attached to the name Celtic that in our own time the Irish language was, so to speak, smuggled into the curricula of the Royal University and of the Intermediate Board under that name.[23]

If we accept the truth of MacNeill's assertion, it points to an early Irish recognition of the utility of pan-Celticism for achieving its cultural and political goals, increasingly expressed in the 1890s (see the following chapter).

Celticism was an important factor in the thought of Michael Davitt, the central figure of Irish land agitation and a committed pan-Celt. Davitt was born in 1846 to a tenant-farming family in County Mayo who were evicted and had their cottage burned down. They emigrated to Lancashire, where eleven-year-old Davitt lost his arm in a factory accident. After joining the Irish Republican Brotherhood and leading the failed raid on Chester Castle in 1867, Davitt was arrested on a treason charge in 1870 for attempting to buy guns. Upon his release in late 1877, he gained fame as a public speaker in Ireland and America as an international economic depression set in. The economic background was a contributing factor to the outbreak of the 'Land War' in 1879, which began in Davitt's home county of Mayo, as bad harvests and shrinking remittances from migrant workers in Britain meant some parts of the country faced starvation. Davitt, among others, saw the agitation not only as important for its own sake but as a platform for rekindling the separatist movement. As he later wrote of the time, 'What was wanted was to link the land or social question to that of Home Rule, by making the ownership of the soil the basis of the fight for self-government'.[24]

This conception underpinned the 'New Departure', which in 1879 united the constitutionalist Home Rule movement, the revolutionary Fenians, and their American counterparts *Clan na Gael*. Led by the alliance of Davitt with the MP Charles Stewart Parnell (1846–1891), the Irish National Land League became the key body for Irish agrarian agitation, but also sought to foment agitation in Scotland and eventually Wales, employing pan-Celtic language to do so. Underlying the ideology of the more radical parts of the movement were the social ideas of Henry George (1839–1897), whose *Progress and Poverty* also appeared in 1879. The argument was the simple one that material 'progress' increased poverty in the modern world because a system of social inequality prevailed. George, who Davitt met on his 1880 American tour, advocated a single tax on land, while Davitt argued for land nationalisation. George would accompany Davitt on a tour of the Highlands a few years later and therefore helped to link up the political arguments in the Celtic lands despite being unswayed by the Celtic historicist case.[25]

While Parnell—an Anglo-Irish landlord—eschewed the more extreme political and cultural arguments made by the radicals if he could help it, Davitt was a committed believer in the utility of Celticism for political purposes. For example, in 1882 Davitt promoted his enlarged National and Industrial Union of Ireland—a federation of land and labour societies—as a 'Celtic Confederation',[26] and in a speech of 1883, Davitt declared that the 'Celtic race' in the west of Ireland knew 'that the land was made for them, and that this land should be theirs', unimpeded by the 'robbing landlord class'.[27] When he came to write his monumental history of the land reform movement, *The Fall of Feudalism in Ireland* (1904), Davitt dedicated it to 'The Celtic Peasantry of Ireland and their Kinsfolk beyond the Seas'. In it he cast the purpose of the Land League as a racial 'struggle for the soil and rule of the Celtic fatherland', raging 'over seven generations'.[28] He would join both the Celtic League of 1886 and the Dublin-based Celtic Association in 1900 and was the vital figure linking the land reform movements in the Celtic nations.

While land politics catalysed nationalist development, Irish nationalists also flirted with pan-Celtic ideas outside of the immediacy of land agitation. Irish-American diaspora nationalism was intense, and American organisers helped to filter money and support to their Fenian counterparts across Europe.[29] One of these was the Philadelphian physician William Carroll (1835–1926)—second in command only to John Devoy (1842–1928) in *Clan na Gael*—who thought the best way of reconciling Ulster Protestants with Irish Catholics was through the *via media* of the Scots, many of whom had feet in both camps as Presbyterian Gaels. He admired John Murdoch's *Highlander* (discussed below), lamenting that 'Nothing half so good ever appears in the *Nation* or *Irishman*', encouraging Irish subscriptions out of 'Celtic sentiment' and organising Murdoch's American trip of 1880.[30] Carroll also suggested the formation of Franco-Irish pan-Celtic links to the Fenian John O'Leary (1830–1907), a former Young Irelander exiled in Paris in 1879. That April, Carroll flirted with the particularly Irish myth of Phoenician origins that stretched back from James Ware (1594–1666) in the seventeenth century through Charles Vallancey in the eighteenth and William Betham in the nineteenth; he suggested to O'Leary that 'Your neighbour Renan should be able to manage that theme intelligently and in a manner to instruct as well as entertain', before asking if he knew 'any of the *Celtic Review* people in Paris'.[31] Whether O'Leary actually knew Renan is unclear—although, given O'Leary's bookishness, it is not out of the question—but if the exchange shows a Fenian sense of opportunism and misunderstanding of the *Revue celtique* (founded to fight against the old spurious myths of things like Phoenicianism), it also reveals an awareness of Celticism's international context and the possible benefits of pan-Celticism. By the 1890s O'Leary too favoured ecumenical pan-Celticism, calling in 1896 for the cooperation of 'Celtic brethren all over the world', and echoing the Home Ruler William O'Brien (1852–1928), who supported the idea of a 'world-wide Celtic league' in 1892.[32]

As will be seen in the following final chapters, pan-Celticism at a global scale never took off, but driven by Irish nationalism and the land agitation in the 1880s it started to gain real converts in other parts of the United Kingdom and the United States. A cultural component that emphasised the Celticity of the people was an important part of the land reform movement, and as agitation increased in intensity so did the importance of Celticity. This led straightforwardly to the recognition of links with the other Celtic nations.

The Highland Land Reform Movement

Although dubbed with a similar name, the 'Crofters' War' in the Scottish Highlands and Islands was nowhere near as violent or dramatic as the Irish Land War.[33] Readers will understand from previous chapters why the Gaelic-speaking Scottish Highlands and Islands were often treated together with Ireland, and shared many of the same problems, but there were key differences.[34] The first one was that, while the British state had had to use force to subdue the Highlands after the Jacobite uprising of 1745–1746, land law and landlord-tenant relations were not rooted in conquest. Highland lairds were hereditary clan chiefs and so still often had at least nominal kinship relations to their tenants. The second major difference was the related one that there was not the same religious fissure between landlords and tenants that generally existed in Ireland. Moreover, many Highland lairds could speak Gaelic and saw themselves as scions of a proud and distinctive Celtic culture preserved in the Highlands but long reconciled to the British state. All of these factors helped to shape a final difference, which was the lack of general resistance to governments and landlords, or the politicisation of land with other purposes, at least in comparison to Ireland.[35] Tom Devine has stressed that the Land Question was just as vexed in the Lowlands as in the Highlands, but the history and identity of Gaelic Scotland gave the question there a particular racial and cultural dimension distinct from the rest of Scotland and most parts of Britain.[36]

In the 'Age of Improvement', Scottish landlords had begun applying economic theories and social engineering in an effort to maximise profits from their land.[37] Since they could make more money from sheep farming or grouse shooting, some landlords—assisted by estate managers (factors) educated in the new field of political economy—began clearing their land of the small-farming peasantry. Some of the earliest and most notorious clearances were carried out in Sutherland in the first two decades of the nineteenth century. The infamous estate manager Patrick Sellar (17580–1851) was rumoured to burn tenants out of their homes, and was deeply prejudiced against them, borrowing the Celtophobic ideas of John Pinkerton and applying them to the crofter 'aborigines' and 'primitives'.[38] These clearances led to mass emigration and were deeply divisive, long lingering in popular memory.

Krisztina Fenyö has investigated the Highland potato famines of the 1840s and 50s, and shown that the predominant press reaction in England, the Lowlands, and even in some Highland newspapers was unsympathetic and even contemptuous.[39] Editorialists routinely pointed to differences in racial character as a chief cause of the distress, contrasting industrious Saxon with lazy Celt. Those who sympathised with the Highlanders also racialised them, but in a positive light; for example, the Highland geologist Hugh Miller (1802–1856) wrote in 1838 that 'The Celt is essentially a different person from the Saxon in the very constitution of his mind', an assertion he drew in part from phrenology.[40] Commentators were careful to draw a distinction along these same lines between the Scandinavian populations in Caithness, Shetland, and the Orkneys, and the Celtic populations in the rest of the Highlands and Islands.[41]

Like Ireland, Scotland received its own commissioner from *The Times* in 1846, who laced his reports with 'disquisitions on the inferiority of the Celtic race', prompting replies from, among others, the editor of the *Inverness Courier* that 'the Celt is not unimprovable', merely wanting the opportunity, rather than the inclination, to work.[42] Others, such as the commissioner of the *Scotsman*, recommended more explicit race-mixing as the only way of counteracting Celtic inferiority by improving the Celtic character.[43] Weary of the relief efforts and debates around them, by 1849 leading commentators increasingly recommended emigration, including Charles Trevelyan (1807–1886), assistant secretary to the Treasury and architect of the famine politics in Ireland and Scotland, who also served as chairman of the Highland Emigration Society and wanted a 'national effort' to 'rid our operatives of the swarming Irish and Scotch Celts'.[44] In sum, Scotland was enveloped in the same racialised discourse as Ireland, but that shared denigration did not yet lead to pan-Celtic cooperation.

Resistance to the prevailing system strengthened in the second half of the nineteenth century, especially in the 1870s when crofters began to riot, rent strike, burn eviction notices, and even, in the 1880s, attack policemen. Political ideas were assisted by a 'Celtic' cultural revival that occurred roughly in conjunction with the rise of the land reform movement. In the early 1870s a number of Gaelic societies, including the flagship Gaelic Society of Inverness, appeared across the Highlands and in major Lowland cities.[45] A Highland press developed in the 1870s, and by 1878 there existed a Federation of Celtic Societies in Glasgow that aimed to connect the various Celtic cultural bodies across Scotland.[46] Adopting a positive image of the Celt, this network helped to stimulate a social movement and politics devoted to remedying the problems in the Highlands, one in which the search for inspiration and support led to pan-Celtic expression.

It has long been recognised that a new Highland press played a vital role in the Highland campaign,[47] and among the most important figures in this landscape was the activist journalist John Murdoch (1818–1903), who produced *The Highlander* weekly journal from 1873 until 1882.[48] He was one of the most advanced social radicals in the Highlands, and ultimately went on to help found the Scottish Labour Party in 1888.[49] Murdoch grew up on a croft in Islay, but his family was eventually evicted from it in tragic circumstances after his father was killed in a shooting accident in 1845. He worked for many years as an excise officer in Dublin, where his pan-Celtic feelings developed. There he began to write for the Irish nationalist paper *The Nation*, which for decades remained a warm supporter of his activities, praising his attempts to establish a 'great and influential brotherhood embracing all the members of the Celtic race'.[50] Already in the 1850s, Murdoch argued that on 'oneness of race, of language and of traditional right, as well as present pressing wrong, let the erstwhile separated Celtic brothers meet with ceud mille failte on the broad ground of the land'.[51] Davitt later called him the 'truest of true Celts',[52] and Murdoch described the aims of his paper as 'sinking the differences between the different members of the great Celtic family . . . bringing them to see face to face and pull "shoulder to shoulder"'.[53]

The Highlander was devised to 'foster enterprise and public opinion in the Highlands and Islands of Scotland', and to advocate 'political, social, and economic measures which appear best calculated to advance the well-being of the people at large'.[54] It featured articles in English and Gaelic, and 'occasionally, Gaelic readers shall be introduced to Irish, Manx, Welsh, &c'.[55] Murdoch toured America with Parnell and John Dillon (1851–1927), and was urged to run for an Irish parliamentary seat by the American Irish nationalist William Carroll. A snub by Parnell put paid to any plans of Irish political involvement by Murdoch, who was nevertheless unfazed, believing political change needed to be forced from outside Parliament.[56] When his paper folded in 1882, Murdoch continued to encourage crofter resistance and travelled around the

Highlands and Islands to offer advice before the approaching parliamentary commission.

Murdoch was the most outspoken journalist and agitator in the Highlands, but there were several other, less radical, journalists who drew much from the intellectual resources of Celticism.[57] One of these was Alexander Mackenzie (1838–1898), who had grown up on a croft in Wester Ross, before working in various trades and settling in Inverness as a draper in 1869.[58] In 1875 he began the monthly periodical *The Celtic Magazine*, which promoted a historical conception of the Gaelic-speaking Highlands by publishing widely on 'Celtic' antiquities, history, literature, music, folklore, and so on.[59] The publication seems to have registered on the international Celtic radar, and the French Celticist Henri d'Arbois de Jubainville later lamented its disappearance and that he could not exchange issues of his *Revue celtique* for it.[60] Articles on Celtic history and culture padded out the central political focus of the periodical in the 1880s, the Land Question, and the political message running through it that ultimately the landlords were responsible.[61] Mackenzie himself serialised historical articles about the clearances that were then published together in his *History of the Highland Clearances* (1883).[62] Importantly, however, Mackenzie was initially anti-Irish and abhorred both the tactics and the goals of the Fenians. He and several of his contributors were, generally speaking, content with the Highlands' place in Britain and especially its empire. Only in the mid-1880s, when the situation in the Highlands intensified, did Mackenzie's views about the Irish begin to shift, along with his views about Scottish home rule.

Mackenzie and the *Celtic Magazine* were supported by the liberal Charles Fraser Mackintosh (1828–1901), 'MP for the Highlands'. Fraser Mackintosh contributed articles to the *Celtic Magazine*, which became increasingly politically charged in the 1880s, reflecting both the escalating stakes over land reform and the germination of a Celtic historicist line as justification for land reform. A series of crofter agitations—beginning on the island of Bernera in 1874—combined with the pressure of the Highland cultural network, and Fraser Mackintosh's continued lobbying in Parliament, all led to the Gladstonian government's appointment of a Royal Commission into the condition of the Crofters in 1882.[63] However, crofter agitation surely played the decisive role, following the height of the conflict on the morning of 19 April 1882, when crofters on the Isle of Skye fought off a ragtag group of Glasgow policemen, local auxiliary authorities, and journalists under the command of the sheriff of Inverness, who was there under the pretext of arresting five rent strikers but was probably really there to quash resistance to the forces of order. Cuts and bruises were sustained on both sides, though no one died, but the episode became widely known as the 'Battle of the Braes' and brought unprecedented attention to the cause. Five 'Crofter MPs' were returned in the elections of 1885, but legislative action stalled until a 'Land War' broke out on Skye in 1885 and a gunboat was sent to restore order, before Gladstone's Crofters' Holdings (Scotland) Act (1886) essentially transposed the Irish Land Act of 1881 onto the Highlands.

Although devised in part to mollify crofter agitation, the Highland land acts were premised on the historicist idea that there existed immemorial Celtic customs completely at odds with what were identified as the tenets of laissez-faire English liberalism.[64] This argument relied on scholarship, particularly that of the philologist and historian William Forbes Skene (1809–1892), whose *Celtic Scotland* (1876–1880) vindicated the ancient Celts as the fount of the Scottish nation possessing its own endogenous national legal system—destroyed by Norman feudalism. But the figure who linked Celtic historicism with the actually existing Land Question was John Stuart Blackie (1809–1895), professor of Latin at Aberdeen and Greek at Edinburgh, Scottish public intellectual, and ardent supporter of land reform. His party politics remained ambiguous, but he was decidedly not a socialist, preferring dual ownership to land nationalisation.[65] Blackie developed an affinity for the Highlands after his trip there in 1847, learning the language and becoming a lifelong devotee of Highland causes.[66] Importantly, he also had an affinity for Ireland, the situation of which he considered one of John Bull's three great blunders, identifying the 'common impress of social misfortune' that the Irish shared with the Highlanders.[67] He therefore supported Irish Home Rule, and when Parnell argued to the U.S. House of Representatives that the English had illegally deprived the Irish of their land, he cited Blackie as his authority.[68] Educated in Germany—like Skene—Blackie worked from the position that 'the historical basis on which all Celtic property in land originally rested' was the principle of common inheritance in the clan system, which the modern legal system had destroyed.[69] It followed that once the Irish had secured 'a legal footing on their native soil . . . their Celtic brethren' in the Highlands could not be denied equal treatment.[70] A related campaign for Celtic culture was Blackie's campaign for a chair of Celtic at Edinburgh University. After the establishment of a Sanskrit chair there, Blackie thought the languages of the westernmost Aryans needed academic vindication, and he campaigned for nearly a decade for the chair's endowment. The Irish philologist Whitley Stokes recognised that it would benefit not only the study of Celtic languages and literature but comparative philology more generally,[71] but it must also be emphasised that raising the study of Gaelic to the university level would elevate the status of the vernacular spoken by the Highland peasantry. The hundreds of contributions from letters across Britain, the Empire, and the United States, held by the National Library of Scotland, attest to Blackie's tireless energy for the cause.[72]

He used these same connections to lobby for land reform, and as early as 1870 the eighth Duke of Argyll (1823–1900)—the largest landowner in the western Highlands and, at this point, an important figure in the Liberal Party—complained to Gladstone that Blackie was fanning the flames with 'Gaelic sentimentalism'.[73] However, Argyll considered himself a Celt and donated to the Celtic Chair Campaign, liaising between Blackie and Queen Victoria in the same cause. Nevertheless, he was one of the most steadfast opponents of Irish and Scottish land legislation, writing to Gladstone as early as 1870 that recourse 'to Irish "History"' or 'Celtic Customs' as justification for reform was 'altogether irrelevant'.[74] Gladstone disagreed, recommending to Argyll a dose of Irish history, ancient and modern. Gladstone read Skene and, when planning his Highland policy with William Vernon Harcourt (1827–1904), deployed a historicist reading of the situation, arguing that the Highlanders had been deprived of Celtic historical rights and were therefore entitled to separate legislation.[75] Support for historicist land rights led to Gladstone's sympathy for Irish Home Rule and embrace of a federal solution for Ireland, which he hinted at for Scotland and Wales too.[76]

The question of Irish influence on the Highlands was long debated, and in 2007 Andrew Newby published a conclusive study determining that the Irish situation and several key individuals inspired rather than instigated Highland resistance. Murdoch was the most famous of these, but several of the other 'Crofter MPs' also had Irish links and sympathies. However, several important figures were quite hostile to the Irish and wanted to maintain a critical distance. The most significant of these was the 'MP for the Highlands', Fraser Mackintosh, but Alexander Mackenzie, editor of the *Celtic Magazine*, was also initially quite inimical to the Irish, and in 1882 he diagnosed the failure of Murdoch's *Highlander* newspaper as due to being 'more Irish than Highland'.[77] But there were clear pan-Celtic links between Ireland and the Highlands, though these often came through the more radical centre of Glasgow. Michael Davitt toured the Highlands three times, once in 1882 and twice in 1887. The Irish Land League sent money to rebelling crofters, and Davitt later claimed that the Dublin branch supplied crofters with guns, though they were used only to kill deer.[78] Such gestures and their resonances led the Irish Home Rule MP T. P. O'Connor (1848–1929) to declare in 1881 that support for a rally in Glasgow indicated 'the strong, ardent and vigorous union of the Celtic race'.[79]

Irish nationalists played up Celtic links in America, and Carroll and Devoy helped to organise trips to the United States for the prominent Highland Celticists Murdoch and Mackenzie, who raised money for their national cause through a speaking tour.[80] American pan-Celtic interest did not go unnoticed by the British press. In 1880, *Blackwood's* printed a letter and accompanying article by 'AN AMERICAN STATESMAN', deploring the treatment of Ireland and threatening a Russo-American intervention. The author let it be known that 'Pan-Celtic societies exist throughout the United States', whose agents were at work 'in Ireland and in the Celtic districts of Scotland and Wales' encouraging tenants to resist eviction. Once the signal was given, American and Russian troops would invade and shear not only Ireland, but the Highlands, Wales, and Cornwall, from England, as had been agreed by the 'Pan-Slavic and Pan-Celtic committees'; the head of the latter was supposedly none other than the former U.S. President Ulysses S. Grant (1822–1885).[81] Clearly such fantasies sprung from the contemporary Eastern Crisis, but John Devoy did meet the Russian foreign minister in America in November 1876, where he presented a report on Irish separatism and lobbied for Russian assistance.[82] Although the article gained some attention across the British press, *Blackwood's* editor had not been sure what to make of it; but even if it was satirical, then the very fact that pan-Celticism was a target attests to its place in parts of the public consciousness. Moreover, popular fears of invasion in the British press were echoed in and strengthened by the speculative invasion-scare fiction produced from *c.* 1870–1914, where the potential vulnerability of the Celtic nations, and especially Ireland, was a common trope. For example, in an anonymous work published in 1885, the narrator 'Posteritas' reveals that a French invading force employs '*Bas Breton* interpreters' to appeal to the Scots regiments as 'kindred Celts'; although the Scots remain loyal in the story, the 'treasonous Irish' betray the English inhabitants of London.[83] If the diverse motivations and shrouded meanings behind these texts were often oblique and allegorical, they nevertheless revealed an awareness of increasing pan-Celticism and, depending on the author, corresponding apprehension.

The Land Question in Wales

The Welsh Land Question has generally received less attention than those of Ireland and Scotland. This is because, although Wales certainly did not lack a tradition of political and social protest, the Land Question there was not as contentious, and the situation remained peaceful. Still, there was a Land Question, which from 1885 until 1893—when a Royal Commission was set up to inquire into the Welsh land system—was one of the most important political issues in Wales, together with the ongoing saga of Church Disestablishment (only achieved in 1920). The Welsh land reform movement never attained the intensity of the Irish or even the Scottish land agitation movements, but it did create some common political ground on which the Welsh, Irish, and Scots could explore their Celticism in common.

Although Welsh pan-Celtic feeling for their fellow ancient Britons in Brittany and to some extent Cornwall was already present at this time, there were considerable barriers to pan-Celtic affection for the Gaels, especially those of Ireland.[84] Large-scale immigration to Wales for jobs in its mines, quarries, and other industrial works generated some xenophobic reactions.[85] Differences of religion, combined with a disapproval of Fenian violence—even among those dissatisfied with Wales's place in the British union—intensified these feelings. Yet the Irish example also inspired Welsh political activism amid a rising popular national consciousness, in line with similar European patterns.[86] Wales had a wealth of national traditions and ideas upon which to draw, one of which was a tradition of Celticism, and this helped more radical political thinkers to link with the cause in Ireland. There are many such expressions in both the Welsh and English languages in the Welsh press over the period. Linguistic matters, whether of the kinship between Irish and Welsh tongues, or the efforts in both countries to maintain their health, featured often. In 1862, Ieuan Ddu (1795–1871) stressed the relations of the Irish and Welsh languages and histories, and asked whether the Celts were fated to always serve foreign masters in their own country.[87] More straightforwardly politicised Celticism absent any historical connection was also evident. In 1887, one writer pointed to the 'Celtic pride' so evident in the Irish defiance of England and urged his compatriots to likewise break their bonds of servility.[88]

The Welsh land reform movement was decentralised but stronger in the north, where some of the more active figures desired to organise on the Irish basis. One of the most vocal and consistent of these was Evan Pan Jones (1834–1922), a Methodist minister who had studied at Marburg. He was a mentee of Michael D. Jones, the Welsh nationalist and leader of the Welsh Patagonian movement. Pan Jones disseminated his views as editor from 1881 to 1884 of *Y Celt*, a weekly journal for the Independent denomination of the church, which became the unofficial organ of the Welsh land movement.[89] Jones promoted a land nationalisation society, 'Cymdeithas y Ddaear i'r Bobl' (Society of Land for the People), which advocated George's single tax and linked the Welsh tenant cause to those further afield, including in the northwest of England (where there was a large Welsh community).[90]

The year 1886 was a major one for Welsh land reform, and one with important Pan-Celtic dimensions (discussed further in the next section).[91] In February, Michael Davitt arrived in Wales at the invitation of Pan Jones and Michael D. Jones, briefly touring with them and the crofter MP Gavin Brown Clark (1846–1930).[92] At Blaenau Ffestiniog, Davitt encouraged the audience to elect able, intelligent MPs to Parliament, who would truly represent the people and drive out landlordism. One of them, David Lloyd George (1863–1945), at the time an unknown twenty-three-year-old lawyer from Criccieth, was very sympathetic to Ireland, Davitt, and the land reform movement. One of the most radical parts of his political platform in years to come was the single tax on land values advocated by Henry George and Evan Pan Jones. At Blaenau Ffestiniog Lloyd George got up to speak, praising Davitt and urging his countrymen—quarrymen rather than farmers though they mostly were—to join the Welsh Land League which was getting started at that time.[93] As has been well noted, Davitt's visit was not received enthusiastically by much of the Welsh press, but it was nevertheless the crucial pan-Celtic episode that began to bring Irish and Welsh 'Celts' closer together.

The year 1886 also brought the election of the most vocal supporter of Welsh land reform in the House of Commons, Thomas Edward Ellis (1859–1899). Himself the son of a tenant farmer, Ellis had done well at school and studied at Oxford before entering politics and becoming the leading voice of Welsh autonomy until his early death. Ellis believed in the 'indestructible influences of race and nationality', whose tenaciousness could be seen 'in the sullen, and necessarily shifting, resistance offered by Celtic peoples like the Welsh and the Irish to the seemingly overwhelming sweep of English ideas, of English law, and of English government'.[94] He had been enthusiastic about Davitt's Welsh tour and wrote to a correspondent at the time that

> We must work for bringing together Celtic reformers and Celtic peoples. The interests of Irishmen, Welshmen and Crofters are almost identical. Their past history is very similar, their present oppressors are the same and their immediate wants are the same—riddance from landlordism and ampler opportunities for developing their own genius and their own powers.[95]

As is evident from the quotation, Ellis's critique was historically rooted. His fundamental argument for reform in 1886 was that 'the ancient land laws of Wales have been forcibly superseded by the English system of land ownership and tenure, and have not been edited in the light of accurate knowledge of early Welsh social history'.[96] Wales deserved separate legislative treatment on this basis.

Although a Welsh League did come into being in 1886, it was founded by Thomas Gee (1815–1898), editor of *Baner ac Amserau Cymru*, the most popular Welsh language newspaper, and the organiser of the anti-tithe league. Gee was not favourable to Davitt, however, and the *Baner* did not discuss his speeches. Pan Jones criticised it frequently and lamented that it had taken the sting out of the Welsh movement. However, a more radical alternative was to emerge in the following year.

Bonar Bridge

The height of Pan-Celtic land politicking came in 1886, when several hundred delegates from various national land reform movements met at Bonar Bridge in Sutherland. Generally dissatisfied with the Crofters' Act, the Crofter MPs and others sympathetic to the cause had agreed at Westminster to invite delegates from Ireland and Wales to the annual convention of the Highland Land Law Reform Association (a pressure group founded earlier in the decade). There they hoped to establish a Celtic League for mutual support. The idea was reported widely in the press, variously billed as a 'Celtic League', 'Celtic Federation', or a 'Pan-Gaelic Conference.[97] A variety of ulterior motives were posited. Some papers wrote that the point was to inaugurate 'a Celtic League which shall embrace all sections of the race', while others prophesied that in addition to 'the usual resolution in favour of land reform, a further resolution demanding Home Rule for Scotland will be proposed, and no doubt adopted'.[98] The Welsh paper *Y Werin* put it in more directly national terms: 'A number of gentlemen have been assembling in Westminster, London, in order to discuss the propriety of forming a Celtic Congress between the Welsh, the Scots, and the Irish, in order to secure the rights of the three nations from the English'.[99]

The main Pan-Celtic force came from John Stuart-Glennie, a barrister, radical philosopher, and well-connected socialist. He was a friend to George Bernard Shaw (1856–1950), for example, and even convinced him to join the Celtic League.[100] Stuart-Glennie acknowledged Pan-Celticism's potential from the 'prodigious political result of historical researches and theories' across Europe over the previous hundred years. Indeed, the Celtic League proposal was rooted in the historicist idea that 'The Celtic race had the first claims on the British government and the first right to the possession of the country, for they were its aboriginal inhabitants'.[101] Various claims like these were made over the course of the congress, which turned out to be more radical than its critics imagined. While it was expected that Scottish Home Rule would be supported, one measure called for Home Rule for Ireland, Scotland, and even Wales.[102]

Evan Pan Jones covered the congress for the Welsh-language press. His old paper *Y Celt* advised its readers to take careful notice of the proceedings, which would surely be 'of great influence in the future politics of Wales'.[103] Jones carefully noted Pan-Celtic sentiment among the Highlanders and aimed to cultivate it in his audience. The Highlanders, we are told, were 'happy to see their brother Celts from Wales' and gave Pan Jones a rousing reception when he spoke. He in turn wrote emotively in Pan-Celtic terms about the significance of the Crofters' War:

> We were standing on a clearing stained with the blood, and consecrated with the tears of our brother and sister Celts, and our sole mission was to sympathise with them, and to join with them in the fight to restore for us and them our natural rights in the earth on which we found ourselves.[104]

Pan Jones likened the crofters to the Welsh peasantry, who asked to speak in their native tongue because they were uncomfortable in English, and whose quiet dignity and determination to their 'natural rights' in the land he desperately wanted the Welsh to adopt for themselves and for the interests of all Celts.[105]

The formation of the Keltic League was the main outcome of the Bonar Bridge conference. John Stuart-Glennie had organised the event and devised the prospectus which outlined the aims of the League, but at some point he invited Pan Jones to be a joint-convener and the secretary for Wales. Welsh commentators particularly welcomed the League because they thought it might amplify Wales's weak voice in Westminster.[106] The main aims of the League were to bring together Scottish, Welsh, and Irish politicians to cooperate on Home Rule and to settle the Land Question; to form the elements for a 'New Radical Party'; and 'to create a spirit of democratic brotherhood and solidarity between the different branches of the Keltic Race'.[107] Federalisation of Britain and its empire was apparently the long-term aspirational political goal.[108] But it would also support the federation of all the Celtic societies the world over and organise literary congresses in support of 'philological and historical Keltic researches', which it recognised as 'of the first importance for

European, and . . . British history', and no doubt for the rationale of the League, revealing once again the links between scholarship, cultural revival, and nascent nationalisms.[109] The *Weekly Mail* accused it of promoting a race war between Celts and Saxons.[110] But although it had grand intentions, the League barely made it into 1887. It organised a response to Irish 'Coercion' by the 'imperial parliament' in the Criminal Law and Procedure (Ireland) Act (1887),[111] but quickly fell into desuetude after that. In a pattern that Pan-Celts would frequently complain of in the twentieth century, the leaders of the Irish movement did not devote attention to it. The Bonar Bridge conference and the resulting Keltic League nevertheless stand out in the history of pan-Celticism for finally bringing together Celtic movements that were mostly political in nature.

Conclusion

The 'Land Question' provided the rationale for connecting first the Scottish and Irish Gaels, and then folding in their Celtic cousins the Welsh. Considering the Land Question encouraged political thinkers in Ireland, Scotland, and Wales to reflect on their national histories and the histories of their legal arrangements and social systems. Although these differed considerably, many came to the conclusion that their own native Celtic system—whatever that might mean or might have been is beside the point—had been corrupted or replaced by an alien English or Anglo-Saxon system. Individuals committed to political change recognised those common patterns and used them to promote their shared cause. They were assisted in these conclusions by the increasing knowledge about the nature of the Celts, and their histories, languages, and cultures. With the linkage of Celtic histories and the Celtic nations in a joint political cause there finally arose a shared sense of Celticism among Ireland, Scotland, and Wales. The pan-Celtic politics of the 1880s provided a crucial step to the fully-fledged Pan-Celticism of the 1890s—*viz.* a Pan-Celtic movement in which the goal was itself Pan-Celticism rather than politics in common—as well as the overtly political, left-leaning Pan-Celticism of the twentieth century.

11

Celtic Daybreak

E. E. FOURNIER D'ALBE, PAN-CELTICISM, AND THE CELTIC ASSOCIATION IN THE *FIN DE SIÈCLE*

ON A BALMY August morning in 1901, a colourfully dressed crowd assembled at the Dublin Mansion House to be welcomed by the Lord Mayor and perform the 'ancient' Druidic *Gorsedd* ceremony, before forming a procession and snaking through the streets of south Dublin to the Antient Concert Rooms. Composed of individuals from across the Celtic nations, the group's diversity was accentuated by the distinctive costumes adorning the participants: the Scots kilted in plaid, the Irish in saffron, the Welsh resplendent in a mixture of green, blue, and white robes, and the Bretons in distinctive black *bragou-braz* pantaloons and broad-brimmed top hats.[1] Heading north on Dawson Street, the multicoloured throng passed through College Green and onto College Street before turning east and marching to its destination at 52 Great Brunswick Street (now Pearse Street). The procession's organiser described it as 'an artistic triumph and an imposing demonstration of Celtic unity', but some spectators reportedly felt 'peculiarly sceptical, and very much out of it . . . this seemed like ritual gone mad'.[2] The Irish-Irelander D. P. Moran (1869–1936) sneered, 'Can a nation be saved by jack-acting?'[3] When the troupe reached the Antient Concert Rooms, its leaders erected a five-foot menhir—the *Lia Cineil*[4]—from five congruent stones, each symbolising a Celtic nation, and then headed inside for three days of debate and celebration. The inaugural Pan-Celtic Congress had begun.

In the previous two chapters I traced the long gestation of informal, 'lowercase p' pan-Celticism, a series of cultural transfers among the Celtic nations based upon increasing familial sentiment and an awareness of shared political goals. Here the focus switches to the emergence of 'uppercase P' Pan-Celticism: a *self-conscious* movement operating on the principle that the Celtic nations are fraternally bonded and should enter into closer cooperation, work together for common goals, and eventually establish a federation. While pan-Celticism recognises shared Celtic links in the past and the cultural and political uses to which they might be put, the explicit aim of Pan-Celticism *is* Pan-Celticism, culturally and politically. The first real Pan-Celtic group, the Dublin-based Celtic Association, viewed itself as the culmination of all previous Celtic revivals and described its Pan-Celtic goals as 'the fostering of mutual sympathy and co-operation between the various branches of the Celtic Race in all matters affecting their language and national characteristics'.[5] As the first institutionalisation of the Pan-Celtic idea, the Celtic Association is at the heart of this chapter. Until recently, it was generally overlooked by scholars and had only appeared fleetingly in surveys of pre-revolutionary Ireland or in short articles by Celticists,[6] but this has happily changed. Christina Murphy-Macinta completed the first detailed study of the Celtic Association on its own terms in 2017, and in 2019 Caoimhín de Barra included several illuminating chapters about it in his book about the links between Welsh and Irish cultural revivalists in the period from roughly 1860 to 1920.[7] My work builds upon theirs while shifting the focus somewhat, examining the association both within the long context of Celticism surveyed in this book, and within the shorter-term development of pan-Celticism examined in the last few chapters.

William Butler Yeats has dominated discussion of the Irish cultural landscape of this era, where his 'Celtic Twilight' was the principal mode of the literary movement in English. Yet Celticism was an important, if nebulous, recourse for all branches of the Irish revival, and there were other outposts of Celtic literary thought, in London and Edinburgh especially. An Anglo-Scottish 'Celtic Renascence' arose in the 1890s, which, though influenced by the Irish Celtic Twilight, was separate from it.[8] An 1897 article on the 'Celtic Renascence' by the Scottish folklorist Andrew Lang (1844–1912) mentioned Yeats only fleetingly, though approvingly, and identified the Scottish leaders as the poet William Sharp (1855–1905), Fiona Macleod (Sharp's pseudonym and alter ego), and the Scottish polymath Patrick Geddes (1854–1932).[9] In the same year, Yeats and his circle made it painfully clear to the Scots that the two movements were distinct. I therefore use 'Celtic Twilight' to refer to the Celtic strand prevalent in the Anglo-Irish movement, and 'Celtic Renascence' to refer to the Anglo-British interest in Celtic topics and materials. Yeats's ubiquity in these cultural milieux makes him inescapable, but, as Roy Foster has emphasised, his Celticism was, for the most part, Hiberno-centric. Rarely for Yeats, he was not the central conduit of Pan-Celticism; some of his relationships that could be considered 'Pan-Celtic'—such as that with the Scottish family of Celtic folklorists, the Carmichaels—only came after the 1901 Pan-Celtic Congress.[10] There is therefore a need to get beyond Yeats—whose gravitational pull continues to be powerful enough to warp most people and things around him—and investigate the different sources that coalesced in the Pan-Celtic movement of the 1900s.[11]

After first examining the limits of Pan-Celticism in the 1890s, the chapter traces the rise of the Celtic Association, its activities, and ideology, with a particular emphasis on its founder and intellectual driver, E. E. Fournier d'Albe. Examining its growth out of the foregoing pan-Celtic currents also sheds light on some international dimensions of the Irish cultural nationalist movements, which have normally been studied from an inward-looking perspective, notwithstanding some strained attempts to find links between nationalists from other Celtic nations and the Easter Rising.[12] Despite enthusiasm from supporters across the Celtic nations, the Pan-Celtic movement can hardly be considered to have been a great triumph. Nevertheless, the Celtic Association laid the blueprint for the form that the twentieth-century Pan-Celtic movement would take, and in which it still exists, and it is therefore a milestone in the history of Celticism.

Celticism in *Fin de siècle* Ireland and Scotland

The Pan-Celtic movement emerged in the late 1890s out of a number of long- and short-term contexts. Important longer-term trends were the rise of pan-Celtic sentiment over the course of the nineteenth century and the multifaceted Irish nationalist tradition. Within the latter strand lay the reemergence of a robust Irish cultural nationalism in the 1880s, which in the 1890s split into roughly two movements:[13] the Gaelic, which argued that a true national literature could only be written in Irish, and the Anglo-Irish, which continued national writing in English. In the short-term political context, Parnell's death in 1891 left the constitutional nationalists rudderless, but even among some unionists there developed a sense that Ireland was overtaxed and should form a 'Pan-Celtic League' to stand up to English hegemony.[14]

Foster has carefully emphasised that the Irish cultural nationalist movement emerged in the 1880s and not, as Yeats later had it, as a result of Parnell's downfall in 1891.[15] Nationalists of all stripes—including Yeats—participated in the cultural fervour of the 1880s, during which Irish figures became more confident in their Celtic national enthusiasms. Celtic interest sustained groups like the Contemporary Club (f. 1885), a literary-political salon featuring 'advanced' nationalist figures like Michael Davitt, John O'Leary, and the Yeatses, among others.[16] Another participant was the future Pan-Celt T. W. Rolleston (1857–1920), a poet and journalist under O'Leary's spell in the 1880s, whose youthful interest in the Romantic nationalism of Young Ireland was tempered by imperial enthusiasms and gelled into a tepid cultural Celticism by 1900. But as co-founder of the *Dublin University Review* in 1885, Rolleston published Yeats for the first time and ensured a steady stream of Celticism mixed into the wider nationalist currents.

Especially against the background of the land agitation in the Celtic nations, pan-Celtic interest increased in the 1880s, with many of these same figures in touch with John Murdoch and indirectly involved with the Highlands. Alongside articles on Welsh language and literature—a common comparator used to inspire Irish cultural revival[17]—one contributor published a piece in the *Dublin University Review* welcoming an impending 'Pan-Celticism ever confronting Landlordism and demanding a swift and ready reckoning'.[18] A Pan-Celtic Society featuring Douglas Hyde, O'Leary, and the future Celtic Association member A. P. Graves (1846–1931) was founded in Dublin in 1888 and interested Yeats, who lived in London at the time.[19] But it was an odd appellation as there was nothing 'pan' about the group beyond a passive interest in things like the Welsh *eisteddfod* and French Pan-Celtic rumours—its common literary and linguistic goals were geared to Irish interest and suggest it was really a manifestation of the Celtic Twilight *avant la lettre*.[20] When its *Lays and Lyrics* were published, the editor made explicit that the group's interest lay primarily in what other countries had contributed to Irish literature, rather than any international Celticism.[21]

While there would have been little opposition to the general Irish cultural movement of the 1880s being referred to as 'Celtic',[22] in the mid-1890s the label came to have associations—if not a definite meaning—that made it contested linguistic terrain.[23] The controversy reflected the rift that had developed within the cultural nationalist movements over whether literature written in English by Irish authors could still be 'Irish'; for Yeats and other Anglo-Irish writers the answer was yes, for the Gaelic movement it was a reluctant no.[24] Although these cracks had existed in the eighties, they widened considerably in the nineties as each group grew in popularity and established institutional bases. However, they overlapped considerably: these individuals still lived in the same spaces, interacted in the same milieux, and shared many things in common, if not their linguistic stance.[25] For example, both groups revered Celtic mythology and resented continental Celtologists for dissecting Celtic myths like a corpse on a table, rather than trying to breathe new life into them.[26]

The Anglo-Irish movement continued the established nationalist tradition, which had existed for at least a century, of writing in the English language; it should be remembered that the Gaelic proponents were the neophytes in the 1890s, a fact occasionally obscured by the Free State's subsequent adoption of their ethos. Of course its roots were deep, but the emergence of the Gaelic stem can be dated to 25 November 1892, when Douglas Hyde spoke to the National Literary Society (f. 1892) on 'The Necessity for De-Anglicising Ireland'.[27] He argued that, in imitating England, Ireland had lost its own character while not becoming English; but being of the Celtic, Gaelic, or Irish race (used interchangeably in the address) precluded full Anglicisation, so assimilation attempts were pointless and should be jettisoned in favour of cultivating a true Irish nationality: 'this island *is* and will *ever* remain Celtic at the core'.[28] Hyde and several others formed the Gaelic League in the following year; while its leaders were fairly sympathetic to the Anglo-Irish movement, a harder-line 'Irish Ireland' branch developed around the turn of the century, embodied by the Catholic polemicist D. P. Moran, Pan-Celticism's greatest antagonist. In the most famous essay of his manifesto—written in 1900 against an increasingly splintered cultural nationalist background—Moran drew attention to the amorphousness of the concept of 'the Celts—a word which is supposed to stand for a people, but who that people are no one seems to know, and indeed very few care'. The use of 'Celtic', according to Moran, was nothing more than an Arnoldian gloss given by Yeats to Ireland's bastard English literature.[29] Moran's rejection of 'Celtic' reflected an increasing idealisation of the peasants of western Ireland, the 'Gaels', who were not any purer racially or nationally, but were more authentically Irish, because supposedly untainted by English civilization. Although both the Gaelic League and the Irish Ireland vanguard came to reject the Celtic Association—to Fournier's bitter disappointment and despite the involvement of figures like the Gaelic League co-founder Thomas O'Neill Russell—all three groups shared similar anti-English and anti-imperial outlooks and looked to native language revival as a way to general cultural revitalisation.

The 'Celtic Twilight' became a discernible strand within the Irish literary revival, though pinpointing where and when may be futile. Yeats's eulogy of

Samuel Ferguson—his first published prose piece—concisely illustrates the difficulty of delineating between the Irish literary revival and the Celtic mode adopted by many of its literati: '[Samuel Ferguson] is the greatest poet Ireland has produced, because the most central and most Celtic'. By Celtic, Yeats clarified that he meant a sensitivity to Ireland's native mythology, which he exhorted 'every Irish reader' to study.[30] There were Celtic streaks to every literary group into the 1890s, from the moderate National Literary Society to the Fenian-inflected Celtic Literary Society (1893–1902), which the founder of Sinn Féin Arthur Griffith (1871–1922) attended. But of all the related groups, those inhabited by Yeats and his circle made the most of the available cultural capital in the modern Celtic tradition; from early on, Yeats had seized upon Arnold's idea of the spiritual singularity of Celticism as opposed to materialistic English philistinism, signing off early newspaper columns as 'A Celt in London'—thereby presenting himself as, in Foster's words, an 'avatar of a new national literature, exiled among the Sassenachs'.[31]

The defining feature of Yeats and his coterie's Celticism of the 1890s was the mystic disposition many of them adopted. Yeats and his friend George Russell (1867–1935), 'Æ', mixed their occult interests with their nationalist positions, trawling through folklore and antiquarian research into the Irish Gods—the *Túatha Dé Danaan*—whose very existence seemed to set off the Irish Celt's anti-materialism as irreconcilable with the rest of British society.[32] The construction of a Celtic Mystical Order from 1895 led to some pan-Celtic suggestions with the French via the Paris-based Maud Gonne (1866–1953)—a nationalist activist best known as Yeats' muse and unrequited lover—and Jacobite MacGregor Mathers (1854–1918). However, this was at root an Irish national mysticism—awakening the Irish Gods would lead to the spiritual restoration of the nation—which Russell jealously guarded.[33]

There was also a wider interest in 'Celtic' literature and art outside of the Irish context. The London-based Rhymers' Club (*c.* 1890–1895) featured a number of self-identified Celtic members, like Yeats, Rolleston, and their friend Ernest Rhys (1859–1946), and was less artistically constricting than the Irish national literary scene. Its members harboured pan-Celtic interests and the group's second anthology contained a pair of poems about Brittany and an ode to 'The Celtic Speech'.[34] Hovering around this and similar literary groups were also a number of British editors and critics like Alfred Nutt (1856–1910), whose scientific approach to folklore Yeats found priggish and repellent, and the novelist and poet George Meredith (1829–1909), who considered himself half-Irish and half-Welsh and wrote his anti-materialist novel *Celt and Saxon*

(1910) in 1895 at the height of the 1890s Celtic enthusiasm. Celticism was also mixed into the work of the practitioners of art for art's sake, who stripped the word of any meaning beyond a vague Arnoldian hatred of philistinism. For example, in 1891 the novelist Grant Allen waxed lyrical about one (English) Pre-Raphaelite Arts & Crafts designer: 'Only a Celt, and only a Celt of our time, could have put so much spirituality into the broidery of a robe.'[35] Two years later, in response to Lord Salisbury's coining of the conceptual 'Celtic Fringe'—originally the 'Celtic edges'—Allen awkwardly countered that there was no such thing as a Celtic race, only British peoples unconquered by the Saxons, who would soon absorb the latter.[36] For proclamations like these, Fiona Macleod flattered Allen in 1894 as the 'most brilliant champion of the Celtic genius now living'; the anthropologist Edward Clodd (1840–1930) in turn praised Macleod's work, which would 'help the Celt to make further conquest of the dullard Saxons'.[37] But this last quote gives the game away—that for many of these figures Celticism meant nothing more than an insipid post-Arnoldian aesthetic sensibility and anti-materialism. The political background is important here, as most of these figures were unionists and therefore hoping to use Celticism to reconcile England and the Celtic nations, rather than drive them apart.

Within this British context, a 'Celtic Renascence' emerged in Scotland, where the eccentric sociologist Patrick Geddes began a publishing firm and hired William Sharp as managing editor in 1895. The Edinburgh movement grouped around the short-lived *Evergreen* (1895–1896) journal, edited by Geddes and shaped by the literary voice of William Sharp's alter ego, Fiona Macleod. Like the Irish cultural nationalist movement, the Scottish Celtic Renascence had its roots in wider cultural trends of the preceding decades, most specifically the Arts & Crafts movement.[38] Geddes envisioned the Celtic Revival as the latest in a line of artistic vogues stretching from the beginning of history: 'Egypt–Chaldea–Greek–Gothic–Renaissance–Celtic'.[39] Though it sought to cultivate a national outlook, the Scottish Celtic Renascence was not nationalist and adopted a Celtic unionist perspective, advanced most forcefully by Sharp/Macleod as the group's public persona. Sharp's wife later wrote that as Fiona Macleod, Sharp had 'deplored' uniting a political purpose to the Celtic Renascence, a key breach with the Irish Celtic movement.[40]

Until the 1890s Sharp had pursued a relatively ordinary literary career as a poet and editor, whose break had come in the early 1880s when the Pre-Raphaelite Dante Gabriel Rossetti (1828–1882) took him under his wing.[41] The details are hazy, but in the early 1890s Sharp underwent an identity crisis during a passionate love affair that produced a female Celtic alter ego bordering on a split personality—Fiona Macleod—the embodiment of the Renanian feminine Celt; the upshot was a burst of creativity that garnered more praise from the literary community than anything Sharp had previously produced. Macleod was clearly influenced by the Irish movement, and above all Yeats, who Sharp named in the introduction to the Celtic anthology *Lyra Celtica* (1896) as 'pre-eminently representative of the Celtic genius of to-day'.[42] Sharp gave a lucid summary of Celtic literature and scholarship, and gently pushed the Pan-Celtic, unionist line of the Scottish Celtic Renascence. Indeed, the work seemed to inspire a Pan-Celtic streak in Yeats, who wrote to Sharp that *Lyra Celtica* would advance 'the mutual understanding & sympathy of the Scotch Welsh & Irish Celts', which Yeats said was near his heart.[43] Pleased with Macleod's commercial success, Sharp worked to ingratiate her with Yeats and his Celtic circle,[44] writing to him in 1897 of an assumed project with Pan-Celtic dimensions: 'We are on the verge of vitally important developments. And all the heart, all the brain, of the Celtic races shall be stirred'.[45] He must therefore have been thrilled by Yeats's letter encouraging Macleod to send her collected works to an Irish editor who wanted 'to work with the Celtic as apart from the merely Irish movement'.[46] This statement indicated Yeats's recognition that they worked in a joint Celtic project; however, differentiating it from the Irish movement also foreshadowed the intra-Celtic cleavages to come.

The foundation of what became the Abbey Theatre laid bare the limits of the Yeatsian circle's Pan-Celticism. Initially conceived of as a 'Celtic' theatre, it was quickly retitled the 'Irish Literary Theatre', because this was deemed to be 'less dangerous', reflecting the fraught Irish cultural situation of the time.[47] Yeats (who suspected the identity of Macleod/Sharp) had used Pan-Celticism to entice the participation of Macleod, writing that plays 'might do more than anything else, we can do, to make the Irish, Scotch, & Other, celts recognize their solidarity',[48] but the inclusion of 'Celtic' in the title seemed to be only a move to accommodate her, as Sharp was present at its formation in Coole.[49] In reality the theatre movement was nationally focused and Sharp's odd behaviour on the trip to Coole would have done nothing to help his Celtic cause. At the time Lady Gregory (1852–1932) described their desire to make Dublin the 'Mecca of the Celt', but she later drily noted that the '"Celtic Movement"' was 'meant to persuade the Scotch to begin buying our books, while we continued not to buy theirs', and she had no qualms about telling Sharp that his movement had to remain separate.[50] Shortly afterward, Yeats responded to Andrew Lang's previously mentioned article on the Scottish 'Celtic Renascence' with a deafening silence in his celebrated speech on 'The Celtic Movement' in December 1897.[51] Sinead Garrigan-Mattar and, less forcefully, Foster, have both stressed the speech as marking Yeats's and his circle's turn away from wider Celtic outreach—symbolically demonstrated by the request that Sharp step down from chairing the meeting.[52] I agree with the broad thrust of this interpretation;[53] however, as discussed in the following section, there was still (limited) space for Pan-Celticism in Yeats's mind—never one to prematurely close a potential avenue for advancement—as well as (crucially) Maud Gonne's, if not in sceptical Lady Gregory's. But it was not just that the Irish Celtic movement wanted to go it alone; above all, the Anglo-Scottish Celtic Renascence lacked the national edge that animated Irish writing in this era. Sharp/Macleod considered themselves variously Saxon, Scandinavian, and British, as well as Celtic, and Sharp's Arnoldian closing line in the introduction to *Lyra Celtica* that 'The Celt falls, but his spirit rises in the heart and the brain of the Anglo-Celtic peoples' was emphatically not the mentality of the Irish national movements, and would have rung a loud warning bell for Yeats.[54]

The flurry of Celtic interest that came with the national literary movements of the 1880s and 90s laid the immediate groundwork for the Pan-Celtic movement of the late 1890s and 1900s. Yet, despite increasing sentiment and declarations, Pan-Celticism remained rather staid. In Britain this was partly due to an Arnoldian desire for spiritual reconciliation between the different ethnic populations of the British Isles, as articulated by Sharp. The art for art's sake viewpoint of many figures precluded any commitment beyond the aesthetic; it turned out the Yeatsian principle that literary output came from strong national feeling was a particularly Irish belief.

E. E. Fournier d'Albe and the Pan-Celtic Movement

The overlapping contexts in which Pan-Celticism arose are vital, but the foundation of a coherent dynamic movement should be attributed to the vigour of one man: the English physicist Edmund Edward Fournier d'Albe.[55] Born in 1868 to a German émigré and his English wife in Bloomsbury, Fournier was educated in Germany but moved back to London and graduated from the Royal College of Science in 1891, before settling in Dublin, where he was a physicist by day and Irish nationalist by evening. Fournier's English birth was a constant source of embarrassment in Ireland, where he was ridiculed by Moran—that Fournier was a *Gaeilgeoir* made the Anglophone monoglot Moran's derision all the more unjust—and so he played up his French name as

Breton and claimed connections to Scotland.[56] He floated around the major Irish cultural groups between 1895 and 1909, when he left Ireland for England and a successful career as a university lecturer, inventor, and popular scientific journalist.

Fournier's colleague, the mineralogist and amateur ethnologist J. P. O'Reilly (1829–1905), likely introduced him to the cultural movement around 1895, the year in which they published an antiquarian paper in the *Proceedings of the Royal Irish Academy*.[57] He helped to found the Gaelic League's musical branch, the *Feis Ceoil*—with, among others, Edith Oldham (1865–1950), the future wife of R. I. Best—and joined the National Literary Society and the Society for the Preservation of the Irish Language soon thereafter.[58] Fournier later identified 1896 as the year he adopted a 'Celtic faith, which I have found the source of the greatest inspiration of my life', after hearing Welsh used as the exclusive means of communication at the 1896 Llandudno *Eisteddfod*.[59] He was inducted into the *Gorsedd* and became the main channel between the Irish and Welsh cultural nationalist movements,[60] as well as the Irish contact for Scotland and Brittany. No doubt his grasp of all the Celtic languages aided his case, and in 1899 and 1900 he won essay prizes at the Gaelic League national festival, the *Oireachtas*.[61] Around the same time Fournier founded the Dalkey branch of the Gaelic League and ensured that Dalkey Station was the first to be signposted in Irish as well as English;[62] he underscored his commitment to Ireland by gaelicising his name—*Éamonn Mac Albann*—and dedicating his books with the convention *Do chum glóire Dé agus onóra na h-Éireann*: 'To the glory of God and the honour of Ireland'. Seduced by what he later described as 'the glamour of the Celtic renaissance', Fournier clearly possessed a deep feeling for things Celtic;[63] but many had similar Celtic affinities, and Fournier's English birth underlines that what was needed for a genuine Pan-Celticism was not so much anything endemically Celtic, but simple enthusiasm and organisational skills.

In 1897 Fournier was elected registrar for the *Feis* and began a correspondence with the Gaelic noble Lord Castletown (1849–1937). Born in London, Bernard Edward Barnaby Fitzpatrick grew up at the family house in County Laois, before attending Eton and Oxford, and then joining the British Army. Upon his father's death in 1883, he succeeded as the second Baron Castletown, inheriting one of the largest estates in Ireland and taking a seat in the House of Lords.[64] Despite his staunch unionism, Castletown was irked by what he saw as England's mistreatment of Ireland, namely overtaxation. At a speech in Cork in 1896, he made reference to the Boston Tea Party, saying that if at any point in the Union's ninety-six-year existence the Irish had resorted to the 'Boston Method' they would have been fully justified in doing so.[65] He pressed the claim over the next few years, and gained notoriety after a fiery speech calling for a 'Pan-Celtic League' in June 1898. Given against the background of a House of Commons debate over the eventual Local Government (Ireland) Act (1898), the oratory attracted comment in the press and in the Commons, but Home Rulers were worried that, fronted by a unionist noble, any such Pan-Celtic League would only support Irish landlords and not the people.[66]

Nevertheless, Castletown's rhetoric impressed Fournier, who immediately invited him to join the committee to host a Pan-Celtic Congress in Dublin.[67] Fournier explained that representatives of the 'four chief Celtic peoples'—Ireland, Wales, Brittany, and the Scottish Highlands (chosen because their native languages still survived)—had decided at the 1898 Belfast *Feis Ceoil* to form a provisional committee for holding a Pan-Celtic Congress in 1900. Fournier took on the role of honorary secretary and informed Castletown that he had 'taken the liberty of proposing Your Lordship as President of the Irish Committee'.[68] Though Castletown was a member of the Gaelic League and even claimed to know some Irish—learned through childhood holidays to Connemara[69]—as a landlord and British officer he was perhaps not an obvious choice for the presidency of a Celtic organisation. However, Castletown hobnobbed with the great and the good in Irish and British society and brought name recognition to the movement—he put Fournier in touch with Douglas Hyde and Lady Gregory, for example, and he invited Sir John Rhys to the 1901 Pan-Celtic Congress.[70] Crucially, Castletown also had (at this time) deep pockets, and went on to fund the lion's share of the Celtic Association's projects. In that same summer of 1898, Fournier set out the goals for the Pan-Celtic Congress and presented a draft programme on trips to Cardiff, London, Oban, and Morlaix to gather support.[71] He also approached prominent figures in the Irish national movements and asked Castletown to promote the cause among the Dublin Castle elite.[72] Castletown was also co-opted into speaking to the National Literary Society on 'Our Celtic Inheritance' by Fournier, who collected the material and edited the speech—an episode revealing the internal dynamics of the association's leadership.[73]

In November 1898 Fournier invited Lady Gregory to join the Irish Pan-Celtic Committee, informing her that Yeats had already agreed to it.[74] As discussed above, it has been argued that Yeats had by this point turned away from Celticism and toward the Irish theatre, though William Halloran has cited Yeats's 1898 involvement with the Celtic Association as evidence that his idea of the Celtic Revival in the 1890s was inherently Pan-Celtic, and that he 'did all he could to foster solidarity between the Irish and their Celtic brethren'.[75] The reality seems somewhere in between. In a wonderfully ambivalent letter to Gregory about the Pan-Celtic Committee—which he attended briefly in 1898—Yeats optimistically averred that the Pan-Celtic Congress might make 'Irish people realize the value of old celtic things', but he quickly added an ulterior motive: 'I dare say we may be able to make it help our second year of the theatre if we get so far'.[76] But a little over a month later he was threatening to resign, finding Fournier 'enthusiastic' but 'altogether without tact or judgement'; both he and Gregory also objected to Castletown's desire for tight control over the Pan-Celtic Committee, but Yeats missed the special meeting held to address their concerns because Maud Gonne summoned him.[77] In the end Yeats stuck around, and Fournier remained hopeful of convincing Gregory to become further involved, appealing to her along Celtic cultural lines:

> I quite agree with you that the organisation of the Congress is a matter requiring great tact and circumspection. Many prejudices—some of them rather ludicrous—have to be overcome, and most people are at a loss what to make of it all—But such difficulties attend every new enterprise. After all, we are fighting a great battle, and our various forces are advancing all along the line. It has always been difficult to make the Celts pull together, and we have been blamed for attempting the impossible. But has not the Gaelic League been laughed at for the same reason? Besides, I would rather be in the wrong with my fellow Irish speakers than with those who believe that 'the rising tide' is English rather than Celtic. My travels have shown me that the best and finest and nicest people in Ireland are the *Gaedhilgeóridhe*. They are worth all the rest. And I believe the future lies with them.[78]

This letter is characteristic of Fournier's boundless enthusiasm for things Celtic, and in it he also expressed similar sentiments about the Highlanders. Nevertheless, it did not persuade Gregory, who—despite her donation to it—skipped out on the Pan-Celtic Congress in 1901.[79]

Gregory's scepticism reflected wider unease within the Irish cultural movement over the Pan-Celts. Though many prominent Gaelic Leaguers were sympathetic, others feared that the Irish Pan-Celts were muscling in on their territory.[80] Hyde reported to Lady Gregory that both the Gaelic League and *Feís* committee saw the Pan-Celts as a financial threat, and that he had been forbidden to join.[81] It was eventually resolved that the League would not support the Celtic Association officially, though members were free to associate with it in a personal capacity. Patrick Pearse (1879–1916) joined the Pan-Celtic Committee in 1899 and travelled with it to the Cardiff *Eisteddfod,* where he gave a speech presenting the Irish and Welsh as 'two branches of the same great race . . . two warriors in a ford fighting against the violence of the foreigner'.[82] However, increasing pressure and a nasty press campaign forced him and Hyde to disassociate from the group. But as with Lady Gregory, Fournier tried to keep Pearse interested, sensitively reassuring the twenty-one-year-old that he understood his deepest sentiments were with 'Our own native language'.[83] Fournier was partly successful, as Pearse paid his ten-shilling annual membership fee and was elected to the Pan-Celtic Executive Committee in 1902;[84] in the same year he joined the Pan-Celtic summer trip to Connemara, though his involvement waned after this point.[85] Pearse later lamented the Gaelic League's harsh anti–Pan-Celtic stance, reflecting on Fournier in 1906 as someone who gave 'as unselfish and brilliant service to the Irish language movement as anyone I know'.[86] Petty personal rivalries mixed with ideological differences and (especially with Moran) religious and class resentments into a toxic national chauvinist brew in the opposition to the Pan-Celts, but this resistance suggests that Pan-Celticism had hit a nerve because there was something to it.

Of all the other Celtic nations, the Pan-Celtic clarion was most successful in Brittany, where the movement was taken very seriously by a new generation of Breton nationalists.[87] Regionalism had been gaining strength as a political movement across France over the past few decades, and in Morlaix on 13 August 1898, a number of activists founded the *Union régionaliste bretonne.*[88] Fournier was there and opened the evening's gala proceedings by inviting the Bretons to the Pan-Celtic Congress. Among those present were Régis-Marie-Joseph, Marquis de l'Estourbeillon (1858–1946), a future vice-president of the Celtic Association and the moving force behind the *Union;* the young and dynamic François Jaffrennou (1879–1956; also known by his Bardic name Taldir), who corresponded with Fournier, and other kindred spirits in Ireland and Wales; Lionel Radiguet (1857–1936), who had been present at the June meeting in Belfast's Grand Hotel, where the committee to hold a Pan-Celtic Congress was formed;[89] and Jean le Fustec (1885–1910), a journalist and the first Archdruid of the Breton *Gorsedd,* founded in 1901. All of these men would journey to the Cardiff 'Pan-Celtic' *Eisteddfod* of 1899 and would join the Celtic Association, in which Estourbeillon, Jaffrennou, and Le Fustec would play prominent roles.[90]

Fournier's participation in the foundation of the *Union régionaliste bretonne* was a key moment for the Bretons. A year later Jaffrennou proclaimed that

Fournier had 'kindled a greater fire amongst us. . . . I am a pan-Celt. We in Brittany are all Pan-Celts'.[91] Maud Gonne was invited to the Breton festival in 1899, and reported to Yeats that Fournier sounded like 'a wonderful man & [whose?] Celtic imagination is strong'; nevertheless, she worried her new Breton friends had overestimated Pan-Celtic influence in Ireland, but had 'in no way undeceived them for I *hope* it will grow into what they think it is & what we all would like it to be'.[92] Gonne had her own Pan-Celtic streak and assured American allies 'that the Celts feel themselves united by racial kinship'.[93] In 1900 Charles le Goffic (1863–1932), a Breton poet and regionalist close to the conservative nationalist Maurice Barrès (1862–1923) and the monarchist Charles Maurras (1868–1952), wrote a long article in the *Revue des deux mondes* introducing the Pan-Celtic movement to a French audience.[94] To be sure, Le Goffic pointed out, there were clear difficulties in forming a united movement in light of the cultural and political differences of each Celtic nation, but in the end he decided that it was possible because 'that which animates the Celtic conscience . . . is the sentiment of the race and of the rights of this race to the integral life of superior races'.[95] The Pan-Celtic Congress would, he hoped, be the turning point to bring the Celtic nations closer together in this racial bond.

Fournier also won over the Welsh movement and the principality's press in a charm offensive, participating in meetings of the Cymmrodorion and on *eisteddfod* committees, at one of which he declared Wales to be the Celtic race's 'standard-bearer. . . . A victory for Welsh is a victory for Irish Gaelic and Breton'.[96] He, Castletown, and a number of Pan-Celtic delegates—including Pearse, Hyde, a dozen Highlanders, and over twenty Bretons—attended the 1899 Cardiff *Eisteddfod*, where Castletown delivered a speech inviting the *Gorsedd* to the first Pan-Celtic Congress in Dublin the following year.[97] In a clever bit of Celtic *Kabuki*, Fournier had the beginning of the address translated into '10th Century Old Irish' by the philologist Heinrich Zimmer (1851–1910).[98] In part this was a shrewd manoeuvre bypassing Castletown's linguistic deficiencies: 'You can do this more easily than you could read Modern Irish. For nobody knows how it was really pronounced'. But Fournier (who included diacritical marks just in case) justified the selection's symbolic value as the version of the language supposedly spoken before it split into the two modern branches (Irish and Scots Gaelic), thereby appealing to unity in collective historical memory.[99] The trick worked, conferring a sacrality on the proceedings that gained the approval of the Welsh press, but Fournier himself stole the limelight; he was described as 'just the type of man for the work. At once courteous, eager, and well-informed, he carries with him an atmosphere of enthusiasm highly charged with contagion'.[100] He and Castletown travelled to the Highland *Mòd* to invite the Scots as well, where, presumably, the same trick was repeated.

The Celtic Association

The efforts of Fournier and his colleagues led to the constitution of the Celtic Association on 12 October 1900.[101] However, this was in part a move to regroup after what Fournier described to Castletown as a 'mutiny' that had occurred in the Irish committee.[102] In addition to the heat being taken from the Gaelic League, Castletown's participation in the Boer War had forced the Congress slated for summer 1900 to be postponed, a serious setback as the organisation lost the momentum and buzz it had generated since its inception in 1898. Of course, the fact that its president was fighting for the British Empire against the Boers provided even more ammunition for the group's enemies. Support for the Boers was the litmus test for advanced Irish nationalists, so any concerns about Castletown's desire for control over the Celtic Association would have been compounded by his participation in the war. Mercifully, he eventually returned, and the first of three Pan-Celtic Congresses—in Dublin (1901), Caernarfon (1904), and Edinburgh (1907)—was held the following year.

Despite the hostility of the Gaelic League, the Celtic Association managed for a time to attract many of the leading Irish cultural figures, including most of Yeats's circle. Edward Martyn (1859–1923), George Moore (1852–1933), and T. P. Gill (1858–1931) remained members throughout the association's lifespan and sat on its executive committee, as did members of the older nationalist generation such as Michael Davitt—who was 'an active Pan-Celt' according to Fournier[103]—and John O'Leary. A. P. Graves, father of Robert Graves, played a considerable part behind the scenes and attempted to keep the association afloat during its final sinking years in London, drafting another son to help edit *Celtia*. Other prominent Celtic cultural figures included the Jesus Professor of Celtic at Oxford, John Rhys, the eccentric Australian-Scottish Jacobite Theodore Napier (1845–1924), and Horace Plunkett (1854–1932), the leader of the Irish Agricultural Movement. Patrick Geddes floated in and out of the association, but he was the chief organiser of the (disappointing) Edinburgh Pan-Celtic Congress in 1907. Vice-presidents of the association included Henri Gaidoz; the Marquis de l'Estourbeillon; Hwfa Môn (1823–1905), the Arch-Druid of the Welsh *Gorsedd*; Count George Plunkett (1851–1948), father of the future revolutionary Joseph

Mary Plunkett (1887–1916); the prominent Scottish folklorist Alexander Carmichael (1832–1912), whose daughter Elizabeth or 'Ella' (1870–1928) served on the Executive Committee; A. W. Moore (1853–1909), leader of the Manx House of Keys; and eventually, when Cornwall was admitted as a Celtic nation in 1904, its cultural leader Henry Jenner (1848–1934).[104]

It is worth lingering on the participation of the Isle of Man and Cornwall, both of whose national revivals date from this period, and whose Pan-Celtic participation gave them a certain amount of cultural legitimacy and direction. Fournier had since 1898 carefully cultivated Manx attention, publishing articles in Manx papers on the revival of the language, sponsoring prizes for compositions in it, and visiting the island.[105] These links strengthened over time, and when *Celtia* was constrained by financial difficulties in 1905–1906, Fournier published Pan-Celtic columns in Manx papers. It seems evident from this patchwork that the Celtic Association had finally managed to tap into the well of Pan-Celtic sentiment that by now apparently existed below the surface in each of the Celtic nations. Given the political, religious, and social differences between them, the significance of this feat should not be underestimated; it speaks to the cultural diplomacy and ecumenical skill of Fournier.

He had an intuitive sense for nation building, demonstrated most clearly in the map titled 'Celtia'—with which this book opened (Fig. 1)—which Fournier began circulating in 1898, and which depicted the Pan-Celtic imagined community. Discussed excitedly in the Welsh press and in *Fáinne an Lae* and looked on with amused scepticism in English periodicals,[106] the map challenged geographical conceptions of Britain, Ireland, and France and indicated a sense of Pan-Celtic plans: 'Celtia' could be either a space for international cooperation or, more radically, an entirely new polity that turned the idea of a 'Celtic Fringe' on its head. Also visible on the map were proposed ferry routes, including a line from Cork to St. Malo, indicating an understanding that national feeling could be spurred by material means and was not just a romantic vision. Fournier clearly understood the utility of a visual conception of 'Celtia', and he delineated precise boundaries based upon language: '"Celtia" has an actual existence in the hearts of those who speak and love their Celtic language, and are in sympathy with the parallel efforts of their kinsfolk across the sea.'[107] Cornwall's conspicuous absence in 1899 reflected the belief that its language was dead, but this also reveals the inextricable link between language and race in Pan-Celtic thought.

Among other things, Fournier noted the importance of the 'modern press' and 'education policy' as drivers of national sentiment since 'the national

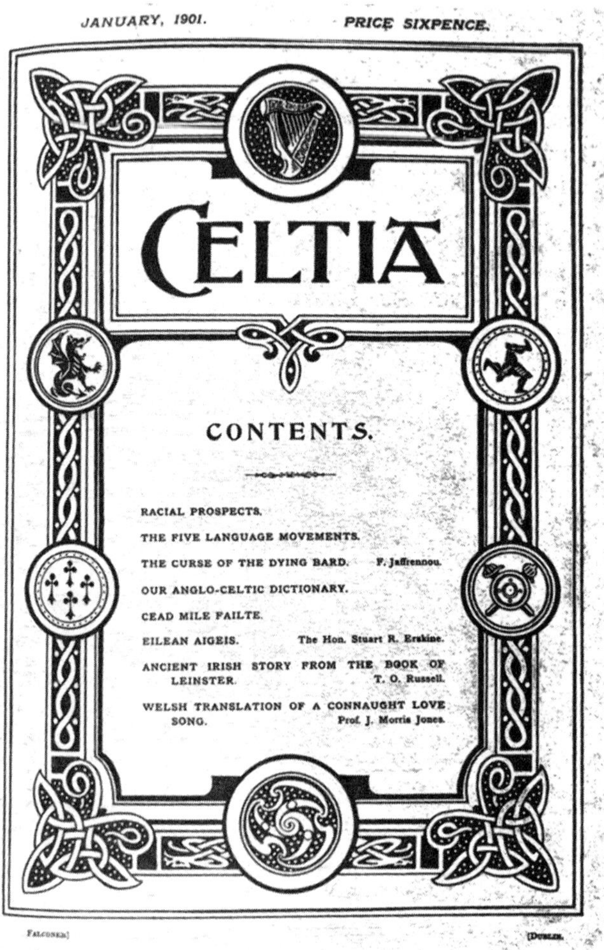

JANUARY, 1901. PRICE SIXPENCE.

CELTIA

CONTENTS.

RACIAL PROSPECTS.
THE FIVE LANGUAGE MOVEMENTS.
THE CURSE OF THE DYING BARD. F. Jaffrennou.
OUR ANGLO-CELTIC DICTIONARY.
CEAD MILE FAILTE.
EILEAN AIGEIS. The Hon. Stuart R. Erskine.
ANCIENT IRISH STORY FROM THE BOOK OF LEINSTER. T. O. Russell.
WELSH TRANSLATION OF A CONNAUGHT LOVE SONG. Prof. J. Morris Jones.

FALCONER] [DUBLIN.

FIG. 13. First issue of *Celtia*.

awakening of Europe', which he dated to 1813 and the 'German war of independence'.[108] 'Celtia' accordingly inspired the name of the association's journal, which Fournier founded in 1901 after first flirting with the idea of taking over the Gaelic League periodical *Fáinne an Lae*.[109] He would edit *Celtia* (Fig. 13) through 1904 and again briefly in 1907, before handing over editorship to the Welshman S. R. John (1886–1909), who only stayed on until May 1908 due to his declining health.[110] The 'Celtia' map illustrated the 'imagined community' that Fournier posited for the Celtic countries, while its journal *Celtia* was an attempt to construct a 'public sphere', later supplemented by the Congresses. Fournier editorialised as the standard-bearer of the Pan-Celtic movement, proclaiming *Celtia* to be 'the organ of militant Celticism, directed mainly against the deadening and demoralising influences of modern Anglo-Saxondom, and working to raise the self-respect and strengthen the cohesion of the Celtic race'.[111]

The Celtic Association was of course also engaged in the very prosaic activities that characterized cultural revivals at this time.[112] It held monthly meetings in its Dublin offices on St Stephens Green, where the Executive Committee met on the first Friday of every month. There was language instruction as well as dancing and the rehearsals of a Celtic choir. In her comprehensive study of the organization, Murphy-Macinta counts 462 total members, which she points out is comparable with some related contemporary organisations like An Comunn Gaidhealach.[113] She also finds that more than a third of that membership was Catholic and pushes back against the perception of the group as dominated by an Anglo-Protestant elite.[114] While Irish Anglican Dubliners made up the largest number of members, Murphy-Macinta shows that the group was more plural than has been assumed, though it seems clear that whatever the other demographics, it was obviously dominated by the well-educated middle class. Only five of the twenty-five members of the Executive Committee were allowed to live outside of Dublin, effectively ensuring Irish dominance.[115]

Pan-Celtic Congresses

The triennial Pan-Celtic Congresses were the Celtic Association's centrepieces and were judged vital to cultivating Pan-Celtic fraternal sentiment. Just the act of meeting face-to-face was important, but this took place within a carefully cultivated background, especially at the Dublin Congress, which garnered attention for its pageantry. After the procession and *Gorsedd* rites discussed in the introduction (Fig. 14), the Congress consisted of academic papers and practical Pan-Celtic discussion, and was punctuated by bits of ceremony and nightly concerts. Fournier—already skilled in fabricating historical memory—had consulted the pan-Celtic historical record, harking back to the 1838 Abergavenny *Eisteddfod* and the 1867 *Congrès celtique* in Saint-Brieuc, in both *Celtia* and in the second and third Congress programmes,[116] thereby reminding the Pan-Celts that they had an associational history with its own ceremonial provenance. The Congress was pitched as another link in the Celtic historical chain, an event 'whose memory will endure as long as the Race itself'.[117] The *Gorsedd*

FIG. 14. *Gorsedd* ceremony, *Illustrated London News*, 31 August 1901, 316.

resurrected the Hirlas Horn—given to Villemarqué by the Welsh in 1838—and the ceremony in which two sword halves were reconnected, with one half representing the Welsh, the other the Bretons. Fournier's own unique contribution was the *Lia Cineil* (Fig. 15), an ogham stone that was broken into five pieces—each representing a Celtic nation—and was only to be erected when members from all nations were present.

The first Pan-Celtic Congress held in Dublin in the summer of 1901 attracted an impressive attendance. Most of the 'Celtic' luminaries were already members of the association, and a number of them spoke. William Sharp attended pseudonymously, according to his wife, though not as Fiona Macleod, suggesting the tantalising possibility of a third alter ego.[118] Six years later, Castletown would remember the Congress for its first-class Celtic scholarship, the main events on the Congress's second and fourth days, which included papers by the German philologists Kuno Meyer (1858–1919) and Heinrich Zimmer, with several others in attendance.[119] Delegates from all the Celtic nations spoke on antiquities, literature, art, and their respective languages. The radical sociologist John Stuart-Glennie, who will be remembered from the previous chapter for beginning a political Pan-Celtic league to col-

FIG. 15. The *Lia Cineil*, from *Celtia*, Congress Number (1904). There is 'ogham' on the side of the pillar.

lectively address the land question, spoke on this and on the Celtic legendary inheritance, after which his friend Patrick Geddes gave a summary of Celtic art and its revival in Scotland.[120] Cornwall's status as a Celtic nation stimulated vigorous debate, but the motion for its official inclusion among the other members of the association was, to Fournier's disappointment, defeated. National dress proved another contentious issue, discussed under the chairmanship of the eccentric William Gibson (1868–1942), future Lord Ashbourne, who attended the Congress dressed in his self-made Irish costume, which

FIG. 16. E. E. Fournier d'Albe in Irish costume at the 1904 Pan-Celtic Congress, in Marion Löffler (ed.), *'A Book of Mad Celts': John Wickens and the Celtic Congress of Caernarfon 1904* (Llandysul, 2000), 23.

Fournier also wore (Fig. 16). The consensus seemed to be that a better costume was needed, and Yeats, of all people, suggested the Irish could wear a national dress on Sundays and Mondays.

There was predictable ridicule from Irish Gaelic purists—Moran later characterised the Congress as a 'sort of circus procession fiasco' perpetrated by 'some irresponsible busy-bodies'[121]—and Saxon chauvinists. Kuno Meyer reported that 'scoffers' called it the 'Pankiltic' Congress, but he described it as 'very picturesque', with 'excellent music' and 'interesting people', though he was unsure what 'the lasting result' would be.[122] The Congress was certainly successful in generating buzz and was reported on in papers across Ireland, Britain, France, and the United States.[123] Even Yeats was pleasantly surprised, and gossiped to Lady Gregory with evident *Schadenfreude* about the ribbing a 'Cornish miner' gave to Castletown over the Boer War, but he was also impressed with the ceremony and speakers. All in all, said Yeats, it was 'a very considerable success'.[124]

The Caernarfon Pan-Celtic Congress (1904) reportedly attracted thousands of observers—Castletown later claimed there were ten-thousand—and even managed to turn a profit.[125] The prospectus announced that the Congress would be 'held on the same lines, but on a larger scale' than the 1901 event, but that the 'principles and policy of the Pan-Celtic movement' were to be newly agreed upon and 'more clearly formulated'.[126] One of the issues to be discussed was the position of the 'minor national languages', and after several years of protesting, the Cornish were finally recognised as kindred members of the Celtic Association, led by the foremost revivalist, the British Museum's librarian Henry Jenner.[127] The scholarly turnout was again impressive, and Kuno Meyer recommended his student J. Glyn Davies (1870–1953) go for networking opportunities. David Lloyd George, MP for Caernarfon at the time, showed up towards the end to attest to 'his personal interest in and sympathy with the congress'.[128] It probably helped that his brother William George (1865–1967) was a Pan-Celt and friends with Fournier, who he introduced to Lloyd George—they all discussed politics and in 1907 David wrote to his brother that Fournier had written him an 'interesting letter on the state of parties in Ireland'.[129] Despite the Congress's superficial success, the association had stagnated since 1901, and the attention garnered by the Caernarfon Congress likely had more to do with Welsh cultural enthusiasm and curiosity than genuine Pan-Celtic interest. It took place right before the national *eisteddfod*, to which it then sent a delegation.

In 1907 the association perfunctorily held a Congress in Edinburgh, organised by Patrick Geddes. The highlight was the opening *Gorsedd*, which took place on the dramatic esplanade in front of the castle;[130] the rest was more mundane, despite Geddes's efforts to select only those speakers with 'something to say'.[131] One attendee with absolutely nothing to say was the newly retired Lord Rosebery (1847–1929) who, when recognised in the crowd by Castletown and asked for an impromptu address, bolted from the room.[132] Castletown repeated his usual Pan-Celtic stump speech, but there was a dearth of compelling presenters and few participants from outside of Scotland and Wales.[133] Bretons had been stalwart in their prior Pan-Celtic attendance, but although the Marquis de l'Estourbeillon appeared, he tried to impress upon Fournier beforehand that the estimated cost of attendance of 400 francs was well out of the reach of most other Bretons.[134] Part of the Congress's failure must also be down to Fournier's diminished attention to Pan-Celticism from around 1905 as a result of the success of his scientific career. With the Association in debt, it was forced to stop printing *Celtia*, and Fournier suggested moving the entire operation to London, which it did in 1907 when *Celtia* briefly started up again.[135] It was therefore not an auspicious year in which to hold another Congress, and although Fournier advised Geddes, his suggestion to copy the *eisteddfod* was hardly revelatory. Nevertheless, the Congresses each succeeded in bringing attention to the movement, and themselves became hallowed *lieux de mémoire* in the reconstituted Pan-Celtic movement later in the twentieth century.

'Tír gan teanga, tír gan anam': Race, Language, and Pan-Celtic Ideology

While the Congresses were an integral part of the Pan-Celtic agenda and the kind of public spectacle necessary to gain notoriety, the Celtic Association also had a sophisticated ideology.[136] It is through *Celtia* that this can best be traced, revealing at once the febrile energy of Fournier and his grand plans for the Pan-Celtic movement. The central principles outlined for the Association in the inaugural *Celtia* relied on three related ideas. The first, which underpinned everything, was a Celtic racial bond. The second was the notion that Celtic racial feeling had been preserved in its native languages: 'the cultivation of the Celtic languages means the regeneration of the Celtic race'. The final principle was the belief in an impending united Celtic future: 'the Celtic race, when unified . . . will exert a great and beneficent influence in the advancement of mankind'.[137] The elephant in the Pan-Celtic room was the Irish nationalist situation, which was purposefully evaded in Celtic Association literature; Fournier had to tiptoe around unionists like Castletown, whose involvement would have signalled to Irish nationalists the group's lack of an advanced nationalist dimension.

Race was the ontological root of Pan-Celticism, and *Celtia*'s first editorial opened with the proclamation that the Celtic race was newly reinvigorated: 'The opening of the twentieth century finds the Celtic race in the beginning of a new phase of existence . . . the racial instinct is asserting itself in manifold forms'. Cultivating this racial feeling was therefore the association's main goal, as racial unity would lead to a brighter future for the Celts, Europe, and the world.[138] Here was a break with the romantic, fatalistic view of Renan and Arnold, who were 'almost ludicrously at fault' for missing the 'practical side' and indefatigable spirit of the Celtic character that often achieves '"the impossible"'.[139] Fournier explicitly rejected links between Pan-Celticism as a racial revival and the 'Celtic Twilight', which he trivialised as merely a 'flavour' in English literature.[140] Instead, the Pan-Celtic outlook was distinctly modernist—'the civilising and beautifying influence of modern progress must be utilised'[141]—optimistic, and forward facing, looking back only to a vague past when the Celtic race was supposedly whole.

The Pan-Celtic narrative tweaked the familiar model of national catastrophe as a result of foreign invasion to be more inclusive; thus, whereas Irish nationalists recognised disaster extending from the twelfth-century Anglo-Norman invasion, the Pan-Celts pushed their catastrophic narrative back to the Romans, who forced the beginning of changes in 'politics and religion' that catalysed 'twenty centuries of division and disaster' and the contemporary 'wide gaps between the Celtic sister nations'.[142] But racial sentiment was strong enough to connect people 'across generations and centuries', providing a 'guarantee of permanence' for the Celtic family.[143] This reading formed the basis for the millenarian sense that Pan-Celticism was part of the 'modern revival of submerged nationalities all over Europe' that would soon burst into a 'new racial life' that 'will beautify the world with new forms of literary splendour and racial vigour'.[144] Since racial struggle was thought to be salutary, *Celtia* welcomed 'racial rivalry', supposedly seen on 'the Celtic borderland', because it was the kind of dynamic that had 'produced the finest gems of literature and the most vigorous advance of civilisation'.[145]

It was primarily through linguistic revival that the race would be rejuvenated. *Celtia* proclaimed languages to be 'the most powerful bond between nations as between individuals',[146] which ultimately led back to the racial root of the Celts. Languages had long been seen as the most important Celtic feature, but the situation had deteriorated to the point where the issue in every Celtic nation was at best preservation, at worst resurrection. In 1903 Fournier described the association's goal as 'The establishment of the Celtic languages as the dominant languages in their respective countries',[147] which it pursued through a number of strategies. As it was a Dublin-based organisation, most of the emphasis was on Irish, and Fournier claimed that the association had pioneered the immersion colony for Irish learners, organising trips to *Gaeltachta* in Connemara and Tory Island. Colonies were also planned in the other Celtic nations, but they never materialised.[148] The association had been founded with a plan to publish an English-Celtic dictionary, with all (at the time) five Celtic languages represented; however, it was likely only Fournier undertaking this monumental task, and he did not get past the letter 'C'. He did manage to publish one of the first English-Irish dictionaries, which became an important early text for the standardisation of the language.[149] In addition to the English-Irish dictionary, he also published *First Lessons in Manx*, a Breton Grammar, a Cornish Grammar, and a collection of Irish music and folktales.[150] Irish and Welsh lessons were offered at the association's offices, and members were urged to join the language associations of the other Celtic nations. In 1907 the Association joined with the Gaelic League and the Society for the Preservation of the Irish Language to form the Dublin Corporation's Gaelic Committee of Reference, for naming streets in Irish.[151] Despite attacks from Gaelic Leaguers, the Celtic Association had therefore succeeded in garnering some clout in Irish circles. The language campaign was symptomatic of the wider project of modernising Irish, wholly supported by the Association. Thomas O'Neill Russell, a founder of the Gaelic League and honorary secretary of the Celtic Association, stressed in *Celtia* the necessity for modernising the language if it were to survive, noting that English and French had both been perpetually updated, while Irish was stuck in its older forms. Fournier wrote in 1902 of the need to develop an Irish scientific vocabulary, excavating words from ancient manuscripts and altering them to suit modern purposes.[152] The modernisation project had begun in the mid-1890s, and the Gaelic League sponsored a contest for the creation of modern Irish technical terms at the 1899 *Oireachtas*; Fournier claimed first prize.[153]

Pan-Celticism relied more heavily on scholarship than some of the other movements, as it was only through comparative philology that the very existence of a Celtic race had been proven, a point Fournier himself emphasised in his early campaigning for the movement.[154] Scholarly Celtic works—mostly on ethnology and philology—were reviewed in *Celtia*, and some evidence that the journal had registered with the scholarly community can be taken from the fact that when Edward Nicholson (1849–1912) was about to publish his book *Keltic Researches*, he listed *Celtia* among the journals to receive a review copy (although it was second from the bottom of an extensive list).[155] Fournier wrote to him about the book in May 1904, inviting him to the Pan-Celtic Congress later that year, which he attended.[156] The scholar closest to the movement was Kuno Meyer (discussed more in the following chapter), but Fournier had also cultivated links with Heinrich Zimmer, professor of Celtic at Berlin.

Despite the universal goal of language revival, commitment and efforts varied by Celtic nation. Kuno Meyer lamented the lack of Highland Celtic scholarship, declaring that even the Isle of Man put the region to shame.[157] Marion Löffler has argued that Wales was 'the most vital part of the [Pan-Celtic] movement', but while the Welsh language's strength made it inspirational, its supporters' perceived lack of a political edge was frustrating, and for a short time in 1903 Fournier advocated a Gaelic empire composed of Ireland, the Isle of Man, and the Scottish Highlands—'Scotia Minor must again become part of Scotia Major'.[158] He considered the Gael to be the 'strongman of these Islands' who would 'put a thing or two in order' when free of Wales, who 'feebly struggles in the dark'.[159] This idea was short-lived, as it unsurprisingly encountered resistance from Scottish and Welsh nationalists,[160] and *Celtia* editorials returned to calling for a Celtic federation rather than a Gaelic empire.

Despite the fact that the Celtic Association took seriously its commitment to linguistic revival, there was no escaping the reality that English was the most practical choice. The great irony was that very few could understand a Celtic language other than their own, if that. Fournier acknowledged as much in the inaugural *Celtia*: 'Pending the evolution of some Celtic *lingua franca*, be the same Irish or Welsh, we shall use English as our chief weapon of war and instrument of propaganda'.[161] Such militaristic rhetoric punctuated the more banal majority of the magazine's content, but it faded as Pan-Celtic enthusiasm failed to match the desired cultural mobilisation for battle. The use of English was obviously problematic to a group with a central goal of de-anglicising the Celtic countries, so in 1902 Fournier began to advocate for Esperanto.[162] As a synthetic language, Esperanto did not have any of the cultural baggage of English or French; it would therefore serve to connect the Celtic peoples while combating the perfidious 'imperial' languages. Esperanto passages were published in *Celtia* from 1902, and at the 1904 and 1907 Congresses Fournier moved unsuccessfully to make it the official language of the Pan-Celtic movement, though his comrades at least humoured him with a discussion of its merits. Fournier went on to found the Irish Esperanto Association with Joseph Mary Plunkett (1887–1916), and he has the unique distinction of being the first to translate a classical Irish text into Esperanto, which still retains a Pan-Celtic presence: a Pan-Celtic Esperanto Conference took place in 2014.[163]

A 'Hansa of Small Nations': Pan-Celticism and International Utopia

Terrestrially, the Celtic Association pursued most of the goals of the other Irish cultural nationalist movements, but it also advanced a remarkably ambitious global utopian vision, a 'Hansa of Small Nations' to oppose imperialist powers.[164] Fournier had been particularly inspired by an address that William O'Brian (who became a member) gave in 1892, in which he called for a 'world-wide Celtic league', connecting not just the core Celtic nations but their diasporic populations in the New World.[165] Building on O'Brian's call, anti-imperialism was at the heart of Fournier's vision. *Celtia* editorials shifted from the optimistic and determined strategy of racial revival in 1901 to exasperation with colonial occupation, stimulated in part by the French government's suppression of Breton: 'The forcible extinction of the language of a conquered people . . . is the strict equivalent in the world of nations of "murder" in the world of individuals'.[166] But a history of similar oppression had sharpened the Celtic racial instinct, which arose due to 'the [Celtic] fight for national existence'.[167] In response to the suppressive linguistic policies of the French government, Fournier issued the somewhat ridiculous warning:

> an attack upon a Celtic language raises a racial issue, and brings forces into play whose power it is impossible to gauge, and which had better not be played with. . . . The race is feeling its renewed strength, and will not hesitate to use it if provoked beyond endurance.[168]

Cultural imperialism would find its 'automatic antidote' in the 'natural law' of 'rivalry and war of existing species'.[169] Fournier argued that although individuals had become enlightened, international relations still existed in 'feudal times', in that great powers overtook and assimilated smaller nations by force:[170] 'A strong individual may deprive a weaker one of his possessions. . . . In the life of nations the same thing happens', but the goal was to 'replace the doctrine of the Superior Race by that of the Liberty of the Subject Nation'.[171]

He predicted the twentieth century would be the 'Century of Small Nations', wherein the principles of individual liberty would be extended to entire nations: 'Individual liberty and nationality are the watchwords of modern progress',[172] and French encroachment on the Breton language was 'a declaration of relentless war upon the Breton language and nationality', which in turn was a 'violation of the rights of Brittany as one of the Celtic nations'.[173] The Celtic Association called a special general meeting as a result of the Breton situation and elected to send a deputation to Paris in order to make their opposition clear to the government, but after several deputies mysteriously found themselves unavailable to make the journey, the Marquis de l'Estourbeillon diplomatically curtailed it.[174] However, Fournier argued that 'future scientific progress', especially air power, would soon democratise international relations by threat of force, and old-fashioned political delegations would no longer be needed.[175] In another veiled threat to the French government, Fournier wrote that the ability to bomb from the air would make the most centralised powers the most vulnerable: 'The greatest power will be as vulnerable as the least, and even more so, since the greater the concentration of wealth in large capitals the greater is the havoc that can be wrought by a flying enemy'.[176] States would cease to exist as no one power would have a monopoly on violence, and the world would be reorganised by racial affinity as state frontiers vanished.[177]

The 'Celtic federation' would be joined by a multitude of other small nations in the construction of this new world order:

> Central and south America, [the] Balkans, Sweden, Norway, Holland, Denmark, Belgium, Portugal and Greece . . . The federation of minor states would soon become itself the greatest power in the world, and would lead . . . to general decentralisation and disarmament.[178]

Each state would be organised on racial lines, speaking its own national language and using Esperanto for international communication. The coalition would operate as a league of nations, ensuring that no one state could oppress another. Clearly, other small nations were looked upon as allies in the growing 'race-and-nation' principle,[179] and *Celtia* reported on the situation of European national movements, protesting against the suppression of Polish by Germany and Finnish by Russia.[180] There were International Sections at both the 1901 and 1904 Pan-Celtic Congresses, where the Polish philologist Alfons Parczewski (1849–1943) presented his own plan for a European federation for the protection of language minorities.[181]

Celtia also reported on other European pan-nationalist movements, but rejected Pan-Germanism and Pan-Slavism for their objectives of subordinating smaller nations to a central power, while Pan-Latinism was seen as an academic pipe dream.[182] To a certain extent Germany, along with Italy and

Greece, was looked on as an example to be emulated, as a country that had established the German-speaking nation and state as co-terminous. But Germany was also treated with disdain for its assimilationist aims and suppression of smaller nationalities like the Poles. Pan-Celticism, on the other hand, advanced a democratic international federation based on the 'moral and intellectual alliance of a half-dozen small nations for mutual support and encouragement, on the basis of national self-reliance and mutual respect'.[183] The Pan-Celtic vision was set in the context of a Europe about to fracture into a number of smaller nations; it was thought this 'national specialisation' would be combined with 'racial cooperation' to form 'the guiding principles in the evolution of future civilisation'.[184]

There was one more important source for Pan-Celtic ideology: science fiction. In an early issue of *Celtia,* Fournier cited Jules Verne (1828–1905) as an example of the 'Franco-Breton genius',[185] whose *Robur the Conqueror* (1886) likely inspired some of his ideas on air power. But the greatest influence was H. G. Wells (1866–1946), with whom Fournier would become friends later in life. *Anticipations* was serialised over the course of 1901—*Celtia*'s first year of production—and contained ideas similar to those espoused by Fournier, particularly the millenarianism of technological change, the decentralisation of cities, the looming promise of airpower, the utility of a world language, and a future central world government.[186] Wells rejected dogmatic racialism and argued that all races were intermixed, criticising Pan-Slavism, Pan-Germanism, Pan-Latinism, and 'Pan-this-and-that movements'.[187] He was particularly disdainful of 'Pan-Kelticism', having seen reports of the Dublin Pan-Celtic Congress:

> Under the intoxication of the Keltic Renascence the most diverse sorts of human beings have foregathered and met face to face, and been photographed Pan-Keltically, and have no doubt gloated over these collective photographs, without any of them realizing, it seems, what a miscellaneous thing the Keltic race must be.[188]

The tenth issue of *Celtia*—published just as the serialisation of *Anticipations* was ending—was likely a response to Wells, as its leading editorial justified the Pan-Celtic racial focus and differentiated itself from the other Pan-nationalist movements that Wells had criticised on the basis that it was the only one 'based on mutual justice, toleration, and equality'.[189] Wells's inclination towards international socialism rejected 'Kelticism' and racialism more generally as legitimate organisational frameworks. Nevertheless, Wells's ideas were almost certainly a template from which Fournier organised his federation of

Celtic nations and its part in the global federation of small nations—his own version of World Government.

Conclusion

The Celtic Association did not achieve its international goals; there was to be no Celtic-led League of Nations. On the contrary, the association nosedived after the Caernarfon Congress. *Celtia* regressed from monthly to quarterly publication, going under in 1905, briefly resurfacing in 1906, and moving to London in 1907, where it lasted a year before it was wound up for good. Without the magazine, the association had no real public sphere. The Association's decline mirrored Fournier's own waning interest in Pan-Celticism as his scientific books began to sell and he met with success in other areas of his life. He departed Ireland for a lectureship at Birmingham University in 1909, which he later described to Castletown as the point when he left his 'Celtic dreams behind for good'.[190] In 1909, A. P. Graves invited Fournier to join a new Pan-Celtic committee that included, among others, Castletown, Nutt, Rolleston, and the Watsons, but Fournier seems to have declined.[191] The Belgian *Union celtique* organised a Pan-Celtic Congress in 1910 in conjunction with the Brussels International Exhibition, but it featured few former members of the association.[192] Maud Gonne warned Yeats away from it (not that he needed persuading), while Lord Inchiquin (1864–1929) wrote to Castletown complaining that he had agreed to chair it—Pan-Celtic enthusiasm had truly ebbed.[193]

However, the fact that such a Congress could take place without Fournier's dynamism behind it showed the movement could exist without him. In 1901, Fournier had written to Castletown that he thought 'sentiment' to be 'the most powerful force in human affairs'; accordingly, the association's 'Chief Function' was to create a 'Pan-Celtic Sentiment'.[194] So, although it failed to live up to its impossible goals, it seems to have succeeded in creating a Pan-Celtic sentiment. Pan-Celtic Congresses began again in 1917 (see the following chapter), restarted by a body that continues to this day.

Contrary to popular belief, when W. B. Yeats referred to the 'Celtic Twilight' he meant the hour before dawn, *not* dusk; however, in many ways Yeats's Celtic Twilight signalled the end of a particular kind of Celticism—evident from the sixteenth century—in which individuals from 'Celtic' nations across Europe argued over the claim to be considered the most Celtic. Yeats's promotion of the Abbey Theatre forced him to finally lay his cards on the table, and they came up all Ireland. I chose to call this chapter 'Celtic Daybreak' because with the Celtic Association came a new kind of genuinely international Celticism, whose goal was Pan-Celticism for its own sake, not for any proxy national, religious, or political reasons. Of course, nationalists—especially those from Ireland and Brittany—continued to draw upon Celticism throughout the twentieth century, but from now on there existed a clique of devoted Pan-Celts, for whom the collective rights of all Celtic nations were more important than any nation's individual Celtic past.

12

From the Pan-Celtic Moment to the Present

'NINETY-NINE IS THE BEGINNING of the Celtic Renaissance', declared Edward Martyn in conversation with W. B. Yeats and George Moore. 'I am glad to hear it', quipped Moore, 'the Celt wants a renaissance and badly; he has been going down in the world for the last two thousand years'.[1] All three tried to save 'the Celt' by participating in revivalist groups—such as the Celtic Association—and writing about related themes in their journalistic and artistic works, but whether they and their like-minded friends managed to stop the downward slide of 'the Celt' is an open question. Considered in the long sweep of ideas examined in this book, the Celtic Revival that happened around 1900 appears as a moment of intense interest, but did it reset the rhythms of Celticism?

The answer varies by nation, but broadly speaking Celticism as it exists today is in many ways indebted to the Celtic Revival at the dawn of the twentieth century. I have approached the question from two angles: popular interest and academic research. The effects were greatest in the two respective leaders in these aspects, Ireland and Germany. Irish nationalists mobilised knowledge in their political pursuits, buoying the field of Celtic studies domestically and internationally. But Germany was the leader. Joachim Lerchenmüller points to the 'irischen Faktor' in the development of German Celtology, but it is just as true to speak of the 'German Factor' in the development of Irish Celtic studies.[2] There was a special relationship between German Celticists and Ireland, one consciously cultivated by the Free State. The Irish Legation in Berlin was effectively set up by young Irish students studying Celtic in Germany in the 1920s, and the Irish government sponsored work by German Celticists when the post-war inflationary crisis started to bite.[3] *Dail Éireann* helped to finance Julius

Pokorny's (1887–1970) *Die älteste Lyrik der grünen Insel* (1923), which might have had something to do with his preface praising the Irish as 'the most gifted branch of the Celtic stem'.[4] Even with the Irish lifeline, Germany lost its status as the Mecca of Celtology in a slide that was already underway in the 1930s but made irreversible by the Second World War.

After Ireland, Brittany was the most turbulent Celtic nation. Its literature was of great interest to French Celticists such as Henri Gaidoz, Henri d'Arbois de Jubainville, and Joseph Vendryès, but the nationalist movement that emerged with the Celtic Revival at the end of the nineteenth century was more popular and quickly became militant.[5] Bretons were probably the most committed Pan-Celts of the twentieth century, but the opportunity offered by the Second World War forced some strange arguments and dubious decisions. Some Breton extremists collaborated with the Nazis, and a Breton unit of the SS was formed briefly near the end of the war. These collaborators chose to emphasise their racial proximity to the Germans: 'the modern Celtic peoples by race, language, and culture, are of the indogermanic family the closest relations of the Germans'.[6] The frenetic politics of the interwar period and the rise of fascism led to other surprising Celtic racial connections. In General Franco's Spain, the Celtic past was harnessed for the politicised purpose of giving Spain an Aryan pedigree.[7]

In the British Celtic nations—Wales, Scotland, Cornwall, and the Isle of Man—Celticism also became increasingly politicised. While the cultural focus characteristic of the Celtic Revival remained a point of interest to people within and without those nations, Home Rule became a goal for activists in all of them, many of whom joined a new Celtic Congress headed by the Welsh politician Edward Thomas John (1857–1931). Pan-Celtic feelings underlay many of the new nationalist movements, especially as activists looked to independent Ireland for inspiration. Yet Ireland's own peculiar historical and political trajectory meant that Irish nationalists were absorbed above all in their own national struggle, and that—as Caoimhín de Barra has shown in convincing detail—Pan-Celtic interests were always ancillary.[8] Nevertheless, as the century progressed, the Irish example shone brightly for nationalist activists, who fused leftist and anti-colonial politics in a movement for Celtic republicanism, often buttressed by the vision of a federal Pan-Celtic union. This was the view of the Celtic League, which has been the most active and visible branch of the Pan-Celtic movement since its foundation in 1961.

The radical Pan-Celticism of the second half of the twentieth century was increasingly out of step with academic Celtic studies, which became firmly established as an international and interdisciplinary field distinguished by a steep gradient of intellectual and scholarly rigour. Mary-Ann Constantine memorably describes modern Celtic studies as characterised by a 'scrupulousness bordering on mania'.[9] This is pointedly inverse to the earlier vein of Celtomania exaggerating the significance of the ancient Celts, and especially their language, to the extent of turning them into the original world-historical people. During the twentieth century, the tone shifted towards the forensic precision that now characterises the discipline. The opinions and criticisms of scholars were still often voiced in correspondence, but this too was rarer in comparison with earlier eras.

An important change of the twentieth century was that women started to play a larger role in the academic field, whereas—the Charlottes, Brooke and Guest, being the exceptions—they had earlier been largely limited to the cultural revivalist sphere. It was female Celtic scholars who kept Celtic studies alive in some of the field's most important places after the Second World War. Celtic studies was spearheaded at Cambridge for several decades in the mid-twentieth century by two women, Nora Chadwick (1891–1972) and Rachel Bromwich (1915–2010). Annie Heiermeier (1908–1985) founded the only new Celtic studies centre in Germany after the cataclysm of the war, while Hildegarde Tristram (1941–2020) ensured that Celtic retained a toehold at Freiburg (though from the English Department). Finally, Maartje Draak (1907–1995) was appointed to the first lectureship devoted solely to Celtic at Utrecht in 1949, before being promoted to special professor there in 1955 and the University of Amsterdam in 1957. Still, it is only very recently that the place of women in the field has become the subject of serious investigation.[10]

The gulf that now exists between Celtic scholars and Celtic activists dates to the postwar period, although the rift was already present in the early twentieth century. This was especially the case in England, where, for example, upon the Bodleian librarian Edward Nicholson's election as an honorary member of Oxford's Gaelic League, he had to ask what it was.[11] However, the same was not true for Cambridge's first Celtic lecturer, Edmund Crosby Quiggin (1875–1920), who took notes on scrap Gaelic League stationary and went through modern Irish articles underlining unknown words and querying spellings.[12] The firm establishment of Celtic at Oxbridge reflects the fact that, in the twentieth-century Anglophone world, Celtic studies went from strength to strength, with the foundation of university chairs, departments, journals, degrees, students, and everything else that comes with professionalisation. It was also established in some of North America's leading universities.

Celtic studies has been supported by new waves of Celtic revivalists, who have been inspired by the heroic depictions of the Celts in antiquity and in their literature and history from the Middle Ages to the present day. Others have looked to Celtic cultures for spiritual renewal, which underpinned the New Age 'Celtic Christianity' movement of the late twentieth century.[13] Although these two branches—the scholarly discipline and the cultural politics—had grown from the same trunk, they were now almost entirely distinct. Today they are occasionally almost antagonistic. Celtic studies lived by killing off the myths on which political activists and religious revivalists depended, and if they do read the material produced by Celtic scholars at all, revivalists and New Age Celtic mystics often do so with their fingers in their ears.

Yet wherever one sits in relation to these different strands of Celticism, they have certain views in common, the most fundamental of which is the vital importance of the Celtic languages. Whether in the most rigorous works of scholarship or the loudest political protests, there is nearly universal agreement that the languages are the key to the Celts, whether one is studying their past or envisioning their future. Because of these recurring patterns, I have decided not to give this book a traditional conclusion, and in this final chapter I instead trace the wider outlines of a story that is still evolving.

The Professionalisation of Celtic Studies, Kuno Meyer, and the School of Irish Learning

I complained in the preface of this book that there exists no synoptic history of Celtic studies.[14] There is a general acceptance that Zeuß's *Grammatica* laid the groundwork for modern Celtology in 1853, but the professionalisation of the field only came in fits and starts over the next half century. In previous chapters we have examined some of the university lectureships and chairs founded for Celtic—in Ireland, England, Scotland, and France—as well as the context in which the *Revue celtique* provided a focal point for the Celtic scholars dotted around Europe from the early 1870s. Over the next few decades momentum continued to gather in each of the Celtic nations as well as in Europe and the United States, as Celticists found university positions. The major shift that took place in the twentieth century was the rise of Ireland to the heights of the field and the decline of German scholarship, which was largely a result of geopolitics. Although personal rivalries and petty jealousies were common—as in any scholarly field—one noticeable difference from earlier eras is that the problems addressed by scholars (the Celto-Germanism of the Nazi era excepted) were generally less politically and ideologically charged, and there is a sense that international cooperation would be vital in order to survey, collect, publish, and analyse all of the material known to exist. The British and Irish scholarly worlds were coming into closer contact with continental scholarship, and because he more than anyone else bridged these worlds, Kuno Meyer, professor of Teutonic and then Celtic at Liverpool from 1884 until 1911, will appear throughout this section.

In the period that Kenneth Jackson and David Ellis Evans memorably described as 'The Heroic Age of Celtic Philology', most of the heroes were German, and those who were not went to Germany to study or published in German.[15] German preeminence was, as Kuno Meyer grumbled, not because of any popular interest in things Celtic, in sharp contrast with Ireland, but because of the quality of German universities and particularly their superior study of *Sprachwissenschaft* (linguistics).[16] Celtic was useful for, among other things, comparative purposes, and German Celticists—such as Ernst Windisch (1844–1918), professor at Leipzig—were also often great Sanskritists or Indo-Europeanists.[17] The case was the same with Meyer's former student and rival Heinrich Zimmer; however, he was able to focus on Celtic for the last decade of his life after he was appointed in 1901 to the chair of Celtic at the University of Berlin, the first in Germany and briefly the flagship international position.[18] According to his latest editor, the Swiss Rudolf Thurneysen, who taught comparative philology at Freiburg and then Bonn, did not think of himself as a Celtologist at all and in 1916 wrote that as intellectually interesting as the problems were, their 'significance is not strong enough' for the devotion of a whole scholarly life.[19] The statement is all the more ironic considering that he was considered the best Celticist of his age and is the 'greatest Celtic scholar of all time', according to one of the greatest of our time.[20] However, by his iconic paper of 1930, 'Why Do Germans Study Celtic Philology?', Thurneysen accepted that he had in fact accidentally devoted his life to it. That was almost the point of the paper: German university education was liberal, refined, and elevated enough to support students interested in what seemed an obscure subject (Thurneysen had come to it while trying to find the origins of the French language).

Kuno Meyer would likely have disagreed with Thurneysen's assessment because at the age of twenty-four he vowed to make Irish the 'principal object of my life's work'.[21] As seen below, his greatest contribution was to Irish scholarship, and principally its medieval literature, but he was also committed to Welsh, and made a lasting contribution to the international Celtic community by co-founding the *Zeitschrift für celtische Philologie* with Ludwig Christian Stern.[22] The journal first appeared in 1897 and was so successful that, in 1905, Meyer wrote to Edward Nicholson that he and Stern were 'overwhelmed with copy'.[23] One point to note about the Germans of this era is that although they were interested in and occasionally published on the Brittonic languages, their focus was firmly on Old and Middle Irish because it was, in Meyer's paraphrase of August Schleicher, 'the Gothic of the Celtic family of speech—that is, the most primitive and original of all Celtic languages', and as such it was thought to provide the oldest view of society and culture in Western Europe.[24]

As if underlining the point, the best Irish scholar of the nineteenth century, Whitley Stokes, could apparently not speak modern Irish, devoting his attention to its ancient forms. Unquestionably, the development of Celtic studies had the most far-reaching political consequences for Ireland, and the Irish pursued the subject more vigorously than any of the other six 'core' Celtic nations. Irish and German philologists developed a particularly close relationship, led by the arrival of Bopp's student Rudolf Thomas Siegfried, and carried on by his successor Carl Lottner (1834–1873). Through these figures Stokes became closely acquainted with German comparative philology and a devoted follower of Zeuß.[25] He explained the state of continental Celtic studies to John O'Donovan, who was irritated by Stokes's aversion to antiquarian studies and his devotion to 'Grammatical theories'.[26] Siegfried wrote to Pictet that Stokes 'knows the <u>grammar</u> of old Irish best of any man, better than O'Donovan & Curry'.[27] This was the largest difference between Stokes and his predecessors: whereas they specialised in Irish philology and did not have a thorough familiarity with the historical grammar of other languages, Stokes was a zealot of comparative grammar and showed that a thorough knowledge of older Indo-European forms could shed greater light on Irish etymology than working backwards from modern dialects. Following the deaths of figures like Zeuß and Ebel in Germany, and O'Donovan and O'Curry in Ireland, along with the departure of Stokes for Madras, there was a real sense of despondency in Irish Celtic studies. Lottner wrote that the 'overwhelming difficulty' of the subject and the absence of a true scientific approach meant that little progress was likely to be made for some time.[28] However, the stumbling block remained money, and scholars in Ireland pleaded with their continental counterparts to write in support of Irish because they would actually be listened to by the British.

Leaving Ireland aside for a moment, scholarship in the Celtic lands lagged behind that in Germany. Scotland stood out in this respect. In 1890 the Irish scholar Standish Hayes O'Grady (1832–1915) wrote to John Rhys that he wished 'the Scots would take up these studies a little. Any of them I wd gladly help, but a hand's turn I never again will do for a German'.[29] Various commentators, among them Kuno Meyer at the 1901 Pan-Celtic Congress, also complained of Scottish lethargy.[30] Folklore was a popular focus there, where collectors like J. F. Campbell (1821–1885) and the exciseman Alexander Carmichael were connected much more firmly with and sensitive to actual Celtic speakers, but somewhat distant from Celtic scholarship.[31] Acknowledging the relatively slow development of Scottish Celtic scholarship in their prospectus, Ella Carmichael and Donald Mackinnon (1839–1914), the first Celtic professor at Edinburgh, launched the *Celtic Review* in 1904, a successful journal that lasted until 1916.[32] But still in 1938 John Fraser (1882–1945), at the time Jesus Professor of Celtic, complained that Celtic students at Edinburgh and Glasgow were all prospective clergyman who wanted to 'get a shine on their native Gaelic for purposes of sermon-writing and general publicity'.[33] After a bequest left by a clergyman in 1893, Glasgow maintained a part-time lectureship in Celtic—held briefly by Kuno Meyer—before a Celtic chair was founded in 1956.[34] Derick Thomson occupied it during Kenneth Jackson's (1909–1991) tenure at Edinburgh, during which time Celtic studies in Scotland strengthened considerably.

Welsh scholars also had something of a local focus, though they had a historical link to Oxford, but even there energy seemed to stall. In 1902, Meyer wrote to Nicholson that he often wondered 'at the lack of British enterprise in scholarship. Surely Oxford—with a Celtic professor—should be able to finance a Celtic Review or the like. So little money is needed . . . I shd start something of the kind to-morrow, but my hands are full'.[35] Perhaps sensing something similar, the historian J. E. Lloyd (1861–1947) founded the *Bulletin Board of Celtic Studies* in 1921, which has continued under the name *Studia Celtica*. Lloyd and the grammarian John Morris-Jones (1864–1929)—'the Cubist of Celtic grammarians', according to Fraser[36]—both modernised their subjects by incorporating the latest Celtic scholarship for comparative and historical purposes.[37] Morris-Jones accelerated the destruction of Iolo Morganwg's invented traditions, while some reviewers criticised the 'un-Celtic coldness' with which Lloyd treated historical sources.[38]

Celtic studies had come a long way in a relatively short time. To be sure, the petty jealousies, personal rivalries, and narcissism of small differences that characterise scholarship in all eras continued, and there were still nationally minded disputes. There was something of a distance between the Celtic scholarly community in Britain, Ireland, and Germany on the one hand, and the French on the other. The chairs in Celtic philology at the *École pratique des hautes études* and at the *Collège de France*—created in 1876 and 1882 for Gaidoz and d'Arbois de Jubainville, respectively—came into existence at a time of deep French anguish over an acknowledged inferiority to German science.[39] Both men, but especially d'Arbois de Jubainville, used Celtic philology to attack German nationalist pretensions, although rivalry did not always split neatly along national lines. D'Arbois de Jubainville carried on a correspondence with Ernst Windisch for decades, during which they bonded over their mutual antagonism towards Heinrich Zimmer.[40] Zimmer swore revenge on them and Whitley Stokes, but the latter apparently did not hold a high opinion of d'Arbois de Jubainville, who he made fun of with Kuno Meyer. Meyer was forthright in his statement that the French had produced 'no great Celtic scholar'.[41] John Rhys, who had belittled Jubainville's phonology for decades, wrote that he would always trust Grimm and Zeuß over d'Arbois de Jubainville.[42] The normal polemics of scholarship often transcended national rivalries, but these were always lingering in the background. After d'Arbois de Jubainville died, his friend Camille Jullian (1859–1933) made an impassioned speech arguing that the Celtic chair at the *Collège de France* was of international political significance; if it was not maintained, then Theodor Mommsen (1817–1903), 'un homme terrible', and the other German nationalists had won.[43] Nevertheless, after its second holder Joseph Loth (1847–1934) retired in December 1930, the chair was transformed into a position for medieval philosophy on 7 December 1931.[44] Related work was undertaken by the holders of the chair in the archaeology and history of Gaul, first held by Jullian, which is perhaps a reflection of the shift towards archaeology in French Celtic studies that has occurred over the last century.

National jealousy played a part in the foundation of the School of Irish Learning, the most important centre for Celtic studies outside of Germany. 'While we think it shows good sense in the Germans to study Gaelic', wrote a member of the Oxford Gaelic League to Edward Nicholson, 'we object very strongly to the idea now so prevalent here that the Germans are the necessary arbiters in all points connected with Gaelic'.[45] Complaints and exhortations like this one had been common for decades. Reviewing a new German work in 1881, Alfred Nutt had written that surely 'Irish scholars will be roused to the scandal and shame of allowing Germans to annex the whole of their rich and precious literature'.[46] Similar sentiments were widespread in the Irish press, but action did not follow complaint, and ultimately and ironically it took a German to bring things together.

On 14 May 1903, Meyer delivered an epoch-making lecture during *Oireachtas* week on the 'Necessity for Establishing a School of Irish Literature, Philology, and History'.[47] The title was an homage to his friend Douglas Hyde's famous speech, and Meyer began by praising the commitment to and strength of the Irish linguistic revival, but stressed 'the necessity of bringing the movement into direct and intimate relations with scholarship', in order to produce a battalion of native scholars, and thereby 'bring about a second golden age of Irish learning'.[48] In short, the aim was to make Ireland the global centre for Celtic scholarship. Irish students, hopefully native speakers, were to be trained up in the best practices of philological scholarship so that they could be set loose upon the abundant Irish manuscript remains. For while Meyer had been trained at the best university for linguistics in Europe, Leipzig University, he was firmly focused on literature—broadly understood—and emphasised that a linguistic revival needed a literary revival on which to feed. The school would produce a journal and encourage its students to publish their findings, otherwise 'the work of publication will go wholly to Germany'.[49]

Meyer and his associates were particularly successful in attracting donations from wealthy supporters of the cultural movement, including the Celtic Association's president, Lord Castletown. The historian Alice Stopford Green (1847–1929) was both zealous—fundraising in America for the school—and generous, funding a scholarship for Osborn Bergin (1873–1950) to study with Zimmer in Berlin and Thurneysen in Freiburg.[50] The actual teaching and learning that took place under the aegis of the school occurred during summers and spring breaks, when Meyer and John Strachan (1862–1907), a comparative philologist at Manchester, would come to Dublin and teach a few dozen students. Other eminent teachers included Rhys, Thurneysen, and Zimmer, and the products of the school included Bergin, Richard Best (1872–1959), and T. F. O'Rahilly (1882–1953). Reports of its activities were published every few years in the in-house journal *Ériu*. In 1908 Welsh was added to the teaching provision, reflecting the fact that the aim of the school was really to be 'the head centre of *Celtic* studies in Ireland'.[51]

Meyer and his allies continued the fight for Irish and Celtic studies more generally, and achieved a victory after the National University was founded in 1908. Two of the leading lights of the Gaelic movement—Douglas Hyde and Eoin MacNeill—were appointed to professorships, in modern Irish and early Irish history, respectively. Through Meyer's brokerage, University College Dublin acquired Heinrich Zimmer's library and University College Cork bought d'Arbois de Jubainville's, securing first-rate collections of reference materials for Celtic in Ireland.[52] In 1910, however, Meyer was recruited by the University of Berlin to fill Zimmer's vacant chair, and the outbreak of war a few years later stifled the School of Irish Learning somewhat.

The Great War redrew lines of affinity and rivalry in Celtic studies. Meyer was ostracised for his obnoxious German nationalism, and it has been a recent point of contention among scholars whether he was a spy.[53] The breaking point came during his American tour that began in late 1914, for which he was chosen by the German government in order to promote the cause among Americans. A speech he gave at a *Clan na Gael* meeting in early December generated controversy and led, as he wrote to his friend Roger Casement (1864–1916), to Harvard withdrawing an invitation to lecture.[54] Meyer's 'cancellation' by Harvard made the front page of the *New York Times*, but the speech that led to it reverberated across the Atlantic and led to an irreparable fallout with many friends and institutions.[55] He was induced shortly afterwards to step down from directing the School of Irish Learning and editing *Ériu*, but was able to reconcile with some of his friends after the war and before his death in 1919.[56]

The war had a debilitating effect on Celtic scholarship more generally. It killed Celticists,[57] among others Joseph Déchelette, author of the standard French archaeological study of the Celts (see chapter 7), who was 'killed by the enemy at the head of the company' he commanded after volunteering well past the age of service.[58] *Ériu*'s 1923 report on the proceedings of the School of Irish Learning noted that the seven-year gap in its publication was not a favourable period for the 'calm pursuit of learning', and the loss of momentum was probably fatal to the school, which was incorporated into the Royal Irish Academy in 1926, although the appointment of its finest academic products to various research and teaching positions in the most elite Irish institutions was also clear evidence of its success.[59] To some extent the war divided German scholars, most of all Meyer, from the international community, and the prewar energy for Celtic scholarship ebbed and only gradually returned.[60] More ominously, Meyer's propaganda efforts and fall from grace foreshadowed the coming entanglements of German scholars with nationalist politics that would seriously damage German Celtology. Ireland's tricky political position encouraged Celticists in the fledgling Free State to start looking beyond Germany towards other sympathetic international audiences.

Eoin MacNeill, the Harvard Survey, and the School of Celtic Studies

The Easter Rising and the subsequent conflict in Ireland seems to have had surprisingly little effect upon Celtic studies. Political commentary rarely features in the correspondence of Irish Celticists of the period—though they must have frequently discussed things in person—and is more evident in the letters of foreign correspondents asking about the Irish situation. Views on the Rising broke down along national lines. As Lerchenmüller notes, German Celticists were stronger Irish nationalists than their Irish counterparts, welcoming the Irish independence struggle for self-interested geopolitical reasons as well as from an ideological commitment.[61] Even the Swiss Thurneysen had written in vivid terms that it was up to Germany to ignite the Celtic dynamite around Britain in the form of Irish nationalist rebellion.[62] French scholars like Henri Gaidoz looked on confused. Gaidoz wrote to Best despondently that 'we can hardly talk of Pan-Celtism when the Sinn Feiners refuse to follow a government directed by a true Celt, Lloyd George'.[63] Yet, as a famous anecdote records, Lloyd George weaponised his Celticity against the Irish delegation in 1921, when he asked Éamon de Valera (1882–1975) with pointed nonchalance what the Irish word for 'republic' was, noting that Welsh had none.[64] But there appears to have been some Pan-Celtic feeling among Irish revolutionaries. Sean Prendergrast, for example, who was imprisoned in Frongoch after taking part in the Rising, recalled the thrill of travelling through 'a Celtic country inhabited by a Celtic people who had withstood the ravages of time to preserve their own national characteristics, traditions, and culture'.[65]

The swelling of national feeling in Ireland and the creation of the Free State generated momentum for Celtic studies, in which many nationalists felt Ireland should take the lead. The historian and statesman Eoin MacNeill is a figure of central importance in this context for two reasons: the first is his work as a historian and the critical (though not hostile) approach he took to the history and idea of Celticity, and the second is the cultural diplomacy that he exercised over the course of the 1920s and 30s. MacNeill is famous for many things, but our interest here is in his ideas on Celtic history. From County Antrim, MacNeill studied law and history in Dublin in the late 1880s, where he also took up Irish; however, in contrast with most of his nationalist peers, MacNeill was initially drawn to the older forms of the language, which required careful philological attention, although he soon learned to speak modern Irish over many trips to the Aran Islands.[66] He helped to found the Gaelic League in 1893 and worked hard for it over the next few years, editing the *Gaelic Journal*, then *Fáinne an Lae* and *An Claidheamh Soluis*. In 1909 he was appointed to the chair in early Irish history at University College Dublin.

Remarkably, considering what else was going on, MacNeill produced some of his most important works over the next dozen years, the two most notable being *Phases of Irish History* (1919) and *Celtic Ireland* (1921), both reworked lecture series. It is generally acknowledged that MacNeill inaugurated a new, more rigorous early medieval Irish historiography based on his facility with all historical forms of the Irish language, and here our focus must be on the critical approach he took to Celticism and Celticity.[67] Importantly, MacNeill pointed out that 'Celtic' was something of a modern academic reinvention. 'There is no small amount of pride in the notion of being Celtic', he pointed out in *Phases of Irish History*; however, 'It is somewhat remarkable, then, to find that throughout all their early history and tradition the Irish and the Britons alike show not the slightest atom of recognition that they were Celtic peoples'.[68] What was the relevant criterion for being Celtic? 'The answer is undoubted—every ancient people that is known to have spoken any Celtic language is said to be a Celtic people. The term Celtic is indicative of language, not of race'.[69] Crucially, MacNeill knew how that understanding had developed. He had pointed this out already in an article of 1913 suggestively called 'The Re-Discovery of the Celts', which he opened with the assertion that 'The honours of the pioneer in Celtic philology belong to a man of Gaelic race, George Buchanan, the Scottish historian'.[70] MacNeill then drew a line from Buchanan to Lhwyd and many of the figures examined in this book, sketching the academic origins of what he called 'the wholly modern development of the Celtic consciousness'.[71] Variations on this sketch have appeared in all of the standard overviews about the Celts ever since. With MacNeill therefore begins the study of the history of Celticism.

MacNeill's awareness that 'Celtic' was a somewhat artificial and retrospective linguistic label did not mean he failed to see its utility or stopped using it. In fact, his important later book *Early Irish Laws and Institutions* (1935) defended 'Celtic Ireland' from 'Celtophobes' who depicted pre-Norman Ireland and other early Celtic societies from reductive theories drawn from evolutionary sociology that put them in a uniformly barbarous Celtic 'tribal' system of warrior nomads not yet advanced to settled agriculturalism. But though he defended Celtic cultures from the charge that the Roman Empire had done them a favour by conquering and civilizing them, MacNeill continued to be critical of a reductive one-society-fits-all approach that ignored differences between the Celtic societies of ancient and medieval Europe. Medieval Ireland had a wealth of primary sources, most spectacularly the Brehon laws, upon which historians could draw. They showed that Irish society had always been regulated by laws, beginning with the Druids, who MacNeill argued were not Celtic, but were the jurists of an indigenous population that inhabited Europe before the arrival of the Celts and other Aryans. Here again MacNeill cast critical light on the Irish as a monolithic Celtic culture, pointing out that beyond language the idea was extremely unclear: 'nearly every generalisation that has passed current about things Celtic or things supposed to be Celtic—the Celtic race, the Celtic temperament, Celtic art, the Celtic Church, Celtic society—stands equally in need of revision and rectification'.[72] The field of Irish history therefore also needed to be defended from 'Celtophiles', because 'the social complex which is commonly spoken of as "Celtic" with reference to Ireland, Britain, and the western parts of the Continent was far from being purely Celtic, and derived much of its character from West-European antecedents'.[73]

MacNeill had given what became *Early Irish Laws* as a set of lectures at New York University in 1930, part of several American trips that he made in the 1920s and 30s to support Irish studies abroad. His cultural diplomacy came during a general interest in Celtic subjects in American culture and universities that had begun at the turn of the century. It is beyond the scope of this book, but the literary revival in Ireland and the other Celtic nations made waves in North America, which attracted attention to Celtic. Its most famous advocate was president Theodore Roosevelt (1858–1919), who (while a sitting president!) in 1907 published a sumptuously illustrated article on 'The Ancient Irish Sagas', regretting how little Americans had contributed to the study and research of ancient Celtic literature (Fig. 17).[74] Letters agreeing with him arrived from Europe and America, including from a Harvard academic named Frederick Norris Robinson (1871–1966), to whom Roosevelt in reply admitted it was unlikely that many students would learn the Celtic languages, but felt 'that Celtic literature should be competently represented at our great universities'.[75] Robinson ensured that was the case at his own university. After studying for a year with Thurneysen in Freiburg, he had returned to his teaching post at Harvard in 1896 and began to give courses in the Celtic languages.[76] Robinson was a Chaucer specialist and based in the English Department, but devoted what time he could to teaching Celtic subjects and ran a Celtic seminar out of his house. Upon his retirement he endowed a Chair at Harvard, which Kenneth Jackson took up in 1940. Elsewhere in the United States, the Ancient Order of Hibernians succeeded in establishing a Celtic position at the Catholic University of America in Washington, D.C., and other posts popped up in wealthier universities across the United States. The University of Wisconsin recruited Myles Dillon (1900–1972) to teach early Irish history and literature in 1937, and he made up a midwestern node of Celtic Studies with professors at Northwestern and Chicago.[77] Similar positions came and went around the U.S. and Canada, but only Harvard has a fully-fledged Department of Celtic

FIG. 17. 'Queen Meave', in Theodore Roosevelt, 'The Ancient Irish Sagas', *The Century* 73 (1907), 331.

Languages and Literature, though Berkeley has the longest running degree-granting program in Celtic Studies in the country, dating from 1911–12, and Wisconsin still has its Center for Celtic Studies.[78]

Outside of Celtic studies proper, the largest Celtic-related American project was the Harvard 'Irish Survey' carried out in the 1930s.[79] It was facilitated by the Austrian archaeologist Adolf Mahr (1887–1951), who was appointed keeper of Irish Antiquities at the National Museum of Ireland in September 1927 and promoted to director in 1934. He had joined the Nazi Party the year before and became the leader of the Nazis based in Dublin. Mahr had pushed for large-scale Celtic archaeological studies since his arrival:

> The whole work of the Irish Antiquities Section of the Museum is in urgent need of legislation or regulations for a monumental survey of the country. The outstanding feature of Ireland's cultural development and of her position in the civilised world may be stated thus: She is not the cradle of the Celtic stock, but she was its foremost stronghold at the time of the decline of the Celts elsewhere; she is the most wonderful artistic province of the Celtic spirit, its centre of missionary enterprise, its last refuge; preeminently *the* Celtic country. Ireland is now the only self-governing State with an uninterrupted Celtic tradition, and has the duty of becoming *the* country for Celtic studies.[80]

Mahr was instrumental in securing permission and aid for the project.[81]

The survey was a joint project between Harvard's Division of Archaeology and the Peabody Museum of Ethnology and Anthropology, under the direction of the physical anthropologist Earnest A. Hooton (1887–1954). It had three strands: social anthropology, physical anthropology, and archaeology. Apart from Hallam Movius (1907–1987), who had written his Cambridge PhD dissertation on Stone Age archaeology in Devon and Cornwall, the Harvard team did not have any special interest in Celts or even Ireland as such. Instead, the project departed from the desire to examine 'a small country from a total anthropological perspective', as 'No modern state, nor any large population group, has ever been subjected to intensive cooperative study by social and biological scientists'.[82] In addition to being a manageable size, the Irish Free State was an ideal case also because, 'though politically new', it was 'culturally old', and because of its position in the extreme northwest of Europe it had 'preserved much of the older culture . . . lost by the continental countries and England due to their vulnerability to outside invasion'. For example—overlooking Wales and therefore signalling the leaders'

Celtic ignorance—it was only in Ireland 'and in Brittany that one still finds a large population using the Celtic tongue, an archaic Aryan language once spoken over a large part of Europe'. Finally, Ireland was the 'country of origin of more than one-fifth of the population of the United States', which would hopefully encourage Bostonians and Americans more generally to reach for their wallets. The project was pitched effectively, and the team was able to raise funds from the Rockefeller Foundation, the Council of Learned Societies, Harvard's Milton Fund, as well as from the governments of the Free State and Northern Ireland.

After a preliminary survey in 1931, members of the Harvard team returned every summer for the next five years. Some initial resistance came from Eoin MacNeill and R.A.S. Macalister (1870–1950; archaeologist and president of the Royal Irish Academy), who were worried that Harvard would strip Ireland of its antiquities. Even after repeated assurances, Macalister remained obstinate, while Mahr worked hard for the Harvard team. After it turned up some impressive material—principally a Viking gaming-board from the ninth or tenth century—one team member wrote to Hooton in late 1932 that 'I saw several rabid de Valera people in Dublin and they are wildly enthusiastic over the prospect of having Harvard dig up Ireland's "glorious past"'.[83] In the following year, a number of American academics, including those not linked to the Anthropology Department—like Fred Norris Robinson, who returned to Ireland for the first time in three decades—or even to Harvard, travelled to Ireland and inspected the progress of the project. One literary scholar from Texas suggested the foundation of an American School in Ireland, linked to the National Museum.[84] The *Irish Times* liked the idea and posed it to other American academics, who kicked the can down the road without ever quashing the rumours.[85] The 'American School of Celtic Studies' would cost the Irish taxpayer nothing because it would be funded by a £10,000 American grant. The idea was never real and vanished quickly, although it may have stimulated Éamon de Valera's interest in a national school for Celtic studies financed by Ireland's own government (see below).[86]

Despite generating considerable interest, the survey's overarching aims were a little unclear. Ireland was 'put into a giant test tube' to discover 'What makes an Irishman?', according to the various press reports in the United States.[87] The *Boston Globe* spelled out that this actually meant 'establishing definitely the racial identity of hitherto almost mythical early inhabitants of Erin', by investigating the 'Remains of an early Pre-Celtic people' from as early as 2000 BCE through the Christian era.[88] For those interested in Celtic questions, however, the Harvard Survey was a disappointment.[89] It was generally assumed that invading Celts had inaugurated the Iron Age—associated with the Hallstatt and La Tène sites in continental Europe—in Ireland at some point in the first millennium BCE, but, according to a report from the second Harvard expedition,

> little Iron Age pottery and indeed scarcely any Iron Age sites have been found before in the country, but inasmuch as the Celts are clearly identified with the Iron Age elsewhere, this has been difficult to reconcile with the known character of the Irish population from the dawn of history.[90]

The team went out of the way to be as apolitical as possible, and the reports of excavations show that the archaeological team was already well on the way to making the economic and social turn away from the ethno-cultural style of archaeology interested in the Celts and the chronology of their invasions or migrations.

While the principal institutional beneficiary of the Harvard Survey was the National Museum, the Royal Irish Academy's Irish Studies Committee was, at de Valera's invitation, devising a plan to place Irish studies on a sounder footing.[91] Its reports of the late 1930s noted that the foundation of Celtic studies faculties within the National University was supposed to lead to significant progress in Irish studies, but after '25 years the burden and reputation of Irish scholarship' was still in the hands of the 'recognised leaders in 1909'.[92] According to the legal scholar D. A. Binchy (1899–1989), there was 'nearly everything' left to be done, and the committee accordingly proposed 'that the Government should revive the School of Irish Learning, but on a much vaster scale'. The new body should be a 'national Institute like the College de France', aimed at 'research and publication' and financed by an annual grant rather than temporary endowments.[93] The government was amenable to the idea, and the Department of Education bounced ideas back and forth over the next few years until de Valera, acting as his own Minister of Education, made a crucial intervention. In the Advanced Studies Bill first introduced to the *Dáil* on 6 July 1939, the School of Irish Studies had been changed to a 'school of Celtic Studies'.[94] A later letter explained: 'The intention is that this school, while primarily concerning itself with the study of the Irish language and its literature, philology, lexicography, grammar, etc. should not be debarred from a similar study of other Celtic languages, literatures, etc.' De Valera did not want 'the grammar and lexicography of the other Celtic languages' to be precluded.[95] He had been promoting the idea at least since the Celtic Congress of 1934, and apparently saw the Irish Studies Committee's suggestion as the opportunity to establish it.[96] He signed the Institute for Advanced Studies Act into law on 19 June 1940, establishing the School of Celtic Studies alongside the School of Theoretical Physics—famously directed by Erwin Schrödinger (1887–1961) after his career was stifled by the Nazis—under the Dublin Institute for Advanced Studies. De Valera's was probably the most high-profile political support that Celtic studies has ever received. Wrote E. J. Gwynn (1868–1941) to Richard Best, one of the school's first senior professors, 'I always said there was some good in de Valera'.[97]

Celts and Celtic Studies in the Third Reich

Ironically, considering their ideology depended on the idea that Germans were the 'Master Race', the Nazis opened up new space for Celticism in Germany. For Pan-German nationalists in the first decades of the century it had been important to delineate ancient Celts from Germans and point to the eternal strength and independence of the German *Volk*, in order to counter assertions of the kind made by d'Arbois de Jubainville and MacNeill that, before the third century, the Germans 'were much under Celtic domination that they were not recognised as a distinct people of importance'.[98] However, the Nazi investment in the primordial superiority of the European race created space for the Celts as a great European nation within the 'Nordic' culture of Northern Europe. By far the strangest example of this was offered by Adolf Hitler (1889–1945) himself on 30 November 1944.[99] Refusing to believe that Jesus had been a Semite, he ginned up an etymological connection between Galilee and Gallia, suggesting that Galileans were a colony of Gaulish legionaries. Incredibly, it seems Hitler's Jesus was Celtic. Yet, as this section illustrates, as with German *Wissenschaft* more generally, the Nazis—including several prominent Celticists—and the Second World War destroyed German preeminence in the field.

Although the work of Zeuß had proven once and for all that the ancient Celts and Germans were distinct peoples, the extent of their interaction and influence over one another remained open questions, especially in places like Austria, Switzerland, and Southern Germany. The famous German archaeologist Gustaf Kossinna (1858–1931), for example, worked on the problem for many years, and found Celtic influence on German material culture, even though he is generally recognised as having emphasised German racial coherence for nationalist purposes.[100] Kossinna's counterpart, the professor of German antiquity at Vienna, Rudolf Much (1862–1936), examined the question repeatedly, always angling against d'Arbois de Jubainville's idea that the Celts had ruled over the Germans. In the suggestively titled illustrated monthly *Volk und Rasse,* he concluded forcefully that 'A prehistorical Celtic domination [*Keltenherrschaft*] over German tribes there was not'.[101] Much's student Julius Pokorny continued his teacher's works and argued against the heresy that 'German' itself had a Celtic etymology.[102] He did so *ex cathedra,* having taken over the Berlin Celtic professorship in 1920.

Pokorny's identity was complicated.[103] Born in Prague to Jewish-descended Germans who had assimilated as Catholics then moved to Austria, he attended the University of Vienna from 1905 to 1910, where he studied law but was most attracted to Celtic. Trips to Wales and Ireland, where in 1910 he studied at the School of Irish Learning summer session and participated in the Gaelic Revival, solidified his interest, and turned him into an ardent Irish nationalist. Pokorny managed to convince the University of Vienna of the importance of Celtic subjects—one of the most important supposedly Celtic settlements had been discovered in Austria at Hallstatt, after all—and began teaching there in 1912 before switching to Berlin. Pokorny is sometimes regarded as the last member of the heroic period of Celtology, although many of his peers did not see him that way. Upon his appointment to the Berlin position, more than one Celticist expressed disapproval. The Dutch Celticist Anton van Hamel (1886–1945) asked Richard Best rhetorically if the appointment of 'P. O'Korny' to the Celtic chair signalled a 'désastre to Celtic Studies?'[104] Josef Baudis (1883–1933), a Czech nationalist, wrote that he hoped Pokorny would take over the *Zeitschrift* and run it into the ground, and thus 'destroy the german reputation altogether'.[105] Pokorny became known for his theories that Druidism was not originally a Celtic religion and had probably originated with a pre-Celtic population that might have been 'eskimos',[106] but his scholarly achievements lay eventually rather in Indo-European etymology.

Pokorny's eventual sacking and persecution by the Nazis have made him a more sympathetic figure, but he was apart from that a pretty unsympathetic figure.[107] Like Meyer, he was both a German nationalist and an Irish nationalist and saw no contradiction in that, and he worked consistently from about 1910 into the 1930s on behalf of the Irish national cause. His biographer has shown that Pokorny had a voluntaristic conception of the nation but believed in the biological reality of race and in racial hierarchy. Pokorny was, however, to be a victim of this racialised view of the world, and as a result of the Nuremberg Race Laws of 1933 he was suspended by his university. After protests and repeated requests to Irish academics and the government to intercede—which it did eventually, but half-heartedly—Pokorny was briefly reinstated, only to be forcibly retired at the end of 1935.[108] He continued to lobby for Irish support, but an internal memo suggests he had no chance:

> It is quite clear that Pokorny has no friends here and we have no benevolent society for the relief of foreign professors of Celtic Languages. The general feeling seems to be that as foreigners take up Celtic languages as a study subject, and a means of livelihood, there is no reason why they should be supported by us as if they were Irishmen.[109]

Stripped of the normal window dressing that accompanied interactions between German Celticists and the Irish State, the memo shows with brutal clarity that Celtic work undertaken by non-Irish people was only worth supporting up to a point. Ultimately, Pokorny escaped to Switzerland in 1943, and later tried to convince de Valera to help found a Celtic studies centre there, since it was the 'original racial home of the Celts . . . ethnologically almost 70% of her population is of pure Celtic origin'.[110] It is tempting to conclude that he learned nothing.

When Pokorny was first suspended, a card-carrying Nazi and SA member named Ludwig Mühlhausen (1888–1956) began sniffing around his chair, and after a sustained campaign was finally appointed in 1936.[111] Having gained his doctorate at Leipzig in 1914, Mühlhausen's academic hopes were halted by the war, and he only gained a precarious post lecturing on Celtic at the University of Hamburg in 1922. Initially more interested in Middle Welsh, Mühlhausen learned Modern Irish over the course of several trips there in the 1920s and 30s, and he became interested in folklore—an interesting and distinct break from the usual German focus on historical forms of the languages. In a letter of 1941 Mühlhausen ridiculed the 'earth-shattering questions' addressed by Celtic philologists, such as 'if, when, how etc. a long *o* came to be transformed into a long *u*'.[112] Folkloristics also gave him the excuse to travel all over the country, and from August to October 1937 Mühlhausen collected folklore in Donegal while spying for Germany, photographing beaches and measuring the depths of harbours.[113] The episode has attracted attention recently, but it was only one of many instances in which Mühlhausen used his Celtic interests for political purposes.[114]

Another such venture was the *Deutsche Gesellschaft für Keltische Studien* (DGKS), which he co-founded in December 1936. Adolf Mahr was a member, as were other younger Nazis such as the secretary Gerhard von Tevenar (1912–

1943), who had spent time in Brittany and other areas with minority nationalist movements.[115] Tevenar was part of the mystic far-right circle around Friedrich Hielscher (1902–1990), and together during these years the pair liaised between militant Breton nationalists and the Nazi regime.[116] The purpose of the DGKS was to get beyond linguistics by mobilising folklorists, historians, geographers, and prehistorians 'to help restore German science's outstanding place in Celtic Research'.[117] Germans could be proud that they had pioneered the field of *Keltenforschung*, but that also created a patriotic responsibility to continue it, wrote a young member of the society as he surveyed the field's history.[118] However, the DGKS was also obviously a political and intelligence-gathering organisation for Nazi outreach to the Celtic nations. As if symbolising these twin purposes, the director of the Irish Folklore Commission, Séamus ó Duilearga (1889–1980), was invited to deliver a lecture at the society's first official meeting on 22 January 1937, where one member of the audience, Wolfram Sievers (1905–1948), was particularly impressed.[119]

Sievers was managing director of the SS's *Ahnenerbe* division, a scientific research centre set up by Heinrich Himmler (1900–1945) in 1935 to undertake historical studies in support of Nazi ideology.[120] Among other things, this division sought to harness Celtic studies as a bridge to winning hearts and minds in Western Europe and proposed to refit the University of Strasbourg for the purpose.[121] Mühlhausen was named a member of the *Ahnenerbe* in July 1942 as head of the section 19 'Teaching and Research Centre of the Celtic Volksforschung', and expressed the purpose of his work in this respect as the spiritual reawakening of the living Celtic peoples.[122] He saw the Celts as one of the great culture-bearers of Northern Europe, who with the Germans exercised a great influence on the course of European history. This was clearly making room for the Celtic race in the Nazi historical worldview: one of the aims of the research would concentrate on 'the Celtic substratum in South and Central Germany as racially and culturally enhancing', a striking break with earlier German nationalist aspirations to refute charges of Celtic influence.[123]

What to make of all this? Though always tempered by a ruthless eye for practical potential, there was a genuine interest in the Celtic nations, their histories, and their cultural and political aspirations.[124] Aside from the obvious and constant current of German supremacy, the ideology that underlay this interest was the one consistent with the Nazi belief that the 'high culture' nations were entitled to geographical space and political autonomy.[125] These views can be seen in the work of Celtic scholars at the time, such as that of Leo Weisgerber (1899–1985), a linguist of high reputation who somehow managed to avoid negative consequences from his work with the *Ahnenerbe* during the war.[126] Essentially, Weisgerber believed—like many across Europe at the time—that nations were organic racial communities whose culture, especially language, had developed over time in a particular place. These things were therefore indelibly linked. To nationalists who believed in this principle, the Celtic nations were victims of English imperialism. Weisgerber highlighted this in a public lecture in 1941. The 'kernel of British history', according to him, was 'England's confrontation with the Celtic lands [*Keltentum*]'.[127] The Celtic nations were divided in space but united in origins and the crucial political factor, English incursion, which made them natural allies of anyone fighting against the 'Western powers', in this case, Germany.[128] It was German scholarship, Weisgerber pointed out, that had helped Ireland to rediscover its historical significance and cultural dignity. Alluding to Thurneysen's 1915 speech about igniting the fuse of the Celtic dynamite of Irish rebellion, he stressed that it was now Germany's duty to light the fuse in the other Celtic nations, so that they could enjoy the right to national autonomy and take their place in the Europe to come.[129]

History and ideology aside, one of the main benefits to studying the living Celtic languages was in their usefulness for propaganda, notably in radio broadcasting. Mühlhausen delivered the first Irish-language broadcast in December 1939, urging Ireland to stay neutral and assuring his audience that an English defeat meant 'the Celtic race will come into its own again'.[130] However, the main focus of Nazi Celtologists during the War was Brittany.[131] The key Nazi figure was Werner Best (1903–1989), a member of the DGKS and the leader of the security forces in occupied France from 1940 to 1942.[132] Best saw Celtic studies as a way to 'bind the Celtic nations of western Europe to the new European order', and in 1941 he supported the formation of a Celtic Institute in Rennes.[133] Best recruited Weisgerber for propaganda purposes, mainly to oversee radio broadcasts to Brittany, which he did with the Breton nationalist Roparz Hemon (1900–1978), editor of the nationalist paper *Gwalarn* and director of the new Celtic Institute.[134] The DGKS, and principally von Tevenar, had already forged links with Breton nationalists in the late 1930s, a few of which were shepherded to Berlin and provided information to the *Ahnenerbe*.[135] One of these was Olier Mordrel (1901–1985), editor of the Breton nationalist journal *Breiz Atao* (Brittany Forever) and a convinced Pan-Celt, who already held far-right political views and was antisemitic.[136] An *Ahnenerbe* file says he had promoted 'ideas in favour of racial and Nordic studies in favour of national socialism since 1935' and 'theories . . . of Celto-Germanic fraternity in an enlarged conception of Nordism'.[137]

However, many Breton nationalists simply looked toward Germany as the best source of support for their independence struggle. One draft document contained in the papers of Louis Feutren (?-2009) was almost apologetic in its justification that collaborating with the Germans represented the best chance for securing a world in which 'we the Celts will have our place'. But some leaders of the movement were racial believers.[138] Celestin Lainé (1908–1983), the leader of a Breton paramilitary force, wrote in his autobiography that he believed in a 'German culture related to Celtic culture' and had an appreciation of 'Nordism'.[139] In the midst of leading the violent arm of the Breton movement in the 1930s, Lainé abandoned Christianity and developed a pagan 'Celtic faith' that he would preserve for the rest of his life.[140] Lainé's group renamed itself the *Bezen Perrot* and notoriously became an official part of the SD (the security police of the SS) in 1944. Mühlahusen, who had been posted to Brittany by Sievers, apparently played some role in this.[141] After operating for less than a year, the group fled with the retreating Germans in August 1944 and gradually disintegrated, but many members remained around the Black Forest from the end of 1944 into the middle of 1945. At what must have been one of their final meetings, Lainé addressed his men, stating that they were part of a common struggle against 'l'internationalisme capitalo-marxiste' and that

> Gerhart [von Tevenar] taught us that our fight was not unique . . . our struggle against France, Latinity, the Mediterranean, the East, Judaism, was also the struggle of other peoples who, to the north of the Loire and the Alps, were creating an Empire under German direction, an Empire whose goal would be to protect the expansion of different nationalities of Nordic culture, an Empire in which Brittany and the other Celtic nations could claim their place.[142]

While some were caught and executed by the French government, most made it into exile, helped by those such as Hielscher, who managed to whitewash his reputation by his involvement in the 20 July plot to kill Hitler.[143]

The Nazi period destroyed German preeminence in Celtic studies. Already in 1935, Adolf Mahr had warned that Germany's primacy in Celtic philology was crumbling. 'German Celtology was world-leading for decades', and although Germans still outshone the French ('themselves of Celtic descent'), the British, and the Americans in the subject, that 'great legacy' was nevertheless dying.[144] That in 1936 Mühlhausen and the members of the DGKS thought Germany needed to 'recapture' its preeminence in Celtic research obviously suggests decline.[145] They failed, and in the words of the pioneering student of the subject, 'Under the direction of the DGKS and the Ahnenerbe Celtology became purely Applied Science'.[146] Mühlhausen lost his chair and never seriously returned to scholarship after the war, but Weisgerber retained his post at Bonn, which, along with Marburg, and eventually Freiburg, became Celtic holdouts.[147] In 1947 Max Förster failed to convince the University of Munich to found a Celtic chair, but in 1949 he assisted Annie Heiermeier in her attempts to make Würzburg '<u>the</u> University of Celtic, esp. Irish, Studies in Germany'.[148] She was met with fierce resistance by Pokorny, who tried to 'destroy [her] womanly dignity' with rumours.[149] 'How he hates her & despises her scholarship!!', wrote Richard Best to Eleanor Knott (1886–1975). Nevertheless, Heiermeier weathered the storm and set up the centre, although it cannot be said to have succeeded on the terms she set out and was eventually folded into comparative linguistics. However, the ultimate symbol of German Celtology's fall is that the flagship Celtic chair at Berlin that was founded at the beginning of the twentieth century did not survive it.[150]

Pan-Celticism in the Twentieth Century: Home Rule and Republicanism, the Celtic Congress and the Celtic League

Pan-Celticism was reborn in the second decade of the twentieth century. Founded by the Welsh liberal E. T. John and managed with the Irish nationalist and Celtic scholar Agnes O'Farrelly (1874–1951), the Celtic Congress—otherwise known as the 'International Union of Celtic Societies'—pursued many of the same cultural goals as had the Celtic Association.[151] Yet, as Caoimhín de Barra has written, this second iteration of Pan-Celticism differed in two important respects: it was shorn of the more theatrical aspects of Fournier's Celtic Association and it was more political.[152] John and many of his supporters advocated Celtic Home Rule, but Pan-Celticism subsequently became harnessed to more radical political visions, including republicanism, socialism, and communism.

After a successful career in the iron industry, E. T. John entered politics and was elected MP for East Denbighshire between 1910 and 1918. Pointing often to the Irish example, while resenting how Irish issues dominated Westminster's attention, John revived the cause of Welsh Home Rule, which he supported for all of the Celtic nations. Already the president of the Union of Welsh Societies, John aimed at an even larger union of all Celtic societies, inviting representatives to discuss the formation of a permanent organization to achieve 'more effective co-operation in the future among the Celtic peoples' at the Birkenhead *Eisteddfod* of 1917.[153]

The congress was an 'International Union of Celtic Societies, consisting of representatives of affiliated Societies, with provision for the inclusion of individual Celts and Celtic sympathisers'.[154] It was thus an umbrella organisation rather than one Celtic society among many. This allowed it to be conceived on a global scale, with spots on the General Council and Executive Committee for members from North and South America, South Africa, and the Antipodes, or what John called 'Celtia Overseas'.[155]

A great deal of energy went into planning the first official congress, slated to take place in Edinburgh in 1919, only for it to be postponed by the Great Rail Strike.[156] When the congress was finally held in May 1920, John delivered a boilerplate inaugural address, running from ancient Celtic military prowess, to the spiritual and Christian sensitivity of medieval Ireland, to the talents for literature, art, and music in the living members of the Celtic race, borrowed from Renan and Arnold.[157] However, John then grafted a new future onto this familiar past. Every Celtic nation that wanted it should have 'complete national government' (i.e., Home Rule), and there would be 'the complete elimination of the element of physical force for the solution of all problems of national and international government'.[158] This second utopian goal can be explained by John's commitment to the pacifist movement, but by renouncing physical force he was also signalling to those listening that the Welsh and other members of the Celtic Congress would not go the way of Ireland.

John's more open political stance created the extremely foreseeable problem that nationalists and unionists would be annoyed by each other.[159] Advanced nationalists felt that the congress was not political enough. The left-wing Scottish Gaelic nationalist Rhuaraidh Erskine (1869–1960) wrote to John that if the organisation were to live it would have to 'recognise Celtic politics, or you will be obliged to make the Congress a fully cultural body. The middle course you suggest, is, I fear, impracticable'.[160] Scottish unionists had kicked a hornet's nest by inviting the government's chief secretary for Ireland—currently at war with the IRA—to preside over the Celtic Concert at the Edinburgh Congress. The Scots led by Erskine—who wanted independence and not Home Rule—left the group before the initial congress even took place, and started planning a rival group for promoting 'Celtic Communism'. In part because Erksine's nationalist clique pulled out, the Gaelic League again refused to associate with the Pan-Celtic movement.[161] The London Branch secretary chastised its lack of political edge: 'whilst the leading Celtic country was in a life and death struggle for its own civilisation and culture, the other Celtic countries were doing nothing to render any effective assistance to their sister nation', and until the congress could deal 'with the essential politics' of the Celtic nations it was a hindrance to them and those 'dealing positively with the preservation of Celtic civilisation and culture'.[162] Eventually, in order to avoid political tensions at the congresses, John mooted a Celtic Federal Union, which would meet separately and address political questions specifically.[163]

These early hiccups aside, the congress as an institution was surprisingly successful. It would be difficult to point to tangible accomplishments, but in some sense the organisation's continued existence was achievement enough. It managed to hold attention in annual congresses that rotated equally between all of the Celtic nations, and attracted contributors of a high calibre. Celticists not only attended the congresses but joined the Executive Committee and helped to organise them. The Dublin Congress of 1925, run by Hyde and O'Farrelly, was a banner event, attended by Thurneysen and Georges Dottin (1863–1928), Saunders Lewis (1893–1985), and John Morris Jones, among others, with R.A.S. Macalister leading the archaeological excursion to Tara.[164] Instead of withering after E. T. John committed suicide in 1931, the congress was strengthened and improved under Agnes O'Farrelly, who was made president for life.[165] At the congress of 1934, which returned to Dublin, both Éamon de Valera and Eoin MacNeill spoke, and de Valera hinted at the financial support he was willing to give, and ultimately did in the form of the School of Celtic Studies.[166] Although the congress lost momentum around 1950, as a generation of Celtic cultural nationalists passed away, the Celtic Congress continued through the rest of the century and still operates today.

The interwar period also saw the rise of Celtic republicanism, which fused left-wing and nationalist politics in Scotland and Wales. We saw in Part I of this book that some early modern authors believed that there had existed Celtic republics in antiquity, but the only modern republic was (and is) the Irish one. Anti-imperialist sentiment was already present with some early members of the Celtic Congress. Ruaridh Erskine, for example, wanted to 'get our race generally to think in racial instead of imperial lines'.[167] It was a fellow Scot, Christopher Grieve (1892–1978), better known by his pen name Hugh MacDiarmid, who articulated a view of Celtic republicanism in a leftist frame that became influential. MacDiarmid fashioned himself an intellectual genealogy from poets like Milton and Blake, explaining that he regarded himself

> in this way as in others (although not in language) as a purely Celtic poet, carrying on . . . the ancient bardic traditions of a very intricate and scholarly poetry, and with all the bardic powers of savage satire and invective as well as the bardic concern for the Celtic countries—Scotland, Ireland,

> Wales, and Cornwall—and for Celtic history and the continuity of Celtic civilization.[168]

Mixing politics and poetics, MacDiarmid explained that he also descended intellectually 'via Marx and Lenin and Stalin', and as such sought 'to get rid of the English Ascendancy and work for the establishment of Workers' Republics in Scotland, Ireland, Wales and Cornwall, and, indeed, make a sort of Celtic Union of Socialist Soviet Republics in the British Isles'.[169] He inspired the Welsh Republican movement, which had a Pan-Celtic undercurrent promoted by Clifford Bere (1915–1997), who approached MacDiarmid for comment on the *Welsh Republican* newspaper. MacDiarmid responded that 'For many years now I have believed that the solution in these islands lies in a Union of independent Celtic Republics, and I hail "The Welsh Republican" as a significant step in that direction'.[170] Sentiments along these lines inspired radical political movements in the Celtic nations, but MacDiarmid was too erratic and idiosyncratic to commit to them anything more than rhetoric.

With its increasing alignment with radical nationalist politics, Pan-Celticism strengthened after the war.[171] Capitalising on the rising tide of energy, on 9 August 1961 more politically committed activists founded a new Celtic League at the Llangollen *Eisteddfod*. It is one of the most interesting Pan-Celtic groups and has arguably been the chief Pan-Celtic organisation since then. Previous Pan-Celts defined themselves in cultural terms and flirted with politics, but the Celtic League was resolutely political from the start.[172] It described its 'fundamental aim' in 1973 as 'to secure or win [for the Celtic nations] political, cultural, social and economic freedom'.[173] Straightforwardly enough, another statement said, 'the purpose is chiefly political because it is recognised that the solution to the cultural and economic problems of the Celtic countries lies in self-government'.[174]

The most important figure was the general secretary, Alan Heusaff (1921–1999), a Breton living in Irish exile. He had been a lieutenant in the *Bezen Perrot* and stayed on in Germany after the war, fearing a death sentence from the French government or reprisals in Brittany, before settling in Ireland in the early 1950s, where he became a meteorologist. It was probably only down to Heusaff's efforts that the league survived.[175] He worked hard to establish contacts not only among the nationalist groups in the Celtic countries, but also with the various minor nationality movements around Europe, and pressed the case for their rights with the Council of Europe.[176] He was also still in touch with the Germans who had helped him into exile, such as the mystic Friedrich Hielscher, who wanted to know what the league's position on Druidic philosophy would be.[177] A memo about the group's early publication, *Celtic Voice*, suggests that Heusaff was aiming to get away from this sort of thing; he did not want 'a magazine of obscure history drawn from the mists of Celtic Twilight, but one that will mirror life in the six Celtic nations in the twentieth century', although articles on Druidism and Celtic spirituality, including by Heusaff's former commanding officer Lainé, occasionally also appeared in the league's periodicals.[178] There were some academics involved, such as the Welsh lecturer Ceinwen Thomas (1911–2008), who edited the league's early periodicals, and Heusaff corresponded with some notable Celticists such as Derick Thomson—who Petra Johana Poncarová has recently shown was influenced by Erskine, Marr, and MacDiarmid, and who was also involved with the Scottish branch of the Celtic Congress[179]—about raising awareness among Scots, who were generally less interested in Celtic-based nationalism.[180] But in general it should be stressed that the league was self-consciously uninterested in what it saw as the academic debates that had characterised previous Pan-Celtic movements.

The league's political framework became firmly postcolonial as a new generation joined and looked beyond Europe at the crumbling structures of the old imperial world.[181] Arguably the most important of these was Peter Berresford Ellis (1943–), who emerged as a dynamic publicist for the movement in the late 1960s and became its de facto historian.[182] His *Creed of the Celtic Revolution* (1969) defined 'the essence of Celtic nationalism or what it should be' as 'freedom from imperialism; more specifically, (a) freedom of the Celtic mind from cultural imperialism and (b) freedom of the Celtic peoples from political and economic imperialism'.[183] Freeing the Celtic mind meant 'Re-Celtisation' through restoring the Celtic languages: 'The task of making a Celtic speaking Celtica must be accomplished at all costs'.[184] Once re-Celtisation was accomplished, self-government would naturally follow; the form envisioned was a union of socialist republics, because historically 'Celtic society was always a socialist society'.[185] 'Celtica' would be interlinked culturally, economically, and politically 'on the same basis as Scandinavia', while folding in Celtic outposts in Patagonia and Nova Scotia (overlooking their colonial foundations). Ellis was followed by the Breton Branch secretary Jakez Derouet (1944–) with calls in the 1970s for a greater social and political message to be promoted by the league, while various left-leaning viewpoints, and also some critiques of them, were voiced by other members.[186]

The linguistic commitment has remained central and helped to move Pan-Celticism beyond the now problematic racial concept that had grounded the

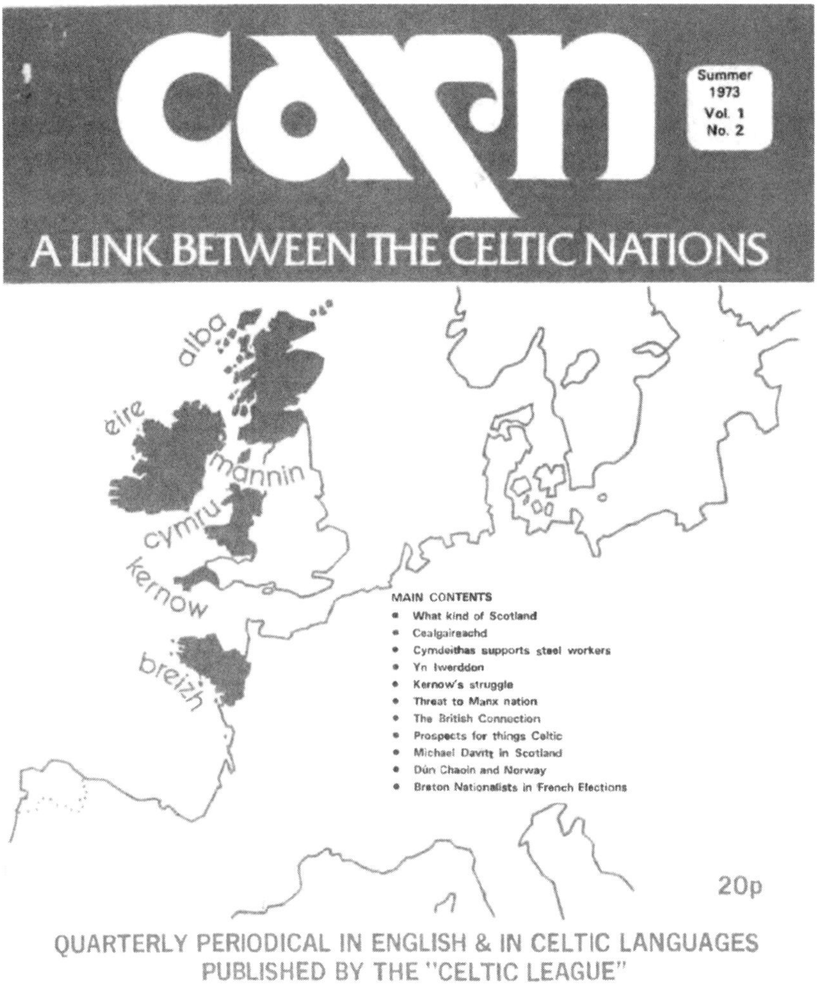

FIG. 18. *Carn* 1 (1973).

idea in the nineteenth century. The league's position has always been that 'the Celtic languages today constitute their least disputable mark of nationality', and articles in the group's long-running journal *Carn* (Fig. 18) have for five decades appeared in all Celtic languages.[187] Amid the political news and internal disputes hashed out in *Carn*, language was the central point of discussion and attracted widespread comment. Victor Durkacz (1952–1993), who produced a major sociolinguistic work well-known in Celtic studies on *The Decline of the Celtic Languages* (1983), published a preview of his thesis in 1977.[188] However, already in 1962 it had been conceded that the league would have to use

English as it was the most commonly used idiom, and it has accordingly been flexible on this point.[189] Most notably, in the mid-1980s, Galicians and Asturians requested to form a branch but, while treated sympathetically, were not admitted because doing so would have violated the linguistic principle (though Galicia has a prevalent Celtic musical tradition).[190] Their campaigns for admission have continued to be refused, but have drawn wider attention, recently in the *Economist* of all places.[191] The episode is reminiscent of the Celtic Association's 1900 refusal to admit Cornwall because its language was dead, but a noticeable distinction of the league is the strong presence of Cornish nationalists and articles written in the Cornish language.

Beyond the many calls for greater Celtic awareness among the nations, the league took on political issues relevant to the territory of the Celtic countries. It adopted an anti-nuclear stance, monitoring military bases and nuclear pollution, and fought a campaign against submarine activity in the Celtic Sea, which had led to several fatalities among fishing crews.[192] More recently the league has taken up ecological positions aligning it with the Green movement, and has fought campaigns to decolonise the internet. In 1983, Ellis looked back on Heusaff's tenure and asserted that the league had managed to achieve a 'modern Celtic consciousness', but whether that is really the case is doubtful, and how much credit the league could take for it is also questionable.[193] Given the difficulties we have seen in maintaining Pan-Celtic interest, however, arguably the Celtic League's greatest achievement is that it survived and continues to promote Pan-Celticism.[194]

While Pan-Celts have claimed victory in some measure for Devolution in the 1990s, these developments owed little to Celticism and everything to models of civic nationalism.[195] However, the potential of Pan-Celticism—though one devoid of anything really 'Celtic'—has started to surface in mainstream politics since the Brexit vote of 2016. Ecological issues are the latest ground on which representatives from the Celtic countries are meeting, and in the summer of 2023 the inaugural Celtic Forum on Green Energy was held in Rennes.[196] As England freefalls and ecological crisis looms, perhaps there is a future yet for Pan-Celticism.

Conclusion: Celticism and Celtic Studies to the Present

The radical Pan-Celtic politics of the later twentieth century were increasingly out of step with the academic field of Celtic studies. Celtic studies has always been decentralised, but in the postwar period there was no recognised leader in the way that German universities, especially whichever one at which Thurneysen happened to be, had previously been. The School of Celtic Studies in Dublin's Institute for Advanced Studies aimed 'to encourage the development of Celtic scholarship in other countries', and was proud that 'Almost everyone now active in Celtic studies [around the world] is in touch with the School in one way or another'.[197] But despite de Valera's underlying belief that Ireland was a 'natural centre for Celtic studies', it was only one centre among many.[198] In 1969, the *Centre de recherche bretonne et celtique* opened in Brest, and in 1985, the University of Wales inaugurated a Centre for Advanced Welsh and Celtic Studies in Aberystwyth. Beyond these there are Celtic studies departments and chairs in Celtic in the four largest Celtic nations and further afield, such as in Utrecht, while Celtic studies has retained a presence in Russia and Poland since the early twentieth century.[199] One of the most successful centres is, ironically, not in a Celtic country, nor is it a purely Celtic department. Despite always playing second or even third fiddle within the Department of Anglo-Saxon, Norse, and Celtic—which tellingly evolved from 'Anglo-Saxon and Kindred Studies' under the direction of H. M. Chadwick (1870–1947)—at Cambridge, many of today's leading scholars are its products.[200] But the professorship of Celtic at Jesus College, Oxford, stands out as probably still the most prestigious post in the field.

The second half of the twentieth century witnessed a gradual but distinct split between Celtologists and Celtic enthusiasts. Celtic studies and Celtic politics both flourished, but they were increasingly pursued by different groups of people. While there had always been a space for Celtic scholars at the Celtic congresses, these finally established their own International Congress of Celtic Studies in 1959, which is now the largest and longest-running gathering of Celticists in existence.[201] The first International Congress was a joint organisation of Trinity College Dublin, University College Dublin, the Royal Irish Academy, and the Dublin Institute of Advanced Studies. Kenneth Jackson, whose work is an excellent example of the rigour of the 'new Celtomania', delivered the keynote. Wholly English in origin and education, Jackson studied at Cambridge before taking up the first professorship at Harvard and then moving to Edinburgh. His *Language and History in Early Britain* (1953) is characteristic of the breadth and rigour of the field, which he was keen to guard against charlatans. 'Celtic Studies are peculiarly dangerous for the amateur', he wrote in 1976 as he surveyed the field's development in the prior half-century. But he was also concerned with dilettantes from neighbouring fields who 'dream up and publish ideas which the Celticist knows to be absurd speculations'.[202] The politicised views of Celtic history advanced in places like the Celtic League were far away from this attitude, which is still present in the field, if usually expressed in less stringent terms.

Despite such warnings, Celtic studies was still itself an interdisciplinary field, and problems eventually arose from the syntheses on 'Celtic Civilization' that were being written even by the best Celticists. As discussed in earlier chapters, the nineteenth-century marriage of ancient history, philology, archaeology, and racial sciences like craniology produced a composite picture of the ancient Celts stretching from Central Europe west into Spain and north into the islands of Britain and Ireland, sharing a material culture and speaking related languages. Archaeology took a central place in these books, with the Celtic art thesis connecting the La Tène people of the Iron Age with a civilization stretching over space and time through medieval Ireland.[203] Yet even the most sophisticated of these popular books, written by two serious scholars, Nora Chadwick and Myles Dillon, identified something more metaphysical connecting these different Celtic societies. They hesitated to name it themselves but noted that Matthew Arnold called it 'the Celtic magic'.[204] Arnold, as we know from the discussion of his *Celtic Literature* in chapter 8, believed in racial essences, and so we can see that this kind of thinking lingered into the postwar period, even if skull shapes are nowhere to be found. Chadwick produced another popular book—titled *The Celts*—for the affordable Pelican Books series in 1971. Again focusing on art and archaeology, Chadwick's book presented an exciting account of an ancient people stretching across Europe, whose 'Common political institutions gave them a unity bordering on nationality'.[205]

Although books like Chadwick's *Celts* remain in print, the new synthesis of Celtic civilization was not to last in the academic world. In the midst of a wider shift in their discipline, in the 1980s archaeologists started to point out serious gaps in the Celtic art thesis, which was based on layer upon layer of conjecture. There was 'no such thing as "Celtic Society"', wrote John Collis already in 1985, an interpretation he has supported ever since.[206] I have already discussed this debate in the introduction, and examined its nineteenth-century archaeological origins in chapter 7, but the point to raise here is that a crude version of the archaeological critique emerged at the end of the 1990s in the popular sphere, exemplified in the work of Simon James. Supported by the British Museum, James ostensibly meant to translate the archaeological argument for a popular audience in his *Atlantic Celts: Ancient People or Modern Invention?*, but his modern sketch of Celticism was also inspired by the 'invention of tradition' thesis.[207] The obnoxiousness of James's intervention briefly made waves in the press, but until Simon Jenkins recently revived its central points for his own purposes in *The Celts: A Sceptical History*, it had largely lain dormant. Many archaeologists have continued to publish books for a popular audience on the Celts that acknowledge the problem but stick with the standard story anyway.[208] The image projected into the popular domain is bipolar: on one side is the traditional picture of a nearly Europe-wide Celtic civilization sharing cultural features across space and time, and on the other is an argument that this never existed, or at least not as it is currently described. Scholars have been left to clean up the mess.

Patrick Sims-Williams has devoted the most attention to the issue, introducing 'Celtoscepticism'—a term that has stuck for those such as Collis who doubt whether old-style Celtic syntheses are possible—into English in an iconic paper of 1998.[209] Pointing out that Celticists routinely refine and, if need be, discard their own categories and paradigms, Sims-Williams has examined in careful detail what can be considered to have been customs particular to ancient Celtic cultures, and thus perhaps held in common, and whether these survived into the Middle Ages.[210] A similar examination was undertaken by the Irish scholar Kim McCone in a robust reply to the Celtosceptic critique in 2008. He suggested that 'Celts' was a self-descriptive term related to militancy that was used not only by the ancient Celts but their Indo-European ancestors. If his etymologies are correct, 'It follows that speakers of Proto-Celtic actually called themselves **Keltoi* "Celts"'.[211] It is a powerful answer that Celticity is rooted in the Celtic languages themselves and has been from the language family's earliest history. Though with characteristic caution, Sims-Williams has also endorsed a view of linguistic identity: 'Applying a single term both to a population and to a language should never be done lightly, but in the case of the Celts they do seem, at least from the middle of the first millennium BC onwards, to constitute a valid "ethno linguistic group"'.[212]

With the academic disintegration of the general history of Celtic civilization came the serious loss of a unified narrative that combined evidence from many fields in an attractive and lively history. That loss was only half-digested in the popular sphere when a new synthetic theory came along: Celtic from the West. The development of this theory is one of the most attention-grabbing Celtic-related developments in the twenty-first century. It is an attractively simple hypothesis: 'Celtic probably evolved in the Atlantic Zone during the Bronze Age'.[213] Advanced since the late 2000s principally by Barry Cunliffe and John T. Koch—among the leaders in their respective fields of archaeology and historical linguistics—this 'Celtic from the West' theory encourages us to consider the possibility that the Celtic languages may have evolved within a community stretching along the Atlantic edges of Western Europe from Iberia to Ireland during the Bronze Age. Although this contrasts starkly with the long-held and now defunct narrative of an Eastern Celtic invasion of Gaul, Iberia, Britain, and Ireland from the Alpine regions of Hallstatt and La Tène, readers who have made it this far will notice a certain symmetry with the traditional Irish account drawing the Gaels from the invasion of Ireland by Míl Espagne. Particularly notable is the interdisciplinary approach of archaeology, linguistics, and genetics. Linguists have long pointed out the dangers of aligning material culture with assumed ethno-linguistic communities, and while the jury is still out on the results of ancient DNA analyses of the ancient Celts, the new hypothesis hinges on linguistic evidence and Koch's argument that Tartessian (an ancient language of southwestern Iberia) is the 'earliest attested Celtic language'.[214] However, while 'Celtic from the West' remains an interesting and stimulating hypothesis, it has encountered considerable resistance.[215]

Yet wherever one now falls on the question of 'Who were the Celts?', with which this book opened, it seems that with the 'revolution' in ancient DNA there is cause for optimism all round. The international project to synthesise ancient DNA, now far more affordable than it was even two decades ago, may yet lead to solutions to questions that have stood for centuries if not millennia.[216] In the Celtic sphere the most recent studies suggest that there was a large population influx to Britain during the late Bronze Age—approximately from 1000 to 875 BCE—with close genetic links to the inhabitants of France at the time.[217] The findings look compatible with a theory published by Patrick Sims-Williams in 2020, 'Celtic from the Centre', which hypothesises that the Celtic languages developed in what is now France around 1000 BCE and subsequently spread across the Channel to Britain, Ireland, and throughout Europe.[218] If the theory is correct, then as Sims-Williams says, 'The big remaining question is: "Did Celtic reach Ireland via Britain or direct from the continent?"'[219] There is a chance that Edward Lhwyd was right all along.

NOTES

Preface and Acknowledgments

1. Eoin MacNeill, *Phases of Irish History* (1919: Dublin, 1920), 5, 38.

2. Remarkably, as far as I know, the only attempt at an overview of Celtic studies remains Victor Tourneur, *Esquisse d'une histoire des études celtiques* (Liège, 1905).

3. Kenneth Jackson, 'Fifty Years of Celtic Philology', *Modern Language Review* 71 (1976), xxiii.

Note on the Celtic Languages

1. 'Brittonic' is equivalent to 'Brythonic', coined by Sir John Rhys [see Kenneth Jackson, *Language and History in Early Britain* (London, 1953), 3].

Introduction

1. Underlining the linguistic point is the conspicuous absence of Cornwall, delimited from the rest of England but unshaded because its Celtic language was assumed to be extinct. On that same day the cartographer delivered a paper on the 'Present Condition of the Five Living Celtic languages' (*Y Cymro*, 28 July 1898, 6).

2. Unless otherwise drawing attention to the issue, I do not normally use quotation marks around Celts, Celtic, and other lexical variants. The idea behind these terms has always been in flux, and explaining why that is the case is one of the main aims of this book.

3. See, for example, Graham Robb, *Ancient Paths: Discovering the Lost Map of Celtic Europe* (London, 2013); Alice Roberts, *The Celts: Search for a Civilization* (London, 2015). Marcus Tanner, *The Last of the Celts* (New Haven, CT, 2004), employs the same trope but features original research and reflections.

4. For academic treatments by specialists, see, for example, Barry Cunliffe and John T. Koch (eds.), *Exploring Celtic Origins: Archaeology, Linguistics, and Genetics* (Oxford, 2019), and their three-volume collection of essays, *Celtic from the West* (3 vols., Oxford, 2010–2016). For overviews from non-specialists, see Jean Manco, *Blood of the Celts: The New Ancestral Story* (London, 2015); Simon Young, *The Celtic Revolution: In Search of 2000 Forgotten Years That Changed the World* (London, 2009).

5. For a clear and exciting overview of Celtic mythology—really medieval literature—see Mark Williams, *The Celtic Myths That Shape the Way We Think* (London, 2021); for Irish mythology, see his brilliant *Ireland's Immortals: A History of the Gods of Irish Myth* (Princeton, NJ, 2016).

Other recent overviews include Philip Freeman, *Celtic Mythology: Tales of Gods, Goddesses, and Heroes* (Oxford, 2017); and James MacKillop, *Myths and Legends of the Celts* (London, 2005). There are of course also dozens of articles published every year in specialist academic journals.

6. The respective accompanying volumes are Julia Farley and Fraser Hunter (eds.), *Celts: Art and Identity* (London, 2015); and Roberts, *Celts*.

7. In addition to the many works of Jean-Louis Brunaux, recent books include Laurent Olivier, *Le pays des Celtes: Mémoires de la Gaule* (Paris, 2018); Katherine Gruel and Olivier Buchsenschutz (eds.), *Réinventer les Celtes* (Paris, 2019).

8. Venceslas Kruta (ed.), *The Celts* (London, 1997); Michael Dietler, '"Our Ancestors the Gauls": Archaeology, Ethnic Nationalism, and the Manipulation of Celtic Identity in Modern Europe', *American Anthropologist* 96 (1994), 584–605.

9. For a classic review, see Rudolf Thurneysen, 'Why Do Germans Study Celtic Philology?' *Studies: An Irish Quarterly Review* 19 (1930), 20–32. The works of the archaeologist and scholar of comparative religions Bernhard Maier continue to do well, and his overview is now in its third edition (Bernhard Maier, *Die Kelten: Ihre Geschichte von den Anfängen bis zur Gegenwart* [2000: 3rd ed., Munich, 2016]).

10. See, for example, Martín Almagro-Gorbea and Gonzalo Ruiz Zapatero (eds.), *Los Celtas: Hispania y Europa* (Madrid, 1993).

11. Peter Berresford Ellis, *Celtic Dawn: The Dream of Celtic Unity* (1993: Tal-y-Bont, 2002), 20–30.

12. Cunliffe and Koch, *Celtic from the West*, vol. 1.

13. For example, the Nova Scotia–based *Celtic Life International* magazine aims to connect the 'hundreds of millions' descended from the 'nomadic Celts' who '2500 years ago . . . roamed across Europe', and has created an international marketplace for Celtic-themed art, clothing, and jewellery ('400 Million Celts. One Voice', accessed 30 December 2020, https://celticlifeintl.com/400-million-celts-one-voice/).

14. Joep Leerssen, 'On the Edge of Europe: Ireland in Search of Oriental Roots (1650–1850)', *Comparative Criticism* 1 (1986), 92.

15. See, for example, Barry Cunliffe, *The Ancient Celts* (1997: 2nd ed., Oxford, 2018), 1–51; Helmut Birkhan, *Kelten: Versuch einer Gesamtdarstellung ihrer Kultur* (Vienna, 1997), 3–21; Gisbert Hemprich, 'Nachleben', in Stefan Zimmer (ed.), *Die Kelten: Mythos und Wirklichkeit* (2004: 3rd ed., Stuttgart, 2012), 199–213.

16. Most works that do address the modern construction of Celtic ideas have been written by scholars who specialise in the ancient and medieval periods; accordingly, their work tends to trace out the reception of ancient ideas rather than to examine the ways those ideas changed in different modern contexts. For good works in this genre see John Collis, *The Celts: Origins, Myths & Inventions* (Stroud, 2003); *idem*, 'Die Entwicklung des Kelten-Konzepts in Britannien während des 18. Jahrhunderts', in Helmut Birkhan (ed.), *Kelten-Einfälle an der Donau* (Vienna, 2007), 111–23; Michael Morse, *How the Celts Came to Britain: Druids, Ancient Skulls and the Birth of Archaeology* (Stroud, 2005); Helmut Birkhan, *Nachantike Keltenrezeption: Projektionen keltischer Kultur* (Vienna, 2009); Jean-Louis Brunaux, *Les Celtes: Histoire d'un mythe* (Paris, 2014).

17. Robert Cecil, Lord Salisbury (1830–1903), is attributed with coining the concept of the 'Celtic fringe' ['Celtic edges'] in 1890, but it was the writer Grant Allen (1848–1899) who used the phrase itself in 1894 [see 'Celtic fringe', in *OED*].

18. For the most recent, stimulating theory on Celtic ethnogenesis, see Patrick Sims-Williams, 'An Alternative to "Celtic from the East" and "Celtic from the West"', *Cambridge Archaeological Journal* 30 (2020), 511–29.

19. For a fresh approach, see Rachel Pope, 'Re-approaching the Celts: Origins, Society, and Social Change', *Journal of Archaeological Research* 30 (2021), 1–67.

20. David Reich, *Who We Are and How We Got Here: Ancient DNA and the New Science of the Human Past* (Oxford, 2018); Kristian Kristiansen, Guus Kroonen, and Eske Willerslev (eds.), *The Indo-European Puzzle Revisited: Integrating Archaeology, Genetics, and Linguistics* (Cambridge, 2023).

21. See Joep Leerssen's perceptive essay, 'Celticism', in Terence Brown (ed.), *Celticism* (Amsterdam, 1996), 1–20, esp. 3–4.

22. These are the controversial views that emerge out of Hugh Trevor-Roper, 'The Invention of Tradition: The Highland Tradition of Scotland', in Eric Hobsbawm and Terence Ranger (eds.), *The Invention of Tradition* (Cambridge, 1983), 15–41; *idem*, *The Invention of Scotland: Myth and History* (New Haven, CT, 2008); Malcolm Chapman, *The Celts: The Construction of a Myth* (Basingstoke, 1992); Simon James, *The Atlantic Celts: Ancient People or Modern Invention?* (London, 1999); Simon Jenkins, *The Celts: A Sceptical History* (London, 2022).

23. The etymologies of Keltoi/Celtae and Galatae/Galli are uncertain, but many suggest a Celtic etymology for one or more of them. See, for example, Kim McCone, *The Celtic Question: Modern Constructs and Ancient Realities* (Dublin, 2008); John T. Koch, 'Celts, Britons, and Gaels: Names, Peoples, and Identities', *Transactions of the Honourable Society of Cymmrodorion*, New Series 9 (2002), 42.

24. For a lively overview of Tacitus's impact, see Christopher B. Krebs, *A Most Dangerous Book: Tacitus's* Germania *from the Roman Empire to the Third Reich* (New York, 2011).

25. Good examples of that former consensus are T.G.E. Powell, *The Celts* (London, 1958); Nora Chadwick, *The Celts* (London, 1971); Myles Dillon and Nora K. Chadwick, *The Celtic Realms* (London, 1967).

26. Little is new under the Celtic sun, and Celtosceptics have existed for a long time. Their spiritual godfather is the Scot John Pinkerton [see chapter 4], but James Cruickshank Roger's *Celticism: A Myth* (London, 1884), has a title that would not be out of place in today's publishing market. For a detailed overview of the early debate, see Patrick Sims-Williams, 'Celtomania and Celtoscepticism', *Cambrian Medieval Celtic Studies* 36 (1998), 1–35. For a recent assessment, see John R. Collis, 'Celts Ancient and Modern: Recent Controversies in Celtic Studies', *Studia Celtica Fennica* XIV (2017), 58–71. 'Celtoscepticism' is sometimes also called 'New Celticism', though this has not really caught on.

27. J.V.S. Megaw and M. R. Megaw, 'Ancient Celts and Modern Ethnicity', *Antiquity* 70 (1996), 175–81; John Collis, 'Celtic Myths', *Antiquity* 71 (1997), 195–201.

28. See, for example, Patrick Sims-Williams, 'Genetics, Linguistics, and Prehistory: Thinking Big and Thinking Straight', *Antiquity* 72 (1998), 505–27; *idem*, 'An Alternative', esp. 511–12; *idem*, *Ancient Celtic Place-Names in Europe and Asia Minor* (Oxford, 2006). See John Mackinnon Robertson, *The Saxon and the Celt: A Study in Sociology* (London, 1897), for a prescient nineteenth-century critique that skewers a casual alignment of archaeological and linguistic evidence with racial theories.

29. Trevor-Roper, 'Invention of Tradition'.

30. Letters from Hugh Trevor-Roper to Nan Dunbar in Christ Church, Oxford, Soc. Dacre, 1/3/27, Dunbar Correspondence. Thank you to Blair Worden for permission to consult the Literary Estate of Lord Dacre of Glanton.

31. James, *Atlantic Celts*. James gestured at the situation in Northern Ireland as a justification for the book, and in one section pointed out that both republicans and loyalists appropriated the Celtic past and used it for nefarious purposes. Citing the imagery of Cú Chulainn in Dublin's General Post Office sculpture and in Ulster loyalist murals, he apparently missed the entire point of the 'invention of tradition' thesis, *viz.* if the mythological character Cú Chulainn had not existed, he or someone like him would have had to be invented [see James, *Atlantic Celts* 11, 23–25]. For a good critique, see Patrick Sims-Williams, 'How Are You Finding It Here?' *London Review of Books*, 28 October 1999.

32. Chapman, *Celts*, 69.

33. Patrick Sims-Williams, '"The Visionary Celt: The Construction of an "Ethnic Preconception"', *Cambridge Medieval Celtic Studies* 11 (1986), 77.

34. Francesca Kaminski-Jones and Rhys Kaminski-Jones (eds.), *Celts, Romans, Britons: Classical and Celtic Influence in the Construction of British Identities* (Oxford, 2020).

35. The point is underlined in Sam Smiles, *The Image of Antiquity: Ancient Britain and the Romantic Imagination* (New Haven, CT, 1994).

36. Leerssen, 'Celticism', 3.

37. Maev Kennedy's article 'From Monsters to Manga: Golden Age of Art by the Celtic Race That Never Was', *Guardian*, 10 July 2015, discusses the British Museum Exhibition of 2015–2016, which is typically representative and also typically confused (accessed 12 October 2020, https://www.theguardian.com/artanddesign/2015/jul/10/from-monsters-to-manga-golden-age-of-art-by-the-celtic-race-that-never-was).

38. On the problematic distinction between academic and popular ideas and debates, see Martha Vandrei, *Queen Boudica and Historical Culture: An Image of Truth* (Oxford, 2018).

39. Patrick Sims-Williams comes the closest to dealing with the impact of race on the development of Celtic studies in his reflections on the discipline [see, for example, Sims-Williams, '"The Visionary Celt"'].

40. The ideas of nation and race have generated huge literatures and I wish to avoid a tedious discussion of them. Basically, I take a 'constructive' approach to nations, trying as far as possible to identify what this protean idea meant to the individuals examined and how it was treated within the context of their times. One way of reading this book would be as a vindication of the ethno-symbolist theory of nationalism—*viz.* 'nation-builders' drew on a broad range of existing narratives, myths, symbols, and historical materials in the intellectual construction of nations—developed by Anthony Smith and John Hutchinson, among others.

41. Benedict Anderson, *Imagined Communities: Reflections on the Origin and Spread of Nationalism* (London, 1983).

42. This is the broad thrust of Anthony D. Smith's work. See, for example, *Myths and Memories of the Nation* (Oxford, 1999).

43. David Bell, *The Cult of the Nation in France: Inventing Nationalism, 1680–1800* (Cambridge, MA, 2003), 15.

44. For a summarization of these developments, see Anderson, *Imagined Communities*; Ernest Gellner, *Nations and Nationalism* (Oxford, 1983). On the political questions, see Richard

Tuck, *The Sleeping Sovereign: The Invention of Modern Democracy* (Cambridge, 2016); John Dunn, *Setting the People Free: The Story of Democracy* (2nd ed., Princeton, NJ, 2018).

45. In his *Qu'est-ce que le tiers état?*, the Abbé Emmanuel Sieyès (1748–1836) fused the organicist conception of the nation with its political claims: 'The nation exists prior to everything; it is the origin of everything. Its will is always legal. It is the law itself. Prior to the nation and above the nation there is only natural law.' See Emmanuel Joseph Sieyès, 'What is the Third Estate?' in Michael Sonenscher (ed. and trans.), *Emmanuel Joseph Sieyès: Political Writings, Including the Debate between Sieyès and Tom Paine in 1791* (Indianapolis, IN, 2003), 136. More generally, see Michael Sonenscher, *Before the Deluge: Public Debt, Inequality, and the Intellectual Origins of the French Revolution* (Princeton, NJ, 2009).

46. Istvan Hont, *Jealousy of Trade: International Competition and the Nation-State in Historical Perspective* (Cambridge, MA, 2005), 499–509, pointed out that the use of the term *nationalismus* or *nationalisme* in the late eighteenth century was a geopolitical idea referring to the wars between European states during the height of absolutism; its meaning expanded in the following century. If it is generally agreed that nationalism is a modern political phenomenon dating from the era of the French Revolution, the question of whether nations existed prior to this time has been much more vexed. To cut a long story short, I believe that if we can recognise many ideas of liberty before modern political conceptions of it like liberalism, we should also be able to identify nations before nationalism. Nations existed as intellectual and ideological abstractions long before the political doctrine of nationalism placed the nation at the heart of its claims for political legitimacy.

47. Ian B. Stewart, 'Celticism and the Four Nations in the Long Nineteenth Century', in Naomi Lloyd-Jones and Margaret M. Scull, *Four Nations Approaches to Modern 'British' History* (Basingstoke, 2018), 135–59.

48. This was a topic of huge popularity in the 1990s and early 2000s but it has since trailed off. See, for example, Anne-Marie Thiesse, *La creation des identités nationales: Europe xviiie-xixe siècle* (Paris, 1999); Joep Leerssen, *National Thought in Europe: A Cultural History* (Amsterdam, 2006); Linda Colley, *Britons: Forging the Nation 1707–1837* (New Haven, CT, 1992); Colin Kidd, *British Identities before Nationalism: Ethnicity and Nationhood in the Atlantic World* (Cambridge, 1999); William Ferguson, *The Identity of the Scottish Nation: An Historic Quest* (Edinburgh, 1998).

49. Susan Reynolds, 'Medieval *Origines Gentium* and the Community of the Realm', *History* 68 (1983), 375–90.

50. Colin Kidd, 'Teutonist Ethnology and Scottish Nationalist Inhibition, 1780–1880', *Scottish Historical Review* 74 (1995), 45–68.

51. Claude Nicolet, *La fabrique d'une nation: la France entre Rome et les Germains* (Paris, 2003).

52. See the excellent recent book by Matthew D'Auria, *The Shaping of French National Identity: Narrating the Nation's Past, 1715–1830* (Cambridge, 2020).

53. See discussion in Steven G. Ellis, 'Why the History of the "Celtic Fringe" Remains Unwritten', *European Review of History* 10 (2003), 221–31. To a certain extent this book is a contribution to the 'New British History' or 'Four Nations History', but this is more a result of my conviction that contexts should be expanded as far as necessary in order to properly appreciate the subject at hand, rather than of any particular attachment to this framework. Ideas cross borders more easily than humans, so it is especially vital to take a transnational approach to

intellectual history. On the New British History, see J.G.A. Pocock, 'British History: A Plea for a New Subject', *Journal of Modern History* 47 (1975), 601–21; Hugh Kearney, *The British Isles: A History of Four Nations* (Cambridge, 1987); Naomi Lloyd-Jones and Margaret M. Scull, *Four Nations Approaches to Modern 'British' History* (Basingstoke, 2018).

54. 'Race', in Samuel Johnson, *A Dictionary of the English Language* (2 vols., London, 1755), vol. 2, p. 1628. See Nicholas Hudson, 'From "Nation" to "Race": The Origin of Racial Classification in Eighteenth-Century Thought', *Eighteenth-Century Studies* 29 (1996) 247–64. On the history of race and genealogy, see Claude-Olivier Doron, *L'homme altéré: races et dégénérescence (xviie-xixe siècles)* (Ceyzérieu 2016).

55. A review of Victorian ideas of race-mixing is out of place here, but there were complicated ideas on the topic [see chapter 8].

56. Edward Said, *Orientalism* (New York, 1978). Said's *Culture and Imperialism* (New York, 1993) incorporates Ireland into his critical view (esp. 220–30). See Leerssen, 'Celticism', for discussion.

57. Michael Hechter, *Internal Colonialism: The Celtic Fringe in British National Development, 1536–1966* (London, 1975). For an important early critique, see Tom Nairn, *The Break-Up of Britain: Crisis and Neo-Nationalism* (1977: 2nd ed., London, 1981), 201.

58. Murray G. H. Pittock, *Celtic Identity and the British Image* (Manchester, 1999); Robert J. C. Young, *The Idea of English Ethnicity* (Oxford, 2008); Katie Trumpener, *Bardic Nationalism: The Romantic Novel and the British Empire* (Princeton, NJ, 1997). For a historical treatment that adopts Hechter's schematic, see Norman Davies, *The Isles: A History* (London, 1999).

59. See Colley, *Britons*; Kidd, *British Identities*; Gerard Carruthers and Alan Rawes (eds.), *English Romanticism and the Celtic World* (Cambridge, 2003); Gerard Carruthers and Colin Kidd, *Literature and Union: Scottish Texts, British Contexts* (Oxford, 2018).

60. Ian McBride, *Eighteenth-Century Ireland: The Isle of Slaves* (Dublin, 2009), 8.

61. Quoted in S. Wallace, *John Stuart Blackie: Scottish Scholar and Patriot* (Edinburgh, 2006), 304.

62. *Y Cymro*, 23 April 1903, 4 [Un o'r pethau rhyfeddaf ar y ddear *yma* yw 'Celtyddiaeth'].

63. This idea was articulated most clearly in the still ubiquitous L. P. Curtis, *Anglo-Saxons and Celts: A Study of Anglo-Irish Prejudice in Victorian England* (Bridgeport, 1968).

64. See discussion in Stephen Howe, *Ireland and Empire: Colonial Legacies in Irish History and Culture* (Oxford, 2000).

65. By this I mean that I treat pan-Celticism as much as I can as a phenomenon across all of the Celtic nations. Pan-Celticism has featured in a few popular works, most notably Ellis, *Celtic Dawn*, but was skated over in the only academic study devoted to pan-nationalisms, Louis L. Snyder, *Macro-Nationalisms: A History of the Pan-Movements* (Westport, CT, 1984). Erwan Chartier-Le Floch, *Histoire de l'interceltisme en Bretagne* (Spézet, 2013), examines pan-Celticism in Brittany, as does Philip Le Stum, *Le néo-druidisme en Bretagne: origine, naissance et développement* (Mayenne, 1998). Caoimhín de Barra, *The Coming of the Celts, AD 1860: Celtic Nationalism in Ireland and Wales* (Notre Dame, 2018), focuses on Ireland and Wales.

66. Our focuses are very different, but I have adopted this from Philip O'Leary, *The Prose Literature of the Gaelic Revival, 1881–1921: Ideology and Innovation* (University Park, PA, 1994), 375–94.

67. 'The Pan-Celtic Movement', *An Treas Comhchruinneachadh nan Celtich Uile* (Edinburgh, 1907), 47, University of Strathclyde Archives, Patrick Geddes Papers, T-Ged5/2/18.

68. Most fruitfully in Andrew G. Newby, *Ireland, Radicalism and the Scottish Highlands, c.1870–1912* (Edinburgh, 2007).

69. MacNeill, *Phases of Irish History*, 5

Chapter One: Source Traditions

1. Abraham Ortelius, 'Europa', *Theatrum Orbis Terrarum* (1570: 2nd ed., Antwerp, 1595). I am grateful to John Considine for assisting me with Ortelius.

2. Thomas Pownall, *An Antiquarian Romance* (London, 1795), 134n. The list is borrowed and condensed from Johann Daniel Schoepflin, *Alsatiae Illustratae* (2 vols., Colmar, 1751–1761), vol. 1, 110–11.

3. Kaminski-Jones and Kaminski-Jones, *Celts, Romans, Britons.*

4. For summaries of these source traditions, see William Dinan, *Monumenta historica celtica* (London, 1911); Philip M. Freeman, 'The Earliest Greek Sources on the Celts', *Études celtiques* 32 (1996), 11–48; Collis, *Celts*, 13–26.

5. For a textured picture of the ancient Celtic world through Hellenistic eyes, see Arnoldo Momigliano, *Alien Wisdom: The Limits of Hellenization* (Cambridge, 1975), 50–73.

6. This fragment survived as reported by Strabo [see Freeman, 'Earliest Greek Sources', 35]. Sims-Williams, 'An Alternative', 525, cautions against the assumption that ancient Greeks used 'Celt' simply as a term for western barbarians without differentiating between the tribes.

7. Dinan, *Monumenta*, 325, 327–29.

8. Freeman, 'Earliest Greek Sources', 23–24.

9. Freeman, 'Earliest Greek Sources', 31–32.

10. Strabo, *Geography*, trans. Duane W. Roller (Cambridge, 2014), 297.

11. Livy, *History of Rome*, trans. B. O. Foster (14 vols., Cambridge, MA, 1919–1959), vol. 3, 127, 155.

12. Polybius, *The Histories*, trans. W. R. Paton, rev. Frank W. Walbank and Christian Habicht (6 vols., Cambridge, MA, 2010–2012).

13. Diodorus Siculus, *Library of History* (12 vols., Cambridge, MA, 1933–1967), vol. 6, 303–19.

14. On the Greek and Roman encounters with the Celts in this era, see J.H.C. Williams, *Beyond the Rubicon: Romans and Gauls in Republican Italy* (Oxford, 2001).

15. Livy, *History*, vol. 5, 117–19.

16. Polybius, *Histories*, vol. 1, 309–61, quote at 311.

17. Livy, *History*, vol. 5, 121–73.

18. Polybius, *Histories*, vol. 2, 453; Livy, *History*, vol. 11, 49–55.

19. Livy, *History*, vol. 11, 55.

20. Polybius, *Histories*, vol. 1, 359–61. The Roman respect for the Gauls in war registered strongly in the early modern period. See, for example, François Hotman, *Francogallia*, trans. J.M.H. Salmon (Cambridge, 1972), 173.

21. Julius Caesar, *Seven Commentaries on the Gallic War*, trans. Carolyn Hammond (Oxford, 1996), 3.

22. Caesar, *Gallic War*, 93, 102.

23. Caesar, *Gallic War*, 116.

24. Caesar, *Gallic War*, 127.

25. However, in 5.48 Caesar sends a message in Greek so that the Nervii could not read it (Caesar, *Gallic War*, 113). Although not known at the time, the oldest Celtic alphabet (probably adapted Etruscan) and texts are from the sixth-century BCE 'Lepontic' culture around the northern Italian lakes. Gaulish inscriptions—in an adapted Greek alphabet—appear from the second century BCE. See Michel Lejeune, *Lepontica* (Paris, 1971); Jean-Yves Lambert, *La langue gauloise: Description linguistique, Commentaire d'inscriptions choisies*, (1994: Revised ed., Paris, 2003); Javier de Hoz, 'The Mediterranean Frontier of the Celts and the Advent of Celtic Writing', *Cambrian Medieval Celtic Studies* 53–54 (2007), 1–22.

26. Caesar, *Gallic War*, 128.

27. On Boudica's long afterlife, see Vandrei, *Queen Boudica*.

28. He later elaborated on these episodes in the *Annals*.

29. Tacitus, *Agricola*, trans. Harold Mattingly, ed. J. B. Rives (1948: London, 2009), 9.

30. Josephus, *Jewish Antiquities, Vol. 1: Books 1–3*, trans. H. St. J. Thackeray (9 vols., Cambridge, MA, 1930–1965), vol. 1, 59 [1.6.1].

31. Collis, *Celts*, 23.

32. Isidore, *The Etymologies of Isidore of Seville*, trans. Stephen A. Barney, W. J. Lewis, J. A. Beach, and Oliver Berghof (Cambridge, 2006), 198 ['ex Gallis, qui Celtici dicebantur'].

33. Robertson, *Saxon and Celt*, 46–47; Powell, *Celts*, 21; Chapman, *Celts*, 32–35.

34. Continental Celtic languages like Celtiberian, Lepontic, and Galatian all died out, though they left their mark in place names.

35. Sims-Williams, Patrick, *Irish Influence on Medieval Welsh Literature* (Oxford, 2010); *idem*, 'Celtomania', 8, 12. Underlining the point is that in medieval Welsh the words for *English*, *Irish*, and *Jew* were all terms of abuse. Nevertheless, this should not detract from the fact that the two cultures *were* cognate, as Sims-Williams discusses elsewhere: 'the name of the Welsh hero *Gwyn* ap Nudd is cognate with the name of the Irish hero *Finn* Mac Cumaill. Both can be derived from a Common Celtic *Windos* "The White One"' (Sims-Willliams, 'Some Celtic Otherworld Terms', in A.T.E. Matonis and Daniel F. Melia [eds.], *Celtic Language, Celtic Culture: A Festschrift for Eric P. Hamp* [Van Nuys, CA, 1990], 57–58).

36. Edward Gibbon, *History of the Decline and Fall of the Roman Empire* (6 vols., London, 1776–1789), vol. 1, 220–21.

37. Williams, *Ireland's Immortals*, 136.

38. See Reynolds, 'Medieval *Origines Gentium*'; Walter Goffart, *The Narrators of Barbarian History (A.D. 550–800): Jordanes, Gregory of Tours, Bede, and Paul the Deacon* (Princeton, NJ, 1988).

39. Gregory of Tours, *The History of the Franks*, trans. Lewis Thorpe (London, 1974); Goffart, *Narrators*, 426.

40. Gildas, *The Works of Gildas*, trans. J. A. Giles (London, 1841), 7–23; Huw Pryce, *Writing Welsh History: From the Early Middle Ages to the Twenty-First Century* (Oxford, 2022), 19–22.

41. Nennius, *Historia Brittonum*, trans. A. W. Wade-Evans (London, 1938), 38–45; Pryce, *Writing Welsh History*, 27–34.

42. Geoffrey of Monmouth, *The History of the Kings of Britain*, trans. Lewis Thorpe (London, 1966). See also T. D. Kendrick, *British Antiquity* (London, 1950). For an overview of origin legends in Britain, see Hugh MacDougall, *Racial Myth in English History: Trojans, Teutons, and Anglo-Saxons* (Montreal, 1982).

43. Williams, *Ireland's Immortals*, 3.

44. Huw Pryce, 'Introduction', in Huw Pryce (ed.), *Literacy in Medieval Celtic Societies* (Cambridge, 1998), 1–13.

45. Anders Ahlqvist, *The Early Irish Linguist* (Helsinki, 1983), 48. On Fénius, see John Carey, 'The Ancestry of Fénius Farsaid', *Celtica* 21 (1990), 104–12.

46. John Carey, *The Irish National Origin-Legend: Synthetic Pseudohistory* (Cambridge, 1994), 4n8, points out that Eoin MacNeill seems to have been the first to use the term in 1921.

47. Nennius, *Historia Brittonum*, 40–41; Carey, *Irish National Origin-Legend*, 5–6. On the connections between Irish and British origin stories, see Lindy Brady, *The Origin Legends of Early Medieval Britain and Ireland* (Cambridge, 2022).

48. The standard modern translation is *Lebor Gabála Érenn: The Book of the Taking of Ireland*, ed. and trans. R. A. Stewart Macalister (5 parts, Dublin, 1938–1956). For the sources behind the work, see Carey, *Irish National Origin-Legend*.

49. See the discussion and helpful narrative diagrams in Williams, *Ireland's Immortals*, 128–39, esp. 132–33.

50. Kenneth Jackson, 'The Duan Albanach', *SHR* 36 (1957), 125–37; Sir James Fergusson, *The Declaration of Arbroath 1320* (Edinburgh, 1970).

51. Colin Kidd, *Subverting Scotland's Past: Scottish Whig Historians and the Creation of an Anglo-British Identity, 1689–c. 1830* (Cambridge, 1993), 18.

52. Nicholas Hardy, *Criticism and Confession: The Bible in the Seventeenth Century Republic of Letters* (Oxford, 2017); Nicholas Hardy and Dmitri Levitin (eds.), *Confessionalisation and Erudition in Early Modern Europe: An Episode in the History of the Humanities* (Oxford, 2019).

53. Caspar Hirschi, *The Origins of Nationalism: An Alternative History from Ancient Rome to Early Modern Germany* (Cambridge, 2011).

54. For the intellectual background of politics in the Reformation, see Quentin Skinner, *The Foundations of Modern Political Thought* (2 vols., Cambridge, 1978), vol. 2.

55. Anthony Grafton, *Forgers and Critics: Creativity and Duplicity in Western Scholarship* (London, 1990).

56. Anthony Grafton's *Joseph Scaliger: A Study in the History of Classical Scholarship* (2 vols., Oxford, 1983–1993) is the work most often identified at the heart of this scholarly revolution. On the history of scholarship, see C. R. Ligota and J.-L. Quantin, *History of Scholarship* (Oxford, 2006), and on the history of knowledge, see Peter Burke, *A Social History of Knowledge* (2 vols., Cambridge, 2000–2012).

57. Anthony Grafton, *Defenders of the Text: The Traditions of Scholarship in an Age of Science, 1450–1800* (Cambridge, MA, 1994); Anthony Grafton and Joanna Weinberg, *'I Have Always Loved the Holy Tongue': Isaac Casaubon, the Jews, and a Forgotten Chapter in Renaissance Scholarship* (Cambridge, MA, 2011); James Turner, *Philology: The Forgotten Origins of the Modern Humanities* (Princeton, NJ, 2014).

58. Anthony Grafton, *New Worlds, Ancient Texts: The Power of Tradition and the Shock of Discovery* (Cambridge, MA, 1992).

59. On English interest in the Near East, see G. J. Toomer, *John Selden: A Life in Scholarship* (Oxford, 2009); *idem*, *Eastern Wisedome and Learning: The Study of Arabic in Seventeenth-Century England* (Oxford, 1996). On European intellectual interest in the Near East, see Dmitri Levitin, *Ancient Wisdom in the Age of the New Science: Histories of Philosophy in England, c. 1640–1700* (Cambridge, 2015); *idem*, 'From Sacred History to the History of Religion: Paganism,

Judaism, and Christianity in European Historiography from Reformation to "Enlightenment"', *HJ* 55 (2012), 1117–60.

60. John Leyden to Lt. Col. Richardson, n.d. [1806], British Library (hereafter BL), Add MS 26565, f. 4v.

61. Jean Bodin, *Method for the Easy Comprehension of History*, trans. Beatrice Reynolds (1566: New York, 1945), 346.

62. Arno Borst, *Der Turmbau von Babel: Geschichte der Meinungen über Ursprung und Vielfalt der Sprachen und Völker* (4 vols. in 6, Stuttgart, 1957–1963), esp. vols. 3.1 and 3.2.

63. Anthony T. Grafton, 'Joseph Scaliger and Historical Chronology: The Rise and Fall of a Discipline', *History and Theory* 14 (1975), 156–85.

64. Grafton, 'Joseph Scaliger', 164–66.

65. Annius's commentaries on the Pseudo-Berosus fragments are extracted and translated in R. A. Asher, *National Myths in Renaissance France: Francus, Samothes and the Druids* (Edinburgh, 1993), 194–226.

66. Asher, *National Myths*, 205.

67. Anthony Grafton, 'Invention of Traditions and Traditions of Invention in Renaissance Europe: The Strange Case of Annius of Viterbo', in Anthony Grafton and Ann Blair (eds.), *The Transmission of Culture in Early Modern Europe* (Philadelphia, PA, 1990), 9. For the use of the Gauls and Celts in Germany, see Frank L. Borchardt, *German Antiquity in Renaissance Myth* (Baltimore, MD, 1971), 89–121.

68. See Herfried Münkler, Hans Grünberger, and Kathrin Mayer, *Nationenbildung: Die Nationalisierung Europa im Diskurs humanistischer Intellektueller. Italien und Deutschland* (Berlin, 1998), 244 [see 242–61 for Annius's impact on German humanism].

69. Borst, *Der Turmbau*, vol. 3.1, 1119–34; Nicolet, *La fabrique*, 40–56.

70. Borst, *Der Turmbau*, vol. 3.1, 1053–55.

71. Bodin, *Method*, 346, complains of exactly this.

72. Colette Beaune, *Naissance de la nation France* (Paris, 1985), 33.

73. For a masterful overview, on which I rely throughout this section, see Toon Van Hal, 'From *Alauda* to *Zythus*. The Emergence and Uses of Old-Gaulish Word Lists in Early Modern Publications', *Keltische Forschungen* 6 (2014), 219–77.

74. For an overview, see Claude-Gilbert Dubois, *Celtes et Gaulois au XVIe siècle: Le développement littéraire d'un mythe nationaliste* (Paris, 1972); Asher, *National Myths*; Beaune, *Naissance*, 19–54.

75. Jean le Maire de Belges, *Les Illustrations de Gaule et singularitez de Troye* (Lyon, 1549), 24–27. This detail was apparently present from an essay of Paolo Emili's composed around 1487 but now lost, which is identified by several historians as an important pre-Annian work that calls attention to France's Gaulish past (Beaune, *Naissance*, 34). See also 'Emili, Paolo', in *Treccani*, accessed 25 July 2023, https://www.treccani.it/enciclopedia/paolo-emili_(Dizionario-Biografico)/.

76. Daniel Droixhe, *L'Étymon des dieux: Mythologie gauloise, archéologie et linguistique à l'âge Classique* (Geneva, 2002), 15–17.

77. Asher, *National Myths*, 47.

78. See John Considine, *Dictionaries in Early Modern Europe: Lexicography and the Making of Heritage* (Cambridge, 2008), 61–63. Estienne's denial of French's Latin roots should not be

overlooked. Joachim Périon, *Dialogues de l'origine du français et de sa parenté avec le grec*, trans. Geneviève Demerson and Alberte Jacquetin (Paris, 2003); Bodin, *Method*, 344, 352.

79. Léon Trippault, *Celt'-hellenisme ou, Etymologie des mots françois tirez du græc* (Orléans, 1580), esp. 302–5. Bodin, *Method*, 108, also noted the etymological idea of milky-white Gaulish skin.

80. Kees Meerhoff, *Rhétorique et Poétique au XVI*[e] *siècle en France* (Leiden, 1986), 276–77.

81. See, for example, Guillaume Postel, *Histoire memorable des expditions depuys le Deluge faictes par les Gauloys ou Françoys depuis la France jusque en Asie* (Paris, 1552); Meerhoff, *Rhétorique*, 276–88; William J. Bouwsma, *Concordia Mundi: The Career and Thought of Guillaume Postel (1510–1581)* (Cambridge, MA, 1957), 220–22, 261. For a further list of works arguing that the Hellenistic civilizations derived their learning from Gaul, see Marian Rothstein, 'The Reception of Annius of Viterbo's Forgeries', *Renaissance Quarterly* 71 (2018), 596–97.

82. Asher, *National Myths*, 24–25; Jacques Barzun, *The French Race: Theories of Its Origins and Their Social and Political Implications prior to the Revolution* (New York, 1932), 66–70.

83. Stefan Donecker, 'Re-inventing the "Germanic" in the Early Modern Era: *Omnes Germani sunt, contra fabulas quorundam*', in Matthias Friedrich and James M. Harland (eds.), *Interrogating the 'Germanic': A Category and Its Use in Late Antiquity and the Early Middle Ages* (Berlin, 2021), 67–88.

84. Noel L. Brann, 'Conrad Celtis and the "Druid" Abbot Trithemius: An Inquiry into Patriotic Humanism', *Renaissance and Reformation* 3 (1979), 16–28; Borchardt, *German Antiquity*, 107–8.

85. Borst, *Der Turmbau*, vol. 3.1, 1058–59.

86. Matthias von Lexer and Sigmund von Riezler (eds.), *Johannes Turmair's genannt Aventinus Sämmtliche Werke* (6 vols., Munich, 1881–1886), vol. 4, 207–10, 412. Heinrich Bebel held a similar position [Borchardt, *German Antiquity*, 108].

87. John F. D'Amico, *Theory and Practice in Renaissance Textual Criticism: Beatus Rhenanus between Conjecture and History* (Berkeley, CA, 1988), 197–99; Paul Joachimsen, *Geschichtsauffassung und Geschichtsschreibung in Deutschland unter dem Einfluss des Humanismus* (1910: Aalen, 1968), 127–28; Borst, *Der Turmbau*, vol. 3.1, 1073.

88. Beatus Rhenanus, *Rerum Germanicarum libri tres (1531)*, trans. Felix Mundt (Tübingen, 2008), 257–69, Gaulish section at 267–69.

89. Rhenanus, *Rerum Germanicarum*, 195.

90. Toon Van Hal, 'When Quotation Marks Matter: Rhellicanus and Boxhornius on the Differences between the *lingua Gallica* and *lingua Germanica*', *Historiographia Linguistica* 38 (2011), 241–52.

91. François Hotman was probably the most famous scholar influenced by Beatus. See Donald R. Kelley, *Foundations of Modern Historical Scholarship: Language, Law, and History in the French Renaissance* (New York, 1970), 201–11; George Huppert, *The Idea of Perfect History: Historical Erudition and Historical Philosophy in Renaissance France* (Urbana, IL, 1970), 78–81; Hotman, *Francogallia*, 167.

92. Sebastian Münster, *La Cosmographie universelle, contenant la situation de toutes les parties du monde avec leurs proprietez & appartenances* (Paris, 1552), 361.

93. Conrad Gessner, *Mithridates*, ed. and trans. Bernard Colombat and Manfred Peters (Geneva, 2009), 142–60.

94. Bernard Colombat and Manfred Peters, 'Introduction', in *Mithridates*, 35–39.

95. Gessner, *Mithridates*, 258. For a general overview, see Erich Poppe, 'The Celtic Languages in Conrad Gessner's *Mithridates* (1555)', *Zeitschrift für Celtische Philologie* 45 (1992), 240–50.

96. Kelley, *Foundations*; Sophie Nicholls, *Political Thought in the French Wars of Religion* (Cambridge, 2021), 62–93.

97. Guillaume Postel, *La Loy salique* (Paris, 1552), esp. Ch. 6.

98. Bodin, *Method*, 351.

99. Bodin, *Method*, 352. Van Hal identifies Bodin as an early examplar of a more systematic use of language and linguistic comparisons for history writing (Van Hal, 'From *Alauda*', 232–33).

100. See Petrus Ramus, *Traitté des meurs et facons des anciens Gauloys*, trans. Michel de Castenau (Paris, 1581).

101. Hotman, *Francogallia*, 147–55, 181, 209, 217.

102. Many more examples of French humanists stressing France's Gallic origins and, not unrelatedly, the extent of ancient Gaulish/Celtic conquest [here the equation of the two terms was helpful], could be adduced—Dubois includes some sixty works in his bibliography (Dubois, *Celtes*, 177–82)—but this would be redundant.

103. On humanist linguistic scholarship in the Low Countries, see Toon Van Hal, *'Moedertalen en taalmoeders'. Het vroegmoderne taalvergelijkende onderzoek in de Lage Landen* (Brussels, 2010).

104. Van Hal, *'Moedertalen'*, 92.

105. Hadrianus Junius, *Batavia* (Leiden, 1588), 375–81.

106. Van Hal, *'Moedertalen'*, 151–54; Van Hal 'From *Alauda*', 239–40.

107. Van Hal, *'Moedertalen'*, *passim*; *idem*, 'A Man of Eight Hearts: Hadrianus Junius and Sixteenth-Century Plurilingualism', in Dirk van Miert (ed.), *The Kaleidoscopic Scholarship of Hadrianus Junius (1511–1575): Northern Humanism at the Dawn of the Dutch Golden Age* (Leiden, 2011), 209n75; *idem*, 'Reviving the Old Teutonic Language: An Unpublished Preface by Abraham Mylius (1563–1637) retrieved in Gottfired Wilhelm Leibniz's Heritage', *Lias* 38 (2011), 129–47, esp. 145–46.

108. For Germano-Celtic theories and Clüver, see Daniel Droixhe, *La Linguistique et l'appel de l'histoire (1600–1800): rationalisme et révolutions positivistes* (Geneva, 1978), 126–42.

109. Philipp Clüver, *Germania antiqua libre tres* (Lugduni Batavorum, 1616), 41.

110. Clüver, *Germania antiqua*, 55, and see 29–40 for his strictures against Bodin. On Clüver's linguistic ideas, see Toon Van Hal, 'One Continent, One Language?: *Europa Celtica* and Its Language in Philippus Cluverius' *Germania antiquia* (1616) and Beyond', *European Review of History* 21 (2014), 889–907; George J. Metcalf, *On Language Diversity and Relationship from Bibliander to Adelung*, ed. Toon Van Hal and Raf Van Rooy (Amsterdam, 2013), 105–22. Historians agree that Clüver developed a sophisticated method for uncovering similarities across European languages, and that he recognised certain families, but that he saw them as residing within a monogenetic comparative framework that tried to reconcile European to unrelated linguistic families.

111. Philipp Clüver, *An Introduction into Geography, both Ancient and Moderne, comprised in sixe books* (Oxford, 1657), 49–50, 126–27.

112. Clüver, *Germania antiqua*, 38.

113. Toon Van Hal, 'On "the Scythian Theory": Reconstructing the Outlines of Johannes Elichmann's (1601/1602–1639) Planned Archaeologia Harmonica', *Language & History* 53 (2010), 70–80.

114. See Toon Van Hal, 'A Precursor and Successor to William Jones: Marcus Zuerius van Boxhorn's Contribution to the Scythian Theory and Comparative Linguistics', *Erudition and the Republic of Letters* 7 (2022), 302–53; Droixhe, *L'Étymon, passim*; *idem*, *La Linguistique*, 93–99.

115. Marcus Zuerius van Boxhorn, *Antwoord van Marcus Zuerius van Boxhorn, Gegeven Op de Vraaghen, hem voorgestelt over de Bediedinge van de Afgodinne Nehalennia* (Leiden, 1647), 90, 94.

116. Marcus Zuerius van Boxhorn, *Originum Gallicarum liber* (Leiden, 1654), 5, 49–52.

117. Prys Morgan, 'Boxhorn and the Welsh: Some Cambro-Dutch Contacts in the Seventeenth Century', *Dutch Crossing* 24 (2000), 183–90.

118. For a fascinating philological examination of Boxhorn's Celto-Germanic assumption, see Van Hal, 'When Quotation Marks Matter', 241–52.

119. Graham Parry, *The Trophies of Time: English Antiquarians of the Seventeenth Century* (Oxford, 1995).

120. Felicity Heal, 'What Can King Lucius Do for You? The Reformation and the Early British Church', *EHR* 120 (2005), 593–614.

121. Glynn Parry, 'Berosus and the Protestants: Reconstructing Protestant Myth', *Huntingdon Library Quarterly* 64 (2001), 1–21.

122. John Bale, *Illustrium maioris Britanniae scriptorium* (London, 1548), 'centuria prima', sig. Bii ['terras Celticas, quas postea Britanniam ac Gallia vocabant'].

123. Kendrick, *British Antiquity*, 72–79.

124. Holinshed, *Chronicles of England, Scotlande, and Irelande* (4 vols., London, 1577), vol. 1, 1, 13 (accessed 26 July 2022, http://english.nsms.ox.ac.uk/holinshed/texts.php?text1=1577_0045&text2=1587_0061).

125. Anthony Munday, *The Triumphes of re-vnited Britania* (London, 1605), sig. Aii^{r-v}.

126. David Armitage, *The Ideological Origins of the British Empire* (Cambridge, 2000), 36–39.

127. Roger A. Mason, 'Scotching the Brut: Politics, History and National Myth in Sixteenth-Century Britain', in Roger A. Mason (ed.), *Scotland and England, 1286–1815* (Edinburgh, 1987), 60–84.

128. George Buchanan, *History of Scotland*, (1582: 2 vols., London, 1733), vol. 1, 47–99. John Major (*c.* 1467–1550) also dropped the Gathelus myth.

129. On Buchanan's understanding and use of 'Celtic', see John Collis, 'George Buchanan and the Celts in Britain', in Ronald Black, William Gillies, and Roiebeard Ó Maolalaigh (eds.), *Celtic Connections* (East Linton, 1999), 91–107.

130. Kidd, *Subverting Scotland's Past*, 12–29; *idem*, *British Identities*, 123–45.

131. Parry, *Trophies*, 22–48.

132. William Camden, *Britain, or a Chorographicall Description of the Most flourishing Kingdomes, England, Scotland, and Ireland, and Islands adioyning, out of the depth of Antiquitie*, trans. Philémon Holland (London, 1610), 1–23. Camden dismissed the 'Milesian fables' with an asterisked marginal note reading 'Old wives tales' on page 16.

133. Camden, *Britain*, 16–17. Importantly, Camden praised authors like Rhenanus and Hotman, who separated Gaulish from German.

134. See, for example, Samuel Bochart, *Geographia sacrae, seu Phaleg et Canaan* (3rd ed., 2 vols., Leiden, 1707), vol. 1, 660.

135. Kidd, *British Identities*, 99–122.

136. Caryl Davies, *Adfeilion Babel: Agweddau ar Syniadaeth Ieithyddol y Ddeunawfed Ganrif* (Caerdydd, 2000), *passim*, but esp. 1–30.

137. Quotation in Davies, *Adfeilion Babel*, 13–14.

138. John Davies, *Antique linguae Britannicae* (London, 1632), 'ad lectorem', sig. **r.

139. van Boxhorn, *Antwoord*, 92; *idem*, *Originum*, 89–94.

140. John Wallis, *Grammaticae linguae Anglicanae* (London, 1653); see John Considine, *Small Dictionaries and Curiosity: Lexicography and Fieldwork in Post-Medieval Europe* (Oxford, 2017), 123–24.

141. 'Celt, Celtiad, Ceiltiaid', in *Geiriadur Prifysgol Cymru*, accessed 5 August 2022, https://geiriadur.ac.uk/gpc/gpc.html.

142. Kidd, *British Identities*, 83

143. Kidd, *British Identities*, 62–63, 75–98, 185–210.

144. Richard Verstegan, *A Restitution of Decayed Intelligence* (1605: London, 1634), 28. He was drawing on the observation of Johann Carion, *Mathematici chronicorum* (Lyon, 1554), 135.

145. John Speed, *The history of Great Britaine* (London, 1611), 162.

146. Robert Sheringham, *De Anglorum gentis origine disceptatio* (London, 1670), 58 ['Cimbros alia quoque cum aliis gentibus communia nomina habuisse, quos aliquando Celtas, aliquando Germanos, aliquando Gallos, aliquando Galatas, veteres appellavere'].

147. George Berkeley, *A Word to the Wise; Or, the Bishop of Cloyne's Exhortation to the Roman Catholick Clergy, of Ireland* (4th ed., Boston, 1750), 2–4.

148. Clare O'Halloran, *Golden Ages and Barbarous Nations: Antiquarian Debate and Cultural Politics in Ireland, c. 1750–1800* (Cork, 2004), 3.

149. Elizabethanne Boran, *The Correspondence of James Ussher, 1600–1656* (3 vols., Dublin, 2015), vol. 2, 684. On this exchange, see Joep Leerssen, 'Archbishop Ussher and Gaelic Culture', *Studia Hibernica* 22/23 (1982/1983), 50–58.

150. Boran, *Correspondence of James Ussher*, vol. 2, 716–17.

151. Bernadette Cunningham, *The Annals of the Four Masters: Irish History, Kingship and Society in the Early Seventeenth Century* (Dublin, 2010).

152. Bernadette Cunningham, *The World of Geoffrey Keating: History, Myth and Religion in Seventeenth-Century Ireland* (Dublin, 2004).

153. Eventually the book was translated into English by Dermot O'Connor (*c.* 1690–*c.* 1730) and published in 1723.

154. Geoffrey Keating, *The General History of Ireland* (1723: 2nd ed., London, 1732), 89–97.

155. See, for example, Morse, *Celts*. But this is a widespread misconception found often in the popular overviews of the Celts.

Chapter Two: Celtic Linguistic Antiquarianism

1. Michael Fryer (ed.), *The Trial and Life of Eugene Aram* (Richmond, 1832), 66.

2. Fryer, *Eugene Aram*, 78–79.

3. Tobias Smollett, *The History of England, From the Revolution in 1688, to the Death of George II* (1785: 5 vols., London, 1805), vol. 5, 531.

4. Edward Lhuyd, *Archaeologia Britannica: Vol. 1 Glossography* (Oxford, 1707). Lhwyd varied the spelling of his name, but I have opted for 'Lhwyd' in the text and only use 'Lhuyd' when that it is how it appears on a published work.

5. Prys Morgan, 'The Abbé Pezron and the Celts', *THSC* (1965), 286–95; Davies, *Adfeilion Babel*, 60–153, *passim*; Daniel R. Davis (ed.), *Celtic Linguistics* (8 vols, London, 2000), vol. 1, xi.

6. For an excellent work on the conjuncture of early modern physical and linguistic antiquarianism [roughly 'archaeology' and 'philology'], see Droixhe, *L'Étymon des dieux*.

7. John H. Davies (ed.), *The Letters of Lewis, Richard, William, and John Morris* (2 vols., Aberystwyth, 1907–1909), vol. 2, 126.

8. G. Bonfante, 'A Contribution to the History of Celtology', *Celtica* 3 (1956), 17; Droixhe, *La linguistique*, 61.

9. Johanne Ihre, *Glossarium suiogothicum* (2 vols., Uppsala, 1769), vol. 1, ii. Thanks to John Considine for this reference.

10. Morgan, 'Abbé Pezron', 286.

11. *Mercure Galant*, December 1706, 69–72.

12. Though his works have been discussed frequently by scholars interested in the history of chronology and Celticism, Pezron has never received a thorough biographical treatment. For aspects of his scholarship, see Morgan, 'Abbé Pezron'; Kidd, *British Identities*, 66–70; Grafton, 'Joseph Scaliger', 178–79; Adam Sutcliffe, *Judaism and Enlightenment* (Cambridge, 2003), 64.

13. P. Pezron, 'Copie d'une Lettre de Mr. l'Abbé de la CHARMOYE, à Mr. l'Abbé Nicaise', *Nouvelles de la République des lettres* (1699), 627–39; G. W. Leibniz, *Sämtliche Schriften und Briefe*, Reihe 1 (Berlin, 2000), vol. 16, 782–89.

14. The work might have grown out of the etymologies, because in 1698 Pezron told Martin Lister (1639–1712) that 'he had *800* Greek Words perfect *Celtique*' (Martin Lister, *A Journey to Paris in the Year 1698* [London, 1699], 96).

15. See P. Pezron, *Antiquité de la nation et de la langue des Celtes, autrement appellez Gaulois* (Paris, 1703), 155–63.

16. Bizarrely, Pezron included almost no discussion of the Gomerian/Titan settlement of Gaul and merely stated that it happened [see, for example, *Antiquité*, 186].

17. Pezron, *Antiquité*, sig. e iii^{r-v}; see also 329–30.

18. Pezron, *Antiquité*, 181–328.

19. Well before his work on the Celts, Pezron had seen the Scythians as of central importance for the history of Eurasian migrations. See Pezron, *Essay d'un commentaire litteral et historique sur les prophetes* (Paris, 1693).

20. See Droixhe, *La linguistique*, 90–92, for a discussion of Salmasius.

21. Pezron aligning himself with Salmasius rather than Boxhorn is a little ironic, considering that Salmasius thought that searching for Celtic origins was futile due to ancient Greek ethnographic confusion, and that Boxhorn had folded Welsh, and therefore Breton, into his Scythian theory [see Claudius Salmasius, *De Hellenistica commentarius* (Leiden, 1643), 371].

22. Pezron, *Antiquité*, 239. Pezron stated it was a general rule that a greater quantity of monosyllables equated to greater antiquity, an idea he might have picked up from his reading of Salmasius (Salmasius, *De Hellenistica commentarius*, 390).

23. Julien Maunoir, *Le Sacré college de Jesus, divisé en cinq classes, ou l'on enseigne en langue Armorique les leçons Chrestiennes avec les 3. clefs pour y entrer, un Dictionnaire, une Grammaire & Syntaxe en méme langue* (Quimper-Corentin, 1659), 10–12.

24. There were of course earlier works on the Gauls, for example Antoine Gosselin, *Historia Gallorum veterum* (Caen, 1636), which began with Caesar and focused on the Gauls and their Greek connections. This inspired a refutation from Bochart, who targeted Gosselin in an early

essay outlining his Phoenician theory of 1637 that was known in the world of letters; Pierre Bayle (1647–1706) was, for example, aware of Bochart's essay in 1678 before it was printed in Bochart's collected works in 1692 [see *Nouvelles lettres de Mr P. Bayle* (2 vols., The Hague, 1739), vol. 2, 55].

25. Bochart, *Geographia sacra*, vol. 1, 660–82.

26. This pattern can be found in, for example, François Eudes de Mézeray, *L'histoire de France*, 2nd ed. (3 vols., Paris, 1685), vol. 1, 3–21.

27. Pezron, *Antiquité*, 394.

28. Pezron, 'Copie d'une Lettre', 631.

29. Pezron, *Antiquité*, 15–19.

30. Pezron, *Antiquité*, 53, 82, 111.

31. Paul-Yves Pezron, *The Rise and Fall of States and Empires* (London, 1809).

32. For Pezron's influence on the British, see Kidd, *British Identities*, 66–72. For his impact on Welsh antiquarianism, see esp. Davies, *Adfeilion Babel*, *passim*; Pryce, *Writing Welsh History*, 186–204.

33. See, for example, Nancy Edwards, 'Edward Lhuyd and the Origins of Early Medieval Celtic Archaeology', *Antiquaries Journal* 87 (2007), 165–96.

34. For the first full biography of Lhwyd, see Brynley Roberts, *Edward Lhwyd: c. 1660–1709, Naturalist, Antiquary, Philologist* (Cardiff, 2022).

35. Lhwyd to John Aubrey, [12 Feb 1687?], Bodlein Library Archives, MS Aubrey 12, fol. 240, in Howard Hotson and Miranda Lewis (eds.), *Early Modern Letters Online*, accessed 26 June 2022, http://emlo.bodleian.ox.ac.uk. The Edward Lhwyd correspondence has been digitised on this invaluable database, hereafter cited as *EMLO*. These letters were all consulted in June and July of 2022. Wyld seems to have had a good collection of books on the 'Celtic' languages and Lhwyd later wrote that it was Wyld who first encouraged him to study 'British Antiquities' (Lhwyd to Aubrey, 16 November 1693, *EMLO*).

36. Joep Leerssen, *Mere Irish and fíor-ghael: Studies in the Idea of Irish Nationality, Its Development and Literary Expression prior to the Nineteenth Century* (1986: 2nd ed., Cork, 1996), 281–93; Considine, *Small Dictionaries*, 123–24.

37. William Temple, *An Introduction to the History of England* (London, 1695), 26–27. Emphasis in original.

38. John Toland, 'A Specimen of the Critical History of the Celtic Religion and Learning', in *A Collection of Several Pieces of John Toland* (2 vols., London, 1726), vol. 1, 1–183, Lhwyd at 32.

39. Lhwyd to Richard Jones, 1688, *EMLO*. Biscay here refers to Basque.

40. On Bernard, see John Considine, 'Stephen Skinner's *Etymologicon* and Other English Etymological Dictionaries, 1650–1700', *Studia Etymologica Cracoviensia* 14 (2009), 123–51.

41. van Boxhorn, *Originum*, 86.

42. 'Mredydh Owen' (Lhwyd) to Robert Plot, 20 May 1690, *EMLO*.

43. Lhwyd to Martin Lister, 17 April 1692(?), *EMLO*.

44. Edward Lhwyd to John Aubrey, Oxford, 9 January 1694, *EMLO*.

45. On Toland's self-inflated retrospection, see also Considine, *Small Dictionaries*, 131.

46. Edward Lhwyd, 'A design of a British dictionary, historical and geographical; with an essay, entitled, *Archaeologia Britannica*: and a natural history of Wales' (1695), in Dewi Wyn Evans and Brynley F. Roberts, *Edward Lhuyd: Archaeologia Britannica. Texts and Translations* (Aberystwyth, 2007), 35–39.

47. Lhwyd, 'A design'.

48. See R. T. Gunther (ed.), *Life and Letters of Edward Lhuyd* (Oxford, 1945); J. L. Campbell and Derick Thomson (eds.), *Edward Lhuyd in the Scottish Highlands, 1699–1700* (Oxford, 1963).

49. On Lhwyd's time in Ireland, see J. L. Campbell, 'The Tour of Edward Lhuyd in Ireland in 1699 and 1700', *Celtica* 5 (1960), 218–28; Richard Sharpe (ed.), *Roderick O'Flaherty's Letters: To William Molyneux, Edward Lhwyd, and Samuel Molyneux, 1696–1709* (Dublin, 2013), 93–110.

50. Edward Lhwyd to Henry Rowlands, 10 March 1701, *EMLO*.

51. This paragraph owes much to Considine's excellent and fresh summary in *Small Dictionaries*, 127–46.

52. William Nicolson, *The Scottish Historical Library* (London, 1702), 346; Edward Lhwyd to Josiah Babington, Oxford, 14 October 1703, *EMLO*. See Considine, *Small Dictionaries*, 137–38, for discussion.

53. David Cram, 'Edward Lhuyd and the Doctrine of the Permutation of Letters', in Gerde Haßler and Peter Schmitter (eds.), *Sprachdiskussion und Beschreibung von Sprachen im 17. und 18. Jahrhundert* (Münster, 1999), 317–35.

54. Edward Lhuyd, 'The Preface', in Evans and Roberts, *Edward Lhwyd*, 55. For Lhwyd's historical purpose and its context, see Pryce, *Writing Welsh History*, 175–85.

55. Lhwyd, 'The Preface', 56.

56. van Boxhorn, *Originum*, 86–89.

57. 'Mredydh Owen' to Robert Plot, 20 May 1690, *EMLO*.

58. Lhwyd to Lister, 5 June 1698, *EMLO*.

59. van Boxhorn, *Originum*, 86 [Id potius ex illo sermonis consensu sequitur, ex eadem gente, tamquam matre, id est Scythica, prodiisse has nationes, et ab eadem eundem sermonem, sed dialecto fere tantum distantem, didicisse].

60. *Pace* Janet Sorensen, '"Genuine Remains": The Celtic Linguistic Artifact in Eighteenth-Century Britain', *Modern Philology* 113 (2016), 388–89, who suggests that a belief in a 'shared ancestral, no longer known, language' underwrote Lhwyd's evolutionary model of linguistic kinship of the Celtic languages with others like Latin.

61. Another possibility is that 'Old Latin' referred to a language anterior to Latin.

62. Edward Lhwyd to John Morton, Oxford, 2 March 1703/4, *EMLO*.

63. Lhwyd, *Archaeologia*, 263.

64. Evans and Roberts, *Edward Lhwyd*, 173.

65. Lhwyd to Aubrey, Oxford, 3 April [1692?], *EMLO*.

66. Lhwyd to John Ray, 25 November 1690, *EMLO*.

67. John Ray to EL, 10 July 1694, *EMLO*.

68. Richard L. Harris (ed.), *A Chorus of Grammars: The Correspondence of George Hickes and His Collaborators on the* Thesaurus linguarum septentrionalium (Toronto, 1992), 151–53.

69. See, for example, William Stonestreet to Lhwyd, 4 November 1703, *EMLO*.

70. See, for example, Morse, *Celts*, 24–26; Sharpe, *Roderick O'Flaherty's Letters*, 214–15.

71. See, for example, Evans and Roberts, 'Introduction', in *Edward Lhwyd*, 19.

72. Edward Lhwyd to Lister, Pembroke, 5 June 1698, *EMLO*; *Pace* Sharpe, *Roderick O'Flaherty's Letters*, 214–15n24.

73. In 1764, Evan Evans wrote that he had some of Lhwyd's papers and 'his abridgment of the contents of Pezron's book' [see Daniel Silvan Evans (ed.), *Gwaith y Parchedig Evan Evans* (Caernarfon, 1876), 187].

74. Evans and Roberts, *Edward Lhwyd*, 9–11.

75. 'A letter from Mr William Baxter to Dr Hans Sloane', in Evans and Roberts, *Edward Lhwyd*, 233–36.

76. Sigrid von der Schulenberg, *Leibniz als Sprachforscher* (Frankfurt, 1973); Maria Rosa Antognazza, *Leibniz: An Intellectual Biography* (Cambridge, 2009), 323–30; Michael C. Carhart, *Leibniz Discovers Asia: Social Networking in the Republic of Letters* (Baltimore, MD, 2019).

77. There are many statements to this effect throughout his massive corpus of writings, but the canonical one is the 'Brevis designatio meditationum de Originibus Gentium, ductis potissimum ex indicio linguarum', read to the Berlin Academy of Sciences in 1710 [see *Miscellanea berolinensia* 1 (1710), 1–16]. See also Toon Van Hal, 'Sprachen, die Geshcichte schreiben. Zu Leibniz' sprachhistorischem Forschungsprogramm und dessen Nachwirkung', in Wenchao Li (ed.), *Einheit der Vernunft und Vielfalt der Sprachen: Beiträge zu Leibnizens Sprachforschung und Zeichentheorie* (Stuttgart, 2014), 177–206; Droixhe, *La linguistique*, 132–38.

78. For Leibniz and Bernard, see Michael C. Carhart, 'Practices of Intellectual Labor in the Republic of Letters: Leibniz and Edward Bernard on Language and European Origins', *JHI* 80 (2019), 365–86.

79. G. W. Leibniz, *Sämtliche Schriften und Briefe*, R. 1, (Berlin, 1964), vol. 7, 416.

80. Leibniz, *Sämtliche Schriften*, R. 1, vol. 7, 365–67; John T. Waterman (ed.), *Leibniz and Ludolf on Things Linguistic: Excerpts from Their Correspondence (1688–1703)* (Berkeley, CA, 1978), 21. N.B. that Waterman confused the lingua Britannica with English.

81. Leibniz, *Sämtliche Schriften*, R. 1, (Berlin, 1992), vol. 9, 650.

82. Leibniz, *Sämtliche Schriften*, R. 1 (Berlin, 1970), vol. 8, 297, 402, 417

83. Leibniz, *Sämtliche Schriften*, R. 1, vol. 9, 268, 330, 650.

84. Leibniz, *Sämtliche Schriften*, R. 1 (Berlin, 1982), vol. 11, 491.

85. Leibniz, *Sämtliche Schriften*, R. 1 (Berlin, 1993), vol. 14, 561.

86. G. W. Leibniz, 'Unvorgreifliche Gedanken, betreffend die Ausübung und Verbesserung der detuschen Sprache', in G. W. Leibniz, *L'harmonie des langues*, ed. and trans. M. Crépon (Paris, 2000), 68–70.

87. Leibniz, *Sämtliche Schriften*, R. 1 (Berlin, 1998), vol. 15, 465 [Ego sub Celtarum nomine comprehendo Germanos Gallosque veteres, atque adeo etiam quod hodie est in Cambrica vel Aremorica. Quod ergo commune Germanico, Latino, vel Cambrico, id Celticum mihi: Latino, inquam, qua Graeco differt].

88. Leibniz, *Sämtliche Schriften*, R. 1, vol. 15, 481 [Ich nenne zeltisch, was Teutsch und Gallisch und das alte Gallische suche ich theils im Cambrischen oder Britannischen theils in dem lateinischen und denen aus dem lateinischen Verderbten Sprachen . . . Ich vermuthe aber daß das uhralte teutsch dem Cambrischen und Lateinischen näher gewesen, als es iezo ist, und daß das Gallische gleichsam ein Mittel gewesen zwischen teutsch und lateinisch. Ich verstehe das Latein, so viel es nicht aus den Griechischen]. I am grateful to John Considine for assistance with this translation.

89. 'Einleitung', in Leibniz, *Sämtliche Schriften*, R. 1 (Berlin, 2000), vol. 16, xliii.

90. Leibniz, *Sämtliche Schriften*, R. 1, vol. 16, 677, 705–7; R. 1, (Berlin, 2001), vol. 17 A, 142; R. 1 (Berlin, 2001), vol. 17 B, 470, 472, 598.

91. On Leibniz and Irish, see Erich Poppe, 'Leibniz and Eckhart on the Irish Language', *Eighteenth-Century Ireland/Iris an dá chultúr* 1 (1986), 65–84, which I have relied on here. However, my account includes new evidence showing Leibniz's earlier engagement with Irish that

Poppe did not have access to because Leibniz's correspondence to that point had not yet been published.

92. Leibniz, *Sämtliche Schriften*, R. 1 (Berlin, 1979), vol. 10, 183.

93. Leibniz, *Sämtliche Schriften*, R. 1, vol. 10, 654; R. 1, vol. 11, 273–74.

94. Leibniz, *Sämtliche Schriften*, R. 1 (Berlin, 2013), vol. 23, 182–83.

95. Leibniz, *Sämtliche Schriften*, R. 1, vol. 23, 503–4.

96. G. W. Leibniz, 'Nouveaux essais sur l'entendement humain', in Leibniz, *Sämtliche Schriften*, R. 6 (Berlin, 1990), vol. 6, 280.

97. Leibniz, *Sämtliche Schriften*, R. 1, vol. 23, 182–83.

98. *Philosophical Transactions of the Royal Society* 20 (31 August 1698), 279–80.

99. Leibniz, *Sämtliche Schriften*, R. 1, vol. 23, 772 [Edvardus Lhuydius Cambrobritannus . . . Opus aeque grande ac Hickesianum jam memoratum, molitur, in enucleandas pertinent accuratissime illustrabit].

100. Leibniz, *Sämtliche Schriften*, R. 1 (Berlin, 2015), vol. 24, 779–80. Translation from Poppe, 'Leibniz and Eckhart', 81.

101. Leibniz, *Sämtliche Schriften*, R. 1, vol. 24, 737.

102. Gottfried Wilhelm Leibniz Bibliothek, MS IV 469, ff. 220–25; Stefan Luckscheiter, 'Leibniz' Schriften zur Sprachforschung', in Li, *Einheit*, 317–432, at 343.

103. The P and C distinction appears on f. 221r (corresponding to Lhwyd, *Archaeologia*, 35) and the bottom of f. 224v (which might correspond to Lhwyd, *Archaeologia*, 20 and 38).

104. Gottfried Wilhelm Leibniz Bibliothek, MS IV 469, ff. 221–23 corresponds roughly to Lhwyd, *Archaeologia*, 30–37.

105. von der Schulenberg, *Leibniz*, 93–95.

106. G. W. Leibniz, 'Nouveaux essais sur l'entendement humain', 280–81.

107. Leibniz, 'Brevis designatio', esp. 9–12.

108. G. W. Leibniz, *Collectanea etymologica*, ed. J. G. Eckhart (Hannover, 1717), 153–54.

109. 'Abstract of M. P. Pezron', Classified Papers of the Royal Society, 22i/48, London.

110. Nearly a century and a half later, this still irked Thomas Price (Thomas Price to Taliesin Williams, 24 March 1840, National Library of Wales, 21275E). Some scholars attribute Lhwyd's lack of impact to later antiquarians being unable to comprehend his virtuoso study. See, for example, Chapman, *The Celts*, 208; Prys Morgan, 'A Death to a View: The Hunt for the Welsh Past in the Romantic Period', in Hobsbawm and Ranger, *Invention of Tradition*, 68–69.

111. Scott Mandelbrote, 'The Bible and National Identity in the British Isles, *c.*1650–1750', in Tony Claydon and Ian McBride (eds.), *Protestantism and National Identity: Britain and Ireland, c. 1650–c. 1850* (Cambridge, 1998), 162.

112. Pryce, *Writing Welsh History*, 191–92.

113. Rowlands to Lhwyd, 5 February 1702/3, *EMLO*.

114. On Rowlands, see Davies, *Adfeilion Babel*, 110–23; Pryce, *Writing Welsh History*, 193–96.

115. Henry Rowlands, *Mona Antiqua Restaurata* (1723: London, 1766), 19–22, 31–32.

116. Rowlands, *Mona Antiqua*, 295–96.

117. Rowlands, *Mona Antiqua*, 33–39, 296–97, 264–70.

118. Davies, *Adfeilion Babel*, 126–34; Morgan, 'Abbé Pezron', 286–87. The pioneering French Celticist Henri Gaidoz read the text with his Welsh philology class at the École des hautes

études in 1899–1900 [see 'Drych y Prif Oesoedd', Archives du Collège de France, Fonds Joseph Vendryès, 56 CDF 1/4].

119. B. L. Jones, 'Drych y Prif Oesoedd', *Y Traethodydd* 118 (1963), 30–47. On Evans, see Geraint H. Jenkins, *Theophilus Evans: Y Din, ei Deulu, a'i Oes* (Aberystwyth, 1993).

120. Huw Jones (ed.), *Diddanwch Teuluaidd* (London, 1763), iii.

121. Lewis Morris, *Celtic Remains* (London, 1878), lxii.

122. David Malcolme, *An Essay on the Antiquities of Great Britain and Ireland* (Edinburgh, 1738), 'Letter to W.E.M. of M.', 1.

123. Malcolme, *Essay*, 'Letter to Archimedes', 2, 20–21.

124. Alexander M'Donald, *A Galick and English Vocabulary* (Edinburgh, 1741); Considine, *Small Dictionaries*, 206–11.

125. Alexander MacDonald, *Ais-Eiridh na Sean Chánoin Albannaich* (Edinburgh, 1751), vi–viii.

126. Lesa Ní Mhunghaile, 'Ossian and the Gaelic World', in Dafydd Moore (ed.), *The International Companion to James Macpherson and* The Poems of Ossian (Edinburgh, 2017), 26–38.

127. For biographical details, see the *Oxford Dictionary of National Biography* [hereafter *ODNB*] and Donald Mackinnon, 'Collection of Ossianic Ballads of Jerome Stone', *Transactions of the Gaelic Society of Inverness* 14 (1887–1888), 314–19.

128. *Scots Magazine* 17 (1755), 91–93.

129. *Scots Magazine* 18 (1756), 15–17.

130. Jerome Stone to Thomas Tullidelph, 20 September 1755, Edinburgh University Library [hereafter EUL], La.III.251, f. 5v.

131. The unfinished manuscript is held in EUL, La.III.251.

132. Jerome Stone, 'An Enquiry Into the Original of the Nation and Language of the ancient Scots, with Conjectures about the primitive State of the Celtic, and other European Nations,' EUL, La.III.251, f. 41r, f. 39v.

133. Stone, 'An Enquiry,' f. 43r, ff. 69r-70r. Though he provided no references, it seems Stone derived his information on the settlement of Ireland from William Petty, *The Political Anatomy of Ireland* (London, 1691), 103–4, and Leibniz, *Collectanea etymologica*, 153–54. This is the same passage around which Malcolme centred his diffusionist account.

134. See, for example, Leerssen, 'Archbishop Ussher', 54; Leersen, *Mere Irish*, 321–22.

135. Sharpe, *Roderick O'Flaherty's Letters*, 215–16. This was also a direct rejection of Pezron's derivation of Greek from Celtic. Instead, O'Flaherty thought them to be original and distinct languages.

136. Sharpe, *Roderick O'Flaherty's Letters*, 43–44.

137. Toland 'Specimen', 118.

138. Alan Harrison, *The Dean's Friend: Anthony Raymond 1675–1726, Jonathan Swift and the Irish Language* (Caisleán an Bhúrcaigh, 1999).

139. Alan Harrison, 'Who Wrote to Edward Lhuyd?', *Celtica* 16 (1984), 175–78.

140. Anthony Raymond, *A Short Preliminary Discourse to the History of Ireland* (London, 1725), 6–8.

141. [Charles O'Conor], *Dissertations on the Antient History of Ireland: wherein an Account is given of the Origine, Government, Letters, Sciences, Religion, Manners and Customs, of the antient Inhabitants* (Dublin, 1753), v.

142. *Dissertations on the Antient History of Ireland*, 35–38.

143. Norman Vance, 'Celts, Carthaginians and Constitutions: Anglo-Irish Literary Relations, 1780–1820', *IHS* 22 (1981), 216–38; O'Halloran, *Golden Ages*.

144. John O'Brien, *Focalóir Gaoiodhigle-sax-bhéarle, or an Irish-English Dictionary* (Paris, 1768), i.

145. Francis Wise, *Some Enquiries concerning the First Inhabitants, Language, Religion, Learning and Letters of Europe* (Oxford, 1758), 29–30.

146. John Cleland, *The Way to Things by Words, and To Words by Things; being a Sketch of An Attempt at the Retrieval of the Antient Celtic, or, Primitive Language of Europe* (London, 1766), 7, 9 [emphasis in original]; Hal Gladfelder, *Fanny Hill in Bombay: The Making and Unmaking of John Cleland* (Baltimore, MD, 2012), 224.

147. Rowland Jones, *A Postscript to the Origin of Language and Nations* (London, 1767), 31; *idem*, 'An Universal English Grammar', 41, in *The Circles of Gomer, or, an Essay towards an Investigation and Introduction of the English as an Universal Language* (London, 1771).

148. For the Celtic origins of the Isle of Man, see William Sacheverell, *An Account of the Isle of Man* (London, 1702); Thomas Brown, *A Short Dissertation About the Mona of Caesar and Tacitus* (London, 1702).

149. Thomas Hearne, *Remarks and Collections of Thomas Hearne* (10 vols., Oxford, 1885–1915), vol. 7, 59.

150. William Baxter to Lhwyd, 27 January 1702/3, *EMLO*.

151. Grégoire de Rostrenen, *Dictionnaire François-Celtique ou François-Breton* (Rennes, 1732), 'Préface', np.

152. de Rostrenen, 'Préface'.

153. Louis le Pelletier, *Dictionnaire de la langue bretonne*, ed. Charles Taillandier (Paris, 1752), viii.

154. For Furetière, Richelet, and the Académie Françoise, see John Considine, *Academy Dictionaries 1600–1800* (Cambridge, 2014), 28–50.

155. Grégoire de Rostrenen, *Grammarie Françoise-Celtique, ou Françoise-Bretonne; qui contient Tout ce qui est nécessaire pour apprendre par les Regles la Langue Celtique, ou Bretonne* (Rennes, 1738), xv.

156. See, above all, d'Auria, *Shaping*.

157. Raymond Mas, 'Recherches sur les Gaulois et sentiment national en france au XVIIIe siecle', in Chantall Grell and Jean-Michel Dufays (eds.), *Pratiques et concepts de l'histoire en Europe XVIe-XVIIIe Siècles* (Paris, 1990), 161–221, esp. 174; Catherine Volpilhac, 'Les Gaulois à l'Académie des Inscriptions et Belles-Lettres de 1701 à 1791', in Jean Ehrard and Paul Viallaneix (eds.), *Nos ancêtres les Gaulois* (Clermont-Ferrand, 1982), 77–83, esp. 77.

158. Quoted in Mas, 'Recherches', 182–84.

159. The literature is substantial, but see, for example, Nicolet, *La fabrique*, 57–96.

160. D'Auria, *Shaping*, 87–95.

161. Thomas E. Kaiser, 'The Abbé Dubos and the Historical Defence of Monarchy in Early Eighteenth-Century France', *Studies on Voltaire & the Eighteenth Century* 267 (1989), 92–101; D'Auria, *Shaping*, 119–25.

162. See, for example, D'Auria, *Shaping*, 199–213, and *passim*; Annelien de Dijn, *French Political Thought from Montesquieu to Tocqueville: Liberty in a Levelled Society?* (Cambridge, 2008), esp. 11–39.

163. Mas, 'Recherches', 182.

164. This paragraph relies on J. Lüdtke, 'Die Debatte um die Herkunft des Französischen 1733–1757', in H.-J. Niederehe and B. Schlieben-Lange (eds.), *Die Frühgeschichte der Romanischen Philologie von Dante bis Diez* (Tübingen, 1987), 151–76; Droixhe, *La linguistique*, 144–54. See esp. the essays collected in vol. 1, 'Origines; préliminaires de l'histoire de France', and vol. 14, section 1, 'Histoire de la langue française', of C. Leber, J. B. Salgues, and J. Cohen (eds.), *Collection des meilleurs dissertations, notices et traites particuliers relatifs à l'histoire de France* (20 vols., Paris, 1826–1838).

165. Charles Pinot Duclos, *Discours sur l'origine et les révolutions des langues celtique et françoise* (Paris, 1780), esp. viii, xxiv.

166. 'Sur la langue vulgaire de la gaule', *Histoire et mémoires de l'académie royale des inscriptions et belles-letters* 23 (1756), 244–49, quotations on 244.

167. [Anne Turgot], 'Etymologie', in Denis Diderot and Jean le Rond d'Alembert (eds.), *Encyclopédie, ou dictionnaire raisonné des sciences, des arts et des metiers* (17 vols., Paris, 1751–1765), vol. 6, 98–111.

168. [Nicholas Beauzée], 'Langue', in *Encyclopédie* (17 vols., Paris, 1751–1765), vol. 9, 259.

169. Daniel Droixhe, 'Impasse du commerce: Fréret linguiste', in Chantal Grell and Catherine Volpilhac-Auger (eds.), *Nicolas Fréret, légende et verité* (Oxford, 1994), 165–75.

170. Silvan Evans, *Evan Evans*, 182–83.

171. Jean-Baptiste Bullet, *Mémoires sur la langue Celtique* (3 vols., Besançon, 1754–60), vol. 1, 6.

172. Bibliothèque nationale de France [hereafter BNF], Manuscrits français, 22132, LXXII, ff. 27–30.

173. Jean-Baptiste Bullet, *Dissertations sur différens sujets de l'histoire de France* (Bescançon, 1759), 4.

174. Evans, *Evan Evans*, 182–83; Catherine Coogan Ward and Robert E. Ward (eds.), *The Letters of Charles O'Conor of Belanagare* (2 vols., Ann Arbor, MI, 1980), vol. 1, 184–86.

175. Simon Pelloutier, *Histoire des Celtes* (2 vols., The Hague, 1740–1750), vol. 1, 155–90.

176. Pelloutier, *Histoire des Celtes*, vol. 1, 161–65.

177. Pelloutier, *Histoire des Celtes*, vol. 1, 176.

178. Pelloutier, *Histoire des Celtes*, vol. 1, 'Preface', 9.

179. J. P. Süssmilch, 'Reflexions sur la convenance de la langue celtique, et en particulier de la teutonique avec celles de l'orient', *Histoire de l'académie royale des sciences et des belles lettres de Berlin* (Berlin, 1746), 188–203. Süssmilch also contributed to Le Pelletier's Breton dictionary and carried on a correspondence with its editor (Taillandier, 'Preface', in Le Pelletier, *Dictionnaire de la Langue bretonne*, ii–iii).

180. J. G. Herder, 'Treatise on the Origin of Language', in Michael N. Forster (ed. and trans.), *Herder: Philosophical Writings* (Cambridge, 2002), 161.

181. *Pace* Morgan, 'Abbé Pezron', 286–88.

Chapter Three: Gods, Druids, and Stonehenge

1. Diogenes Laertius, *Lives of the Eminent Philosophers* (2 vols., Cambridge, MA, 1925), vol. 1, 3.

2. Jacob Brucker, *The History of Philosophy*, trans. William Enfield (2 vols., London, 1791), vol. 1, 84–85.

3. Brucker, *History of Philosophy*, vol. 1, 84–85.

4. Williams, *Ireland's Immortals*, 9–12, explains how the Celtic peoples thought of their gods locally and might not have considered them in terms of a pantheon in the Greek or Roman sense.

5. T. D. Kendrick, *The Druids: A Study in Keltic Prehistory* (London, 1927), 73–103; A. L. Owen, *The Famous Druids: A Survey of Three Centuries of English Literature on the Druids* (Oxford, 1926), 15–26; and Ronald Hutton, *Blood and Mistletoe: The History of the Druids in Britain* (New Haven, CT, 2009), 1–48 all emphasise that the classical record is not only depressingly slight but also seriously problematic and unreliable.

6. Rowlands, *Mona Antiqua*, 55; John Aubrey, *Monumenta Britannica*, ed. John Fowles and Rodney Legg (2 vols., Sherborne, 1980), vol. 1, 146.

7. William Stukeley, *Stonehenge, a temple restor'd to the British Druids* (London, 1740), preface, sig. a[2][r].

8. Kendrick, *Druids*, 8; Kelsey Jackson Williams, *The Antiquary: John Aubrey's Historical Scholarship* (Oxford, 2016), 13; Rosemary Sweet, *Antiquaries: The Discovery of the Past in Eighteenth-Century Britain* (London, 2004), 125.

9. Smiles, *Image of Antiquity*.

10. Bernard de Montfaucon, *L'Antiquité expliquée et representée en figures* (5 vols. in 10, Paris, 1722–1724), vol. 2.2, 412.

11. Asher, *National Myths*, 3.

12. Parry, *Trophies*, 34–35.

13. Rowlands, *Mona Antiqua*, 137.

14. Quoted in Owen, *Famous Druids*, 56. This remained a popular position into the nineteenth century.

15. Tom Pye, 'Histories of Liberty in Scottish Thought, 1747–1787', PhD dissertation (University of Cambridge, 2018), 39–41.

16. Here we can see how arguments for the close relationship of Hebrew and Welsh developed by figures such as John Davies and Henry Rowlands fit in: if their languages were similar and had once been identical, the same principle applied to their religions.

17. D. P. Walker, *The Ancient Theology: Studies in Christian Platonism from the Fifteenth to the Eighteenth Century* (London, 1972).

18. On the potential religious and philosophical benefits of studying ancient Near Eastern philosophy, see Levitin, *Ancient Wisdom*.

19. Kendrick, *Druids*, 16.

20. Owen, *Druids*, 31–32; D. P. Walker, 'The *Prisca Theologia* in France', *Journal of the Warburg and Courtauld Institutes* 17 (1954), 204–59, esp. 212–17.

21. [Noël Taillepied], *Histoire de l'estat et republique des druides* (Paris, 1585), 3–6. The Celts appear very little in this book, though it is clear that Taillepied understands them to be the same as the Gauls. *Celte* appears more often as a proper name.

22. Owen, *Famous Druids*, 34–35.

23. The definitive biography is Toomer, *John Selden*. For Selden and the Druids, see 84–85, 93, 115 of this work.

24. Michael Drayton, *Poly-Olbion* (London, 1612), 96–98. Around the same time Selden devoted considerable attention to pre-Roman Britain, which he understood to be related to

ancient 'Celtica' in his work on the ancient constitution [see John Selden, *The reverse or back-face of the English Janus*, trans. Redman Westcot (1610: London, 1682), 2]. Selden, perhaps influenced by the jurist Edward Coke, found in the ancient Britons the tradition of deliberative assemblies, said to be the ancestors of Parliament [see Hutton, *Blood*, 62–63].

25. Gerardus Vossius, *De theologia gentili* (Amsterdam, 1641), 259, 264. The professor of divinity at King's College Aberdeen, James Garden (1645–1726), picked up on this etymology and shared it with Aubrey in 1693 [see Michael Hunter (ed.), *The Occult Laboratory: Magic, Science, and Second Sight in Seventeenth-Century Scotland* (Woodbridge, 2001), 139–40].

26. Alexander Ross, *Pansebeia, or, a View of all the Religions in the World* (1653: 2nd ed., 1655), 148–49.

27. Thomas Smith, *Syntagma de Druidum moribus* (London, 1664), 7–8.

28. See esp. Owen, *Famous Druids*; Hutton, *Blood*.

29. 'Introduction générale', in Honoré d'Urfé, *L'Astrée*, ed. Delphine Denis (Paris, 2011), vol. 1, 48.

30. On Aubrey, see Anthony Powell, *John Aubrey and His Friends* (London, 1948); Michael Hunter, *John Aubrey and the Realm of Learning* (London, 1975); Williams, *The Antiquary*; Parry, *Trophies*, 275–307.

31. Kendrick, *Druids*, 8–9; Williams, *The Antiquary*, 20–45.

32. Aubrey, *Monumenta Brittannica*, vol. 1, 21.

33. Jackson Williams, *The Antiquary*, 33–4.

34. The etymology was incorrect.

35. Aubrey, *Monumenta Bittannica*, vol. 1, 25.

36. Aubrey, *Monumenta Britannica*, vol. 1, 31–32.

37. Aubrey, *Monumenta Britannica*, vol. 1, 128–29.

38. Aubrey, *Monumenta Britannica*, vol. 1, 124–27.

39. Aubrey, *Monumenta Britannica*, 131–50 [for Druids], 151–69 [for Bards]. See, for example, the letter from James Garden to Aubrey of 6 March 1693, where he tries to assuage some of Aubrey's fears about his theory by suggesting that the present lack of oak groves near stone circles did not mean that they had not been there in antiquity [see Hunter, *Occult Laboratory*, 135–42].

40. Aubrey, *Monumenta Britannica*, vol. 1, 528–29. Cf. Aubrey's similar passage in his 'Villare Anglicanum,' (1687) reproduced in Sims-Williams, *Ancient Celtic Place-Names*, 6.

41. It should be noted that arguments for Roman or Saxon construction continued to be made [see, for example, Sweet, *Antiquaries*, 124–25].

42. But see above all Justin Champion, *Republican Learning: John Toland and the Crisis of Christian Culture, 1696–1722* (Manchester, 2003); *idem*, *The Pillars of Priestcraft Shaken: The Church and Its Enemies, 1660–1730* (Cambridge, 1992).

43. John Toland, 'A Specimen of the Critical History of the Celtic Religion and Learning', in *A Collection of Several Pieces of John Toland* (2 vols., London, 1726), 4.

44. The most complete treatments of the work are Justin Champion, 'John Toland, the Druids, and the Politics of Celtic Scholarship', *IHS* 32 (2001), 321–42; *idem*, *Republican Learning*, 213–35.

45. Toland, 'Specimen', 8, 59.

46. Toland, 'Specimen', 8.

47. Toland, 'Specimen', 15.

48. Two such vocabularies were included in Toland, 'Specimen', 204–11 and 212–19.

49. See esp. Caryl Davies, *Adfeilion Babel: Agweddau ar Syniadaeth Ieithyddol y Ddeunawfed Ganrif* (Caerdydd, 2000), 143–46.

50. Toland, 'Specimen', 133. Though by this point Toland had the benefit of Lhwyd's exhaustive study of the other Celtic languages.

51. Similarly to the way he had depicted himself as a generative influence upon Lhwyd, Toland claimed that he had shown Aubrey 'authorities' to confirm his opinions (Toland, 'Specimen', 112).

52. Champion, 'John Toland', 328–29.

53. Toland, 'Specimen', 4–7; Champion, 'John Toland', 333–35.

54. This story stretched back to Adamnan's life of Columba, and the etymology is still accepted [Toland, 'Specimen', 4–5n].

55. For Toland's historical vision, see O'Halloran, *Golden Ages*, 74–78.

56. Toland, 'Specimen', 33–40.

57. Toland, 'Specimen', 9.

58. Champion, 'John Toland', 335.

59. Toland, 'Specimen', 13.

60. Toland, 'Specimen', 102.

61. Champion, 'John Toland', 336–41.

62. Hutton, *Blood*, 111.

63. See Stuart J. Piggott, *William Stukeley: An Eighteenth-Century Antiquary* (1950: 2nd ed., London, 1985), which was superseded by David Boyd Haycock, *William Stukeley: Science, Religion and Archaeology in Eighteenth-Century England* (Woodbridge, 2002). Aubrey Burl and Neil Mortimer (eds.), *Stukeley's Stonehenge: An Unpublished Manuscript, 1721–1724* (New Haven, CT, 2005), 2–3, 12–14, prefers Piggott's version, but a more historically sensitive interpretation has won out in Hutton, *Blood*, 86–102, and Paul Kléber Monod, *Solomon's Secret Arts: The Occult in the Age of Enlightenment* (New Haven, CT, 2013), 157–88.

64. W. C. Lukis (ed.), *Family Memoirs of Rev. William Stukeley* (3 vols., Durham, 1882–1887), vol. 1, 216, 228.

65. Lukis, *Family Memoirs*, vol. 1, 32; Diana and Michael Honeybone (eds.), *Stukeley and Stamford, Part 1: Cakes and Curiosity: The Sociable Antiquarian, 1710–1737* (Boydell, 2021), 15, 23.

66. Diana and Michael Honeybone (eds.), *The Correspondence of William Stukeley and Maurice Johnson 1714–1754* (Woodbridge, 2014), 1–6.

67. Burl and Mortimer, *Stukeley's Stonehenge*, 8; Honeybone, *Correspondence*, 14, 17.

68. William Stukeley, *An Account of a Roman Temple, and other Antiquities, near Graham's Dike in Scotland* (London, 1720), 23–24.

69. J. Guenebault, *Le réveil de Chyndonax prince des vacies druydes celtiques dijonois* (Dijon, 1621). Aubrey also took notice of him in *Monumenta Britannica*, vol. 1, 144. Bernard de Montfaucon, discussed below, doubted the authenticity of the inscription (Montfaucon, *L'Antiquité expliquée*, vol. 5, 428–32).

70. Burl and Mortimer, *Stukeley's Stonehenge*, 21.

71. Burl and Mortimer, *Stukeley's Stonehenge*, 37, 39.

72. Burl and Mortimer, *Stukeley's Stonehenge*, 127.

73. For Chyndonax, see Stukeley, *Stonehenge*.

74. N.B.: this was 1724 in British Old-Style dates.

75. William Stukeley, *Itinerarium curiosum: Or, An account of the Antiquities, and Remarkable Curiosities in Nature or Art, Observed in Travels Through Great Britain* (1724: 2nd ed., 2 vols, London, 1766), vol. 1, 'Preface', np.

76. Lukis, *Family Memoirs*, vol. 1, 228.

77. Stukeley, *Stonehenge*, 5.

78. Stukeley, *Stonehenge*, 2.

79. Stukeley, *Stonehenge*, 8, 5, 47–48.

80. Stukeley, *Stonehenge*, 9.

81. Stukeley, *Stonehenge*, 17.

82. Stukeley dedicated an entire notebook to drafting the letter to Anne. See Bodleian Library, MS Eng. Misc., e. 403.

83. *Publications of the Surtees Society* 80 (1887), 210–11.

84. Stukeley, *Origines Britannicae*, Society of Antiquaries of London, MS 793, f. 20.

85. Hutton, *Blood*, 101; Sweet, *Antiquaries*.

86. Charles Pinot Duclos, 'Mémoire sur les Druides', *Mémoires de literature, tirés registres de l'académie royale des inscriptions et belles-lettres* 19 (1753), 483–94. This line was borrowed by Jaucourt in his article 'Druides' in the *Encyclopédie*.

87. The exception that proves the rule was Johann Georg Keyßler (1693–1743)—a German antiquarian who travelled to England, was inducted into the Royal Society, and saw Stonehenge—who included an explanation of Stonehenge as a Germanic monument, noting he did not distinguish between Germans and Celts, and using 'Celt' as an umbrella term for the original Europeans (Johann Georg Keyßler, *Antiquitates selectae septentrionale et Celticae* [Hanover, 1720], x, 1–12).

88. Duclos, 'Mémoire', 490, 492.

89. This paragraph and the several that follow it rely on Droixhe, *L'Étymon*.

90. Stephanus Vinandus Pighius, *Hercules prodicius* (Antwerp, 1587), 264–66.

91. Droixhe, *L'Étymon*, 89.

92. Paul-Marie Duval, 'Le groupe de bas-reliefs des <<Nautae Parisiaci>>', *Monuments et mémoires de la Fondation Eugène Piot* 48 (1954), 63–90.

93. Stéphane Van Damme, 'The Pillar of Metropolitan Greatness: The Long Making of Archaeological Objects in Paris (1711–2001)', *History of Science* 55 (2017), 302–35.

94. Charles-César Baudelot de Dairval, *Description des bas-reliefs anciens trouvez depuis peu dans l'Eglise Cathedrale de Paris* (Paris, 1711), 2.

95. Baudelot de Dairval, *Description*, 32.

96. Philibert-Bernard Moreau de Mautour, *Observations sur des monuments d'antiquité trouvez dans l'eglise cathedrale de Paris* (Paris, 1711), 15.

97. Moreau de Mautour, *Observations*, 24; *Journal des Sçavans*, 17 August 1711, 513–18.

98. G. W. Leibniz, *Opera omnia*, ed. L. Dutens (6 vols., Paris, 1768), vol. 5, 500–501.

99. Leibniz, *Collectanea*, 76–77.

100. Leibniz, *Collectanea*, 80.

101. See Blandine Barrett-Kriegel, *Les historiens et la monarchie* (4 vols., Paris, 1988), vol. 3.

102. Montfaucon, *L'antiquité expliquée*, vol. 2.2, 416, 423–27.

103. Michel Félibien, *Histoire de la ville de Paris* (5 vols., Paris, 1725), vol. 1, cxxix-clii.

104. Caylus, *Recueil d'antiquités égyptiennes, étrusques, grecques, romains, et gauloises* (7 vols., Paris, 1752–1767), vol. 2, 367–70.

105. Jacques Martin, *La religion des gaulois, tirée des plus pures sources de l'antiquité* (2 vols., Paris, 1727), vol. 1, iii.

106. Martin, *La religion*, vol. 1, 9, 46, 58–61.

107. Martin, *La religion*, vol. 1, 15–16. This is also the view adopted, more or less, in R. Goscinny and A. Uderzo, *Astérix chez les Bretons* (Paris, 1966).

108. Thomas Pennant, *The Journey to Snowdon* (London, 1781), 112. Thanks to Rhys Kaminski-Jones for this reference.

109. See Volpilhac, 'Les Gaulois'.

110. Duclos, 'Mémoire', 489.

111. Duclos, 'Mémoire', 483–84.

112. 'Sur l'usage des sacrifices humains, établi chez différentes Nations & particulièrement chez les Gaulois', *Mémoires de literature, tirés registres de l'académie royale des inscriptions et belles-lettres* 18 (1753), 178–81.

113. 'Sur la nature et les dogmes les plus connus de la religion gauloise', *Mémoires de literature, tirés registres de l'académie royale des inscriptions et belles-lettres* 18 (1753), 183.

114. Jean Ehrard, 'Les Gaulois dans l'*Encyclopédie*', in Ehrard and Viallaneix, *Nos ancêtres les Gaulois* (Clermont-Ferrand, 1982), 99–106.

115. [Abbé Yvon], 'Celtes', *Encyclopédie*, vol. 2, 808–11.

116. Mary-Ann Constantine, *Curious Travellers: Writing the Welsh Tour 1760–1820* (Oxford, 2024); Nigel Leask, *Stepping Westward: Writing the Highland Tour, c. 1720–1830* (Oxford, 2020).

117. Hutton, *Blood*, 125–45.

118. Joseph de Maistre, *Considerations on France*, trans. Richard Lebrun (Cambridge, 1994), 63.

119. Benjamin Constant, *Political Writings*, trans. Biancamaria Fontana (Cambridge, 1988), 309–10.

Chapter Four: Civilization, Savagery, and the Celts

1. [James Macpherson], *Fragments of Ancient Poetry, Collected in the Highlands of Scotland, and translated from the Galic or Erse language* (Edinburgh, 1760); *idem*, *Fingal, an ancient epic poem in six books* (London, [December 1761] 1762); *idem*, *Temora, an ancient poem in eight books* (London, 1763). *The Works of Ossian, the Son of Fingal* (2 vols., London, 1765), contains all of Macpherson's works and Hugh Blair's revised *Critical Dissertation*. I follow the convention of referring to the poems collectively as Ossian.

2. William Stukeley, *A Letter from Dr. Stukeley to Mr. Macpherson, On his Publication of Fingal and Temora* (London, 1763), 6–7. Macpherson said little about these things, but Stukeley read into them what he wanted to.

3. Stukeley, *A Letter*, 19.

4. Howard Gaskill (ed.), *Ossian in Europe* (London, 2004).

5. Edward D. Snyder, *The Celtic Revival in English Literature, 1760–1800* (Cambridge, MA, 1923), 4.

6. Ian Stewart, 'The Mother Tongue: Historical Study of the Celts and Their Language(s) in Eighteenth-Century Britain and Ireland', *P&P* 243 (2019), 71–107.

7. Howard Weinbrot, *Britannia's Issue: The Rise of British Literature from Dryden to Ossian* (Cambridge, 1993); Trumpener, *Bardic Nationalism*. See also Jeff Strabone, *Poetry and British Nationalisms in the Bardic Eighteenth Century: Imagined Antiquities* (London, 2018).

8. Kristine Louise Haugen, 'Ossian and the Invention of Textual History', *JHI* 59 (1998), 309–27; Fiona J. Stafford, *The Sublime Savage: A Study of James Macpherson and the Poems of Ossian* (Edinburgh, 1988), 163–78.

9. James Macpherson, 'A Dissertation concerning the Antiquity, &c. of the Poems of Ossian the Son of Fingal', in *Fingal*, ii.

10. See, among others, Ronald L. Meek, *Social Science and the Ignoble Savage* (Cambridge, 1976); J.G.A. Pocock, *Barbarism and Religion* (Cambridge, 1999), vol. 2.

11. Michael Brown, *The Irish Enlightenment* (Cambridge, MA, 2016).

12. Colin Kidd, 'Gaelic Antiquity and National Identity in Enlightenment Ireland and Scotland', *EHR* 109 (1994), 1197–214; Clare O'Halloran, 'Irish Re-Creations of the Gaelic Past: The Challenge of Macpherson's Ossian', *P&P* 124 (1989), 69–85; *idem*, 'The Island of Saints and Scholars': Views of the Early Church and Sectarian Politics in Late-Eighteenth Century Ireland', *Eighteenth-Century Ireland* 5 (1990), 7–20; *idem*, *Golden Ages*, *passim*.

13. James Macpherson, *Introduction to the History and Antiquities of Great Britain* (London, 1771), 202–3.

14. Aneirin Lewis (ed.), *The Correspondence of Thomas Percy & Evan Evans* (Baton Rouge, LA, 1957), 174.

15. Henry Mackenzie (ed.), *Report of the Committee of the Highland Society of Scotland, Appointed to Inquire into the Nature and Authenticity of the Poems of Ossian* (Edinburgh, 1805). This is the key set of primary sources on which virtually all subsequent accounts have been based. See also Susan Manning, 'Henry Mackenzie's *Report on Ossian*: Cultural Authority in Transition', *Modern Language Quarterly* 68 (2007), 517–39.

16. See, for example, J. F. Campbell's verdict on the 'pestilent Scotchman' in J. F. Campbell, *Leabhar Na Feinne* (London, 1872), 180.

17. L. C. Stern, 'Die ossianischen Heldenlieder', *Zeitschrift für vergleichende Litteraturgeschichte* 8 (1895), 51–86, 143–74, esp. 63–71; Derick S. Thomson, *The Gaelic Sources of Macpherson's 'Ossian'* (Edinburgh, 1952); Howard Gaskill (ed.), *Ossian Revisited* (Edinburgh, 1991). As far as I am aware, the most recent accusation of forgery is Thomas M. Curley, *Samuel Johnson, the* Ossian *Fraud, and the Celtic Revival in Great Britain and Ireland* (Cambridge, 2009).

18. For recent summations, see Sebastian Mitchell (ed.) 'Special Issue: Ossian in the Twenty-First Century', *Journal for Eighteenth-Century Studies* 39 (2016), 157–250; Dafydd Moore, *The International Companion to James Macpherson and* The Poems of Ossian (Edinburgh, 2017).

19. On Macpherson, see Stafford, *Sublime Savage*; Paul J. de Gategno, *James Macpherson* (Boston, MA, 1989); Bailey Saunders, *The Life and Letters of James Macpherson* (London, 1895). On Macpherson's (vague) early politics, see Melvin Kersey, 'The Pre-Ossianic Politics of James Macpherson', *Journal for Eighteenth-Century Studies* 27 (2004), 61–76.

20. Stafford, *Sublime Savage*, 24–39.

21. Stafford, *Sublime Savage*, 40–43. It should be said that their emphasis on hunting and invasion are in line with the traditional Gaelic poetry that existed in the Highlands at the time.

22. Richard Sher traces the evidence for this first Macpherson-Ferguson meeting only as far back as an article in the *Celtic Magazine* of 1880 [this publication is discussed below chapter 10]. See Richard B. Sher, *Church and University in the Scottish Enlightenment: The Moderate Literati of Edinburgh* (1985: Edinburgh, 2015), 243n138.

23. Mackenzie, *Report*, 27.

24. Macpherson, *Fingal*, sig. a-a1.

25. Mackenzie, *Report*, 8–9.

26. On these relationships, see J.N.M. Maclean, 'The Early Political Careers of James "Fingal" Macpherson (1736–1796) and Sir John Macpherson, Bart. (1744–1821)', unpublished PhD dissertation (University of Edinburgh, 1967).

27. See the following essays, all of which appear in Gaskill, *Ossian in Europe*: Dafydd Moore, 'The Reception of *The Poems of Ossian* in England and Scotland', 21–37; Mary-Ann Constantine, 'Ossian in Wales and Brittany', 67–90; Mícheál Mac Craith, '"We Know All These Poems": The Irish Response to *Ossian*', 91–108.

28. He published two collected editions of the *Poems of Ossian* in 1765 and 1773.

29. Mackenzie, *Report*, 15–18; Ní Mhunghaile, 'Ossian and the Gaelic World', in Daffyd Moore (ed.), *The International Companion*, 26–38.

30. Mackenzie, *Report*, 15–16.

31. Victoria Henshaw, 'James Macpherson and His Contemporaries: The Methods and Networks of Collectors of Gaelic Poetry in Late Eighteenth-Century Scotland', *Journal for Eighteenth-Century Studies* 39 (2016), 197–209; Celestina Savonius-Wroth, 'Bardic Ministers: Scotland's Gaelic-Speaking Clergy in the Ossian Controversy', *Eighteenth-Century Studies* 52 (2019), 225–43.

32. Sher, *Church and University*, 242–61; Hugh Blair, 'Appendix', in *Works of Ossian*, ii, 446.

33. See, for example, Silvia Sebastiani, *The Scottish Enlightenment: Race, Gender, and the Limits of Progress*, trans. Jeremy Carden (Basingstoke, 2013), esp. 6–9.

34. Adam Smith, *Lectures on Jurisprudence*, ed. R. L. Meek, D. D. Raphael, and P. G. Stein (Oxford, 1978), 14.

35. Kidd, *Subverting*, 101–28; John Robertson, *The Scottish Enlightenment and the Militia Issue* (Edinburgh, 1985).

36. [Hugh Blair], 'Preface', in [James Macpherson], *Fragments of Ancient Poetry, Collected in the Highlands of Scotland, and Translated from the Galic or Erse Language* (1760: 2nd ed., Edinburgh, 1760), iii.

37. Adam Smith, *Lectures on Jurisprudence*, 239, 573.

38. See Adam Ferguson, *Analysis of Pneumatics and Moral Philosophy* (Edinburgh, 1766), 11, and the second section 'Of Rude Nations prior to the Establishment of Property', in Part II of *idem*, *An Essay on the History of Civil Society*, ed. Fania Oz-Salzberger (1767: Cambridge, 1995), 80–94; Meek, *Social Science*, 152–53.

39. Mackenzie, *Report*, 8.

40. *The Critical Review* 12 (1761), 409.

41. J.Y.T. Greig (ed.), *The Letters of David Hume* (2 vols., Oxford, 1932), vol. 1, 330. This 'country surgeon' may have been Dr Donald Smith, some of whose letters on Ossianic poetry, which he affirmed he had heard and learned from childhood, are preserved in EUL, La.II.474.

42. Mackenzie, *Report*, 4–11; Richard B. Sher, *The Enlightenment and the Book: Scottish Authors & Their Publishers in Eighteenth-Century Britain, Ireland, & America* (Chicago, IL, 2006),

90. Blair incorporated the information gleaned at Hume's urging in the appendix to his *Critical Dissertation* in the 1765 *Works of Ossian.*

43. [Hugh Blair], *A Critical Dissertation on the Poems of Ossian, Son of Fingal* (London, 1763), 1–4.

44. [Blair], *Critical Dissertation*, 13–14.

45. [Blair], *Critical Dissertation*, 11–12.

46. [Blair], *Critical Dissertation*, 4–12, referred the reader to Wormius and Hickes for examples of Gothic poetry. Ossian remained a fixture of Blair's lectures [see Hugh Blair, *Lectures on Rhetoric and Belles-Lettres* (2 vols., London, 1783), vol. 2, 319, for comments on Gothic poetry].

47. Hugh Blair to [Becket], 17 March 1763, EUL, Coll-1405, E2012.35.

48. On Macpherson's historical politics, see esp. Kidd, *Subverting*, 219–39; Dafydd Moore, 'James Macpherson and "Celtic Whiggism"', *Eighteenth-Century Life* 30 (2006), 1–24. It seems likely that Macpherson wrote all or part of the preface to the Rev. John Macpherson's *Critical Dissertations* (1768), and he had repeatedly affirmed since *Fingal* that he shared the opinions of the latter, so the preface can be counted with the works under James's name [Macpherson, *Introduction*, viii; John Macpherson to Thomas Becket, 13 Dec 1766, BL Add MS 40166, ff. 104–5]. Gibbon treated them together and so did John Whitaker, *The Genuine History of the Britons Asserted* (London, 1772), 5–6.

49. Macpherson, *Fingal*, ii.

50. Macpherson, *Fingal*, ii–ix.

51. Macpherson, *Introduction*, 154–55.

52. See Maclean, 'Political Careers', 195.

53. James Macpherson, *Introduction to the History of Great Britain and Ireland* (1771: London, 2nd ed., 1772), 244–45. For comments on the importance of language in this respect, see 19–20, 241–57.

54. Macpherson, *Introduction* (2nd ed., 1772), 249, 9. The Rev. Donald McLagan also thought highly of Bullet's [almost completely spurious] work (EUL Laing.II.511, ff. 181–82).

55. Macpherson, *Introduction* (2nd ed.), 272, 322.

56. Macpherson, *Introduction* (2nd ed.), 9–10.

57. Kidd, *Subverting*, 219–39.

58. Stern, 'Die ossianischen Heldenlieder', 55; Dafydd Moore, '"Caledonian Plagiary": The Role and Meaning of Ireland in the Poems of *Ossian*', in Ben Dew and Fiona Price (eds.), *Historical Writing in Britain, 1688–1830: Visions of History* (Basingstoke, 2014), 92–108.

59. James Macpherson to George Laurie, 27 February 1760, Yale University Library, Boswell Collection, GEN MSS 89, Box 27, Folder 650. Caledonians fighting off foreign invaders form much of the subject matter of Ossian as well as Macpherson's earlier poetry.

60. See Kelsey Jackson Williams, *The First Scottish Enlightenment: Rebels, Priests, and History* (Oxford, 2020); Kidd, *Subverting*; Ferguson, *Identity*.

61. Macpherson, 'Preface', in Macpherson, *Critical Dissertations*, xx.

62. Macpherson, *Temora*, xi, xx.

63. Macpherson, *Temora*, xxi.

64. Macpherson, *Temora*, xii.

65. Macpherson, *Temora*, xii.

66. Macpherson, *Temora*, v–vi.

67. Macpherson, 'Dissertation', in *Fingal*, x; Macpherson, 'A Dissertation', in *Temora*, ii.

68. Macpherson, *Introduction*, 10–12, 30. See discussion in Mary-Ann Constantine, *The Truth against the World: Iolo Morganwg and Romantic Forgery* (Cardiff, 2007), 89–90.

69. Constantine, 'Ossian', 69–70.

70. David Hume, *The History of England* (6 vols., London, 1754–1761), vol. 1, 2–3.

71. Ferguson, *An Essay*, 102–4, 192.

72. Alexander Fraser Tytler, *Memoirs of the Life and Writings of Lord Kames* (2 vols., Edinburgh, 1807), vol. 2, 90–91. Henry Home, *Sketches of the History of Man* (1774: 3 vols., Indianapolis, IN, 2007), vol. 1, 424–27, 453–54.

73. John Millar, *The Origin of the Distinction of Ranks, or, Inquiry into the Circumstances which give rise to Influence and Authority, in the Different Members of Society* (1771: Indianapolis, IN, 2006), 126.

74. Edward Gibbon, *The History of the Decline and Fall of the Roman Empire*, (1776–1789: 2 vols., London, 1890), vol. 1, 88, 669n2. This puzzled Trevor-Roper, *Invention of Scotland*, 141, and Pocock, *Barbarism and Religion*, vol. 6, 236–43.

75. See Paul Van Tieghem, *Ossian en France* (Paris, 1917); Rudolf Tombo, *Ossian in Germany* (New York, 1901); Gaskill, *Ossian in Europe*.

76. Julian P. Boyd (ed.), *The Papers of Thomas Jefferson* (43– vols., Princeton, 1950–), vol. 1, 96–97.

77. Boyd, *Papers of Thomas Jefferson*, vol. 1, 100–101.

78. John Murray to the Highland Society of London, National Library of Scotland [hereafter NLS], Highland Society of London Papers, Dep. 268/1.

79. Constantine, 'Ossian', 68. See also Constantine, *Truth*, 85–91.

80. Lewis, *Correspondence*, 149.

81. Constantine, 'Ossian', 74.

82. Davies, *Letters of Lewis*, vol. 2, 240–42, 273.

83. Lewis, *Correspondence*, 161.

84. Lewis, *Correspondence*, 100.

85. Saunders Lewis, *A School of Welsh Augustans* (London, 1924), 134–35.

86. Hugh Owen, *Additional Letters of the Morrises of Anglesey* (2 vols., London, 1947–1949), vol. 2, 467; Lewis Morris, 'On the Cambro-British Music', in Hugh Owen (ed.), *Additional Letters of the Morrises of Anglesey (1735–1786)* (2 vols., London, 1947–1949), vol. 1, 72–80. Thanks to Rhys Kaminski-Jones for this reference.

87. Owen, *Additional Letters*, vol. 1, 144; Jones, *Diddanwch Teuluaidd*.

88. See Morris's letter of 1761 to Samuel Pegge in *Cambrian Register*, vol. 1 (1795), 367–72.

89. Silvan Evans, *Evan Evans*, contains his work and a selection of letters.

90. Davies, *Adfeilion Babel*, 174–76, 195–98.

91. Silvan Evans, *Evan Evans*, 162–70.

92. Evan Evans, *Some Specimens of the Poetry of the Ancient Welsh Bards* (London, 1764), i–ii.

93. Lewis, *Correspondence*, 1–5.

94. Lewis, *Correspondence*, 92.

95. Morris, *Celtic Remains*, xix; Lewis, *Correspondence*, 66 [Evans used the phrase 'Celtic Empire' at p. 91].

96. Silvan Evans, *Evan Evans*, 135.

97. See, for example, *Critical Review* 18 (1764), 81–87; *Monthly Review*, 31 (1764), 22–25.

98. Evans, *Specimens*, 49–50 note h, 54.

99. Evans, *Specimens*, 30–31.

100. Evans, *Specimens*, 63, 104–5. Evans derived his information from William Lloyd, *An Historical Account of Church-Government As it was in Great Britain and Ireland, When they first received the Christian Religion* (London, 2nd ed., 1684), 31. See also Lewis, *Correspondence*, 35–36.

101. Kidd, *British Identities*, 95–96; Sweet, *Antiquaries*, 146–47. For ancient British commerce, see John Whitaker, *The History of Manchester* (2 vols., London, 1771–1773), vol. 1, 69–70, 284–88, 384–91; for the origins of British feudalism, see 262–68.

102. Whitaker, *History of Manchester*, vol. 1, 16–17.

103. Whitaker, *History of Manchester*, vol. 1, 6–7, 16n6; Whitaker, *Genuine History*, 3.

104. Whitaker, *Genuine History*, 154–293, deals with the origin of the Scots, but a summation is at 283–93, the quote at 283. Whitaker also repeatedly went out of his way to pour scorn on Irish historical tradition.

105. Diary of William Erskine, BL Add MS 39, 945, f. 32v.

106. Kidd, *British Identities*, 95–96, 199.

107. Hume, *Letters*, vol. 1, 400.

108. On the Irish reaction, see O'Halloran, 'Irish Re-Creations'; Leerssen, *Mere Irish*, 338–49; Mac Craith, 'The Irish Response to *Ossian*'; *idem*, 'Charles O'Conor of Ballinagare and the Macpherson Controversy', in Luke Gibbons and Kieran O'Connor (eds.), *Charles O'Conor of Ballinagare, 1790–91: Life and Works* (Dublin, 2015), 165–85.

109. *Critical Review* 10 (July 1760), 28–30; *Dublin Journal*, 1 December 1761, 3.

110. Sylvester O'Halloran, *Ierne Defended* (Dublin, 1774), 29. See also J. B. Lyons (ed.), 'The Letters of Sylvester O'Halloran', *Northern Munster Antiquarian Journal* 8 (1961), 171.

111. See, for example, the abrasion Hume's history—particularly his account of 1641—caused to Charles O'Conor and his network [Ward and Ward, *Letters, passim*].

112. O'Halloran, 'Irish Re-Creations'; *idem*, *Golden Ages*, 97–124.

113. [Daniel Webb], *Fingal Reclaimed* (London, 1763); Misos-dolos [Sylvester O'Halloran], 'The Poems of Ossine, the son of Fionne Mac Comhal, Re-Claimed', *Dublin Magazine* (January 1763), 21–23, in Moore, *Ossian and Ossianism* (4 vols., London, 2004), vol. 3, 87.

114. Fernando Warner, *Remarks on the History of Fingal, and other Poems of Ossian* (London, 1762), 4, 11.

115. O'Conor wrote to others of his correspondence with Warner. See Ward and Ward, *Letters*, vol. 1, 113–14, 133.

116. Ferdinando Warner, *The History of Ireland* (London, 1763), vol. 1, xix, xvii.

117. Warner, *History*, 42–48, plagiarising Berkeley.

118. Diarmaid Ó Catháin, 'An Irish Scholar Abroad: Bishop John O'Brien of Cloyne and the Macpherson Controversy', in Patrick O'Flanagan and Cornelius G. Buttimer (eds.), *Cork: History & Society* (Dublin, 1993), 499–533; McBride, *Eighteenth-Century Ireland*, 254–55, 258.

119. [John O'Brien], 'Mémoire de M. de C. à Messieurs les auteurs, Du Journal des Sçavans, au Sujet des Poëmes de M. Macpherson', *Journal des Sçavans* (1764), 277, 553. Charles O'Conor repeated the jibe more subtly in his preface to Roderic O'Flaherty, *The Ogygia Vindicated: Against the Objections of Sir George Mackenzie*, ed. Charles O'Conor (Dublin, 1775), xv.

120. [O'Brien], 'Mémoire', *Journal des Sçavans* (1764), 279–80, 417, 548–49.

121. O'Brien, *Focalóir.*

122. O'Conor, *Dissertations on the Antient History of Ireland*, 14, 22–24, 35–36, 42.

123. O'Conor, *Dissertations on the Antient History of Ireland* (2nd ed., Dublin, 1766), 23n, 38–39, 184–88n; Ward and Ward, *Letters*, vol. 1, 197.

124. Charles O'Conor, 'Observations on Mr. Mac Pherson's Dissertations and Notes on the Poems, intitled, Fingal and Temora', in *idem*, *Historical Dissertations* (2nd ed., 1766), 23–24; on this point, see O'Halloran, 'Irish Re-Creations', 76–77.

125. O'Conor, 'Observations', 57.

126. Ward and Ward, *Letters*, vol. 1, 134–35.

127. Walter D. Love, 'Charles O'Conor of Belanagare and Thomas Leland's "Philosophical" History of Ireland', *Irish Historical Studies* 13 (1962), 1–25; see, for example, O'Halloran, *Ierne Defended*, 18–19.

128. Claire Lyons, 'Sylvester O'Halloran's *General History* (1778): Irish Historiography and the Late Eighteenth-Century British Empire', PhD dissertation (University of Galway, 2011); J. B. Lyons, 'Sylvester O'Halloran, 1728–1807', *Eighteenth-Century Ireland* 4 (1989), 65–74.

129. J. B. Lyons (ed.), 'The Letters of Sylvester O'Halloran: I', *Northern Munster Antiquarian Journal* 8 (1961), 175.

130. O'Halloran to Sir James Caldwell, 13 December 1777, reproduced in Lyons, 'Sylvester O'Halloran's *General History*', 276.

131. Sylvester O'Halloran, *Insula Sacra* (Limerick, 1770).

132. O'Halloran, *Insula Sacra*, 6.

133. O'Halloran, *Insula Sacra*, 16–17. Claire E. Lyons, 'An Imperial Harbinger: Sylvester O'Halloran's *General History* (1778)', *IHS* 39 (2015), 357–77, argues that the purpose of the *General History* was to convince the British that Irish Catholics could be able and willing agents of empire.

134. Ward and Ward, *Letters*, vol. 1, 292.

135. Lyons, 'Letters', 171.

136. See, for example, *Monthly Review* 49 (1773), 193–202; *Critical Review* 35 (1773), 198–202; *L'esprit des journaux* 4 (1773), 180–82.

137. Charles O'Conor, 'Dissertation', in Roderic O'Flaherty, *The Ogygia Vindicated*, xxvii.

138. Ward and Ward, *Letters*, vol. 1, 254, 256, 261 62; O'Halloran, *Golden Ages*, 38–40.

139. Charles Vallancey, *A Grammar of the Iberno-Celtic or Irish Language* (Dublin, 1773), v.

140. Vallancey, *A Grammar*, xvii, xxvii–xxviii.

141. O'Halloran, *Golden Ages*, 169.

142. Whitaker, *History of Manchester*, vol. 1, 308.

143. O'Halloran, *Ierne Defended*, esp. 22–29.

144. Hume wrote to Dalrymple to assuage Gray's doubts (Greig, *Letters of David Hume*, vol. 1, 328). Gray and Macpherson corresponded, but the letters are lost.

145. Hume, *Letters*, vol. 1, 399.

146. James Boswell, *Life of Johnson* (1791: Oxford, 2008), 280, 443.

147. Fiona Stafford, 'Doctor Johnson and the Ruffian: New Evidence in the Dispute between Samuel Johnson and James Macpherson', *Notes & Queries* 36 (1989), 70–77.

148. Bertram H. Davis, *Thomas Percy: A Scholar-Cleric in the Age of Johnson* (Philadelphia, PA, 1989). On this context, see Philip Connell, 'British Identities and the Politics of Ancient Poetry in Later Eighteenth-Century Britain', *Historical Journal* 49 (2006), 161–92.

149. Margaret Clunies Ross and Amanda J. Collins, *The Correspondence of Edward Lye* (Toronto, 2004).

150. This section relies on Colin Kidd's pioneering chapter 'Constructing the Pre-Romantic Celt', in *British Identities*, 186–210.

151. Thomas Percy (ed.), *Five Pieces of Runic Poetry Translated from the Islandic Language* (London, 1763); Nick Groom, *The Making of Percy's* Reliques (Oxford, 1999).

152. Groom, *Percy's* Reliques, 95–96.

153. Lewis, *Correspondence*, 88.

154. Van Hal, 'One Continent, One Language?'; Stewart, 'The Mother Tongue'.

155. Thomas Percy, *Northern Antiquities* (2 vols., London, 1770), vol. 1, ii.

156. Percy, *Northern Antiquities*, vol. 1, sig. A3^{r}, iv, ix.

157. Percy, *Northern Antiquities*, vol. 1, ii–iii.

158. Percy, *Northern Antiquities*, vol. 1, xix.

159. Percy, *Northern Antiquities*, vol. 1, xxiv–xlvii.

160. Percy, *Northern Antiquities*, I, xlv. For example, both Macphersons used Bullet [Macpherson, *Critical Dissertations*, 26; Macpherson, *Introduction*, 34, 39, 52], and so did Lewis Morris and Charles O'Conor [O'Conor, 'Observations', 57; Ward and Ward, *Letters*, 184, 186]. [Charles Vallancey], *An Essay on the Antiquity of the Irish Language* (Dublin, 1772), viii, noted Percy's dismantling of Bullet.

161. Davis, *Thomas Percy*, 222–23.

162. Patrick O'Flaherty, *Scotland's Pariah: The Life and Work of John Pinkerton, 1758–1826* (Toronto, 2014), 77–80.

163. His notebooks for this period are found in NLS, MSS 1718–1720. Many of the letters in his correspondence from this period are also concerned with his linguistic theories [see Dawson Turner (ed.), *The Literary Correspondence of John Pinkerton* (2 vols., London, 1830), vol. 1, *passim*].

164. 'The Pictish poetry furnished the language, and therein the chief fund, of Scotish poetry', [John Pinkerton], *Ancient Scotish Poems* (2 vols., London, 1786), vol. 1, lx.

165. [Pinkerton], *Ancient Scotish Poems*, vol. 1, li–lii.

166. [Pinkerton], *Ancient Scotish Poems*, vol. 1, xliv.

167. [Pinkerton], *Ancient Scotish Poems*, vol. 1, xxi–xxiii, n.

168. John Pinkerton, *A Dissertation on the Origin and Progress of the Scythians or Goths* (London, 1787), 9–23, 30. For criticisms of Gibbon, see NLS MS 1718, f. 70; NLS MS 1720, f. 5v.

169. Pinkerton, *Dissertation*, 27.

170. Pinkerton, *Dissertation*, 91.

171. Pinkerton, *Dissertation*, vi, 17–19.

172. O'Flaherty, *Scotland's Pariah*, 47–48.

173. Pinkerton, *Dissertation*, 91–99.

174. Pinkerton, *Dissertation*, 45, 51.

175. See, for example, Smith, *Lectures on Jurisprudence*, 239, where the Ossianic Caledonians and the Native Americans are considered together.

176. Pinkerton, *Dissertation*, 69.

177. 'Philistor' [John Pinkerton], 'Letters to the People of Great Britain, on the Cultivation of their National History', *Gentleman's Magazine*, 58 (1788), 500.

178. Robert MacFarlan, *George Buchanan's Dialogue concerning the Rights of the Crown of Scotland translated into English* (London, 1799), 40.

179. O'Flaherty, *Scotland's Pariah*, 225–26n144.

180. James McLagan to John M'Naughton, 27 February 1771, EUL La.II.511, f. 181v. The letter is reprinted in *Blackwood's Magazine* 1 (1817), 256–60.

181. [William Shaw], *Memoirs of the Life and Writings of the Late Dr. Samuel Johnson* (1785: London, 1974), 42–48; Boswell, *Life of Johnson*, 797–99; William Shaw, *An Analysis of the Galic Language* (Edinburgh, 1778), xvi–xvii; William Shaw, *A Galic and English Dictionary* (2 vols., London, 1780); William Shaw, *An Enquiry into the Authenticity of the Poems Ascribed to Ossian* (London, 1781); John Clark, *An Answer to Mr Shaw's Inquiry into the Authenticity of the Poems of Ossian* (Edinburgh, 1781), 33–34.

182. Raonuill Macdomhnuill, *Comh-Chruinneachidh Orannaigh Gaidhealach* (Duneidiunn, 1776), v–viii; Eoin Gillies (ed.), *Sean Dain, agus Orain Ghaidhealach* (Perth, 1786), 'advertisement', np.

183. The plan to publish the 'originals' is first mentioned in an advertisement in *Fingal*. On his death, Macpherson did leave money in his will for their publication (Mackenzie, *Report*, 45–46).

184. Vincenzo Merolle, *Correspondence of Adam Ferguson* (2 vols., London, 1995), vol. 2, 352.

185. Merolle, *Correspondence*, vol. 2, 353. To be fair, the orthography of the Celtic languages was at this time highly unstable, and it was not uncommon for Welsh writers to use the Greek characters χ (for 'ch') or δ (for 'dd' or 'th').

186. Leask, *Stepping Westward*.

Chapter Five: Celts in the Age of Revolution and Empire

1. John Pinkerton, *Recollections of Paris, in the years 1802–3–4–5* (2 vols., London, 1806), vol. 1, 102–3.

2. Archives nationales, F/17/1214/B, dossier 11.

3. John Pinkerton, *Modern Geography* (1804: 3 vols., London, 1807), vo. 1, xxxvi n., 268n.

4. Sieyès, 'What Is the Third Estate?', 99.

5. See Sieyès, 'An Essay on Privileges', in Sonenscher, *Sieyès*, 68–88; D'Auria, *Shaping*, 234–46, 266–67.

6. See, for example, Alexander Murray to Archibald Constable, 22 August 1806, NLS, MS 681, 133r: 'his Imperial Majesty of the Gauls'.

7. Although the foundations of Irish Celticism were laid during this period, there were still some holdouts who defended Scythian or Phoenician theories. As chapter 7 shows, these interpretations were finally definitively uprooted in the 1830s and 40s.

8. [Edward Davies], *Mr Davies's Letters* (London, 1802), 3rd Letter, 3.

9. Keith Baker, *Inventing the French Revolution* (Cambridge, 1990), 252–305.

10. See esp. Jean-Yves Guiomar, 'La Révolution Française et les origines celtiques de la France', *Annales historiques de la révolution française* 287 (1992), 63–85.

11. Jacques Le Brigant, *Élémens de la langue des Celtes Gomérites, ou Bretons: Introduction a cette langue et par elle à celles de tous les peuples connus* (Strasbourg, 1779), 1.

12. Jacques Le Brigant, *Observations fondamentales sur les langues anciennes et modernes; ou Prospectus de l'Ouvrage intitulé: La langue primitive conservée* (Paris, 1787).

13. Advertisements for the demonstration and its results appeared in the *Journal de Paris*, on 27 March, 4 April, and 10 April 1789.

14. Jacques Le Brigant, *Lettre a monsieur l'Abbé du Crotz, Au sujet du jeune homme qui étoit chez M. Deltuso; qu'on a cru, sur les mots nombreux de cette Langue, dont il se servoit, être de l'isle de Taïti* (Paris, 1789).

15. Theodore Besterman (ed.), *The Complete Works of Voltaire* (Oxford, 1975), vol. 34, letter D17867, 27–28; René Pomeau, *Voltaire en son temps* (2 vols., Paris, 1995), vol. 2, 212–13.

16. Jacques Le Brigant to Benjamin Franklin, 16 August 1780, American Philosophical Society, Franklin Papers, Mss B.F85, inventory 05.

17. *Gazette de France*, 23 October 1787; *Monthly Magazine, or British Register*, June 1797, 416–18.

18. Claude-Urbain de Retz de Servières to Jacques Le Brigant, 14 March 1773, BNF, NAF 14898, f. 285.

19. Marquis de Condorcet to Jacques Le Brigant, 24 February 1788, Archives nationales, AE/I/2/9.

20. Olympe de Gouges, *Le bonheur primitif de l'homme, ou les rêveries patriotiques* (Paris, 1789), 32.

21. Abbé Grandidier to J. J. Oberlin, 26 May 1778, in Aug. Kroeber (ed.), 'Correspondance de l'Abbé Grandidier, et autres documents relatifs a cet historien, a sa famille et ses ouvrages', *Revue d'Alsace* 17, t. 12 (1866), 473.

22. Anne-Marie Mercier-Faivre, *Un supplement à "L'Encyclopédie": Le "Monde primitif" d'Antoine Court de Gébelin* (Paris, 1999).

23. Sophia Rosenfeld, *A Revolution in Language: The Problem of Signs in Late Eighteenth-Century France* (Stanford, CA, 2001), 113.

24. Antoine Court de Gébelin, *Le Monde primitif, analysé et comparé avec le monde moderne* (9 vols., Paris, 1773–1782), vol. 8, xlvi–xlviii.

25. Guiomar, 'La Révolution française', 63.

26. Guiomar, 'La Révolution française', 63–65.

27. Bonneville admitted he had not read Gébelin's massive work, but he assured readers of its excellence based on its title alone. See Nicolas de Bonneville, *De l'Esprit des Religions* (1791: Paris, 1792), 26–28.

28. See, for example, J. A. Dulaure, *Histoire critique de la noblesse depuis le commencement de la monarchie jusqu'à nos jours* (Paris, 1790); Suzanne Citron, *Le mythe national: l'histoire de France revisitée* (Paris, 2008), 159–63.

29. *Mémoires de l'Académie celtique* (1807), vol. 1, 322–52.

30. On the revolutionary politics of language, see above all Michel de Certeau, Dominique Julia, and Jacques Revel, *Une politique de la langue, la Revolution française et les patois: l'enquête de Grégoire* (1975: Paris, 2002); Bell, *Cult of the Nation*, 169–97.

31. M. J. Guillaume (ed.), *Procès-verbaux du comité d'instruction publique de la convention nationale* (7 vols., Paris, 1891–1957), vol. 5, 384.

32. [Abbé Henri] Grégoire, *Rapport sur la nécessité et les moyens d'anéantir les patois, et d'universaliser l'usage de la langue française* (Paris, 1794), 2, 13.

33. David A. Bell, 'Tearing Down the Tower of Babel: Grégoire and French Multilingualism', in Jeremy D. Popkin and Richard H. Popkin (eds.), *The Abbé Grégoire and his World* (Dordrecht, 2000), 113.

34. Certeau et al., *Une politique*, 87.

35. A. Gazier (ed.), *Lettres à Grégoire sur les patois de France, 1790–1794* (1880: Geneva, 1969), 167–69.

36. Gazier, *Lettres à Grégoire*, 286, 207.

37. Guiomar, 'La Révolution française', 81–82.

38. Guiomar, 'La Révolution française', 70–71; Marc Regaldo, '<<La Décade,>> revue bretonne?', *Annales de Bretagne et des pays de l'Ouest* (1976), 605–17.

39. [M.A.B. de Mangourit], *De la Tyrannie de Carnot, ou des Carnutes: Anecdote druidique, écrite il y a 2000 ans* (Paris, an 6 [1797–1798?]), 36–52.

40. Théophile Malo-Corret de La Tour d'Auvergne to [?], 7 November 1783, Médiathèque Alain-Gérard, MS 214.

41. *Mémoires de l'Académie celtique* (1809) vol. 4, 466.

42. Théophile Malo Corret de la Tour d'Auvergne, *Nouvelles recherches sur la langue, l'origine & les antiquités des Bretons* (Bayonne, 1792), 19–20.

43. de la Tour d'Auvergne, *Nouvelles recherches*, 27–36n2.

44. L. Buhot de Kersers (ed.), *Correspondance de La Tour d'Auvergne (Corret)* (Bourges, 1908), 263–66.

45. Théophile Malo Corret de la Tour d'Auvergne, *Origines gauloises, celles des plus anciens peuples de l'Europe* (Paris, 1796), 213–14; cf. Tour d'Auvergne, *Nouvelles recherches*, 77–78, 83.

46. *Gazette national ou Le Moniteur universel*, 4 April 1797, 780.

47. de Kersers, *Correspondance*, 273–74.

48. Annie Jourdan, 'The Image of Gaul during the French Revolution', in Brown, *Celticism*, 183–206.

49. Antoine Mongez, 'Mémoire sur les gladiateurs', *Mémoires de l'Institut national des sciences et arts: Littérature et Beaux arts* (Paris, 1799) 423–68, quote at 465.

50. 'Barbare mourant', in T. Piroli and Louis Petit-Radel, *Les Monumens antiques du Musée Napoleon* (4 vols., Paris, 1806), vol. 4, 51–52. For general information, see Francis Haskell and Nicholas Penny, *Taste and the Antique: The Lure of Classical Sculpture 1500–1900* (New Haven, CT, 1981), 224–27.

51. Generally, this section relies on Leerssen, *Mere Irish*, 294–376, and O'Halloran, *Golden Ages*, *passim*, but esp. 158–81.

52. Monica Nevin, 'General Charles Vallancey 1725–1812', *Journal of the Royal Society of Antiquaries of Ireland* 123 (1993), 19–58; Clare O'Halloran, 'An English Orientalist in Ireland: Charles Vallancey (1726–1812)', in Joep Leerssen, A. H. van der Weel, and Bart Westerweel (eds.), *Forging in the Smith: National Identity and Representation in Anglo-Irish Literary History* (Amsterdam, 1995), 161–73; *idem*, *Golden Ages*, *passim*.

53. O'Halloran, *Golden Ages*, 42.

54. [Charles Vallancey] *An Essay on the Antiquity of the Irish Language* (Dublin, 1772), viii, 1–2.

55. Celticus [Charles O'Conor], 'Remarks on the Essay on the Antiquity of the Irish Language', reprinted in *Collectanea de Rebus Hibernicis* 2 (Dublin, 1786), 337–48.

56. Leerseen, *Mere Irish*, 347–49.

57. Walter D. Love, 'The Hibernian Antiquarian Society: A Forgotten Predecessor to the Royal Irish Academy', *Studies* 51 (1962), 419–31.

58. See, for example, R. F. Foster, 'History and the Irish Question', *TRHS* 33 (1983), 171–72.

59. R. B. McDowell, 'The Main Narrative: Before 1800', in T. Ó Raifeartaigh (ed.), *The Royal Irish Academy: A Bicentennial History, 1785–1985* (Dublin, 1985), 12.

60. Vallancey, *Grammar*, v.

61. McDowell, 'The Main Narrative', 19–20.

62. Walter D. Love, 'Edmund Burke, Charles Vallancey, and The Sebright Manuscripts', *Hermathena* 95 (July 1961), 21–35.

63. Charles Vallancey, 'Observations on the Alphabet of the Pagan Irish', *Archaeologia* 7 (1785), 276–85, quote at 283.

64. Theophilus O'Flanagan, 'An Account of an antient Inscription in Ogam Character on the Sepulchral Monument of an Irish Chief', *Transactions of the Royal Irish Academy* 1 (1787), Antiquities Section, 3–17.

65. O'Halloran, *Golden Ages*, 169–72.

66. She was not the first to translate and publish Irish poetry, but she was unquestionably the most popular.

67. Charlotte Brooke, *Reliques of Irish Poetry* (Dublin, 1789), vii.

68. Brooke, *Reliques*, 3.

69. Brooke, *Reliques*, 5.

70. Brooke, *Reliques*, 137.

71. Brooke, *Reliques*, 139.

72. Lawrence Parsons, *Observations on the Bequest of Henry Flood* (Dublin, 1795), 13–16; Leerssen, *Mere Irish*, 361–62; O'Halloran, *Golden Ages*, 161.

73. Leerssen, *Mere Irish*, 363.

74. Parsons, *Observations*, 38–39.

75. *Transactions of the Gaelic Society of Dublin*, vol. 1 (1808), iii–ix; Leerssen, *Mere Irish*, 365–66.

76. Edward O'Reilly to William Betham, 17 April 1820, National Library of Ireland [hereafter NLI] MS 24, 587(7).

77. O'Reilly to Betham, 17 July 1821, NLI, MS 24, 587(7).

78. R. F. Foster, *Words Alone: Yeats and His Inheritances* (Oxford, 2011), 1–44.

79. On the Gorsedd's invention, see Dillwyn Miles, *The Secret of the Bards of the Isle of Britain* (Llandybie, 1992); Geraint Bowen, 'Gorsedd y Beirdd: From Primrose Hill 1792 to Aberystwyth 1992', *THSC* (1992), 115–39.

80. A major University of Wales and AHRC project titled 'Iolo Morganwg and the Romantic Tradition in Wales, 1740–1918' resulted in several important monographs and an extremely valuable edition of his correspondence. The standard English-language biography is now Geraint H. Jenkins, *Bard of Liberty: The Political Radicalism of Iolo Morganwg* (Cardiff, 2012). Geraint H. Jenkins (ed.), *A Rattleskull Genius: The Many Faces of Iolo Morganwg* (Cardiff, 2009), captures Iolo's diverse range of interests and his influence.

81. National Library of Wales [hereafter NLW], MS 13144A, ff. 228–29.

82. Constantine, *Truth*, 6–8.

83. Hutton, *Blood*, 146–82.

84. Cathryn Charnell-White, *Bardic Circles: National, Regional, and Personal Identity in the Bardic Vision of Iolo Morganwg* (Cardiff, 2007), 15–16.

85. Prys Morgan, 'Iolo Morganwg and Welsh Historical Traditions', in Jenkins, *Rattleskull Genius*, 251–68.

86. See numerous letters and fragments aimed at Macpherson and Pinkerton in Iolo's 'Literary Papers', NLW 21419E; Charnell-White, *Bardic Circles*, 51–58.

87. Charnell-White, *Bardic Circles*, 34–35, 82–117; Jenkins, *Bard of Liberty*, 46, 63; Geraint Phillips, *Dyn heb ei gyffelb yn y byd: Owain Myfyr a'i gysylltiadau llenyddol* (Caerdydd, 2010), 43–74.

88. Geraint H. Jenkins, Ffion Mair Jones, David Ceri Jones, and Andrew Davies, *The Correspondence of Iolo Morganwg* (3 vols., Cardiff, 2007), vol. 1, 104; NLW, MS 21419E, f. 6.

89. Jenkins et al., *Correspondence*, vol. 1, 84–85.

90. NLW, MS 13144A, ff. 226–27.

91. Jenkins et al., *Correspondence*, vol. 1, 103, 110, 455, 486, 498–501; NLW, MS 21419E, ff. 1–2.

92. The standard biographies are Geraint Phillips, *Dyn*; Glenda Carr, *William Owen Pughe* (Caerdydd, 1983). William Owen took the surname 'Pughe' in 1806 when he came into an inheritance.

93. Iolo's former mentor John Williams wrote to Pughe. He was worried about rumours that Iolo exercised 'a papal authority over your judgement' [see John Williams to William Owen Pughe, 19 June 1793, NLW, MS 13224B, 116].

94. Phillips, *Dyn*, 17–42.

95. Phillips, *Dyn*, 56.

96. The work and its context are described and analysed with clarity in Mary-Ann Constantine, 'Welsh Literary History and the Making of the "The Myvyrian Archaiology of Wales"', *European Studies* 26 (2008), 109–28.

97. For the 'Third Series' of triads, see [Owen Jones, William Owen Pughe, Edward Williams], *The Myvyrian Archaiology of Wales* (3 vols., London, 1801–1807), vol. 2, 57–75. For an edition of Iolo's translation of them, see Rachel Bromwich, 'Trioedd Ynys Prydain: The *Myvyrian* "Third Series"', *THSC* (1968), 299–338; (1969), 127–56.

98. See esp. Rachel Bromwich, *'Trioedd Ynys Prydain' in Welsh Literature and Scholarship* (Cardiff, 1969).

99. Geraint H. Jenkins, *Facts, Fantasy and Fiction: The Historical Vision of Iolo Morganwg* (Aberystwyth, 1997).

100. Charnell-White, *Bardic Circles*, 104–10, makes this clear. On the historical versus the mythological Taliesin, see Williams, *Celtic Myths*, 23–24, 28–30.

101. Hutton, *Blood*, 157.

102. Charnell-White, *Bardic Circles*, 18. It was only published posthumously in 1829 (Iolo Morganwg, *Cyfrinach Beirdd Ynys Prydain*, ed. Taliesin Williams [Abertawe, 1829]), and it attempted to establish Glamorgan verse conventions as those best preserving Wales's medieval bardic tradition.

103. William Owen [Pughe], *The Heroic Elegies and other pieces of Llywarç Hen, Prince of the Cumbrian Britons* (London, 1792), xxxiv.

104. Owen [Pughe], *The Heroic Elegies*, xxiv.

105. *Morning Chronicle*, 26 September 1792.

106. Charnell-White, *Bardic Circles*, 119–21.

107. *Gentleman's Magazine* 59 (1789), 976–77; Thomas Davis, *Awdlau ar destynau Cymdeithas y Gwyneddigion i'r Eisteddfodau* (London, 1791), 46. The only inkling of the first *Gorsedd* is in Edward Williams, *Poems Lyric and Pastoral* (2 vols., London, 1794), vol. 2, 193.

108. *The Times*, 1 January 1793, 4. Bowen, 'Gorsedd y Beirdd', 119, suggests Primrose Hill was chosen because it was the location where John Toland held the first meeting of the 'Ancient Druid Order' in 1717.

109. Williams, *Poems*, vol. 2, 39.

110. See, for example, the account in *Gentleman's Magazine* 62 (1792), 956–75.

111. Geraint Jenkins presents Iolo as a disciple of Paine [see Jenkins, *Bard of Liberty*, esp. 90–105]; Victoria Myers, David O'Shaughnessy, and Mark Philp (eds.), *The Diary of William Godwin* (Oxford Digital Library, 2010), 2 January 1795, 3 January 1795, accessed 30 December 2020, http://godwindiary.bodleian.ox.ac.uk.

112. Charnell-White, *Bardic Circles*, 20–21.

113. Williams, *Poems*, vol. 1, xxvi, xxxiv.

114. NLW, MS 21419E, f. 10.

115. NLW, MS 21419E, f. 18.

116. For detailed explanations, see Jenkins et al., *Correspondence*, vol. 1, 482–87, 498–507. For a summary, see Constantine, *Truth*, 106–11.

117. Caesar, *Gallic War*, 339.

118. Jenkins et al., *Correspondence*, vol. 1, 456, 485–86.

119. Jenkins et al., *Correspondence*, vol. 1, 519–20.

120. Moira Dearnley, '"Mad Ned" and the "Smatter-Dasher": Iolo Morganwg and Edward "Celtic" Davies', in Jenkins, *A Rattleskull Genius*, 429. Edmund Fry, *Pantographia* (London, 1799), 205, 305–6.

121. Jenkins et al., *Correspondence*, vol. 2, 302.

122. William Owen [Pughe], *A Grammar of the Welsh Language* (London, 1803), 3–6.

123. Marion Löffler, *The Literary and Historical Legacy of Iolo Morganwg, 1826–1926* (Cardiff, 2007), 96.

124. Jenkins et al., *Correspondence*, vol. 1, 560–62; Dearnley, '"Mad Ned"'.

125. Edward Davies, *Mythology and Rites of the British Druids* (London, 1809).

126. Quoted in Dearnley, '"Mad Ned"', 429.

127. Edward Davies to Pughe, 4 November 1799, NLW, MS 145C.

128. Edward Williams, *Prospectus of collections for a new history of Wales based upon Manuscript Sources* (Carmarthen, 1819).

129. Huw Walters, 'Myfyr Morganwg and the Rocking-Stone Gorsedd', in Jenkins, *A Rattleskull Genius*, 481–500.

130. Löffler, *Literary and Historical Legacy*.

131. Carr, *William Owen Pughe*, 103.

132. George Ellis to Pughe [n.d., 1803], NLW, MS 13221E, 163. See Carr, *William Owen Pughe*, 115–20.

133. Jenkins et al., *Correspondence*, vol. 2, 446.

134. Carr, *William Owen Pughe*, 100. I am grateful to Rhys Kaminski-Jones for pointing out this material for me.

135. Jenkins et al., *Correspondence*, vol. 2, 447.

136. Jenkins et al., *Correspondence*, vol. 2, 450–51.

137. William Owen [Pughe] to George Chalmers, 10 January 1803, EUL, La.II.474, ff. 48r-50v.

138. *Mémoires de l'Académie celtique*, vol. 1, 15.

139. For a recent article analysing the relationship between scholarship and the politicised Celtic past, see Ian Stewart, 'Language and the National Past in Napoleonic France: Reassessing the Académie celtique, 1805–1813', *French History* 35 (2021), 219–42.

140. Louis Dujardin, *La vie et les oeuvres de Jean-François-Marie-Maurice-Agathe Le Gonidec, grammairien et lexicographe breton, 1775–1838* (Brest, 1949), 44.

141. G. Basc-Bautier and B. de Chancel-Bardelot, *Un musée révolutionnaire: le Musée des Monuments français d'Alexandre Lenoir* (Paris, 2016).

142. R. R. Palmer, 'A Revolutionary Republican: M.A.B. Mangourit', *William & Mary Quarterly* 9 (1952), 483–96; Anne de Mathan (ed.), *Jacques Cambry, 1749–1807: un Breton des Lumières au service de la construction nationale* (Brest, 2007).

143. See Stewart, 'Language and the National Past'.

144. Stuart Woolf, 'French Civilization and Ethnicity in the Napoleonic Empire', *P&P* 124 (1989), 96–120.

145. *Mémoires de l'Académie celtique*, vol. 1, 'Épitre dédicatoire', np.

146. *Mémoires de l'Académie celtique*, vol. 1, 1–3.

147. *Mémoires de l'Académie celtique*, vol. 1, 42.

148. *Mémoires de l'Académie celtique*, vol. 1, 22.

149. This is a common theme throughout, but see esp. *Mémoires de l'Académie celtique*, vol. 1, 1–64.

150. *Mémoires de l'Académie celtique*, vol. 1, 63–64.

151. Stewart McCain, 'Our Ancestors Were Not Celts: History, Folklore, and the Celtic Past in Napoleonic France', *European Review of History* 29 (2022), 674–94.

152. See, for example, N. Belmont, 'L'Académie celtique et George Sand: les débuts des recherches folkloriques en France', *Romantisme* 9 (1975), 29–38; H. Senn, 'Folklore Beginnings in France, the Académie celtique:1804–1813', *Journal of the Folklore Institute* 18 (1981), 23–33; M. Ozouf, 'L'invention de l'ethnographie française: le questionnaire de l'Académie celtique', *Annales. Histoire, Sciences Sociales* 36 (1981), 210.

153. The questionnaire and responses are conveniently collected in Nicole Belmont, *Aux sources de l'ethnologie française: L'Académie celtique* (Paris, 1995).

154. Belmont, *Aux sources*, 31.

155. J. Cambry, *Monumens celtiques, ou recherches sur le culte des pierres, précédées d'une notice sur les Celtes et sur les Druides, et suivies d'étymologies celtiques* (Paris, 1805), xxvii–xxviii.

156. Éloi Johanneau, 'Réflexions sur la langue celtique', in Cambry, *Monumens celtiques*, 377.

157. *Gazette nationale ou le Moniteur universel*, 2 March 1806, 242.

158. Stewart, 'Language and the National Past'.

159. In reality, Celtiberian and Proto-Basque were separate languages from different families. See F. Beltrán and C. Jordán, 'Writing and Language in Celtiberia', in Alejandro G. Sinner and Javier Velaza (eds.), *Paleohispanic Languages and Epigraphies* (Oxford, 2019), 240–303.

160. Éloi Johanneau, 'Avertissement du traducteur', in Don J. de Erro y Aspiroz, *La langue primitive de l'Espagne et explication de ses plus anciens monumens, en inscriptions et medailles*, trans. Éloi Johanneau (Paris, 1808), 1–8.

161. J.F.M.M.A. Le Gonidec, *Grammaire Celto-Bretonne* (Paris, 1807).

162. On 'Celtomanie' in late eighteenth-century language study, Droixhe, *La Linguistique,* 142–56.

163. On 'Celtomanie' and the Académie see Stewart, 'Language and the National Past', 236–42.

164. Johanneau, 'Réflexions', 379–81; *Mémoires de l'Académie celtique,* vol. 6, 5–27.

165. The term was coined by J.-M. Baudouin de Maison-Blanche (1742–1812) in *Mémoires de l'Académie celtique,* vol. 4, 351. See also Johanneau's use of 'manie' and 'Celtomane' to describe the work of some of his predecessors, vol. 2, 430, and vol. 6, 11, 15.

166. Archives nationales, 36 AS 1, fo. 14.

167. O'Halloran, *Golden Ages.*

Chapter Six: From Philology to Ethnology

1. Thomas Hodgkin, 'Obituary of Dr. Prichard', *Journal of the Ethnological Society of London* 2 (1850), 185.

2. Jean-Frédéric Schaub and Silvia Sebastiani, *Race et histoire dans les sociétés occidentales (xve-xviiie siècle)* (Paris, 2021); Justin E. H. Smith, *Nature, Human Nature, and Human Difference in Early Modern Philosophy* (Princeton, NJ, 2015); Doron, *L'Homme altéré.*

3. See Silvia Sebastiani, 'Civilization and Perfectibility: Conflicting Views of the History of Humankind?', in John Robertson (ed.), *Time, History, and Political Thought* (Cambridge, 2023), 196–97; Ian Stewart, 'Racialising the World: Civilisation, Knowledge, and the Crystallisation of Race in European Thought', in Sarah C. Dunstan and Ian Stewart, *Race: Histories of an Idea in the Modern World* (forthcoming).

4. Linda Andersson Burnett and Bruce Buchan, *Race and the Scottish Enlightenment: A Colonial History, c. 1750–1820* (New Haven, CT, forthcoming).

5. The terms 'monogenesis' and 'polygenesis' were coined by the racist, pro-slavery American polygenists J. C. Nott and G. R. Gliddon, in *Indigenous Races of the Earth* (Philadelphia, PA, 1857), 402–602.

6. William Jones, 'The Third Anniversary Discourse, on the Hindus, delivered 2[d] February 1786', in John Shore, Baron Teignmouth, *The Works of Sir William Jones* (13 vols., London, 1807), vol. 3, 34.

7. As we saw in the previous chapter, it is highly ironic that 'Celtomania' was coined by those in the *Académie celtique,* against whom the epithet has been wielded ever since.

8. James Cowles Prichard, *The Eastern Origin of the Celtic Nations: Proved by a Comparison of their Dialects with the Sanskrit, Greek, Latin, and Teutonic Languages* (London and Oxford, 1831), 23.

9. See, for example, Erich Poppe, 'Lag es in der Luft?: Johann Kaspar Zeuß und die Konstituierung der Keltologie', *Beiträge zur Geschichte der Sprachwissenschaft* 2 (1992), 41–56; *idem,* 'Das weite Feld der "keltischen Philologie(n)"', *Beiträge zur Geschichte der Sprachwissenschaft* 11 (2001), 302–17; Toon Van Hal, 'From Jones to Pictet: Some Notes on the Early History of Celtic Linguistics', *Beiträge zur Geschichte der Sprachwissenschaft* 15 (2005), 219–43; Thomas Charles-Edwards, 'The Lure of the Celtic Languages, 1850–1914', in Marios Costambeys, Andrew Hamer, and Martin Heale (ed.), *The Making of the Middle Ages* (Liverpool, 2007), 15–35.

10. See, for example, *New London Review* 1 (1799), 508–10; *Edinburgh Review* 2 (1803), 116–28. See Alexander Murray's verdict of Vallancey's book in 1803 as 'pure nonsense' (Murray to Archibald Constanble, 20 April 1803, NLS, MS 681, f. 60r.).

11. Peter Roberts (trans.), *The Chronicle of the Kings of Britain* (London, 1811), 251.

12. See esp. William Betham, *The Gael and Cymbri* (Dublin, 1834), 328; *idem*, *Etruria-Celtica* (2 vols., Dublin, 1842). It is possible that it was Betham who wrote in the *Dublin Penny Journal* (1832), 94, that Gaelic might be 'radically different' from the Brittonic branch.

13. William K. Sullivan, 'Celtic Studies', *The Atlantis* 3 (1863), 49.

14. For a summary of Rask's criticisms, see Alderik H. Blom, 'Rasmus Rask's Study of Celtic', *Beiträge zur Geschichte der Sprachwissenschaft* 19 (2009), 223–51, esp. 225–32. I am grateful to the author for providing me with an offprint of this article during the height of the Covid-19 pandemic.

15. Christoph Meiners, *Grundriss der Geschichte der Menscheit* (Lemgo, 1785), 30–5. For a summary, see Sabine Vetter, *Wissenschaftlicher Reduktionismus und die Rassentheorie von Christophe Meiners* (Mainz, 1996), 195–207. See also Morgan Golf-French, 'Teaching Race in the German Enlightenment: Christoph Meiners' History of Humanity in Institutional Context', *History of Universities* 34 (2023), 243–60, and the author's other works.

16. Christoph Meiners, 'Of the Beauty of the Human Form, and of the propensity in all ugly nations to render themselves still more ugly', in *Selections from the most celebrated Foreign Literary Journals and other Periodical Publications* (2 vols., London, 1798), vol. 1, 343.

17. Britta Rupp-Eisenreich, 'The "Société des Observateurs de l'Homme" and German Ethno-Anthropology at the End of the 18th Century', *History of Anthropology Newsletter* 10 (1983), 5–11.

18. Bibliothèque de l'Académie nationale de médecine, Paris, MS 165/81, f. 1, f. 207.

19. J. J. Virey, *Histoire naturelle du genre humain* (2 vols., Paris, 1800), vol. 1, 129, 145–47.

20. It must be noted that in the second edition of the work published in 1824 Virey more assiduously separated Celts and Germans.

21. Schoepflin, *Alsatiae Illustratae*; J. C. Adelung and J. S. Vater, *Mithridates* (4 vols., Berlin, 1806–1817), vol. 2, 31.

22. Martin-Jean de Bast, *Recherches historiques et littéraires sur la langue celtique, gauloise, et tudesque* (2 vols., Gand, 1815); Van Hal, 'From Jones to Pictet', 225.

23. See, for example, Christian Gottlieb von Arndt, *Ueber den Ursprung und die verschiedenartige Verwandschaft der Europaeischen Sprachen* (Frankfurt, 1818), 17–57, esp. 43; he included not only Basque but also Albanian as a Celtic language.

24. Vans Kennedy, *Researches into the Origin and Affinity of the Principal Languages of Asia and Europe* (London, 1828), 66n. On Kennedy, see Ludo Rocher, 'Vans Kennedy (1784–1846): A Preliminary Bio-Bibliography', *Journal of the American Oriental Society* 109 (1989), 621–25.

25. Kennedy, *Researches*, 85.

26. Prichard, *Researches into the Physical History of Mankind*, (3rd ed., London, 1841), vol. 3, 136n.

27. Garland Cannon (ed.), *The Letters of Sir William Jones* (2 vols., Oxford, 1970), vol. 1, 285.

28. Jones, 'Third Anniversary Discourse', 34–35.

29. T. E. Colebrooke, *The Life of H. T. Colebrooke* (London, 1867), 84.

30. The modern authority is Anna Morpurgo Davies, *History of Linguistics: Volume IV: The Nineteenth Century* (London, 2000). However, on developments in Britain at the time, see Ian

Stewart, 'After Sir William Jones: British Linguistic Scholarship and European Intellectual History', *Journal of Modern History* 95 (2023), 808–46.

31. Friedrich Schlegel, *Ueber die Sprache und Weisheit der Indier* (Heidelberg, 1808), 81–84. He mentions consulting Le Brigant, Pinkerton, and Vallancey, along with some of the Scottish Gaelic grammarians, in the note on page 81.

32. See, however, Blom, 'Rasmus Rask's Study of Celtic'.

33. *Göttingische Gelehrte Anzeigen* (1824), 114.

34. A synthetic work detailing Celticism in nineteenth-century German scholarship is a desideratum, but see the essays of Erich Poppe on Welsh and Irish studies in Germany.

35. *British Review and London Critical Journal* 6 (1815), 510.

36. The standard biographies are Hannah Franziska Augstein, *James Cowles Prichard's Anthropology: Remaking the Science of Man in Early Nineteenth-Century Britain* (Amsterdam, 1999); George W. Stocking Jr., 'From Chronology to Ethnology: James Cowles Prichard and British Anthropology, 1800–1850', in *idem* (ed.), James Cowles Prichard, *Researches into the Physical History of Mankind* (1813: Chicago, 1973), xxxiv–xl. The biographical details in these works are based primarily on obituaries, but Margaret Crump is writing the definitive life of Prichard based upon a large corpus of his own writings. I am very grateful to her for sharing her research and many sources with me. See Margaret Crump, *Dr Prichard of the Red Lodge: A Life of Science during the Age of Improvement* (Lincoln, NE, forthcoming).

37. Hodgkin, 'Obituary of Dr. Prichard', 185.

38. J. C. Prichard, 'On the Varieties of the Human Race', *Royal Medical Society Dissertations*, 58 (1807–1808), 87–133.

39. Bill Jenkins, 'Race before Darwin: Variation, Adaptation and the Natural History of Man in Post-Enlightenment Edinburgh, 1790–1835', *British Journal of the History of Science* 53 (2020), 333–50; Kidd, *The Forging of Races: Race and Scripture in the Protestant Atlantic World, 1600–2000* (Cambridge, 2006), 101–4.

40. Prichard, *Researches* (1813), ii–iii; Augstein, *James Cowles Prichard's Anthropology*, 106–7. See Ian Stewart, 'Dugald Stewart and Racial Theory at the University of Edinburgh in the Late Scottish Enlightenment' (forthcoming).

41. Prichard, *Researches* (1813), 61, 71.

42. There was a long history of similar assumptions; see esp. David Bindman, *Ape to Apollo: Aesthetics and the Idea of Race in the 18th Century* (London, 2002). That climate and the 'state of society' had produced racial variation was a common view in Edinburgh at the time Prichard studied there.

43. Prichard, *Researches* (1813), 232–33.

44. Edward Davies, *Celtic Researches on the Origins, Traditions and Language of the Ancient Britons* (London, 1804), lviii.

45. J. C. Prichard to Iolo Morganwg, 2 February 1815, NLW, MS 21282E, f. 387; J. C. Prichard to Taliesin Williams, NLW, MS 21275E, f. 593. I am grateful to Margaret Crump for information about Edward Davies's visit to the Prichards in 1802. Taliesin went to see Prichard when he was ill in 1843 [William Williams to Taliesin Williams, 4 March 1843, NLW, MS 21278E, no. 994 and no. 995].

46. *British Review and London Critical Journal* 6 (1815), 507–8.

47. On Prichard's Celtic scholarship, see Ian Stewart, 'James Cowles Prichard and the Linguistic Foundations of Ethnology', *Berichte zur Wissenschaftsgeschichte* 46 (2023), 76–91.

48. Prichard, *Researches* (1813), 473.

49. Prichard, *Researches* (1813), 534.

50. *Edinburgh Review* 13 (1809), 366–84.

51. Rosane Rocher, *Alexander Hamilton (1762–1824): A Chapter in the Early History of Sanskrit Philology* (New Haven, CT, 1968).

52. See also *Edinburgh Review* 33 (1820), 432.

53. Prichard, *Researches* (1813), 534–35n.

54. Prichard's review strongly suggests that he had read Schlegel's *Über die Sprache und Weisheit der Indier*, because their idealisations of the inflecting Indo-European languages and ambiguity on how they reached such perceived refinement are strikingly similar.

55. *British Review and London Critical Journal* 6 (1815), 507–8.

56. *British Review and London Critical Journal* 6 (1815, 507–8.

57. *British Review and London Critical Journal* 6 (1815), 507–8.

58. *British Review and London Critical Journal* 6 (1815), 511.

59. Prichard, *Researches* (2nd ed., 2 vols., London, 1826), vol. 2, 105–49.

60. Thanks to Margaret Crump, who provided me with data from Prichard's Bristol Library Society records.

61. Prichard, *Eastern Origin*, 23; *Göttingische Gelehrte Anzeigen*, 18 February 1832, 257–62.

62. Prichard, *Eastern Origin*, 8.

63. Prichard, *Eastern Origin*, 9–13, 17.

64. Prichard, *Eastern Origin*, 19–23.

65. *British Review and London Critical Journal* 6 (1815), 507–8.

66. Prichard, *Eastern Origin*, 27–64, quote at 36.

67. Prichard, *Eastern Origin*, 28–29. In Sanskrit, this process (*sandhi*) is apparently almost universally triggered by phonological causes, while in the Celtic languages there are grammatical elements in play.

68. Prichard, *Eastern Origin*, 120–25. Welsh makes up for this in some ways with the prepositional pronoun system common to the Celtic languages.

69. Prichard, *Eastern Origin*, 191.

70. Prichard, *Disputatio inauguralis de generis humani varietate* (Edinburgh, 1808), 138: [Nec minus notabilis congruentia est, inter linguas Hebraeam et Cambriae populi, non in vocabulis solum, sed quod multo magis momenti est, et ipsa sermonis compositione, et declinationibus verborum]. Ironically, the comment is important in its own right for containing a fairly early recognition in the importance of grammatical morphology in proving linguistic kinship.

71. Augstein, *James Cowles Prichard's Anthropology*; Hannah Franziska Augstein, 'Aspects of Philology and Racial Theory in Nineteenth Century Celticism: The Case of James Cowles Prichard', *Journal of European Studies* 28 (1998), 359–60; *idem*, 'Linguistics and Politics in the Early Nineteenth Century: James Cowles Prichard's Moral Philology', *History of European Ideas* 23 (1997), 10–11.

72. William Whewell, *The Philosophy of the Inductive Sciences, Founded upon their History* (2 vols., London, 1840), vol. 2, 108; Arthur Stanley, *The Life and Correspondence of Thomas Arnold* (2 vols., London, 1844), vol. 2, 202.

73. Richard Garnett, 'Prichard on the Celtic Languages', reprinted in Richard Garnett, *The Philological Essays of the Late Rev. Richard Garnett, of the British Museum* (London, 1859), 78–110, quote at 80; Richard Garnett to Taliesin Williams, 25 January 1838, NLW 21272E, f. 189. For

examples of Prichard's use by other English philologists, see Joseph Bosworth, *A Dictionary of the Anglo-Saxon Language* (London, 1838), esp. v; W. B. Winning, *A Manual of Comparative Philology* (London, 1838), viii.

74. Daniel Hack Tuke, *Prichard and Symonds in Especial Relation to Mental Science with Chapters on Moral Insanity* (London, 1891), 6–7.

75. *Göttingische Gelehrte Anzeigen*, 18 February 1832, 257–62.

76. Nicholas Wiseman, *Twelve Lectures on the Connexion Between Science and Revealed Religion* (1837: 2nd ed., London, 1842), 37.

77. *Dublin Review* 2 (1837), 293–329.

78. 'Extract of letter from Mme Bunsen', 17 March 1841, NLW, MS 13182C, f. 19.

79. Augstein, 'Aspects', 359, is aware of the relationship between Prichard and Bunsen but does not connect it to Prichard's Celtic work.

80. C.C.J. Bunsen, 'On the results of the recent Egyptian researches in reference to Asiatic and African Ethnology, and the Classification of Languages', in *Three Linguistic Dissertations read at the meeting of The British Association in Oxford* (London, 1848), 257, 261, 265.

81. Charles Meyer, 'On the Importance of the Study of the Celtic Language as exhibited by the Modern Celtic Dialects still extant', in *Three Linguistic Dissertations*, 301–2. Diefenbach published his etymological work *Celtica* in 1839–1840.

82. Poppe, 'Lag es in der Luft?', 50.

83. *Jahrbücher der Literatur* 103 (1843), 118–48. Further evidence for the continental influence of Prichard can be found in Van Hal, 'From Jones to Pictet', and Poppe, 'Lag es in der Luft?', esp. 51.

84. Theodor Benfey, *Geschichte der Sprachwissenschaft und orientalischen Philologie in Deutschland* (Munich, 1869), 510n3, 655.

85. As seen below, Pictet must have known about Prichard's Celtic book and Bopp owned a copy of it, which is now in the Cornell University Library. William Sullivan, 'Preface', in Hermann Ebel, *Celtic Studies* (London, 1863), vi–vii, suggests that Prichard's work stimulated the works of Pictet, Bopp, and Diefenbach.

86. Prichard, *Researches* (3rd ed., London, 1841), vol. 3.1, 49–200.

87. Prichard, *Researches* (3rd ed., London, 1841), vol. 3.1, 139.

88. Madame Bunsen to the Cymreigyddion, 17 March 1841, NLW, MS 13182E11.

89. J. C. Prichard to Charles Bunsen, 7 October 1842, Geheimes Staatsarchiv Preußischer Kulturbesitz, Berlin, VI. HA Bunsen, B 36. Thanks to Margaret Crump for these sources.

90. J. C. Prichard to Bunsen, 20 October 1842, Geheimes Staatsarchiv Preußischer Kulturbesitz, Berlin, VI. HA Bunsen, B 36.

91. Claude Blanckaert, 'On the Origins of French Ethnology: William Edwards and the Doctrine of Race', in George W. Stocking Jr. (ed.), *Bones, Bodies, Behavior: Essays on Biological Anthropology* (Madison, WI, 1988), 18–55

92. For a biography, see Ian B. Stewart, 'William Frédéric Edwards and the Study of Human Races in France, from the Restoration to the July Monarchy', *History of Science* 58 (2020), 275–300.

93. W. F. Edwards, *De l'Influence des agens physiques sur la vie* (Paris, 1824) made his scientific reputation.

94. Jules Michelet, *Écrits de jeunesse: journal (1820–1823)—Mémorial journal des idées*, ed. Paul Viallaneix (Paris, 1959), 244, 247.

95. Stewart, 'William Frédéric Edwards', 285.

96. M. Seliger, 'Race-Thinking during the Restoration', *JHI* 19 (1958): 273–82, esp. 275–76; M. Seliger, 'The Idea of Conquest and Race-Thinking during the Restoration', *The Review of Politics* 22 (1960), 544–67.

97. Amédée Thierry, *Histoire des Gaulois, depuis les temps plus reculés jusqu'a l'entière soumission de la Gaule á la dominion Romaine* (3 vols., Paris, 1828), vol. 1, lxix–lxx.

98. W. F. Edwards, *Des caractères physiologiques des races humaines considérés dans leurs rapports avec l'histoire* (Paris, 1829), 5, 11–21, 21–29, 30–35.

99. Edwards, *Des caractères physiologiques*, 47–48.

100. Edwards, *Des caractères physiologiques*, 44n68.

101. Edwards, *Des caractères physiologiques*, 5n68.

102. See Stewart, 'William Frédéric Edwards'.

103. Edwards, *Des caractères physiologiques*, 99.

104. Edwards, *Des caractères physiologiques*, 100–102.

105. W. F. Edwards, *Recherches sur les langues celtiques* (Paris, 1844), iii.

106. Edwards, *Recherches*, 32.

107. Edwards, *Recherches*, ix–xi.

108. Edwards, *Recherches*, 13, 56.

109. Edwards, *Recherches*, 14–16.

110. W. F. Edwards, 'De l'influence réciproque des races sur le caractère national', *Mémoires de la Société ethnologique* 2 (1845), 1–12.

111. W. F. Edwards, 'Fragments d'un mémoire sur les Gaëls', *Mémoires de la Société Ethnologique de Paris* 2 (1845), 13–43, at 42n117.

112. Poppe, 'Lag es in der Luft?', 48–49.

113. A. W. Schlegel, 'Sur l'Origine des Hindous', *Transactions of the Royal Society of Literature* 2 (1834), 405–46.

114. Schlegel, 'Sur l'Origine', 442–44. August Pott favoured a similar explanation in 1836.

115. See, for example, a piece of doggerel from 1835 ridiculing the Académie française's plans for a new edition of its dictionary, in which he again singled out the Celtomaniac villains 'Court de Gebelin . . . Pezron, Pelloutier, Lebrigand' and joked that their ancestors the Gauls had all been cuckolded by the Franks (A. W. Schlegel, 'Examen des quarante', in Édouard Böcking (ed.), *Oeuvres de Auguste-Guillaume de Schlegel, écrites en francais* [3 vols., Leipzig, 1846), vol. 1, 35–36]).

116. Adolph Pictet, 'Lettres à M. A.W. de Schlegel sur l'affinité des langues celtiques avec le sanscrit', *Journal asiatique* 3.1 (1836), 263–90, 417–48; 3.2 (1836), 440–66.

117. Remarkably, there is no biography of Pictet, but see Maurice Olender, *Les langues du paradis* (Paris, 1989), 177–97.

118. See Pictet to his father, 4 December 1820, Bibliothèque de Genève [hereafter BGE], Papers d'Adolphe Pictet, Ms. fr. 4222, f. 34^{r}; Pictet to his father, 29 February 1823, BGE, Ms. fr. 4222, f. 62^{r}.

119. Pictet to his father, 17 April 1823, BGE, Ms. fr. 4222, ff. 65^{v}-66^{r}.

120. Pictet to his father, 17 April 1823, BGE, Ms. fr. 4222, f. 66^{r}.

121. Pictet to his father, 17 April 1823, BGE, Ms. fr. 4222, f. 66^{r}. See also Pictet to his father, 18 May 1823, BGE, Ms. fr. 4222, f. 67^{r}.

122. Adolphe Pictet, *Du culte des Cabires chez les anciens irlandais* (Geneva and Paris, 1824), iv, 5.

123. Pictet, 'Lettres', 3.1, 264.

124. Since Pictet was responding to Schlegel's article 'Sur l'origine des Hindous', in which Schlegel included comments on Prichard's Celtic work, Pictet must have known about it.

125. Pictet, 'Lettres', 3.1, 264–65.

126. A. W. von Schlegel, 'Vorrede', in J. C. Prichard, *Darstellung der Aegyptischen Mythologie*, trans. L. Haymann (Bonn, 1837), v–vi.

127. Pictet, 'Lettres', 3.1, 264. Pictet's eventual magnum opus was a major study of the ancient Indo-Europeans (Adolphe Pictet, *Les origins indo-européennes, ou les Aryas primitifs: essai de paléontologie linguistique* [2 vols., 1859–1863]).

128. Adolph Pictet, 'Lettres', 3.2, 453–56.

129. Paragraph contained in Robert Macadam to John O'Donovan, 21 April 1859, Royal Irish Academy [hereafter RIA], 24 O 39/JOD/191(xxxv).

130. Franz Bopp, 'Über die celtischen Sprachen vom Gesichtspunkte der vergleichenden Sprachforschung', *Abhandlungen der Königlichen Akademie der Wissenschaften zu Berlin, Aus dem Jahre 1838* (Berlin, 1839), [Philologische und historische Abhandlungen], 187–272.

131. Franz Bopp, 'Vergleichende Zergliederung des Sanskrits und der mit ihm verwandten Sprachen', *Abhandlungen der historisch-philologischen Klasse der Königlichen Akademie der Wissenschaften zu Berlin aus dem Jahre 1824* (Berlin, 1826), 123.

132. Bopp, 'Über die celtischen Sprachen', 187–89. It should be noted that Bopp's emphasis is firmly on what Celtic can reveal about Sanskrit and its early history, not vice versa.

133. Bopp, 'Über die celtischen Sprachen', 190.

134. The Brittonic languages have the most mutations. For example, in Welsh *plant* (children) can be spelled *blant, mhlant*, or *phlant* based on the rule in operation, with corresponding sound changes.

135. Bopp, 'Über die celtischen Sprachen', 206–9.

136. Bopp, 'Über die celtischen Sprachen', 209.

137. The biography from which most subsequent accounts have derived is Christian Wilhelm Glück, *Erinnerung an Kaspar Zeuss* (Munich, 1857). See also Francis Shaw, 'Johann Kaspar Zeuss', *Studies* 43 (1954), 194–206; Hans Hablitzel, *Prof. Dr. Johann Kaspar Zeuss: Begründer der Keltologie und Historiker aus Vogtendorf/Oberfranken* (Kronach, 1987); Hans Hablitzel and David Stifter, *Johann Kaspar Zeuß im kultur-und sprachwissenschaftlichen Kontext (19.bis21.Jahrhundert)* (Vienna, 2007).

138. Hablitzel, *Prof. Dr. Johann Kaspar Zeuss*, 316–17.

139. Francis Shaw, 'The Background to *Grammatica Celtica*', *Celtica* 3 (1956), 1–16, is a pioneering article in this regard, but see also Poppe, 'Lag es in der Luft?'.

140. [Johann] K. Zeuß, *Die Herkunft der Baiern von den Markomannen* (Munich, 1839), iv.

141. Erich Poppe, 'Johann Kaspar Zeuß und die Keltomanie', in Michael Wollenschläger, Eckhard Kreßel, and Johann Egger (eds.), *Recht-Wirtschaft-Kultur: Herausforderungen an Staat und Gesellschaft im Zeitalter der Globalisierung* (Berlin, 2005), 239–50; *idem*, 'The Welsh Language in German Philology around 1850', in Bernhard Maier (ed.), *150 Jahre "Mabinogion"—Deutsch-Walisische Kulturbeziehungen* (Tübingen, 2001), esp. 208–10. Poppe uses the German spelling of 'Kelt', which I have rendered 'Celt' in line with the rest of this book.

142. For some background on this, see Brent Maner, *Germany's Ancient Pasts: Archaeological and Historical Interpretation since 1700* (Chicago, 2018), 88–96.

143. Adolf Holtzmann, *Kelten und Germanen: Eine Historische Untersuchung* (Stuttgart, 1855), 1–8.

144. Those with a taste for irony might remember that James Macpherson made the same tripartite split.

145. [Johann] Kaspar Zeuß, *Die Deutschen und die Nachbarstämme* (Munich, 1837), 17–18. A similar line is repeated in Zeuß, *Die Herkunft*, iv–v.

146. Zeuß, *Die Deutschen*, 20n.

147. Cf. Thurneysen, 'Why Do Germans Study Celtic Philology?', 23.

148. Poppe, 'Lag es in der Luft?', 52.

149. Zeuß, *Die Herkunft*, ix. Bullet's book was a 'fantastic Mishmash' (xv).

150. Zeuß, *Die Herkunft*, xi–xx, esp. xi, xvii.

151. For discussion, see Anna Helene Feulner, '"Geschichtsforcher und Sprachkenner": Zu Zeuß' Markomannentheorie', in Hablitzel and Stifter, *Johann Kaspar Zeuß*, 49–93, esp. 54.

152. Andreas Hüther, 'Keltische Forschungen im 19. Jahrhundert zum Zweck regionaler Identitätskonstruktionen: Eine Forschungsskizze', in Ingo Wiwjorra and Dietrich Hakelberg (eds.), *Archäologie und Nation: Kontexte der Erforschung 'vaterlandischen Alterthums'* (Heidelberg, 2021), 253–60.

153. See, for example, J. M. Kemble's reference in Raymond A. Wiley (ed.), *John Mitchell Kemble and Jakob Grimm: A Correspondence, 1832–1852* (Leiden, 1971), 183.

154. Passages quoted in Poppe, 'Johann Kaspar Zeuss', 112–13.

155. Charles-Edwards, 'Celtic Languages', provides an especially clear account of the construction and significance of the book.

156. Zeuß, *Grammatica Celtica* (2 vols., Leipzig, 1853), vol. 2, 911.

157. Zeuß, *Grammatica Celtica*, vol. 1, xii.

158. Shaw, 'Johann Kaspar Zeuss', 198; Charles-Edwards, 'Celtic Languages', 21. Zeuß also consulted all the modern sources he could get his hands on, including the recently published Endlicher's glossary [Zeuß, *Grammatica Celtica*, vol. 1, 13], the *Myvyrian Archaiology*, and the *Mabinogion*.

159. L. Delâtre, *Revue archaeologie* 10 (1853), 762–64.

160. Dáibhí Ó Cróinín, 'The Reception of Johann Kaspar Zeuss's *Grammatica Celtica* in Ireland and Britain, and on the Continent: Some New Evidence', in Wollenschläger, Kreßel, and Egger (eds.), *Recht-Wirtschaft-Kultur*, 85–91.

161. See NLW, MS 922C.

162. *Cambrian Journal* (1854), 291–94.

163. *Archaeologia Cambrensis*, New Series 5 (1854), 230.

164. Pól Ó Dochartaigh, '"A Shadowy but Important Figure"': Rudolf Thomas Siegfried', in Elizabeth Boyle & Paul Russell, *The Tripartite Life of Whitley Stokes (1830–1909)* (Dublin, 2011), 29–43.

165. R. T. Siegfried to Adolphe Pictet, BGE Ms. fr. 4229, f. 138r.

166. John O'Donovan, 'Zeuss's "Grammatica Celtica"', *Ulster Journal of Archaeology* 7 (1859), 11; Michael Herity, 'Whitley Stokes's Correspondence with John O'Donovan, 1857–1861', *Studia*

Hibernica 36 (2009–2010), 9–89; see also the correspondence between John O'Donovan and William Reeves at University College Dublin [hereafter UCD].

167. Herity, 'Whitley Stokes's Correspondence', 69. O'Donovan was referring to Mone and Leo.

168. Ludwig Chr. Stern, 'Briefe von J. K. Zeuss an Chr. W. Glück', *Zeitschrift für Celtische Philologie* 3 (1901), 363–64.

169. Verena Schwartz, 'Kelten bei dem Laienforscher Christian Keferstein (1784–1866)', in Simeone Kahlow, Judith Schachtmann, and Cathrin Hähn (eds.), *Grenzen überwinden: Archëologie zwischen Disziplin und Disziplinen* (Rahden, 2021), 85–92.

170. Poppe, 'Johann Kaspar Zeuß', 245–47.

171. Holtzmann, *Kelten und Germanen*, ix–xiv, 1–7.

172. H.B.C. Brandes, *Das ethnographische verhältniss der Kelten und Germanen* (Leipzig, 1857), 87.

173. William K. Sullivan, 'Preface', in Ebel, *Celtic Studies*, iii.

174. Sullivan, 'Celtic Studies', 49.

175. Pedersen's classic *Linguistic Science in the Nineteenth Century* takes no notice of either Prichard or Pictet.

176. *The Saturday Review*, vol. 6, 7 August 1858, 139.

177. Joep Leerssen, *Remembrance and Imagination: Patterns in the Historical and Literary Representation of Ireland in the Nineteenth Century* (Cork, 1996), 90–91.

Chapter Seven: The Celtic Past in the Age of Romantic Nationalism

1. See, for example, Pittock, *Celtic Identity*, chapter 2; Davies, *Isles*, 78–79; Tanner, *Last of the Celts*, 17–18; Morse, *Celts*, 47–48; Chapman, *Celts*, 120–45; Richard McMahon, *The Races of Europe: Construction of National Identities in the Social Sciences, 1839–1939* (Basingstoke, 2016), 169.

2. Joep Leerssen, 'Notes towards a Definition of Romantic Nationalism', *Romantik* 2 (2013), 28.

3. Thiesse, *La création*; Leerssen, *National Thought*; *idem*, *Encyclopedia of Romantic Nationalism in Europe* (2 vols., Amsterdam, 2018).

4. See, for example, O'Halloran, *Golden Ages*; *eadem*, 'Harping on the Past: Translating Antiquarian Learning into Popular Culture in Early Nineteenth-Century Ireland', in Melissa Calaresu, Filippo de Vivo, and Joan-Pau Rubiés (eds.), *Exploring Cultural History: Essays in Honour of Peter Burke* (Farnham, 2010), 327–43; Constantine, *Truth*. See also Joep Leerssen, 'Literary Historicism: Romanticism, Philologists, and the Presence of the Past', *Modern Language Quarterly* 65 (2004), 221–43.

5. O'Halloran, *Golden Ages*, 186. See also Vance, 'Celts'.

6. Lionel Gossman, *Between History and Literature* (Cambridge, MA, 1990).

7. Kidd, 'Teutonist Ethnology'.

8. Marinell Ash, *The Strange Death of Scottish History* (Edinburgh, 1980); Kidd, *Subverting*.

9. Graeme Morton, *Unionist Nationalism: Governing Urban Scotland, 1830–60* (East Linton, 1999).

10. George Grierson, *The Letters of Sir Walter Scott* (12 vols., London, 1932–1937), vol. 1, 324.

11. Walter Scott, *Sir Tristrem* (1804: Edinburgh, 1819), lv.

12. Walter Scott, *Sir Tristrem*, lxv.

13. Malcolm Laing to John Pinkerton, 9 February 1799, Edinburgh, NLS, MS.1709, f. 78.

14. [Walter Scott], 'The Poetical Works of James Macpherson, &c., containing the Poems of Ossian', *Edinburgh Review* 6 (1805), 459, 462.

15. Hutton, *Blood*, 159.

16. Walter Scott, *Marmion; A Tale of Flodden Field* (Edinburgh, 1808), 242.

17. Walter Scott, *Marmion*, 247.

18. Grierson, *Letters*, vol. 1, 319–25.

19. Ferguson, *Scottish Nation*, 274–79.

20. George Chalmers, *Caledonia, Or an Account, Historical and Topographical of North Britain* (4 vols., Edinburgh, 1807–1824) vol. 1, 1–103, 198–234.

21. Walter Scott, *Sir Tristrem, a Metrical Romance of the Thirteenth Century* (1804: London, 1811), li, n.

22. Walter Scott, *The Antiquary* (1816: Oxford, 2002), 64.

23. [Walter Scott], 'Review of Joseph Ritson, *Annals of the Caledonians, Picts, and Scots*', *Quarterly Review* 41 (1829), 120–62.

24. [Scott], 'Review of Joseph Ritson', 143–44.

25. See, for example, Peter Womack, *Improvement and Romance: Constructing the Myth of the Highlands* (Basingstoke, 1989); Kenneth McNeil, *Scotland, Britain, Empire: Writing the Highlands, 1760–1860* (Columbus, OH, 2007); Leask, *Stepping Westward*.

26. 'Celtic Society Minute Book', Vol. I, 1820–1824, NLS, Royal Celtic Society Archives [hereafter RCSA], TD-3690 1, ff. 1, 11, 98.

27. 'Celtic Society Minute Book', f. 98.

28. John Sinclair, *An Account of the Highland Society of London, From its Establishment in May 1778, to the Commencement of the Year 1813* (London, 1813), 7.

29. John Prebble, *The King's Jaunt* (London, 1988).

30. NLS, RCSA, Box 17(i).

31. 'Celtic Society Minute Book', ff. 54–55.

32. Walter Scott to Graham Stirling, 24 August 1822, NLS, RCSA, Box 17(i).

33. McNeil, *Scotland*, 73–81; Pittock, *Celtic Identity*, 42.

34. W. P. Colyear Roberton to Highland Society of London, 21 February 1807, NLS, Dep.268, 1.

35. The archetypal work is Stanley Mellon, *The Political Uses of History: A Study of Historians in the French Restoration* (Stanford, CA, 1958). See also Sylvain Venayre, *Les origines de la France: Quand les historiens racontaient la nation* (Paris, 2013), Shirley M. Gruner, 'Political Historiography in Restoration France', *History and Theory* 8 (1969), 346–65; Ceri Crossley, *French Historians and Romanticism: Thierry, Guizot, the Saint-Simonians, Quinet, Michelet* (London, 1993), esp. 1–44; D'Auria, *Shaping*, 249–358.

36. On Thierry, see D'Auria, *Shaping*, 291–321; Gossman, *Between History*, 83–151.

37. Augustin Thierry, 'Introduction', in Armand Carrel, *Résume de l'histoire d'Écosse* (Paris, 1825), ii–iii.

38. Augustin Thierry, *Lettres sur l'histoire de France, pour servir d'introduction à l'étude de cette histoire*, ed. Aude Déruelle (1827: Paris, 2012), 109, 97.

39. Thierry, *Histoire des Gaulois*, vol. 1, i–ii.

40. Thierry, *Histoire des Gaulois*, vol. 1, lxix.

41. Thierry, *Histoire des Gaulois*, vol. 1, xii, lxii.

42. Gervais de la Rue, *Recherches sur les ouvrages des bardes de la Bretagne armoricaine dans le moyen age* (Caen, 1815), 3, 17–18.

43. [Claude Fauriel], Review of *The Myvyrian Archaiology of Wales*, in *Archives philosophiques, politiques, et littéraires* 3 (1818), 88–116.

44. Fauriel, Review of *The Myvyrian Archaiology*, 96–97.

45. Fauriel, Review of *The Myvyrian Archaiology*, 98.

46. Constantine, *Truth*, 145–46.

47. Thierry, *Histoire des Gaulois*, vol. 1, lxiii, n. 1.

48. Thierry, *Histoire des Gaulois*, vol. 1, lxv.

49. Jules Michelet, *Histoire de France* (17 vols., Paris, 1833–1841), vol. 1, 48.

50. Jules Michelet, *Origines du droit français* (Paris, 1837), lxxxiv–lxxxvii.

51. Michelet, *Histoire de France*, vol. 1, 142–43n1. On Edwards and Michelet, see Stewart, 'William Frédéric Edwards', 295.

52. Michelet, *Histoire de France*, vol. 1, 145.

53. Michelet, *Histoire de France*, vol. 1, 43n1.

54. Michelet, *Histoire de France*, vol. 1, 150–51. This was also Edwards's view.

55. Michelet, *Histoire de France*, vol. 1, 460–72.

56. For examples of his familiarity with British evidence, see Michelet, *Histoire de France*, vol. 1, 460–72, 482–85.

57. Gabriel Hanotaux, *Henri Martin: sa vie—ses oeuvres—son temps, 1810–1883* (Paris, 1885); Charles Rearick, 'Henri Marti: From Druidic Traditions to Republican Politics', *Journal of Contemporary History* 7 (1972), 53–64.

58. Jean-Charles Geslot, 'Un inestimable succès: l'*Histoire de France* d'Henri Martin et ses publics', *Revue d'histoire du XIXe siècle* 69 (2020–2021), 239–55.

59. David Albert Griffiths, *Jean Reynaud, Encyclopediste de l'époque romantique, d'après sa correspondence inedite* (Paris, 1965), 275–77.

60. Jean Reynaud, *Considérations sur l'esprit de la Gaule* (Paris, 1847), 5–6.

61. Reynaud, *Considérations*, 303–6.

62. Henri Martin, *Histoire de France* (1833: 4th ed., 17 vols., Paris, 1855–1860), vol. 1, 479–81.

63. Martin, *Histoire de France*, vol. 1, xvi–xvii.

64. Hanotaux, *Henri Martin*, 235.

65. Martin, *Histoire de France*, vol. 1, 47–48.

66. Martin to Pictet, 17 September 1861, BGE Ms. fr. 4228, ff. 250r-v.

67. Martin to Johnes, 1 October 1868, NLW Dolaucaothi Records, L 3355.

68. Martin to Pictet, 17 September 1861, BGE Ms. fr. 4228, ff. 260r.

69. Thiesse, *La création*.

70. Émile Bourdon, *La forge gauloise de la nation: Ernest Lavisse et la fabrique des ancêtres* (Lyon, 2017).

71. Löffler, *Literary and Historical Legacy*.

72. Brynley F. Roberts, '"The Age of Restitution": Taliesin ab Iolo and the Reception of Iolo Morganwg', in Jenkins, *Rattleskull Genius*, 461–79; Hutton, *Blood*, 241–86.

73. [Thomas Price] Carnhuanawc, 'Hiliogaeth Gomer', *Y Seren Gomer* (1823), 81–83.

74. Jane Williams (ed.), *The Literary Remains of the Rev. Thomas Price* (2 vols., Llandovery, 1854–1855), vol. 2, 40–48, 52. Davies offered to recommend his curacy for Price on his retirement.

75. Williams, *Literary Remains*, vol. 2, 83–84, 93.

76. Williams, *Literary Remains*, vol. 2, 112.

77. Price to Taliesin Williams, 28 August 1826, NLW, MS 21275, f. 552.

78. Williams, *Literary Remains*, vol. 2, 265.

79. Williams, *Literary Remains*, vol. 2, 265–66.

80. Williams, *Literary Remains*, vol. 2, 83.

81. [Thomas Price] Carnhuanawc, 'Yr Iaith Geltaeg', *Seren Gomer* 64 (1821), 13 [yn taenu nid yn unig dros Brydain Fawr, ond hefyd dros holl Ffrainc, a'r rhan fwyaf o Ewropa].

82. [Thomas Price] Carnhuanawc, 'Yr Iaith Geltaeg', *Seren Gomer* 123 (1825), 361–63 [o fereu hyd nos].

83. Thomas Price, 'Philological Remarks on Greek, Latin and Celtic Words', *The Classical Journal* XXXVIII (1828), 269.

84. Price, 'Philological Remarks', 267–73; Williams, *Literary Remains*, vol. 2, 99–100.

85. Thomas Price, *An Essay on the Physiognomy and Physiology of the present Inhabitants of Britain; with reference to their origin as Goths and Celts* (London, 1829), 1–2.

86. Price, *An Essay*, 2, 51.

87. Price, *An Essay*, 3.

88. Price, *An Essay*, 13. Price pointed to figures like the Scottish geologist John MacCulloch (1773–1835) as having uncritically accepted Pinkerton's arguments. Five years previously, Price had called MacCulloch 'an inveterate enemy to the Celts' (Williams, *Literary Remains*, vol. 2, 86).

89. Price, *Essay*, 35.

90. See Pryce, *Writing Welsh History*, for a detailed description of the book.

91. Pryce, *Writing Welsh History*, 239–40.

92. Thomas Price, *Hanes Cymru* (Crughywel, 1842), 1. For the triad, see *Myvyrian Archaiology*, vol. 2, 57.

93. See Price's rejection of 'Lhuyd's speculation' in Price to Taliesin Williams, NLW 21275E, f. 568.

94. For a biography, see Revel Guest and Angela V. John, *Lady Charlotte Guest: An Extraordinary Life* (Stroud, 2007).

95. NLW, Lady Charlotte Guest MSS, XI, 2–3.

96. NLW, Lady Charlotte Guest MSS, XI, 10, 41, 103.

97. Lady Charlotte Guest, *The Mabinogion* (3 vols., London, 1849), vol. 1, xxii–xxiii.

98. See, for example, Adam Coward, *The Correspondence of Thomas Stephens: Revolutionising Welsh Scholarship in the Mid-Nineteenth Century through Knowledge Exchange* (Aberystwyth, 2020), 219.

99. For biographical information, see 'A few notes for the Biography of Thomas Stephens,' MS notebook in NLW, MS 966C.

100. Stephens won the contest judged by his neighbour from Neath, William Williams of Aberpergwm, and at least one person accused the latter of favoritism [see William Williams to Taliesin Williams, 27 August 1840, NLW, MS 21278E, no. 970].

101. Marion Löffler and Hywel Gethin Rhys, 'Thomas Stephens and the Abergavenny Cymreigyddion: Letters from the Cambrian 1842–3', *National Library of Wales Journal* 34 (2009), 399–451, at 407.

102. Taliesin had had to search out Stephens in 1840 on behalf of a friend of his who wanted to offer the young Stephens advice on competing in his first *eisteddfod* [see William Williams to Taliesin Williams, 29 February 1840, NLW 21278E, no. 950]. Price cautioned Taliesin to keep his cool [see Price to Taliesin, 14 February 1843, NLW, MS 21275E, no. 582].

103. NLW, MS 937B, 90–92.

104. Coward, *Correspondence*, 72.

105. Thomas Stephens, *The Literature of the Kymry*, ed. D. Silvan Evans (1849: London, 1876), x.

106. Coward, *Correspondence*, 152.

107. B. T. Williams, 'Life of Thomas Stephens,' in Stephens, *Literature of the Kymry*, xxv.

108. Coward, *Correspondence*, 107–10.

109. Coward, *Correspondence*, 113.

110. Coward, *Correspondence*, 115–27.

111. Coward, *Correspondence*, 153.

112. Löffler and Rhys, 'Thomas Stephens', 412–13, 449; NLW, MS 937B, 92.

113. *Guardian*, 30 November 1850, in NLW 966C.

114. Bromwich, 'Trioedd', 34–42.

115. Löffler, *Literary and Historical Legacy*, 67–70, 95.

116. See, for example, *Cambrian Journal* 2 (1855), 32.

117. Löffler, *Literary and Historical Legacy*, 97–98.

118. T. Price to Taliesin Williams, 12 July 1830, NLW 21275E, f. 558, f. 568.

119. Price to Taliesin Williams, 24 March 1840, NLW 21275 E, f. 568. Price scolded Taliesin fairly regularly that an antiquarian of his stature should always be citing originals and never secondary works or opinions [e.g., Price to Taliesin Williams, 8 May 1844, NLW 21275E, no. 587].

120. Löffler and Rhys, 'Thomas Stephens', 432.

121. Thomas Stephens, 'An Essay on the Bardic Alphabet Called "Coelbren Y Beirdd"', *Archaeologia Cambrensis* 4th Ser., v. 3 (1872), 181–210.

122. Stephens, 'An Essay'.

123. *Saturday Review*, 12 October 1861.

124. William Williams to Taliesin Williams, 17 April 1838, NLW 21278E, no. 911.

125. William Williams to Taliesin Williams, 21 April 1838, NLW 21278E, no. 912; William Williams to Taliesin Williams, 19 January 1839, NLW 21278E, no. 926.

126. William Williams to Taliesin Williams, 29 March 1840, NLW 21278E, no. 954; William Williams to Taliesin Williams, 19 June 1840, NLW 21278E, no. 966; William Williams to Taliesin Williams, 30 November 1841, NLW 21278E, no. 981.

127. *The Cambrian*, 13 June 1840, 4 July 1840, 18 July 1840.

128. A second volume was published in London in 1874.

129. Coward, *Correspondence*, 166.

130. Dean Powell, *Dr William Price: Wales's First Radical* (Stroud, 2012).

131. *Y Cymmrodor* I (1877), 46; Löffler, *Literary and Historical Legacy*, 58–59.

132. Löffler, *Literary and Historical Legacy*, 58–61.

133. Coward, *Correspondence*, 155.

134. John Peter to Henri Gaidoz, 31 August 1871, Bangor University Archives, BMSS/718.

135. Coward, *Correspondence*, 219.

136. Quoted in B. T. Williams, 'Life of Thomas Stephens', xxviii.

137. Foster, 'History and the Irish Question', 171–72.

138. Thanks to Friedrich Engels for this reference: *Karl Marx and Frederick Engels on Ireland* (London, 1971), 192n. See Roger O'Connor, *Chronicles of Eri; being the History of the Gaal Sciot Iber: or, the Irish People; translated from the original manuscripts in the Phoenician dialect of the Scythian language* (2 vols., London, 1822), vol. 1, cclxi.

139. The classic account is Charles Gavan Duffy, *Young Ireland: A Fragment of Irish History, 1840–1850* (2 vols., London, 1880–1883). For a good modern summary, see Richard Davis, *The Young Ireland Movement* (London, 1987).

140. See, for example, James Quinn, *Young Ireland and the Writing of Irish History* (Dublin, 2015); David Dwan, *The Great Community: Culture and Nationalism in Ireland* (Dublin, 2008).

141. Leerssen, *Remembrance*, *passim*, esp. 12.

142. Kevin Collins, *Catholic Churchmen and the Celtic Revival in Ireland, 1848–1916* (Dublin, 2002), 9–10.

143. J. H. Andrews, *A Paper Landscape: The Ordnance Survey in Nineteenth-Century Ireland* (Oxford, 1975).

144. He himself claimed expertise in 'the science (if it may be so called) of architectural antiquities' (George Petrie, *The Ecclesiastical Architecture of Ireland* [Dublin, 1845], 1); William Stokes, *The Life and Labours in Art and Archaeology, of George Petrie* (London, 1868); John Waddell, *Foundation Myths: The Beginnings of Irish Archaeology* (Bray, 2005), 103–113.

145. Stokes, *Life and Labours*, 23.

146. Betham was at least assisted by the lexicographer Edward O'Reilly, and even Eugene O'Curry offered him the use of Peter O'Connell's 'perfect' Irish glossary. See the letters between O'Reilly and Betham in NLI, MS 24, 587(7); Owen Curry [Eugene O'Curry] to William Betham, April(?) 1827, NLI, MS 24, 587(4).

147. Leerssen, *Remembrance*, 68–156.

148. Stokes, *Life and Labours*, 146–47.

149. Leerssen, *Remembrance*.

150. Petrie, *Ecclesiastical Architecture*, 2.

151. *Dublin Penny Journal* I (1832), 93–94.

152. William J. O'Neill Daunt, *A Catechism of the History of Ireland: Ancient and Modern* (Dublin, 1844), iii, 1.

153. Betham, *The Gael and the Cymbri*, viii, 328. The *Dublin Penny Journal* III (1834), 154–56, was unsure what to make of this.

154. Williams, *Remains*, vol. 2, 228.

155. Stokes, *Life and Labours*, 117–18; Wiseman, *Twelve Lectures*, 48–51. For a positive review, however, see *Belfast Newsletter*, 9 May 1834, 1.

156. Peter Rowley-Conway, *From Genesis to Prehistory: The Archaeological Three Age System and Its Contested Reception in Denmark, Britain, and Ireland* (Oxford, 2007), 200.

157. John O'Donovan, *A Grammar of the Irish Language* (Dublin, 1845), lxxxi–lxxxv. He noted in a letter of 1848 that he also owned Pictet's book (O'Donovan to Reeves, 14 July 1848, UCD Special Collections).

158. Letter printed in *Revue celtique* 6 (1883–1885), 416.

159. Quinn, *Young Ireland*.

160. Quinn, *Young Ireland*, 29.

161. See, for example, RIA, 24 O39/JOD 18/xiii.

162. Gavan Duffy, *Young Ireland*, 528.

163. Gavan Duffy, *Thomas Davis: The Memoirs of an Irish Patriot, 1840–1846* (London, 1890), 339.

164. Gavan Duffy, *Thomas Davis*, 295.

165. 'Our National Language', *The Nation* (1 April 1843), 12.

166. Thomas Davis, *The Poems of Thomas Davis*, ed. Thomas Wallis (Dublin, 1846), 27–29.

167. See also *The Nation* (4 November 1843), 3.

168. Davis, *Poems*, 27. Emphasis in original.

169. Thomas Davis, 'Ballad Poetry of Ireland', in *Prose Writings of Thomas Davies*, ed. T. W. Rolleston (London, 1890), 193.

170. O'Donovan to William Reeves, 26 July 1845, John O'Donovan and William Reeves Correspondence, UCD Special Collections.

171. O'Donovan to William Reeves, 13 May 1848, UCD, JO'D L 32; O'Donovan to Reeves, 14 July 1848, UCD, JO'D L 33.

172. W. E. Hudson to O'Donovan, 2 September 1848, RIA, 24 O39/18/iv, f. 1

173. Edward Berwick to O'Donovan, 6 August 1849, RIA, 24 O39/18/i.

174. W. H. Allen to O'Donovan, 19 October 1850, RIA, 24 O39/JOD/2(iii).

175. MacAdam to O'Donovan, 12 April 1850, RIA, 24 O39/JOD/191(i).

176. D. Murray, *Romanticism, Nationalism and Irish Antiquarian Societies, 1840–80* (Maynooth, 2000), 8–13.

177. Ciaran McDonough, 'Investigating Irish Antiquarianism: A Comparative Study of Protestant and Catholic Antiquarian Cultures, 1830–1876', PhD dissertation (University of Galway, 2017), chapter 2.

178. Nicholas O'Kearney to Smith O'Brien, 15 September 1858, NLI, MS G 1244/1.

179. Eugene O'Curry to W. S. O'Brien, 28 July 1862, NLI, MS G 1244/1.

180. See the entertaining biography in John O'Donvan to J. T. Gilbert, 2 December 1853, NLI, MS 1426.

181. John O'Donovan to J. T. Gilbert, 2 December 1853, NLI, MS 1426.

182. John O'Donovan to J. T. Gilbert, 2 December 1853, NLI, MS 1426.

183. O'Curry to [?], n.d., UCD Archives, LA 38/34.

184. Gaidoz to Pictet, 2 May 1869, BGE, Ms. fr. 4228/2, f. 183^{v}.

185. J. Vendryès, 'Keltisch von Herr Prof. Ord. Thurneysen vorgetragen' (1898–1899), Collège de France, Fonds Joseph Vendryès, 56 CDF 1/3, f. 37r.

186. O'Donovan to Reeves, 14 July 1848, UCD.

187. Stokes, *Life and Labours*, 405.

188. O'Donovan Rossa to O'Donovan, 4 October 1857, RIA, 24 O39/JOD/270 (xiv).

189. O'Donovan Rossa to O'Curry, 12 November 1861, UCD, LA 38/2.

190. Gaidoz to Pictet, BGE, MS fr. 4228/2.

191. J. T. Gilbert to Adolphe Pictet, BGE, Ms. fr. 4229, f. 61v.

192. Jean-Yves Guiomar, *Le Bretonisme: Les historiens bretons au xix*[e] *siècle* (Mayenne, 1987).

193. Ernest Renan, *Cahiers de Jeunesse: 1845–1846* (Paris, 1906), 326–27.

194. Biographers, including Renan himself, have placed strong emphasis on his Breton upbringing. See, for example, Ernest Renan, *Souvenirs d'enfance et de jeunesse* (Paris, 1883); Jean-Pierre van Deth, *Ernest Renan: Simple chercheur de vérité* (Paris, 2012), esp. chapter 1, 'une enfance bretonne'; Jean Balcou, *Ernest Renan: Une biographie* (Paris, 2017), 25–45.

195. Ernest Renan, *Correspondance générale*, ed. Anne-Marie de Brem, and Jean Balcou (3 vols., Paris, 1995–2008), vol. 2, 224.

196. Ernest Renan, 'La Poésie des races celtiques', *Revue des deux mondes* (1854), 473–506, subsequently updated and republished in Ernest Renan, *Essais de Morale et de Critique* (Paris, 1859), 375–456, [hereafter 'La Poésie' is cited from the *Revue des deux mondes*].

197. Renan, 'La Poésie', 474.

198. Renan, 'La Poésie', 475.

199. Renan, 'La Poésie', 473–74.

200. Renan, 'La Poésie', 475.

201. Renan, 'La Poésie', 479.

202. Renan, 'La Poésie', 495–505.

203. Cf. Young, *English Ethnicity*, 21. See also depictions of the Celts as feminine in Pittock, *Celtic Identity*, 62–93.

204. Renan, 'La Poésie', 478.

205. Renan, 'La Poésie', 478.

206. Renan, 'La Poésie', 475, 483.

207. Renan, 'La Poésie', 491.

208. Robert D. Priest, *The Gospel According to Renan: Reading, Writing, & Religion in Nineteenth-Century France* (Oxford, 2015).

209. Ernest Renan, *Vie de Jésus* (Paris, 1863), 5.

210. Renan, 'La Poésie', 476.

211. Renan, *Correspondance*, vol. 2, 84.

212. Renan, *Correspondance*, vol. 2, 203.

213. Ernest Renan, *Recollections and Letters of Ernest Renan*, trans. Isabel F. Hapgood (New York, 1892), 8.

214. Renan, 'La Poésie', 506.

215. Phillippa Levine, *The Amateur and the Professional: Antiquarians, Historians and Archaeologists in Victorian England, 1838–1886* (Cambridge, 1986); Ève Gran-Aymerich, *Naissance de l'archéologie moderne, 1798–1945* (Paris, 1998).

216. Rowley-Conway, *From Genesis.*

217. In some ways, the question was about whether ancient European society was better characterised by war or by commerce.

218. Timothy Champion, 'The Celt in Archaeology', in Brown (ed.), *Celticism*, 61–78; Morse, *Celts*, esp. 127–50.

219. Samuel Birch, 'On the Torc of the Celts', *The Archaeological Journal* 2 (1846), 368. Morse, *Celts*, 128–29.

220. Birch, 'Torc', 380.

221. Karel Sklenář, *Archaeology in Central Europe: The First 500 Years*, trans. Iris Lewitová (Leicester, 1983), esp. 91–93.

222. Marc-Antoine Kaeser, 'Antiquare, Pfahlbauten und die Entstehung der urgeschichtlichen Wissenschaft: Die nationale und internationale Ausstrahlung der Antiquarischen Gesellschaft in Zürich', in Marianne Flüeler-Grauwiler and Josef Gisler (eds.), *Pfahlbaufieber* (Zürich, 2004), 128.

223. Ferdinand Keller, 'Die keltischen Grabhügel im Burghölzi und die Gräber auf der Forch', *Mittheilungen der Zürcherischen Gesellschaft für Vaterländische Alterthümer* 1 (1837), 1–8, esp. 8.

224. For a good overview, see Dietrich Hakelberg, 'Nationalismus einer Elite "Heidnisches Teutschland" und "vaterländisches Altertumskunde" in der ersten Hälfte des 19. Jahrhunderts', in Elisabeth Vogel (ed.), *Zwischen Ausgrenzung und Hybridisierung: zur Konstruktion von Identitäten aus kulturwissenschaftlicher Perspektive* (Würzburg, 2003), 15–35; Maner, *Germany's Ancient Pasts*, 88–96.

225. Friedrich Garscha, 'Heinrich Schreiber (1793–1872): Ein Beitrag zur Geschichte der Keltomanie im 19. Jahrhundert', in A. Kirchner (ed.), *Ur-und Frühgeschichte als historische Wissenschaft* (Heidelberg, 1950), 3–18.

226. Heinrich Schreiber, *Die Neuentdeckten Hünengräber im Breisgau* (Freiburg, 1826), 50.

227. Hakelberg, 'Nationalismus', 27.

228. Garscha, 'Heinrich Schreiber', 16–17.

229. Heinrich Schreiber, *Die ehrenen Streikeile zumal in Deutschland* (Freiburg, 1842), 83.

230. Hüther, 'Keltische Forschungen', 259.

231. Werner Leitz, *Das Gräberfeld von Bel-Air bei Lausanne: Frédéric Troyon (1815–1866) und die Anfänge der Frühmittelalterarchäologie* (Lausanne, 2002), 35.

232. Frédéric Troyon, 'Antiquités de Bel-Air, près Lausanne, de Nordendorf, près Augsbourg et de Leux, dans le département du Pas-de-Calais', *Allgemeine Zeitschrift für Geschichte* 5 (1846), 272–85.

233. Margarita Pertlwieser, 'Johann Georg Ramsauer (1795–1874): Der Ausgräber des Hallstätter Gräberfeldes', *Oberösterreichische Heimatblätter* 34 (1980), 3–14.

234. Matthias Koch, 'Aufklärung über die Schlacht zu Fridolfing durch die neusten antiquarischen Funde', *Oberbayerisches Archiv für vaterländische Geschichte* 6 (1845), 77–112.

235. *Allgemeine Zeitung*, 20 January 1845, 153–54.

236. Joseph Gaisberger, *Die Gräber bei Hallstadt im Österreichischen Salzkammergut* (Linz, 1848), 43–54.

237. Ferdinand Keller, 'Die keltischen Pfahlbauten in den Schweizerseen', *Mittheilungen der Antiquarischen Gesellschaft in Zürich* 9 (1853–1856), 65–100.

238. Keller, 'Die keltischen Pfahlbauten', 67.

239. Keller, 'Die keltischen Pfahlbauten', 67.

240. William Wilde, *A Descriptive Catalogue of the Antiquities of Stone, Earthen, and Vegetable Materials in the Museum of the Royal Irish Academy* (Dublin, 1857), 233–35.

241. Salomon Reinach, 'Esquisse d'une histoire de l'archaéologie gauloise', *Revue celtique* 19 (1898), 301.

242. See, for example, Jean-Baptiste Verchère de Reffye, 'Les armes l'Alise', *Révue archéologique* 10 (1864), 337–49, at 347.

243. Marc-Antoine Kaeser, *Les lacustres: archéologie et mythe national* (Lausanne, 2004); Marc-Antoine Kaeser, 'Des fantasmes d'une Suisse insulaire: le mythe de la <<civilisation lacustre>>', *Perspective* 2 (2006), 1–10.

244. Marc-Antoine Kaeser, *L'Univers du préhistorien: Science, foi et politique dans l'oeuvre et la vie d'Édouard Desor (1811–1882)* (Paris, 2004), 229–356.

245. Frédéric Troyon, *Habitations lacustres des tèmps anciens et modernes* (Lausanne, 1860).

246. Ferdinand Keller, 'Pfahlbauten. Dritter Bericht', *Mittelungen der Antiquarischen Gesellschaft in Zürich* 13.2.3 (Zürich, 1860).

247. Édouard Desor, *Les palafittes: ou, constructions lacustres du lac de Neuchatel* (Paris, 1865), 79–80, 131–34. Kaeser, *L'Univers*, 306–7, suggests that Desor's use of the plural 'races' is telling.

248. *Materiaux pour l'histoire positive et philosophique de l'homme* (Paris, 1866), 526.

249. J. M. Kemble, *Horae Ferales, or, Studies in the Archaeology of the Northern Nations*, ed. R. G. Latham and A. W. Franks (London, 1863), 79.

250. Kemble, *Horae Ferales*, 79.

251. Kemble, *Horae Ferales*, 125.

252. Kemble, *Horae Ferales*, 172–77, 184–89.

253. Ferdinand Keller, 'Pfahlbauten. Sechster Bericht', *Mittheilungen der antiquarischen Gesellschaft in Zürich* 15.7 (Zürich, 1866), 303.

254. Hans Hildebrand, 'Sur les commencements de l'âge du Fer en Europe', *Congrès international d'anthropologie et d'archéologie préhistoriques 1874* (2 vols., Stockholm, 1876), 592–601, esp. 599.

255. Henri d'Arbois de Jubainville, *Les premiers habitants de l'europe* (2nd ed., 2 vols., Paris, 1889), vol. 1, 255, 369–73.

Chapter Eight: Race, History, and the Irish Question

1. David Stack, 'Phrenological Friends: Cobden and His "Father Confessor" George Combe', in Anthony Howe and Simon Morgan (eds.), *Rethinking Nineteenth-Century Liberalism: Richard Cobden Bicentenary Essays* (Aldershot, 2006), 31–32.

2. [underlined in letter] Combe to Cobden, 31 January 1848, BL, Combe Papers, Add. MS 43,660, f. 99.

3. Georgios Varouxakis, *Victorian Political Thought on France and the French* (Basingstoke, 2002), 13.

4. 'The Saxon, The Celt, and The Gaul', *Economist*, 29 April 1848.

5. Edwards, 'Fragments d'un mémoire', 42n117. Irish commentators felt the same way at the time. See *Leinster Express*, 2 October, 1841, 4: 'The mass of Irish people, like their kindred Celts of France, must always have something to excite them'.

6. Augustin Thierry, *Histoire de la conquête de l'Angleterre par les Normands* (3 vols., Paris, 1825), vol. 3, 482.

7. Gustave de Beaumont, *Ireland: Social, Political and Religious*, ed. W. C. Taylor (2 vols., London, 1839), vol. 1, 1–3.

8. Beaumont, *Ireland*, vol. 1, 6.

9. Beaumont, *Ireland*, vol. 1, 6–7; vol. 2, 16–36.

10. *Caledonian Mercury*, 10 January 1828; McMahon, *Races of Europe*, 253–54.

11. See Kidd, 'Teutonist Ethnology', for the wider patterns of Lowland Saxonism.

12. See James Stafford, *The Case of Ireland: Commerce, Empire and the European Order, 1750–1848* (Cambridge, 2022).

13. Even though he was uninterested in such things, O'Conell was occasionally referred to in the Irish press as a 'Celt', in contrast to his 'Saxon' parliamentary opponents. See, for example, *Carlow Morning Post*, 20 October 1831, 2.

14. Stefan Collini, *Public Moralists: Political Thought and Intellectual Life in Britain, 1850–1930* (Oxford, 1993).

15. For works building on Curtis, see Ned Lebow, *White Britain and Black Ireland: The Influence of Stereotypes on Colonial Policy* (Philadelphia, PA, 1976); Luke Gibbons, 'Race Against Time: Racial Discourse and Irish History', in Catherine Hall (ed.), *Cultures of Empire: A Reader* (Manchester, 2000), 207–23; Steve Garner, *Racism in the Irish Experience* (London, 2004); Michael de Nie, *The Eternal Paddy: Irish Identity and the British Press, 1798–1882* (Madison, WI, 2004); Pittock, *Celtic Identity*.

16. Curtis, *Anglo-Saxons*, 103.

17. Curtis, *Anglo-Saxons*, 19.

18. Sheridan Gilley, 'English Attitudes to the Irish in England, 1780–1900', in Colin Holmes (ed.), *Immigrants and Minorities in British Society* (London, 1978), 81–110; D. G. Paz, 'Anti-Catholicism, Anti-Irish Stereotyping, and Anti-Celtic Racism in Mid-Victorian Working-Class Periodicals', *Albion* 18 (1986), 601–16; R. F. Foster, *Paddy and Mr Punch: Connections in Irish and English History* (London, 1993), 171–94.

19. *North Wales Chronicle*, 15 December 1866.

20. J.E.E. Dalberg-Acton, 'Goldwin Smith's Irish History', in J. N. Figgis and R. V. Laurence (eds.), *The History of Freedom and Other Essays* (London, 1907), 240.

21. George Combe to Richard Cobden, 25 October 1848, BL Add. MS 43, 660/f. 164. On phrenology's Celtic implications, see Colin Kidd, 'Medicine, Race, and Radicalism in the Later Scottish Enlightenment', in Margaret Pelling and Scott Mandelbrote (eds.), *The Practice of Reform in Health, Medicine, and Science, 1500–2000* (Aldershot, 2005), esp. 207–9, 219–21.

22. Frances Kingsley (ed.), *Charles Kingsley, His Letters and Memories of His Life* (1877: 2 vols., London, 1894), vol. 2, 111, 200.

23. R. W. Emerson, *English Traits* (London, 1857), 27–28.

24. See also Foster, 'History and the Irish Question'.

25. Probably most famously in Curtis. See also Young, *English Ethnicity*, 14–39.

26. Mandler, *The English National Character: The History of an Idea from Edmund Burke to Tony Blair* (New Haven, CT, 2006), 59–60.

27. *The Globe*, 5 August 1841, 3.

28. *London Quarterly Review* 31 (1869), 48.

29. The passage is often trotted out to strengthen evidence of Arnold as the godfather of anti-Celtic, or anti-Catholic, feeling, but both characterizations are simply incorrect. For an example, see Léon Poliakov, *The Aryan Myth: A History of Racist and Nationalist Ideas in Europe*, trans. Edmund Howard (New York, 1974), 51.

30. Thomas Arnold, 'Inaugural Lecture', *Introductory Lectures on Modern History* (1843: London, 1845), 23–24.

31. The use of the 'K' is telling of the influence of German scholarship on him, but not significant of anything more.

32. Thomas Arnold, *The Christian Duty of Granting the Claims of the Roman Catholics* (Oxford, 1829), 23–24.

33. Duncan Forbes, *The Liberal Anglican Idea of History* (Cambridge, 1952), 51.

34. Arnold, *Christian Duty*, 38–42, esp. 42.

35. Arthur Penrhyn Stanley, *Life and Correspondence of Thomas Arnold* (1844: 3rd ed., 2 vols., London, 1845), vol. 1, 410.

36. Stanley, *Life*, vol. 2, 202.

37. Thomas Arnold, *History of Rome* (3 vols., London, 1838–1843), vol. 1, 527.

38. Stanley, *Life*, vol. 1, 265.

39. Herbert Butterfield, *The Whig Interpretation of History* (London, 1931).

40. Peter Ghosh, 'Macaulay and the Heritage of the Enlightenment', *EHR* 112 (1997), 358–60.

41. J. W. Burrow, *A Liberal Descent: Victorian Historians and the English Past* (Cambridge, 1981), 36, 69–70.

42. Burrow, *A Liberal Descent*, 92–93.

43. Young, *English Ethnicity*, 51, 103–5; Robert E. Sullivan, *Macaulay: The Tragedy of Power* (Cambridge, MA, 2009), 330–36.

44. Thomas Babington Macaulay, *The History of England from the Accession of James the Second*, in Hannah Trevelyan (ed.), *The Works of Lord Macaulay* (8 vols., London, 1866), vol. 1, 13.

45. Macaulay, *The Works of Lord Macaulay*, vol. 3, 48.

46. Macaulay, *Works of Lord Macaulay*, vol. 3, 93.

47. Macaulay, *Works of Lord Macaulay*, vol. 1, 53.

48. Ironically, the Chartists and O'Connell hated one another; see Matthew Roberts, 'Daniel O'Connell, Repeal, and Chartism in the Age of Atlantic Revolutions', *JMH* 90 (2018), 1–39.

49. Thomas Carlyle, *Chartism* (December 1839: London, 1840), 27–28.

50. Carlyle, *Chartism*, 30–31.

51. Carlyle's image in this respect has been redressed in Julie M. Dugger, 'Black Ireland's Race: Thomas Carlyle and the Young Ireland Movement', *Victorian Studies* 48 (2006), 461–85; John Morrow, 'Thomas Carlyle, "Young Ireland" and the "Condition of Ireland Question"', *Historical Journal* 51 (2008), 643–67.

52. *Carlyle Letters Online*, vol. 13, 278–279, online at https://carlyleletters.dukeupress.edu/volume/13/letters_to_carlyles. Emphasis in original.

53. Friedrich Engels, *The Condition of the Working Class in England*, ed. D. McLellan (Oxford, 1993), 102.

54. Friedrich Engels, 'History of Ireland', in I. L. Golman and V. Kunina (eds.), *Karl Marx and Friedrich Engels: Ireland and the Irish Question* (Moscow, 1971), 209.

55. Engels does refer to the 'Irish race' here, but the main point is their resistance to centuries of oppression [see I. L. Golman and V. Kunina, *Karl Marx*, 210–11].

56. Friedrich Engels, *Origin of the Family and Private Property* (London, 2010), 166.

57. Golman and Kunina, *Karl Marx*, 162.

58. Cf. Aidan Beatty, 'Marx and Engels, Ireland, and the Racial History of Capitalism', *JMH* 91 (2019), 815–47.

59. For a summary of Mill's anti-racialism, see Georgios Varouxakis, *Mill on Nationality* (London, 2002), 38–52.

60. John Stuart Mill, *The Principles of Political Economy with some of their Applications to Social Philosophy*, ed. William Ashley (1848: London, 1920), 324.

61. Mill, *Principles of Political Economy*, 376. On Mill's anti-racism, see Varouxakis, *Mill*, 38–52.

62. George Poulett Scrope, *How is Ireland to be Governed?* (1834: London, 1836), 35.

63. Henry Thomas Buckle, *History of Civilization in England* (1857–1861: Cambridge, 2011), 61–62n51.

64. See also de Barra, *Celts*, 21–23.

65. *Hansard*, HC Deb, 16 June 1843, vol. 70, c. 63.

66. Thomas Campbell Foster, *Letters on the Condition of the People of Ireland* (London, 1846), vii, 1.

67. Campbell Foster, *Letters*, viii.

68. Campbell Foster, *Letters*, x.

69. Campbell Foster, *Letters*, 44. Emphasis in original.

70. Campbell Foster, *Letters*, 44–48n126.

71. Campbell Foster, *Letters*, 288–89.

72. Little is known about McElheran, but see Diarmid A. Fennigan, 'Race, Space, and Politics in Mid-Victorian Ireland: The Ethnologies of Abraham Hume and John McElheran', *Historical Geography* 42 (2014), 152–70. For McElheran and the Celtic Union, see *Carlow Morning Post*, 17 December 1853, 3.

73. John McElheran, *Celt and Saxon* (Belfast, 1852), 8. See also 'Irish Impudence', *The Times*, 7 October 1852, 5.

74. *The Times*, 7 October 1852.

75. *Punch*, 16 October 1852, 165.

76. The various contributions and comments are collected in McElheran, *Celt and Saxon*.

77. John McElheran, *The Condition of Women and Children among the Celtic, Gothic, and other Nations* (Boston, 1858), 24.

78. James Secord, *Visions of Science: Books and Readers at the Dawn of the Victorian Age* (Chicago, 2015).

79. On the collection and phrenology in a global context, see James Poskett, *Materials of the Mind* (Chicago, IL, 2019).

80. George Combe, *The Constitution of Man, considered in relation to external objects* (Edinburgh, 1828), 154, 167.

81. 'National Skulls', EUL/Gen. 608/2/ff. 99–101.

82. Charles Gibbon, *The Life of George Combe*, (2 vols, London, 1878), vol. 2, 255–56.

83. Gibbon, *Life*, vol. 2, 263.

84. Stack, 'Phrenological Friends', 31–32.

85. Gibbon, *Life*, vol. 2, 268–69.

86. Gibbon, *Life*, vol. 2, 311.

87. McMahon, *Races of Europe*, 93–167, gives a good summary of how classification worked.

88. Edwards, *Des caractères physiologiques*, 60 and *passim*.

89. 'Indice céphalique' was coined by Paul Broca in 1861 (Paul Broca, 'Sur des crânes provenant d'un cimetière de la Cité, antérieur au treizième siècle', *BSAP* [1861], 501–13, at 505).

90. Anders Retzius, 'Mémoire sur les forms du crane des habitants du nord', trans. G. Courty, *Mémoires d'histoire naturelle* S3.6 (1846), 133–72.

91. Anders Retzius, 'On the Ethnographical Distribution of Long and Elongated Crania', *Report of the Sixteenth Meeting of the British Association for the Advancement of Science* (London,

1847), part 2, 116; *idem*, *Coup d'oeil sur l'état actuel de l'ethnologie au point de vue de la forme du crane osseux*, trans. E. Claparède (Geneva, 1860), 3.

92. Anders Retzius, *Ethnologische Schriften* (Stockholm, 1864), 62–64, 99–111; Retzius, *Coup d'oeil*, 6.

93. For a (hagiographic) biography, see Francis Schiller, *Paul Broca: Founder of French Anthropology, Explorer of the Brain* (1978: Oxford, 1992). The best examination of Broca's anthropology—which is fully aware of his scientific racism—is Claude Blanckaert, *De la race à l'évolution: Paul Broca et l'anthropologie française (1850–1900)* (Paris, 2009), esp. 17–21 for comments on Broca in myth. See also Carole Reynaud-Paligot, *La République raciale: Une histoire, 1860–1940* (2nd ed., Paris, 2021).

94. Stephen J. Gould, *The Mismeasure of Man* (New York, 1981).

95. Blanckaert, *De la race*, 13–14.

96. Paul Broca, *Mémoires de l'anthropologie* (Paris, 1871), vol. 1, 278.

97. Broca, *Mémoires de l'anthropologie*, vol. 1, esp. 247, 275–76.

98. See, generally, Blanckaert, *De la race*, 67–107.

99. Blanckaert, *De la race*, 35–65.

100. Paul Broca, *Recherches sur l'hybridité animale en general et sur l'hybridité humain en particulier, considérés dans leur rapports avec la question de la pluralité des espèces humaines* (Paris, 1860), 594.

101. Paul Broca, *Recherches sur l'hybridité*, 610–11, 614–16.

102. *Bulletins de la société d'anthropologie de Paris* 1 (1860), 5–15.

103. Broca, *Mémoires de l'anthropologie*, vol. 1, 284–85.

104. Broca, *Mémoires de l'anthropologie*, vol. 1, 330–31.

105. Broca, *Mémoires de l'anthropologie*, vol. 1, 300.

106. Broca, *Mémoires de l'anthropologie*, vol. 1, 304.

107. McMahon, *Races of Europe*, 214n4.

108. Broca, *Mémoires de l'anthropologie*, vol. 1, 370–76.

109. Broca, *Mémoires de l'anthropologie*, vol. 1, 234–35.

110. Broca, *Mémoires de l'anthropologie*, vol. 1, 282–84; Paul Broca, 'La race celtique ancienne et moderne', *Revue d'anthropologie* 2 (1873), 579.

111. Broca, *Mémoires de l'anthropologie*, vol. 1, 282–84.

112. This is a fundamental argument of modern Celtosceptics. See Paul Broca, 'Sur les textes relatifs aux Celtes dans la Grande-Bretagne', in *Bulletins de la société d'anthropologie de Paris* S.II 12 (1877), 509–15.

113. Broca, 'La race celtique', 579.

114. Alexandre Bertrand, 'Celtes, Gaulois et Francs: Lettres au Docteur Paul Broca', *Revue d'anthropologie* 2 (1873), 235–50, 422–35; 629–43.

115. Henri Martin, 'Les celtes selon M. le docteur Broca', *BSAP* 9 (1874), 614–18.

116. Efram Sera-Shriar, *The Making of British Anthropology, 1813–1871* (London, 2013). On anthropology in this period generally, see George W. Stocking Jr., *Victorian Anthropology* (New York, 1987).

117. Robert Knox, *The Races of Men: A Fragment* (Philadelphia, PA, 1850), 23. Knox repeatedly targeted Blumenbach and Prichard as having produced nothing of value and misleading the public as to the facts of race [Knox, *Races*, 11, 14, 25, 39, 40, 43, 242].

118. Knox, *Races*, 19, 27.

119. Knox, *Races*, 222.

120. Knox, *Races*, 217–18.

121. Knox, *Races*, 11, 26, 27, 212–27.

122. Knox, *Races*, 214–15.

123. Knox, *Races*, 21–22.

124. Knox, *Races*, 27.

125. Robert Knox, *The Races of Men: A Philosophical Enquiry into the Influence of Race over the Destinies of Nations* (London, 1862), 379.

126. *Perthshire Advertiser*, 28 November 1848, 4; Knox, *Races*, 83–84.

127. J. W. Burrow, 'Evolution and Anthropology in the 1860's: The Anthropological Society of London, 1863–71', *Victorian Studies* 7 (1963), 143.

128. [James Hunt], 'Knox on the Celtic Race', *Anthropological Review* 6 (1868), 175–91.

129. [Hunt], 'Knox on the Celtic Race', 181n. Emphasis in the original.

130. James Higgin, *The Irish Government Difficulty Considered as a Race Question* (Manchester, 1867), 2–4.

131. This entire episode appeared collected and reprinted in 'Professor Huxley on Political Ethnology', *Anthropological Review* 8 (1870), 197–216.

132. 'Professor Huxley on Political Ethnology', 197–204.

133. 'Professor Huxley on Political Ethnology', 207–8.

134. Leonard Huxley (ed.), *Life and Letters of Thomas Henry Huxley* (2 vols., New York, 1900), vol. 1, 346–50.

135. D = Dark brown hair, N = Black or intense brown hair (Niger), R = Red hair, and F = Fair hair (John Beddoe, *The Races of Britain: A Contribution to the Ethnology of Western Europe* [Bristol and London, 1885], 4).

136. Horace G. Hutchinson, *Life of Sir John Lubbock* (2 vols., London, 1914), vol. 1, 253–59.

137. 'British Race-Types of Today', *The Times*, 12 October 1887.

138. Robertson, *The Saxon and the Celt*.

139. Vincent P. Pecora, 'Arnoldian Ethnology', *Victorian Studies* 41 (1998), 355–79.

140. Rachel Bromwich, *Matthew Arnold and Celtic Literature: A Retrospect, 1865–1965* (Oxford, 1965), 6.

141. He was also a schools inspector for thirty-five years [Stefan Collini, *Matthew Arnold: A Critical Portrait* (Oxford, 1994), 18–24].

142. Cecil Y. Lang (ed.), *The Letters of Matthew Arnold* (6 vols., Charlottesville, VA, 1996–2001), vol. 3, 17 (hereafter *Letters of M. A.*). Their mother was Cornish (*Letters of M. A.*, vol. 1, 515).

143. Arnold, *Celtic Literature*, 21, 135–81.

144. Arnold, *Celtic Literature*, vii–viii.

145. Arnold, *Celtic Literature*, xviii.

146. *Reports of the Commissioners of Inquiry into the State of Education in Wales* (London, 1848), 401.

147. Viscountess Emily Strangford (ed.), *Original Letters and Papers of the Late Viscount Strangford upon Philological and Kindred Subjects* (London, 1878), 224.

148. Arnold, *Celtic Literature*, 16.

149. Arnold, *Celtic Literature*, 17–22.

150. Arnold, *Celtic Literature*, 8.

151. Arnold, *Celtic Literature,* 85.

152. Arnold, *Celtic Literature,* 116.

153. This idea was taken, of course, from Henri Martin [Arnold, *Celtic Literature,* 102–3]. Henri Martin, *De la France, de son génie, et de ses destinées* (Paris, 1847), 107.

154. Arnold, *Celtic Literature,* 101, 108–9.

155. Arnold, *Celtic Literature,* 108–9.

156. Arnold, *Celtic Literature,* 135. On the last of these themes, see Patrick Sims-Williams, 'The Invention of Celtic Nature Poetry', in Brown, *Celticism,* 97–124.

157. Arnold, *Celtic Literature,* 141, 153.

158. Arnold, *Celtic Literature,* 166–67.

159. Arnold, *Celtic Literature,* 159. Emphasis in original.

160. Arnold, *Celtic Literature,* 153.

161. Arnold, *Celtic Literature,* xi, 14.

162. Arnold, *Celtic Literature,* 177.

163. Arnold, *Celtic Literature,* 181.

164. Arnold, *Celtic Literature,* 12–13.

165. Strangford, *Original Letters,* 224.

166. Arnold refuted the letter at length in the introduction of *Celtic Literature,* ix–xii.

167. *The Examiner,* 24 August 1867.

168. Google Books Ngram Viewer, 'Celtic', accessed 31 May 2024, https://books.google.com/ngrams/graph?content=Celtic&year_start=1800&year_end=2019&corpus=en-2019&smoothing=3.

169. Max Müller to John Rhys, 18 June 1874, NLW, Sir John Rhys Papers, A1/1/5.

170. See John Rhys, *The Early Ethnology of the British Isles* (London, 1882).

171. John Rhys, *Lectures on Welsh Philology* (London, 1877), viii–ix. Inscriptions and oghams occupy much space in the early letters in NLW, Sir John Rhys Papers, A1/1/1-A1/1/xxx

172. Huxley noted that Irish national papers caricatured the Saxon in the same way. See 'Professor Huxley on Political Ethnology', *Pall Mall Gazette,* 10 January 1870.

173. Freeman's cognitive dissonance has been highlighted by Burrow, *Liberal Descent,* 188–92.

174. W.R.W. Stephens, *The Life and Letters of Edward A. Freeman* (2 vols., London, 1895), vol. 2, 242.

175. Norfolk Record Office, Y/D27/13.

Chapter Nine: *Nos ancêtres les Gallois*

1. See, for example, *Elgin Courier,* 27 September 1867, 4; *Nottingham Journal,* 26 September 1867, 2.

2. There is no scholarly history of pan-Celticism. Chartier-Le Floch, *Histoire de l'interceltisme en Bretagne,* is maybe the closest, but it focuses on Brittany, with the other Celtic nations entering and exiting accordingly. Ellis, *Celtic Dawn,* provides a short overview.

3. Robert Graves, *The Crowning Privilege: Collected Essays on Poetry* (London, 1955), 155.

4. Williams, *Literary Remains,* vol. 1, x.

5. For comparisons with other (pan-)national movements, see Thiesse, *La création;* Leerssen, *National Thought.*

6. Hobsbawm and Ranger, *Invention.*

7. Hywel Teifi Edwards, *The Eisteddfod* (Cardiff, 1990), 2; Prys Morgan, *The Eighteenth Century Renaissance: A New History of Wales* (Llandybie, 1981), 57.

8. William Whewell to Julius Charles Hare, 17 February 1833, Trinity College, Cambridge, Add. Ms. a/215/27.

9. For Price's Pan-Celtic status, see Leersen, 'Celticism', in Brown, *Celticism,* 19n28; Marion Löffler, 'Der Pankeltismus vor dem Ersten Weltkreig im europäisschen Kontext', in Erich Poppe (ed.), *Keltologie heute: Themen und Fragestellungen* (Münster, 2004), 276.

10. Williams, *Literary Remains,* vol. 2, 149–50.

11. 'A Tour through Brittany' was first printed in *The Cambrian Quarterly Magazine and Celtic Repertory* in 1830–1831 and later in Williams, *Literary Remains,* vol. 1, 1–111.

12. Le Baron Silvestre du Sacy, *Notice sur la vie et les ouvrages de M. Saint-Martin* (1836), 1–15.

13. Williams, *Literary Remains,* vol. 2, 149.

14. John Hughes, *Horae Britannicae* (London, 1819), ix, 378–88.

15. Williams, *Literary Remains,* vol. 2, 151–52.

16. Louis Dujardin, *La vie et les oeuvres,* 77–81.

17. 'Je consigne ici le memoire du Voyage de angleterre' (*c.* 1802–1814), Notebooks of Jean-François-Marie-Maurice-Agatha Le Gonidec, Box 1, Notebook Small 1, Manuscripts Division, Department of Rare Books and Special Collections, Firestone Library, Princeton University.

18. Williams, *Literary Remains,* vol. 2, 164–66.

19. Price, 'A Tour through Brittany', in Williams, *Literary Remains,* vol. 1, 11.

20. Price, 'A Tour through Brittany', in Williams, *Literary Remains,* vol. 1, 105.

21. John White, *Guide to the Town and Neighbourhood of Abergavenny* (Abergavenny, 1845), 39.

22. See Celyn Gurden-Williams, 'Lady Llanover and the Creation of a Welsh Cultural Utopia', PhD dissertation (Cardiff University, 2008); Maxwell Fraser, 'Lady Llanover and Her Circle', *THSC* (1968), 170–96.

23. For a general biography of Rio, see Léon Lefébure, *Portraits de Croyants au XIXe siècle* (Paris, 1905), 155–284. Rio later wrote a history of the uprising, Alexis-François Rio, *La petite chouannerie ou Histoire d'un college breton sous l'Empire* (London, 1842).

24. On Rio and Brittany, see L. Gougaud, 'Alexis-François Rio et la Bretagne', *Annales de Bretagne* 29 (1913), 439–63; Alexis-François Rio, *Épilogue a l'art chrétien* (2 vols., Freiburg im Breisgau, 1870), vol. 2, 150.

25. Rio to Gladstone, 28 July 1838, BL, Add. MS 44,355, f. 103.

26. Rio to Gladstone, 29 October 1838, BL, Add. MS 44,355, ff. 139–40.

27. The prize could run to over £60 [White, *Guide to the Town,* 41].

28. Frank Foerster, *Christian Carl Josias Bunsen: Diplomat, Mäzen und Vordenker in Wissenschaft, Kirche und Politik* (Bad Arolsen, 2001).

29. Frances Bunsen, *A memoir of Baron Bunsen, late minister, plenipotentiary and envoy extraordinary of his Majesty Frederic William IV at the Court of St. James* (2 vols., London, 1868), vol. 1, 129–30.

30. Madame Bunsen to the Cymreigyddion Society, 17 March 1841, NLW, MSS 13182E11.

31. Marion Löffler, 'Prince Albert's "Celtic" Librarian: Culture, Diplomacy and Politics', in Friedegund Freitag (ed.), *Dynastie-Wissenschaft-Kunst: Die Verbindungen der Dynastien Sachsen-Gotha-Altenburg und Sachsen-Coburg und Gotha zum Britischen Empire* (Würzburg, 2020), 145–61.

32. Bunsen, *A memoir*, vol. 2, 119–20.

33. Victoria, quoted in Löffler, 'Prince', 150.

34. NLW, MS 13184E, f. 6; Henry Hallam to Thomas Bevan, 5 September 1838, NLW, MS 13183 EII, f. 117r-v.

35. A. J. Johnes, *Philological Proofs of the Original Unity and Recent Origin of the Human Race, derived from a Comparison of the Languages of Asia, Europe, Africa, and America* (London, 1843); Marian Henry Jones, 'The Letters of Arthur James Johnes, 1809–71', *National Library of Wales Journal* 10 (1958), 264.

36. Thomas Price, 'An Essay on The Comparative Merits of the Remains of Ancient Literature in the Welsh, Irish, and Gaelic Languages, and their value in elucidating the ancient history, and the mental cultivation of the inhabitants of Britain, Ireland and Gaul', in Williams, *Literary Remains*, vol. 1, 116–232.

37. Price, 'An Essay', in Williams, *Literary Remains*, vol. 1, 168.

38. Richard Garnett to Taliesin Williams, 25 January 1838, NLW, MS 21272E, f. 189.

39. Sinéad Garrigan-Mattar, *Primitivism, Science, and the Irish Revival* (Oxford, 2004).

40. *Monmouthshire Merlin*, 22 October 1842.

41. See, for example, Stephens, *Literature of the Kymry*; Albert Schulz, *An Essay on the influence of Welsh tradition upon the literature of Germany, France, and Scandinavia*, trans. Frances Berrington (London, 1841).

42. They were Théoodre Hersart de la Villemarqué, Louis de Jacquelot du Boisruvray, Jules de Francheville, Auguste-Félix du Marchallac'h, and Antoine de Mauduit.

43. Rio, *Épilogue a l'art chrétien*, vol. 2, 322.

44. See accounts in Louis Charles Marie de Jacquelot du Boisrouvray (1798–1881) to le Chevalier de Blois, 29 October 1838, in Archives départementales, Quimper, Côtes extreme 67 J 48; Pierre de la Villemarqué, *La Villemarqué: Sa vie & ses oeuvres* (Paris, 1926), 49–50.

45. Williams, *Literary Remains*, vol. 2, 174, 223–25; Price to Villemarqué, 11 April 1837, 22 June 1838, NLW, Facs 854.

46. On Villemarqué generally, see Villemarqué, *La Villemarqué*; Francis Gourvil, *Théodore-Claude-Henri Hersart de La Villemarqué (1815–1895) et le 'Barzaz-Breiz' (1839–1845–1867)* (Rennes, 1960).

47. On this exchange, see Fañch Postic, 'Prémiers échanges interceltiques: Le voyage de La Villemarqué au pays de Galles', *ArMen* 125 (2001), 34–43; Mary-Ann Constantine, '"Impertinent Structures": A Breton's Adventures in Neo-Gothic Wales', *Studies in Travel Writing* 18 (2014), 134–47; Villemarqué, *La Villemarqué*, 41–42.

48. Villemarqué, *La Villemarqué*, 19–20.

49. L. Gougaud, 'A propos d'une lettre de Brizeux à Alexis-François Rio', *Annales de Bretagne* 28 (1912), 203–7.

50. Williams, *Literary Remains*, vol. 2, 235.

51. 'Extract of a letter from Dr J. C. Prichard', 26 October 1838, American Philosophical Society, lld.

52. 'Discours prononcé par Mr Louis Jacquelot du Boisrouvray', Archives départementales, Quimper, Côtes extreme, 67 J 48.

53. Villemarqué, *La Villemarqué*, 52–53.

54. Villemarqué, *La Villemarqué*, 53–55.

55. Price to Taliesin Williams, 14 December 1838, NLW 21275E, no. 562, no. 563.

56. NLW, Lady Charlotte Guest Diaries, XI, 24 December 1838, 105.

57. Constantine, *Truth*, 156–60.

58. Constantine, *Truth*, 183–85.

59. See NLW Facs 854, esp. Thomas Stephens to Villemarqué, 23 September 1861.

60. Théodore Hersart de la Villemarqué, *Barzaz Breiz: Chants populaires de la Bretagne* (1839: 4th ed., 2 vols., Paris, 1846), vol. 1, lxxvii–lxxviii.

61. *Monmouthshire Merlin*, 27 October 1838; *The Glamorgan Monmouth and Brecon Gazette and Merthyr Guardian*, 6 October 1838.

62. Villemarqué, *La Villemarqué*, 43.

63. 'Abergavenny Eisteddvod', *Morning Post*, 18 October 1838.

64. *Gazette de France*, 22 October 1838.

65. Chartier-Le Floch, *Histoire de l'interceltisme*.

66. *Journal des débats politiques et littéraires*, 19 October 1838.

67. Guiomar, *Le Bretonisme*, 19; Morgan, *Eighteenth Century Renaissance*, 57.

68. This and the following paragraph owe much to Kathryn N. Jones, Carol Tully, and Heather Williams, *Hidden Texts, Hidden Nation: (Re)Discoveries of Wales in Travel Writing in French and German (1780–2018)* (Liverpool, 2020), 67–112.

69. *The Cardiff and Merthyr Guardian*, 24 August 1861, 6.

70. See, for example, *South Wales Daily News*, 28 August 1885, 3.

71. Martin to Pictet, 17 September 1861, BGE, Ms. 4228, ff. 250r-v.

72. Henri Martin, *Études d'archéologie celtique* (Paris, 1872), 42.

73. For a biography, see Nelly Blanchard and Fañch Postic, 'Charles de Gaulle (1837–1880): inventeur du movement Breton? Une approache par sa correspondence avec Théodore Hersart de Le Villemarqué (1861–1872)', *HAL*, University of Western Brittany, Breton and Celtic Research Center (2021).

74. Chartier-le-Floch, *Histoire de l'interceltisme*, 75.

75. Charles de Galle to Henri Martin, 12 November 1870, BNF, NAF-21597, ff. 104–5.

76. See letters in NLW, Sir John Rhys Papers, B1/1.

77. Charles de Gaulle, 'Les Celtes au XIXe siècle: Appel aux Représentants actuels de la race celtique', *Revue de Bretagne et de Vendée* 6 (1864), 262.

78. de Gaulle, 'Les Celtes', 257–66.

79. de Gaulle, 'Les Celtes', 260.

80. de Gaulle, 'Les Celtes', 348–49.

81. de Gaulle, 'Les Celtes', 351–53

82. de Gaulle, 'Les Celtes', 361–63.

83. Charles de Gaulle to M. D. Jones, 21 April 1865, Bangor University Archives, BMSS/7564.

84. See, for example, John Peter to Henri Gaidoz, 18 November 1871, Bangor University Archives, BMSS/718; De Gaulle to Elspeth Rhys, 23 May 1870, in NLW, Sir John Rhys Papers, B1/1.

85. Charles de Gaulle, *The Celts of the Nineteenth Century, An Appeal to the Living Representatives of the Celtic Race*, trans. J. Davenport Mason (London, 1865), 1.

86. De Gaulle, 'Les Celtes', 351, 368.

87. Notes de Charles de Gaulle, Archives départementales, Finistère, Fonds Théodore Hersart de La Villemarqué, 263 K 2/3782.

88. *Baner ac Amserau Cymru*, 24 July 1867, 13.

89. Coward, *Correspondence*, 141.

90. *The Nation*, 7 September 1867, 40–41. In the end *The Nation* was disappointed with the lack of Irish involvement [*The Nation*, 9 November 1867, 184].

91. *Elgin Courier*, 27 September 1867, 4.

92. *Nottingham Journal*, 26 September 1867, 2.

93. Henri Martin to Pictet, 30 July 1867, BGE, Ms. fr. 4228, f. 254r.

94. *Congrès Celtique International tenu À Saint-Brieuc (Côtes du Nord), Bretagne, En Octobre 1867: Séances.—Mémoires.* (Saint-Brieuc, 1868), 14–18.

95. *Congrès Celtique International*, 27.

96. Martin to Pictet, 2 December 1867, BGE, Ms. fr. 4228/2, f. 256v.

97. Martin to Pictet, 10 February 1868, BGE, Ms. fr. 4228/2, f. 257v.

98. Henri Martin to Johnes, 31 August 1867, NLW, Dolaucothi Estate Papers, L3354.

99. Extract from Luzel in d'Arbois de Jubainville to Paul Meyer, 26 October 1867, BNF, NAF 24417, f. 171r. On the controversy, see Fañch Postic, 'Le Beau contre le Vrai? La "Querrelle du Barzaz Breiz" (1866–1868)', in *Bérose—Encyclopédie internationale des histoires de l'anthropologie*.

100. See, for example, Constantine, *Truth*, 192.

101. Martin to Johnes, 1 October 1868, NLW, Dolaucothi Estate Papers, L3355.

102. Martin to Johnes, 28 July 1869, NLW, Dolaucothi Estate Papers, L3357.

103. Johnes to Norman MacColl, NLW, Dolaucothi Estate Papers, L3357, L10313.

104. Charles-Edwards, 'Celtic Languages', in Costambeys et al., *The Making of the Middle Ages*, 15.

105. For recognitions of German preeminence see, for example, Henri d'Arbois de Jubainville, 'Rapport sur les progress de la philologie celtique en France', in Joseph-Daniel Guigniaut (ed.), *Progrès des études classiques et du moyen âge, philologie celtique, numismatique* (Paris, 1868), 144.

106. Martin to Pictet, 16 December 1869, BGE, Ms. fr. 4228/2, f. 263r-v.

107. Gaidoz to Richard Best, 5 September 1917, NLI, MS 11000(27)iv.

108. Stewart, 'Language', 241.

109. Gaidoz to Pictet, 22 February 1869, BGE, Ms. fr. 4228/2, ff. 181r-v.

110. Gaidoz to Pictet, 22 February 1869, BGE, Ms. fr. 4228/2, f. 181v. Gaidoz also sent out prospectuses to the United States, Canada, and Australia [Gaidoz to Pictet, 2 May 1869, CH BGE, Ms. fr. 4228/2, f. 183r].

111. Gaidoz to Rhys, 8 July 1874, NLW, Sir John Rhys Papers, A1/1/5.

112. Gaidoz to Pictet, 22 February 1869, BGE, Ms. fr. 4228/2, f. 181r.

113. The content of his lectures seems to have remained largely the same, beginning with phonetics, moving to morphology, and then reading a key text with students [see, for example, Collège de France, 56 CDF 1.1, the lecture notes on Welsh philology taken by Joseph Vendryès].

114. 'Petition pour les langues provincials au corps legislative de 1870', accessed 13 June 2017, http://www.berose.fr/IMG/pdf/Gaidoz_petition-2.pdf, accessed 13 June 2017.

115. See Ian Stewart, 'Celtic Philology, French Nationalism, and Science in the Pan-German Shadow, 1868–1932' (forthcoming).

116. de Gaulle to Martin, 12 November 1870, BNF, NAF-21597, f. 104.

117. Henri Gaidoz, 'Les Revendications du Pangermanisme', *Revue des Deux Mondes* 91 (1871), 385–405.

118. Gaidoz to Rhys, 15 January 1874, NLW, Sir John Rhys Papers, A1/1/5.

119. Gaidoz, 'Pangermanisme', 387–88.

120. Ernest Renan, *Qu'est-ce qu'une nation?* (Paris, 1882).

121. NLW, MS 6251D, f. 4.

Chapter Ten: Politics and pan-Celticism

1. G. V. McNeill (ed.), *Full Report of the Highland Reform Association Conference, Held at Bonar Bridge On 22nd and 23rd September, 1886* (1886), 7.

2. *Provisional Prospectus of the Keltic League* [1887] in Lionel Robbins Library at the London School of Economics and Political Science (hereafter LSE), JC/A23.

3. Matthew Cragoe and Paul Readman (eds.), *The Land Question in Britain, 1750–1950* (Basingstoke, 2010), 2.

4. Paul Readman, *Land and Nation in England: Patriotism, National Identity, and the Politics of Land, 1880–1914* (Woodbridge, 2008).

5. *Leeds Times*, 4 November 1843, 4.

6. Newby, *Ireland*, 1, 38, *passim*.

7. W. B. Yeats, *Autobiographies* (London, 1955), 438; Newby, *Ireland*, 38.

8. Clive Dewey, 'Celtic Agrarian Legislation and the Celtic Revival: Historicist Implications of Gladstone's Irish and Scottish Land Acts, 1870–86', *Past & Present* lxiv (1974), 43.

9. *Cork Examiner*, 15 November 1843, 4.

10. This conclusion is based upon keyword searches in the *British Newspaper Archive* (https://www.britishnewspaperarchive.co.uk/) and the *Irish Newspaper Archives* (https://www.irishnewsarchive.com/).

11. Michael Davitt, *The Fall of Feudalism in Ireland* (London, 1904), 54.

12. Stafford, *Case of Ireland*.

13. Davitt, *Fall*, 58. This is somewhat ironic because Lalor did not use the language of Celticism.

14. John Mitchel, *Jail Journal* (1913: Reading, 1983), xxix.

15. J. F. Tormy, 'The Ancient Race', in Martin MacDermott (ed.), *The New Spirit of the Nation* (London, 1894), 5–7.

16. *The Celt* I (Dublin, 1857), 1–9.

17. Isaac Butt, *Land Tenure in Ireland: A Plea for the Celtic Race* (Dublin, 1866), 6, 93.

18. Butt, *Land Tenure in Ireland*, 65–66, 94.

19. Butt, *Land Tenure in Ireland*, 101.

20. Ciaran McDonough, 'Investigating Irish Antiquarianism'.

21. de Barra, *Celts*, 32–42.

22. Quoted in de Barra, *Celts*, 58.

23. MacNeill, *Phases*, 3–4. See also Brian Hughes (ed.), *Eoin MacNeill: Memoir of a Revolutionary Scholar* (Dublin, 2016), 15.

24. Davitt, *Fall*, 121.

25. George was unconvinced by the historicist argument that Ireland was a special case: 'England, too, is a conquered country; her soil has been confiscated again and again; and, [in] spite of all talk about the Saxon oppressor and the down-trodden Celt, it is not probable that,

after the admixture of generations, the division of landholder and non-landholder any more coincides with distinction of race in the one country than in the other' (Henry George, *The Irish Land Question* [New York, 1881], 4).

26. *The Nation*, 23 September 1882, 3.

27. *Freeman's Journal*, 10 December 1883, 7.

28. Davitt, *Fall*, xii–xiii.

29. R. F. Foster, *Modern Ireland, 1600–1972* (London, 1988), 345–428.

30. William O'Brien and Desmond Ryan (eds.), *Devoy's Post Bag, 1871–1928* (2 vols., Dublin, 1948–1953), vol. 1, 335; Newby, *Ireland*, 39.

31. William Carroll to John O'Leary, 29 April 1879, NLI, MS 18,002/18/2.

32. John O'Leary, *Recollections of Fenians and Fenianism* (2 vols., London, 1896), vol. 1, 225; William O'Brien, *The Influence of the Irish Language on Irish National Literature and Character* (Cork, 1892), 23; Newby, *Ireland*, 5.

33. I.M.M. Macphail, *The Crofters' War* (Stornoway, 1989); T. M. Devine, *Clanship to Crofters' War: The Social Transformation of the Scottish Highlands* (Manchester, 1994).

34. Newby, *Ireland*, 7.

35. H. J. Hanham, 'The Problem of Highland Discontent, 1880–1885', *TRHS* 19 (1969), 23–24.

36. T. M. Devine, *The Scottish Clearances: A History of the Dispossessed* (London, 2018).

37. Fredrik Albritton Jonsson, *Enlightenment's Frontier: The Scottish Highlands and the Origins of Environmentalism* (New Haven, CT, 2013).

38. Devine, *Scottish Clearances*, 316.

39. Krisztina Fenyö, *Contempt, Sympathy and Romance: Lowland Perceptions of the Highlands and the Clearances During the Famine Years, 1845–1855* (East Linton, 2000).

40. Quoted in Fenyö, *Contempt, Sympathy and Romance*, 7.

41. Fenyö, *Contempt, Sympathy and Romance*, 54–55.

42. *Inverness Courier*, 21 October 1846, 2. Fenyö, *Contempt, Sympathy and Romance*, 56–57, 66.

43. Fenyö, *Contempt, Sympathy and Romance*, 60–63.

44. T. M. Devine, *The Great Highland Famine: Hunger, Emigration, and the Scottish Highlands in the Nineteenth Century* (Edinburgh, 1988), 251.

45. Hanham, 'Problem', 38; Macphail, *Crofters' War*, 8–10.

46. Ewen A. Cameron, 'Journalism in the Late Victorian Scottish Highlands: John Murdoch, Duncan Campbell, and the "Northern Chronicle"', *Victorian Periodicals Review* 40 (2007), 281–306.

47. Hanham, 'Problem', 34.

48. A year before its demise, the journal moved to monthly publication.

49. See James Hunter (ed.), *For the People's Cause: From the Writings of John Murdoch, Highland and Irish Land Reformer* (Edinburgh, 1986).

50. *The Nation*, 14 December 1878, 12.

51. Hunter, *People's Cause*, 99.

52. Davitt, *Fall*, 228.

53. *The Highlander*, 15 May 1875, quoted in James Hunter, 'The Gaelic Connection: The Highlands, Ireland and Nationalism, 1873–1922', *Scottish Historical Review* 54 (1975), 184.

54. *The Highlander*, 24 May 1873, 16.

55. *The Highlander*, 24 May 1873, 16.

56. William Carroll to John Devoy, 11 May 1880, NLI, MS 18,002/23/2.

57. A. G. Newby, 'The *Oban Times* and the Early Land Agitation in the Highlands, 1877–81', *Scottish Local History* 54 (2002), 13–19; Ewen Cameron, 'Journalism'.

58. Ben Thomas, '"The Clach": Alexander Mackenzie and the Land Question in the Late-Nineteenth Century Highlands and Islands', *Northern Scotland* 8 (2017), 68–86.

59. Ian B. Stewart, 'Of Crofters, Celts, and Claymores: The *Celtic Magazine* and the Highland Cultural Nationalist Movement, 1875–88', *Historical Research* 89 (2016), 88–113.

60. D'Arbois de Jubainville to George Metcalfe, 2 July 1889, NLS, MS 3654, ff. 73r-74r. He cannot have been paying very close attention, for he thought the editor was Alexander MacBain (1855–1907), the philologist, not Alexander Mackenzie the activist journalist.

61. Stewart, 'Of Crofters', 13–14.

62. Eric Richards, *Debating the Highland Clearances* (Edinburgh, 2007), 19; Devine, *Clanship*, 224.

63. *Royal Commission of Inquiry into the Condition of Crofters and Cottars in the Highlands and Islands* (4 vols., Edinburgh, 1884).

64. On historicism, see Dewey, 'Celtic Agrarian Legislation'.

65. Wallace, *John Stuart Blackie*, 282.

66. See, for example, J. S. Blackie, 'The Education of the Highlanders', *Celtic Magazine* II (1877), 385–91.

67. John Stuart Blackie, *The Language and Literature of the Scottish Highlands* (Edinburgh, 1876), 1; *idem*, *Gaelic Societies, Highland Depopulation and Land Law Reform* (Edinburgh, 1880), 3.

68. Davitt, *Fall*, 199–200.

69. John Stuart Blackie, *The Scottish Highlanders and the Land Laws: An Historico-Economical Enquiry* (London, 1885), 9–11.

70. Blackie, *Land Laws*, 205.

71. Whitley Stokes to J. S. Blackie, 31 March 1876, NLS, MS 2653(1).

72. These letters also attest to Highland enthusiasm and the elite's recognition of philology's prestige and scholarly importance [NLS, MS 2653 (1&2)].

73. Cited in Dewey, 'Celtic Agrarian Legislation', 54n58.

74. Argyll to Gladstone, 7 January 1870, BL Add. MSS. 44, 101, ff. 185–86. The Liberal MP—and first Black Scottish MP—Peter McLagan (1823–1900) rejected the historicist argument for restoring the 'Tribal tenure . . . under which the land was held by the Celts both in Ireland and in the north of Scotland', because conquest had led to the institution of prescriptive rights which it would be unjust to override (Peter Maclagan, *Land Culture and Land Tenure in Ireland* [Edinburgh, 1869], 51–52).

75. H.C.G. Matthew (ed.), *The Gladstone Diaries* (14 vols., Oxford, 1968–1994), vol. 9, 136; vol. 11, 279.

76. W. E. Gladstone, *Home Rule: The Unity of the Empire and the Authority of Parliament* (1887), 8–9, Lionel Robbins Library, LSE, JF(42)/405.

77. *Celtic Magazine* VII (1882), 295.

78. *Celtic Magazine* VII, 228.

79. Andrew G. Newby, *The Life and Times of Edward McHugh (1853–1915): Land Reformer, Trade Unionist, and Labour Activist* (Lewiston, 2004), 25.

80. Carroll to John Devoy, 11 September 1879, NLI, MS 18,002/19/2.

81. 'An American Statesman on Irish Atrocities', *Blackwood's Magazine* 127 (1880), 279–82.

82. John Devoy, *Recollections of an Irish Rebel* (New York, 1929), 399–400.

83. 'Posteritas', *The Siege of London* (London, 1885), 42. I am indebted to Christian Melby for this reference. See also Christian K. Melby, 'Empire and Nation in British Future-War and Invasion-Scare Fiction, 1871–1914', *Historical Journal* 63 (2020), 389–410.

84. de Barra, *Celts*, 69–102.

85. Paul O'Leary, *Immigration and Integration: The Irish in Wales, 1798–1922* (Cardiff, 2002).

86. Kenneth Morgan, *Rebirth of a Nation: Wales 1880–1980* (Oxford, 1980).

87. *Y Gwladgarwr*, 28 February 1863, 2.

88. *North Wales Express*, 30 September 1887, 5.

89. Peris Jones-Evans, 'Evan Pan Jones—Land Reformer', *Welsh History Review* 4 (1968), 143–59.

90. *Y Celt*, 18 January 1884, 2.

91. This paragraph and the following owe much to J. Graham Jones, 'Michael Davitt, David Lloyd George, and T. E. Ellis: The Welsh Experience, 1886', *Welsh History Review* 18 (1997), 450–82.

92. Jones-Evans, 'Evan Pan Jones', 152; Graham Jones, 'Michael Davitt', 461–62.

93. David H. Howell, 'The Land Question in Nineteenth-Century Wales, Ireland and Scotland: A Comparative Study', *Agricultural History Review* 61 (2013), 97.

94. T. E. Ellis, 'Welsh Land Laws', in Annie Ellis, *Speeches and Addresses by the late Thomas E. Ellis, M.P.* (Wrexham, 1912), 228.

95. Quoted in Graham Jones, 'Michael Davitt', 450.

96. T. E. Ellis, 'Welsh Land Laws', 227–28.

97. *Glasgow Herald*, 7 September 1886, 5.

98. *London Evening Standard*, 7 September 1886, 2; *Glasgow Evening Post*, 7 September 1886, 2.

99. *Y Werin*, 11 September 1886, 3.

100. Byron Tyson (ed.), *Bernard Shaw's Book Reviews* (2 vols., Philadelphia, PA, 1996), vol. 2, 229.

101. McNeill, *Full Report*, 4, 8.

102. *Y Celt*, 8 October 1886, 4.

103. *Y Celt*, 1 October, 1886, 6. In addition to *Y Celt*, *Tarian Y Gweithiwr* and *Y Drych* carried accounts of the meeting.

104. *Y Celt*, 8 October 1886, 3.

105. *Y Celt*, 8 October 1886, 3–4.

106. *North Wales Express*, 22 April 1887, 5.

107. *The Keltic League* (first proof), in Bangor University Special Collections, BMSS/3033.

108. *Provisional Prospectus of the Keltic League*, i–ii.

109. *Provisional Prospectus of the Keltic League*, iii.

110. *Weekly Mail*, 30 July 1887, 6.

111. *Freeman's Journal*, 7 April 1887.

Chapter Eleven: Celtic Daybreak

1. The Manx deputation did not have a national costume (to the other Pan-Celts' disapproval), while Cornwall would only be officially recognised as a Celtic nation at the Pan-Celtic Congress of 1904.

2. *Celtia* I, 129; *Manchester Courier and Lancashire General Advertiser*, 26 August 1901.

3. 'Some Pan-Celtic Comicalities', *The Leader*, 31 August 1901.

4. Literally 'race/family stone'.

5. Celtic Association Circular, 12 October 1900, NLI, MS 35,305(4).

6. For popular works, see Ellis, *Celtic Dawn*; Chartier-Le Floch, *Histoire de l'interceltisme*. For a short scholarly treatment, see Löffler, 'Der Pankeltimus'. Kaori Nagai, '"Tis Optophone Which Ontophanes": Race, the Modern and Irish Revivalism', in Len Platt (ed.), *Modernism and Race* (Cambridge, 2011), 58–76, examines the Pan-Celtic movement as a 'modernist' pet project of Fournier d'Albe, but I find this lens (as well as the accompanying Freudianism) unconvincing.

7. Christina Eileen Murphy-Macinta, 'Pan-Celtic Nationalism at the Fin de Siècle: A History of the Celtic Association, 1898–1911', PhD dissertation (Brandeis University, 2017); De Barra, *Celts*. For a literature review of scholarly treatments of the Celtic Association—and their shortcomings—see Murphy-Macinta, 'Pan-Celtic Nationalism', 8–43.

8. Cf. Murray Pittock and Isla Jack, 'Patrick Geddes and the Celtic Revival', in Ian Brown, Susan Manning, Thomas Owen Clancy, and Murray Pittock (eds.), *The Edinburgh History of Scottish Literature* (3 vols., Edinburgh, 2007), vol. 2, 338–46, who conflate the Irish and Scottish Celtic 'Revivals' with the Pan-Celtic movement more generally; Pittock, *Celtic Identity*, 77.

9. Andrew Lang, 'The Celtic Renascence', *Blackwood's Magazine* CLXI (1897), 181–91.

10. R. F. Foster, 'Yeats and Scotland', unpublished lecture, University of Edinburgh, 2 May 2015.

11. Yeats's presence—real, imagined, and historiographical—has been addressed eloquently in Foster, *Words Alone*.

12. See, for example, Ruán O'Donnell (ed.), *The Impact of the 1916 Rising: Among the Nations* (Dublin, 2008).

13. John Hutchinson, *The Dynamics of Cultural Nationalism: The Gaelic Revival and the Creation of the Irish Nation State* (London, 1987).

14. 'Ireland's Taxes', *Daily Mail*, 15 June 1898, 15.

15. R. F. Foster, *W. B. Yeats: A Life* (2 vols., Oxford, 1997–2003), vol. 1, 41. For Yeats's refashioning, see Yeats, *Autobiographies*, 199–250.

16. Foster, *W. B. Yeats*, vol. 1, 41–42; Mary L. Macken, 'W. B. Yeats, John O'Leary, and the Contemporary Club', *Studies: An Irish Quarterly Review* 28 (1939), 136–42.

17. Caoimhín de Barra, 'A Gallant Little "Tírín": The Welsh Influence on Irish Cultural Nationalism', *IHS* 39 (2014), 58–75; *idem*, *Celts*.

18. Hugh H. Johnson, 'Rent and Tithes in Wales', *Dublin University Review* II, no. 10 (1886), 838–41.

19. John Kelly and Eric Domville (eds.), *The Collected Letters of W. B. Yeats, Volume I: 1865–1895* (Oxford, 1986), 83, 185–86.

20. *The Nation*, 28 September 1889; 13 September 1890; J. B. Hughes, 'The Pan-Celtic Society (1888–1891)', *Irish Monthly* 81 (1953), 17–19; Murphy-Macinta, 'Pan-Celtic Nationalism', 140–41.

21. Andrew Russell St. Ritsh, *Lays and Lyrics of the Pan-Celtic Society* (Dublin, 1889), 1.

22. See, for example, *The Nation*, 25 September 1886, 14; 11 January 1890, where the Irish language movement is loosely referred to as the 'Celtic movement'.

23. Historians continue to debate its legitimacy [see, for example, Collins, *Catholic Churchmen*].

24. Philip O'Leary points out that Gaelic Leaguers praised the intentions of figures like Yeats, George Russell, and Lady Gregory, disagreeing with them nonetheless (O'Leary, *Ideology*, 226).

25. The point is well made in Timothy G. McMahon, *Grand Opportunity: The Gaelic Revival and Irish Society, 1893–1910* (Syracuse, NY, 2008), 29–31.

26. See, for example, Douglas Hyde, 'A Plea for the Irish Language', *Dublin University Review* II, no. 6 (1886), 666–76; Garrigan-Mattar, *Primitivism*, 226–32.

27. Douglas Hyde, 'The Necessity for De-Anglicising Ireland', in *The Revival of Irish Literature* (London, 1894), 155–61.

28. Hyde, 'The Necessity', 159.

29. D. P. Moran, *The Philosophy of Irish Ireland*, ed. Patrick Maume (1905: Dublin, 2006), 104–6.

30. W. B. Yeats, 'The Poetry of Sir Samuel Ferguson', *Dublin University Review* II (1886), 940–41.

31. Foster, 'Yeats and Scotland'.

32. Williams, *Ireland's Immortals*, esp. chapter 8.

33. Foster, *W. B. Yeats*, vol. 1, 197–98; Warwick Gould, John Kelly, and Deirdre Toomey (eds.), *The Collected Letters of W. B. Yeats, Volume II: 1896–1900* (Oxford, 1997), 663–69.

34. *The Second Book of the Rhymers' Club* (London, 1894), 28–32, 123.

35. Grant Allen, 'The Celt in English Art', *Fortnightly Review* 49 (1891), 267–77.

36. Grant Allen, 'The Celtic Fringe', *Westminster Gazette* (1893), 1–2.

37. Cited in Elizabeth A. Sharp (ed.), *William Sharp (Fiona Macleod)* (1910: 2 vols., London, 1912), vol. 1, 16, 47.

38. Ferguson, 'Patrick Geddes and the Celtic Renascence'.

39. 'Celtic Art', University of Strathclyde Archives, Patrick Geddes Papers [hereafter PGP], T-GED 5/2/5.

40. Sharp, *William Sharp*, 320.

41. Sharp, *William Sharp*, 53.

42. William Sharp, 'Introduction', in E. A. Sharp and W. Sharp (eds.), *Lyra Celtica: An Anthology of Celtic Poetry* (Edinburgh, 1896), xliv.

43. Yeats, *Collected Letters*, vol. 2, 37.

44. William F. Halloran, 'W. B. Yeats, William Sharp, and Fiona Macleod: A Celtic Drama, 1897', in Warwick Gould (ed.), *Yeats and the Nineties: Yeats Annual No. 14, A Special Number* (Basingstoke, 2001), 159.

45. 'Fiona Macleod' [William Sharp] to W. B. Yeats, NLS, MS 8783, ff. 5–8.

46. Yeats, *Collected Letters*, vol. 2, 118.

47. Yeats, *Collected Letters*, vol. 2, 277.

48. Yeats, *Collected Letters*, vol. 2, 73.

49. Augusta Gregory, *Our Irish Theatre: A Chapter of Autobiography* (New York, 1913), 9.

50. Gregory, *Our Irish Theatre*, 9–10; James Pethica, *Lady Gregory's Diaries, 1892–1902* (Gerrards Cross, 1996), 153–57.

51. W. B. Yeats, 'The Celtic Element in Literature' *Cosmopolis* X (1898), 675–86.

52. Pethica, *Lady Gregory's Diaries*, 156–57.

53. Garrigan-Mattar, *Primitivism*, 72–74; Foster, 'Yeats and Scotland'.

54. Sharp, 'Introduction', in Sharp and Sharp (eds.), *Lyra Celtica*, li.

55. For a biography, see Ian Stewart, 'E. E. Fournier d'Albe's *Fin de siècle*: Science, Nationalism and Monistic Philosophy in Britain and Ireland', *Cultural & Social History* 14 (2017), 599–620.

56. See, for example, *The Leader* 9 (1904), 33.

57. J. P. O'Reilly and E. E. Fournier D'Albe, 'On a Pandean Pipe from Tanna Island, New Hebrides', *Proceedings of the Royal Irish Academy* 3 (1893–1896), 511–15.

58. *Freeman's Journal*, 20 March 1896; 21 August 1896. He was part of the Society for the Preservation of the Irish Language's council by 1903.

59. *Carnarvon and Denbigh Herald and North and South Wales Independent*, 17 March 1899.

60. Fournier to Castletown, 17 June 1898, NLI, MS 35,305(1).

61. S. J. Barrett (ed.), *Imtheachta an Oireacthais, 1899* (Dublin, 1899), 165–66; *idem* (ed.), *Imtheachta an Oireacthais, 1900* (Dublin, 1900), 45–48.

62. Fournier to Castletown, 19 October 1900, NLI, MS 34,178(1).

63. Fournier to Castletown, 27 December 1923, NLI, MS 35,305(7).

64. See Castletown's autobiography: Bernard Fitzpatrick, *"Ego": Random Records of Sport, Service, and Travel in Many Lands* (London, 1923).

65. *Freeman's Journal*, 16 December 1896.

66. See, for example, *Morning Post*, 15 June 1898; *Hansard*, HC Debate, 14 July 1898, v. 68, c. 979.

67. Fournier to Castletown, 17 June 1898, NLI, MS 35,305(1).

68. Fournier to Castletown, 13 July 1898, NLI, MS 35,305(1).

69. Castletown recorded learning Irish through summer romances with a local girl, 'Arrah' (*"Ego"*, 6).

70. Castletown to Rhys, 17 July 1901, NLW, Sir John Rhys Papers, A1/1/32(ii).

71. Letters to Castletown, 13 July, 5 August, 19 August, and 29 October 1898, NLI, MS 35,305(1).

72. Fournier to Castletown, 26 November 1898, NLI, MS 35,305(2).

73. Fournier to Castletown, 24 December 1898, NLI, MS 35,305(2); for early drafts of the speech, see NLI, MS 35,307(6), MS 35,307(7), and MS 35,307(10).

74. Fournier d'Albe to Lady Gregory, 8 November 1898, New York Public Library, Berg Collection, Lady Gregory Papers [hereafter NYPL, Berg Collection, LGP].

75. William F. Halloran, 'W. B. Yeats, William Sharp, and Fiona Macleod: A Celtic Drama: 1887 to 1897', in Warwick Gould (ed.), *Yeats Annual No. 13* (Basingstoke, 1998), 63n4.

76. Yeats, *Collected Letters*, vol. 2, 300.

77. Yeats, *Collected Letters*, vol. 2, 329, 337–38.

78. Fournier to Lady Gregory, 10 October 1899, NYPL, Berg Collection, LGP.

79. Lady Gregory to Lord Castletown, n.d., NLI, MS 35,306(2).

80. Ruth Dudley Edwards, *Patrick Pearse: The Triumph of Failure* (New York, 1977), 26–36; Philip O'Leary, '"Children of the Same Mother": Gaelic Relations with the Other Celtic Revival Movements, 1882–1916', in *Proceedings of the Harvard Celtic Colloquium* 6 (1986), 101–30.

81. Pethica, *Lady Gregory's Diaries*, 197.

82. *Weekly Mail*, 22 July 1899.

83. Fournier to Patrick Pearse, 26 April 1900, NLI, MS 21,053/5/7 [ár dteanga duthchais féin].

84. Fournier to Pearse, 5 May 1902, NLI, MS 21,047/6/3, f. 689; Fournier to Pearse, 3 June 1902, NLI, MS 21,047/7/3.

85. *Celtia* II, 65.

86. *An Claidheamh Soluis*, 31 March 1906.

87. For a general overview, see Jack E. Reece, *The Bretons against France: Ethnic Minority Nationalism in Twentieth-Century Brittany* (Chapel Hill, NC, 1977); Le Stum, *Le néo-druidisme.*

88. Reece, *Bretons,* 54–79.

89. Le Stum, *Le néo-druidisme,* 27.

90. Le Stum, *Le néo-druidisme,* 29–34.

91. *Weekly Mail,* 22 July 1899.

92. Anna MacBride White and A. Norman Jeffares (eds.), *The Gonne-Yeats Letters 1893–1938* (Syracuse, NY, 1994), 101–2. Emphasis in original.

93. Serge Sculfort de Beaurepas, *Rénovation celtique* (Paris, 1903), 11.

94. Charles Le Goffic, 'Le Mouvement panceltique', *Revue des deux mondes* 159 (1900), 141–74.

95. Le Goffic, 'Le Mouvement panceltique', 172.

96. See, for example, *London Kelt,* 23 July 1898; *Carnarvon and Denbigh Herald and North and South Wales Independent,* 17 March 1899.

97. *Le Figaro,* 24 July 1899.

98. In the previous year, Zimmer had written an article explaining Pan-Celticism to a German audience that was sympathetic but somewhat sceptical about whether religious fissures could be bridged (Heinrich Zimmer, 'Der Pan-Keltismus in Großbritannien und Irland', *Preussische Jahrbücher* 93 [1898], 59–93).

99. Fournier to Castletown, 1 July 1899, NLI, MS 35,305(3).

100. *Weekly Mail,* 29 July 1899.

101. Celtic Association Circular, NLI, MS 35,305(4).

102. Fournier to Castletown, 19 October 1900, NLI, MS 34,178(1).

103. Quoted in Murphy-Macinta, 'Pan-Celtic Nationalism', 186.

104. Fournier to Jenner, 24 September 1904, Kresen Kernow, DC 1141/5/3811.

105. Murphy-Mactinta, 'Pan-Celtic Nationalism', 154n379.

106. See, for example, 'The Pan-Celtic Movement', *Pall Mall Gazette,* 17 July 1899, 8.

107. 'Celtia', *Fáinne an Lae,* 6 January 1900.

108. These are some of the key arguments of Anderson, *Imagined Communities;* see *Celtia* I, 14.

109. 'The Break of Day'; the decision not to take over the paper was regretted when it merged with *An Claidheamh Soluis* ['The Sword of Light'], and launched attacks on the Pan-Celtic movement and Fournier personally [Fournier to Castletown, 22 April 1899, NLI, MS 35,305(3)].

110. Murphy-Macinta, 'Pan-Celtic Nationalism', 18.

111. *Celtia* I, 15.

112. For an overview of these activities and events, see Murphy-Macinta, 'Pan-Celtic Nationalism.'

113. Murphy-Macinta, 'Pan-Celtic Nationalism', 165.

114. Although he was nominally Protestant, Fournier was resolutely anticlerical, and there were also four self-identified theosophists in the group (Murphy-Macinta, 'Pan-Celtic Nationalism', 176).

115. Murphy-Macinta, 'Pan-Celtic Nationalism', 159.

116. Programme of the 1904 Pan-Celtic Congress, 14, Cambridge University Library, Needham, A.144; Programme of the Third Pan-Celtic Congress (1907), 47, University of Strathclyde, PGP, T-GED 5/2/18.

117. *Celtia* I, 129.

118. Sharp, *William Sharp*, 310.

119. For Lord Castletown's recollections, see Bernard Fitzpatrick, 'Address to the Pan-Celtic Congress of 1907', *Scotia: The Journal of the St. Andrew Society* I (1907), 325–28; for the Pan-Celtic Programme of 1901, see NLI, MS 35,307(6).

120. *Manchester Guardian*, 24 August 1901.

121. *The Leader* 9 (1904), 33.

122. Quoted in Seán Ó Lúing, *Kuno Meyer, 1858–1919* (Dublin, 1991), 15–16.

123. *Le Petit Parisien* 28 August 1901; *Athenaeum*, 31 August 1901; *New York Times*, 25 August 1901.

124. John Kelly and Ronald Schuchard (eds.), *The Collected Letters of W. B. Yeats, Volume III: 1901–1904* (Oxford, 1994), 109–10. On Yeats at the conference, see Foster, *W. B. Yeats*, vol. 1, 247.

125. See Marion Löffler, *'A Book of Mad Celts': John Wickens and the Celtic Congress of Caernarfon 1904* (Llandysul, 2000), for an account of the Congress and a fun set of photographs.

126. Prospectus in Bodleian Library, MS Eng. misc., c. 71, f. 496.

127. *The Times*, 5 September 1904.

128. *The Times*, 3 September 1904.

129. William George to Fournier, 5 January 1909, E. E. Fournier d'Albe Papers (private collection); George to Fournier, 11 December 1916, Fournier d'Albe papers; Lloyd George to William George, 13 August 1907, NLW, William George (Solicitor) Papers, f. 1924.

130. *The Times*, 25 September 1907.

131. Patrick Geddes to Fournier, 10 August 1907, Fournier d'Albe Papers.

132. *The Times*, 27 September 1907.

133. Programme of the Third Pan-Celtic Congress (1907), University of Strathclyde, PGP, T-GED 5/2/18.

134. Le Marquis de l'Estourbeillon to Fournier, 30 August 1907, Fournier d'Albe Papers.

135. Fournier to Castletown, 6 October 1905, NLI, MS 35,305(6).

136. *Tír gan teanga, tír gan anam:* 'A country without a language, a country without a soul', *Celtia* I, 49.

137. *Celtia* I, 15.

138. *Celtia,* I, 1.

139. *Celtia* I, 195.

140. *Celtia,* III, 1.

141. *Celtia* IV, 18.

142. See Lord Castletown, 'Our Celtic Inheritance', NLI, MS 35,307(10); *Celtia* I, 97, 3.

143. *Celtia* I, 149.

144. *Celtia* III, 70.

145. *Celtia* IV, 17.

146. *Celtia* I, 17.

147. *Celtia* III, 33.

148. *Celtia* II, 69–71.

149. E. E. Fournier d'Albe, *An English-Irish Dictionary and Phrase Book* (Dublin, 1903); Liam Mac Amhlaigh, 'Foclóireacht na nua-ghaeilge—tábhacht agus traidisiún', *Comhar* LXIX (2009), 16–19.

150. *Celtia* VII, 2.

151. *Celtia* VII, 8–9.

152. *Celtia* II, 34.

153. Barrett, *Imtheachta, 1899*, 165–66.

154. See, for example, his speech reported in *Y Clorianydd*, 4 August 1898, 4.

155. 'Keltich Researches, copies given away', Bodleian Library, MS Eng. misc., c. 71, 340v.

156. Fournier to Nicholson, 18 May 1904, Bodleian Library, MS Eng. misc., c. 71, ff. 494–95. He also invited Nicholson to the 1907 Congress, but it is unclear whether Nicholson was there [see Fournier to Nicholson, 24 September 1907, Bodleian Library, MS Eng. misc., c. 71, ff. 178r–179]. Fournier's review of Nicholson's book appeared in *Celtia* IV, 59–60.

157. *Celtia* I, 168–69.

158. *Celtia* III, 90.

159. *Celtia* III, 91.

160. *Celtia* III, 121–23.

161. *Celtia* I, 15.

162. *Celtia* II, 90.

163. E. E. Fournier, *Eachtra Laoghaire Mic Criomthain go maigh meall. The visit of Leary, son of Criffan, to the plain of delight: An ancient Irish story from the Book of Lismore translated into modern Irish and Esperanto*, trans. R. B. White (Dublin, 1908).

164. *Celtia* II, 115.

165. *Celtia* I, 126; William O'Brian, *Irish Ideas* (London, 1893), 72.

166. *Celtia* I, 17.

167. *Celtia* I, 3.

168. *Celtia* II, 161–62.

169. *Celtia* II, 162–63.

170. *Celtia* I, 99.

171. *Celtia* I, 17.

172. *Celtia* II, 98.

173. *Celtia* II, 161–62.

174. *Celtia* II, 178.

175. *Celtia* II, 162–63.

176. *Celtia* III, 70.

177. *Celtia* III, 70.

178. *Celtia* II, 98.

179. *Celtia* III, 71.

180. *Celtia* IV, 107.

181. *Celtia* III, 81; Alfons Parczewski, *A Survey of the Language Map of Europe and a Sketch of an International Peace Union for the Protection of Linguistic Minorities: Submitted to the Pan-Celtic Congress at Carnarvon* (Caernarvon, 1904).

182. *Celtia* I, 149; II, 83.

183. *Celtia* I, 149.

184. *Celtia* II, 162–63.

185. *Celtia* I, 36.

186. H. G. Wells, *Anticipations of the Reaction of Mechanical and Scientific Progress Upon Human Life and Thought* (London, 1902).

187. Wells, *Anticipations*, 248.

188. Wells, *Anticipations*, 218n44.

189. *Celtia* I (1901), 149–50.

190. Fournier to Castletown, 27 December 1923, NLI, MS 35,305(7). Fournier continued to live on in Irish cultural memory however, as the eponym of the Celticist and inventor 'le Fournier' as well as partial inspiration for 'de Selby' in Flann O'Brien's (1911–1966) masterpiece *The Third Policeman* (1966).

191. A. P. Graves to Fournier, 27 July 1909, Fournier d'Albe Papers.

192. *The Tablet*, 18 June 1910, 31.

193. MacBride White and Jeffares, *Gonne-Yeats Letters*, 289.

194. Fournier to Castletown, 6 May 1901, NLI, MS 35,305(5).

Chapter Twelve: From the Pan-Celtic Moment to the Present

1. George Moore, *Hail and Farewell* (3 vols., London, 1911–1914), vol. 1, 42.

2. Joachim Lerchenmüller, 'Keltologie', in Frank-Rutger Hausmann (ed.), *Die Rolle der Geisteswissenschaften im Dritten Reich 1933–1945* (Munich, 2002), 137–63.

3. Joachim Fischer and John Dillon (eds.), *The Correspondence of Myles Dillon, 1922–1925: Irish-German Relations and Celtic Studies* (Dublin, 1999), 21, 38, 77.

4. Julius Pokorny, *Die älteste Lyrik der grünen Insel* (Halle, 1923), 3.

5. Reece, *Bretons*. See also Ian Stewart, 'Celtic Philology, French Nationalism, and Science in the Pan-German Shadow, 1868–1932' (forthcoming).

6. 'Exposé sur la question Bretonne', NLW, GB2010, Feutren 4/1, folder 1.

7. Aarón Alzola Romero and Eduardo Sánchez-Moreno, 'Fabricating Celts: How Iron Age Iberians Became Indo-Europeanized during the Franco Regime', *Proceedings of the Harvard Celtic Colloquium* 29 (2009), 1–29.

8. de Barra, *Celts*.

9. Constantine, 'Welsh Literary History', 112.

10. For a good start, see Bernard Maier, 'The Female Quest for the Celtic Tongues of Ireland, Scotland, and Wales', in Wendy Ayres-Bennett and Helena Sanson (eds.), *Women in the History of Linguistics* (Oxford, 2020), 305–18; Christina Cleary and Chantal Kobel (eds.), *Essays in Memory of Eleanor Knott* (Dublin, 2023). The 2023–2024 series of the Bonn/Marburg Celtic Seminar was on the subject of 'Women in Celtic Studies'.

11. Bodleian Library, MS, Eng. misc., 71.

12. CUL, GBR/0012/MS Add. 78000/C/7, Add. 7800/C/4. These are from the *Derry People*, presumably picked up during his fieldwork in Donegal.

13. Donald Meek, *The Quest for Celtic Christianity* (Edinburgh, 2000).

14. There are of course many fine studies of individual scholars, important works, and networks, but Tourneur's *Esquisse* is still the only overview. This was already 'very disappointing' to Kuno Meyer in 1906 (Bernhard Maier (ed.), *Kuno Mayer and Wales: Letters to John Glyn Davies, 1892–1919* [Würzburg, 2017], 109).

15. David Ellis Evans, 'The Heroic Age of Celtic Philology', *ZCP* 54 (2004), 1–30. On German Celtology specifically, see Karl Horst Schmidt, 'Stand und Aufgaben der deutschsprachigen

Keltologie', in Martin Rockel and Stefan Zimmer (eds.), *Akten des ersten Symposiums Deutschsprachiger Keltologen* (Tübingen, 1993), 1–36; Sean Ó Lúing, 'Celtic Scholars of Germany', *ZCP* 46 (1994), 249–70.

16. See, for example, Ó Lúing, *Kuno Meyer*, 110–11.

17. On the scholarly utility of Celtic, see Gero Will, 'Die Anfänge der Deutschen Keltologie und ihre Insittutionalisierung bis 1901', in Sabine Heinz (ed.), *Die Deutsche Keltologie und ihre Berliner Gelehrten bis 1945* (Frankfurt, 1999), 25–38.

18. On this chair, see Ute Fickelscherer, 'Autoren Keltologischer Forschungensarbeiten in Berlin von den Anfängen bis 1945', in Heinz, *Deutsche Keltologie*, 39–49.

19. Patrizia de Bernardo Stempel, 'Rudolf Thurneysen (1857–1940) und sein sprachwissenschaftliches Werk', *ZCP* 46 (1994), 219.

20. Charles-Edwards, 'Celtic Languages', 26.

21. Ó Lúing, *Kuno Meyer*, 3.

22. On the genesis of the *Zeitschrift*, see Ó Luing, *Kuno Meyer*, 13–14.

23. Kuno Meyer to Edward Nicholson, 15 September 1905, Bodleian Library, MS Eng. misc., c. 72, f. 57r.

24. Kuno Meyer, 'The Necessity for Establishing a School of Irish Literature, Philology, and History', *Celtia* III (1903).

25. See the essays in Boyle and Russell, *Tripartite Life of Whitley Stokes*; Dáibhí Ó Cróinín, *Whitley Stokes (1830–1909): The Lost Celtic Notebooks Rediscovered* (Dublin, 2011), 7–25.

26. Whitley Stokes, 'Notes (for O'Donovan) on Celtic Researches', University College London Special Collections, MS Add. 300, Whitley Stokes Papers, Box 4. For O'Donovan's comment, see O'Donovan to Reeves, 4 August 1858, UCD Special Collections.

27. R. T. Siefried to Pictet, 19 February 1859, BGE, Ms. fr. 4229, f. 135^{v}.

28. Carl Lottner to Pictet, 6 July 1863, BGE, Ms. fr. 4229, ff. 89^{v}-91^{r}.

29. O'Grady to Rhys, 31 March 1891, NLW, Sir John Rhys Papers, 31 March 1891.

30. Meyer then took up a part-time lectureship at Glasgow from 1905.

31. Domhnall Uilleam Stiùbhart (ed.), *The Life & Legacy of Alexander Carmichael* (Port of Ness, 2008).

32. Prospectus in Bodleian Library, Ms. Eng. misc., c. 71, f. 436.

33. Fraser to R. Best, 28 May 1938, NLI, MS 11000(24).

34. See 'The Gaelic Story at the University of Glasgow', accessed 21 June 2024, https://sgeulnagaidhlig.ac.uk/?lang=en.

35. Kuno Meyer to E. Nicholson, 20 February 1902, Bodleian Library, MS Eng. misc., c. 71, f. 239^{r}.

36. Fraser to Best, 29 January 1914, NLI, MS 11000(17)i.

37. See Huw Pryce, *J. E. Lloyd and the Creation of Welsh History: Renewing a Nation's Past* (Cardiff, 2011); Patrick Sims-Williams, 'John Morris-Jones and his *Welsh Grammar*', *THSC*, New Series 22 (2016), 134–53.

38. Cited in Huw Prys, 'J. E. Lloyd's *History of Wales* (1911)', in Neil Evans and Huw Pryce (eds.), *Writing a Small Nation's Past: Wales in Comparative Perspective, 1850–1950* (Farnham, 2013), 49–64, at 62.

39. See Stewart, "Celtic Philology".

40. Heinrich Zimmer, *Keltische Studien* (2 vols., Berlin, 1881–1884), vol. 2, vi. See, for example, D'Arbois de Jubainville to Windisch, 9 June and 16 June 1884, Universitätsarchiv, Leipzig University, Nachlass Ernst Windisch, 2.7.2–2.7.3.

41. Ó Lúing, *Kuno Meyer*, 13–14, 111.

42. See, for example, Rhys to Gaidoz, 15 February 1879, NLW, Sir John Rhys Papers, A1/1/10; Rhys to Gaidoz, 26 June 1880, NLW, Sir John Rhys Papers, A1/1/11; Rhys to Nicholson, 23 February 1906, Bodleian Library, MS Eng. misc., c. 72, f. 95$^{r\text{-}v}$.

43. Collège de France, 14 CDF 18-a, B-II, a-5, 'Exposé de C. Jullian', esp. 14–15.

44. Collège de France, 14 CDF 18-a, B-II Celtique.

45. C. A. Chavasse to E. Nicholson, 11 April 1910, Bodleian Library, MS Eng. misc., c. 73, ff. 37$^{r\text{-}v}$.

46. *The Academy*, 20 August 1911.

47. Dáibhí Ó Cróinín, 'Letters of Kuno Meyer to Douglas Hyde, 1896–1919', *Studia Hibernica* 42 (2016), 30–31.

48. The speech was published by Fournier in *Celtia* and is reprinted in Ó Lúing, *Kuno Meyer*, 240–46.

49. Quoted in Lúing, *Kuno Meyer*, 36.

50. Ó Cróinín, 'Letters of Kuno Meyer to Douglas Hyde', 32–33, 53; 'Report on the Work of the School of Irish Learning', *Ériu* III (1907), i; Ó Lúing, *Kuno Meyer*, 37–42.

51. Ó Lúing, *Kuno Meyer*, 60, 71.

52. Ó Lúing, *Kuno Meyer*, 89.

53. Joachim Lerchenmüller, *>Keltischer Sprengstoff<: Eine wissenschaftsgeschichtliche Studie über die deutsche Keltologie von 1900 bis 1945* (Tübingen, 1997), arraigns Meyer on charges of perverting Celtic scholarship for political purposes, but the issue is more complicated than that. An example of Meyer's nationalism is his tasteless joke to Richard Best while sailing past Ireland 'whether there will be a new chapter to the *Gabála Érenn*' (quoted in Ó Lúing, *Kuno Meyer*, 167).

54. See Kuno Meyer to Roger Casement, 10 January 1915, NLI, MS 13,073/10ii/6.

55. *New York Times*, 18 December 1914, 1; *Gaelic American* 11, 26 December, 1914, 4; *New York Times*, 13 March 1915, 4; *New York Times*, 28 April 1915, 3; *The Times*, 24 December 1914, 10; *The Times*, 7 January 1915, 9.

56. Ó Lúing, *Kuno Meyer*, 176–82.

57. See A. G. Van Hamel to R. I. Best, 18 February 1916, NLI, MS 11004(7)ii.

58. Joseph Loth to R. I. Best, 20 October 1914, NLI, MS 11001(21)i.

59. *Ériu* IX (1921–1923), 188; *Ériu* X (1926–1928), i–iv.

60. Though see the many letters of frustrated concern by Henri Gaidoz to Richard Best about Meyer in NLI, MS 11000(27).

61. Lerchenmüller, 'Keltologie', 140.

62. Rudolf Thurneysen, 'Irland und England', in Rudolf Thurneysen, *Gesammelte Schriften*, ed. Patrizia de Bernardo Stempel and Rolf Ködderitzsch (3 vols., Tübingen, 1991–1995), vol. 2, 240.

63. Gaidoz to Best, 24 June 1918 and 29 July 1918, NLI, MS 11000(27)iv. Gaidoz's letters to Best on the subject are amusing because he was at that time conducting anthropological work on the Irish race and wanted to know about events as well as the skull shapes of those involved.

See Gaidoz to Best, 3 July 1916, NLI, MS 11000(27)ii; Gaidoz to Best, 6 July 1917, NLI, MS 11000(27)iv.

64. de Barra, *Celts*, 250–51.

65. Quoted in de Barra, *Celts*, 236.

66. Julius Pokorny, 'MacNeill's Place in Celtic Studies', in F. X. Martin and F. J. Byrne, *The ScholaRevolutionary: Eoin MacNeill and the Making of the New Ireland, 1867–1945* (Shannon, 1973), 13–14.

67. See the essays on his scholarship in Conor Mulvagh and Emer Purcell (eds.), *Eoin MacNeill: The Pen and the Sword* (Cork, 2022).

68. MacNeill, *Phases*, 4.

69. MacNeill, *Phases*, 3.

70. Eoin MacNeill, 'The Re-Discovery of the Celts', *Irish Review* 3 (1913), 522–32, at 522.

71. MacNeill, *Phases*, 9.

72. Eoin MacNeill, *Early Irish Laws and Institutions* (Dublin, 1935), 25–26.

73. MacNeill, *Early Irish Laws*, 54–55.

74. Theodore Roosevelt, 'The Ancient Irish Sagas', *The Century* 73 (1907), 327–37.

75. Theodore Roosevelt to F. N. Robinson, 29 January 1907, Houghton Library, Harvard University, MS AM. 1792 (2). Roosevelt also corresponded with, among others, Kuno Meyer.

76. For Celtic studies in North America, see Roland Blenner-Hassett, 'A Brief History of Celtic Studies in North America', *Publications of the Modern Language Association of America* 69 (1954), supplement, 3–21.

77. Arthur Brown to Best, 9 October 1937, NLI, 11000(4)ii.

78. Michael Linkletter, 'The Early Establishment of Celtic Studies in North American Universities', *Proceedings of the Harvard Celtic Colloquium* 29 (2009), 138–53.

79. For a history of the project, see Mairéad Carew, *The Quest for the Irish Celt: The Harvard Archaeological Mission to Ireland, 1932–1936* (Dublin, 2018).

80. *Irish Times*, 15 October 1927, 5.

81. Carew, *Quest*.

82. 'The Harvard Study of the Irish Free State', 1, Harvard Peabody Museum Archives, Hooton Papers, 995-1, Box 21.9.

83. Hencken to Hooton, 4 July 1932, Harvard Peabody Museum Archives, Hooton Papers, 995-1, Box 21.10.

84. *Irish Times*, 24 August 1933, 4. This section relies on Carew, *Quest*, 79–86, though I place little stock in the reality of the idea.

85. *Irish Times*, 26 August 1933, 8; 1 September 1933, 8; 2 September 1933.

86. See, for example, *New York Herald Tribune*, 18 February 1934.

87. See various press clippings in Harvard Peabody Museum Archives, Hooton Papers, 995-1, Box 21.1. For the more circumspect statement actually released by the Harvard Team, see Hooton Papers, 995-1, Box 21.7, 'Harvard University Irish Expedition'.

88. *Boston Globe*, 6 November 1932.

89. Cf. Carew, *Quest*, which overplays the 'Celtic' significance of the survey.

90. 'Report of the Second Harvard Archaeological Expedition to Ireland, 1933', 4, Harvard Peabody Museum Archives, Hooton Papers, 995-1, Box 21.1.

91. *Twenty Year Report: School of Celtic Studies, Dublin Institute for Advanced Studies* (Dublin, 1962), vii.

92. 'The Endowment of Irish Scholarship', 2, NLI, MS 11005(2).

93. D. A. Binchy, 'Report on the present position of Irish Studies and suggestions for future developments', second draft, 1, 9, NLI, MS 11005(3).

94. *Evening Herald*, 6 July 1939, 5. *Irish Press*, 7 July 1939, 2, shows that de Valera relied on Binchy's report when he introduced the bill.

95. Proinsias Ó Dubhthaigh to R. I. Best, 16 April 1940, NLI, MS 11005(5).

96. *Irish Press*, 11 July 1934, 7.

97. E. J. Gwynne to R. I. Best, 30 October 1940, NLI, MS 11001(9)ii.

98. MacNeill, *Phases*, 16. See also Henri d'Arbois de Jubainville, 'Les origines gauloises: L'empire celtique au IVe siècle avant notre ère', *Revue Historique* 30 (1886), 1–48.

99. Adolf Hitler, *Monologue im Führer-Hauptquarter, 1941–1944*, ed. Heinrich Heim and Werner Jochmann (Hamburg, 1980), 355.

100. See, for example, Gustaf Kossinna, *Die Herkunft der Germanen* (Würzburg, 1911).

101. Robert Much, 'Die angebliche Keltenherrschaft in Germanien', *Volk und Rasse* (1926), 100–105, at 105.

102. Julius Pokorny, 'Ist der Germanenname Keltisch?', *ZCP* 20 (1936), 461–75, esp. 475.

103. This paragraph relies on Pól Ó Dochartaigh, *Julius Pokorny, 1887–1970: Germans, Celts and Nationalism* (Dublin, 2004), and Lerchenmüller, *>Keltischer Sprengstoff<*, 243–303.

104. Van Hamel to Best, 11 November 1919, NLI, MS 11004(6)i

105. Baudis to Best, 10 December 1919, NLI, MS 11000(5)ii. See also Baudis to Best, 30 October 1919, NLI, MS 11000(5)ii.

106. Julius Pokorny, 'The Origins of Druidism', *Celtic Review* 5 (1908), 1–20; *Irish Times*, 27 October 1925, 5; Julius Pokorny, *A History of Ireland*, trans. Séana D. King (London, 1933), 16–17. Pokorny's ideas may have been the origin of MacNeill's similar argument.

107. In addition to other ugly qualities, such as racism and lechery, Pokorny was antisemitic and seems to have been more upset by being 'treated exactly like a Jew' rather than by the treatment of the Jews by the Nazis. Günther Haseloff to Richard Best, NLI, MS 11001(11), asked about the rumours of 'unpleasant influence . . . in personal and moral matters' that Pokorny had on Irish students.

108. Lerchenmüller, *>Keltischer Sprengstoff<*, 282. Some Irish diplomats, like Charles Bewley, worked for Pokorny's supersession by Ludwig Mühlhausen.

109. Quoted in Ó Dochartaigh, *Julius Pokorny*, 129.

110. Quoted in Lerchenmüller, *>Keltischer Sprengstoff<*, 418.

111. For biographical information, see Lerchenmüller, *>Keltischer Sprengstoff<*, 264–69, 273–75, 351–57, 383.

112. Quoted in Christopher Hutton, *Linguistics and the Third Reich: Mother-Tongue Fascism, Race and the Science of Language* (New York, 1998), 128.

113. Lerchenmüller, *>Keltischer Sprengstoff<*, chapter 13; George Broderick, 'Celtic Studies and Their Function in Germany during and after the Period of the Third Reich', *Keltische Forschungen* (2021).

114. See the BBC Northern Ireland documentary 'Nazi sa Ghaeltacht' (first broadcast 26 July 2020).

115. Lerchenmüller, >*Keltischer Sprengstoff*<, 384–88.

116. Sebastien Carney, *Breiz Atao! Mordrel, Delaporte, Lainé, Fouéré: une mystique nationale (1901–1948)* (Rennes, 2015).

117. Gervard von Tevenar, 'Zur Gründung der "Deutschen Gesellschaft für keltische Studien"', *ZCP* 22 (1941), 440–41.

118. Helmut Bauersfeld, *Die Entwicklung der keltischen Studien in Deutschland* (Berlin, 1937), 3, 20.

119. Lerchenmüller, >*Keltischer Sprengstoff*<, 396.

120. Michael H. Kater, *Das "Ahnenerbe" der SS 1935–1945* (Stuttgart, 1974); Heather Pringle, *The Master Plan: Himmler's Scholars and the Holocaust* (London, 2006).

121. Lerchenmüller, >*Keltischer Sprengstoff*<, 405–6.

122. Kater, *Das "Ahnenerbe"*, 196; Lerchenmüller, >*Keltischer Sprengstoff*<, 405–6; Hutton, *Linguistics*, 131–33; Lerchenmüller, 'Keltologie', 142–43.

123. Quoted in Hutton, *Linguistics*, 132.

124. See, for example, Hutton, *Linguistics*, 128–32.

125. See, for example, Lerchenmüller, >*Keltischer Sprengstoff*<, 369.

126. On Weisgerber, see Nelly Blanchard, *Un agent du Reich à la rencontre des militants bretons: Leo Weisgerber* (Brest, 2003); Hutton, *Linguistics*, 106–43.

127. Leo Weisgerber, *Die Keltischen Völker im Umkreis von England* (Marburg, 1941), 7.

128. Weisgerber, *Die Keltischen Völker*, 7, 48.

129. Weisgerber, *Die Keltischen Völker*, 54.

130. David O'Donoghue, *Hitler's Irish Voices: The Story of German Radio's Wartime Irish Service* (Belfast, 1998).

131. Lerchenmüller, >*Keltischer Sprengstoff*<, 402.

132. Lerchenmüller, >*Keltischer Sprengstoff*<, 404.

133. For the Best quote, see Lerchenmüller, >*Keltischer Sprengstoff*<, xii, n. 4; Gerhard von Tevenar, 'Ein keltisches Institut in der Bretagne', *ZCP* 22 (1941), 443.

134. On *Gwalarn* and the Breton movement, see, for example, Ronan Calvez, 'Le réenchantement d'un monde: Mouvement Breton, nazisme et émissions de radio en breton', in Sabine Heinz (ed.), *Die Deutsche Keltologie und ihre Berliner Gelehrten bis 1945* (Frankfurt, 1999), 101–37; Blanchard, *Un agent*, 47–54.

135. Daniel Leach, '"A Sense of Nordism": The Impact of Germanic Assistance upon the Militant Interwar Breton Nationalist Movement', *European Review of History* 17 (2010), 639.

136. Carney, *Breiz Atao!*, 190–96, 263–96, 438–39. Carney, *Breiz Atao!*, 38–41, shows that at seventeen, Mordrel was already well versed in racial theory and craniology (though he was at this point anti-German!).

137. Olier Mordrel files in Ursinus College Special Collections, accessed 15 November 2023, https://digitalcommons.ursinus.edu/breton/.

138. Leach, '"A Sense of Nordism"'.

139. 'Notre position', in NLW, Feutren 4/1, folder 1; Celestin Lainé, 'Biographie-Mémoires', trans. Daniel Leach and Guillaume Legros, *E-Keltoi* 4 (2012), 92. Lainé managed to have an article published in Mühlhausen's *ZCP* in 1943.

140. Carney, *Breiz Atao!*, 263–68.

141. Hutton, *Linguistics*, 132–33; Lerchenmüller, >*Keltischer Sprengstoff*<, 407.

142. Document dated 5 March 1945 in Tübingen, NLW, Feutren 4/1, folder 4.

143. Alan Heursaff to Raymond Jegaden, 8 January 1994, NLW, Feutren 4/1, folder 1.

144. Letter extracted in Lerchenmüller, >*Keltischer Sprengstoff*<, 280.

145. Quoted in Lerchenmüller, >*Keltischer Sprengstoff*<, 351.

146. Lerchenmüller, >*Keltischer Sprengstoff*<, 409.

147. Hildegard L. C. Tristram, 'Celtic Studies in West Germany', *Celtic Cultures Newsletter* 4 (1986), 5–12.

148. Max Förster to Richard Best, 13 January 1947, NLI, MS 11000(23); Annie Heiermeier to Best, 11 February 1949, NLI, MS 11001(13); Annie Heiermeier to R. Best, 2 September 1949, NLI, MS 11001(13); Günther Haseloff to Richard Best, 30 July 1949, NLI, MS 11001(11).

149. Heiermeier to Best, 21 January 1950, NLI, MS 11001(13).

150. Sabine Heinz, 'Foreword', in *eadem*, *Die Deutsche Keltologie*, 10–11. It was officially eliminated in 1998 but had been unfilled since Mühlhausen left. The Irish government offered to come to the aid of Celtic studies at Berlin on the condition that it would be joined by other Celtic nations, but it came to nothing [see *Irish Times*, 15 July 2003, accessed 5 December 2023, https://www.irishtimes.com/culture/the-slow-curtain-on-celtic-studies-1.366161].

151. O'Farrelly had been involved in the Pan-Celtic movement of the early 1900s [see, for example, *Celtia*, IV: 'Congress Number', 97].

152. de Barra, *Celts*, 195–96. Fournier was uninvolved with the new Pan-Celtic movement, and when Castletown was invited to the Birkenhead meeting of 1917 he did not reply [Letter to E. T. John, 30 June 1919, NLW, ETJ 5558].

153. 'Proposed Pan-Celtic Conference', NLW, ETJ 5556.

154. *The Celtic Congress: Constitution*, 3. Copy in NLS, Acc. 9736/99.

155. *The Celtic Congress: Constitution*, 5–6; E. T. John, 'Celtic Congress Edinburgh: Inaugural Address' (Bangor, 1921), 18, in NLS, Acc. 9736/100.

156. 'Y Cynghrair Celtaidd', *Y Darian*, 9 October 1919, 1. See the plans for 1919 in NLW, ETJ 5558.

157. John, 'Inaugural Address by the President Edw. T. John', in NLS, Acc. 9736/100. See also NLW, ETJ 5559 for congress paraphernalia.

158. John, 'Inaugural Address by the President Edw. T. John', 20, 22–23.

159. de Barra, *Celts*, 206–11.

160. Ruaridh Erskine to E. T. John, 4 September [1919], NLW, ETJ 2877.

161. Liaim O'Briain to E. T. John, 6 September 1919, NLW, ETJ 2293.

162. Art Ó Brian to John, 3 September 1919, NLW, ETJ 2284.

163. See papers in NLW, ETJ 5562 and ETJ 5563.

164. *Manchester Guardian*, 10 July 1925, 6.

165. *Scotsman*, 30 August 1950.

166. Mícheál Briody, *The Irish Folklore Commission, 1935–1970: History, Ideology, Methodology* (Helsinki, 2008), 307–9.

167. Ruaridh Erskine to E. T. John, [1919], NLW, ETJ 2302.

168. Hugh MacDiarmid, *Lucky Poet: A Self-Study in Literature and Political Ideas* (London, 1943), 166.

169. MacDiarmid, *Lucky Poet*, 26.

170. NLS, Acc. 9337, 3.

171. See Ellis, *Celtic Dawn*, 108–38.

172. 'A League for the Freedom of the Celtic Peoples' [1962?], NLW, Celtic League Archives, S1/1. The only academic history of the league, so far as I am aware, is Héloïse Verissi, 'The Celtic League and Its Vision on the French and English Colonization of the Celtic Countries and Territories since 1961', unpublished MA thesis (Université Paris Cité/UCD, 2023). I'm grateful to her for sharing it with me.

173. *Carn* 1 (1973), 1.

174. Celtic League membership application found in *Celtic League Annual* [this from 1969].

175. This is the verdict of Peter Berresford Ellis, '"We Only Want the Earth"', in Cathal Ó Luain (ed.), *For a Celtic Future* (Dublin, 1983), 328.

176. See the correspondence files in NLW, Celtic League Archives, S1.

177. Hielscher to Heusaff, 1 December 1966, NLW, Celtic League Archives, S1/3 Correspondence 1965–66.

178. 'Celtic Voice', in NLW, Celtic League Archives, S1/1. See Neven Henaff, 'Prospects for Things Celtic', *Carn* 2 (1973), 13; *Carn* 6 (1974), 21–22; *Carn* 17 (1977), 21–22.

179. See the 1953 Celtic Congress programme in NLI, MS 22,111. Petra Johana Poncarová, *Derick Thomson and the Gaelic Revival* (Edinburgh, 2024), esp. 49–54.

180. Later, scholars of Celtic subjects such as George Broderick and Kevin Collins contributed articles to *Carn*.

181. Peter Berresford Ellis, 'The Celtic League—Twenty Years A-Growing', *Carn* 35/36 (1981), 24.

182. See the autumn and winter issues of *Carn* 1981 for some early histories of the league, and the later chapters of Ellis's *Celtic Dawn*.

183. Peter Berresford Ellis, *The Creed of the Celtic Revolution* (London, 1969), 11. The pamphlet came with a disclaimer that the views expressed in it were not necessarily those of the league, but it also contained Heusaff's contact information for those who were interested.

184. Ellis, *Creed*, 11.

185. Ellis, *Creed*, 23.

186. See the issues of *Carn* in the 1970s.

187. *Carn* 1 (1973), 1.

188. Victor Durkacz, 'Historical Connections in the Development of Celtic Education', *Carn* 17 (1977), 19–21.

189. *Carn* 1 (1973), 1; 'A League for the Freedom of the Celtic Peoples', NLW, Celtic League Archives, S1/1.

190. For a retrospective summary, see Alan Heusaff, 'Relations with Galicia', *Carn* 98 (1997), 22. He had long had a soft spot for Galician Celtic enthusiasts [see Heussaff to M. Davies, 25 May 1963, NLW, Celtic League Archives, S1/1].

191. 'Galicia's Disputed Celtic Heritage', *Economist*, 9 May 2017.

192. See Verissi, 'Celtic League', for these platforms.

193. Ellis, '"We Only Want the Earth"', in Luain, *For a Celtic Future*, 323.

194. The league does not release its membership numbers, but Verissi's interviews suggested that a few hundred people are probably enrolled.

195. Nairn, *Break-Up*, 71.

196. 'Celtic Forum on Green Energy, Culture and Youth Mobility: Memorandum of Understanding and Declaration', accessed 3 December 2023, https://www.gov.scot/publications/celtic-forum-on-green-energy-culture-and-youth-mobility-memorandum-of-understanding-and

-declaration/pages/memorandum-of-understanding/. Curiously, representatives of all of the Celtic nations bar the Isle of Man were present, as well as those from Galicia and Asturia.

197. *Twenty Year Report*, vii, 6.

198. *Irish Times*, 7 July 1959, 9.

199. Bart Jaski, Lars Nooij, Sanne Nooij-Jongeleen, and Nike Stam (eds.), *A Man of Two Worlds: A. G. van Hamel, Celticist and Germanist* (Utrecht, 2023). On Celtic studies in Russia, see Séamus Mac Mathúna, 'The History of Celtic Scholarship in Russia and the Soviet Union', *Studia Celto-Slavica* 1 (2006), 3–41; Piotr Stalmaszczyk, 'Celtic Studies in Poland: Recent Themes and Developments', *Studia Celto-Slavica* 1 (2006), 43–59.

200. Michael Lapidge (ed.), *H. M. Chadwick and the Study of Anglo-Saxon, Norse and Celtic in Cambridge* (Aberystwyth, 2015).

201. Brian Ó Cuív, 'Celtic Studies–An Appraisal', in Cyril J. Byrne, Margaret Harry, and Pádraig Ó Siadhail (eds.), *Celtic Languages and Celtic Peoples* (Halifax, 1992), 1–9.

202. Jackson, 'Fifty Years', xxiii–xxiv.

203. See, for example, Powell, *The Celts*.

204. Dillon and Chadwick, *Celtic Realms*, preface.

205. Chadwick, *The Celts*, 42.

206. John Collis, Review of Barry Cunliffe, *Danebury: An Iron Age Hillfort in Hampshire* (2 vols., London, 184), *Proceedings of the Prehistoric Society* 51 (1985), 348–49.

207. See my comments in the introduction on Simon James's misunderstanding of the 'invention of tradition'.

208. See, for example, Roberts, *Celts*.

209. Sims-Williams, 'Celtomania and Celtoscepticism'.

210. See esp. Patrick Sims-Williams, 'Celtic Civilization: Continuity or Coincidence?', *CMCS* 64 (2012), 1–45.

211. McCone, *The Celtic Question*, 39, 46. Though cf. Patrick Sims-Williams, 'Celto-Etruscan Speculations', in Eugenio R. Luján and Juan Luis García Alonson (eds.), *A Greek Man in the Iberian Street: Papers in Linguistics and Epigraphy in Honor of Javier de Hoz* (Innsbruck, 2011), 275–84.

212. Sims-Williams, 'An Alternative', 511. N. B. Sims-Williams does not necessarily accept McCone's etymologies. His picture is based on his own extensive work on Celtic place and personal names attested across ancient Europe.

213. Cunliffe and Koch, *Celtic from the West*, vol. 1, 1.

214. Cunliffe and Koch, *Celtic from the West*, vol. 1, 1.

215. See, for example, Sims-Williams, 'An Alternative'; *idem*, 'The Location of the Celts According to Hecataeus, Herodotus, and other Greek Writers', *Études celtiques* 42 (2016), 7–32.

216. See Reich, *Who We Are*, for an accessible introduction.

217. Nick Patterson, Michael Isakov, Thomas Booth, et al., 'Large-Scale Migration into Britain during the Middle to Late Bronze Age', *Nature* 601 (2022), 588–94.

218. Sims-Williams, 'Celtic from the Centre'. See also his summary of the DNA and linguistic arguments in *idem*, 'Pryd y death y Gymraeg i Ynys Prydain?', *Barn* 709 (2022), 20–22.

219. Franz Lidz, '3,000 Years Ago, Britain Got Half Its Genes From . . . France?', *New York Times*, 22 December 2021, accessed 3 October 2023, https://www.nytimes.com/2021/12/22/science/archaeology-britain-migration-dna-reich.html?searchResultPosition=1.

BIBLIOGRAPHY

Archives

France

Archives départementales, Finistère
Archives départementales, Quimper
Archives municipales, Rennes
Archives nationales, Paris
Bibliothèque nationale de France, Paris
Bibliothèque de l'Académie nationale de médecine, Paris
Collège de France, Paris
E. E. Fournier d'Albe Papers (Private Collection)
Médiathèque Alain-Gérard, Quimper
Muséum d'histoire naturelle, Paris

Germany

Geheimes Staatsarchiv Preußischer Kulturbesitz, Berlin
Gottfried Wilhelm Leibniz Bibliothek, Hanover
Universitätsarchiv, Leipzig

Ireland

National Library of Ireland, Dublin
Royal Irish Academy, Dublin
University College Dublin, Dublin

Switzerland

Bibliothèque de Genève, Geneva

United Kingdom

Bangor University Archives, Bangor
Bodleian Library, Oxford

British Library, London
Cambridge University Library, Cambridge
Christ Church, Oxford
Edinburgh University Library, Edinburgh
Kresen Kernow, Redruth
Lionel Robbins Library, The London School of Economics and Political Science, London
National Library of Scotland, Edinburgh
National Library of Wales, Aberystwyth
Norfolk Record Office, Norwich
Royal Medical Society, Edinburgh
Society of Antiquaries of London, London
The Royal Society, London
Trinity College, Cambridge
University of Aberystwyth, Aberystwyth
University College London, London
University of Strathclyde, Glasgow

United States of America

American Philosophical Society, Philadelphia, PA
Firestone Library, Princeton University, Princeton, NJ
Harvard Peabody Museum Archives, Cambridge, MA
Houghton Library, Harvard University, Cambridge, MA
New York Public Library, New York
Ursinus College, Collegeville, PA
Yale University Library, New Haven, CT

Newspapers and Periodicals

The Academy
Allgemeine Zeitung
An Claidheamh Soluis
Anthropological Review
Archaeologia Cambrensis
Athenaeum
Baner ac Amserau Cymru
Belfast Newsletter
Blackwood's Magazine
Boston Globe
British Review and London Critical Journal
Bulletins de la société d'anthropologie de Paris
Caledonian Mercury
The Cambrian

Cambrian Journal
Cambrian Register
Cambro-Britain
The Cardiff and Merthyr Guradian
Carlow Morning Post
Carn
Carnarvon and Denbigh Herald and North and South Wales Independent
The Celt
Celtia
Celtic Life International
Celtic Magazine
The Critical Review
Daily Mail
Dublin Journal
Dublin Penny Journal
Dublin Review
The Economist
Edinburgh Review
Elgin Courier
Ériu
Evening Herald
The Examiner
Fáinne an Lae
Freeman's Journal
Gaelic American
Gazette de France
Gazette national ou Le Moniteur universel
Gentleman's Magazine
The Glamorgan Monmouth and Brecon Gazette and Merthyr Guardian
Glasgow Evening Post
Glasgow Herald
The Globe
Göttingische Gelehrte Anzeigen
The Guardian
The Highlander
Histoire et mémoires de l'académie royale des inscriptions et belles-letters
Inverness Courier
Irish Examiner
Irish Press
Irish Times
Jahrbücher der Literatur
Journal de Paris
Journal des débats politiques et littéraires
Journal des Sçavans

The Leader
Leeds Times
L'esprit des journaux
Le Figaro
Le Petit Parisien
London Evening Standard
London Kelt
London Quarterly Review
London Review of Books
Manchester Courier and Lancashire General Advertiser
Manchester Guardian
Mémoires de l'Académie celtique
Mémoires de literature, tirés registres de l'académie royale des inscriptions et belles-lettres
Mercure Galant
Monmouthshire Merlin
Monthly Magazine, or British Register
Monthly Review
Morning Chronicle
Morning Post
The Nation
New London Review
New York Herald Tribune
New York Times
North Wales Chronicle
North Wales Express
Nottingham Journal
Nouvelles de la république des lettres
Pall Mall Gazette
Perthshire Advertiser
Philosophical Transactions of the Royal Society
Publications of the Surtees Society
Punch
Revue archaeologie
Revue celtique
Revue des deux mondes
The Saturday Review
Scots Magazine
Scotsman
South Wales Daily News
The Tablet
Tarian Y Gweithiwr
The Times
Transactions of the Gaelic Society of Dublin
Weekly Mail

Westminster Review
Y Celt
Y Cymmrodor
Y Cymro
Y Darian
Y Drych
Y Gwladgarwr
Yn Clorianydd
Y Werin

Unpublished Theses and Lectures

Ferguson, Megan, 'Patrick Geddes and the Celtic Renascence of the 1890s', PhD dissertation (University of Dundee, 2011).
Foster, R. F., 'Yeats and Scotland', unpublished lecture, University of Edinburgh, 2 May 2015.
Gurden-Williams, Celyn, 'Lady Llanover and the Creation of a Welsh Cultural Utopia', PhD dissertation (Cardiff University, 2008).
Maclean, J.N.M., 'The Early Political Careers of James "Fingal" Macpherson (1736–1796) and Sir John Macpherson, Bart. (1744–1821)', unpublished PhD dissertation (University of Edinburgh, 1967).
McDonough, Ciaran, 'Investigating Irish Antiquarianism: A Comparative Study of Protestant and Catholic Antiquarian Cultures, 1830–1876', PhD dissertation (University of Galway, 2017).
Murphy-Macinta, Christina Eileen, 'Pan-Celtic Nationalism at the Fin de Siècle: A History of the Celtic Association, 1898–1911', PhD dissertation (Brandeis University, 2017).
Lyons, Claire, 'Sylvester O'Halloran's *General History* (1778): Irish Historiography and the Late Eighteenth-Century British Empire', PhD dissertation (University of Galway, 2011).
Pye, Tom, 'Histories of Liberty in Scottish Thought, 1747–1787', PhD dissertation (University of Cambridge, 2018).
Verissi, Héloïse, 'The Celtic League and Its Vision on the French and English Colonization of the Celtic Countries and Territories since 1961', unpublished MA thesis (Université Paris Cité/UCD, 2023).

Online Reference Works and Databases

Bérose, Encyclopédie internationale des histoires de l'anthropologie: https://www.berose.fr/?lang=fr
British Newspaper Archive: https://www.britishnewspaperarchive.co.uk/
Early Modern Letters Online (EMLO): http://emlo.bodleian.ox.ac.uk
Geiriadur Prifysgol Cymru: https://geiriadur.ac.uk/gpc/gpc.html
Hansard: https://api.parliament.uk/historic-hansard/index.html
Irish Newspaper Archives: https://www.irishnewsarchive.com/
Oxford English Dictionary: https://www.oed.com/
Treccani: https://www.treccani.it/enciclopedia/

Published Works

Adelung, J. C., and Vater, J. S., *Mithridates oder Allgemeine Sprachenkunde* (4 vols., Berlin, 1806–1817).

Ahlqvist, Anders, *The Early Irish Linguist* (Helsinki, 1983).

Allen, Grant, 'The Celt in English Art', *Fortnightly Review* 49 (1891).

Allen, Grant, 'The Celtic Fringe', *Westminster Gazette* (1893).

Almagro-Gorbea, Martín, and Ruiz Zapatero, Gonzalo (eds.), *Los Celtas: Hispania y Europa* (Madrid, 1993).

Anderson, Benedict, *Imagined Communities: Reflections on the Origin and Spread of Nationalism* (London, 1983).

Andersson Burnett, Linda, and Buchan, Bruce, *Race and the Scottish Enlightenment: A Colonial History, c. 1750–1820* (New Haven, CT, forthcoming).

Andrews, J. H., *A Paper Landscape: The Ordnance Survey in Nineteenth-Century Ireland* (Oxford, 1975).

Antognazza, Maria Rosa, *Leibniz: An Intellectual Biography* (Cambridge, 2009).

Armitage, David, *The Ideological Origins of the British Empire* (Cambridge, 2000).

Arnold, Matthew, *On the Study of Celtic Literature* (London, 1867).

Arnold, Thomas, *The Christian Duty of Granting the Claims of the Roman Catholics* (Oxford, 1829).

Arnold, Thomas, *History of Rome* (3 vols., London, 1838–1843).

Arnold, Thomas, *Introductory Lectures on Modern History* (1843: London, 1845).

Ash, Marinell, *The Strange Death of Scottish History* (Edinburgh, 1980).

Asher, R. A., *National Myths in Renaissance France: Francus, Samothes and the Druids* (Edinburgh, 1993).

Aubrey, John, *Monumenta Britannica*, ed. John Fowles and Rodney Legg (2 vols., Sherborne, 1980).

Augstein, Hannah Franziska, 'Linguistics and Politics in the Early Nineteenth Century: James Cowles Prichard's Moral Philology', *History of European Ideas* 23 (1997), 1–18.

Augstein, Hannah Franziska, 'Aspects of Philology and Racial Theory in Nineteenth-Century Celticism: The Case of James Cowles Prichard', *Journal of European Studies* 28 (1998), 355–372.

Augstein, Hannah Franziska, *James Cowles Prichard's Anthropology: Remaking the Science of Man in Early Nineteenth-Century Britain* (Amsterdam, 1999).

Baker, Keith, *Inventing the French Revolution* (Cambridge, 1990).

Balcou, Jean, *Ernest Renan: Une biographie* (Paris, 2017).

Bale, John, *Illustrium maioris Britanniae scriptorium* (London, 1548).

Barrett, S. J. (ed.), *Imtheachta an Oireacthais, 1899* (Dublin, 1899).

Barrett, S. J. (ed.), *Imtheachta an Oireacthais, 1900* (Dublin, 1900).

Barrett-Kriegel, Blandine, *Les historiens et la monarchie* (4 vols., Paris, 1988).

Barzun, Jacques, *The French Race: Theories of Its Origins and Their Social and Political Implications prior to the Revolution* (New York, 1932).

Basc-Bautier, G., and de Chancel-Bardelot, B., *Un musée révolutionnaire: Le Musée des Monuments français d'Alexandre Lenoir* (Paris, 2016).

Baudelot de Dairval, Charles-César, *Description des bas-reliefs anciens trouvez depuis peu dans l'Eglise Cathedrale de Paris* (Paris, 1711).

Bauersfeld, Helmut, *Die Entwicklung der keltischen Studien in Deutschland* (Berlin, 1937).

[Bayle, Pierre], *Nouvelles lettres de Mr P. Bayle* (2 vols., The Hague, 1739).

Beatty, Aidan, 'Marx and Engels, Ireland, and the Racial History of Capitalism', *JMH* 91 (2019), 815–47.

Beaune, Colette, *Naissance de la nation France* (Paris, 1985).

[Beauzée, Nicholas], 'Langue', in Denis Diderot and Jean le Rond d'Alembert (eds.), *Encyclopédie, ou dictionnaire raisonné des sciences, des arts et des metiers* (17 vols., Paris, 1751–1765).

Beddoe, John, *The Races of Britain: A Contribution to the Ethnology of Western Europe* (Bristol and London, 1885).

Bell, David A., 'Tearing Down the Tower of Babel: Grégoire and French Multilingualism', in Jeremy D. Popkin and Richard H. Popkin (eds.), *The Abbé Grégoire and His World* (Dordrecht, 2000), 109–28.

Bell, David, *The Cult of the Nation in France: Inventing Nationalism, 1680–1800* (Cambridge, MA, 2003).

Belmont, Nicole, 'L'Académie celtique et George Sand: Les débuts des recherches folkloriques en France', *Romantisme* 9 (1975), 29–38.

Belmont, Nicole, *Aux sources de l'ethnologie française: L'Académie celtique* (Paris, 1995).

Beltrán, F., and Jordán, C., 'Writing and Language in Celtiberia', in Alejandro G. Sinner and Javier Velaza (eds.), *Paleohispanic Languages and Epigraphies* (Oxford, 2019), 240–303.

Benfey, Theodor, *Geschichte der Sprachwissenschaft und orientalischen Philologie in Deutschland* (Munich, 1869).

Berkeley, George, *A Word to the Wise; Or, the Bishop of Cloyne's Exhortation to the Roman Catholick Clergy, of Ireland* (4th ed., Boston, 1750).

Bertrand, Alexandre, 'Celtes, Gaulois et Francs: Lettres au Docteur Paul Broca', *Revue d'anthropologie* 2 (1873), 235–50, 422–35; 629–43.

Besterman, Theodore (ed.), *The Complete Works of Voltaire* (205 vols., Oxford, 1968–2022).

Betham, William, *The Gael and Cymbri* (Dublin, 1834).

Betham, William, *Etruria-Celtica* (2 vols., Dublin, 1842).

Bindman, David, *Ape to Apollo: Aesthetics and the Idea of Race in the 18th Century* (London, 2002).

Birch, Samuel, 'On the Torc of the Celts', *The Archaeological Journal* 2 (1846), 368–80.

Birkhan, Helmut, *Kelten: Versuch einer Gesamtdarstellung ihrer Kultur* (Vienna, 1997).

Birkhan, Helmut, *Nachantike Keltenrezeption: Projektionen keltischer Kultur* (Vienna, 2009).

Blackie, John Stuart, *The Language and Literature of the Scottish Highlands* (Edinburgh, 1876).

Blackie, John Stuart, *Gaelic Societies, Highland Depopulation and Land Law Reform* (Edinburgh, 1880).

Blackie, John Stuart, *The Scottish Highlanders and the Land Laws: An Historico-Economical Enquiry* (London, 1885).

[Blair, Hugh], *A Critical Dissertation on the Poems of Ossian, Son of Fingal* (London, 1763).

Blair, Hugh, *Lectures on Rhetoric and Belles-Lettres* (2 vols., London, 1783).

Blanchard, Nelly, *Un agent du Reich à la rencontre des militants bretons: Leo Weisgerber* (Brest, 2003).

Blanchard, Nelly, and Postic, Fañch, 'Charles de Gaulle (1837–1880): Inventeur du movement Breton? Une approache par sa correspondence avec Théodore Hersart de Le Villemarqué (1861–1872)', *HAL*, Breton and Celtic Research Center, University of Western Brittany (2021).

Blanckaert, Claude, 'On the Origins of French Ethnology: William Edwards and the Doctrine of Race,' in George W. Stocking Jr. (ed.), *Bones, Bodies, Behavior: Essays on Biological Anthropology* (Madison, WI, 1988), 18–55.

Blanckaert, Claude, *De la race à l'évolution: Paul Broca et l'anthropologie française (1850–1900)* (Paris, 2009).

Blenner-Hassett, Roland, 'A Brief History of Celtic Studies in North America', *Publications of the Modern Language Association of America* 69 (1954), supplement, 3–21.

Blom, Alderik H., 'Rasmus Rask's Study of Celtic', *Beiträge zur Geschichte der Sprachwissenschaft* 19 (2009), 223–51.

Bochart, Samuel, *Geographia sacra, seu Phaleg et Canaan* (3rd ed., 2 vols., Leiden, 1707).

Bodin, Jean, *Method for the Easy Comprehension of History*, trans. Beatrice Reynolds (1566: New York, 1945).

Bonfante, G., 'A Contribution to the History of Celtology', *Celtica* 3 (1956), 17–34.

Bopp, Franz, 'Vergleichende Zergliederung des Sanskrits und der mit ihm verwandten Sprachen', *Abhandlungen der historisch-philologischen Klasse der Königlichen Akademie der Wissenschaften zu Berlin aus dem Jahre 1824* (Berlin, 1826), 117–48.

Bopp, Franz, 'Über die celtischen Sprachen vom Gesichtspunkte der vergleichenden Sprachforschung', *Abhandlungen der Königlichen Akademie der Wissenschaften zu Berlin, Aus dem Jahre 1838* (Berlin, 1839), [Philologische und historische Abhandlungen], 187–272.

Boran, Elizabethanne, *The Correspondence of James Ussher, 1600–1656* (3 vols., Dublin, 2015).

Borchardt, Frank L., *German Antiquity in Renaissance Myth* (Baltimore, MD, 1971).

Borst, Arno, *Der Turmbau von Babel: Geschichte der Meinungen über Ursprung und Vielfalt der Sprachen und Völker* (4 vols. in 6, Stuttgart, 1957–1963).

Boswell, James, *Life of Johnson* (1791: Oxford, 2008).

Bosworth, Joseph, *A Dictionary of the Anglo-Saxon Language* (London, 1838).

Bourdon, Émile, *La forge gauloise de la nation: Ernest Lavisse et la fabrique des ancêtres* (Lyon, 2017).

Bouwsma, William J., *Concordia Mundi: The Career and Thought of Guillaume Postel (1510–1581)* (Cambridge, MA, 1957).

Bowen, Geraint, 'Gorsedd y Beirdd: From Primrose Hill 1792 to Aberystwyth 1992', *THSC* (1992), 115–39.

Boyd, Julian P. (ed.), *The Papers of Thomas Jefferson* (43– vols., Princeton, NJ, 1950–).

Brady, Lindy, *The Origin Legends of Early Medieval Britain and Ireland* (Cambridge, 2022).

Brandes, Heinrich, *Das ethnographische verhältniss der Kelten und Germanen* (Leipzig, 1857).

Brann, Noel L., 'Conrad Celtis and the "Druid" Abbot Trithemius: An Inquiry into Patriotic Humanism', *Renaissance and Reformation* 3 (1979), 16–28.

Briody, Mícheál, *The Irish Folklore Commission, 1935–1970: History, Ideology, Methodology* (Helsinki, 2008).

Broca, Paul, *Recherches sur l'hybridité animale en general et sur l'hybridité humain en particulier, considérés dans leur rapports avec la question de la pluralité des espèces humaines* (Paris, 1860).

Broca, Paul, 'Sur des crânes provenant d'un cimetière de la Cité, antérieur au treizième siècle', *BSAP* (1861), 501–13.

Broca, Paul, *Mémoires de l'anthropologie* (Paris, 1871).

Broca, Paul, 'La race celtique ancienne et moderne', *Revue d'anthropologie* 2 (1873), 577–628.

Broca, Paul, 'Sur les textes relatifs aux Celtes dans la Grande-Bretagne', in *BSAP* S.II, 12 (1877), 509–15.

Broderick, George, 'Celtic Studies and Their Function in Germany during and after the Period of the Third Reich', *Keltische Forschungen* (2021).

Bromwich, Rachel, *Matthew Arnold and Celtic Literature: A Retrospect, 1865–1965* (Oxford, 1965).

Bromwich, Rachel, 'Trioedd Ynys Prydain: The *Myvyrian* "Third Series"', *THSC* (1968), 299–338; (1969), 127–56.

Bromwich, Rachel, *'Trioedd Ynys Prydain' in Welsh Literature and Scholarship* (Cardiff, 1969).

Brooke, Charlotte, *Reliques of Irish Poetry* (Dublin, 1789).

Brown, Michael, *The Irish Enlightenment* (Cambridge, MA, 2016).

Brown, Terence (ed.), *Celticism* (Amsterdam, 1996).

Brown, Thomas, *A Short Dissertation about the Mona of Caesar and Tacitus* (London, 1702).

Brucker, Jacob, *The History of Philosophy*, trans. William Enfield (2 vols., London, 1791).

Brunaux, Jean-Louis, *Alésia* (Paris, 2012).

Brunaux, Jean-Louis, *Les Celtes: Histoire d'un mythe* (Paris, 2014).

Buchanan, George, *History of Scotland* (1582: 2 vols., London, 1733).

Buckle, Henry Thomas, *History of Civilization in England* (1857–1861: Cambridge, 2011).

Bullet, Jean-Baptiste, *Mémoires sur la langue Celtique* (3 vols., Besançon, 1754–1760).

Bullet, Jean-Baptiste, *Dissertations sur différens sujets de l'histoire de France* (Bescançon, 1759).

Bunsen, Charles, Meyer, Rev. Charles, and Muller, Max. *Three Linguistic Dissertations Read at the Meeting of the British Association in Oxford* (London, 1848).

Bunsen, Frances, *A Memoir of Baron Bunsen, Late Minister, Plenipotentiary and Envoy Extraordinary of His Majesty Frederic William IV at the Court of St. James* (2 vols., London, 1868).

Burke, Peter, *A Social History of Knowledge* (2 vols., Cambridge, 2000–2012).

Burl, Aubrey, and Mortimer, Neil (eds.), *Stukeley's Stonehenge: An Unpublished Manuscript, 1721–1724* (New Haven, CT, 2005).

Burrow, J. W., 'Evolution and Anthropology in the 1860's: The Anthropological Society of London, 1863–71', *Victorian Studies* 7 (1963), 137–54.

Burrow, J. W., *A Liberal Descent: Victorian Historians and the English Past* (Cambridge, 1981).

Butt, Isaac, *Land Tenure in Ireland: A Plea for the Celtic Race* (Dublin, 1866).

Butterfield, Herbert, *The Whig Interpretation of History* (London, 1931).

Caesar, Gaius Julius, *Seven Commentaries on the Gallic War*, trans. Carolyn Hammond (Oxford, 1996).

Calvez, Ronan, 'Le réenchantement d'un monde: Mouvement Breton, nazisme et émissions de radio en breton', in Sabine Heinz (ed.), *Die Deutsche Keltologie und ihre Berliner Gelehrten bis 1945* (Frankfurt, 1999), 101–37.

Cambry, Jacques, *Monumens celtiques, ou recherches sur le culte des pierres, précédées d'une notice sur les Celtes et sur les Druides, et suivies d'étymologies celtiques* (Paris, 1805).

Camden, William, *Britain, or a Chorographicall Description of the Most flourishing Kingdomes, England, Scotland, and Ireland, and Islands adioyning, out of the depth of Antiquitie*, trans. Philémon Holland (London, 1610).

Cameron, Ewen A., 'Journalism in the Late Victorian Scottish Highlands: John Murdoch, Duncan Campbell, and the "Northern Chronicle"', *Victorian Periodicals Review* 40 (2007), 281–306.

Campbell, J. F., *Leabhar Na Feinne* (London, 1872).

Campbell, J. L., 'The Tour of Edward Lhuyd in Ireland in 1699 and 1700', *Celtica* 5 (1960), 218–28.

Campbell, J. L., and Thomson, Derick (eds.), *Edward Lhuyd in the Scottish Highlands, 1699–1700* (Oxford, 1963).

Cannon, Garland (ed.), *The Letters of Sir William Jones* (2 vols., Oxford, 1970).

Carew, Mairéad, *The Quest for the Irish Celt: The Harvard Archaeological Mission to Ireland, 1932–1936* (Dublin, 2018).

Carey, John, 'The Ancestry of Fénius Farsaid', *Celtica* 21 (1990), 104–12.

Carey, John, *The Irish National Origin-Legend: Synthetic Pseudohistory* (Cambridge, 1994).

Carhart, Michael C., *Leibniz Discovers Asia: Social Networking in the Republic of Letters* (Baltimore, MD, 2019).

Carhart, Michael C., 'Practices of Intellectual Labor in the Republic of Letters: Leibniz and Edward Bernard on Language and European Origins', *JHI* 80 (2019), 365–86.

Carion, Johann, *Mathematici chronicorum* (Lyon, 1554).

Carlyle, Thomas, *Chartism* (December 1839: London, 1840).

Carney, Sebastien, *Breiz Atao! Mordrel, Delaporte, Lainé, Fouéré: Une mystique nationale (1901–1948)* (Rennes, 2015).

Carr, Glenda, *William Owen Pughe* (Caerdydd, 1983).

Carruthers, Gerard and Kidd, Colin, *Literature and Union: Scottish Texts, British Contexts* (Oxford, 2018).

Carruthers, Gerard, and Rawes, Alan (eds.), *English Romanticism and the Celtic World* (Cambridge, 2003).

Caylus, *Recueil d'antiquités égyptiennes, étrusques, grecques, romains, et gauloises* (7 vols., Paris, 1752–1767).

Chadwick, Nora, *The Celts* (1971: London, 1992).

Chalmers, George, *Caledonia, Or an Account, Historical and Topographical of North Britain* (4 vols., Edinburgh, 1807–1824).

Champion, Justin, *The Pillars of Priestcraft Shaken: The Church and Its Enemies, 1660–1730* (Cambridge, 1992).

Champion, Justin, 'John Toland, the Druids, and the Politics of Celtic Scholarship', *IHS* 32 (2001), 321–42.

Champion, Justin, *Republican Learning: John Toland and the Crisis of Christian Culture, 1696–1722* (Manchester, 2003).

Champion, Timothy, 'The Celt in Archaeology', in Terence Brown (ed.), *Celticism* (Amsterdam, 1996), 61–78.

Chapman, Malcolm, *The Celts: The Construction of a Myth* (Basingstoke, 1992).

Charles-Edwards, Thomas, 'The Lure of the Celtic Languages, 1850–1914', in Marios Costambeys, Andrew Hamer, and Martin Heale (ed.), *The Making of the Middle Ages* (Liverpool, 2007), 15–35.

Charnell-White, Cathryn, *Bardic Circles: National, Regional, and Personal Identity in the Bardic Vision of Iolo Morganwg* (Cardiff, 2007).

Chartier-Le Floch, Erwan, *Histoire de l'interceltisme en Bretagne* (Spézet, 2013).

Citron, Suzanne, *Le mythe national: L'histoire de France revisitée* (Paris, 2008), 159–63.

Clark, John, *An Answer to Mr Shaw's Inquiry into the Authenticity of the Poems of Ossian* (Edinburgh, 1781).

Cleary, Christina, and Kobel, Chantal (eds.), *Essays in Memory of Eleanor Knott* (Dublin, 2023).

Cleland, John, *The Way to Things by Words, and To Words by Things; being a Sketch of An Attempt at the Retrieval of the Antient Celtic, or, Primitive Language of Europe* (London, 1766).

Clüver, Philipp, *Germaniae antiquae libri tres* (Lugduni Batavorum, 1616).

Clüver, Philipp, *An Introduction into Geography, both Ancient and Moderne, comprised in sixe books* (Oxford, 1657).

Colebrooke, T. E., *The Life of H. T. Colebrooke* (London, 1867).

Colley, Linda, *Britons: Forging the Nation 1707–1837* (New Haven, CT, 1992).

Collini, Stefan, *Public Moralists: Political Thought and Intellectual Life in Britain, 1850–1930* (Oxford, 1993).

Collini, Stefan, *Matthew Arnold: A Critical Portrait* (Oxford, 1994).

Collins, Kevin, *Catholic Churchmen and the Celtic Revival in Ireland, 1848–1916* (Dublin, 2002).

Collis, John, Review of Barry Cunliffe, *Danebury: An Iron Age Hillfort in Hampshire* (2 vols., London, 184), *Proceedings of the Prehistoric Society* 51 (1985), 348–49.

Collis, John, 'Celtic Myths', *Antiquity* 71 (1997), 195–201.

Collis, John, 'George Buchanan and the Celts in Britain', in Ronald Black, William Gillies, and Roiebeard Ó Maolalaigh (eds.), *Celtic Connections* (East Linton, 1999), 91–107.

Collis, John, *The Celts: Origins, Myths & Inventions* (Stroud, 2003).

Collis, John, 'Die Entwicklung des Kelten-Konzepts in Britannien während des 18. Jahrhunderts', in Helmut Birkhan (ed.), *Kelten-Einfälle an der Donau* (Vienna, 2007), 111–23.

Collis, John 'Celts Ancient and Modern: Recent Controversies in Celtic Studies', *Studia Celtica Fennica* XIV (2017), 58–71.

Combe, George, *The Constitution of Man, Considered in Relation to External Objects* (Edinburgh, 1828).

Congrès Celtique International tenu À Saint-Brieuc (Côtes du Nord), Bretagne, En Octobre 1867: Séances.—Mémoires. (Saint-Brieuc, 1868).

Connell, Philip, 'British Identities and the Politics of Ancient Poetry in Later Eighteenth-Century Britain', *Historical Journal* 49 (2006), 161–92.

Considine, John, *Dictionaries in Early Modern Europe: Lexicography and the Making of Heritage* (Cambridge, 2008).

Considine, John, 'Stephen Skinner's *Etymologicon* and Other English Etymological Dictionaries, 1650–1700', *Studia Etymologica Cracoviensia* 14 (2009), 123–51.

Considine, John, *Academy Dictionaries 1600–1800* (Cambridge, 2014).

Considine, John, *Small Dictionaries and Curiosity: Lexicography and Fieldwork in Post-Medieval Europe* (Oxford, 2017).

Constant, Benjamin, *Political Writings*, trans. Biancamaria Fontana (Cambridge, 1988).

Constantine, Mary-Ann, 'Ossian in Wales and Brittany,' in Gaskill, Howard (ed.), *Ossian in Europe* (London, 2004), 67–90.

Constantine, Mary-Ann, *The Truth against the World: Iolo Morganwg and Romantic Forgery* (Cardiff, 2007).

Constantine, Mary-Ann, 'Welsh Literary History and the Making of the "The Myvyrian Archaiology of Wales"', *European Studies* 26 (2008), 109–28.

Constantine, Mary-Ann, '"Impertinent Structures": A Breton's Adventures in Neo-Gothic Wales', *Studies in Travel Writing* 18 (2014), 134–47.

Constantine, Mary-Ann, *Curious Travellers: Writing the Welsh Tour, 1760–1820* (Oxford, 2024).

Court de Gébelin, Antoine, *Le Monde primitif, analysé et comparé avec le monde moderne* (9 vols., Paris, 1773–1782).

Coward, Adam, *The Correspondence of Thomas Stephens: Revolutionising Welsh Scholarship in the Mid-Nineteenth Century through Knowledge Exchange* (Aberystwyth, 2020).

Cragoe, Matthew, and Readman, Paul (eds.), *The Land Question in Britain, 1750–1950* (Basingstoke, 2010).

Cram, David, 'Edward Lhuyd and the Doctrine of the Permutation of Letters', in Gerde Haßler and Peter Schmitter (eds.), *Sprachdiskussion und Beschreibung von Sprachen im 17. und 18. Jahrhundert* (Münster, 1999), 317–35.

Crossley, Ceri, *French Historians and Romanticism: Thierry, Guizot, the Saint-Simonians, Quinet, Michelet* (London, 1993).

Crump, Margaret, *Dr Prichard of the Red Lodge: A Life of Science during the Age of Improvement* (Lincoln, NE, forthcoming).

Cunliffe, Barry, *The Ancient Celts* (1997: 2nd ed., Oxford, 2018).

Cunliffe, Barry, and Koch, John T. (eds.), *Celtic from the West* (3 vols., Oxford, 2010–2016).

Cunliffe, Barry, and Koch, John T. (eds.), *Exploring Celtic Origins: Archaeology, Linguistics, and Genetics* (Oxford, 2019).

Cunningham, Bernadette, *The World of Geoffrey Keating: History, Myth and Religion in Seventeenth-Century Ireland* (Dublin, 2004).

Cunningham, Bernadette, *The Annals of the Four Masters: Irish History, Kingship and Society in the Early Seventeenth Century* (Dublin, 2010).

Curley, Thomas M., *Samuel Johnson, the* Ossian *Fraud, and the Celtic Revival in Great Britain and Ireland* (Cambridge, 2009).

Curtis, L. P., *Anglo-Saxons and Celts: A Study of Anglo-Irish Prejudice in Victorian England* (Bridgeport, CT, 1968).

Dalberg-Acton, J.E.E., 'Goldwin Smith's Irish History', in J. N. Figgis and R. V. Laurence (eds.), *The History of Freedom and Other Essays* (London, 1907).

D'Amico, John F., *Theory and Practice in Renaissance Textual Criticism: Beatus Rhenanus between Conjecture and History* (Berkeley, CA, 1988).

d'Arbois de Jubainville, Henri, 'Rapport sur les progress de la philologie celtique en France', in Joseph-Daniel Guigniaut (ed.), *Progrès des études classiques et du moyen âge, philologie celtique, numismatique* (Paris, 1868), 131–44.

d'Arbois de Jubainville, Henri, 'Les origines gauloises: L'empire celtique au IVe siècle avant notre ère', *Revue Historique* 30 (1886), 1–48.

d'Arbois de Jubainville, Henri, *Les premiers habitants de l'europe* (2nd ed., 2 vols., Paris, 1889).

D'Auria, Matthew, *The Shaping of French National Identity: Narrating the Nation's Past, 1715–1830* (Cambridge, 2020).

Davies, Caryl, *Adfeilion Babel: Agweddau ar Syniadaeth Ieithyddol y Ddeunawfed Ganrif* (Caerdydd, 2000).

[Davies, Edward], *Mr Davies's Letters* (London, 1802).
Davies, Edward, *Celtic Researches on the Origins, Traditions and Language of the Ancient Britons* (London, 1804).
Davies, Edward, *Mythology and Rites of the British Druids* (London, 1809).
Davies, John, *Antiquae linguae Britannicae* (London, 1632).
Davies, John H. (ed.), *The Letters of Lewis, Richard, William, and John Morris* (2 vols., Aberystwyth, 1907–1909).
Davies, Norman, *The Isles: A History* (London, 1999).
Davis, Bertram H., *Thomas Percy: A Scholar-Cleric in the Age of Johnson* (Philadelphia, PA, 1989).
Davis, Daniel R. (ed.), *Celtic Linguistics* (8 vols., London, 2000).
Davis, Richard, *The Young Ireland Movement* (London, 1987).
Davis, Thomas, *Awdlau ar destynau Cymdeithas y Gwyneddigion i'r Eisteddfodau* (London, 1791).
Davis, Thomas, *The Poems of Thomas Davis*, ed. Thomas Wallis (Dublin, 1846).
Davis, Thomas, *Prose Writings of Thomas Davies*, ed. T. W. Rolleston (London, 1890).
Davitt, Michael, *The Fall of Feudalism in Ireland* (London, 1904).
Dearnley, Moira, '"Mad Ned" and the "Smatter-Dasher": Iolo Morganwg and Edward "Celtic" Davies', in Geraint H. Jenkins (ed.), *A Rattleskull Genius: The Many Faces of Iolo Morganwg* (Cardiff, 2005), 425–42.
de Barra, Caoimhín, 'A Gallant Little "Tírín": The Welsh Influence on Irish Cultural Nationalism', *IHS* 39 (2014), 58–75.
de Barra, Caoimhín, *The Coming of the Celts, AD 1860: Celtic Nationalism in Ireland and Wales* (Notre Dame, IN, 2018).
de Bast, Martin-Jean, *Recherches historiques et littéraires sur la langue celtique, gauloise, et tudesque* (2 vols., Gand, 1815).
de Beaumont, Gustave, *Ireland: Social, Political and Religious*, ed. W. C. Taylor (2 vols., London, 1839).
de Bernardo Stempel, 'Rudolf Thurneysen (1857–1940) und sein sprachwissenschaftliches Werk', *ZCP* 46 (1994), 216–48.
de Bonneville, Nicolas, *De l'esprit des religions* (1791: Paris, 1792).
de Certeau, Michel, Julia, Dominique, and Revel, Jacques, *Une politique de la langue, la Revolution française et les patois: L'enquête de Grégoire* (1975: Paris, 2002).
de Dijn, Annelien, *French Political Thought from Montesquieu to Tocqueville: Liberty in a Levelled Society?* (Cambridge, 2008).
de Elio y Aspiroz, Don J., *La langue primitive de l'Espagne et explication de ses plus anciens monumens, en inscriptions et medailles*, trans. Éloi Johanneau (Paris, 1808).
de Gategno, Paul J., *James Macpherson* (Boston, MA, 1989).
de Gaulle, Charles, 'Les Celtes au XIXe siècle: Appel aux Représentants actuels de la race celtique', *Revue de Bretagne et de Vendée* 6 (1864), 257–84, 337–68.
de Gaulle, Charles, *The Celts of the Nineteenth Century, An Appeal to the Living Representatives of the Celtic Race*, trans. J. Davenport Mason (London, 1865).
de Gouges, Olympe, *Le bonheur primitif de l'homme, ou les rêveries patriotiques* (Paris, 1789).
de Hoz, Javier, 'The Mediterranean Frontier of the Celts and the Advent of Celtic Writing', *CMCS* 53–54 (2007), 1–22.
de Kersers, L. Buhot (ed.), *Correspondance de La Tour d'Auvergne (Corret)* (Bourges, 1908).

de la Rue, Gervais, *Recherches sur les ouvrages des bardes de la Bretagne armoricaine dans le moyen age* (Caen, 1815).

de la Tour d'Auvergne, Théophile Malo Corret, *Nouvelles Recherches sur la Langue, l'Origine & les Antiquités des Bretons, pour servir à l'Histoire de ce Peuple* (Bayonne, 1792).

de la Tour d'Auvergne, Théophile Malo Corret, *Origines gauloises, celles des plus anciens peuples de l'Europe* (Paris, 1796).

de la Villemarqué, Pierre, *La Villemarqué: Sa vie & ses oeuvres* (Paris, 1926).

de la Villemarqué, Thédore Hersart, *Barzaz Breiz: Chants populaires de la Bretagne* (1839: 4th ed., 2 vols., Paris, 1846)

de Maistre, Joseph, *Considerations on France*, trans. Richard Lebrun (Cambridge, 1994).

[de Mangourit, M.A.B.], *De la Tyrannie de Carnot, ou des Carnutes: Anecdote druidique, écrite il y a 2000 ans* (Paris, an 6 [1797–1798]).

de Mathan, Anne (ed.), *Jacques Cambry, 1749–1807: Un Breton des Lumières au service de la construction nationale* (Brest, 2007).

de Mézeray, François Eudes, *L'histoire de France* (2nd ed., 3 vols., Paris, 1685).

de Montfaucon, Bernard, *L'Antiquité expliquée et representée en figures* (5 vols. in 10, Paris, 1722–1724).

de Nie, Michael, *The Eternal Paddy: Irish Identity and the British Press, 1798–1882* (Madison, WI, 2004).

de Rostrenen, Grégoire, *Dictionnaire François-Celtique ou François-Breton* (Rennes, 1732).

de Rostrenen, Grégoire, *Grammarie Françoise-Celtique, ou Françoise-Bretonne; qui contient Tout ce qui est nécessaire pour apprendre par les Regles la Langue Celtique, ou Bretonne* (Rennes, 1738).

Desor, Édouard, *Les palafittes: Ou, constructions lacustres du lac de Neuchâtel* (Paris, 1865).

Devine, T. M., *The Great Highland Famine: Hunger, Emigration, and the Scottish Highlands in the Nineteenth Century* (Edinburgh, 1988).

Devine, T. M., *Clanship to Crofters' War: The Social Transformation of the Scottish Highlands* (Manchester, 1994).

Devine, T. M., *The Scottish Clearances: A History of the Dispossessed* (London, 2018).

Devoy, John, *Recollections of an Irish Rebel* (New York, 1929).

Dewey, Clive, 'Celtic Agrarian Legislation and the Celtic Revival: Historicist Implications of Gladstone's Irish and Scottish Land Acts, 1870–86', *Past & Present* LXIV (1974), 30–70.

Dietler, Michael, '"Our Ancestors the Gauls": Archaeology, Ethnic Nationalism, and Manipulation of Celtic Identity in Modern Europe', *American Anthropologist* 96 (1994), 584–605.

Dillon, Myles, and Chadwick, Nora K., *The Celtic Realms* (London, 1967).

Dinan, William, *Monumenta historica Celtica* (London, 1911).

Diodorus Siculus, *Library of History* (12 vols., Cambridge, MA, 1933–1967).

Donecker, Stefan, 'Re-Inventing the "Germanic" in the Early Modern Era: *Omnes Germani sunt, contra fabulas quorundam*', in Matthias Friedrich and James M. Harland (eds.), *Interrogating the 'Germanic': A Category and Its Use in Late Antiquity and the Early Middle Ages* (Berlin, 2021), 67–88.

Doron, Claude-Olivier, *L'homme altéré: Races et dégénérescence (xviie-xixe siècles)* (Ceyzérieu 2016).

Drayton, Michael, *Poly-Olbion* (London, 1612).

Droixhe, Daniel, *La Linguistique et l'appel de l'histoire (1600–1800): Rationalisme et révolutions positivistes* (Geneva, 1978).

Droixhe, Daniel, 'Impasse du commerce: Fréret linguiste', in Chantal Grell and Catherine Volpilhac-Auger (Eds.), *Nicolas Fréret, légende et verité* (Oxford, 1994), 165–75.

Droixhe, Daniel, *L'Étymon des dieux: Mythologie gauloise, archéologie et linguistique à l'âge Classique* (Geneva, 2002).

Dubois, Claude-Gilbert, *Celtes et Gaulois au XVIe siècle: Le développement littéraire d'un mythe nationaliste* (Paris, 1972).

Duclos, Charles Pinot, 'Mémoire sur les Druides', *Mémoires de literature, tirés registres de l'académie royale des inscriptions et belles-lettres* 19 (1753), 483–94.

Duclos, Charles Pinot, *Discours sur l'origine et les révolutions des langues celtique et françoise* (Paris, 1780).

Dudley Edwards, Ruth, *Patrick Pearse: The Triumph of Failure* (New York, 1977).

Dugger, Julie M., 'Black Ireland's Race: Thomas Carlyle and the Young Ireland Movement', *Victorian Studies* 48 (2006), 461–85.

Dujardin, Louis, *La vie et les oeuvres de Jean-François-Marie-Maurice-Agathe Le Gonidec, grammairien et lexicographe breton, 1775–1838* (Brest, 1949).

Dulaure, J. A., *Histoire critique de la noblesse depuis le commencement de la monarchie jusqu'à nos jours* (Paris, 1790).

Dunn, John, *Setting the People Free: The Story of Democracy* (2nd ed., Princeton, NJ, 2018).

d'Urfé, Honoré, *L'Astrée*, ed. Delphine Denis (Paris, 2011–).

Durkacz, Victor, 'Historical Connections in the Development of Celtic Education', *Carn* 17 (1977), 19–21.

du Sacy, Silvestre, *Notice sur la vie et les ouvrages de M. Saint-Martin* (1836).

Duval, Paul-Marie, 'Le groupe de bas-reliefs des <<Nautae Parisiaci>>', *Monuments et mémoires de la Fondation Eugène Piot* 48 (1954), 63–90.

Dwan, David, *The Great Community: Culture and Nationalism in Ireland* (Dublin, 2008).

Ebel, Hermann, *Celtic Studies* (London, 1863).

Edwards, Hywel Teifi, *The Eisteddfod* (Cardiff, 1990).

Edwards, Nancy 'Edward Lhuyd and the Origins of Early Medieval Celtic Archaeology', *Antiquaries Journal* 87 (2007), 165–96.

Edwards, W. F., *De l'Influence des agens physiques sur la vie* (Paris, 1824).

Edwards, W. F., *Des caractères physiologiques des races humaines considérés dans leurs rapports avec l'histoire* (Paris, 1829).

Edwards, W. F., *Recherches sur les langues celtiques* (Paris, 1844).

Edwards, W. F., 'De l'influence réciproque des races sur le caractère national', *Mémoires de la Société ethnologique de Paris* 2 (1845), 1–12.

Edwards, W. F., 'Fragments d'un mémoire sur les Gaëls', *Mémoires de la Société Ethnologique de Paris* 2 (1845), 13–43.

Ehrard, Jean, and Viallaneix, Paul (eds.), *Nos ancêtres les Gaulois* (Clermont-Ferrand, 1982).

Ellis, Annie, *Speeches and Addresses by the late Thomas E. Ellis, M.P.* (Wrexham, 1912).

Ellis, Peter Berresford, *The Creed of the Celtic Revolution* (London, 1969).

Ellis, Peter Berresford, 'The Celtic League—Twenty Years A-Growing', *Carn* 35/36 (1981).

Ellis, Peter Berresford, '"We Only Want the Earth"', in Cathal Ó Luain (ed.), *For a Celtic Future* (Dublin, 1983).

Ellis, Peter Berresford, *Celtic Dawn: The Dream of Celtic Unity* (1993: Tal-y-Bont, 2002).

Ellis, Steven G., 'Why the History of the "Celtic Fringe" Remains Unwritten', *European Review of History* 10 (2003), 221–31.

Emerson, R. W., *English Traits* (London, 1857).

Engels, Friedrich, *The Condition of the Working Class in England*, ed. D. McLellan (Oxford, 1993).

Engels, Friedrich, *Origin of the Family and Private Property* (London, 2010).

Evans, David Ellis 'The Heroic Age of Celtic Philology', *ZCP* 54 (2004), 1–30.

Evans, Dewi Wyn, and Roberts, Brynley F., *Edward Lhuyd: Archaeologia Britannica. Texts and Translations* (Aberystwyth, 2007).

Evans, Evan, *Some Specimens of the Poetry of the Ancient Welsh Bards* (London, 1764).

Farley, Julia, and Hunter, Fraser (eds.), *Celts: Art and Identity* (London, 2015).

[Fauriel, Claude], Review of *The Myvyrian Archaiology of Wales*, in *Archives philosophiques, politiques, et littéraires* 3 (1818), 88–116.

Félibien, Michel, *Histoire de la ville de Paris* (5 vols., Paris, 1725).

Fenyö, Krisztina, *Contempt, Sympathy and Romance: Lowland Perceptions of the Highlands and the Clearances during the Famine Years, 1845–1855* (East Linton, 2000).

Fennigan, Diarmid A., 'Race, Space, and Politics in Mid-Victorian Ireland: The Ethnologies of Abraham Hume and John McElheran', *Historical Geography* 42 (2014), 152–70.

Ferguson, Adam, *Analysis of Pneumatics and Moral Philosophy* (Edinburgh, 1766).

Ferguson, Adam, *An Essay on the History of Civil Society*, ed. Fania Oz-Salzberger (1767: Cambridge, 1995).

Ferguson, William, *The Identity of the Scottish Nation: An Historic Quest* (Edinburgh, 1998).

Fergusson, James, *The Declaration of Arbroath, 1320* (Edinburgh, 1970).

Feulner, Anna Helene, '"Geschichtsforcher und Sprachkenner": Zu Zeuß' Markomannentheorie', in Hans Hablitzel and David Stifter (eds.), *Johann Kaspar Zeuß im kultur-und sprachwissenschaftlichen Kontext (19.bis21.Jahrhundert)* (Vienna, 2007), 49–93.

Fickelscherer, Ute, 'Autoren Keltologischer Forschungensarbeiten in Berlin von den Anfängen bis 1945', in Sabine Heinz (ed.), *Die Deutsche Keltologie und ihre Berliner Gelehrten bis 1945* (Frankfurt, 1999), 39–49.

Fischer, Joachim, and Dillon, John (eds.), *The Correspondence of Myles Dillon, 1922–1925: Irish-German Relations and Celtic Studies* (Dublin, 1999).

Fitzpatrick, Bernard, 'Address to the Pan-Celtic Congress of 1907', *Scotia: The Journal of the St. Andrew Society* I (1907), 325–28.

Fitzpatrick, Bernard,*"Ego": Random Records of Sport, Service, and Travel in Many Lands* (London, 1923).

Foerster, Frank, *Christian Carl Josias Bunsen: Diplomat, Mäzen und Vordenker in Wissenschaft, Kirche und Politik* (Bad Arolsen, 2001).

Forbes, Duncan, *The Liberal Anglican Idea of History* (Cambridge, 1952).

Forster, Michael N. (ed. and trans.), *Herder: Philosophical Writings* (Cambridge, 2002).

Foster, R. F., 'History and the Irish Question', *TRHS* 33 (1983), 169–94.

Foster, R. F., *Modern Ireland, 1600–1972* (London, 1988).

Foster, R.F. *Paddy and Mr. Punch: Connections in Irish and English History* (London, 1993).

Foster, R. F., *W. B. Yeats: A Life* (2 vols., Oxford, 1997–2003).

Foster, R. F., *Words Alone: Yeats and His Inheritances* (Oxford, 2011).

Foster, Thomas Campbell, *Letters on the Condition of the People of Ireland* (London, 1846).

Fournier d'Albe, E. E., *An English-Irish Dictionary and Phrase Book* (Dublin, 1903).

Fournier, E. E., *Eachtra Laoghaire Mic Criomthain go maigh meall. The visit of Leary, son of Criffan, to the plain of delight: An ancient Irish story from the Book of Lismore translated into modern Irish and Esperanto*, trans. R. B. White (Dublin, 1908).

Fraser, Maxwell, 'Lady Llanover and Her Circle', *THSC* (1968), 170–96.

Freeman, Philip M., 'The Earliest Greek Sources on the Celts', *Études celtiques* 32 (1996), 11–48.

Freeman, Philip, *Celtic Mythology: Tales of Gods, Goddesses, and Heroes* (Oxford, 2017).

Fry, Edmund, *Pantographia* (London, 1799).

Fryer, Michael (ed.), *The Trial and Life of Eugene Aram* (Richmond, 1832).

Gaidoz, Henri, 'Les Revendications du Pangermanisme', *Revue des deux mondes* 91 (1871), 385–405.

Gaisberger, Joseph, *Die Gräber bei Hallstadt im Österreichischen Salzkammergut* (Linz, 1848).

Garner, Steve, *Racism in the Irish Experience* (London, 2004).

Garnett, Richard, *The Philological Essays of the Late Rev. Richard Garnett, of the British Museum* (London, 1859).

Garrigan-Mattar, Sinéad, *Primitivism, Science, and the Irish Revival* (Oxford, 2004).

Garscha, Friedrich, 'Heinrich Schreiber (1793–1872): Ein Beitrag zur Geschichte der Keltomanie im 19. Jahrhundert', in A. Kirchner (ed.), *Ur-und Frühgeschichte als historische Wissenschaft* (Heidelberg, 1950), 3–18.

Gaskill, Howard (ed.), *Ossian Revisited* (Edinburgh, 1991).

Gaskill, Howard (ed.), *Ossian in Europe* (London, 2004).

Gavan Duffy, Charles, *Young Ireland: A Fragment of Irish History, 1840–1850* (2 vols., London, 1880–1883).

Gavan Duffy, Charles, *Thomas Davis: The Memoirs of an Irish Patriot, 1840–1846* (London, 1890).

Gazier, A. (ed.), *Lettres à Grégoire sur les patois de France, 1790–1794* (1880: Geneva, 1969).

Gellner, Ernest, *Nations and Nationalism* (Oxford, 1983).

Geoffrey of Monmouth, *The History of the Kings of Britain*, trans. Lewis Thorpe (London, 1966).

George, Henry, *The Irish Land Question* (New York, 1881).

Geslot, Jean-Charles, 'Un inestimable succès: L'*Histoire de France* d'Henri Martin et ses publics', *Revue d'histoire du XIXe siècle* 69 (2020–2021), 239–55.

Gessner, Conrad, *Mithridates*, ed. and trans. Bernard Colombat and Manfred Peters (Geneva, 2009).

Ghosh, Peter, 'Macaulay and the Heritage of the Enlightenment', *EHR* 112 (1997), 358–95.

Gibbon, Charles, *The Life of George Combe* (2 vols, London, 1878).

Gibbon, Edward, *The History of the Decline and Fall of the Roman Empire* (6 vols., London, 1776–1789).

Gibbons, Luke, 'Race Against Time: Racial Discourse and Irish History', in Catherine Hall (ed.), *Cultures of Empire: A Reader* (Manchester, 2000), 207–23.

Gildas, *The Works of Gildas*, trans. J. A. Giles (London, 1841).

Gilley, Sheridan, 'English Attitudes to the Irish in England, 1780–1900', in Colin Holmes (ed.), *Immigrants and Minorities in British Society* (London, 1978), 81–110.

Gillies, Eoin (ed.), *Sean Dain, agus Orain Ghaidhealach* (Perth, 1786).

Gladfelder, Hal, *Fanny Hill in Bombay: The Making and Unmaking of John Cleland* (Baltimore, MD, 2012).

Glück, Christian Wilhelm, *Erinnerung an Kaspar Zeuss* (Munich, 1857).

Goffart, Walter, *The Narrators of Barbarian History (A.D. 550–800): Jordanes, Gregory of Tours, Bede, and Paul the Deacon* (Princeton, NJ, 1988).

Golf-French, Morgan, 'Teaching Race in the German Enlightenment: Christoph Meiners' History of Humanity in Institutional Context', *History of Universities* 34 (2023), 243–60.

Golman, I. L., and Kunina, V. (eds.), *Karl Marx and Friedrich Engels: Ireland and the Irish Question* (Moscow, 1971).

Goscinny, R. and Uderzo, A., *Astérix chez les Bretons* (Paris, 1966).

Gosselin, Antoine, *Historia Gallorum veterum* (Caen, 1636).

Gossman, Lionel, *Between History and Literature* (Cambridge, MA, 1990).

Gougaud, L., 'A propos d'une lettre de Brizeux à Alexis-François Rio', *Annales de Bretagne* 28 (1912), 203–7.

Gougaud, L., 'Alexis-François Rio et la Bretagne', *Annales de Bretagne* 29 (1913), 439–63.

Gould, Stephen J., *The Mismeasure of Man* (New York, 1981).

Gould, Warwick, Kelly, John, and Toomey, Deirdre (eds.), *The Collected Letters of W. B. Yeats: Volume II: 1896–1900* (Oxford, 1998).

Gourvil, Francis, *Théodore-Claude-Henri Hersart de La Villemarqué (1815–1895) et le 'Barzaz-Breiz' (1839–1845–1867)* (Rennes, 1960).

Grafton, Anthony T., 'Joseph Scaliger and Historical Chronology: The Rise and Fall of a Discipline', *History and Theory* 14 (1975), 156–85.

Grafton, Anthony, *Joseph Scaliger: A Study in the History of Classical Scholarship* (2 vols., Oxford, 1983–1993)

Grafton, Anthony, *Forgers and Critics: Creativity and Duplicity in Western Scholarship* (London, 1990).

Grafton, Anthony, 'Invention of Traditions and Traditions of Invention in Renaissance Europe: The Strange Case of Annius of Viterbo', in Anthony Grafton and Ann Blair (eds.), *The Transmission of Culture in Early Modern Europe* (Philadelphia, PA, 1990), 8–38.

Grafton, Anthony, *New Worlds, Ancient Texts: The Power of Tradition and the Shock of Discovery* (Cambridge, MA, 1992).

Grafton, Anthony, *Defenders of the Text: The Traditions of Scholarship in an Age of Science, 1450–1800* (Cambridge, MA, 1994).

Grafton, Anthony, and Weinberg, Joanna, *'I Have Always Loved the Holy Tongue': Isaac Casaubon, the Jews, and a Forgotten Chapter in Renaissance Scholarship* (Cambridge, MA, 2011).

Graham Jones, J., 'Michael Davitt, David Lloyd George, and T. E. Ellis: The Welsh Experience, 1886', *Welsh History Review* 18 (1997), 450–82.

Gran-Aymerich, Ève, *Naissance de l'archéologie moderne, 1798–1945* (Paris, 1998).

Graves, Robert, *The Crowning Privilege: Collected Essays on Poetry* (London, 1955).

Grégoire, [Henri] *Rapport sur la nécessité et les moyens d'anéantir les patois, et d'universaliser l'usage de la langue française* (Paris, 1794).

Gregory, Augusta, *Our Irish Theatre: A Chapter of Autobiography* (New York, 1913).

Gregory of Tours, *The History of the Franks*, trans. Lewis Thorpe (London, 1974).

Greig, J.Y.T. (ed.), *The Letters of David Hume* (2 vols., Oxford, 1932).

Grierson, George, *The Letters of Sir Walter Scott* (12 vols., London, 1932–1937).

Griffiths, David Albert, *Jean Reynaud, Encyclopediste de l'époque romantique, d'après sa correspondence inedite* (Paris, 1965).

Groom, Nick, *The Making of Percy's* Reliques (Oxford, 1999).

Gruel, Katherine, and Buchsenschutz, Olivier (eds.), *Réinventer les Celtes* (Paris, 2019).

Gruner, Shirley M., 'Political Historiography in Restoration France', *History and Theory* 8 (1969), 346–65.

Guenebault, J., *Le réveil de Chyndonax prince des vacies druydes celtiques dijonois* (Dijon, 1621).

Guest, Charlotte, *The Mabinogion* (3 vols., London, 1849).

Guest, Revel, and John, Angela V., *Lady Charlotte Guest: An Extraordinary Life* (Stroud, 2007).

Guillaume, M. J. (ed.), *Procès-verbaux du comité d'instruction publique de la convention nationale* (7 vols., Paris, 1891–1957).

Guiomar, Jean-Yves, *Le Bretonisme: Les historiens bretons au xix*[e] *siècle* (Mayenne, 1987).

Guiomar, Jean-Yves, 'La Révolution Française et les origines celtiques de la France', *Annales historiques de la révolution française* 287 (1992), 63–85.

Gunther, R. T. (ed.), *Life and Letters of Edward Lhuyd* (Oxford, 1945).

Hablitzel, Hans, *Prof. Dr. Johann Kaspar Zeuss: Begründer der Keltologie und Historiker aus Vogtendorf/Oberfranken* (Kronach, 1987).

Hablitzel, Hans, and Stifter, David, *Johann Kaspar Zeuß im kultur-und sprachwissenschaftlichen Kontext (19.bis21.Jahrhundert)* (Vienna, 2007).

Hakelberg, Dietrich, 'Nationalismus einer Elite "Heidnisches Teutschland" und "vaterländisches Altertumskunde" in der ersten Hälfte des 19. Jahrhunderts', in Elisabeth Vogel (ed.), *Zwischen Ausgrenzung und Hybridisierung: Zur Konstruktion von Identitäten aus kulturwissenschaftlicher Perspektive* (Würzburg, 2003), 15–35.

Halloran, William F., 'W. B. Yeats, William Sharp, and Fiona Macleod: A Celtic Drama: 1887 to 1897', in Warwick Gould (ed.), *Yeats Annual No. 13* (Basingstoke, 1998), 62–109.

Halloran, Willam F., 'W. B. Yeats, William Sharp, and Fiona Macleod: A Celtic Drama, 1897', in Warwick Gould (ed.), *Yeats and the Nineties: Yeats Annual No. 14, A Special Number* (Basingstoke, 2001), 159–208.

Hanham, H. J., 'The Problem of Highland Discontent, 1880–1885', *TRHS* 19 (1969), 21–66.

Hanotaux, Gabriel, *Henri Martin: Sa vie—ses oeuvres—son temps, 1810–1883* (Paris, 1885).

Hardy, Nicholas, *Criticism and Confession: The Bible in the Seventeenth Century Republic of Letters* (Oxford, 2017).

Hardy, Nicholas, and Levitin, Dmitri (eds.), *Confessionalisation and Erudition in Early Modern Europe: An Episode in the History of the Humanities* (Oxford, 2019).

Harris, Richard L. (ed.), *A Chorus of Grammars: The Correspondence of George Hickes and His Collaborators on the* Thesaurus linguarum septentrionalium (Toronto, 1992).

Harrison, Alan, 'Who Wrote to Edward Lhuyd?', *Celtica* 16 (1984), 175–78.

Harrison, Alan, *The Dean's Friend: Anthony Raymond 1675–1726, Jonathan Swift and the Irish Language* (Caisleán an Bhúrcaigh, 1999).

Haskell, Francis, and Penny, Nicholas, *Taste and the Antique: The Lure of Classical Sculpture, 1500–1900* (New Haven, CT, 1981).

Haugen, Kristine Louise, 'Ossian and the Invention of Textual History', *JHI* 59 (1998), 309–27.

Haycock, David Boyd, *William Stukeley: Science, Religion, and Archaeology in Eighteenth-Century England* (Woodbridge, 2002).

Heal, Felicity, 'What Can King Lucius Do for You? The Reformation and the Early British Church', *EHR* 120 (2005), 593–614.

Hearne, Thomas, *Remarks and Collections of Thomas Hearne* (10 vols., Oxford, 1885–1915).

Hechter, Michael, *Internal Colonialism: The Celtic Fringe in British National Development, 1536–1966* (London, 1975).

Hemprich, Gisbert, 'Nachleben', in Stefan Zimmer (ed.), *Die Kelten: Mythos und Wirklichkeit* (2004: 3rd ed., Stuttgart, 2012), 199–213.

Henshaw, Victoria, 'James Macpherson and His Contemporaries: The Methods and Networks of Collectors of Gaelic Poetry in Late Eighteenth-Century Scotland', *Journal for Eighteenth-Century Studies* 39 (2016), 197–209.

Herity, Michael, 'Whitley Stokes's Correspondence with John O'Donovan, 1857–1861', *Studia Hibernica* 36 (2009–2010), 9–89.

Higgin, James, *The Irish Government Difficulty Considered as a Race Question* (Manchester, 1867).

Hildebrand, Hans, 'Sur les commencements de l'âge du Fer en Europe', *Congrès international d'anthropologie et d'archéologie préhistoriques 1874* (2 vols., Stockholm, 1876), 592–601.

Hirschi, Caspar, *The Origins of Nationalism: An Alternative History from Ancient Rome to Early Modern Germany* (Cambridge, 2011).

Hitler, Adolf, *Monologue im Führer-Hauptquarter, 1941–1944*, ed. Heinrich Heim and Werner Jochmann (Hamburg, 1980).

Hobsbawm, Eric, and Ranger, Terence (eds.), *The Invention of Tradition* (Cambridge, 1983).

Hodgkin, Thomas, 'Obituary of Dr. Prichard', *Journal of the Ethnological Society of London* 2 (1850), 182–207.

Holinshed, Raphael, *Chronicles of England, Scotlande, and Irelande* (4 vols., London, 1577).

Holtzmann, Adolf, *Kelten und Germanen: Eine Historische Untersuchung* (Stuttgart, 1855).

Honeybone, Diana and Michael (eds.), *The Correspondence of William Stukeley and Maurice Johnson, 1714–1754* (Woodbridge, 2014).

Honeybone, Diana and Michael (eds.), *Stukeley and Stamford, Part 1: Cakes and Curiosity: The Sociable Antiquarian, 1710–1737* (Boydell, 2021).

Hont, Istvan, *Jealousy of Trade: International Competition and the Nation-State in Historical Perspective* (Cambridge, MA, 2005).

Hotman, François, *Francogallia*, trans. J.M.H. Salmon (Cambridge, 1972).

Howe, Stephen, *Ireland and Empire: Colonial Legacies in Irish History and Culture* (Oxford, 2000).

Howell, David H., 'The Land Question in Nineteenth-Century Wales, Ireland and Scotland: A Comparative Study', *Agricultural History Review* 61 (2013), 83–110.

Hudson, Nicholas, 'From "Nation" to "Race": The Origin of Racial Classification in Eighteenth-Century Thought', *Journal for Eighteenth-Century Studies* 29 (1996) 247–64.

Hughes, Brian (ed.), *Eoin MacNeill: Memoir of a Revolutionary Scholar* (Dublin, 2016).

Hughes, J. B., 'The Pan-Celtic Society (1888–1891)', *Irish Monthly* 81 (1953), 17–19.

Hughes, John, *Horae Britannicae* (London, 1819).

Hume, David, *The History of England* (6 vols., London, 1754–1761).

[Hunt, James], 'Knox on the Celtic Race', *Anthropological Review* 6 (1868), 175–91.

Hunter, James, 'The Gaelic Connection: The Highlands, Ireland and Nationalism, 1873–1922', *SHR* 54 (1975), 178–204.

Hunter, James (ed.), *For the People's Cause: From the Writings of John Murdoch, Highland and Irish Land Reformer* (Edinburgh, 1986).

Hunter, Michael, *John Aubrey and the Realm of Learning* (London, 1975).

Hunter, Michael (ed.), *The Occult Laboratory: Magic, Science, and Second Sight in Seventeenth-Century Scotland* (Woodbridge, 2001).

Huppert, George, *The Idea of Perfect History: Historical Erudition and Historical Philosophy in Renaissance France* (Urbana, IL, 1970).

Hutchinson, Horace G., *Life of Sir John Lubbock* (2 vols., London, 1914).

Hutchinson, John, *The Dynamics of Cultural Nationalism: The Gaelic Revival and the Creation of the Irish Nation State* (London, 1987).

Hüther, Andreas, 'Keltische Forschungen im 19. Jahrhundert zum Zweck regionaler Identitätskonstruktionen: Eine Forschungsskizze', in Ingo Wiwjorra and Dietrich Hakelberg (eds.), *Archäologie und Nation: Kontexte der Erforschung 'vaterlandischen Alterthums'* (Heidelberg, 2021), 253–60.

Hutton, Christopher, *Linguistics and the Third Reich: Mother-Tongue Fascism, Race and the Science of Language* (New York, 1998).

Hutton, Ronald, *Blood and Mistletoe: The History of the Druids in Britain* (New Haven, CT, 2009).

Hyde, Douglas, 'A Plea for the Irish Language', *Dublin University Review* II, no. 6 (1886), 666–76.

Hyde, Douglas, 'The Necessity for De-Anglicising Ireland', in *The Revival of Irish Literature* (London, 1894), 155–61.

Ihre, Johanne, *Glossarium suiogothicum* (2 vols., Uppsala, 1769).

Isidore, *The Etymologies of Isidore of Seville*, trans. Stephen A. Barney, W. J. Lewis, J. A. Beach, and Oliver Berghof (Cambridge, 2006).

Jackson, Kenneth, *Language and History in Early Britain* (London, 1953).

Jackson, Kenneth, 'The Duan Albanach', *SHR* 36 (1957), 125–37.

Jackson, Kenneth, 'Fifty Years of Celtic Philology', *Modern Language Review* 71 (1976).

James, Simon, *The Atlantic Celts: Ancient People or Modern Invention?* (London, 1999).

Jaski, Bart, Nooij, Lars, Nooij-Jongeleen, Sanne, and Stam, Nike (eds.), *A Man of Two Worlds: A. G. van Hamel, Celticist and Germanist* (Utrecht, 2023).

Jenkins, Bill, 'Race before Darwin: Variation, Adaptation and the Natural History of Man in Post-Enlightenment Edinburgh, 1790–1835', *British Journal of the History of Science* 53 (2020), 333–50.

Jenkins, Geraint H., *Theophilus Evans: Y Din, ei Deulu, a'i Oes* (Aberystwyth, 1993).

Jenkins, Geraint H., *Facts, Fantasy and Fiction: The Historical Vision of Iolo Morganwg* (Aberystwyth, 1997).

Jenkins, Geraint H. (ed.), *A Rattleskull Genius: The Many Faces of Iolo Morganwg* (Cardiff, 2009).

Jenkins, Geraint H., *Bard of Liberty: The Political Radicalism of Iolo Morganwg* (Cardiff, 2012).

Jenkins, Geraint H., Jones, Ffion Mair, Jones, David Ceri, and Davies, Andrew, *The Correspondence of Iolo Morganwg* (3 vols., Cardiff, 2007).

Jenkins, Simon, *The Celts: A Sceptical History* (London, 2022).

Joachimsen, Paul, *Geschichtsauffassung und Geschichtsschreibung in Deutschland unter dem Einfluss des Humanismus* (1910: Aalen, 1968).

Johnes, A. J., *Philological Proofs of the Original Unity and Recent Origin of the Human Race, Derived from a Comparison of the Languages of Asia, Europe, Africa, and America* (London, 1843).

Johnson, Hugh H., 'Rent and Tithes in Wales', *Dublin University Review* II, no. 10 (1886), 838–41.

Johnson, Samuel (ed.), *A Dictionary of the English Language* (2 vols., London, 1755).

Jones, B. L., 'Drych y Prif Oesoedd', *Y Traethodydd* 118 (1963), 30–47.

Jones, Huw (ed.), *Diddanwch Teuluaidd* (London, 1763).

Jones, Kathryn N., Tully, Carol, and Williams, Heather, *Hidden Texts, Hidden Nation: (Re)Discoveries of Wales in Travel Writing in French and German (1780–2018)* (Liverpool, 2020).

Jones, Marian Henry, 'The Letters of Arthur James Johnes, 1809–71', *National Library of Wales Journal* 10 (1958), 233–64.

Jones, Owen, Owen Pughe, William, and Williams, Edward, *The Myvyrian Archaiology of Wales* (3 vols., London, 1801–1807).

Jones, Rowland, *A Postscript to the Origin of Language and Nations* (London, 1767).

Jones, Rowland, *The Circles of Gomer, or, an Essay towards an Investigation and Introduction of the English as an Universal Language* (London, 1771).

Jones-Evans, Peris, 'Evan Pan Jones—Land Reformer', *Welsh History Review* 4 (1968), 143–59.

Jonsson, Fredrik Albritton, *Enlightenment's Frontier: The Scottish Highlands and the Origins of Environmentalism* (New Haven, CT, 2013).

Josephus, *Jewish Antiquities, Vol. 1: Books 1–3*, trans. H. St. J. Thackeray (9 volumes, Cambridge, MA, 1930–1965).

Jourdan, Annie, 'The Image of Gaul during the French Revolution', in Terence Brown (ed.), *Celticism* (Amsterdam, 1996), 183–206.

Junius, Hadrianus, *Batavia* (Leiden, 1588).

Kaeser, Marc-Antoine, 'Antiquare, Pfahlbauten und die Entstehung der urgeschichtlichen Wissenschaft: Die nationale und internationale Ausstrahlung der Antiquarischen Gesellschaft in Zürich', in Marianne Flüeler-Grauwiler and Josef Gisler (eds.), *Pfahlbaufieber* (Zürich, 2004).

Kaeser, Marc-Antoine, *Les lacustres: Archéologie et mythe national* (Lausanne, 2004).

Kaeser, Marc-Antoine, *L'Univers du préhistorien: Science, foi et politique dans l'oeuvre et la vie d'Édouard Desor (1811–1882)* (Paris, 2004).

Kaeser, Marc-Antoine, 'Des fantasmes d'une Suisse insulaire: Le mythe de la <<civilisation lacustre>>', *Perspective* 2 (2006), 1–10.

Kaiser, Thomas E., 'The Abbé Dubos and the Historical Defence of Monarchy in Early Eighteenth-Century France', *Studies on Voltaire & the Eighteenth Century* 267 (1989), 92–101.

Kames, Henry Home, *Sketches of the History of Man* (1774: 3 vols., Indianapolis, IN, 2007).

Kaminski-Jones, Francesca, and Kaminski-Jones, Rhys, (eds.), *Celts, Romans, Britons: Classical and Celtic Influence in the Construction of British Identities* (Oxford, 2020).

Kater, Michael H., *Das "Ahnenerbe" der SS 1935–1945* (Stuttgart, 1974).

Kearney, Hugh, *The British Isles: A History of Four Nations* (Cambridge, 1987).

Keating, Geoffrey, *The General History of Ireland* (1723: 2nd ed., London, 1732).

Keller, Ferdinand, 'Die keltischen Grabhügel im Burghölzi und die Gräber auf der Forch', *Mittheilungen der Zürcherischen Gesellschaft für Vaterländische Alterthümer* 1 (1837), 1–8.

Keller, Ferdinand, 'Die keltischen Pfahlbauten in den Schweizerseen', *Mittheilungen der Antiquarischen Gesellschaft in Zürich* 9 (1853–1856), 65–100.

Keller, Ferdinand, 'Pfahlbauten. Dritter Bericht', *Mittelungen der Antiquarischen Gesellschaft in Zürich* 13.2.3 (Zürich, 1860).

Keller, Ferdinand, 'Pfahlbauten. Sechster Bericht', *Mittheilungen der antiquarischen Gesellschaft in Zürich* 15.7 (Zürich, 1866).

Kelley, Donald R., *Foundations of Modern Historical Scholarship: Language, Law, and History in the French Renaissance* (New York, 1970).

Kelly, John, and Domville, Eric (eds.), *The Collected Letters of W. B. Yeats, Volume I: 1865–1895* (Oxford, 1986).

Kelly, John, and Schuchard, Ronald (eds.), *The Collected Letters of W. B. Yeats, Volume III: 1901–1904* (Oxford, 1994).

Kemble, J. M., *Horae Ferales, or, Studies in the Archaeology of the Northern Nations*, ed. R. G. Latham and A. W. Franks (London, 1863).

Kendrick, T. D., *The Druids: A Study in Keltic Prehistory* (London, 1927).

Kendrick, T. D., *British Antiquity* (London, 1950).

Kennedy, Vans, *Researches into the Origin and Affinity of the Principal Languages of Asia and Europe* (London, 1828).

Kersey, Melvin, 'The Pre-Ossianic Politics of James Macpherson', *Journal for Eighteenth-Century Studies* 27 (2004), 61–76.

Keyßler, Johann Georg, *Antiquitates selectae septentrionale et Celticae* (Hannover, 1720).

Kidd, Colin, *Subverting Scotland's Past: Scottish Whig Historians and the Creation of an Anglo-British Identity, 1689–c. 1830* (Cambridge, 1993).

Kidd, Colin, 'Gaelic Antiquity and National Identity in Enlightenment Ireland and Scotland', *EHR* 109 (1994), 1197–214.

Kidd, Colin, 'Teutonist Ethnology and Scottish Nationalist Inhibition, 1780–1880', *SHR* 74 (1995), 45–68.

Kidd, Colin, *British Identities before Nationalism: Ethnicity and Nationhood in the Atlantic World* (Cambridge, 1999).

Kidd, Colin, 'Medicine, Race, and Radicalism in the Later Scottish Enlightenment', in Margaret Pelling and Scott Mandelbrote (eds.), *The Practice of Reform in Health, Medicine, and Science, 1500–2000* (Aldershot, 2005), 207–22.

Kidd, Colin, *The Forging of Races: Race and Scripture in the Protestant Atlantic World, 1600–2000* (Cambridge, 2006).

Kingsley, Frances (ed.), *Charles Kingsley, His Letters and Memories of His Life* (1877: 2 vols., London, 1894).

Koch, John T., 'Celts, Britons, and Gaels: Names, Peoples, and Identities', *THSC*, New Series 9 (2002), 41–56.

Koch, John T., *Celtic Culture: A Historical Encyclopedia* (5 vols., Santa Barbara, CA, 2006).

Koch, Matthias, 'Aufklärung über die Schlacht zu Fridolfing durch die neusten antiquarischen Funde', *Oberbayerisches Archiv für vaterländische Geschichte* 6 (1845), 77–112.

Kossinna, Gustaf, *Die Herkunft der Germanen* (Würzburg, 1911).

Knox, Robert, *The Races of Men: A Fragment* (Philadelphia, PA, 1850).

Knox, Robert, *The Races of Men: A Philosophical Enquiry into the Influence of Race over the Destinies of Nations* (London, 1862).

Krebs, Christopher B., *A Most Dangerous Book: Tacitus's* Germania *from the Roman Empire to the Third Reich* (New York, 2011).

Kristiansen, Kristian, Kroonen, Guus, and Willerslev, Eske (eds.), *The Indo-European Puzzle Revisited: Integrating Archaeology, Genetics, and Linguistics* (Cambridge, 2023).

Kroeber, Aug. (ed.), 'Correspondance de l'Abbé Grandidier, et autres documents relatifs à cet historien, à sa famille et ses ouvrages', *Revue d'Alsace* 17, t. 12 (1866).

Kruta, Venceslas (ed.), *The Celts* (London, 1997).

Laertius, Diogenes, *Lives of the Eminent Philosophers* (2 vols., Cambridge, MA, 1925).

Lainé, Celestin, 'Biographie-Mémoires', trans. Daniel Leach and Guillaume Legros, *E-Keltoi* 4 (2012), 39–180.

Lambert, Jean-Yves, *La langue gauloise: Description linguistique, Commentaire d'inscriptions choisies* (1994: Revised ed., Paris, 2003).

Lang, Andrew, 'The Celtic Renascence', *Blackwood's Magazine* CLXI (1897), 181–91.

Lang, Cecil Y. (ed.), *The Letters of Matthew Arnold* (6 vols., Charlottesville, VA, 1996–2001).

Lapidge, Michael (ed.), *H. M. Chadwick and the Study of Anglo-Saxon, Norse and Celtic in Cambridge* (Aberystwyth, 2015).

Leach, Daniel, '"A Sense of Nordism": The Impact of Germanic Assistance upon the Militant Interwar Breton Nationalist Movement', *European Review of History* 17 (2010), 629–46.

Leask, Nigel, *Stepping Westward: Writing the Highland Tour, c. 1720–1830* (Oxford, 2020).

Leber, C., Salgues, J. B., and Cohen, J. (eds.), *Collection des meilleurs dissertations, notices et traites particuliers relatifs à l'histoire de France* (20 vols., Paris, 1826–1838).

Lebow, Ned, *White Britain and Black Ireland: The Influence of Stereotypes on Colonial Policy* (Philadelphia, PA, 1976).

Le Brigant, Jacques, *Élémens de la langue des Celtes Gomérites, ou Bretons: Introduction a cette langue et par elle à celles de tous les peuples connus* (Strasbourg, 1779).

Le Brigant, Jacques, *Observations fondamentales sur les langues anciennes et modernes; ou Prospectus de l'Ouvrage intitulé: La langue primitive conservée* (Paris, 1787).

Le Brigant, Jacques, *Lettre a monsieur l'Abbé du Crotz, Au sujet du jeune homme qui étoit chez M. Deltuso; qu'on a cru, sur les mots nombreux de cette Langue, dont il se servoit, être de l'isle de Taïti* (Paris, 1789).

Leerssen, Joep 'Archbishop Ussher and Gaelic Culture', *Studia Hibernica* 22/23 (1982/1983), 50–58.

Leerssen, Joep, 'On the Edge of Europe: Ireland in Search of Oriental Roots (1650–1850)', *Comparative Criticism* 1 (1986), 91–112.

Leerssen, Joep, *Mere Irish and fíor-ghael: Studies in the Idea of Irish Nationality, Its Development and Literary Expression prior to the Nineteenth Century* (1986: 2nd ed., Cork, 1996).

Leerssen, Joep, 'Celticism', in Terence Brown (ed.), *Celticism* (Amsterdam, 1996), 1–20.

Leerssen, Joep, *Remembrance and Imagination: Patterns in the Historical and Literary Representation of Ireland in the Nineteenth Century* (Cork, 1996).

Leerssen, Joep, 'Literary Historicism: Romanticism, Philologists, and the Presence of the Past', *Modern Language Quarterly* 65 (2004), 221–43.

Leerssen, Joep, *National Thought in Europe: A Cultural History* (Amsterdam, 2006).

Leerssen, Joep, 'Notes towards a Definition of Romantic Nationalism', *Romantik* 2 (2013), 9–35.

Leerssen, Joep (ed.), *Encyclopedia of Romantic Nationalism in Europe* (2 vols., Amsterdam, 2018).

Lefébure, Léon, *Portraits de Croyants au XIXe siècle* (Paris, 1905).

Le Goffic, Charles, 'Le Mouvement panceltique', *Revue des deux mondes* 159 (1900), 141–74.

Le Gonidec, J.F.M.M.A., *Grammaire Celto-Bretonne* (Paris, 1807).

Leibniz, G. W., 'Brevis designatio meditationum de Originibus Gentium, ductis potissimum ex indicio linguarum', *Miscellanea Berolinensia* 1 (1710), 1–16.

Leibniz, G. W., *Collectanea etymologica*, ed. J. G. Eckhart (Hannover, 1717).

Leibniz, G.W., *Opera omnia*, ed. L. Dutens (6 vols., Paris, 1768).

Leibniz, G. W. *Sämtliche Schriften und Briefe*, Reihe 1 (27 vols., Berlin, 1957–).

Leibniz, G. W., *L'harmonie des langues*, ed. and trans. M. Crépon (Paris, 2000).

Leitz, Werner, *Das Gräberfeld von Bel-Air bei Lausanne: Frédéric Troyon (1815–1866) und die Anfänge der Frühmittelalterarchäologie* (Lausanne, 2002).

Lejeune, Michel, *Lepontica* (Paris, 1971).

le Maire de Belges, Jean, *Les Illustrations de Gaule et singularitez de Troye* (Lyon, 1549).

le Pelletier, Louis, *Dictionnaire de la langue bretonne*, ed. Charles Taillandier (Paris, 1752).

Lerchenmüller, Joachim, *>Keltischer Sprengstoff<: Eine wissenschaftsgeschichtliche Studie über die deutsche Keltologie von 1900 bis 1945* (Tübingen, 1997).

Lerchenmüller, Joachim, 'Keltologie', in Frank-Rutger Hausmann (ed.), *Die Rolle der Geisteswissenschaften im Dritten Reich 1933–1945* (Munich, 2002), 137–63.

Le Stum, Philippe, *Le néo-druidisme en Bretagne: Origine, naissance et développement* (Mayenne, 1998).

Levine, Philippa, *The Amateur and the Professional: Antiquarians, Historians and Archaeologists in Victorian England, 1838–1886* (Cambridge, 1986).

Levitin, Dmitri, 'From Sacred History to the History of Religion: Paganism, Judaism, and Christianity in European Historiography from Reformation to "Enlightenment"', *The Historical Journal* 55 (2012), 1117–160.

Levitin, Dmitri, *Ancient Wisdom in the Age of the New Science: Histories of Philosophy in England, c. 1640–1700* (Cambridge, 2015).

Lewis, Aneirin (ed.), *The Correspondence of Thomas Percy & Evan Evans* (Baton Rouge, LA, 1957).

Lewis, Saunders, *A School of Welsh Augustans* (London, 1924).

Lhwyd, Edward, *Archaeologia Britannica: Vol. 1, Glossography* (Oxford, 1707).

Ligota, C. R., and Quantin, J.-L., *History of Scholarship* (Oxford, 2006).

Linkletter, Michael, 'The Early Establishment of Celtic Studies in North American Universities', *Proceedings of the Harvard Celtic Colloquium* 29 (2009), 138–53.

Lister, Martin, *A Journey to Paris in the Year 1698* (London, 1699).

Livy, *History of Rome*, trans. B. O. Foster (14 vols., Cambridge, MA, 1919–1959).

Lloyd, William, *An Historical Account of Church-Government As it was in Great Britain and Ireland, When they first received the Christian Religion* (London, 2nd ed., 1684).

Lloyd-Jones, Naomi, and Scull, Margaret M., *Four Nations Approaches to Modern 'British' History: A (Dis)united Kingdom?* (Basingstoke, 2018).

Löffler, Marion, *'A Book of Mad Celts': John Wickens and the Celtic Congress of Caernarfon, 1904* (Llandysul, 2000).

Löffler, Marion, 'Der Pankeltismus vor dem Ersten Weltkreig im europäisschen Kontext', in Erich Poppe (ed.), *Keltologie heute: Themen und Fragestellungen* (Münster, 2004), 271–89.
Löffler, Marion, *The Literary and Historical Legacy of Iolo Morganwg, 1826–1926* (Cardiff, 2007).
Löffler, Marion, 'Prince Albert's "Celtic" Librarian: Culture, Diplomacy and Politics', in Friedegund Freitag (ed.), *Dynastie-Wissenschaft-Kunst: Die Verbindungen der Dynastien Sachsen-Gotha-Altenburg und Sachsen-Coburg und Gotha zum Britischen Empire* (Würzburg, 2020), 145–61.
Löffler, Marion, and Rhys, Hywel Gethin, 'Thomas Stephens and the Abergavenny Cymreigyddion: Letters from the Cambrian 1842–3', *National Library of Wales Journal* 34 (2009), 399–451.
Love, Walter D., 'Edmund Burke, Charles Vallancey, and the Sebright Manuscripts', *Hermathena* 95 (July 1961), 21–35.
Love, Walter D., 'Charles O'Conor of Belanagare and Thomas Leland's "Philosophical" History of Ireland', *IHS* 13 (1962), 1–25.
Love, Walter D., 'The Hibernian Antiquarian Society: A Forgotten Predecessor to the Royal Irish Academy', *Studies: An Irish Quarterly Review* 51 (1962), 419–31.
Luckscheiter, Stefan, 'Leibniz' Schriften zur Sprachforschung', in Wenchao Li (ed.), *Einheit der Vernunft und Vielfalt der Sprachen: Beiträge zu Leibnizens Sprachforschung und Zeichentheorie* (Stuttgart, 2014), 317–432.
Lüdtke, Jens, 'Die Debatte um die Herkunft des Französischen 1733–1757', in H.-J. Niederehe and B. Schlieben-Lange (eds.), *Die Frühgeschichte der Romanischen Philologie von Dante bis Diez* (Tübingen, 1987), 151–76.
Lukis, W. C. (ed.), *Family Memoirs of Rev. William Stukeley* (3 vols., Durham, 1882–1887).
Lyons, Claire E., 'An Imperial Harbinger: Sylvester O'Halloran's *General History* (1778)', *IHS* 39 (2015), 357–77.
Lyons, J. B. (ed.), 'The Letters of Sylvester O'Halloran', *Northern Munster Antiquarian Journal* 8 (1961), 168–81.
Lyons, J. B., 'Sylvester O'Halloran, 1728–1807', *Eighteenth-Century Ireland* 4 (1989), 65–74.
Macalister, R. A. Stewart (ed. and trans.), *Lebor Gabála Érenn: The Book of the Taking of Ireland* (5 parts, Dublin, 1938–1956).
Mac Amhlaigh, Liam, 'Foclóireacht na nua-ghaeilge—tábhacht agus traidisiún', *Comhar* LXIX (2009), 16–19.
Macaulay, Thomas Babington, *The Works of Lord Macaulay*, ed. Hannah Trevelyan (8 vols., London, 1866).
MacBride White, Anna, and Jeffares, A. Norman (eds.), *The Gonne-Yeats Letters, 1893–1938* (Syracuse, NY, 1994).
Mac Craith, Mícheál, '"We Know All These Poems": The Irish Response to *Ossian*', in Howard Gaskill (ed.), *Ossian in Europe* (London, 2004), 91–108.
Mac Craith, Micheál, 'Charles O'Conor of Ballinagare and the Macpherson Controversy', in Luke Gibbons and Kieran O'Connor (eds.), *Charles O'Conor of Ballinagare, 1790–91: Life and Works* (Dublin, 2015), 165–85.
MacDiarmid, Hugh, *Lucky Poet: A Self-Study in Literature and Political Ideas* (London, 1943).
Macdomhnuill, Raonuill, *Comh-Chruinneachidh Orannaigh Gaidhealach* (Duneidiunn, 1776).
MacDonald, Alexander, *Ais-Eiridh na Sean Chánoin Albannaich* (Edinburgh, 1751).

MacDougall, Hugh, *Racial Myth in English History: Trojans, Teutons, and Anglo-Saxons* (Montreal, 1982).

MacFarlan, Robert, *George Buchanan's Dialogue concerning the Rights of the Crown of Scotland translated into English* (London, 1799).

Macken, Mary L., 'W. B. Yeats, John O'Leary, and the Contemporary Club', *Studies: An Irish Quarterly Review* 28 (1939), 136–42.

Mackenzie, Henry (ed.), *Report of the Committee of the Highland Society of Scotland, Appointed to Inquire into the Nature and Authenticity of the Poems of Ossian* (Edinburgh, 1805).

MacKillop, James, *Myths and Legends of the Celts* (London, 2005).

Mackinnon, Donald, 'Collection of Ossianic Ballads of Jerome Stone', *Transactions of the Gaelic Society of Inverness* 14 (1887–1888), 314–69.

Maclagan, Peter, *Land Culture and Land Tenure in Ireland* (Edinburgh, 1869).

Maclean, Lachlan, *The History of the Celtic Language* (London, 1840).

Mac Mathúna, Séamus, 'The History of Celtic Scholarship in Russia and the Soviet Union', *Studia Celto-Slavica* 1 (2006), 3–41.

MacNeill, Eoin, 'The Re-Discovery of the Celts', *Irish Review* 3 (1913), 522–32.

MacNeill, Eoin, *Phases of Irish History* (1919: Dublin, 1920).

MacNeill, Eoin, *Celtic Ireland* (Dublin, 1921).

MacNeill, Eoin, *Early Irish Laws and Institutions* (Dublin, 1935).

Macphail, I.M.M., *The Crofters' War* (Stornoway, 1989).

[Macpherson, James], *Fragments of Ancient Poetry, Collected in the Highlands of Scotland, and translated from the Galic or Erse language* (Edinburgh, 1760).

Macpherson, James, *Fingal, an Ancient Epic Poem in Six Books* ([December 1761]: London, 1762).

Macpherson, James, *Temora, an Ancient Poem in Eight Books* (London, 1763).

Macpherson, James, *The Works of Ossian, the Son of Fingal* (2 vols., London, 1765).

Macpherson, James, *Introduction to the History and Antiquities of Great Britain* (London, 1771).

Macpherson, James. *Introduction to the History of Great Britain and Ireland* (1771: London, 2nd ed., 1772).

Macpherson, John, *Critical Dissertations on the Origin, Antiquities, Language, Government, Manners, and Religion, of the Ancient Caledonians, Their Posterity the Picts, and the British and Irish Scots* (London, 1768).

Maier, Bernhard, *Die Kelten: Ihre Geschichte von den Anfängen bis zur Gegenwart* (2000: 3rd ed., Munich, 2016).

Maier, Bernhard (ed.), *Kuno Mayer and Wales: Letters to John Glyn Davies, 1892–1919* (Würzburg, 2017).

Maier, Bernard, 'The Female Quest for the Celtic Tongues of Ireland, Scotland, and Wales', in Wendy Ayres-Bennett and Helena Sanson (eds.), *Women in the History of Linguistics* (Oxford, 2020), 305–18.

Maitland, William, *The History and Antiquities of Scotland from the earliest account of time to the death of James the First, anno 1437* (2 vols., London, 1757).

Malcolme, David, *An Essay on the Antiquities of Great Britain and Ireland* (Edinburgh, 1738).

Manco, Jean, *Blood of the Celts: The New Ancestral Story* (London, 2015).

Mandelbrote, Scott, 'The Bible and National Identity in the British Isles, c. 1650–1750', in Tony Claydon and Ian McBride (eds.), *Protestantism and National Identity: Britain and Ireland, c. 1650–c. 1850* (Cambridge, 1998), 157–81.

Mandler, Peter, *The English National Character: The History of an Idea from Edmund Burke to Tony Blair* (New Haven, CT, 2006).

Maner, Brent, *Germany's Ancient Pasts: Archaeological and Historical Interpretation since 1700* (Chicago, 2018).

Manias, Chris, *Race, Science, and the Nation: Reconstructing the Ancient Past in Britain, France, and Germany* (Abingdon: Routledge, 2013).

Manning, Susan, 'Henry Mackenzie's *Report on Ossian*: Cultural Authority in Transition', *Modern Language Quarterly* 68 (2007), 517–39.

Martin, F. X., and Byrne, F. J., *The Scholar Revolutionary: Eoin MacNeill and the Making of the New Ireland, 1867–1945* (Shannon, 1973).

Martin, Jacques, *La religion des gaulois, tirée des plus pures sources de l'antiquité* (2 vols., Paris, 1727).

Martin, Henri, *Histoire de France* (1833: 4th ed., 17 vols., Paris, 1855–1860).

Martin, Henri, *De la France, de son génie, et de ses destinées* (Paris, 1847).

Martin, Henri, *Études d'archéologie celtique* (Paris, 1872).

Martin, Henri, 'Les celtes selon M. le docteur Broca', *BSAP* 9 (1874), 614–18.

Mas, Raymond, 'Recherches sur les Gaulois et sentiment national en france au XVIIIe siecle', in Chantall Grell and Jean-Michel Dufays (eds.), *Pratiques et concepts de l'histoire en Europe XVIe-XVIIIe Siècles* (Paris, 1990), 161–221.

Mason, Roger A. (ed.), *Scotland and England, 1286–1815* (Edinburgh, 1987).

Materiaux pour l'histoire positive et philosophique de l'homme (Paris, 1866).

Matthew, H.C.G. (ed.), *The Gladstone Diaries* (14 vols., Oxford, 1968–1994).

Maunoir, Julien, *Le Sacré college de Jesus, divisé en cinq classes, ou l'on enseigne en langue Armorique les leçons Chrestiennes avec les 3. clefs pour y entrer, un Dictionnaire, une Grammaire & Syntaxe en méme langue* (Quimper-Corentin, 1659).

McBride, Ian, *Eighteenth-Century Ireland: The Isle of Slaves* (Dublin, 2009).

McCain, Stewart, 'Our Ancestors Were Not Celts: History, Folklore, and the Celtic Past in Napoleonic France', *European Review of History* 29 (2022), 674–94.

McCone, Kim, *The Celtic Question: Modern Constructs and Ancient Realities* (Dublin, 2008).

McDowell, R. B., 'The Main Narrative: Before 1800', in T. Ó Raifeartaigh (ed.), *The Royal Irish Academy: A Bicentennial History, 1785–1985* (Dublin, 1985).

McElheran, John, *Celt and Saxon* (Belfast, 1852).

McElheran, John, *The Condition of Women and Children among the Celtic, Gothic, and Other Nations* (Boston, 1858).

McMahon, Richard, *The Races of Europe: Construction of National Identities in the Social Sciences, 1839–1939* (Basingstoke, 2016).

McMahon, Timothy G., *Grand Opportunity: The Gaelic Revival and Irish Society, 1893–1910* (Syracuse, NY, 2008).

McNeill, G. V. (ed.), *Full Report of the Highland Reform Association Conference, Held at Bonar Bridge on 22nd and 23rd September, 1886* (1886).

McNeil, Kenneth, *Scotland, Britain, Empire: Writing the Highlands, 1760–1860* (Columbus, OH, 2007).

M'Donald, Alexander, *A Galick and English Vocabulary* (Edinburgh, 1741).

Meek, Ronald L., *Social Science and the Ignoble Savage* (Cambridge, 1976).

Meek, Donald, *The Quest for Celtic Christianity* (Edinburgh, 2000).

Meerhoff, Kees, *Rhétorique et Poétique au XVIe siècle en France* (Leiden, 1986).

Megaw, J.V.S., and Megaw, M. R. 'Ancient Celts and Modern Ethnicity', *Antiquity* 70 (1996), 175–81.

Meiners, Christoph, *Grundriss der Geschichte der Menscheit* (Lemgo, 1785).

Melby, Christian K., 'Empire and Nation in British Future-War and Invasion-Scare Fiction, 1871–1914', *Historical Journal* 63 (2020), 389–410.

Mellon, Stanley, *The Political Uses of History: A Study of Historians in the French Restoration* (Stanford, CA, 1958).

Mercier-Faivre, Anne-Marie, *Un supplement à "L'Encyclopédie": Le "Monde primitif" d'Antoine Court de Gébelin* (Paris, 1999).

Merolle, Vincenzo, *Correspondence of Adam Ferguson* (2 vols., London, 1995).

Metcalf, George J., *On Language Diversity and Relationship from Bibliander to Adelung*, ed. Toon Van Hal and Raf Van Rooy (Amsterdam, 2013).

Michelet, Jules, *Histoire de France* (17 vols., Paris, 1833–1841).

Michelet, Jules, *Origines du droit français* (Paris, 1837).

Michelet, Jules, *Écrits de jeunesse: Journal (1820–1823)—Mémorial journal des idées*, ed. Paul Viallaneix (Paris, 1959).

Miles, Dillwyn, *The Secret of the Bards of the Isle of Britain* (Llandybie, 1992).

Mill, John Stuart, *The Principles of Political Economy with some of their Applications to Social Philosophy*, ed. William Ashley (1848: London, 1920).

Millar, John, *The Origin of the Distinction of Ranks, or, Inquiry into the Circumstances which give rise to Influence and Authority, in the Different Members of Society* (1771: Indianapolis, IN, 2006).

Mitchel, John, *Jail Journal* (1913: Reading, 1983).

Mitchell, Sebastian (ed.), 'Special Issue: Ossian in the Twenty-First Century', *Journal for Eighteenth-Century Studies* 39 (2016), 157–250.

Momigliano, Arnoldo, *Alien Wisdom: The Limits of Hellenization* (Cambridge, 1975).

Mongez, Antoine, 'Mémoire sur les gladiateurs', *Mémoires de l'Institut national des sciences et arts: Littérature et Beaux arts* (Paris, 1799) 423–68.

Monod, Paul Kléber, *Solomon's Secret Arts: The Occult in the Age of Enlightenment* (New Haven, CT, 2013).

Moore, Dafydd, *Ossian and Ossianism* (4 vols., London, 2004).

Moore, Dafydd 'The Reception of *The Poems of Ossian* in England and Scotland', in Howard Gaskill (ed.), *Ossian in Europe* (London, 2004), 21–37.

Moore, Dafydd, 'James Macpherson and "Celtic Whiggism"', *Eighteenth-Century Life* 30 (2006), 1–24.

Moore, Dafydd, '"Caledonian Plagiary": The Role and Meaning of Ireland in the Poems of *Ossian*', in Ben Dew and Fiona Price (eds.), *Historical Writing in Britain, 1688–1830: Visions of History* (Basingstoke, 2014), 92–108.

Moore, Dafydd (ed.), *The International Companion to James Macpherson and* The Poems of Ossian (Edinburgh, 2017).

Moore, George, *Hail and Farewell* (3 vols., London, 1911–1914).

Moran, D. P., *The Philosophy of Irish Ireland*, ed. Patrick Maume (1905: Dublin, 2006).

Moreau de Mautour, Philibert-Bernard, *Observations sur des monuments d'antiquité trouvez dans l'eglise cathedrale de Paris* (Paris, 1711).

Morgan, Kenneth, *Rebirth of a Nation: Wales 1880–1980* (Oxford, 1980).

Morgan, Prys, 'The Abbé Pezron and the Celts', *THSC* (1965), 286–95.

Morgan, Prys, *The Eighteenth Century Renaissance: A New History of Wales* (Llandybie, 1981).

Morgan, Prys, 'A Death to a View: The Hunt for the Welsh Past in the Romantic Period', in Eric Hobsbawm and Terence Ranger, *The Invention of Tradition* (Cambridge, 1983), 43–100.

Morgan, Prys, 'Early Victorian Wales and Its Crisis of Identity', in Laurence Brockliss and David Eastwood, *A Union of Multiple Identities: The British Isles, c. 1750–c. 1850* (Manchester, 1997), 93–109.

Morgan, Prys, 'Boxhorn and the Welsh: Some Cambro-Dutch Contacts in the Seventeenth Century', *Dutch Crossing* 24 (2000), 183–90.

Morgan, Prys, 'Iolo Morganwg and Welsh Historical Traditions', in Geraint H. Jenkins (ed.), *A Rattleskull Genius: The Many Faces of Iolo Morganwg* (Cardiff, 2009), 251–68.

Morganwg, Iolo, *Cyfrinach Beirdd Ynys Prydain*, ed. Taliesin Williams (Abertawe, 1829).

Morpurgo Davies, Anna, *History of Linguistics: Volume IV: The Nineteenth Century* (London, 2000).

Morris, Lewis, *Celtic Remains* (London, 1878).

Morrow, John, 'Thomas Carlyle, "Young Ireland" and the "Condition of Ireland Question"', *Historical Journal* 51 (2008), 643–67.

Morse, Michael, *How the Celts Came to Britain: Druids, Ancient Skulls and the Birth of Archaeology* (Stroud, 2005).

Morton, Graeme, *Unionist Nationalism: Governing Urban Scotland, 1830–60* (East Linton, 1999).

Much, Robert, 'Die angebliche Keltenherrschaft in Germanien', *Volk und Rasse* (1926), 100–105.

Mulvagh, Conor, and Purcell, Emer (eds.), *Eoin MacNeill: The Pen and the Sword* (Cork, 2022).

Munday, Anthony, *The Triumphes of re-vnited Britania* (London, 1605).

Münkler, Herfried, Grünberger, Hans, and Mayer, Kathrin, *Nationenbildung: Die Nationalisierung Europa im Diskurs humanistischer Intellektueller. Italien und Deutschland* (Berlin, 1998).

Münster, Sebastian, *La Cosmographie universelle, contenant la situation de toutes les parties du monde avec leurs proprietez & appartenances* (Paris, 1552).

Murray, D., *Romanticism, Nationalism and Irish Antiquarian Societies, 1840–80* (Maynooth, 2000).

Myers, Victoria, O'Shaughnessy, David, and Philp, Mark (eds.), *The Diary of William Godwin* (Oxford Digital Library, 2010).

Nagai, Kaori, '"Tis Optophone Which Ontophanes": Race, the Modern and Irish Revivalism', in Len Platt (ed.), *Modernism and Race* (Cambridge, 2011), 58–76.

Nairn, Tom, *The Break-Up of Britain: Crisis and Neo-Nationalism* (1977: 2nd ed., London, 1981).

Nennius, *Historia Brittonum*, trans. A. W. Wade-Evans (London, 1938).

Nevin, Monica, 'General Charles Vallancey, 1725–1812', *Journal of the Royal Society of Antiquaries of Ireland* 123 (1993), 19–58.

Newby, A. G., 'The *Oban Times* and the Early Land Agitation in the Highlands, 1877–81', *Scottish Local History* 54 (2002), 13–19.

Newby, Andrew G., *The Life and Times of Edward McHugh (1853–1915): Land Reformer, Trade Unionist, and Labour Activist* (Lewiston, 2004).

Newby, Andrew G., *Ireland, Radicalism and the Scottish Highlands, c. 1870–1912* (Edinburgh, 2007).

Nicholls, Sophie, *Political Thought in the French Wars of Religion* (Cambridge, 2021).

Nicolet, Claude, *La fabrique d'une nation: La France entre Rome et les Germains* (Paris, 2003).

Nicolson, William, *The Scottish Historical Library* (London, 1702).

Ní Mhunghaile, Lesa, 'Ossian and the Gaelic World', in Dafydd Moore (ed.), *The International Companion to James Macpherson and* The Poems of Ossian (Edinburgh, 2017), 26–38.

Nott, J. C., and Gliddon, G. R., *Indigenous Races of the Earth* (Philadelphia, PA, 1857).

O'Brian, William, *Irish Ideas* (London, 1893).

O'Brien, John, *Focalóir Gaoiodhigle-sax-bhéarle, or an Irish-English Dictionary* (Paris, 1768).

O'Brien, William, *The Influence of the Irish Language on Irish National Literature and Character* (Cork, 1892).

O'Brien, William, and Ryan, Desmond (eds.), *Devoy's Post Bag, 1871–1928* (2 vols., Dublin, 1948–1953).

Ó Catháin, Diarmaid, 'An Irish Scholar Abroad: Bishop John O'Brien of Cloyne and the Macpherson Controversy', in Patrick O'Flanagan and Cornelius G. Buttimer (eds.), *Cork: History & Society* (Dublin, 1993), 499–533.

O'Connor, Roger, *Chronicles of Eri; being the History of the Gaal Sciot Iber: or, the Irish People; translated from the original manuscripts in the Phoenician dialect of the Scythian language* (2 vols., London, 1822).

[O'Conor, Charles], *Dissertations on the Antient History of Ireland: wherein an Account is given of the Origine, Government, Letters, Sciences, Religion, Manners and Customs, of the antient Inhabitants* (Dublin, 1753).

O'Conor, Charles, *Dissertations on the Antient History of Ireland* (2nd ed., Dublin, 1766).

[O'Conor, Charles], 'Remarks on the Essay on the Antiquity of the Irish Language', reprinted in *Collectanea de rebus Hibernicis* 2 (Dublin, 1786), 337–48.

Ó Cróinín, Dáibhí, 'The Reception of Johann Kaspar Zeuss's *Grammatica Celtica* in Ireland and Britain, and on the Continent: Some New Evidence', in Michael Wollenschläger, Eckhard Kreßel, and Johann Egger (eds.), *Recht-Wirtschaft-Kultur: Herausforderungen an Staat und Gesellschaft im Zeitalter der Globalisierung* (Berlin, 2005), 85–91.

Ó Cróinín, Dáibhí, *Whitley Stokes (1830–1909): The Lost Celtic Notebooks Rediscovered* (Dublin, 2011).

Ó Cróinín, Dáibhí, 'Letters of Kuno Meyer to Douglas Hyde, 1896–1919', *Studia Hibernica* 42 (2016), 1–64.

Ó Cuív, Brian, 'Celtic Studies–An Appraisal', in Cyril J. Byrne, Margaret Harry, and Pádraig Ó Siadhail (eds.), *Celtic Languages and Celtic Peoples* (Halifax, 1992), 1–9.

Ó Dochartaigh, Pól, *Julius Pokorny, 1887–1970: Germans, Celts and Nationalism* (Dublin, 2004).

Ó Dochartaigh, Pól, '"A Shadowy but Important Figure": Rudolf Thomas Siegfried', in Elizabeth Boyle & Paul Russell, *The Tripartite Life of Whitley Stokes (1830–1909)* (Dublin, 2011), 29–43.

O'Donnell, Ruán (ed.), *The Impact of the 1916 Rising: Among the Nations* (Dublin, 2008).

O'Donoghue, David, *Hitler's Irish Voices: The Story of German Radio's Wartime Irish Service* (Belfast, 1998).

O'Donovan, John, *A Grammar of the Irish Language* (Dublin, 1845).

O'Donovan, John, 'Zeuss's "Grammatica Celtica"', *Ulster Journal of Archaeology* 7 (1859), 11–32.

O'Flaherty, Patrick, *Scotland's Pariah: The Life and Work of John Pinkerton, 1758–1826* (Toronto, 2014).

O'Flaherty, Roderic, *The Ogygia Vindicated: Against the Objections of Sir George Mackenzie*, ed. Charles O'Conor (Dublin, 1775).

O'Flanagan, Theophilus, 'An Account of an antient Inscription in Ogam Character on the Sepulchral Monument of an Irish Chief', *Transactions of the Royal Irish Academy* 1 (1787), Antiquities Section, 3–17.

O'Halloran, Clare, 'Irish Re-Creations of the Gaelic Past: The Challenge of Macpherson's Ossian', *P&P* 124 (1989), 69–85.

O'Halloran, Clare, '"The Island of Saints and Scholars": Views of the Early Church and Sectarian Politics in Late-Eighteenth Century Ireland', *Eighteenth-Century Ireland* 5 (1990), 7–20.

O'Halloran, Clare, 'An English Orientalist in Ireland: Charles Vallancey (1726–1812)', in Joep Leerssen, A. H. van der Weel, and Bart Westerweel (eds.), *Forging in the Smith: National Identity and Representation in Anglo-Irish Literary History* (Amsterdam, 1995), 161–73.

O'Halloran, Clare, *Golden Ages and Barbarous Nations: Antiquarian Debate and Cultural Politics in Ireland, c. 1750–1800* (Cork, 2004).

O'Halloran, Clare, 'Harping on the Past: Translating Antiquarian Learning into Popular Culture in early Nineteenth-Century Ireland', in Melissa Calaresu, Filippo de Vivo, Joan-Pau Rubiés (eds.), *Exploring Cultural History: Essays in Honour of Peter Burke* (Farnham, 2010), 327–43.

O'Halloran, Sylvester, *Insula Sacra* (Limerick, 1770).

O'Halloran, Sylvester, *Ierne Defended* (Dublin, 1774).

O'Leary, John, *Recollections of Fenians and Fenianism* (2 vols., London, 1896).

O'Leary, Paul, *Immigration and Integration: The Irish in Wales, 1798–1922* (Cardiff, 2002).

O'Leary, Philip, '"Children of the Same Mother": Gaelic Relations with the Other Celtic Revival Movements, 1882–1916', in *Proceedings of the Harvard Celtic Colloquium* 6 (1986), 101–30.

O'Leary, Philip, *The Prose Literature of the Gaelic Revival, 1881–1921: Ideology and Innovation* (University Park, PA, 1994).

Olender, Maurice, *Les langues du paradis* (Paris, 1989).

Olivier, Laurent, *Le Pays des Celtes: Mémoires de la Gaule* (Paris, 2018).

Ó Lúing, Seán, *Kuno Meyer, 1858–1919* (Dublin, 1991).

Ó Lúing, Seán, 'Celtic Scholars of Germany', *ZCP* 46 (1994), 249–70.

O'Neill Daunt, William J., *A Catechism of the History of Ireland: Ancient and Modern* (Dublin, 1844).

O'Reilly, J. P., and Fournier D'Albe, E. E., 'On a Pandean Pipe from Tanna Island, New Hebrides', *Proceedings of the Royal Irish Academy* 3 (1893–1896), 511–15.

Ortelius, Abraham, *Theatrum Orbis Terrarum* (1570: 2nd ed., Antwerp, 1595).

Owen, A. L., *The Famous Druids: A Survey of Three Centuries of English Literature on the Druids* (Oxford, 1926).
Owen, Hugh, *Additional Letters of the Morrises of Anglesey (1735–1786)* (2 vols., London, 1947–1949).
Owen [Pughe], William, *The Heroic Elegies and other pieces of Llywarç Hen, Prince of the Cumbrian Britons* (London, 1792).
Owen [Pughe], William, *A Grammar of the Welsh Language* (London, 1803).
Ozouf, Mona, 'L'invention de l'ethnographie française: Le questionnaire de l'Académie celtique', *Annales. Histoire, Sciences Sociales* 36 (1981), 210–30.
Palmer, R. R., 'A Revolutionary Republican: M.A.B. Mangourit', *William & Mary Quarterly* 9 (1952), 483–96.
Parczewski, Alfons, *A Survey of the Language Map of Europe and a Sketch of an International Peace Union for the Protection of Linguistic Minorities: Submitted to the Pan-Celtic Congress at Carnarvon* (Caernarvon, 1904).
Parry, Glynn, 'Berosus and the Protestants: Reconstructing Protestant Myth', *Huntingdon Library Quarterly* 64 (2001), 1–21.
Parry, Graham, *The Trophies of Time: English Antiquarians of the Seventeenth Century* (Oxford, 1995).
Parsons, Lawrence, *Observations on the Bequest of Henry Flood* (Dublin, 1795).
Patterson, Nick, Isakov, Michael, Booth, Thomas, et al. 'Large-Scale Migration into Britain during the Middle to Late Bronze Age', *Nature* 601 (2022), 588–94.
Paz, D. G., 'Anti-Catholicism, Anti-Irish Stereotyping, and Anti-Celtic Racism in Mid-Victorian Working-Class Periodicals', *Albion* 18 (1986), 601–16.
Pecora, Vincent P., 'Arnoldian Ethnology', *Victorian Studies* 41 (1998), 355–79.
Pelloutier, Simon, *Histoire des Celtes* (2 vols., The Hague, 1740–1750).
Pennant, Thomas, *The Journey to Snowdon* (London, 1781).
Percy, Thomas (ed.), *Five Pieces of Runic Poetry Translated from the Islandic Language* (London, 1763).
Percy, Thomas (ed.), *Northern Antiquities* (2 vols., London, 1770).
Périon, Joachim, *Dialogues de l'origine du français et de sa parenté avec le grec*, trans. Geneviève Demerson and Alberte Jacquetin (Paris, 2003).
Pertlwieser, Margarita, 'Johann Georg Ramsauer (1795–1874): Der Ausgräber des Hallstätter Gräberfeldes', *Oberösterreichische Heimatblätter* 34 (1980), 3–14.
Pethica, James, *Lady Gregory's Diaries, 1892–1902* (Gerrards Cross, 1996).
Petrie, George, *The Ecclesiastical Architecture of Ireland* (Dublin, 1845)
Petty, William, *The Political Anatomy of Ireland* (London, 1691).
Pezron, Paul-Yves, 'Copie d'une Lettre de Mr. l'Abbé de la CHARMOYE, à Mr. l'Abbé Nicaise', *Nouvelles de la République des lettres* (1699), 627–39.
Pezron, Paul-Yves, *Essay d'un commentaire litteral et historique sur les prophetes* (Paris, 1693).
Pezron, Paul-Yves, *Antiquité de la nation et de la langue des Celtes, autrement appellez Gaulois* (Paris, 1703).
Pezron, Paul-Yves, *The Rise and Fall of States and Empires* (London, 1809).
Phillips, Geraint, *Dyn heb ei gyffelb yn y byd: Owain Myfyr a'i gysylltiadau llenyddol* (Caerdydd, 2010).

Pictet, Adolphe, *Du culte des Cabires chez les anciens irlandais* (Geneva and Paris, 1824).

Pictet, Adolphe, 'Lettres à M. A.W. de Schlegel sur l'affinité des langues celtiques avec le sanscrit', *Journal asiatique* 3.1 (1836), 263–90, 417–48; 3.2 (1836), 440–66.

Pictet, Adolphe, *Les origins indo-européennes, ou les Aryas primitifs: Essai de paléontologie linguistique* (2 vols., 1859–1863).

Piggott, Stuart J., *William Stukeley: An Eighteenth-Century Antiquary* (1950: 2nd ed., London, 1985).

Pighius, Stephanus Vinandus, *Hercules prodicius* (Antwerp, 1587).

Pinkerton, John, *Ancient Scotish Poems* (2 vols., London, 1786).

Pinkerton, John, *A Dissertation on the Origin and Progress of the Scythians or Goths* (London, 1787).

Pinkerton, John, *Recollections of Paris, in the Years 1802–3–4–5* (2 vols., London, 1806).

Pinkerton, John, *Modern Geography* (1804: 3 vols., London, 1807).

Piroli, T., and Petit-Radel, Louis, *Les Monumens antiques du Musée Napoleon* (4 vols., Paris, 1806).

Pittock, Murray G. H., *Celtic Identity and the British Image* (Manchester, 1999).

Pittock, Murray, and Jack, Isla, 'Patrick Geddes and the Celtic Revival', in Ian Brown, Susan Manning, Thomas Owen Clancy, and Murray Pittock (eds.), *The Edinburgh History of Scottish Literature* (3 vols., Edinburgh, 2007).

Pocock, J.G.A., 'British History: A Plea for a New Subject', *JMH* 47 (1975), 601–21.

Pocock, J.G.A., *Barbarism and Religion* (6 vols., Cambridge, 1999–2015).

Pokorny, Julius, 'The Origins of Druidism', *Celtic Review* 5 (1908), 1–20.

Pokorny, Julius, *Die älteste Lyrik der grünen Insel* (Halle, 1923).

Pokorny, Julius, *A History of Ireland*, trans. Séana D. King (London, 1933).

Pokorny, Julius, 'Ist der Germanenname Keltisch?', *ZCP* 20 (1936), 461–75.

Pokorny, Julius, 'MacNeill's Place in Celtic Studies', in F. X. Martin and F. J. Byrne, *The Scholar Revolutionary: Eoin MacNeill and the Making of the New Ireland, 1867–1945* (Shannon, 1973), 13–14.

Poliakov, Léon, *The Aryan Myth: A History of Racist and Nationalist Ideas in Europe*, trans. Edmund Howard (New York, 1974).

Polybius, *The Histories*, trans. W. R. Paton, rev. Frank W. Walbank and Christian Habicht (6 vols., Cambridge, MA, 2010–2012).

Pomeau, René, *Voltaire en son temps* (2 vols., Paris, 1995).

Poncarová, Petra Johana, *Derick Thomson and the Gaelic Revival* (Edinburgh, 2024).

Pope, Rachel, 'Re-Approaching the Celts: Origins, Society, and Social Change', *Journal of Archaeological Research* 30 (2022), 1–67.

Poppe, Erich, 'Leibniz and Eckhart on the Irish Language', *Eighteenth-Century Ireland* 1 (1986), 65–84.

Poppe, Erich, 'The Celtic Languages in Conrad Gessner's *Mithridates* (1555)', *ZCP* 45 (1992), 240–50.

Poppe, Erich, 'Lag es in der Luft?: Johann Kaspar Zeuß und die Konstituierung der Keltologie', *Beiträge zur Geschichte der Sprachwissenschaft* 2 (1992), 41–56.

Poppe, Erich, 'Das weite Feld der "keltischen Philologie(n)"', *Beiträge zur Geschichte der Sprachwissenschaft* 11 (2001), 302–17.

Poppe, Erich, 'The Welsh Language in German Philology around 1850', in Bernhard Maier (ed.), *150 Jahre "Mabinogion"—Deutsch-Walisische Kulturbeziehungen* (Tübingen, 2001).

Poppe, Erich, 'Johann Kaspar Zeuß und die Keltomanie', in Michael Wollenschläger, Eckhard Kreßel, and Johann Egger (eds.), *Recht-Wirtschaft-Kultur: Herausforderungen an Staat und Gesellschaft im Zeitalter der Globalisierung* (Berlin, 2005), 239–50.

Poskett, James, *Materials of the Mind* (Chicago, IL, 2019).

'Posteritas', *The Siege of London* (London, 1885).

Postic, Fãnch, 'Prémiers échanges interceltiques: Le voyage de La Villemarqué au pays de Galles', *ArMen* 125 (2001), 34–43.

Postic, Fañch, 'Le Beau contre le Vrai? La "Querrelle du Barzaz Breiz" (1866–1868)', in *Bérose—Encyclopédie internationale des histoires de l'anthropologie.*

Postel, Guillaume, *Histoire memorable des expeditions depuys le Deluge faictes par les Gauloys ou Françoys depuis la France jusque en Asie* (Paris, 1552).

Postel, Guillaume, *La Loy salique* (Paris, 1552).

Powell, Anthony, *John Aubrey and His Friends* (London, 1948).

Powell, Dean, *Dr William Price: Wales's First Radical* (Stroud, 2012).

Powell, T.G.E., *The Celts* (London, 1958).

Pownall, Thomas, *An Antiquarian Romance* (London, 1795).

Prebble, John, *The King's Jaunt* (London, 1988).

[Price, Thomas] Carnhuanawc, 'Yr Iaith Geltaeg', *Seren Gomer* 64 (1821), 13.

[Price, Thomas] Carnhuanawc, 'Hiliogaeth Gomer', *Seren Gomer* (1823), 81–83.

[Price, Thomas] Carnhuanawc, 'Yr Iaith Geltaeg', *Seren Gomer*, 123 (1825), 361–363.

Price, Thomas, 'Philological Remarks on Greek, Latin and Celtic Words', *The Classical Journal* XXXVIII (1828), 269–73.

Price, Thomas, *An Essay on the Physiognomy and Physiology of the present Inhabitants of Britain; with reference to their origin as Goths and Celts* (London, 1829).

Price, Thomas, *Hanes Cymru* (Crughywel, 1842).

Prichard, James Cowles, 'On the Varieties of the Human Race', *Royal Medical Society Dissertations*, 58 (1807–1808), 87–133.

Prichard, James Cowles, *Disputatio inauguralis de generis humani varietate* (Edinburgh, 1808).

Prichard, James Cowles, *Researches into the Physical History of Man* (London, 1813).

Prichard, James Cowles, *Researches into the Physical History of Mankind* (2nd ed., 2 vols., London, 1826).

Prichard, James Cowles, *The Eastern Origin of the Celtic Nations: Proved by a Comparison of Their Dialects with the Sanskrit, Greek, Latin, and Teutonic Languages* (London, 1831).

Prichard, James Cowles, *Darstellung der Aegyptischen Mythologie*, trans. L. Haymann (Bonn, 1837).

Prichard, James Cowles, *Researches into the Physical History of Mankind* (3rd ed., 5 vols., London, 1837–1847).

Prichard, James Cowles, *Ethnography of the Celtic Race* (London, 1840?).

Priest, Robert D., *The Gospel According to Renan: Reading, Writing, & Religion in Nineteenth-Century France* (Oxford, 2015).

Pringle, Heather, *The Master Plan: Himmler's Scholars and the Holocaust* (London, 2006).

Pryce, Huw (ed.), *Literacy in Medieval Celtic Societies* (Cambridge, 1998).

Pryce, Huw, *J. E. Lloyd and the Creation of Welsh History: Renewing a Nation's Past* (Cardiff, 2011).

Pryce, Huw, 'J. E. Lloyd's *History of Wales* (1911)', in Neil Evans and Huw Pryce (eds.), *Writing a Small Nation's Past: Wales in Comparative Perspective, 1850–1950* (Farnham, 2013), 49–64.

Pryce, Huw, *Writing Welsh History: From the Early Middle Ages to the Twenty-First Century* (Oxford, 2022).

Quinn, James, *Young Ireland and the Writing of Irish History* (Dublin, 2015).

Ramus, Petrus, *Traitté des meurs et facons des anciens Gauloys*, trans. Michel de Castenau (Paris, 1581).

Raymond, Anthony, *A Short Preliminary Discourse to the History of Ireland* (London, 1725).

Readman, Paul, *Land and Nation in England: Patriotism, National Identity, and the Politics of Land, 1880–1914* (Woodbridge, 2008).

Rearick, Charles, 'Henri Marti: From Druidic Traditions to Republican Politics', *Journal of Contemporary History* 7 (1972), 53–64.

Rearick, Charles, *Beyond the Enlightenment: Historians & Folklore in Nineteenth-Century France* (Bloomington, IN, 1974).

Reece, Jack E., *The Bretons against France: Ethnic Minority Nationalism in Twentieth-Century Brittany* (Chapel Hill, NC, 1977).

Regaldo, Marc, '<<La Décade>> revue bretonne?', *Annales de Bretagne et des pays de l'Ouest* (1976), 605–17.

Reich, David, *Who We Are and How We Got Here: Ancient DNA and the New Science of the Human Past* (Oxford, 2018).

Reinach, Salomon, 'Esquisse d'une histoire de l'archaéologie gauloise', *Revue celtique* 19 (1898), 101–17, 292–307.

Renan, Ernest, 'La Poésie des races celtiques', *Revue des deux mondes* (1854), 473–506.

Renan, Ernest, *Essais de Morale et de Critique* (Paris, 1859).

Renan, Ernest, *Vie de Jésus* (Paris, 1863).

Renan, Ernest, *Qu'est-ce qu'une nation?* (Paris, 1882).

Renan, Ernest, *Souvenirs d'enfance et de jeunesse* (Paris, 1883).

Renan, Ernest, *Recollections and Letters of Ernest Renan*, trans. Isabel F. Hapgood (New York, 1892).

Renan, Ernest, *Cahiers de Jeunesse: 1845–1846* (Paris, 1906).

Renan, Ernest, *Correspondance générale*, ed. Anne-Marie de Brem and Jean Balcou (3 vols., Paris, 1995–2008).

Reports of the Commissioners of Inquiry into the State of Education in Wales (London, 1848).

Retzius, Anders, 'Mémoire sur les forms du crane des habitants du nord', trans. G. Courty, *Mémoires d'histoire naturelle* S3.6 (1846), 133–72.

Retzius, Anders, 'On the Ethnographical Distribution of Long and Elongated Crania', *Report of the Sixteenth Meeting of the British Association for the Advancement of Science* (London, 1847).

Retzius, Anders, *Coup d'oeil sur l'état actuel de l'ethnologie au point de vue de la forme du crane osseux*, trans. E. Claparède (Geneva, 1860).

Retzius, Anders, *Ethnologische Schriften* (Stockholm, 1864).

Reynaud, Jean, *Considérations sur l'esprit de la Gaule* (Paris, 1847).

Reynaud-Paligot, Carole, *La République raciale: Une histoire, 1860–1940* (2007: 2nd ed., Paris, 2021).

Reynolds, Susan, 'Medieval *Origines Gentium* and the Community of the Realm', *History* 68 (1983), 375–90.

Rhenanus, Beatus, *Rerum Germanicarum libri tres (1531)*, trans. Felix Mundt (Tübingen, 2008).

Rhys, John, *Lectures on Welsh Philology* (London, 1877).

Rhys, John, *The Early Ethnology of the British Isles* (London, 1882).

Richards, Eric, *Debating the Highland Clearances* (Edinburgh, 2007).

Rio, Alexis-François, *La petite chouannerie ou Histoire d'un college breton sous l'Empire* (London, 1842).

Rio, Alexis-François, *Épilogue a l'art chrétien* (2 vols., Freiburg im Breisgau, 1870).

Robb, Graham, *Ancient Paths: Discovering the Lost Map of Celtic Europe* (London, 2013).

Roberts, Alice, *The Celts: Search for a Civilization* (London, 2015).

Roberts, Brynley F., '"The Age of Restitution": Taliesin ab Iolo and the Reception of Iolo Morganwg', in G. H. Jenkins (ed.), *A Rattleskull Genius: The Many Faces of Iolo Morganwg* (Cardiff, 2005), 461–79.

Roberts, Brynley F., *Edward Lhwyd, c. 1660–1709, Naturalist, Antiquary, Philologist* (Cardiff, 2022).

Roberts, Matthew, 'Daniel O'Connell, Repeal, and Chartism in the Age of Atlantic Revolutions', *JMH* 90 (2018), 1–39.

Roberts, Peter (trans.), *The Chronicle of the Kings of Britain* (London, 1811).

Robertson, J. M., *The Saxon and the Celt: A Study in Sociology* (London, 1897).

Robertson, John, *The Scottish Enlightenment and the Militia Issue* (Edinburgh, 1985).

Rocher, Ludo, 'Vans Kennedy (1784–1846): A Preliminary Bio-Bibliography', *Journal of the American Oriental Society* 109 (1989), 621–25.

Rocher, Rosane, *Alexander Hamilton (1762–1824): A Chapter in the Early History of Sanskrit Philology* (New Haven, CT, 1968).

Roger, James Cruickshank, *Celticism: A Myth* (London, 1884).

Romero, Aarón Alzola, and Sánchez-Moreno, Eduardo, 'Fabricating Celts: How Iron Age Iberians Became Indo-Europeanized during the Franco Regime', *Proceedings of the Harvard Celtic Colloquium* 29 (2009), 1–29.

Roosevelt, Theodore, 'The Ancient Irish Sagas', *The Century* 73 (1907), 327–37.

Rosenfeld, Sophia, *A Revolution in Language: The Problem of Signs in Late Eighteenth-Century France* (Stanford, CA, 2001).

Ross, Alexander, *Pansebeia, or, a View of all the Religions in the World* (1653: 2nd ed., 1655).

Ross, Margaret Clunies, and Collins, Amanda J., *The Correspondence of Edward Lye* (Toronto, 2004).

Rothstein, Marian, 'The Reception of Annius of Viterbo's Forgeries', *Renaissance Quarterly* 71 (2018), 580–609.

Rowlands, Henry, *Mona Antiqua Restaurata* (1723: London, 1766).

Rowley-Conway, Peter, *From Genesis to Prehistory: The Archaeological Three Age System and Its Contested Reception in Denmark, Britain, and Ireland* (Oxford, 2007).

Royal Commission of Inquiry into the Condition of Crofters and Cottars in the Highlands and Islands (4 vols., Edinburgh, 1884).

Rupp-Eisenreich, Britta, 'The "Société des Observateurs de l'Homme" and German Ethno-Anthropology at the End of the 18th Century', *History of Anthropology Newsletter* 10 (1983), 5–11.

Sacheverell, William, *An Account of the Isle of Man* (London, 1702).

Said, Edward, *Orientalism* (New York, 1978).

Said, Edward, *Culture and Imperialism* (New York, 1993).

Salmasius, Claudius, *De Hellenistica commentarius* (Leiden, 1643).

Saunders, Bailey, *The Life and Letters of James Macpherson* (London, 1895).

Savonius-Wroth, Celestina, 'Bardic Ministers: Scotland's Gaelic-Speaking Clergy in the Ossian Controversy', *Eighteenth-Century Studies* 52 (2019), 225–43.

Schaub, Jean-Frédéric, and Sebastiani, Silvia, *Race et histoire dans les sociétés occidentales (xve-xviiie siècle)* (Paris, 2021).

Schiller, Francis, *Paul Broca: Founder of French Anthropology, Explorer of the Brain* (1978: Oxford, 1992).

Schlegel, A. W., 'Sur l'Origine des Hindous', *Transactions of the Royal Society of Literature* 2 (1834), 405–46.

Schlegel, A. W., 'Examen des quarante', in Édouard Böcking (ed.), *Oeuvres de Auguste-Guillaume de Schlegel, écrites en francais* (3 vols., Leipzig, 1846).

Schlegel, Friedrich, *Ueber die Sprache und Weisheit der Indier* (Heidelberg, 1808).

Schmidt, Karl Horst, 'Stand und Aufgaben der deutschsprachigen Keltologie', in Martin Rockel and Stefan Zimmer (eds.), *Akten des ersten Symposiums Deutschsprachiger Keltologen* (Tübingen, 1993), 1–36.

Schoepflin, Johann Daniel, *Alsatiae illustratae* (2 vols., Colmar, 1751–1761).

Schreiber, Heinrich, *Die Neuentdeckten Hünengräber im Breisgau* (Freiburg, 1826).

Schreiber, Heinrich, *Die ehrenen Streikeile zumal in Deutschland* (Freiburg, 1842).

Schulz, Albert, *An Essay on the influence of Welsh tradition upon the literature of Germany, France, and Scandinavia*, trans. Frances Berrington (London, 1841).

Schwartz, Verena, 'Kelten bei dem Laienforscher Christian Keferstein (1784–1866)', in Simeone Kahlow, Judith Schachtmann, and Cathrin Hähn (eds.), *Grenzen überwinden: Archëologie zwischen Disziplin und Disziplinen* (Rahden, 2021), 85–92.

Scott, Walter, *Sir Tristrem* (1804: Edinburgh, 1819).

Scott, Walter, *Sir Tristrem, a Metrical Romance of the Thirteenth Century* (1804: London, 1811).

[Scott, Walter], 'The Poetical Works of James Macpherson, &c., containing the Poems of Ossian', *Edinburgh Review* 6 (1805).

Scott, Walter, *Marmion; A Tale of Flodden Field* (Edinburgh, 1808).

Scott, Walter, *The Antiquary* (1816: Oxford, 2002).

[Scott, Walter], Review of Joseph Ritson, *Annals of the Caledonians, Picts, and Scots*, *Quarterly Review* 41 (1829), 120–62.

Scrope, George Poulett, *How Is Ireland to Be Governed?* (1834: London, 1836).

Sculfort de Beaurepas, Serge, *Rénovation celtique* (Paris, 1903).

Sebastiani, Silvia, *The Scottish Enlightenment: Race, Gender, and the Limits of Progress*, trans. Jeremy Carden (Basingstoke, 2013).

Sebastiani, Silvia, 'Civilization and Perfectibility: Conflicting Views of the History of Humankind?', in John Robertson (ed.), *Time, History, and Political Thought* (Cambridge, 2023), 194–215.

The Second Book of the Rhymers' Club (London, 1894).

Secord, James A., *Visions of Science: Books and Readers at the Dawn of the Victorian Age* (Chicago, 2015).

Selden, John, *The reverse or back-face of the English Janus*, trans. Redman Westcot (1610: London, 1682).

Selections from the most celebrated Foreign Literary Journals and other Periodical Publications (2 vols., London, 1798).

Seliger, M., 'Race-Thinking during the Restoration,' *JHI* 19 (1958), 273–82.

Seliger, M., 'The Idea of Conquest and Race-Thinking during the Restoration', *The Review of Politics* 22 (1960), 544–67.

Senn, H., 'Folklore Beginnings in France, the Académie celtique: 1804–1813', *Journal of the Folklore Institute* 18 (1981), 23–33.

Sera-Shriar, Efram, *The Making of British Anthropology, 1813–1871* (London, 2013).

Sharp, E. A., and Sharp, W. (eds.), *Lyra Celtica: An Anthology of Celtic Poetry* (Edinburgh, 1896).

Sharp, Elizabeth A. (ed.), *William Sharp (Fiona Macleod)* (1910: 2 vols., London, 1912).

Sharpe, Richard (ed.), *Roderick O'Flaherty's Letters: To William Molyneux, Edward Lhwyd, and Samuel Molyneux, 1696–1709* (Dublin, 2013).

Shaw, Francis, 'Johann Kaspar Zeuss', *Studies: An Irish Quarterly Review* 43 (1954), 194–206.

Shaw, Francis, 'The Background to *Grammatica Celtica*', *Celtica* 3 (1956), 1–16.

Shaw, William, *An Analysis of the Galic Language* (Edinburgh, 1778).

Shaw, William, *A Galic and English Dictionary* (2 vols., London, 1780).

Shaw, William, *An Enquiry into the Authenticity of the Poems Ascribed to Ossian* (London, 1781).

[Shaw, William], *Memoirs of the Life and Writings of the Late Dr. Samuel Johnson* (1785: London, 1974).

Sher, Richard B., *Church and University in the Scottish Enlightenment: The Moderate Literati of Edinburgh* (1985: Edinburgh, 2015).

Sher, Richard B., *The Enlightenment and the Book: Scottish Authors & Their Publishers in Eighteenth-Century Britain, Ireland, & America* (Chicago, IL, 2006).

Sheringham, Robert, *De Anglorum gentis origine disceptatio* (London, 1670).

Shore, John (ed.), *The Works of Sir William Jones* (13 vols., London, 1807).

Silvan Evans, Daniel (ed.), *Gwaith y Parchedig Evan Evans* (Caernarfon, 1876).

Sims-Williams, Patrick, 'The Visionary Celt: The Construction of an "Ethnic Preconception"', *CMCS* 11 (1986), 71–96.

Sims-Williams, Patrick, 'Some Celtic Otherworld Terms', in A.T.E. Matonis and Daniel F. Melia (eds.), *Celtic Language, Celtic Culture: A Festschrift for Eric P. Hamp* (Van Nuys, CA, 1990).

Sims-Williams, Patrick, 'The Invention of Celtic Nature Poetry', in Terence Brown, *Celticism* (Amsterdam, 1996), 97–124.

Sims-Williams, Patrick, 'Celtomania and Celtoscepticism', *CMCS* 36 (1998), 1–35.

Sims-Williams, Patrick, 'Genetics, Linguistics, and Prehistory: Thinking Big and Thinking Straight', *Antiquity* 72 (1998), 505–27.

Sims-Williams, Patrick, *Ancient Celtic Place-Names in Europe and Asia Minor* (Oxford, 2006).

Sims-Williams, Patrick, *Irish Influence on Medieval Welsh Literature* (Oxford, 2010).

Sims-Williams, Patrick, 'Celto-Etruscan Speculations', in Eugenio R. Luján and Juan Luis García Alonson (eds.), *A Greek Man in the Iberian Street: Papers in Linguistics and Epigraphy in Honor of Javier de Hoz* (Innsbruck, 2011), 275–84.

Sims-Williams, Patrick, 'Celtic Civilization: Continuity or Coincidence?', *CMCS* 64 (2012), 1–45.

Sims-Williams, Patrick, 'John Morris-Jones and his *Welsh Grammar*', *THSC*, New Series 22 (2016), 134–53.

Sims-Williams, Patrick, 'The Location of the Celts According to Hecataeus, Herodotus, and Other Greek Writers', *Études celtiques* 42 (2016), 7–32.

Sims-Williams, Patrick, 'An Alternative to "Celtic from the East" and "Celtic from the West"', *Cambridge Archaeological Journal* 30 (2020), 511–29.

Sims-Williams, Patrick, 'Pryd y death y Gymraeg i Ynys Prydain?', *Barn* 709 (2022), 20–22.

Sinclair, John, *An Account of the Highland Society of London, From its Establishment in May 1778, to the Commencement of the Year 1813* (London, 1813).

Skinner, Quentin, *The Foundations of Modern Political Thought* (2 vols., Cambridge, 1978).

Sklenár, Karel, *Archaeology in Central Europe: The First 500 Years*, trans. Iris Lewitová (Leicester, 1983).

Smiles, Sam, *The Image of Antiquity: Ancient Britain and the Romantic Imagination* (New Haven, CT, 1994).

Smith, Adam, *Lectures on Jurisprudence*, ed. R. L. Meek, D. D. Raphael, and P. G. Stein (Oxford, 1978).

Smith, Anthony D., *Myths and Memories of the Nation* (Oxford, 1999).

Smith, Justin E. H., *Nature, Human Nature, and Human Difference in Early Modern Philosophy* (Princeton, NJ, 2015).

Smith, Thomas, *Syntagma de Druidum Moribus* (London, 1664).

Smollett, Tobias, *The History of England, From the Revolution in 1688, to the Death of George II* (1785: 5 vols., London, 1805).

Snyder, Edward D., *The Celtic Revival in English Literature, 1760–1800* (Cambridge, MA, 1923).

Snyder, Louis L., *Macro-Nationalisms: A History of the Pan-Movements* (Westport, CT, 1984).

Sonenscher, Michael (ed. and trans.), *Emmanual Joseph Sieyès: Political Writings, Including the Debate between Sieyès and Tom Paine in 1791* (Indianapolis, IN, 2003).

Sonenscher, Michael, *Before the Deluge: Public Debt, Inequality, and the Intellectual Origins of the French Revolution* (Princeton, NJ, 2009).

Sorensen, Janet, '"Genuine Remains": The Celtic Linguistic Artifact in Eighteenth-Century Britain', *Modern Philology* 113 (2016), 373–97.

Speed, John, *The History of Great Britaine* (London, 1611).

Stack, David, 'Phrenological Friends: Cobden and His "Father Confessor" George Combe', in Anthony Howe and Simon Morgan (eds.), *Rethinking Nineteenth-Century Liberalism: Richard Cobden Bicentenary Essays* (Aldershot, 2006), 23–38.

Stafford, Fiona J., *The Sublime Savage: A Study of James Macpherson and the Poems of Ossian* (Edinburgh, 1988).

Stafford, Fiona J., 'Doctor Johnson and the Ruffian: New Evidence in the Dispute between Samuel Johnson and James Macpherson', *Notes & Queries* 36 (1989), 70–77.

Stafford, James, *The Case of Ireland: Commerce, Empire and the European Order, 1750–1848* (Cambridge, 2022).

Stalmaszczyk, Piotr, 'Celtic Studies in Poland: Recent Themes and Developments', *Studia Celto-Slavica* 1 (2006), 43–59.

Stanley, Arthur, *The Life and Correspondence of Thomas Arnold* (2 vols., London, 1844).

Stanley, Arthur Penrhyn, *Life and Correspondence of Thomas Arnold* (1844: 3rd ed., 2 vols., London, 1845).

Stephens, Thomas, *The Literature of the Kymry*, ed. D. Silvan Evans (1849: London, 1876).

Stephens, Thomas, 'An Essay on the Bardic Alphabet Called "Coelbren Y Beirdd"', *Archaeologia Cambrensis* 4th Series, 3 (1872), 181–209.

Stephens, W.R.W., *The Life and Letters of Edward A. Freeman* (2 vols., London, 1895).

Stern, L. C., 'Die ossianischen Heldenlieder', *Zeitschrift für vergleichende Litteraturgeschichte* 8 (1895), 51–86, 143–74.

Stern, L. C. 'Briefe von J. K. Zeuss an Chr. W. Glück', *ZCP* 3 (1901), 334–76.

Stewart, Ian, 'Of Crofters, Celts, and Claymores: The *Celtic Magazine* and the Highland Cultural Nationalist Movement, 1875–88', *Historical Research* 89 (2016), 88–113.

Stewart, Ian, 'E. E. Fournier d'Albe's *Fin de siècle*: Science, Nationalism and Monistic Philosophy in Britain and Ireland', *Cultural & Social History* 14 (2017), 599–620.

Stewart, Ian, 'Celticism and the Four Nations in the Long Nineteenth Century', in Naomi Lloyd-Jones and Margaret M. Scull, *Four Nations Approaches to Modern 'British' History: A (Dis)united Kingdom?* (Basingstoke, 2018), 135–59.

Stewart, Ian, 'The Mother Tongue: Historical Study of the Celts and Their Language(s) in Eighteenth-Century Britain and Ireland', *P&P* 243 (2019), 71–107.

Stewart, Ian, 'William Frédéric Edwards and the Study of Human Races in France, from the Restoration to the July Monarchy', *History of Science* 58 (2020), 275–300.

Stewart, Ian, 'Language and the National Past in Napoleonic France: Reassessing the *Académie celtique*, 1805–1813', *French History* 35 (2021), 219–42.

Stewart, Ian, 'After Sir William Jones: British Linguistic Scholarship and European Intellectual History', *JMH* 95 (2023), 808–46.

Stewart, Ian, 'James Cowles Prichard and the Linguistic Foundations of Ethnology', *Berichte zur Wissenschaftsgeschichte* 46 (2023), 76–91.

Stewart, Ian 'Celtic Philology, French Nationalism, and Science in the Pan-German Shadow, 1868–1910' (forthcoming).

Stewart, Ian, 'Dugald Stewart and Racial Theory at the University of Edinburgh in the Late Scottish Enlightenment' (forthcoming).

Stewart, Ian, 'Racialising the World: Civilisation, Knowledge, and the Crystallisation of Race in European Thought', in Sarah C. Dunstan and Ian Stewart, *Race: Histories of an Idea in the Modern World* (forthcoming).

Stiùbhart, Domhnall Uilleam (ed.), *The Life & Legacy of Alexander Carmichael* (Port of Ness, 2008).

Stocking Jr., George W., 'From Chronology to Ethnology: James Cowles Prichard and British Anthropology, 1800–1850', in George W. Stocking Jr. (ed.), James Cowles Prichard, *Researches into the Physical History of Man* (Chicago, 1973).

Stocking Jr., George W., *Victorian Anthropology* (New York, 1987).

Stokes, William, *The Life and Labours in Art and Archaeology, of George Petrie* (London, 1868).

Strabo, *Geography*, trans. Duane W. Roller (Cambridge, 2014).

Strabone, Jeff, *Poetry and British Nationalisms in the Bardic Eighteenth Century: Imagined Antiquities* (London, 2018).

Strangford, Viscountess Emily (ed.), *Original Letters and Papers of the Late Viscount Strangford upon Philological and Kindred Subjects* (London, 1878).

St. Ritsh, Andrew Russell, *Lays and Lyrics of the Pan-Celtic Society* (Dublin, 1889).

Stukeley, William, *An Account of a Roman Temple, and other Antiquities, near Graham's Dike in Scotland* (London, 1720).

Stukeley, William, *Stonehenge, a temple restor'd to the British Druids* (London, 1740).

Stukeley, William, *A Letter from Dr. Stukeley to Mr. Macpherson, On his Publication of Fingal and Temora* (London, 1763).

Stukeley, William, *Itinerarium curiosum: Or, An account of the Antiquities, and Remarkable Curiosities in Nature or Art, Observed in Travels Through Great Britain* (1724: 2nd ed., 2 vols, London, 1766).

Sullivan, Robert E., *Macaulay: The Tragedy of Power* (Cambridge, MA, 2009).

Sullivan, William K., 'Celtic Studies', *The Atlantis* 3 (1863).

Süssmilch, J. P., 'Reflexions sur la convenance de la langue celtique, et en particulier de la teutonique avec celles de l'orient', *Histoire de l'académie royale des sciences et des belles lettres de Berlin* (Berlin, 1746), 188–203.

Sutcliffe, Adam, *Judaism and Enlightenment* (Cambridge, 2003).

Sweet, Rosemary, *Antiquaries: The Discovery of the Past in Eighteenth-Century Britain* (London, 2004).

Tacitus, *Agricola*, trans. Harold Mattingly, ed. J. B. Rives (1948: London, 2009).

[Taillepied, Noël], *Histoire de l'estat et republique des druides* (Paris, 1585).

Tanner, Marcus, *The Last of the Celts* (New Haven, CT, 2004).

Temple, William, *An Introduction to the History of England* (London, 1695).

Thierry, Amédée, *Histoire des Gaulois, depuis les temps plus reculés jusqu'a l'entière soumission de la Gaule á la dominion Romaine* (3 vols., Paris, 1828).

Thierry, Augustin, *Histoire de la conquête de l'Angleterre par les Normands* (3 vols., Paris, 1825).

Thierry, Augustin, 'Introduction', in Armand Carrel, *Résume de l'histoire d'Écosse* (Paris, 1825), i–xiii.

Thierry, Augustin, *Lettres sur l'histoire de France, pour servir d'introduction à l'étude de cette histoire*, ed. Aude Déruelle (1827: Paris, 2012).

Thiesse, Anne-Marie, *La creation des identités nationales: Europe xviiie-xixe siècle* (Paris, 1999).

Thomas, Ben, '"The Clach": Alexander Mackenzie and the Land Question in the Late-Nineteenth Century Highlands and Islands', *Northern Scotland* 8 (2017), 68–86.

Thomson, Derick S., *The Gaelic Sources of Macpherson's 'Ossian'* (Edinburgh, 1952).

Thurneysen, Rudolf, *Handbuch des Alt-Irischen* (2 vols., Heidelberg, 1909).

Thurneysen, Rudolf, 'Why Do Germans Study Celtic Philology?' *Studies: An Irish Quarterly Review* 19 (1930), 20–32.

Thurneysen, Rudolf, *Gesammelte Schriften*, ed. Patrizia de Bernardo Stempel and Rolf Ködderitzsch (3 vols., Tübingen, 1991–1995).

[Toland, John], *A Collection of Several Pieces of John Toland* (2 vols., London, 1726).

Tombo, Rudolf, *Ossian in Germany* (New York, 1901).

Toomer, G. J., *Eastern Wisedome and Learning: The Study of Arabic in Seventeenth-Century England* (Oxford, 1996).

Toomer, G. J., *John Selden: A Life in Scholarship* (Oxford, 2009).

Tormy, J. F., 'The Ancient Race', in Martin MacDermott (ed.), *The New Spirit of the Nation* (London, 1894), 5–7.

Tourneur, Victor, *Esuisse d'une histoire des études celtiques* (Liège, 1905).

Trevor-Roper, Hugh, 'The Invention of Tradition: The Highland Tradition of Scotland', in Eric Hobsbawm and Terence Ranger (eds.), *The Invention of Tradition* (Cambridge, 1983), 15–41.

Trevor-Roper, Hugh, *The Invention of Scotland: Myth and History* (New Haven, CT, 2008).

Trippault, Léon, *Celt'-hellenisme ou, Etymologie des mots françois tirez du græc* (Orléans, 1580).

Tristram, Hildegard L. C., 'Celtic Studies in West Germany', *Celtic Cultures Newsletter* 4 (1986), 5–12.

Troyon, Frédéric, 'Antiquités de Bel-Air, près Lausanne, de Nordendorf, près Augsbourg et de Leux, dans le département du Pas-de-Calais', *Allgemeine Zeitschrift für Geschichte* 5 (1846), 272–85.

Troyon, Frédéric, *Habitations lacustres des tèmps anciens et modernes* (Lausanne, 1860).

Trumpener, Katie, *Bardic Nationalism: The Romantic Novel and the British Empire* (Princeton, NJ, 1997).

Tuck, Richard, *The Sleeping Sovereign: The Invention of Modern Democracy* (Cambridge, 2016).

Tuke, Daniel Hack, *Prichard and Symonds in Especial Relation to Mental Science with Chapters on Moral Insanity* (London, 1891).

[Turgot, Anne], 'Etymologie', in Denis Diderot and Jean le Rond d'Alembert (eds.), *Encyclopédie, ou dictionnaire raisonné des sciences, des arts et des metiers* (17 vols., Paris, 1751–1765), vol. 6, 98–111.

Turner, Dawson (ed.), *The Literary Correspondence of John Pinkerton* (2 vols., London, 1830).

Turner, James, *Philology: The Forgotten Origins of the Modern Humanities* (Princeton, NJ, 2014).

Twenty Year Report: School of Celtic Studies, Dublin Institute for Advanced Studies (Dublin, 1962).

Tyson, Byron (ed.), *Bernard Shaw's Book Reviews* (2 vols., Philadelphia, PA, 1996).

Tytler, Alexander Fraser, *Memoirs of the Life and Writings of Lord Kames* (2 vols., Edinburgh, 1807).

[Vallancey, Charles], *An Essay on the Antiquity of the Irish Language* (Dublin, 1772).

Vallancey, Charles, *A Grammar of the Iberno-Celtic or Irish Language* (Dublin, 1773).

Vallancey, Charles, 'Observations on the Alphabet of the Pagan Irish', *Archaeologia* 7 (1785), 276–85.

van Boxhorn, Marcus Zuerius, *Antwoord van Marcus Zuerius van Boxhorn, Gegeven Op de Vraaghen, hem voorgestelt over de Bediedinge van de Afgodinne Nehalennia* (Leiden, 1647).

van Boxhorn, Marcus Zuerius, *Originum Gallicarum liber* (Leiden, 1654).

Vance, Norman, 'Celts, Carthaginians and Constitutions: Anglo-Irish Literary Relations, 1780–1820', *IHS* 22 (1981), 216–38.

Van Damme, Stéphane, 'The Pillar of Metropolitan Greatness: The Long Making of Archaeological Objects in Paris (1711–2001)', *History of Science* 55 (2017), 302–35.

van Deth, Jean-Pierre, *Ernest Renan: Simple chercheur de vérité* (Paris, 2012).

Vandrei, Martha, *Queen Boudica and Historical Culture: An Image of Truth* (Oxford, 2018).

Van Hal, Toon, 'From Jones to Pictet: Some Notes on the Early History of Celtic Linguistics', *Beiträge zur Geschichte der Sprachwissenschaft* 15 (2005), 219–43.

Van Hal, Toon, *'Moedertalen en taalmoeders'. Het vroegmoderne taalvergelijkende onderzoek in de Lage Landen* (Brussels, 2010).

Van Hal, Toon, 'On "the Scythian Theory": Reconstructing the Outlines of Johannes Elichmann's (1601/1602–1639) Planned *Archaeologia Harmonica*', *Language & History* 53 (2010), 70–80.

Van Hal, Toon, 'A Man of Eight Hearts: Hadrianus Junius and Sixteenth-Century Plurilingualism', in Dirk van Miert (ed.), *The Kaleidoscopic Scholarship of Hadrianus Junius (1511–1575): Northern Humanism at the Dawn of the Dutch Golden Age* (Leiden, 2011), 188–213.

Van Hal, Toon, 'Reviving the Old Teutonic Language: An Unpublished Preface by Abraham Mylius (1563–1637) Retrieved in Gottfired Wilhelm Leibniz's Heritage', *Lias* 38 (2011), 129–47.

Van Hal, Toon, 'When Quotation Marks Matter: Rhellicanus and Boxhornius on the Differences between the *lingua Gallica* and *lingua Germanica*', *Historiographia Linguistica* 38 (2011), 241–52.

Van Hal, Toon, 'From *Alauda* to *Zythus*. The Emergence and Uses of Old-Gaulish Word Lists in Early Modern Publications', *Keltische Forschungen* 6 (2014), 219–77.

Van Hal, Toon, 'One Continent, one Language?: *Europa Celtica* and Its Language in Philippus Cluverius' *Germania antiquia* (1616) and Beyond', *European Review of History* 21 (2014), 889–907.

Van Hal, Toon, 'Sprachen, die Geshcichte schreiben. Zu Leibniz' sprachhistorischem Forschungsprogramm und dessen Nachwirkung', in Wenchao Li (ed.), *Einheit der Vernunft und Vielfalt der Sprachen: Beiträge zu Leibnizens Sprachforschung und Zeichentheorie* (Stuttgart, 2014), 177–206.

Van Hal, Toon, 'A Precursor and Successor to William Jones: Marcus Zuerius Boxhorn's Contribution to the Scythian Theory and Comparative Linguistics', *Erudition and the Republic of Letters* 7 (2022), 302–53.

Van Tieghem, Paul, *Ossian en France* (2 vols., Paris, 1917).

Varouxakis, Georgios, *Mill on Nationality* (London, 2002).

Varouxakis, Georgios, *Victorian Political Thought on France and the French* (Basingstoke, 2002).

Venayre, Sylvain, *Les origines de la France: Quand les historiens racontaient la nation* (Paris, 2013).

Verchère de Reffye, Jean-Baptiste, 'Les armes l'Alise', *Révue archéologique* 10 (1864), 337–49.

Verstegan, Richard, *A Restitution of Decayed Intelligence* (1605: London, 1634).

Vetter, Sabine, *Wissenschaftlicher Reduktionismus und die Rassentheorie von Christophe Meiners* (Mainz, 1996), 195–207.

Virey, J. J., *Histoire naturelle du genre humain* (2 vols., Paris, 1800).

Volpilhac, Catherine, 'Les Gaulois à l'Académie des Inscriptions et Belles-Lettres de 1701 à 1791', in Jean Ehrard and Paul Viallaneix (eds.), *Nos ancêtres les Gaulois* (Clermont-Ferrand, 1982), 77–83.

von Arndt, Christian Gottlieb, *Ueber den Ursprung und die verschiedenartige Verwandschaft der Europaeischen Sprachen* (Frankfurt, 1818).

von der Schulenberg, Sigrid, *Leibniz als Sprachforscher* (Frankfurt, 1973).

von Lexer, Matthias, and von Riezler, Sigmund (eds.), *Johannes Turmair's genannt Aventinus Sämmtliche Werke* (6 vols., Munich, 1881–1886).

von Tevenar, Gerhard, 'Ein keltisches Institut in der Bretagne', *ZCP* 22 (1941), 443.

von Tevenar, Gervard, 'Zur Gründung der "Deutschen Gesellschaft für keltische Studien"', *ZCP* 22 (1941), 440–41.

Vossius, Gerardus, *De Theologia gentili* (Amsterdam, 1641).

Waddell, John, *Foundation Myths: The Beginnings of Irish Archaeology* (Bray, 2005).

Walker, D. P., 'The *Prisca Theologia* in France', *Journal of the Warburg and Courtauld Institutes* 17 (1954), 204–59.

Walker, D. P., *The Ancient Theology: Studies in Christian Platonism from the Fifteenth to the Eighteenth Century* (London, 1972).

Wallace, S., *John Stuart Blackie: Scottish Scholar and Patriot* (Edinburgh, 2006).

Wallis, John, *Grammaticae linguae Anglicanae* (London, 1653).

Walters, Huw, 'Myfyr Morganwg and the Rocking-Stone Gorsedd', in Geraint H. Jenkins (ed.), *A Rattleskull Genius: The Many Faces of Iolo Morganwg* (Cardiff, 2005), 481–500.

Ward, Catherine Coogan, and Ward, Robert E. (eds.), *The Letters of Charles O'Conor of Belanagare* (2 vols., Ann Arbor, MI, 1980).

Warner, Fernando, *Remarks on the History of Fingal, and Other Poems of Ossian* (London, 1762).

Warner, Ferdinando, *The History of Ireland* (London, 1763).

Waterman, John T. (ed.), *Leibniz and Ludolf on Things Linguistic: Excerpts from Their Correspondence (1688–1703)* (Berkeley, CA, 1978).

[Webb, Daniel], *Fingal Reclaimed* (London, 1763).

Weinbrot, Howard, *Britannia's Issue: The Rise of British Literature from Dryden to Ossian* (Cambridge, 1993).

Weisgerber, Leo, *Die Keltischen Völker im Umkreis von England* (Marburg, 1941).

Wells, H. G., *Anticipations of the Reaction of Mechanical and Scientific Progress upon Human Life and Thought* (London, 1902).

Whewell, William, *The Philosophy of the Inductive Sciences, Founded Upon Their History* (2 vols., London, 1840).

Whitaker, John, *The History of Manchester* (2 vols., London, 1771–1773).

Whitaker, John, *The Genuine History of the Britons Asserted* (London, 1772).

White, John, *Guide to the Town and Neighbourhood of Abergavenny* (Abergavenny, 1845).

Wilde, William, *A Descriptive Catalogue of the Antiquities of Stone, Earthen, and Vegetable Materials in the Museum of the Royal Irish Academy* (Dublin, 1857).

Wiley, Raymond A. (ed.), *John Mitchell Kemble and Jakob Grimm: A Correspondence, 1832–1852* (Leiden, 1971).

Will, Gero, 'Die Anfänge der Deutschen Keltologie und ihre Insittutionalisierung bis 1901', in Sabine Heinz (ed.), *Die Deutsche Keltologie und ihre Berliner Gelehrten bis 1945* (Frankfurt, 1999), 25–38.

Williams, Edward, *Poems Lyric and Pastoral* (2 vols., London, 1794).

Williams, Edward, *Prospectus of Collections for a New History of Wales Based Upon Manuscript Sources* (Carmarthen, 1819).

Williams, Jane (ed.), *The Literary Remains of the Rev. Thomas Price* (2 vols., Llandovery, 1854–1855).

Williams, J.H.C., *Beyond the Rubicon: Romans and Gauls in Republican Italy* (Oxford, 2001).

Williams, Kelsey Jackson, *The Antiquary: John Aubrey's Historical Scholarship* (Oxford, 2016).

Williams, Kelsey Jackson, *The First Scottish Enlightenment: Rebels, Priests, and History* (Oxford, 2020).

Williams, Mark, *Ireland's Immortals: A History of the Gods of Irish Myth* (Princeton, NJ, 2016).

Williams, Mark, *The Celtic Myths That Shape the Way We Think* (London, 2021).
Winning, W. B., *A Manual of Comparative Philology* (London, 1838).
Wise, Francis, *Some Enquiries concerning the First Inhabitants, Language, Religion, Learning and Letters of Europe* (Oxford, 1758).
Wiseman, Nicholas, *Twelve Lectures on the Connexion between Science and Revealed Religion* (1837: London 1842).
Womack, Peter, *Improvement and Romance: Constructing the Myth of the Highlands* (Basingstoke, 1989).
Woolf, Stuart, 'French Civilization and Ethnicity in the Napoleonic Empire', *P&P* 124 (1989), 96–120.
Yeats, W. B., 'The Poetry of Sir Samuel Ferguson', *Dublin University Review* II (1886).
Yeats, W. B., 'The Celtic Element in Literature' *Cosmopolis* X (1898), 675–86.
Yeats, W. B., *Autobiographies* (London, 1955).
Young, Robert J. C., *The Idea of English Ethnicity* (Oxford, 2008).
Young, Simon, *The Celtic Revolution: In Search of 2000 Forgotten Years That Changed the World* (London, 2009).
Zeuß, [Johann], *Die Deutschen und die Nachbarstämme* (Munich, 1837).
Zeuß, [Johann] K., *Die Herkunft der Baiern von den Markomannen* (Munich, 1839).
Zeuß, [Johann] K., *Grammatica Celtica* (2 vols., Leipzig, 1853).
Zimmer, Heinrich, *Keltische Studien* (2 vols., Berlin, 1881–1884).
Zimmer, Heinrich, 'Der Pan-Keltismus in Großbritannien und Irland', *Preussische Jahrbücher* 93 (1898), 59–93.

INDEX

A NOTE ON THE TYPE

This book has been composed in Arno, an Old-style serif typeface in the classic Venetian tradition, designed by Robert Slimbach at Adobe.